NETWORK +
CERTIFICATION
TRAINING GUIDE

Editor in Chief: Stephen Helba
Assistant Vice President and Publisher: Charles E. Stewart, Jr.
Production Editor: Alexandrina Benedicto Wolf
Design Coordinator: Diane Ernsberger
Cover Designer: Michael R. Hall
Cover Art: Michael R. Hall
Illustrations: Michael R. Hall and Cathy J. Boulay
Production Manager: Matthew Ottenweller

This book was set in Times New Roman and Arial by Cathy J. Boulay, Marcraft International, Inc. It was printed and bound by R.R. Donnelley & Sons Company. The cover was printed by Phoenix Color Corp.

Pearson Education Ltd., *London*
Pearson Education Australia Pty. Limited, *Sydney*
Pearson Education Singapore, Pte. Ltd.
Pearson Education North Asia Ltd., *Hong Kong*
Pearson Education Canada, Ltd., *Toronto*
Pearson Educación de Mexico, S.A. de C.V.
Pearson Education–Japan, *Tokyo*
Pearson Education Malaysia, Pte. Ltd.
Pearson Education, *Upper Saddle River, New Jersey*

Written by Randy L. Ratliff

10 9 8 7 6 5 4 3 2 1

ISBN 0-13-112346-7

PREFACE

PURPOSE

Marcraft International has been producing certification courseware for different facets of the electronic, computer architecture, computer repair, and IT industry since 1988. This Network+ book has been designed to prepare students for the CompTIA Network+ Certification exam and prepare them with the necessary tools for grasping the complex technologies of networking computers.

Appropriately, Marcraft's original Network+ Certification Program – Theory and Lab course has changed to reflect the evolving nature of computer networking. The tasks performed by network administrators have changed considerably since the original course was introduced. Networking hardware has advanced and become smarter, and software has been made much more complex and smarter.

NETWORK+ CERTIFICATION

The Network+ Certification exam represents a standard benchmark by which companies, professionals, and students of computer networking can measure their knowledge of the rapid changes taking place in the field of computer networking. This Network+ course has been designed to prepare students to successfully challenge the Network+ certification exam as well as provide a complete training course designed to provide the knowledge base required to establish a career in networking.

The textbook and lab book are intended for anyone interested in pursuing the Network+ certification and contains all of the pedagogical support materials to be used in a classroom environment, but can also be used in a self-study mode by experienced network technicians to prepare for the exam.

Key Revisions

This edition of the Network+ Certification Program has been expanded to include information about all of the new (0/02) objectives. It has been streamlined to more closely follow the CompTIA objectives. Much of the basic information has been combined and/or enhanced with additional technological upgrading.

Key Features

The pedagogical features of this book were carefully developed to provide readers with key content information, as well as review and testing opportunities. A complete Network+ objectives map and Test Tip information boxes are included to help you key in on Network+ specific materials. Each chapter begins with a list of learning objectives that provides a systematic preview of the chapter. Also, each chapter concludes with a chapter summary of the points and objectives that should have been accomplished. A complete Network+ objective map provides content directly related to the Network+ Certification exam. Key terms are presented in bold or italics throughout the text. Background Info sections appear throughout the chapters to add in-depth discussions, which can be used as background information.

Network+ Core Hardware Exam/Operating System Technologies Exam Coverage

The locations of Network+ specific materials are identified with a Test Tip marker in the margin that helps students focus on key content that they will be expected to know for the Network+ certification exam. *Appendix A* provides a comprehensive listing of the Network+ objectives.

Evaluation and Test Material

An abundance of test materials is available with this course. Each chapter contains a 10-question multiple-choice section and a 15-question section of open-ended review questions. Additional Network+ test material can be found on the Interactive CD-ROM that comes with the book. The 10 multiple-choice questions test knowledge of the basic concepts presented in the chapter, while the 15 open-ended review questions are designed to test critical thinking.

Interactive CD-ROM

The *Network+ Certification* book is accompanied by a comprehensive Network+ test bank that is sealed on the back cover of the book. This CD testing material was developed to simulate the Network+ Certification Exam testing process and materials and to allow students to complete practice tests, determine their weak points, and study more strategically.

The ExamGear test engine included on the accompanying CD provides three styles of testing:

- Study Mode – enables you to review questions and check the answers and references from within the test

- Test Mode – simulates the actual fixed-length A+ exams

- Adaptive Mode – enables you to take practice tests in the same adaptive mode that CompTIA eventually converts all of its exams into

During the question review, the correct answer is presented on the screen along with the reference heading where the material can be found in the text. A single mouse click takes you quickly to the corresponding section of the electronic textbook on the CD.

Pedagogical Features

Diagrams and screen dumps are included in each chapter to provide constant visual reinforcement of the concepts being discussed.

Each chapter begins with a list of learning objectives that establishes a foundation and systematic preview of the chapter. Each chapter concludes with a key points review of its material.

Key terms are presented in bold type throughout the text. These terms work in conjunction with the extensive Glossary at the end of the book. Key thoughts in the chapter are presented in special boxes to call special attention to them.

In general, it is not necessary to move through this text in the same order that it is presented. Also, it is not necessary to teach any specific portion of the material to its extreme. Instead, the material can be adjusted to fit the length of your course. As a matter of fact, practicing IT professionals can use the material in the CD test banks to identify the areas where they need to brush up, and then use the text book to study that material directly.

ORGANIZATION

Chapter 1 – *Network Topologies and Media* provides a focus on the physical aspects of a network detailing the intricacies of how the network is physically arranged as well as the physical infrastructure of the network. Information is presented on the physical infrastructure referred to as the network media, and the physical arrangement is identified with the network topology.

Chapter 2 – *IEEE 802.x Protocols* deals with the standards of the Media Access Control (MAC) sublayer of layer two, the Data Link layer, of the ISO OSI Reference Model. The standards are important to understanding local area networks because nearly all LANs are designed and implemented around the standards. A thorough understanding of these protocols will help you make more sense of protocols and practices used in wide area networks.

Chapter 3 – *Networking Hardware* provides an overview of hardware commonly used with networks, as well as the accompanying wiring infrastructures. Because the Network+ Exam assumes a working knowledge of the basic purpose of networking hardware, it is imperative that networking professionals understand the hardware used in networking.

Chapter 4 – *ISO OSI Reference Model* uses the protocol standards as a tool to measure and describe networking systems. The chapter provides a true understanding of the model that is essential both in understanding internetworking, and in taking the Network+ Certification exam.

Chapter 5 – *Network Protocols* discusses the concepts, technologies, standards, and services that comprise the operations that occur on a network, excluding the wide area arena. The intricacies of the Network and Transport layers are examined with regard to what's broadly called internetwork protocols, and specifically the TCP/IP suite of protocols. The physical interconnect technologies are described, along with the methods for carrying data between LANs using different access methods. In addition, several transport services used to increase the performance of networks are also examined.

Chapter 6 – *TCP/IP Utilities* introduces the various utility commands or network tools that are used for checking network connections to the Internet or between intranets. Also provided are the procedures for using a variety of utility tools.

Chapter 7 – *Remote Access and Security Protocols* deals with the protocols related to remote access services, and the protocols and conventions used in setting up and maintaining a connection between a computer and remote servers. Specific protocols related to security for remote access servers are also described.

Chapter 8 – *Network Services* provides an overview of the most common network services used to name networks and then resolve those names to IP addresses, as well as software management tools, which is the parlance of the Network+ exam. Also there is an overview of how the Internet began, the different areas of the Internet, and why the protocols are relevant and important.

Chapter 9 – *WAN Technologies* deals with what a wide area network is and how interconnections of networks are accomplished. As the term implies, a wide area network covers a large geographical area and is a network of interconnected networks. The chapter shows that a WAN is like the Internet, which is a true network of networks, and how those networks are connected together.

Chapter 10 – *Operating Systems* offers an overview of operating system software, including specific configuration settings. As required by the Network+ Exam configuration and troubleshooting of TCP/IP parameters on client computers, instructions are included for configuring the most common networking protocols. Configuration of a variety of operating systems is considered and performed to provide a true understanding of what is needed.

Chapter 11 – *Network Systems* introduces basic concepts of data communications by defining common terms and describing equipment fundamental to the industry. Some of the more common standards and protocols are introduced along with characteristics common to the many areas comprising data communications.

Chapter 12 – *Network Media Losses* discusses the different types of problems associated with the variety of transmission media that is used to connect computers together in networks. The types of problems encountered by data signals are analyzed in this chapter as well as the actions taken to overcome or correct the known conditions.

Chapter 13 – *Network Protection* deals with maintaining data integrity and provides a thorough look at several techniques used to protect network resources. The chapter provides an overview of server hardware to set the stage to examine the need for being prepared for the disastrous loss of network hardware.

Chapter 14 – *Troubleshooting Strategies* provides a basic overview of troubleshooting processes and builds on concepts presented in earlier chapters.

The Lab Guide

Applying the concepts of the chapter to hands-on exercises is crucial to preparing for a successful career as a network technician. The lab guide provides an excellent hands-on component to emphasize the theoretical materials. Each lab in the lab guide provides exercises that reinforce the theory content via hands-on exploration. Questions at the end of each lab enable students to assess their understanding of the lab.

Teacher Support

An instructor's guide accompanies the course. Answers for all of the end-of-chapter questions are included along with a reference point in the chapter where a particular item is covered. Sample schedules are included as guidelines for possible course implementations. Answers to all lab review questions and fill-in-the-blank steps are provided so that there is an indication of what the expected outcomes should be.

An electronic copy of the textbook is included on the CD-ROM disk at the back of the lab book. This copy is electronically linked to the Network+ Practice Test Bank. This permits information concerning test questions to be accessed directly and immediately.

Test Taking Tips

The Network+ exam is an objective-based timed test. It covers the objectives listed in **Appendix A** in a multiple-choice format. There are two general methods of preparing for the test. If you are an experienced technician using this material to obtain certification, use the testing features at the end of each chapter and on the accompanying CD to test each area of knowledge. Track your weak areas and spend the most time concentrating on them.

If you are a newcomer to the subject of serious computer repair, plan a systematic study of the materials, reserving the testing functions until each chapter has been completed.

In either case, after completing the study materials you should use the various testing functions available on the CD to practice taking the test. Use the Study and Exam modes to test yourself by chapter, or on a mixture of questions from all areas of the text. Practice until you are very certain that you are ready. The CD will allow you to immediately refer to the area of the text that covers material that you might miss.

- Answer the questions you know first. You can always go back and work on questions.

- Don't leave any questions unanswered. They will be counted as incorrect.

- There are no trick questions. The correct answer is in there somewhere.

- Be aware of Network+ questions that have more than one correct answer. Questions that have multiple correct answers can be identified by the special formatting applied to the letters of their possible answers. They are enclosed in a square box. When you encounter these questions, make sure to mark every answer that applies.

- Get plenty of hands-on practice before the test, using the time limit set for the test.

- Make certain to prepare for each test category listed above. The key is not to memorize but to understand the topics.

- Take your watch. The Network+ exam is a timed test. You will need to keep an eye on the time to make sure that you are getting to the items that you are most sure of.

- Get plenty of rest before taking the test.

TRADEMARK ACKNOWLEDGMENTS

All terms mentioned in this book that are known to be trademarks or service marks are listed below. Marcraft cannot attest to the accuracy of this information. Use of a term in this book should not be regarded as affecting the validity of any trademark or service mark.

MS-DOS is a registered trademark of Microsoft Corporation.

Windows for Workgroups is a registered trademark of Microsoft Corporation.

Windows 95/98/NT are registered trademarks of Microsoft Corporation.

MARCRAFT is a registered trademark of Marcraft International Corporation.

ACKNOWLEDGMENTS

The author wishes to make the following acknowledgments in appreciation for help obtained in the writing, and preparing, of this book.

No one can write a book of this scope and magnitude without a lot of help. I'm grateful to the following for their expertise, encouragement, criticisms, suggestions, and general good will: Cathy Boulay for finding each and every item that was missing; Michael Hall for incredible graphics created from my indecipherable sketches; Wanda Dawson and Paul Havens for their help with NetWare and many other laboratory experiments; Gary Gregg for showing me what's around the corner; Grant Socal and Shawn Ratliff at Cisco for bearing with me, while still answering my questions as if they made sense; and Chuck Brooks, who was with me a long time ago—when this book was just an idea.

I would like to thank numerous companies for access to their resources: Cisco Systems, Cabletron Systems, 3Com, Bay Networks and Nortel, Rockwell, Intel, Lucent Technologies, Zoltrix, Hayes, Marcraft International, Red Hat, Computer Learning Centers and all the folks at the April 99 Net+ seminar in Virginia, CompTIA and Doug Bastianelli, Microsoft, Novell, and the Branike Corporation for their excellent work with cable modems.

My wife, Jan. My daughter, Phoebe. My son, Nick.

TABLE OF CONTENTS

CHAPTER 3   NETWORKING HARDWARE

CHAPTER 4   ISO OSI REFERENCE MODEL

CHAPTER 5   NETWORK PROTOCOLS

CHAPTER 6   TCP/IP UTILITIES

CHAPTER 7   REMOTE ACCESS AND SECURITY PROTOCOLS

CHAPTER 8   NETWORK SERVICES

CHAPTER 9   WAN TECHNOLOGIES

CHAPTER 10   OPERATING SYSTEMS

CHAPTER 11   NETWORK SYSTEMS

CHAPTER 12   NETWORK MEDIA LOSSES

CHAPTER 13   NETWORK PROTECTION

CHAPTER 14   TROUBLESHOOTING STRATEGIES

APPENDIX A

APPENDIX B

INDEX

CHAPTER

1

NETWORK TOPOLOGIES AND MEDIA

LEARNING
OBJECTIVES

LEARNING OBJECTIVES

Upon completion of this chapter and its related lab procedures, you will be able to perform the following tasks:

1. Draw simple sketches of mesh, star, ring, bus, and hierarchical topologies.

2. State advantages and disadvantages for mesh, star, ring, and bus topologies.

3. Recognize the following logical or physical topologies given a schematic diagram or description: star, bus, mesh, ring, wireless, hierarchical.

4. Discuss the advantages and disadvantages of analog and digital waveforms when used in networking.

5. Define "media" as applied to networking.

6. State several factors that influence the choice of media.

7. Recognize and describe the advantages/disadvantages of coaxial, CAT3, CAT5, fiber-optic, UTP, and STP media.

8. Explain how CAT5 UTP increases bandwidth capabilities of twisted-pair cable.

9. List differences between the various categories of UTP.

10. Identify the use of the (MAU) transceiver network component.

11. Discuss the differences between thicknet and thinnet coaxial cable.

12. Explain the purpose of a terminator, and the problems encountered through improper use of a terminator.

13. Recognize and describe the visual appearance of the following connectors and describe their uses: RJ-11, RJ-45, AUI, BNC, ST, SC.

14. Provide a basic description of how light propagates through a fiber-optic cable.

15. Describe the physical and optical characteristics of fiber-optic cable.

16. Provide a description of how to connect a connector to a fiber-optic cable.

CHAPTER 1

NETWORK TOPOLOGIES AND MEDIA

INTRODUCTION

This chapter focuses on physical aspects of a network—how the network is physically arranged and the physical infrastructure of the network. The physical infrastructure is referred to as the network media, while the physical arrangement is called the network topology.

Topology plays an important role in networking. The topology affects cost, reliability, complexity, and ease of expansion. The various types of topologies are named to describe how the network looks. Hence, in a ring topology, the network is structured to resemble a ring.

Network media is a critical component of networking. Media refers to the type of path that data takes between workstations, as well as the connector interfaces used between the workstations and the media path. The network infrastructure has a huge impact on the performance of a network. Some media types carry data faster than other types, but not all media types work well with certain topologies. For example, fiber-optic cable is the fastest media, but it doesn't work well in a bus topology.

Fiber optics has been hailed as the transmission media totally immune from EMI interference—and it is. Fiber-optic cable can be run side-by-side with industrial grade motors and not be affected by radiated noise. However, fiber remains an expensive option when compared to alternative, copper-based media. The coaxial-cable-based systems of cable television companies will offer an intriguing communication system in the near future. More than half of U.S. households are cable subscribers. Coaxial cable has a bandwidth several times that of telephone twisted wires, which means the time is not so far off when the household subscriber or business office may be able to rent space for transmitting data.

Whereas fiber-optic cable seemed destined to capture the majority of wiring closets, unshielded twisted pair (UTP) cabling that's been configured for networking is now the media of choice for network runs to the desktop. Although structurally identical to telephone wire, UTP cable is designed so that it eliminates most of the noise problems associated with telephone cable. Therefore, UTP cable became the media of choice over fiber-optic cable because of its relatively good noise immunity characteristics and lower cost of installation and maintenance compared to fiber.

The cost of a network can't be minimized. Somewhere, an accountant's teeth will gnash each time you spend money and the cabling infrastructure is a significant investment—about 30% or more of the total network cost. When tens of thousands of feet of cabling are installed in a medium-sized network, you can't make too many cabling mistakes, and still expect to keep your job.

TOPOLOGY

Network topology is the physical arrangement of nodes. A node refers to any device connected to the network—a computer, workstation, switching unit, etc.

Network topologies are significant because they affect the network reliability, flexibility, cost of adding nodes, future growth, and the disruption of data flow when adding or deleting nodes.

You can't realistically separate protocols at the Data Link layer of the OSI model and the interface of the Physical layer. That is, Ethernet is a Data Link layer protocol, but it also crosses the boundary into the Physical layer since the protocol includes specifications for mechanical and electrical characteristics. At the same time, Ethernet is bound by topology (by convention, not necessarily by technology). For the purposes of the Network+ exam, you should view physical topology of a network as separate from protocols.

Originally, the purpose of formulating network topologies was to reduce the workload of workstations spent in routing data. If the routing workload is reduced, then more time can be spent shuttling data frames that carry user data. The basic idea of networks, then, is to more or less distribute the work among all the nodes. The topology—the method chosen to physically connect nodes—directly affects the total time the network system manages itself.

The speed capabilities of end-users have far outpaced speed developments in networking. Although great strides have been made in this area, there remains much to be done. When using 2 GHz microprocessors, any attempt to send a packet of data on a local area network with this same throughput will result in failure, even in the fastest local area networks.

No one topology is best. Some have more advantages than others, and as such, have come to dominate the topology market. But networking changes in a blink, and what was discarded last year may very well be resurrected this year, clothed in a new technology. As with most of electronics in general, and data communications in particular, the best topology is the one that best fills the needs of the user.

It's significant to point out that a formal network isn't always necessary or desirable. A topologically defined network is only needed when production costs, and the consumption of time required to add and manage links, exceed the costs of a network. In the purest implementation, a peer-to-peer topology (and by extension, a point-to-point topology) is the best network because at any one time, only two nodes are communicating. Visualize a personal computer connected to an ISP (Internet Service Provider), for example. Although this connection only directly involves two nodes, it's a full-fledged network in a point-to-point topology.

How will you know when it's time to network beyond the peer-to-peer relationship? By factoring sheer numbers and production costs. Let's take a look at the largest network topology in the world for an example.

Mesh Topology

The most basic type of topology is the **mesh**, shown in Figure 1-1. This represents five computers that have been connected together. In a pure mesh network, each node has a physical link (coax, twisted pair, microwave, fiber optic) connection to all other nodes. This enables the mesh topology to provide a highly-fault tolerant network environment. If one of its physical links fail, there is always another link available for use. Mesh networks are the most fault-tolerant network topologies available.

Ten links are required to connect the five computers shown in Figure 1-1. If a sixth node is added, fifteen links will be required; if a seventh node is added, twenty-one links will be needed.

The number of links required to service a specified number of nodes in a mesh network is found by:

$$Ln = [Nn(Nn - 1)]/2$$

where Ln = number of links required, and Nn = number of nodes in the network.

If an office building has 99 PCs and the network administrator decides to add another, an additional 99 wires will be needed to tie the PCs together, for a total of 4,950 links! Somewhere, in those thousands of links, will be a point at which the cost of purchasing a more efficient network will make a lot of sense. And if we think about the arrangement, there will be a better way to physically organize the nodes that can simplify the thousands of wires needed.

The largest mesh topologies are the public telephone network and the Internet. Interestingly, both the telephone system and the Internet allow users to connect from anywhere in the world at any time with a single and unique addressing scheme—a telephone number for callers, and an IP address for Internet users.

Mesh is the correct choice given the available technology for the Internet and the telephone network. But for smaller networks such as a LAN, they create horrific management nightmares. Even on a wide scale, in which a network is large enough to be classified as a WAN, mesh may not be a good choice. The physical (millions of wired connections needed for the telephone network) and logical (complex addressing schemes such as IP addresses) requirements may represent overkill in terms of cost and complexity.

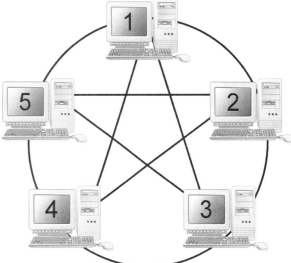

> **NOTE**
>
> A mesh topology is a type of arrangement in which all nodes are physically connected.

Figure 1-1: Mesh Network

> **TEST TIP**
>
> Be aware that the mesh topology is use to provide fault tolerant networking. The other networking topologies commonly available do not offer any built-in fault tolerance.

Bus Topology

When you consider all communications opportunities, the bus topology will predominate. A **bus topology** may be inches long, or miles long. It's the favored architecture for routing data and address information inside computers, and by extension, was one of the first topologies used in networking.

A bus topology is a straight-line connection strategy.

A typical bus topology is illustrated in Figure 1-2. Nodes are attached to the network bus through interface units. Data is transferred and received through specified node addresses. The address requirement is that it must be unique on the network. The address may be a number, name, or symbol. No two nodes on the network can have the same address, no matter the addressing scheme.

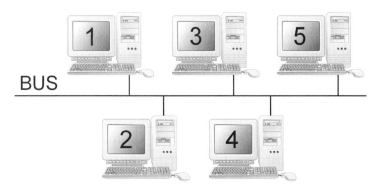

Figure 1-2:
Bus Topology

If the received data packet contains an address that's the same as the address assigned to the node, then the node will accept the packet. If the address doesn't match the address of the node, then the node will reject the data packet.

In a bus network setting, there are several ways to set up data packet routing decisions. The nodes may be connected directly to a central controller and the controller makes all decisions concerning which node get packets and when they get them. (This is what happens inside a computer.) Or, more commonly, the nodes themselves make the decision.

When several computers are networked on a bus topology, the network interface card (NIC) installed in the computer contributes to the decision. The NIC card is responsible for determining if the data to be sent is intended for computers on the same network as the transmitting computer, or if it's intended for a computer on a distant network. If the NIC decides that the packet is intended for a computer on the local network, then the packet is placed on the bus, and the connected nodes accept or reject the packet based upon the address of the destination computer. If the NIC determines that the packet is intended for a computer on another network, then another network device (a router) facilitates the transfer.

With the proper protocol, bus topologies can be one of the best performers. It's easy to add nodes by simply plugging them into the bus, and the reliability of the bus is very high. However, an electrical fault may render a portion of the bus inoperable. If a bus opens, or a short occurs, the entire network could crash, or a node may be damaged.

polling

time slots

contention

There are three common technologies associated with transporting data across the bus: **polling**, **time slots**, and **contention**. With the poll technique, a transmitting station may be asked by the controller if it has a message to send. If the node has nothing, the poll moves on to the next node. In many bus networks, the user can prioritize nodes so that if a node midway along the bus declines to transmit, the poll is reset and the first node on the network is polled. Each time the poll is declined, it's reset and polls the first node. The first node has been assigned the highest priority to transmit.

A simpler technique for granting nodes access to the network is the time slot. A master oscillator in the controller begins a counting sequence, and when the count matches a node's assigned ID count, that node sends a message to the controller to transmit. The master oscillator is turned off, and the node has the network to itself. When combined with a fast switch or router, this method is extremely effective.

The most common access method is the contention-based technique. Nodes that have messages to send compete for control of the channel, and eventually, a winner emerges. This is the type of situation that occurs with collision detection schemes such as Ethernet.

Data communications over cable television systems (used to access the Internet using cable television fiber/coaxial media) use bus topologies with the coaxial cable serving as a backbone to subscribers. Backbone is a term used to describe a common channel that is shared by many users. As in any bus topology, the subscribers share the backbone's bandwidth using one of the methods described above. In the case of using cable modems for Internet access, users are rewarded with a bus connection that is much faster than a dial-up connection over the mesh topology of the telephone system.

The bus topology isn't without drawbacks. It's the only network that can't easily use end-to-end fiber optics, since the bus taps make for an awkward connection. The length of the bus may create problems. The nodes furthest from a server (if used) may be ignored occasionally. The length of the bus creates opportunities for noise to distort control messages, and the cumulative voltage drop can cause messages to be lost altogether. Long buses require that repeaters be selectively placed to boost the signal strength and restore its shape.

Since all users share the bandwidth, speeds are related to the number of users. The more users on a bus topology, the slower it operates. For Ethernet networks as well as cable modem subscribers, more users on the network means that the network will operate slower.

Star Topology

The **star topology** consists of a central hub with spokes extending out from it and terminated in nodes, shown in Figure 1-3. The hub is essentially a complex switch used to connect the nodes. It is the most widely used topology.

The star is one of the older topologies. In the early days of its use, it tended to be used inappropriately; that is, over long distances of many miles. If limited to the distance in a building, or adjacent buildings, and if the central hub retains the original intent as a switch—then it performs well.

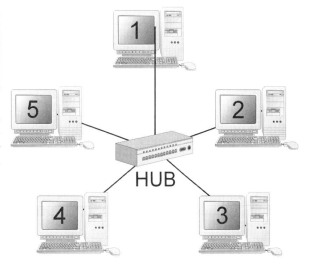

Figure 1-3: Star Topology

The performance factors of a star are paradoxical because for each advantage it has, a draw-back is uncovered. It's one of the cheapest topologies in terms of cost per node. All that's required to expand a star is to add another node to a hub port. This sounds easier than it is. The addition of a node may require a long and awkward wire run, which means it's an expensive expansion. The relative ease of adding nodes makes the star a good contender for networks with good growth opportunities. However, a hub must be installed with the ports ready to be plugged into. In other words, you have to initially pay for a performance level you aren't utilizing.

Star topologies usually have low overhead and high throughput. But this depends on the hub. If the hub can switch only one message at a time, the hub may act like a bottleneck. If the nodes transmit data at a faster rate than the hub can switch it, then the hub buffers may overflow, and data from the nodes may be lost. The hub is the critical network component. Most central hubs incorporate parallel switching for use in high-volume environments.

Since all traffic passes through a hub on the way to its destination, the hub is a useful point for regenerating signal levels. Noise that's acquired from a copper cable run can be eliminated by having the hub work as a repeater in a network. Then, as a repeater, it can also be used to segregate—or extend—the length of a LAN.

Notice that each node in a star topology is connected in a point-to-point arrangement with the hub. A node need only know the physical address of a hub in order to communicate with any other node. The hub, however, needs to know the physical address of all nodes, so that when it receives a data frame it can forward it on to the correct physical location. In other words, the hub may also work as a router in a LAN.

It's typical to have Ethernet running on a star LAN. If a hub is also used as a router or bridge, it can be configured to connect the Ethernet LAN to a Token Ring LAN. In this case, the topology is of a hybrid nature (meaning that two or more physical topologies comprise the network) and nodes on the different types of networks will be able to communicate.

Hubs do all of the above and more. The options available are almost endless, with some hubs having stackable capabilities so that you can add additional ports at a rate equal to the growth of your network. Other hubs consist of circuit cards which slip into slots of a chassis, so you can add functionality—router or gateway capabilities—as needed. And there's no need to bring the network down to add the electronics, since the chassis upgrades are "hot swappable," which means you add or remove the circuit cards without removing power. This keeps the network running while you do the upgrade.

Hubs come in several varieties. The following reviews the most common types:

Passive Hubs

- **Passive Hubs:** A passive hub requires no power and is used to organize wiring in a room or building. A patch panel is a passive hub.

Active Hubs

- **Active Hubs:** Active hubs regenerate data signals. They are used to link coaxial cable segments, or to subdivide larger UTP-based LANs. They require power and typically come with multiple ports for node connections.

Switching Hubs

- **Switching Hubs:** These allow any port on the hub to be logically connected to any other port on a hub. This provides greater use of the available bandwidth on the network by assigning ports their own Ethernet segment.

Finally, the hub requires some sort of management as it grows. The more sophisticated hubs allow you to configure ports on the fly; that is, with software. This saves the time of having to actually go to the wiring closet and move an RJ-45 connector from one port to another.

The reliability of the star is directly related to the hub. It's not unusual for several layers of switching redundancy to be built into the hub. This saves the entire network from crashing. A recent trend in star topologies has been to reduce the complexity of the hub by distributing some of the work to nodes. This degrades an otherwise simple topology by complicating the nodes (and increasing cost), and requiring a more complex routing protocol.

Any of the physical media is suitable for star topologies, and any of the common character and bit-oriented protocols work well.

Ring Topology

Ring topologies offer much versatility. The nodes are connected into a continuous loop, and data is passed from node to node, usually flowing in one direction as shown in Figure 1-4. Message transmission uses one of two techniques. The transmitting node gains access to the ring and sends the message to the receive node, and the receive node removes the message. In the second technique, the sender transmits the message and the receiver makes a copy of the message, rather than removing it from the ring. The message returns to the transmitter and serves as an acknowledgment that it was received.

> **NOTE**
>
> A ring topology connects the nodes in a continuous loop. Data flows around the ring in one direction.

Rings have a high future-growth potential. To add another node, you simply break the ring, and plug in the node. The ease with which changes can be made makes it a very flexible topology.

Speed and throughput are a function of the nodes. This network will only work as well as the poorest performing node. Assuming all nodes are of similar integrity, efficiencies run quite high, with +90% throughput common. Routing decisions are quite simple since data travels in only one direction. The nodes—which monitor routing—can be made simpler, and dedicated to the primary task of transmitting and receiving data.

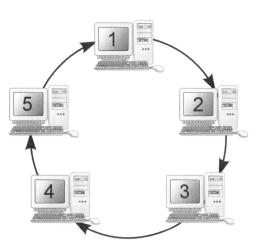

Figure 1-4: Ring Topology

The major disadvantage of ring topologies is their lack of reliability. If one node fails, the whole system may fail. In anticipation of this, ring designers use data-path redundancies. In Figure 1-5, the link between nodes 1 and 2 is broken. Data is rerouted around the break, and onto the spare ring. Once the break is bypassed, data returns to the primary ring.

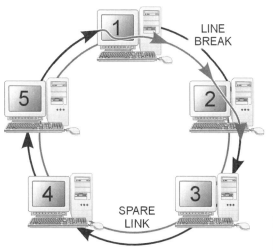

Figure 1-5: Spare Ring Topology

Another drawback of ring networks is that if a node is added, the ring must be broken. Network message flow can continue by bypassing the node, but eventually the node will have to be actively wired into the network to ensure its operational status. During this time, the network is down.

token passing

fixed slots

delay insertion

> Three basic techniques are used for gaining access to a ring network: **token passing**, **fixed slots**, and **delay insertion**.

In token passing, the token presents control of the network to the node holding the token. The token may be offered to each node sequentially, or the nodes may contend for it.

The fixed-slot technique divides the ring channel into fixed slots that circulate around the ring. If a slot arrives at a node that has data to transmit, it fills the slot; or the node may remove data from the slot. If the data is addressed to that node, it removes the data and the now-empty slot moves on to be filled by a node with a message to send.

The delay-insertion technique delays incoming messages. During the delay time, a node can transmit data. Once the delayed messages arrive at the node, the transmitter is turned off and data that didn't get transmitted is stored in a transmit buffer. The node also contains a receive buffer. If the node is unable to process the received messages before the transmitter is turned back on, they are stored in the receive buffer.

Token passing is easy to implement and widely used. Unfortunately, if not carefully monitored, throughput can nosedive with a corresponding increase in overhead. Delay insertion is very efficient, but requires more complex, and expensive, nodes.

Token Ring topologies are attributed to IBM. They have used them successfully for years, and the main reason for that success is that they were used appropriately; that is, in a small environment in which there was a need for predictability and control of which nodes had access to the network. The topology fell out of favor for some years because network managers tried to replace Ethernet LANs with Token Ring (Token Ring LANs were running at 16 Mbps, while Ethernet ran at 10 Mbps) with the intent of speeding up their networks.

It didn't work. On a bit-by-bit basis, a 16M Token Ring LAN will have higher delays than a 10 Mbps Ethernet LAN. On the surface, then, the Token Ring solution didn't make sense. But you have to look a bit deeper than simply speed and delays. The access methods used with Token Ring offer advantages that Ethernet will never have—but things change.

Ring topologies are now an important part of distributed LANs. Typically, several Ethernet LANs connect to the ring, which is used as a backbone for connecting the Ethernet networks. The ring media is fiber optic and runs at a speed of 100 Mbps (FDDI), much faster than 10 Mbps Ethernet "nodes" connected to its ports—and equal to the 100 Mbps data rates of Fast Ethernet.

Any physical media can be used with rings. They lend themselves particularly well to fiber-optic systems.

Wireless Topology

Wireless uses the atmosphere as the communication medium. Wireless technologies have been around for many years, but only in the last several have wireless LANs begun to predominate.

A **wireless topology** is not fixed since the media is the atmosphere. A wireless topology may use one of several methods for generating data signals that propagate through the atmosphere. The most common are radio frequency (RF), microwave, and infrared. RF data signals are closely associated with the IEEE emerging standards for wireless LANs, referred to as the IEEE 802.11 series of standards. Microwaves, normally associated with parabolic antennas mounted on a building, are used to transport data across long distances, such as across a town or campus. Infrared is most commonly associated with the Bluetooth standard used to connect peripherals, as well as other computers, to a computer.

Figure 1-6 shows a typical wireless topology using the IEEE 802.11 protocol. The computer workstations are equipped with a wireless card in an available expansion slot. The card is configured for networking in the same manner as a wired network adapter. That is, it's assigned a unique address and protocol. To send and receive signals, the adapter has a built-in antenna that may protrude from the card or be encapsulated in the casing of the card to avoid damage. The same antenna is used to send and receive data.

An AP performs a function similar to a hub in a wired network. It serves as a common point for routing data signals. There are some notable differences. First, the AP is not passive. It sends signals to all wireless cards within its range and keeps track of who is out there. The AP needs to know because it determines a sequence that the workstations must follow in order to transmit data frames.

Next, the AP does some lower-layer protocol conversions. In a standard Ethernet (wired) network, nodes gain access by detecting collisions on a network. In a wireless Ethernet LAN, nodes gain access by avoiding collisions. The nodes check to see if any other station is sending data. If there is, the node waits and tries later. If no other node is sending data, the node will transmit. Wireless networks rely on collision avoidance. The nodes listen to determine whether the network is in use before transmitting data. If a wireless network will never be connected to a wired LAN, no protocol conversion between a collision detection scheme and a collision avoidance scheme is needed. But, typically, that's not the case.

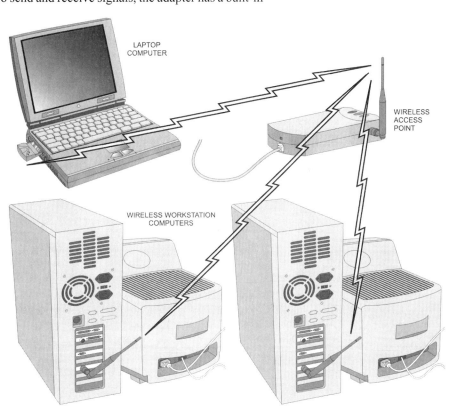

LAPTOP COMPUTER

WIRELESS ACCESS POINT

WIRELESS WORKSTATION COMPUTERS

Figure 1-6: Wireless Topology

Figure 1-7 shows a wireless LAN connected to a wired Ethernet LAN. Notice that the AP has an RJ-45 connection leading back to a wired hub. In order to make the conversion between the different access methods, most APs incorporate a bridge. A bridge is used to convert from one Data Link layer protocol to another, such as from collision detection to collision avoidance, or from collision detection to token-based.

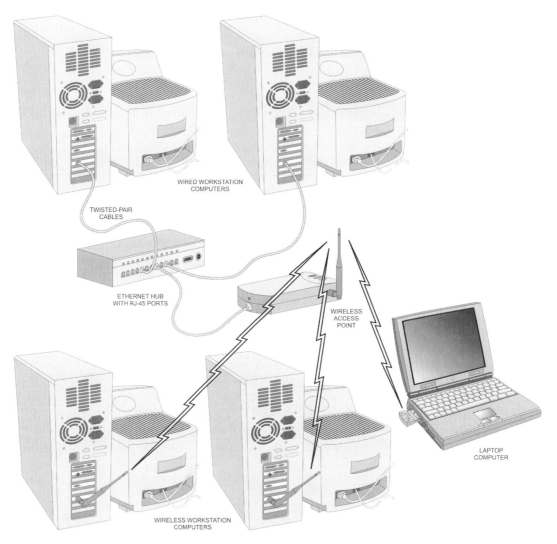

WIRED WORKSTATION
COMPUTERS

TWISTED-PAIR
CABLES

ETHERNET HUB
WITH RJ-45 PORTS

WIRELESS
ACCESS
POINT

LAPTOP
COMPUTER

WIRELESS WORKSTATION
COMPUTERS

Figure 1-7: Wireless LAN Connected to a Wired LAN

Notice that the topology used in a wireless network is a star. All workstations are connected to a central AP.

Nodes in a wireless network connect to an access point.

Wireless LANs using the IEEE 802.11b protocol operate at up to 11 Mbps. This is near the same speed as conventional Ethernet (10 Mbps). Recently, the cost of a wireless solution has dropped to the point that it's competitive with wired solutions. In terms of flexibility, wireless offers the greatest opportunities. A single AP can have a practical maximum of 15 to 30 workstations assigned to it (the standard specifies a theoretical maximum of 64 users). The range of a wireless LAN varies widely according to the vendor. The standard specifies a minimum range at 11 Mbps at 50 meters. At longer ranges, the data rate falls back to lower speeds. A range of 500 meters is not uncommon at a data rate of 2 Mbps. The IEEE 802.11 protocol is described in detail in Chapter 2.

─ NOTE ─

The physical interface used with wireless networks is an antenna.

Bluetooth, also described in Chapter 2, is a competing wireless implementation to IEEE 802.11. Bluetooth holds considerable promise because it can be used to connect about anything to a computer—a digital camera, printer, scanner, or another computer. In fact, the time may come when the connectors (serial, parallel, USB, or P/S2 ports) found on the back of a computer may disappear. Bluetooth sends data at 723.2 kbps. The range of Bluetooth devices are limited to 10 meters.

The topology used with Bluetooth is a star. One Bluetooth device is used to coordinate transmitting slots among the connected devices. A maximum of seven devices can be active at any one time using Bluetooth. More devices can be attached, but only seven at a time can be active.

Range and speed are the limiting factors of Bluetooth. But IEEE 802.11 is range limited as well. If a workstation—such as a notebook computer—is moved too far away from the AP, then it will be out of the network. Both technologies are quite reliable and inexpensive. The cost and effort to add or delete nodes is comparable to adding or deleting nodes in a wired LAN.

Microwave networks encompass an array of topologies. When used in a LAN, or in a CAN, a microwave system is little more than a relay station for data signals. But microwave networks can be used to send data around the globe via satellites.

> For more in-depth information about satellite systems and the techniques used in many microwave technologies refer to the Electronic Reference Shelf—"Satellite Communication" located on the CD that accompanies this book.

hierarchical topology

Hierarchical Topology

A **hierarchical topology** is composed of one or more of the discrete topologies discussed previously (bus, star, ring, or mesh topologies). For example, it's not unusual to have several star networks connected to a ring network. The ring provides a common interconnection for the star networks. Figure 1-8 shows such an example.

> **NOTE**
>
> A hierarchical topology is a combination of bus, star, ring, or mesh topologies.

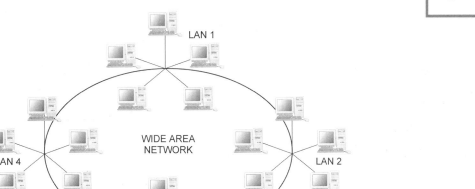

Figure 1-8: Multiple Topologies Comprise a Hierarchical Topology

By connecting networks together in a hierarchical topology, networks can grow as the need arises. Through addressing schemes, a hierarchical network also allows several networks to be physically connected but logically separated.

The cost and reliability considerations for a hierarchical topology are the same as for the discrete topologies. A star network, for example, is only as reliable as the hub connecting the nodes. And if a series of star networks are connected to a ring, the star networks may lose connectivity with one another if the ring goes down.

There's no practical limit to the size or complexity of a hierarchical network. A global company may have many types of topologies in thousands of locations. The various locations can be connected together by a large mesh topology like the Internet, or be connected to a high-speed ring that's administered by a common long distance carrier.

Logical Topology

> A **logical topology** is a reference to the way that data is sent across a network. It can be implemented on any physical topology such as star, ring, or mesh.

A common implementation is a logical bus topology. Most Ethernet LANs use a logical bus on a physical star. Figure 1-9 shows an example.

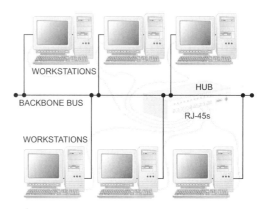

Figure 1-9: Logical Bus Topology

The physical star consists of a hub with nodes connected to it. But within the hub is a common backplane that connects together all of the hub ports. The backplane is a common connection point for all nodes connected to the hub. When a node has data to send, the data packets go to the hub and are available to all nodes via the common backplane. Only the node that the packet is addressed to will accept the packet; all other nodes will reject the packet. So, while the network is structured in a physical star topology, data is sent and received over a logical bus within the hub.

A physical star may also use a logical mesh topology to send and receive data. Some hubs have the capability to dynamically link any two ports at any time. This type of hub is called a switching hub. A switching hub uses a logical mesh to send and receive data. Port connection within the hub can be built and torn down as the need arises. The switching activity is accomplished with software and uses the address of the receiving and sending nodes as the basis for the connection. Since any node on the physical star can be connected to any other node on the star, the network uses a physical mesh topology to transport data.

The Internet is actually a combination of a physical mesh and a logical mesh. The telephone network infrastructure comprises the physical topology while the unique addresses assigned to all computers and devices connected to the Internet comprise the logical mesh topology.

DATA SIGNALS

Digital data is preferred over analog data because noise and distortion are easier to remove, it's in the same format as computer data, and the sharp edges of square waves provide more reliable bit recognition.

In its earliest form, electrical communication was digital. The telegraph of Samuel Morse operated by alternately opening and closing a switch. When the switch was closed, current flowed in the telegraph line. The **Morse code** characters were composed of dots and dashes that, in an open-and-close type circuit, described digital square waves. Oddly, it was the simplicity of telegraphy that ultimately resulted in its demise as a commercial method of communication. As communication systems became more sophisticated, the code associated with Morse code proved to be quite slow and cumbersome for the fast operations of machines.

Morse code

The ASCII and EBCDIC codes described in Chapter 11 as well as a variety of others originated with Morse code. Most of the codes in use today are of a digital nature. These codes were originally in an analog format, usually in the form of speech. To get a clear understanding of why digital communications have had such a special place in data communications, it's necessary to analyze the structure of analog and digital signals.

Analog Signals

An analog signal is shown in Figure 1-10. It has a peak value of 1 V, a frequency of 1 kHz, and a **period** of 1 ms. As an ac waveform, it has positive and negative alternations, and it recurs in time in a predictable manner. It was stated that the period of the signal is 1 ms. This was found by taking the inverse of the frequency, or:

period

$$T = 1/F$$

measured at the 0-degree crossover points. But the conventional method of measuring the pulse width, or time of an alternation, is to measure from the 10% point at the leading edge of the signal and the 90% point at the trailing edge, as shown in Figure 1-10. The pulse width at these points is 0.4 ms. Because of the sine structure of the ac wave, it is extremely difficult to determine how much the voltage level is since the amplitude is different for each moment in time through the alternation. The same can be said of the period, pulse width, or time. If the point at which the pulse width is measured is taken with respect to voltage levels around the alternations, then the pulse width becomes as relative as the amplitude measurements. The extreme variety of change in an analog signal makes it a difficult waveform with which to establish a predictable pattern suitable for digital equipment.

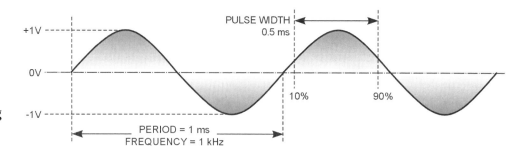

Figure 1-10: Analog Signals of Constant Variation

As a practical example of the problem of analog signals in data communications, consider an ac sine wave with a frequency of 1 kHz and a peak amplitude of 6 volts. If this signal were transmitted through an EIA/TIA-232 interface, it could create a considerable amount of confusion. The interface may not recognize amplitude levels of less than 3 volts, so the amplitude may be cut in half. Now, if a synchronizing pulse had been sent with the signal, it may be lost. The portion of the alternations not cut off will be transmitted as bits. Due to the sine of the alternations, the time between bits will not be equal to the time of a bit and the receiver may fail to correctly identify the proper bit times.

Ac waveforms of any type—analog or digital—are susceptible to **noise distortion** enroute to the receiver. But analog data distorted by noise presents a particularly difficult problem because the noise is difficult to remove without causing further distortion of the signal.

In fact, in some types of channels, the noise may be of a frequency that passes through the line easier than the signal. The receiver may reject the signal and accept only noise—in which case, the receiver will futilely process noise. The constant change of analog signals and the problem with removing noise from these signals are their most serious drawbacks.

An analog signal is not without redeeming qualities. A 1 kHz sine wave has a bandwidth of 1 kHz. As will be shown shortly, a 1 kHz square wave used in digital systems has an 11 kHz bandwidth. An analog system would be the best choice to use in channels with a scarce amount of bandwidth. A channel with a 10 kHz bandwidth can accommodate ten analog signals but can barely contain one digital signal.

Digital Signals

Square waves are used in digital communications because they're representative of the base two, binary number system. **Binary numbers** consist of 1 and 0, and a square wave is either on or off, high or low. It's the equivalency to binary that makes square waves the reasonable choice of data communications. A square wave is relatively easy to generate as well as to code to represent alphanumeric systems. Of course, analog signals can be coded, too; but keep in mind that the first communication systems—telegraph and, later, the Teletype—were digital systems. Much of the development in data processing can be traced back to an effort to improve the transmission and reception of telegraph signals. Since the data being transmitted was digital, it follows that the machines developed to automate telegraphy were digital systems.

Figure 1-11 illustrates a square wave of 1-volt peak amplitude, a frequency of 1 kHz, and a period of 1 ms. In terms of basic specifications it's no different than the sine wave discussed earlier. But those are about the only similarities shared by the two waveforms. The pulse width of a square wave—the time of a single bit—is measured in a manner similar to that of a sine wave, except it doesn't matter whether the measurement is taken on the leading or trailing edge (assuming, of course, that both edges are identical). If the pulse width is measured between 10% and 90%, or 40% and 60%, the pulse width is the same. The vertical slope of leading and trailing edges provides transmitting and receiving equipment with a very predictable waveform. Compare pulse-width measurements of square waves to sine waves, whose pulse widths are open to interpretation, depending on where the measurement is taken.

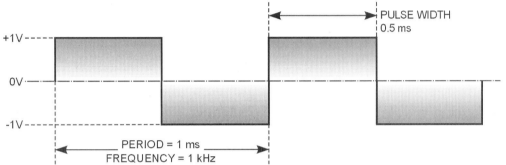

Figure 1-11: Predictable Square Waves

Having said that, consider data bits switched through wide area networking machines—routers, for example—that are clocked at GHz rates. At high data rates, bit edges are all that matters. The bits have been manipulated by coding and modulation beyond recognition so that the 10%/90% measuring points are critical.

Undesired noise may be superimposed on a square wave as shown in Figure 1-12. The square wave has been heavily distorted. The **regenerator**, or **repeater**, is an in-line amplifier that boosts the signal level and restores the square wave to its original shape. Many network hubs on the market today incorporate repeaters as a matter of course. The regenerator can contain an **astable multivibrator** (Schmitt trigger) designed with threshold voltages equal to the original amplitude of the signal. At the output of the regenerator, the square wave is clean of noise and distortion. If the distance from transmitter to receiver is long, there may be many repeaters along the way. Since the repeaters regenerate a new signal at each point, the overall performance of the system and the quality of the data are much higher than for analog systems.

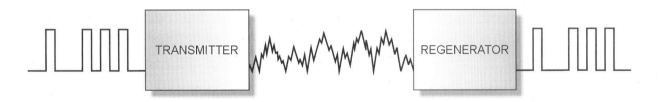

Figure 1-12: Digital Data is Less Sensitive to Noise than Analog Signals

Can repeaters be used with analog systems? They can, and frequently are. But the disadvantage to regenerating an analog signal is that the corrupting noise is amplified along with the signal. At best, analog repeaters serve to compensate for losses resulting from long cable lengths, but do very little to eliminate or decrease noise.

You may wonder why the analog repeater can't simply restore the signal to its original shape, since this is essentially what a digital repeater does. To answer this, think about the definitions of analog and digital. A digital signal is composed of only two states, whereas an analog signal contains an infinite number of states. No matter how complex a digital waveform becomes, only one of two state changes (even if it occurs multiple times within a bit) will ever be used to represent some part of the data. In the analog signal—take your pick as to how many of the infinite possibilities are actually incorporated. The only way to be sure is to know what was originally transmitted, and if you knew that, repeaters wouldn't be needed since the destination node would also know.

Digital square waves have the disadvantage of requiring at least five times as much bandwidth as analog.

The disadvantage of a digital signal is the wide bandwidth required to transmit it. Figure 1-13 depicts the components that are combined to create a 1 kHz square wave. Square waves are composed of an infinite number of odd harmonics of a fundamental frequency. In Figure 1-13, the fundamental frequency is 1 kHz, so the odd harmonics 3 kHz, 5 kHz, 7 kHz, and so forth, are summed together to create the square wave.

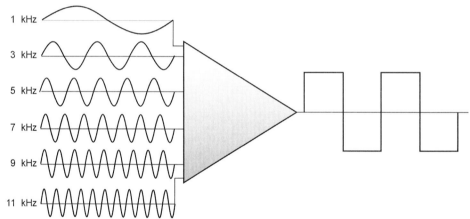

Figure 1-13: Square Wave Produced from a Fundamental Sine Wave and its Odd Harmonics

In practice, harmonics beyond the fifth order (11 kHz, in this example) have a negligible effect on the structure of the square wave and can be ignored. Each alternation of the square wave is composed of two vertical sides (the leading and trailing edges) and the horizontal peak. The sides are representative of a rapid change, which is descriptive of the higher-order harmonics: The higher frequencies are primarily responsible for the vertical slope of the leading and trailing edges.

The flat top of the square wave is representative of the lower-order harmonics: the lower frequencies are responsible for the horizontal peak of a square wave.

In order to transmit the square wave through a channel, it must have a bandwidth at least equal to the fifth harmonic of the frequency of the square wave. If the bandwidth isn't wide enough, one or more of the higher-order harmonics will be attenuated and the square wave distorted. Harmonic distortion is illustrated in Figure 1-14.

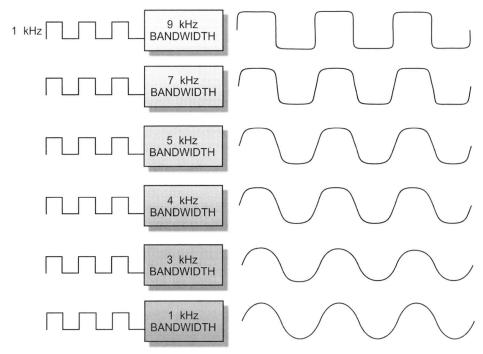

**Figure 1-14:
Inadequate Bandwidth
Causes Harmonic
Distortion**

When the 1 kHz square wave is passed through a circuit (**communication channel**) with a 9 kHz bandwidth, the corners of the square wave are rounded slightly, but the square wave remains flat on top. The loss of the 11 kHz fifth harmonic has caused the rounding of the corners, as well as increased the rise and fall time of the square wave. If the same 1 kHz square wave is transmitted through a channel with a 7 kHz bandwidth, the rounding of the corners is more severe and the rise and fall times increase. The square wave takes on the characteristics of the first-order harmonic when it's applied to a channel with a 1 kHz bandwidth. At this point, what was once a digital signal with sharply defined edges is now an analog signal whose characteristic amplitude and pulse width are open to the interpretation of the receiver.

The wide bandwidth requirements of digital signals are a disadvantage to digital communications. However, the disadvantage can easily be turned into an opportunity to improve the performance of a data system. It was mentioned earlier that channel capacity (the volume of data) is proportional to bandwidth. This means that the greater the bandwidth, the greater is the volume of data that can be transmitted. Various multiplexing schemes have been devised to utilize as much of the available bandwidth as possible to transmit many channels of data through a single, wide-bandwidth channel.

┌─ NOTE ──────────────────
│ Digital data is preferred over analog data be-
│ cause noise and distortion are easier to remove,
│ it's in the same format as computer data, and the
│ sharp edges of square waves provide more reli-
│ able bit recognition.
└──────────────────────────

Increasingly, the terms "data communication" and "digital communication" are used interchangeably. The digital structure of **machine language**, the superior quality and performance of digital systems, and simpler digital multiplexing methods have combined to make digital methods the choice data structure for networks. The telephone system still retains a small segment of analog networks, but these are being gradually replaced with digital networks.

MEDIA INFRASTRUCTURE

Transmission media is the physical path data travels enroute to its destination. There are four basic mediums: twisted-pair wire, coaxial cable, fiber-optic cable, and radio frequencies (microwaves). For each medium, there are characteristics that make it a better choice than another. It would be an oversimplification to say that one is better than another, because there are several factors to consider when selecting a transmission media.

┌─ **NOTE** ──────────────────────┐

Transmission media refers to the channel data travels enroute to the receiving station. Transmission media include coaxial cable, twisted wire pairs, fiber optics, and the atmosphere.

└─────────────────────────────────┘

The cost of media is certainly a primary concern. Too often, the temptation to use the exotic or superior performer is given into, when a cheaper, although less glamorous, medium would have done an acceptable job. An example is to lease satellite time to send data across the country, when the long distance carriers could probably transmit everything at a significantly lower cost.

Compatibility with existing media and machines demands a thoughtful analysis. If an extension to an existing network is under consideration, and the network is wired with coaxial cable, then it probably wouldn't be a good idea to wire the extension with twisted pairs. Existing media, also called the cabling infrastructure, accounts for about 30% of the cost of a network. Considerable thought must be given to the initial infrastructure because future changes that include a different cable type will be expensive.

Signal losses, or attenuation, due to a wrong media selection require an expensive fix: The entire medium has to be replaced, or an extensive amount of repeaters, filters, and shielding must be installed. The effects of noise that a signal may be exposed to can be minimized with the correct media choice.

Attenuation results in a gradual loss of signal strength from one end of a cable to another. The loss is measured in decibels (dB). There are two ways of looking at signal loss in a cable. The first is based on characteristics of the cable and is stated as dB/m, dB/km, or dB/ft. These specs are readily available from cable manufacturers, but they should correspond to certain accepted standards in the networking business. (For an overview of decibels, see Chapter 12.)

The other way of viewing attenuation is to measure the loss of signal integrity across a cable run. For example, the losses from a node placed 100 feet from a hub will be greater than from one placed 10 feet from the hub. When measured within a network, the losses are specific to the protocol and media type.

The **impedance** of a cable directly affects losses. Impedance, measured in ohms, is the total amount of opposition in a cable that a data signal must overcome. The higher the impedance, the higher the losses. Since impedance is influenced by resistive as well as reactive characteristics of the cable, it will vary for each cable type. The frequency (in BPS) will also affect losses.

The **bandwidth characteristics** of the medium are an important factor in making a selection because bandwidth in networking is synonymous with channel capacity and data rates. Twisted pairs are the least expensive cable medium but, depending on their implementation (CAT 3 versus CAT 5 UTP, for example), may also have restricted bandwidth; fiber optics have the widest bandwidth but are also the most expensive cable medium.

Cabling also affects the time that a signal takes to arrive at the receiving node. This characteristic is called propagation delay, and is stated in microseconds. The delay, in either copper-based or optical cables, is appreciable and will ultimately limit the physical size of the network. The implication is that larger networks require cabling with shorter delays, or must come with in-line equipment that has signal regeneration capabilities.

Noise immunity of a cable may be important depending on the environment surrounding the infrastructure. An industrial environment is likely to generate considerably more electrical interference than an office environment. On the other hand, a building that's extensively wired for networking may have a problem with crosstalk. **Crosstalk** is the coupling of electrical energy between wires lying in a parallel plane.

The topology of a network may affect your decision on the type of media. Bus networks, for example, require that the ends of the bus be terminated with a proper resistance so that data signals aren't reflected back through the wire thereby creating distortion.

Other factors to consider when evaluating the cable plant are ambient temperature, the type of data to be exchanged on the network (voice, data, video, etc.), future growth, and mobility of the users. It costs about three times as much to move a network connection as it does to relocate a telephone connection. The reason is that telephone connections are typically already installed, whereas network connections are typically installed when they're needed.

Twisted pairs, coaxial cable, and fiber optics are analyzed in the following sections. The final criteria for selecting the medium are ultimately determined by the level of performance required of the communications system.

Unshielded Twisted Pair

Twisted-pair cables consist of copper wire twisted into a spiral shape as shown in Figure 1-15. They're normally associated with telecommunications because it's the most common type of subscriber loop wiring. **Twisted pairs** have been used extensively in networking since they're a major component of the installed telephone network. Using the existing twisted-pair cables for data communications represents a significant cost savings. However, as you'll see shortly, this isn't a good idea.

Twisted pairs may be 22, 24, or 26 **American Wire Gauge (AWG)**. The copper wire (solid or stranded) is insulated by a polyethylene or polyvinyl chloride jacket. The wires are twisted together to reduce noise and, in particular, crosstalk. Recall that crosstalk is the magnetic induction of a signal from wires lying in a parallel plane. The twisting of the wires causes the unwanted crosstalk signals to cancel.

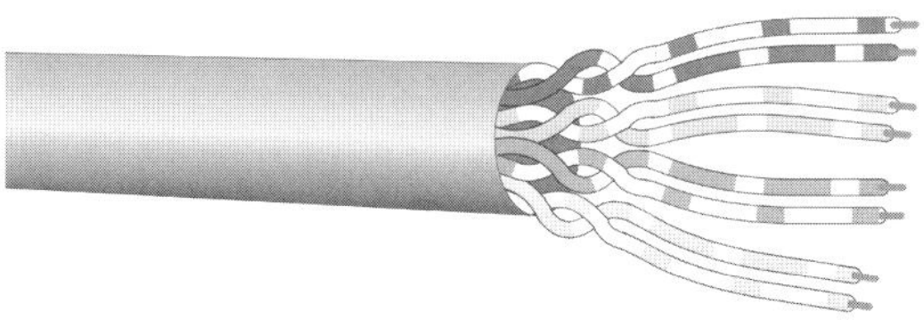

Twisted pairs, referred to in this book as unshielded twisted pairs (UTP), represent the largest installed base of cable media used in networks. Not only is there a lot of it out there, it's also capable of handling data rates from Gbps, all the way down to voice band frequencies.

Figure 1-15: Twisted-Pair Wire

> ┌─ NOTE ───────────────────
> Twisted pair is the most widely installed media. Its size ranges from 16 to 24 AWG, and may be found in a single-pair cable or up to 6,000 pairs may be encased in a single sheath. Unshielded twisted pair (UTP) is the preferred cabling for LANs. UTP is classified by the EIA/TIA according to categories. Whenever possible, use CAT5 UTP.

Twisted-pair wires outside a residence are of a larger gauge. They may be stretched above ground between telephone poles or buried beneath the ground. Buried cable is cable that's buried in the earth without underground conduit. You may also see twisted-pair wires referred to as underground cable. This cable runs through ducts installed underground. The cables running outside, whether above ground or underground, are 16 to 19 AWG. They're designed to carry thousands of telephone channels and, in order to handle such a large volume, the twisted pairs are grouped in as many as 6,000 pairs encased in a plastic sheath.

As mentioned earlier, twisted pairs are the most widely used transmission medium due to the sheer numbers installed in homes and businesses. But of all the media, twisted-pair wire is the easiest to work with as well. In order to make a connection or splice, it's necessary to just strip the insulation, connect the wire, and solder.

When speaking of twisted-pair wiring, it's important to distinguish between voice- and network-grade cabling. Structurally, the two are identical, and voice can be transmitted equally well over either type. The difference is the mechanical connection on each end of the cable. If you have a PC at home connected to the Internet, you're using voice-grade twisted pairs (actually, the wire pair may or may not be twisted).

If you have several PCs connected together in a network, you're using (or should be using) network-grade twisted pairs. We'll take a look at both types of cabling.

There are several disadvantages to consider with voice-grade twisted pairs. The data rates that can be transmitted through the medium are around 1 Mbps for unconditioned cable installed in a residence or business. With conditioning and special care, the data rate can be increased to about 10 Mbps for voice-grade cabling, and in excess of 100 Mbps for data cabling.

Conditioning refers to the deliberate loading of twisted pairs with inductance. The most common loading is 19H-88 loaded pair. This means 19 AWG cable is loaded with 88 mH (millihenrys) of inductance every 6,000 feet.

The effects of 19H-88 loading are shown in Figure 1-16.

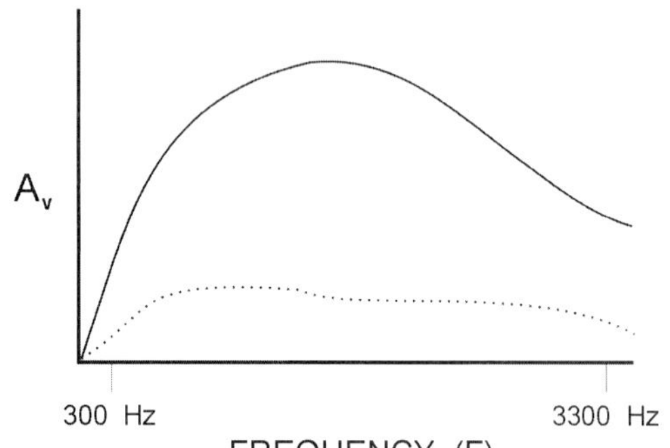

A_v

300 Hz   3300 Hz

FREQUENCY (F)

Figure 1-16: Effects Of 19H-88 Loading

The solid line on the graph illustrates the **frequency response** of an unloaded line. The range of frequencies in a telephone voice channel are from 300 Hz to 3,300 Hz.

The unloaded line shows a sharp increase in signal attenuation over the channel. The dotted line indicates the response of the same channel that's been 19H-88 loaded. The insertion of the induction increases the attenuation over the frequency range of the voice channel, but it also results in a flat response. The graph in Figure 1-16 illustrates one of the several methods of line conditioning.

For more in-depth information about other methods of line conditioning refer to the Electronic Reference Shelf—"The Telephone System" located on the CD that accompanies this book.

Another disadvantage of voice-grade twisted pairs is the rather narrow bandwidth (about 100 kHz). The narrow bandwidth is a serious disadvantage since it ultimately restricts the volume of data that can be transmitted. There are a couple of reasons that voice-grade UTP is bandwidth restricted. The maximum distance from telephone to switching centers is often violated, usually by the telephone subscriber. Connections made within a house or business are often of poor quality resulting in signal losses. But the most important reason is that only two wires are used in a voice-grade connection. Some of the induced noise and crosstalk is eliminated by twisting the wires, which has the effect of canceling much of the noise, but it doesn't eliminate all of it. The single most important reason, though, is that voice-grade UTP was designed for voice communication. As you'll see shortly, network-grade UTP, even though it's structurally identical to voice UTP, extends data rates by taking a preventive approach to eliminating problems.

Figure 1-17 shows a UTP cable used for networking. This is the type of cable used in a typical Ethernet LAN. It's also 22, 24, or 26 AWG unshielded copper (solid or stranded) wire. A connection between two nodes on a network will have eight wires (four cable pairs). Normally, four pairs are sheathed within a polyvinyl chloride jacket.

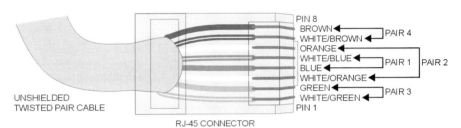

Figure 1-17: UTP Networking Cable

The wires are segregated into pairs, which are then twisted and labeled as transmit and receive pairs. In each pair, one wire carries the transmission, while the other wire carries an inverted copy of the transmission. Hence, when a node sends data, the actual transmission is carried on Tx+ while an inverted copy of the transmission is carried on Tx−. In other words, all transmission on an LAN wired with UTP cable includes an opposite mirror of the original transmission.

When a node transmits, both signals propagate on the cable at the same rate and are influenced by the same factors. This is because the wires are constructed identically and are twisted about one another. If external noise induces a noise signal into the wires, it will be induced into both in an identical manner.

Figure 1-18 shows the sequence of events as a signal is transmitted from a node. As you can see, the signal is first inverted and both signals are sent at the same time. Enroute to the receiver, a noise spike causes distortion of the data bits. Notice that the noise affects both Tx+ and Tx− in the same manner. When the signals arrive at the receiving node, the Tx− signal is inverted back to its original polarity and summed with the Tx+ signal. The induced noise on Tx− is inverted as well, then summed along with the Tx+ noise. The noise spikes are summed as reverse polarity signals that are identical in all aspects except for polarity. The summing action eliminates the noise spikes.

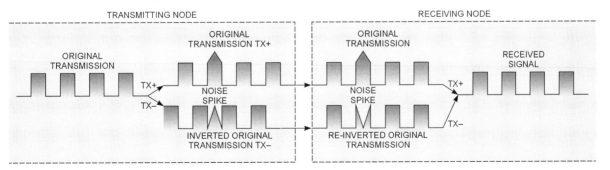

Figure 1-18: Summing Reverse Polarity Noise Spikes

Since UTP uses separate receive and transmit wire pairs, it's important not to connect the Tx+ of one station to the Tx+ of another station. If this happens, both stations will eventually try to transmit to one another on the same wire at the same time.

By using two wires for both the transmit and receive signals, network-grade UTP is able to virtually eliminate noise, including crosstalk.

Ethernet is designed so that, ultimately, the link between the two stations will crash. The IEEE 802.3 protocol (see Chapter 12), as part of the Data Link layer concept, is designed for straight-through wiring from network device (a hub) to network stations (a personal computer). Straight-through wiring means that you attach RJ-45 connectors to the ends of the UTP cable, and then plug the connectors into the station ports. No special precautions are needed on your part. The wire pair switch is built into the hub. A hub that's compliant with the standard will reverse the Tx wires at one end of the cable so that they connect to the Rx wires at the other end. Compliant hubs are marked with an X at each port.

If similar network devices are connected—two hubs, for example—a crossover cable must be connected between them. The crossover is a connector that performs the switch between Tx and Rx. Note that a link requiring a crossover must have an odd number of crossover cables, or the transmit and receive wire pair switch won't occur.

UTP Standards

UTP is differentiated according to specifications published by the Electronic Industry Association (EIA) and the Telecommunications Industry Association (TIA). The standard used most often is EIA/TIA-568. The standard details the types of connectors used with UTP, how far the cable must be located from electrical sources, how to install the cable to prevent damage to personnel or equipment, and other factors that may affect the system's quality.

An often repeated UTP specification is EIA/TIA Categories for UTP. These categories define the minimum quality level requirements for various applications of the cable. The cable is then specified by the category. The categories are as follows:

- **Category 1:** 22 or 24 AWG untwisted wire. This is common telephone cable and is used to connect many telephones to phone drops as well as connect extensions within a building.

- **Category 2:** 22 or 24 solid wire, twisted pairs. CAT2 cable was the first networking UTP but is now considered obsolete. It supports data rates up to 1 Mbps and is not tested for crosstalk distortion.

- **Category 3:** 24 solid wire, twisted pairs. Originally used in IBM Token Ring LANs, CAT3 is seldom used outside an IBM environment, and has been replaced by CAT5 cabling. CAT3 is occasionally used in 10 Mbps Ethernet LANs as well as 4 Mbps Token Ring LANs. It has been tested for data rates up to 16 Mbps. The wire has a characteristic impedance of 100 ohms.

- **Category 4:** 22 or 24 AWG solid wire, twisted pairs. This category has been specified for up to 20 Mbps and is specific to 16 Mbps Token Ring LANs. The wire has a characteristic impedance of 100 ohms.

- **Category 5:** 22 or 24 AWG solid wire, twisted pairs. CAT5 cable has a characteristic impedance of 100 ohms and is specified for data rates up to 100 Mbps. This is the preferred cabling installation for Ethernet and Token Ring, and is recommended for all new installations, even if an existing LAN is running at 10 Mbps (Standard Ethernet speeds). If you choose to upgrade to the 100 Mbps Fast Ethernet, the cabling will already be installed and ready to go.

When you buy UTP, you need to know, in addition to the category, whether the cable is PVC or plenum rated, and whether the cabling scheme is compliant to EIA/TIA-568 A or B. "Plenum" rated UTP has a higher heat resistance rating so that it can be run in HVAC (Heating/Ventilation/Air Conditioning) plenum. PVC UTP without the plenum rating should be used when the cabling will be routed through walls, sub-flooring, or overhead—but not through heat plenum.

EIA/TIA-568A/B compliant refers to which of the four pairs in the UTP cable are designated as transmit, and which are designated as receive. Use the following as a guide:

- **EIA/TIA-568A:** 10Base-T (10 Mbps) and 100Base-TX (100 Mbps) devices transmit over pair 3, and receive over pair 2.

- **EIA/TIA-568B:** 10Base-T and 100Base-TX devices are configured to transmit over pair 2, and to receive over pair 3.

It's important to terminate all cables at a location according to the same standard, either A or B, but not both at the same facility. If you don't, you'll have a situation in which one device is trying to transmit along a wire connected to a transmit side of the receiving device; invariably, the two will try to transmit at the same time and the data will collide, eventually crashing the network.

UTP 4-Pair and 25-Pair Cabling Schemes

UTP in the LAN environment is installed using 4-pair or 25-pair cable. The larger bundle is used to connect together wiring closets or hubs that service different parts of a network. The smaller 4-pair cable is dedicated to network devices such as the connection between a hub and a personal computer. The jackets of either cable will vary in color, and may be orange, green, white, or blue. Table 1-1 illustrates a 4-pair color coding scheme.

Four of the eight wires will be solid colors of brown, blue, orange, and green. The other four wires will consist of a solid white base color and an accent color consisting of rings of the other four colors. When referring to the wires in a jacket, use the following convention:

Solid Color Wires: Blue (BL), Brown (BR), Green (GR), Orange (OR).

White Base Color with Accent: White/Color. For example, a white base with blue accent is written as white/blue (W/BL).

Table 1-1: Four-Pair Color Codes

Wire Color	EIA/TIA Pair	Ethernet Signal Use	
		568A	568B
White / Blue (W-BL)	Pair 1	Not Used	
Blue (BL)			
White / Orange (W-OR)	Pair 2	RX+	TX+
Orange (OR)		RX-	TX-
White / Green (W-GR)	Pair 3	TX+	RX+
Green (GR)		TX-	RX-
White / Brown (W-BR)	Pair 4	Not Used	
Brown (BR)			

As mentioned on the previous page, 25-pair cabling is used where many connections are run between two points. Wiring closets in two different locations will be connected with 25-pair cable. The fifty wires in each cable are identical to their four-pair counterpart in all aspects other than the color coding of the insulation. In Table 1-2, each wire is identified by two colors, and the convention for referring to the color is base color/accent color.

**Table 1-2:
Color Codes for
25 Wire Pairs**

Port Number	+-RX/TX	Color Code	RJ21 Pin Number	Punchdown In Number	Punchdown Out Number
1	RX+	White/Blue	26	A1	B1
	RX-	Blue/White	1	A2	B2
	TX+	White/Orange	27	A3	B3
	TX-	Orange/White	2	A4	B4
2	RX+	White/Green	28	A5	B5
	RX-	Green/White	3	A6	B6
	TX+	White/Brown	29	A7	B7
	TX-	Brown/White	4	A8	B8
3	RX+	White/Gray	30	A9	B9
	RX-	Gray/White	5	A10	B10
	TX+	Red/Blue	31	A11	B11
	TX-	Blue/Red	6	A12	B12
4	RX+	Red/Orange	32	A13	B13
	RX-	Orange/Red	7	A14	B14
	TX+	Red/Green	33	A15	B15
	TX-	Green/Red	8	A16	B16
5	RX+	Red/Brown	34	A17	B17
	RX-	Brown/Red	9	A18	B18
	TX+	Red/Gray	35	A19	B19
	TX-	Gray/Red	10	A20	B20
6	RX+	Black/Blue	36	A21	B21
	RX-	Blue/Black	11	A22	B22
	TX+	Black/Orange	37	A23	B23
	TX-	Orange/Black	12	A24	B24

Table 1-2:
Color Codes for 25
Wire Pairs (continued)

Port Number	+-RX/TX	Color Code	RJ21 Pin Number	Punchdown In Number	Punchdown Out Number
8	RX+	Black/Gray	40	A29	B29
	RX-	Gray/Black	15	A30	B30
	TX+	Yellow/Blue	41	A31	B31
	TX-	Blue/Yellow	16	A32	B32
9	RX+	Yellow/Orange	42	A33	B33
	RX-	Orange/Yellow	17	A34	B34
	TX+	Yellow/Green	43	A35	B35
	TX-	Green/Yellow	18	A36	B36
10	RX+	Yellow/Brown	44	A37	B37
	RX-	Brown/Yellow	19	A38	B38
	TX+	Yellow/Gray	45	A39	B39
	TX-	Gray/Yellow	20	A40	B40
11	RX+	Violet/Blue	46	A41	B41
	RX-	Blue/Violet	21	A42	B42
	TX+	Violet/Orange	47	A43	B43
	TX-	Orange/Violet	22	A44	B44

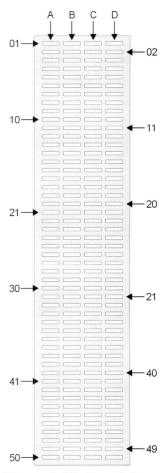

Figure 1-19: Punchdown for 25 Wire Pairs

For example, a wire with a green base color that has white rings imprinted on it is written as white/green (W/GR).

With a 25-pair cable, 12 devices can be connected (one of the wire pairs is not used). Each device requires two pairs designated as Tx+, Tx–, Rx+, and Rx–. In addition, the pairs must be mated. An RJ21 connector is one way to mate cable pairs. In addition to the color scheme used with the cable, Table 1-2 also shows how the cable transmit and receive pairs are mated to specific pins of the connector. Another method for mating cable pairs is to use a punchdown.

A **punchdown** is a device used to connect large cable runs, then to distribute wire pairs to network devices.

The wires are clamped to **bayonet pins** to hold them in place, and are distributed according to the scheme shown in Figure 1-19. All wires entering the punchdown do so on the "A" side and exit on the "B" side.

RJ-11 and RJ-45 Connectors

UTP 4-pair cables use an RJ-45 connector, pictured in Figure 1-20. Physically, it resembles an oversized telephone jack. Telephone connectors are specified as RJ-11. To make a cable, the insulation is stripped from the ends of each wire using a commercial wire stripping tool. The bare wires are then slipped into the connector, and an end piece, or cover, is snapped over the connector to retain the wires. Alternatively, the connector may be installed using a crimping tool.

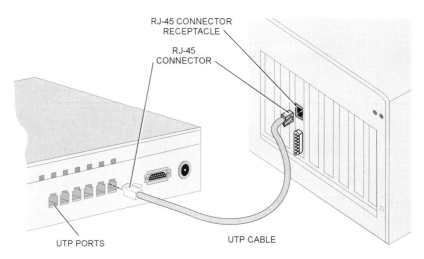

Figure 1-20: UTP RJ-45 Connector

It should be noted that while CAT5 UTP is widely used as networking media, it doesn't necessarily follow that RJ-45 connectors are used only with CAT5 cable. RJ-45 is a generic, 8-pin connector that may be found in any of the other categories of UTP as well. The connector may be used for single wire pairs, or in cases when only two wire pairs are needed.

> UTP may use an RJ-11 or an RJ-45 connector. An RJ-11 connector is used for voice UTP, whereas an RJ-45 connector is used for data UTP.

On a cost-per-foot basis, twisted pair is the cheapest medium. It offers an extensive amount of compatibility with the existing telephone network as well as with devices designed to work with the telephone network. However, it's not an acceptable practice to connect voice devices such as telephones to unused CAT5 UTP. Interference from the network cable may distort voice signals. In addition, using excess pairs for voice prevents their use for network connections if the need arises in the future. A disadvantage of UTP is that it's the least secure of all media types. It's as easy to **tap** a telephone line as it is to make a connection. A **security breach** is also difficult to detect.

Shielded Twisted Pair

STP is an abbreviation for **Shielded Twisted Pair**. It contains a metal shielding fully encircling the twisted pairs that's intended for reducing **ElectroMagnetic Interference** (**EMI**). EMI is produced by sources such as motors, generators, power lines, or high-wattage radio signals. The shielding—when grounded properly—causes a current to be induced in it from the interference. This same current will generate electromagnetic flux that induces an opposite polarity current into the twisted pairs. Since the two noise signals are of opposite polarities, they cancel, thereby eliminating the interfering noise.

The shielding may be either a metal foil (called Foil Twisted Pair, or FTP), or it may consist of a fine mesh of braided metal (called Screened Twisted Pair, or STP). STP using the foil shield is thinner, and somewhat easier to install, than the type that contains a braided shield. The braided shielding contributes to the bulk of the cable, which limits the bending radius in an installation. FTP is cheaper than STP, but the differences in installation savings can be negligible since both types must be carefully installed.

The reason that care must be taken is that STP works only as well as the shielding that encloses the twisted wires. The cable must be properly grounded to an earth ground that's neither too long, nor too short. If, at any point along the length of the cable, the foil becomes disrupted, the effectiveness of the shield diminishes. A disrupted shield may occur due to a tear in the shield, or it could be caused by a manufacturing defect that may not manifest itself until the cable is installed in the field. Other factors contribute to the shield's effectiveness as well. The frequency of the noise, the thickness of the shield, the ground connections, the cable's end connections, and the type of grounding will all affect the ability of the shield to protect the twisted pairs.

STP may be grounded at one or both ends of a connection. For high-frequency applications, both ends must be grounded in order to prevent the signal-carrying twisted pairs from inducing crosstalk into adjacent wires. The ground from end-to-end must be continuous.

If, during installation, the cable is pulled beyond the tensile strength of the shield, or if it's bent to the point that the strength is stressed, EMI will be radiated from the wire pairs, or be induced into them from an outside source.

UTP doesn't have these drawbacks. Its use of two transmit and receive wires virtually eliminates crosstalk, as well as outside magnetic field interference. It's also cheaper and easier to install. The problem associated with grounding doesn't occur.

It makes sense to install STP when it's already installed in a network, and you don't want to spend the money to rewire the media. This is particularly true if the current system is working adequately. However, for new installations, choose CAT5 UTP. If you are adding UTP cabling to an existing STP installation, UTP and STP cables may be interfaced with each other through a device called a media filter.

Coaxial Cable

Networking **coaxial cable** has a maximum data rate of 100 Mbps, and fair noise immunity. In other applications, it has a maximum data rate of 4,000 Mbps, bandwidths of up to 1,000 MHz, and is more expensive to install than twisted wire pairs.

Originally, coaxial cable offered better noise immunity than UTP, and in some situations this remains the case. It consists of two conductors insulated from one another and enclosed in a **polyethylene** jacket. A cut-away view of coax cable is shown in Figure 1-21. The center conductor is surrounded by a flexible polyethylene insulator. Wrapped about the insulator is the second conductor consisting of braided wire, foil, or both. The braid is connected to ground potential. Since it entirely encircles the center conductor, external noise such as crosstalk is effectively shorted to ground. The braided conductor is covered with an outer jacket of polyethylene insulation. Polyethylene is resistant to substances that damage the conductors, such as salt, water, or oil. It retains a high degree of flexibility over broad temperature ranges.

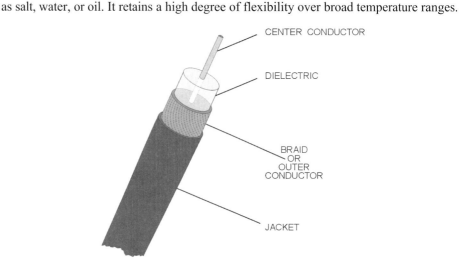

CENTER CONDUCTOR

DIELECTRIC

BRAID
OR
OUTER
CONDUCTOR

JACKET

Figure 1-21:
Coaxial Cable

Coaxial cable is most effective at frequencies over 100 kHz. At lower frequencies, the skin effects are minimal, and external noise "leaks" through the braid to cause distortion of the signal carried on the center conductor. The upper frequency limit for data transmission rates using coaxial cable can exceed 400 Mbps. However, resistive losses increase rapidly with the frequency necessitating the use of repeaters for long distance transmission.

The cable television industry has used coaxial cable extensively. Many local area networks owe their high data rates to cable advancements brought about by the cable TV industry. Cable TV networks can utilize coaxial cable with a 400 MHz bandwidth. At this size bandwidth, 52 TV channels can be carried on a single cable with the assistance of multiplexing. LANs typically transmit on coax from 1 Mbps up to about 100 Mbps.

The disadvantage of coaxial cable is its cost and lack of compatibility with twisted wires. The cost is only slightly more per foot than twisted wire, but this can grow to significant proportions when thousands of feet of cable are needed. Compatibility with UTP is a problem since most Ethernet networks now use UTP.

Thicknet

Originally, many LANs used coax as the transmission medium. The cable was called **thicknet** due to its strength and resistance to bending. Because of its bulkiness (.4 inch thick), thicknet is used primarily as a backbone for interconnecting network devices. Thicknet, also referred to 10Base-5, supports 100 transceivers on each segment. Any unused ends must be terminated with a 50-ohm resistance to prevent signal reflections. The cable is yellow or orange with dark colored rings spaced every 2.5 meters. The rings represent the minimum spacing of in-line transceiver taps to the backbone. The number of connections are limited to prevent signal attenuation and interference. The transceivers, in turn, connect to the coax cable via a 15-pin connector and cable (no longer than 50 feet) through one of two methods—intrusive taps, or nonintrusive taps. Figure 1-22 shows a typical thicknet connection.

Note the terminology used. The MAU, or Medium Attachment Unit, contains the transceiver circuitry along with various digital devices used to format data bits into Ethernet frames. A transceiver, as used with coaxial cable, simply receives and transmits signals. It lacks the sophistication to manage or massage the signal in any way. It doesn't amplify it, or remove noise, and it can't be assigned to another physical device through software configurations. An AUI, or Attachment Unit Interface, is a DB15 connector (either male or female) used to connect a 15-wire AUI cable between an MAU and the computer interface. Figure 1-23 shows the AUI cable and its associated pinout. Notice the reversal of pin number designations between the male and female connectors.

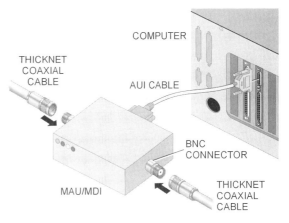

Figure 1-22: Thicknet Connections

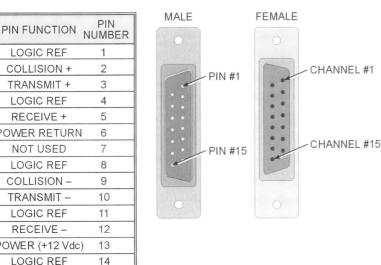

PIN FUNCTION	PIN NUMBER
LOGIC REF	1
COLLISION +	2
TRANSMIT +	3
LOGIC REF	4
RECEIVE +	5
POWER RETURN	6
NOT USED	7
LOGIC REF	8
COLLISION –	9
TRANSMIT –	10
LOGIC REF	11
RECEIVE –	12
POWER (+12 Vdc)	13
LOGIC REF	14
NOT USED	15

Figure 1-23: AUI Connector Point

The frames formatted in the MAU are up and downloaded to the thicknet coaxial cable via the MDI, which stands for Medium Dependent Interface. The MDI is nothing more than a mechanical connection, or interface from the MAU to the coax. There are two types of MDI, **intrusive taps** and **nonintrusive taps**.

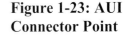

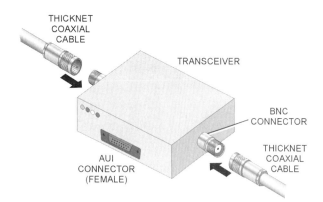

Figure 1-24: Thicknet Intrusive Tap

An intrusive tap, shown in Figure 1-24, requires the coax to be cut and a barrel connector inserted, which allows the transceiver and cable to join the coax backbone. The barrel connector fits to an interface that also joins the transceiver's 15-pin cable from the node.

A nonintrusive tap (also called a "vampire tap") doesn't require the cable to be broken and, therefore, the network doesn't have to be brought down each time another user is added. A hole is pierced through the coax and a bayonet spear inserted into the hole, which contacts the center conductor of the cable. The nonintrusive method is the favored practice because the network continues to run while the procedure takes place. Figure 1-25 illustrates a nonintrusive tap.

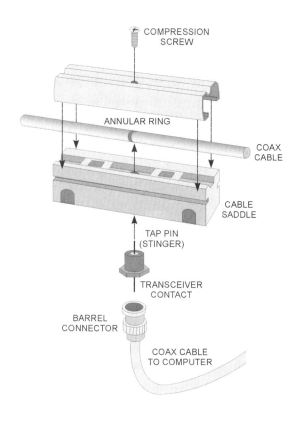

Figure 1-25: Thicknet Nonintrusive Tap

Thinnet

Thinnet, or 10Base-2 (also called cheapernet, RG-58A/U, or thin coaxial) coaxial cable has less shielding than thicknet, and consequently, smaller permissible segment lengths in a LAN. The maximum length of thinnet is 185 meters (compared to 500 meters for thicknet) and each unused segment end must be equipped with a 50-ohm termination to prevent undesired signal reflections. It can support up to 30 transceivers on each segment, but the transceivers can be placed as close together as 0.5 meter.

┌─ NOTE ──────────
Coaxial cable may use either an AUI connector or a BNC connector.
└────────────────

To connect a transceiver, the cable is cut and the ends prepared for BNC connectors and a T-connector installed at the break. One of the leads from the T connects back to the NIC card of the computer (which contains the transceiver circuitry), while the other two leads form an Ethernet bus. Figure 1-26 shows a typical arrangement. Barrel connectors can be used to join two short RG-58 cables, if necessary.

Coaxial cable is seldom used at the LAN level of networking in modern networks. UTP and fiber optics have exceeded it in terms of bandwidth and channel capacity, although in a small peer-to-peer LAN, it may be easier to configure than UTP, and will work just as well.

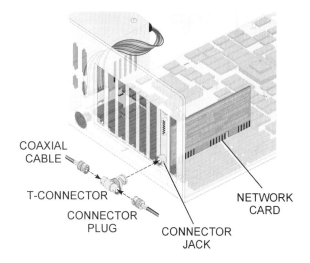

COAXIAL CABLE

T-CONNECTOR

CONNECTOR PLUG

CONNECTOR JACK

NETWORK CARD

Figure 1-26: Thinnet Connections

Fiber Optics

Fiber optics represents a very important stride in the development of data communications systems. A fiber-optic system offers much higher data rates, bandwidth, and noise immunity than do copper-based systems. At present, fiber systems are used in point-to-point configurations using conventional star, ring, and, in some cases, bus topologies. Due to the large capacity of a fiber system, it's installed where it will be expected to carry large volumes of data. Telecommunications and cable television industries have used it for many years because of this.

Within the last ten years, fiber has bubbled down to the local network level due to a drop in prices—although it remains the most expensive media—and broader standardization. The actual cost of fiber cable isn't expensive. The connectors, special tools needed, and hardware to convert signals from electrical to light and vice versa all combine to drive up the cost of an optical system.

Even though it's an expensive choice, there are several reasons to install fiber in a network. Since no copper is used in the cable, data bits won't be corrupted by electromagnetic interference (EMI), crosstalk, or other external noise that may garble bits in a UTP or coaxial system. The optical cable isolates devices connected to either end of it, which makes it a good choice where completely separate systems are linked together. An example is two LANs in different buildings. Connecting them can be tricky because of ground loops caused by common electrical planes. A fiber-optic connection avoids the problem and eliminates the danger to personnel and equipment.

Laboratory experiments with fiber optics have produced data rates as high as 200,000 Mbps. Telecommunication carrier frequencies hover in the 40 Mbps to 8,000 Mbps range. At the local level, data rates are standardized at 10 Mbps and 100 Mbps, using the IEEE 802 protocols and the FDDI (Fiber Distributed Data Interface) protocol. Losses are quite small compared to copper systems. At the long distance carrier level, losses are not to exceed 2 dB/km (over 1 kilometer). Compare this to 11.5 dB/km over 100 meters using UTP. This means that a fiber cable will carry more data further, and with fewer losses, than its copper-based cousin.

Fiber-optic media relay data via light waves through a glass or plastic conductor. It offers the best in noise immunity, but is the most expensive to install. Data rates may run as high as 200,000 Mbps and bandwidths as high as 1,000 GHz. The disadvantage of fiber optics is the expense, special splicing tools, and need for very careful alignment of splices and connections.

How does fiber optics achieve such high data rates and bandwidths? In the next section, the basic structure of light will be reviewed to answer that question.

Light Structure

optical spectrum

Wavelength

Light is electromagnetic radiation that has a wavelength falling within the infrared, visible, or ultraviolet ranges, broadly referred to as the **optical spectrum**. The ranges are illustrated in Figure 1-27.

ULTRAVIOLET (390 nm-10 nm)	Far Ultraviolet 10 nm
	Near Ultraviolet 300 nm
VISIBLE (770 nm-390 nm)	390 nm 770 nm
INFARED (100 µm-3 µm)	Near Infared 3 µm
	Middle Infared 30 µm
	Far Infared 100 µm

Figure 1-27: Optical Spectrum

Typical wavelengths used in fiber-optic networks fall in the near infrared and visible light spectrum.

Wavelength is described as a portion of a meter and will be stated using one of the following units:

- Micron (µm): 10^{-6} meters
- Nanometer (nm): 10^{-9} meters
- Angstrom (A): 10^{-10} meters

Specifications could have described light using frequencies within the optical spectrum, but it would have been inconvenient due to the large numbers used at these high frequencies.

Light is recognized as having two primary properties as it moves, or propagates. It has a wave-like nature and a particle-like nature. When it passes through, or is deflected from, an object (such as a piece of glass), it resembles a wave, much like ac current traveling through a wire. But when it is absorbed by an object (such as semiconductor material), it behaves as particles of energy that strike an object. As far as fiber cable is concerned, think of the light going through it as a single, two-dimensional (direction and amplitude) particle stream.

incident ray

reflected ray

reflected angle

incident angle

Snell's law

Light from any source will disperse, or separate with distance. But it's convenient to think that it doesn't when creating a model to describe how it travels in a fiber cable. Figure 1-28 shows a ray of light (the **incident ray**) striking a surface at an angle. Assume the surface has mirror-like qualities and the ray reflects (**reflected ray**) from it. The incident ray strikes the mirror at some angle called Θ_i (**incident angle**), and is reflected at Θ_r (**reflected angle**).

The relationship between the incident ray and the reflected ray is given by **Snell's law**, which says that when light is reflected the incident angle equals the reflected angle, $\Theta_i = \Theta_r$.

These angles are measured from an imaginary line drawn perpendicular to the incident point. The incident point is the point where the ray of light strikes an object, a mirror in the figure. The imaginary line is called **line normal**, and it provides a reference for measuring both the **angle of incident** and the **angle of reflection**.

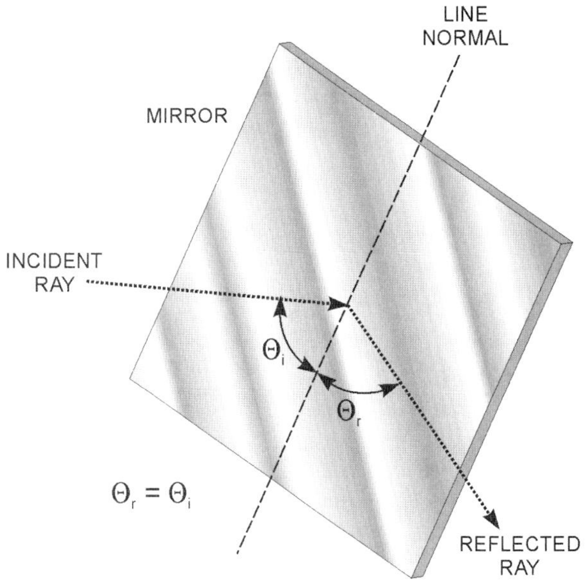

Not all surfaces reflect light. Some surfaces absorb all or part of the light that strikes it, while other surfaces refract light. **Refraction** is the bending of a light ray that occurs when light passes through materials of different densities. Snell has a law for this, too, and it is called **Snell's law of refraction**. The law says that the amount of refraction is determined by the difference in densities of two materials. The greater the relative difference, the greater the refractive angle.

When light passes from air to water, it changes direction (refracts) because the water is denser than the air. You've probably witnessed the effects of this phenomenon by looking at an object at the bottom of a swimming pool. The object looks much closer than it actually is because light entering the pool refracts and slows its rate of propagation in the denser water.

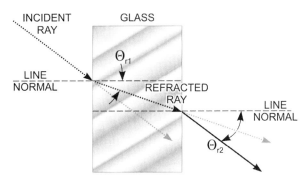

Figure 1-29: Refraction of Light Rays

Figure 1-29 shows a light ray passing from air to glass. The dotted line shows the course that the light ray would take if it didn't refract, while the solid line shows the actual course of the ray due to refraction. The refracted ray travels at a slower rate than the incident ray.

Figure 1-30 is the vector representation of light rays in the dense glass material. Line normal is illustrated as time, and the incident surface is illustrated by describing the amplitude of the light.

Figure 1-28: Reflection of Light Rays

line normal

angle of incident

angle of reflection

Refraction

Snell's law of refraction

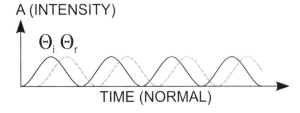

Figure 1-30: Vector Comparison of Incident and Refracted Light

The projected incident ray reaches some maximum amplitude at a time prior to the refracted ray reaching the same amplitude. The only explanation for this is that the refracted ray must be traveling slower than the projected incident ray.

If, after passing through the glass, the light were to reenter air, it would speed up again. This is pictured in Figure 1-29. Notice that the refracted ray bent toward line normal when it entered the denser glass material, but bent away from normal once it reentered the air. This actually makes sense because the velocity of light in air is faster than through the glass. It will now reach its maximum amplitude (called "intensity" in the optical world) at the same rate as the original incident ray, but the event will occur at some later point in time.

A fiber cable makes good use of both reflection and refraction when propagating light. In either case, light must pass through one type of material and strike another type. That is, two types of material (or two materials with differing densities) are needed to manipulate the direction of light. Whether the ray is reflected or refracted, two materials will always be used in the construction of a fiber-optic cable. These materials are called the **core** and the **cladding** and they are further described by their diameter in microns.

The conventional method for specifying fiber cable is to state the diameter of the core versus cladding. For example, a 62.5/125 cable has a 62.5-micron core and a 125-micron cladding.

Fiber Cable Propagation

A cut-away view of a fiber cable is shown in Figure 1-31. The core is composed of either a glass or plastic strand, and the cladding that encircles it is also composed of glass or plastic.

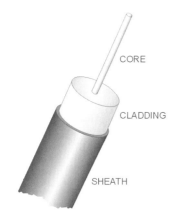

Figure 1-31: Fiber-Optic Cable

The only difference between core and cladding is in the density the two offer to light beams. Examining a fiber cable doesn't help to distinguish between core and cladding, as they are manufactured in the same strand. The density difference is a cable manufacturing specification called refractive index. Refractive index is the ratio of the velocity of light through a material to the velocity of light through a vacuum (300,000,000 m/s). In practice, the refractive index is also influenced by the angle of incidence.

In a fiber-optic cable, the refractive index for the cladding will always be less than the index for the core. Or, in other words, the density of the cladding material will be less than the density of the core. Since the two differ in density, light striking the junction of core and cladding will either reflect or refract. Which phenomenon is used to propagate light is determined by the manner used to construct the cable. There are two basic methods used to construct fiber cable—single-mode and multimode.

Multimode Graded Index Fiber-Optic Cable

Multimode cable is the most commonly used because it's cheaper and will transmit light over distances used in local area networks. Mode refers to the way light traverses a fiber cable, and this, in turn, is partly determined by the manner in which light enters the cable. A working definition of "mode" is the various paths that light takes along the cable.

In a multimode cable means, light will travel in many paths from transmitter to receiver. This is shown graphically in Figure 1-32.

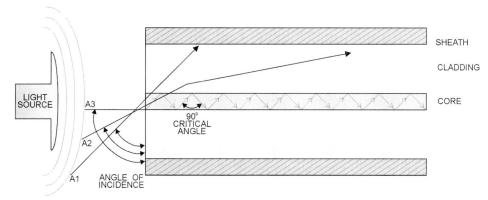

Figure 1-32: Various Light Paths in a Multimode Cable

Light emanating from the source strikes the fiber at many angles. The angle at which light enters the cable is the incident angle. Light wave A1 strikes the fiber end at a very small incident angle. The wave passes through the core, through the cladding, and is absorbed in the sheath, which is opaque. Light wave A2 reaches the core at a much wider angle of incident. As the wave leaves the core and enters the cladding, it's bent from its original path. The core of the cladding is much more dense than the cladding material. The lower cladding density refracts the wave in the direction shown, but the angle of refraction is too wide for the wave to reenter the core and it's subsequently lost in the cladding and sheath.

The third light wave, A3, moves through the core and strikes the cladding interface at a specific angle that, when it strikes the junction of core and cladding, will cause it to refract back into the core. This angle is called the **critical angle**. All light waves that strike the interface will reflect away from the cladding according to Snell's law of reflection.

When the reflected ray once again encounters the core/cladding junction, it is bent back (reflected back) again. This zigzagging continues along the length of the cable. The A3 light wave, or all light waves that fall within the spread of the critical angle, is the beam that will carry data from transmitter to receiver. Information carried in A1 and A2 is lost, which results in an attenuated signal at the receiver.

The critical angle necessary for internal reflection in a fiber covers a range of degrees. The specific range is a function of the composition and physical construction of the fiber, as well as the angle that light enters the fiber cable. Light waves leave the source in many directions, not all of which will cause the rays to reflect within the critical angle. The precise alignment of source to fiber is an important aspect of an optical system.

The manner of propagation in the figure is reflection. As long as light strikes the surface within the critical angle, it will reflect when it encounters the core/cladding interface, and will internally reflect along the length of the cable.

As light enters the core, it does so at many angles of incidence. Some of these will fall within the critical angle necessary for propagation. Consider only those rays that enter within the critical angle. Some will do so at a steeper angle than others and they will zigzag through the cable more times than a ray entering at a slightly wider angle.

A steeper angle means the wave will take longer to get to the end of the cable than the wave that enters at a wide angle. At the receiving end of the cable, the rays arriving at different times cause a variance in phase of the light beams. This effect is called **modal dispersion** since the light rays strike the core at different angles, causing them to propagate through the fiber in different modes, or manners.

The remedy for modal dispersion is to restrict the size (diameter) of the core. If the thickness of the cladding is at least three times the thickness of the core, modal dispersion can be eliminated. Multimode cables should consist of 50/125 μm, 62.5/125 μm, or 100/140 μm. The cable should be tested at a wavelength of 850 nm over 1 km (in an Ethernet application) for losses not to exceed –13 dB, –16 dB, and –19 dB respectively for the core/cladding sizes.

Single-Mode Fiber Cable

The problem with multimode fiber is that more than one path exists for light to travel along the core. This results in **modal distortion** at the receiver that may cause a loss of data bits over long runs. (Visually, the effect of modal dispersion is to stretch a transmitted pulse. The greater the dispersion, the longer it will take for all components of a pulse to arrive at the receiver and the longer the received pulse will be stretched. The result is that data bits will no longer be the prescribed width or data rate, causing a complete signal loss in the system.) To eliminate the problem requires limiting the modal paths. This is accomplished by using a very small core strand so that only one wavelength of light will radiate through the cable. Figure 1-33 shows a **single-mode** cable connected to a laser light source.

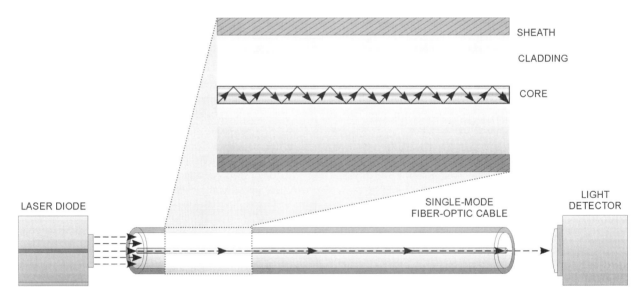

SHEATH

CLADDING

CORE

LASER DIODE

SINGLE-MODE
FIBER-OPTIC CABLE

LIGHT
DETECTOR

**Figure 1-33:
Single-Mode
Fiber-Optic Light
Propagation**

Notice that light travels axially through the cable, and not in the zigzag fashion that's typical of multimode. Since only one wavelength of light is being transmitted, modal dispersion is entirely eliminated. The bits arriving at the receiver will have phase characteristics identical to those of the bits at the transmitting end of the cable.

A laser is necessary to drive single-mode cable because it produces energy that's coherent (in phase), monochromatic (of the same wavelength), and collimated (traveling in the same direction, not radiating in many directions like light from a LED). At the receiving end, the detector is specialized to the wavelength of the transmitted light.

The laser, even if it's a semiconductor device, drives up the cost of a single-mode system. Single-mode cable is also the most expensive and difficult to work with because of its small size, and the precise alignment needed between cable and end connections. It is, however, the most efficient and less distorting of all fiber cable types.

Single-mode cable is limited by the FDDI protocol to a diameter of 8.7/125 microns. The length of the cable is determined by topology. When used in point-to-point configuration, the maximum length is 40 km (24 miles), but in a ring topology the length can be extended to 100 km (62 miles) for dual rings, and 200 km (124 miles) for single rings. It typically uses light with a wavelength of 1,305 nm with cable attenuation of .5 dB/km.

Single-mode fiber cable is used in applications where data speed and distance (limited to 5 km, maximum in an Ethernet network) are the concern. Multimode fiber isn't acceptable over long runs due to excessive modal dispersion.

Fiber-Optic Connections

Fiber-optic connections are considerably more difficult to make than the solder connections of copper wire. Usually, a light source (LED) and the fiber are coupled together with a plastic connector, as shown in Figure 1-32. The same is true of the fiber-to-light detector connection. The two most important considerations of connecting fibers are that the connection offer the proper alignment so as to avoid any more than the minimum amount of connector loss, and that the end of the fiber be unblemished.

The proper alignment of the fiber is accomplished by correctly fitting the cable plug as shown in Figure 1-34(a). Shown is a standard cable plug that can be used to connect the cable to fiber-optic equipment. Figure 1-34(b) shows a breakdown of the plug and a typical fiber cable receptacle. The cable sheath should be stripped to expose approximately 1/4 inch of the fiber. The retention clip is then slid onto the cable with the notched "V" on the exposed end of the fiber. The cable and retention clip assembly are then pressed into the plug. The connector—plug and receptacle—will generally ensure a good alignment of the fibers.

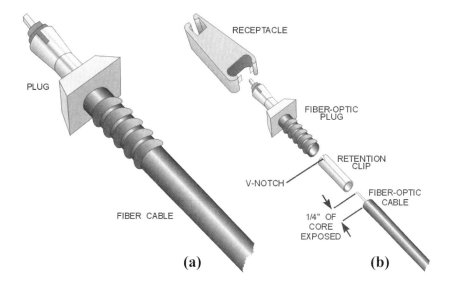

Figure 1-34: Fiber Connections

The end of the fiber must be unblemished (not scratched, nicked, or dirty). There are two methods for preparing the fiber ends. The first method involves polishing the fiber ends.

The other method involves using a **hot knife**. Ideally, the knife should have an adjustable temperature range since different sizes and types of fibers have optimum heat ranges for cutting. The fiber cable is slipped into a cutting fixture that has a flat circular surface on one end, as shown in Figure 1-35. The beveled edge of the hot knife is slid along the flat surface of the cutting tool to make a clean, smooth cut.

If the ends of the fiber are not prepared so they are smooth and clean, the connection loss can be significant. It is analogous to a cold solder joint with copper wires.

The preceding discussion serves to highlight some of the difficulties you encounter when working with fiber. Fortunately, many of the connection problems described for the connector have been eliminated through better designs. The cable shown in Figure 1-34 is called a Sub-Miniature Assembly, or SMA. These are gradually being replaced with connectors that provide better alignment with fewer opportunities for problems. Figure 1-36 shows an ST, or Straight Tip, connector. ST connectors are common in 10 Mbps networks using fiber cable.

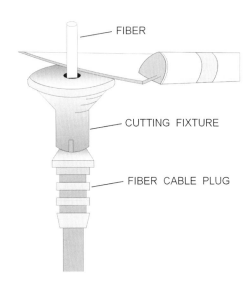

Figure 1-35: Cutting Fixture and Hot Knife

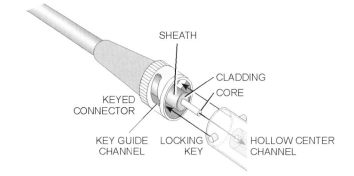

Figure 1-36: Straight Tip Fiber-Optic Connector

The ST has a keyed locking connector that automatically aligns the center strands of the fiber cable to the network device it's connected to. An integral spring helps to keep the fiber strands from being crushed together and damaging the cable ends. There are different ST connector types for single-mode cable and multimode cable, and the two can't be interchanged.

100 Mbps fiber-optic networks require the use of an SC connector, pictured in Figure 1-37. While no standard has been defined for connectors in a 100 Mbps network at the time of this writing, the SC seems to predominate in the industry.

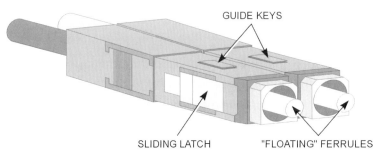

Figure 1-37: SC Fiber-Optic Connector

At the high data rates used with 100 Mbps networks, the fiber strands must be very accurately aligned so as to avoid signal loss. This is done in an SC cable by including floating ferrules, which contact the fiber strands. The ports of devices connected to an SC connector also have floating ferrules. Since the ferrules are floating, they're held loosely in place and will move slightly when contacting the fiber strands. The small amount of movement addresses slight alignment differences found from connector to connector and from port to port.

KEY POINTS REVIEW

- Network topology is the physical arrangement of the nodes (computers, workstations, or other devices) connected to the network.

- A star topology consists of a central hub, or switch, connecting the nodes like spokes extending out from it. It is the most widely used topology.

- A ring topology connects the nodes in a continuous loop. Data flows around the ring in one direction.

- Three basic access techniques for ring networks are token passing, fixed slots, and delay insertion.

- A bus topology is a straight-line connection strategy.

- A mesh topology is an arrangement in which all nodes are physically connected.

- A hierarchical topology is a combination of bus, star, ring, or mesh topologies.

- A logical topology refers to the manner in which data is sent across a network.

- A wireless topology is not fixed since the media is the atmosphere. But the arrangement of nodes resembles a star.

- Nodes in a wireless network connect to an access point.

- Digital data is preferred over analog data because noise and distortion are easier to remove, it's in the same format as computer data, and the sharp edges of square waves provide more reliable bit recognition.

- Digital square waves have the disadvantage of requiring at least five times as much bandwidth as analog.

- Transmission media refers to the channel data travels on enroute to the receiving station. Transmission media include coaxial cable, twisted wire pairs, fiber optics, and the atmosphere.

- Twisted pair is the most widely installed media. Its size ranges from 16 to 24 AWG, and it may be found in a single-pair cable, or up to 6,000 pairs may be encased in a single sheath. Unshielded twisted pair (UTP) is the preferred cabling for LANs. UTP is classified by the EIA/TIA according to categories. Whenever possible, use CAT5 UTP.

- UTP may use an RJ-11 or an RJ-45 connector. An RJ-11 connector is used for voice UTP, whereas an RJ-45 connector is used for data UTP.

- Coaxial cable used in networking has a maximum data rate of 10 Mbps. It offers fair noise immunity. In other applications, it has a maximum data rate of 4,000 Mbps, bandwidths of up to 1,000 MHz, and is somewhat more expensive to install than twisted wire pairs.

- Coaxial cable may use either an AUI connector or a BNC connector.

- Fiber-optic media relay data via light waves through a glass or plastic conductor. It offers the best noise immunity but is the most expensive to install. Data rates may run as high as 200,000 Mbps and bandwidths as high as 1,000 GHz. The disadvantage of fiber optics is the expense, special splicing tools, and need for very careful alignment of splices and connections.

- Fiber-optic cable may use either a ST or a SC connector.

- The physical interface used with wireless networks is an antenna.

At this point, review the objectives listed at the beginning of the chapter to be certain that you understand and can perform them. Afterward, answer the review questions that follow to verify your knowledge of the information.

REVIEW QUESTIONS

The following questions test your knowledge of the material presented in this chapter:

1. What type of network is described by the following statement? The nodes are connected by a central hub.

2. Explain how CAT 5 UTP greatly extends the bandwidth of voice-grade UTP.

3. Describe the difference between intrusive and nonintrusive coaxial cable taps.

4. Why should you know whether a cable plant is compliant to EIA/TIA-568A or B?

5. What are the advantages of UTP over STP?

6. What are the advantages/disadvantages of fiber cable?

7. Describe the difference between multimode and single-mode fiber-optic cable.

8. An RJ-45 connector is only used with CAT5 UTP cable; true or false?

9. In what type of network are all of the nodes physically connected?

10. Which network topology uses the atmosphere for the network media?

11. In what topology do the nodes attach to a single, common backplane?

12. Which topology consists of more than one topology type?

13. What is the difference between thinnet and thicknet cable?

14. Which requires more bandwidth, analog or digital signals?

15. What connector is used for voice communication?

1. In a _____ network, nodes attach to the channel in a daisy-chain manner.
   a. ring
   b. mesh
   c. bus
   d. star

2. What is refraction?
   a. the dispersion of light waves
   b. the bending of light passing through materials of different density
   c. a narrowing of the light wave as it's transmitted
   d. a thickening in the intensity of light as it travels further from the source

3. The polyethylene jacket that encloses a coaxial cable is also called the ____.
   a. center conductor
   b. insulator
   c. shielding
   d. outer insulation

4. A data signal square wave requires ____ times as much bandwidth as an equivalent analog signal.
   a. 2
   b. 3
   c. 4
   d. 5

5. Which of the following connector types would be used with fiber optic cable?
   a. RJ-11
   b. RJ-45
   c. ST
   d. BNC

6. A notebook computer connected to a wireless network can no longer connect to other workstations. Which of the following is the most likely cause?
   a. The cable has a break in it.
   b. The ring is broken.
   c. The bus has shorted.
   d. The notebook is out of range.

7. An AUI is a(n):
   a. DB-15 pin connector
   b. 4-wire RJ-11 connector
   c. BNC connector
   d. 8-wire RJ-45 connector

8. Which of the following UTP cable types are recommended for 100 Mbps networking?
   a. CAT 3
   b. CAT 5
   c. CAT 2
   d. CAT 1

9. Which topology is used to structure the Internet?
   a. star
   b. bus
   c. ring
   d. mesh

10. A star network utilizes a hub that has an internal common backplane. What type of topology is used in the hub?
    a. physical star
    b. logical mesh
    c. logical bus
    d. physical ring

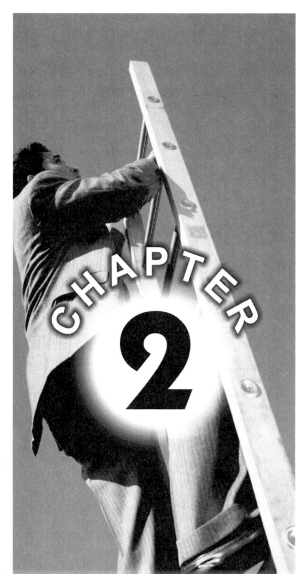

CHAPTER 2

IEEE 802.X PROTOCOLS

LEARNING OBJECTIVES

Upon completion of this chapter and its related lab procedures, you will be able to perform the following tasks:

1. List the IEEE 802 series protocols for Ethernet, Token Bus, Token Ring, and Wireless.

2. Specify speed, access method, topology, and media for the following:
   - 802.2
   - 802.5
   - FDDI
   - 802.3
   - 802.11

3. Specify characteristics of speed, length, topology, and cable type for:
   - 10Base-T
   - 1000Base-TX
   - 10Base-5
   - 100Base-TX
   - 10Base-2
   - 100Base-FX

4. Label a block diagram for the frame format for CSMA/CD.

5. Give an example of a MAC address.

6. State the purpose and length of each field of the IEEE 802.3 CSMA/CD frame.

7. Sketch a typical IEEE 802.3 Ethernet LAN

8. Define slot time, interframe gap, jam, backoff delay, and segment.

9. Discuss the procedure used with CSMA/CD for detecting collisions.

10. State several characteristics of 100VG-AnyLAN.

11. Sketch a typical migration plan from 10Base-T through 1000Base-T.

12. Label a block diagram for the IEEE 802.4 Token Bus frame, and describe the purpose and length of each field.

13. Sketch a typical IEEE 802.4 Token Bus LAN.

14. Discuss token passing and token recovery on a Token Bus network.

15. Label a block diagram of the IEEE 802.5 Token Ring frame.

16. Describe the purpose and length of each frame for the Token Ring.

17. Sketch a typical Token Ring LAN using IEEE 802.5 specifications.

18. Describe the process of token passing on a Token Ring network.

19. State the network access protocol used with 802.11 wireless.

20. Sketch a typical IEEE 802.11 wireless LAN.

21. For an IEEE 802.11 wireless LAN, describe the requirements for connecting to an IEEE 802.3 wired LAN.

22. State several advantages and disadvantages of wireless networks versus wired networks.

23. State the purpose, topology, and specification for the ANSI FDDI protocol.

24. Label a block diagram of the FDDI protocol stack.

25. Discuss the functions/specifications of the Physical Medium Dependent layer, the Physical layer protocol, and the Media Access Control layer.

26. Label a block diagram of a FDDI token and frame, and state each field's purpose.

27. Describe the process of wring-wrapping a fault condition using FDDI.

IEEE 802.x Protocols

INTRODUCTION

The IEEE 802 standards consist of specifications of the Media Access Control sublayer of layer two, the Data Link layer, of the ISO Open System Interconnection (OSI) Reference Model. A detailed description of the model is discussed in Chapter 4. In this chapter, the sublayers of the Data Link layer are detailed because the IEEE 802 series protocols have been adopted directly by the ISO for the OSI model.

Perhaps one of the reasons LANs have been so widely embraced by users is the existence of well-documented standards. In 1985, the IEEE approved a series of LAN standards describing several recommendations for implementing LANs at layers 1 and 2 of the OSI reference mode. Since then, the ISO has adopted the standards, exactly as approved by the IEEE, in the ISO 8803 series of standards. The recommendations are referred to as the IEEE 802 standards.

The 802 series of standards are important to understanding local area networks since nearly all LANs are designed and implemented around these standards. In addition, a thorough understanding of these protocols will help you make more sense of protocols and practices used in wide area networks.

IEEE 802 FAMILY OF LAN STANDARDS

The 802 standard describes three major portions of LANs:

(1) Specifications of the Media Access Control (MAC) sublayer of layer 2, the Data Link layer.

(2) Descriptions of the electrical and physical characteristics at the Physical layer.

(3) Specifications of the Logical Link Control (LLC) sublayer of the Data Link layer.

> **NOTE**
>
> The lower sublayer of the OSI Data Link layer is Media Access Control, while the upper sublayer is called Logical Link Control.

Figure 2-1 details the Data Link layer. The LLC, described by IEEE 802.2, is a software interface from the Data Link layer to the Network layer. The primary function of the LLC is to manage the flow of data from a network device (such as a computer) as the data is sent or received from the device. The particulars of how the LLC accomplishes this task will be discussed after the MAC sublayer is described.

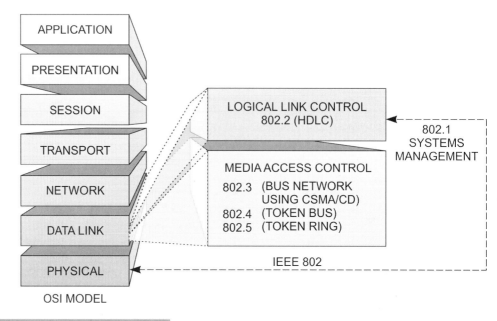

Figure 2-1: IEEE 802 Standards

The Media Access Control is the lower sublayer of the Data Link level. The 802 standards for this sublayer describe how various techniques are used to gain access to a network, as well as electrical and mechanical specifications for various protocols.

IEEE 802.1 describes the system's management between the logical link, the media-access methods, the Physical layer, and a network with the upper OSI levels.

Essentially, it describes the architecture of the system manager. Areas of involvement include protocol initialization, and parameters for error control or security. This standard won't be discussed further.

In practice, IEEE 802.2 is confined to the Data Link layer, as shown in Figure 2-1. But the MAC sublayer protocols (802.3, 802.4, 802.5, etc.) actually cross the boundary to the Physical layer in their scope of operation, and as such, are sometimes referred to as Physical layer protocols. The IEEE 802 standards are summarized in Table 2-1. Many have been adopted by the ISO for the OSI Reference Model.

Table 2-1:
Description of IEEE
802 Standards for
LANs

IEEE 802 Standards	
802.1	Systems standard for local and metropolitan area networks
802.2	Logical Link Control (LLC) sublayer
802.3	CSMA/CD access, including MAC sublayer and Physical layer signaling (10Base-2, 10Base-5, 10Base-T, 100Base-T, 1000Base-T, 10Broad-36)
802.4	Token bus. Included in the Manufacturing Automation Protocol suite (MAP)
802.5	Token Ring
802.6	Metropolitan Area Networks. Specifies a dual fiber optic bus with time slots
802.7	Broadband technology
802.8	Fiber-optic technology
802.9	Integrated Voice and Data. Describes use of ISDN devices with LANs.
802.10	LAN security
802.11	Wireless LANs
802.12	100VG-AnyLAN

Most vendor specifications will refer to one of these standards when describing their LAN product. This chapter emphasizes 802.3, 802.4, 802.5, and 802.11. A thorough understanding of LAN protocols is essential to evaluate networks, and they will be discussed in detail in the following sections.

> **NOTE**
>
> The most widely used media-access protocols are CSMA/CD (Carrier-Sense Multiple Access/Collision Detection), CSMA/CA (Carrier-Sense Multiple Access/Collision Avoidance), token ring passing, and token bus.

Protocols aren't static. They change because there's always a better way to build and manage a network. Also, users want more speed and bandwidth, and vendors want more market share—because we simply aren't content to limit our achievements. You can keep abreast of LAN-level changes by visiting the IEEE web site at *www.ieee.org/*.

> **NOTE**
>
> Media-access control is described by the IEEE 802.3 (CSMA/CD Ethernet), 802.4 (Token Bus), and 802.5 (Token Ring) standards.

IEEE 802.3 ETHERNET

The 802.3 standard for bus networks is based upon the joint efforts of Digital Equipment Corporation, Intel, and Xerox. The original standard was called Ethernet, and the name has been retained although the current versions are not the same as the original. The original is now called Ethernet I, or simply "the DIX standard" after the founding companies.

> **NOTE**
>
> The 802.3 standard (CSMA/CD) was derived from an earlier data-communications effort called Ethernet undertaken jointly by the Xerox, Digital Equipment, and Intel companies.

Based upon experimental work performed in Xerox laboratories, the three companies sought commercial applications of Xerox research. The result, in 1980, was a data communications network called **Ethernet**. Ethernet represented the first nonproprietary network, and vendors were encouraged to design equipment geared toward Ethernet. Many vendors did so. In 1985, the DIX version was revised, and this version, called Ethernet II, was submitted to the IEEE. The IEEE used Ethernet II as the foundation for bus network standards called IEEE 802.3, Carrier Sense Multiple Access with Collision Detection Access Method and Physical Layer Specifications.

Four basic variations of Ethernet are in use today. The distinguishing factor from one to the next is subtle differences in the frame format used to package data so it can be sent onto the network. None is compatible with the others. Table 2-2 lists the types of Ethernet frames and includes brief differences and typical applications.

Table 2-2: Ethernet Frame Types

Ethernet Frame Types		
Frame Types	**Features**	**Applications**
Ethernet 802.3	Also called **raw Ethernet**, the frame begins with a 7-byte Preamble, which is followed by a 1-byte Start Frame Delimiter. Along with Source and Destination Address fields, a 2-byte Length field is included that specifies the length of the data field. Ethernet 802.3 is not in compliance with IEEE 802.3.	Used in NetWare version 2.2 and 3.x networks.
Ethernet 802.2	This frame type includes three fields from the LLC sublayer and is in full compliance with IEEE 802.3.	Used in NetWare version 3.12 and 4.x networks.
Ethernet SNAP	Ethernet SNAP (Sub-Network Address Protocol) is similar to Ethernet 802.3 except the Length field is replaced with a Type field. The Type field specifies network layer protocol in the Data (Information) field.	Used in AppleTalk networks.
Ethernet II	The preamble and start frame delimiter are combined into a single 8-byte Preamble field. A 2-byte Type field is included (but not a Length field), which contains Network layer information and LLC sublayer information.	Typically used in TCP/IP networks. Ethernet running across the Internet is likely to use Ethernet II.

Although not technically correct, IEEE 802.3 CSMA/CD is referred to as Ethernet.

The basis of the standard, at the logical level, is the media-access technique known as **Carrier-Sense Multiple-Access/Collision** (contention) **Detect (CSMA/CD)**. It's operated in both baseband and broadband modes.

The IEEE 802.3 standards specify that the protocol used is Ethernet, and the access method used is CSMA/CD. When CSMA/CD is operating in a baseband mode, it doesn't use a carrier, so the acronym is a little misleading. The terminology derives from using Manchester encoding with CSMA/CD. Recall from earlier chapters that data are frequently encoded to prevent the build-up of a dc component when long strings of 1's and 0's are transmitted (intersymbol interference). The positive and negative transitions of the Manchester code are a continuous event, so the constant repetition is similar to the predictability of a carrier. A CSMA/CD node samples (or senses) the channel for Manchester data. From this process, the "carrier sense" is derived.

All nodes have access to the media; i.e., "multiple access." In a network operating in the baseband mode, only one node can transmit at a time (half duplex). If two nodes attempt to transmit at the same time, the messages will collide. When a collision occurs, it's detected in the first 64 bytes of a transmission. Detection occurs before the signal has had time to be received by any stations on the channel. The terminology "collision detect" comes from this.

The data frame format for CSMA/CD is depicted in Figure 2-2. The 7-byte preamble is a series of alternating 1s and 0s used for synchronization. The start frame delimiter consists of the bit pattern 10101011. The last bit in the preamble is used to designate the start of the frame. It tells the receiving node that the synchronization time is completed and the next bit begins the critical frame information. Depending on the type of Ethernet frame used (see Table 2-2) the preamble and start frame delimiter fields may be combined into a single 8-byte field.

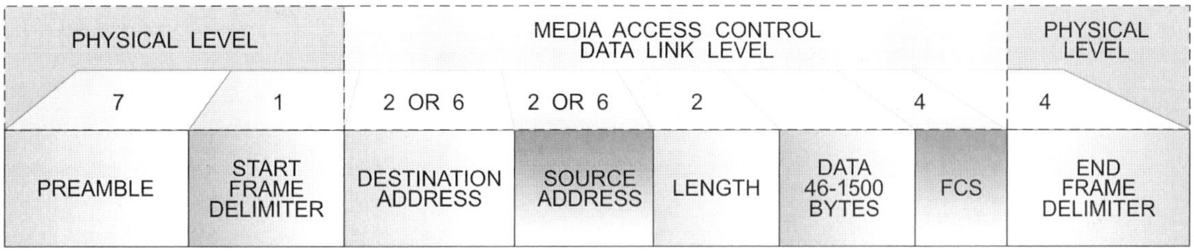

PHYSICAL LEVEL		MEDIA ACCESS CONTROL DATA LINK LEVEL					PHYSICAL LEVEL
7	1	2 OR 6	2 OR 6	2	4		4
PREAMBLE	START FRAME DELIMITER	DESTINATION ADDRESS	SOURCE ADDRESS	LENGTH	DATA 46-1500 BYTES	FCS	END FRAME DELIMITER

When a frame tries to send data, the preamble and delimiter are sent first. The end frame delimiter formally ends the frame. This is physical activity occurring on the network. Because bits are being discussed, the IEEE 802.3 is a Physical layer protocol, as well as a Data Link layer protocol. Remember, implementing the 802 standards results in a crossover between the Physical and Data Link levels.

Figure 2-2: CSMA/CD Data Frame Format

All nodes, or stations, on the network have a unique address. The address is referred to as the MAC (Media Access Control), or hardware address. A 6-byte length is permitted. The original version of Ethernet specified a 6-byte address; IEEE 802.3 permits a 2-byte alternative that is seldom used. At this time, the first three bytes of an address field are assigned by the IEEE, while the last three bytes are assigned by the manufacturer of the network device (such as a network interface card). The first three bytes tend to be vendor-specific, since vendors reserve blocks of addresses for their products. A partial list of the addresses for various vendors is shown in Table 2-3. The addresses are assigned so that the address will remain unique for any Ethernet port. Originally, Xerox supplied the addresses, but has since delegated the responsibility and control to the IEEE. Any addresses assigned prior to the changeover were retained.

Table 2-3:
Vendor MAC
Address

Sample Vendor MAC Addresses	
Hex Address	**Vendor**
00000C	Cisco
00001D	Cabletron
00003D	AT&T (one of several)
00005E	U.S. Department of Defense
000062	Honeywell
00608C	3COM
00C0BE	Alcatel
080006	Apple
080009	Hewlett Packard
08005A	IBM (one of several)
1000D4	DEC

Ethernet addresses are commonly called "MAC addresses" or "physical addresses." This is used to differentiate them from logical addresses assigned at the Network layer (in Network layer software). Since a MAC address is hard-wired into the circuitry of a node, it must go wherever the node goes. The usual implementation occurs in a Network Interface Card (NIC) containing transceiver and frame-formatting electronics. If you remove an NIC card from one PC, and place it in another PC, you have to tell the Network layer software (NetWare, NT, etc.) that you've done so, or run the risk of blocking the node from the network. In larger LANs, this is a requirement.

TEST TIP

Be able to recognize a valid MAC address.

Typically, MAC addresses are displayed in the hexadecimal numbering system. Hexadecimal are base-16 numbers, rather than the the base-10 numbers you are accustomed to use when counting. An example of a MAC address is:

> 00-06-80-00-A1-B6

Each character in a hexadecimal MAC address represents four bits, for a total of 48 bits.

Ethernet frames, as well as all other frame types generated at the Data Link layer, include a source and a destination address. Nodes on the network are considered to be peers. This means that they don't need permission to send or receive data. Since they will send data when they have gained access to the network, the destination address is needed so that the receiving node will recognize that the frame is intended for it. The receiving node will send back a frame that acknowledges receipt.

In order to return an acknowledgment, the receiving station must know the address of the sender. Consequently, the MAC address of the source of the frame as well as the MAC address of the destination for the frame is included in each frame sent over the network.

In a LAN that consists of nodes sharing the same cable infrastructure, getting a frame to its destination is rather straightforward. All nodes on the network receive the frame at the same time. Each node compares the destination address to its own address and, if it matches, reads the frame into the buffers of its own NIC card. If it doesn't match, the frame is ignored. This is the basic process used by all Ethernet networks using a bus topology (the majority of installations).

The Length field contains 2 bytes to indicate the amount of data contained in the data field. This includes any frames from the upper layers of the OSI model, as well as all user data. In short, the Length field indicates the size of the data field. What isn't counted are bytes that may be placed in the Data field—called pads—that are used to pad the frame size, so that it's a minimum of 64 bytes.

Some versions of Ethernet (Ethernet II, for example) omit the Length field and replace it with a Type field. The details of the Type field are given later in the chapter.

Following the Data field is a 32-bit frame-check sequence, using the **Cyclic Redundancy Check (CRC)** algorithm. The FCS is used to detect errors in the frame.

The CSMA/CD protocol operates by continuously monitoring the channel for other transmitting stations. If the channel is being used, the station waits until it's cleared. Once the station detects no carrier, it waits 9.6 µs and then transmits. This is equivalent to 96 bits on a 10 Mbps LAN, and is called the **InterFrame Gap (IFG)**. The delay is necessary to give the other stations time to reset after receiving or transmitting a message.

Once a station begins transmitting, if there's to be a collision, it will happen in the first 512 bits (64 bytes) of the transmission. This bit time is called the slot time (or collision window), and is related to the round-trip propagation delay on the network, which is 51.2 µs. The receive and transmit circuitry in the station detects the collision by measuring the average dc voltage on the network. On the network, a logic 0 = 0 volts, and a logic 1 = –2.05 volts; the average of the two conditions equals 1 volt [(0 + 2.05)/2 = 1 volt]. When two stations transmit at the same time, the average voltage rises to about 1.5 volts, and the collision-detect circuits inform the transmitter that there's been a collision. The IEEE defines a collision as a **Signal Quality Error (SQE)**. This has created some confusion because Ethernet II uses a mechanism called a **heartbeat** that serves the same purpose as the SQE. However, the two mechanisms aren't compatible, and the IEEE 802.3 standard stipulates that, when the two versions of Ethernet are mixed, the heartbeat from Ethernet II must be turned off.

Once the collision occurs, and is detected by the transmitting stations, the transmitter continues to transmit for 32 bits. This bit time is called a **jam.** A jam is necessary to make sure each transmitting station has had time to detect the collision, and 32 bits is the maximum time it takes data to travel the length of a **segment**, 25.6 µs. At the end of 32 bits, the station will stop transmitting.

When a station has stopped transmitting, it backs off from further transmitting by a randomly selected time interval, based on its MAC address. The **backoff delay** varies slightly with each station, since each one has a different address. At the end of the backoff delay, each transmitting station tries again.

If there's another collision, the backoff times will be doubled. After sixteen attempts to transmit, the station generates an error, and stops trying. Because of the exponential binary algorithm used with backoff delays, it's extremely improbable that any two stations will continue to create a jam over the full sixteen tries. However, if this occurs, any data that was in the attempted frame is lost at the MAC layer. Collision detection is shown in Figure 2-3.

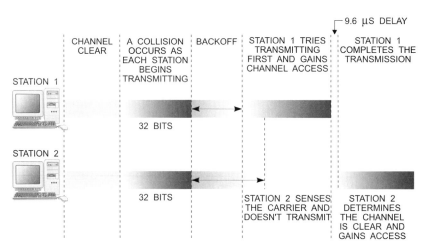

Figure 2-3: CSMA/CD Collision Detection

Note that the nature of a CSMA/CD network is to create collisions. Collisions don't necessarily mean that there's a problem with an Ethernet installation; in fact, they mean that the network is working the way it's supposed to work. But the more nodes on the network, the more collisions will occur. This is why the number of stations on link segments is limited. The same is true for the volume of traffic running on a network. Network traffic is measured as **utilization rates**.

This is the ratio of the amount of time the network is used, to the amount of time that it's idle. The ratio is surprisingly small, averaging between 20% to 40%. But it tends to peak at certain times such as the mornings, when e-mail is checked and responded to. As the utilization rises, collisions will increase nonlinearly—that is, a doubling of the utilization rate will create more than a doubling of collisions. As you might imagine, the network slows down in the same fashion as delays increase. As a rule of thumb, a utilization rate of about 75% is the maximum for networks.

As mentioned earlier, the IEEE 802.3 CSMA/CD protocol is very similar to the original Ethernet. However, there are exceptions. Ethernet contains a Type field prior to the Data field. The Type field specifies the type of frame as information, unnumbered, or supervisory. The Type field is actually a function of the LLC sublayer and is discussed in the IEEE 802.2 section of this chapter. For now, note that IEEE 802.3 has a Length field in the frame, while Ethernet II has a Type field in the frame header. In a pure IEEE 802.3 frame, the equivalent Type field is embedded in the Data field and serves the same function as the Type field placed in the Ethernet header. In place of the Type field in an Ethernet II header, 802.3 has a Length field, and as mentioned previously, it gives the length of the Data field.

IEEE 802.3 CSMA/CD is a mouthful. It should come as no surprise, then, that the term "Ethernet" has been retained in the networking industry, even though Ethernet is, theoretically, obsolete. But the reality is that Ethernet II is widely used, particularly when Ethernet frames are sent over the Internet. Beyond this chapter, consider "Ethernet" to mean the IEEE 802.3 protocol, and not the original DIX, Ethernet I, or Ethernet II versions.

There are many variants of IEEE 802.3. Table 2-4 shows specifications for IEEE 802.3a–t. Refer to the table in the sections ahead as the more common variants are described. These specifications are valid for Ethernet running at 10 Mbps or less.

┌─ **TEST TIP** ─┐

For each of the IEEE 802.3 specifications, memorize the data rate.

Table 2-4: IEEE 802.3a–t Specification

Attempt Limit	16
Backoff Limit	10
Insertion Loss	11.5 dB at 5-10 MHz
Interframe Gap	9.6 μs
Jam Size	32 bits
Maximum Bridge Hops	7
Maximum Propagation Delay	25.6 μs one-way, 51.2 μs round trip
Maximum Repeater Hops	4
Maximum Segments	5 (3 with nodes; 2 as link segments)
Maximum Stations on Network	1024
Maximum Frame Size	1514 bytes
Slot Time	512 bits (64 bytes)
Minimum Frame Size	64 bytes

	10Base-5	10Base-2	10Base-T (STP)	10Base-T (UTP)	AUI	Fiber	
Attenuation	Max 8.5 dB at 10 MHz Max 6.0 dB at 5 MHz		8-10 dB at 20°C		3 dB over frequency range	50/125 μm	≤13 dB
						62.5/125 μm	≤16 dB
						100/140 μm	≤19 dB
						8-12/125 μm	≤10 dB
Impedance	50 ± 2 Ω		150 Ω	85-111 Ω			
Jitter	≤ 8.0 ns		≤ ± 5.0 μS		1.5 nS at receiver		
Limits	≤ 2.5 km between receivers					5 segments max: link segment ≤ 500 m, w/4 segments and 3 repeaters, max segment is 1000 m	
Max Propagation Delay/Link Seg	2165 ns	950 ns	1000 ns		257 ns	5000 ns	
Maximum Cable Length	500 m	185 m	200 m	100 m	50 m	1000 m	
Minimum Cable Length		.5 m					
Min Separation Between MAUs	2.5 m	.5 m					

A typical Ethernet installation is shown in Figure 2-4. In this configuration, three 24-port hubs are running Ethernet in a star topology to 72 nodes. According to the 802.3 standard, this is a small LAN because it could support up to 1,024 nodes.

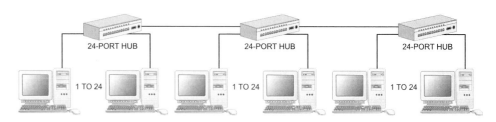

Figure 2-4: Typical Ethernet Installation

The entire LAN as you see it in the figure is a network. A **network**, in the context of Ethernet, means that if a collision occurs, it will be sensed by all nodes. Each of the hubs has a bus wire to which all nodes are connected. Also, notice that the hubs are directly connected. As a result, all nodes are directly connected via the bus in the hubs and the direct connection between hubs.

The LAN could also be called a segment if it was a part of a larger, interconnected network. Figure 2-5 illustrates this scenario. Two identical LANs (A and B) have been linked by a router. A router (discussed in Chapter 3) is used to interconnect different networks. A collision on LAN A will not be sensed by any of the nodes on LAN B since the router filters traffic between the two networks. The total network, then, consists of two segments in an **internetwork**.

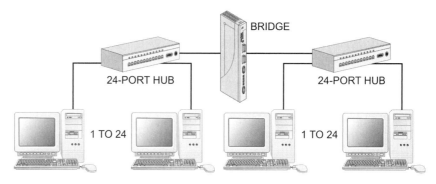

Figure 2-5: Interconnected Ethernet LANs

Note that in a star topology using Ethernet, a **segment** is understood to encompass all nodes that can detect a collision. Ethernet networks using CAT5 UTP cable typically have a single node connected to each hub port. For Ethernet LANs using a different media—coaxial—more than one node is permitted on a length of cable. For coaxial installations, the cable length with several nodes connected is referred to as a **segment**. Regardless of the infrastructure, though, an Ethernet segment occurs across any number of nodes that will detect a collision on the network.

Another scenario is pictured in Figure 2-6. This time, four 48-port repeater hubs (IEEE 802.3 permits a hub size of up to 132 ports) are stacked, presumably in a wiring closet. The four hubs have a total of 192 nodes connected them. Since the hubs are nothing more than signal regenerators, all nodes are in the same network. Because this is a 10 Mbps LAN running on UTP cable, each connection from node to hub port is a maximum length of 100 meters.

If, on the other hand, the LAN shown in Figure 2-6 were cabled with coaxial instead of UTP, we would have a different situation. The hubs may still be linked (stacked) together, but the nodes could be daisy-chained together in a bus arrangement (making it a physical star-bus topology). Coaxial media topologies are driven by the 5-4-3 rule, which states that Ethernet networks can have *five segments*, connected to *four repeaters/hubs*, with only *three of the segments populated* with nodes connected in a bus.

The three Ethernet LANs in the above example are using CAT5 UTP in the cabling infrastructure. At least one (probably two or more) of the nodes is a server. A Network-layer software package, such as Windows NT or Novell NetWare, is managing the flow of packets, as well as providing a level of reliability in the form of acknowledgments at the LLC sublayer. The nodes are all communicating in half duplex; that is, one gains access to the media bandwidth, sends a packet, then vies for access again. If a receiving node has a response to the sending node, it has to wait until it gains access to the media. Or, in other words, 10 Mbps Ethernet—at the node level—is a half-duplex protocol.

It doesn't have to be. IEEE 802.3 allows for full-duplex operation at 20 Mbps, but it's rarely implemented at the LAN level. At the time the standard was being determined, though, the predominant media was coaxial, and full-duplex operation on coax was cost-prohibitive. Since then, technology has changed, prices have dropped, and full duplex is a reality for Ethernet. However, at 10 Mbps data rates, it remains half duplex.

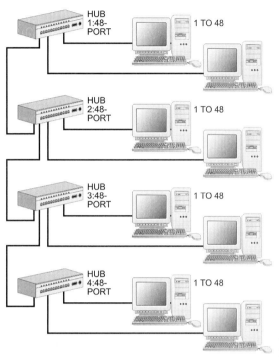

Figure 2-6: Ethernet LAN with Repeater Hubs

IEEE 802.3u Fast Ethernet

IEEE 802.3u Fast Ethernet runs at 100 Mbps.

IEEE 802.3u, also called Fast Ethernet or 100Base-TX, is very similar to the 10 Mbps variety, except it uses a modified physical interface, and runs ten times as fast at 100 Mbps. Why do we need to get faster?

Comparatively speaking, networks are slow when compared to their silicon colleagues in the nodes they connect. A modern microprocessor, for example, runs hundreds of times faster than the data that it generates can be sent to another computer. This means that the servers connected to a LAN or WAN, such as an intranet or the Internet, are prepared to serve users faster than the network technology can bring them the information. A database file, a voice or video file, complex and very graphical engineering or simulation applications, and real-time medical images may all be bottlenecked by the network.

> **NOTE**
>
> Ethernet networks may operate at 10, 100, or 1,000 Mbps data rates, and use UTP, fiber-optic, or coaxial cable in the cabling infrastructure.

Higher speed technologies are easing the network throughput strain, and Fast Ethernet is one that has been widely accepted. Approved by the IEEE as a subgroup of the IEEE 802.3 standards, it has the same frame format and access method (CSMA/CD), and is backward compatible with 10 Mbps, 10Base-T LANs (through an autonegotiation mechanism). The cabling infrastructure may be UTP, fiber, or a 40-pin AUI cable (an option, rather than an implementation for copper-based systems) when the transceiver circuitry is not on the NIC. There are Fast Ethernet specifications for each of the physical connections. These determine the particular method used to achieve the 100 Mbps data rate. They include the following:

- *100Base-TX:* CAT 5 UTP

- *100Base-T4:* CAT 3 UTP

- *100Base-FX:* multimode fiber optic

- *100VG-AnyLAN (IEEE 802.12):* token access

TEST TIP

Be able to relate the IEEE 802.3 specification to specific network media.

100Base-TX and FX are the most widely used. 100VG-AnyLAN was given its own 802 subgroup heading because it may also be used in Token Ring topologies. However, since it resembles Fast Ethernet in all aspects other than the access method, it's included in the section.

100Base-TX uses a coding scheme called 4B5B coding. This means that for each four bits entering the NIC card (during transmit), a 5-bit symbol is encoded. The encoded data is then subjected to MLT3 signaling. In MLT3 encoding (Manchester), a line transition is represented by a logic 1, while no-changes (consecutive logic 1's or 0's) are represented as a logic 0. Data is transmitted at 100 Mbps on two transmit wires (Tx+ and Tx−) and received on two receive wires (Rx+ and Rx−).

This occurs over CAT5 UTP, and the pinout of the RJ-45 connector is shown in Figure 2-7 (for STP wiring, a sub-D9 connector is used). Since it's CAT5, the +/− polarities of transmit and receive wires provide excellent noise immunity. Notice that with two wire pairs, the 100Base-TX is configured for full-duplex operation, although this is typically reserved for 100 Mbps switching hubs or routers. When a hub or router is operating in full duplex, the exchange between them runs at 200 Mbps. The nodes connected to the hubs or routers still send only when they have access to the network, which means they operate at half duplex, 100 Mbps rates.

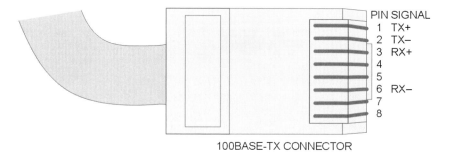

PIN SIGNAL
1 TX+
2 TX−
3 RX+
4
5
6 RX−
7
8

100BASE-TX CONNECTOR

Figure 2-7: 100Base-TX Connector

TEST TIP

Remember the type of physical connector employed in 10Base-T and 100Base-TX connectors.

Since 100Base-TX utilizes most of the characteristics of 10Base-T, it's not uncommon to include both options in node NIC cards. The reason is twofold. First, 100Base-TX is a painless upgrade for 10Base-T networks. The most apparent change is in routers, switching hubs, or repeaters. Each of these need to be physically and logically compatible to the 100 Mbps standard. The NIC card will use the same RJ-45 connector to attach to either type, but will be software configured for either 10 Mbps or 100 Mbps operation.

The second reason is that, with relatively little hardware change, both 10 Mbps and 100 Mbps nodes can be connected to the same repeater. Many vendors offer an option to 10Base-T hubs that includes one or more 100Base-TX ports.

100Base-TX uses the full bandwidth capabilities of CAT5 cable to achieve 100 Mbps data rates. Notice in Table 2-5 that the specifications are very similar to those of 10Base-T.

IEEE 802.3u 100Base-TX Specifications	
Wire Speed	100 Mbps
Cable Type	CAT5
Connector	RJ-45
Maximum Segment Length	100 m
Maximum Taps/Segment	2
Maximum Stations/Network	1024
Maximum Number of Repeaters	2
Typical Topology	Star

Table 2-5: 100Base-TX Specifications

100Base-T4 is an alternate version of 100Base-TX. It uses category 3 (or better), voice-grade twisted pairs for cable links to hubs. Unlike 100Base-TX, T4 must use all eight wires that are attached to a RJ-45 connector. The pinout is shown in Figure 2-8.

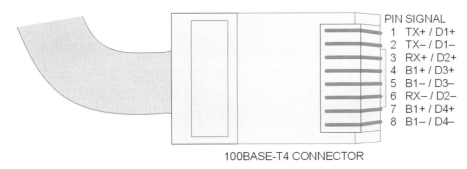

PIN	SIGNAL
1	TX+ / D1+
2	TX– / D1–
3	RX+ / D2+
4	B1+ / D3+
5	B1– / D3–
6	RX– / D2–
7	B1+ / D4+
8	B1– / D4–

100BASE-T4 CONNECTOR

Figure 2-8: 100Base-T4 Connector

Shown are two transmit and two receive wire pairs. Also, there are two pairs of bi-directional wires (B1–D3 and B1–D4). The bi-directional pairs are shared during transmit and receive. When a node wins access to the network, the data bits are organized into 8-bit bytes. Using 8B6T coding, the eight bits are coded so that each byte is converted into a group of six three-level symbols. Each symbol is then sent to the transmit and two bi-directional pairs in a round-robin manner.

The data rate of each wire pair of 100Base-T4 is 33.33 Mbps. Since three pairs are sending one byte of data (encoded into six symbols) one after another, the data is being transmitted at 3×33.33 Mbps = 100 Mbps. If you do the math, you will see that sending eight bits of unencoded data would take more than one pass across each wire pair. But each symbol is carrying an average of 1.33 data bits (eight data bits are used to create six symbols), so a full byte is delivered to the receiving station at a 100 Mbps rate.

100Base-T4 was created so that a company, having installed a base of CAT3 cabling, wouldn't have to pull it all out and replace it with CAT5 in order to run 100 Mbps Ethernet. For a new installation, it makes sense to spend a little extra and install CAT5 to run 100Base-TX. The specifications for 100Base-T4 are shown in Table 2-6.

Table 2-6: 100Base-T4 Specifications

IEEE 802.3u 100Base-T4 Specifications	
Wire Speed	100 Mbps
Cable Type	CAT3 or better
Connector	RJ-45
Maximum Segment Length	100 m
Maximum Taps/Segment	2
Maximum Stations/Network	1024
Maximum Number of Repeaters	2
Typical Topology	Star

100Base-FX is the fiber-optic version 100 Mbps Ethernet. It uses any of the common fiber-optic connectors illustrated in Figure 2-9. The connection between devices includes only two fiber strands, a transmit and a receive strand. Both are running at 100 Mbps.

┌─ TEST TIP ─────
│ Know the visual difference
│ between connector types.
└──────────────────

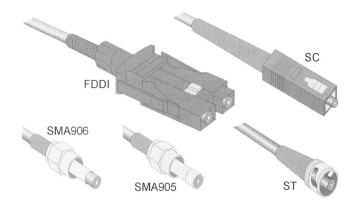

Figure 2-9: 100Base-FX Connectors

Data to be transmitted is first separated into 4-bit groups, then encoded into a 5-bit symbol (a 4B5B coding scheme). Next, the data is encoded using unipolar NRZ. Recall that unipolar NRZ assigns a positive voltage to logic 1's, and 0 volts to logic 0's. Since a fiber channel isn't affected by distributed reactances that cause intersymbol interference, this simple encoding method is all that's needed.

The IEEE specified 62.5/125 μm multimode fiber at a wavelength of 1,300 nm for 100Base-FX. Single-mode isn't in the specification, but if it's used, it will increase distances to around 20 km. Table 2-7 lists the specifications. Notice that when it's run full duplex, allowable distances are far greater. Typically, full-duplex operation will occur between switching hubs or routers, and not from the node to the hub.

IEEE 802.3u 100Base-FX Specifications	
Wire Speed	100 Mbps
Cable Type	Fiber, 62.5/125 µm multimode
Connector	ST, SC, SMA, FDDI
Maximum Segment Length Half Duplex	412 m
Maximum Segment Length Full Duplex	2000 m
Maximum Taps/Segment	2
Maximum Stations/Network	1024
Maximum Number of Repeaters	2
Typical Topology	Star

Table 2-7: 100Base-FX Specification

100VG-AnyLAN is described in the IEEE 802.12 protocol. It operates at 100 Mbps but uses an access method totally different than CSMA/CD. In a 100VG network, a hub determines which nodes transmit by using a **demand priority** access scheme.

Demand priority consists of a poll issued from the hub to each of the nodes asking them if they have frames to send. If they do, the node has full access to the network bandwidth and sends its frame. If not, the poll goes to the next port and does the same. In this way, each node connected to a port hub is given an equal chance to transmit, and there should never be a situation in which one node dominates the network by winning access (a remote, but possible occurrence in CSMA/CD access methods).

A network manager may configure access (through software) so that some ports have a higher priority than others. For example, suppose that node 1 sends large graphical files on a routine basis, while nodes 2 and 3 primarily send text files. Node 1 may be given higher priority to access the media than nodes 2 and 3, so that it's not penalized for sending large files across the LAN. Now, access may be extended as node 1, node 2, node 1, node 3, node 1, etc. Obviously, if all nodes have a high-access priority, the advantage is lost.

100VG-AnyLAN is very similar to Token Ring access methods, except it operates at 100 Mbps and can be used on star topologies (as well as rings), which have historically been reserved for Ethernet. A huge disadvantage to CSMA/CD is that network managers can't prioritize access for bandwidth-intensive users. They compete for access just like a user who sends out one 4-line e-mail message a week.

The downside to 100VG-AnyLAN is that users who don't have priority may complain about a slow connection, because high-priority users will be serviced before them. This situation can get to the point that a high-priority user appears to dominate the network. It's up to the network manager to set the priorities so that this doesn't happen.

One way IEEE 802.12 deals with scaling priorities is to set a maximum time that any node has network access. 100VG contains a timer that can be set from 200–300 ms, limiting the amount of time that a normal-priority request can be kept waiting. If a high-priority node has the media for an amount of time exceeding this, the hub will reset the priorities, giving the normal node a high priority. It then starts accessing ports beginning at port 1. When it gets to the normal port, it's permitted to continue sending frames until it's either finished, or the 200–300 ms timer once again expires. In this way, the protocol tries to ensure that no one port dominates the network.

As mentioned earlier, 100VG-AnyLAN can be used with star and ring topologies, making it independent of the physical infrastructure. CAT5 UTP or fiber cables are used to connect nodes to the hub.

IEEE 802.3z Gigabit Ethernet

IEEE 802.3z Gigabit Ethernet runs at 1,000 Mbps.

IEEE 802.3a, referred to as Gigabit Ethernet or 1000Base-T, means that data is sent at one billion bits a second. The technology uses CSMA/CD as the access method, and is typically installed in a star topology. It's backward compatible with Fast Ethernet, so a network can be easily upgraded from Fast Ethernet to Gigabit Ethernet.

The standard specifies fiber, coaxial cabling, or CAT 5 UTP cabling. Typically, the technology isn't run to desktop computers but is used between switching hubs or routers, and from hubs to farms of super-servers.

The servers contain a 100/1,000 Mbps NIC card to interface the cable and hub. The 100 Mbps option is made available so that existing Fast Ethernet systems can be migrated to Gigabit systems, the same way as many Ethernet cards include a 10/100 Mbps option. Four physical implementations are available with Gigabit Ethernet:

(1) 1000Base-SX: Multimode fiber with diameters of 62.5 μm (220-275 m range) or 50 μm (550 m range), that use 850 nm wavelengths.

(2) 1000Base-LX: Single-mode fiber with diameters of 62.5 μm (500 m range), 50 μm (550 m range), or 9 μm (5 km range), that use 1,300 nm wavelengths.

(3) 1000Base-CX—Coaxial cable, 150 cable (25 m range).

(4) 1000Base-T: CAT5 UTP (100 m range).

1000Base-T uses all four wire pairs in a CAT5 cable to send and receive. This provides two pairs for transmitting and two pairs for receiving. Send and receive may occur simultaneously during full-duplex operation. When data is transmitted, it's organized into groups of eight bits that are then separated into 4-bit nibbles. The nibbles are encoded using a 4B5B scheme. The encoding is done with 5-level Pulse Amplitude Modulation (PAM). The relative modulation levels used are $-2, -1, 0, +1, +2$. Four of the levels are used to represent two bits of data, with the fifth bit used for forward error correction. In other words, a single symbol contains two bits of frame data. Since there are four pairs, then 2 bits × 4 pairs = 8 bits, which is the size of the group that was originally encoded.

Data on each wire is sent at 125 Mbps. There are eight wires in the CAT5 cable, so 125 Mbps × 8 = 1,000 Gbps. Note that 125 Mbps is necessary, because 5-amplitude PAM is used with the fifth bit, or amplitude, for error correcting.

In order to operate at full duplex so that send and receive occur at the same time, a hybrid is used at each wire port to separate send and receive signals on each wire pair. In essence, the transmit signal on the receiving end is eliminated.

Figure 2-10 shows a typical Ethernet installation, which includes many of the Ethernet variants discussed. Notice that it illustrates the practical uses of the faster technologies. The scenario shown is a reasonable migration from 10Base-T to Gigabit Ethernet.

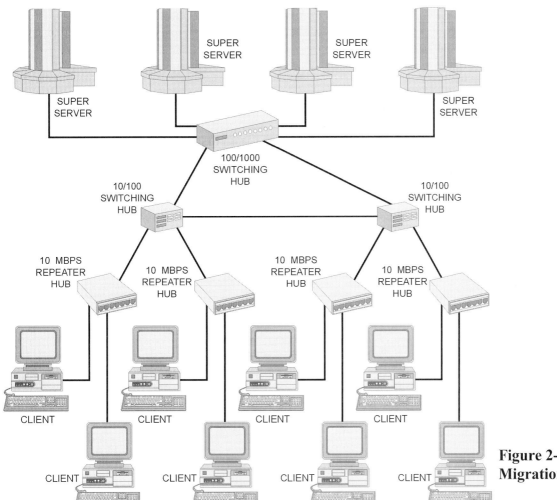

Figure 2-10: Ethernet Migration Strategy

IEEE 802.4 TOKEN BUS

A token-passing network sends a signal to each station, providing it access to the network. The access signal is commonly referred to as a token. The token bus access method differs from CSMA/CD by directly ensuring that a station has time on the network, rather than through a contention method.

The token bus method has several similarities to CSMA/CD. Only one station may transmit at any one time. The network taps are passive, allowing easy station addition or deletion. The token bus doesn't readily lend itself to fiber-optic cable, due to the bus taps. No bus network does. However, it should be noted that although there are many products that facilitate fiber optics in a bus, none is straightforward.

There are also several differences between a token bus and a contention bus. The first is that with each being a bus network—with its general pros and cons—a contention system is less complicated, and generally more reliable. From an applications standpoint, most of the advantages found in a token bus are also found in a token ring, without the bus disadvantages, as will be shown shortly.

In a token bus, the token is transferred to each station based upon **priority tables** contained in the network software, and there is little competition for the token. Stations with heavy traffic are permitted to transmit more frequently than stations with a light work load.

If a station in the token-passing sequence is lost, there are fallback measures to reconfigure the network, but during the reconfiguration, the network is basically at a standstill. This doesn't occur on the CSMA/CD bus.

The frame format for token bus is shown in Figure 2-11. The **preamble** is used to establish station synchronization. The Start Frame Delimiter marks the formal beginning of the data frame, and the End Frame Delimiter marks the end of the frame.

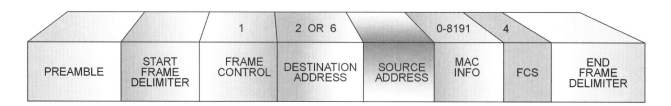

Figure 2-11: Frame Format for Token Bus

As in the CSMA/CD bus, the token bus has destination and source addresses. These are 6 bytes long. IEEE 802.4 allows a 2-byte option, as well. Whichever length is selected, consistency must be maintained throughout the network.

The Frame Control field determines the type of data contained in the **Media Access Control** (**MAC**) Info field. The Frame field is 1 byte long, and specifies if the MAC field contains logical link control data, management instructions for the Media Access Control sublevel, or station-to-station (user) data. The MAC Data field, containing one of the above, is 0 bytes to 8,191 bytes long.

The Frame-Check Sequence (FCS), following the MAC Info field, examines the frame for errors.

A token-bus network operates by identifying a station as a **predecessor**. In Figure 2-12, station 5 receives the token from station 6. To station 5, station 6 is its predecessor. Station 4 is the **successor** to station 5. To say it another way: The station receiving the token from the transmitter is a successor, and the transmitter is the predecessor to the receiving station.

The token usually passes down in a numerically descending order. Although it's shown to pass sequentially in Figure 2-11, the token-bus software contains **table arrays** for selecting which station is first to receive the token, which is second, and so on.

For example, the token route may be programmed for an initial pass of the following stations of Figure 2-12:

11, 7, 5, 3

on the next pass:

11, 9, 5, 1

on the third pass:

10, 8, 5, 4

on the final pass:

10, 6, 5, 2

In this example, station 10 and 11 have two opportunities to transmit, whereas station 5 transmits with each pass of the token through the network. All other stations are permitted time to transmit on every fourth pass of the token. The network may be configured in this fashion because station 5 has a heavy workload, as do stations 10 and 11. The other stations, relatively speaking, aren't expected to transmit as much.

The simplified network of Figure 2-13 illustrates the **token recovery** in a situation where one station in the network has become inoperable.

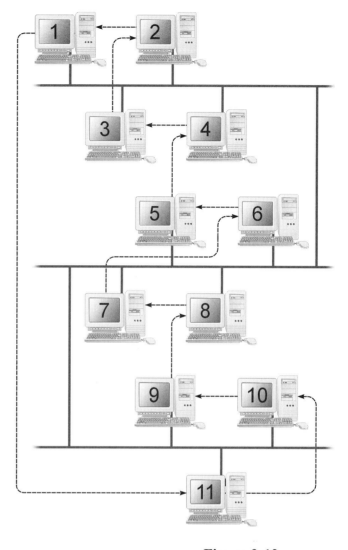

Figure 2-12: Successor and Predecessor

table arrays

token recovery

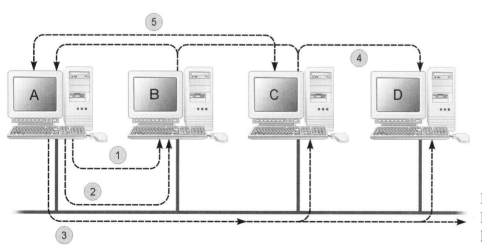

Figure 2-13: Token Bus Fallback Token Recovery Procedure

A transmitting station (station A) monitors the channel after sending the token (step 1) to its successor (station B), and if the successor transmits, it assumes the token pass was successful. If the successor doesn't transmit, it tries a second time (step 2).

who-follows

If the above fallback doesn't work, the transmitter sends a **who-follows** across the network (step 3). The who-follows has the address of the transmitter's successor in the data frame. The network stations compare the address in the frame to see if it is their predecessor's.

routing table

Once a match is made, the station that makes the match (station C) sends its address to the original transmitter (step 4). The transmitter reconfigures the **routing table** to make the matching station (station C) its successor. The station loading the token (station B) is cut out of the network, under the assumption that it contains a fault that requires operator attention.

The example token bus utilizes a continuously shifting FSK carrier, at a data rate of 1 Mbps, using Manchester encoding. The bus cable is 750-ohm coaxial. A multiple-bus network is often connected by regenerative repeaters. Stations connect to the bus via a 50-ohm coaxial cable, no more than 35 cm long. The 1 Mbps data is modulated onto a 5 MHz carrier. Other token-bus networks are available with data rates of 5 and 10 Mbps, at carrier frequencies of 10 MHz and 20 MHz.

IEEE 802.5 TOKEN RING

The IEEE 802.5 standard was adapted from Token Ring access methods developed by IBM in the early 1970s. IBM used the topology and access method in most of its networks, and even today, advances in Token Ring can often be traced to IBM. Second in the number of installations to Ethernet (estimates range from 10% to 20% of all networks), Token Ring is a widely installed network that is constantly finding new applications. Although there are slight differences in IEEE 802.5 and IBM's Token Ring, both access methods are collectively referred to as Token Ring, and this book takes a similar approach.

> Data rates on a IEEE 802.5 Token Ring network are specified for 4 Mbps and 16 Mbps, with the latter being used in all modern networks.

However, all Token Ring NIC cards also support a fallback to 4 Mbps for older networks. There's also a full-duplex mode available with Token Ring at 32 Mbps. This isn't run to the desktop, and when used, it's normally as a connection for superservers. Like Token Bus, the network media is accessed with a small frame called a token. The primary differences are that the Token Ring sends data on a loop architecture, and does so sequentially.

idle token

busy mode

The token is a 3-byte data stream passed from node to node. When the token is in transition from one station to another, it's known as an **idle token**. When a station with data to send receives the token, its mode changes to busy. During the **busy mode**, no other stations have access to the channel.

MultiStation Access Units (MSAUs)

All Token Ring networks are structured in a similar manner by connecting nodes to hubs in a star configuration, then interconnecting hubs in a ring fashion. Token Ring hubs are called **MultiStation Access Units** (**MSAUs**). Figure 2-14(a) illustrates an MSAU with nodes attached. Note that the MSAU-to-node connection is via a Token Ring NIC card.

- NOTE -

A token-passing network passes an access signal, called a token, to each station, based upon a priority table contained in network software. This ensures that each station has time on the network.

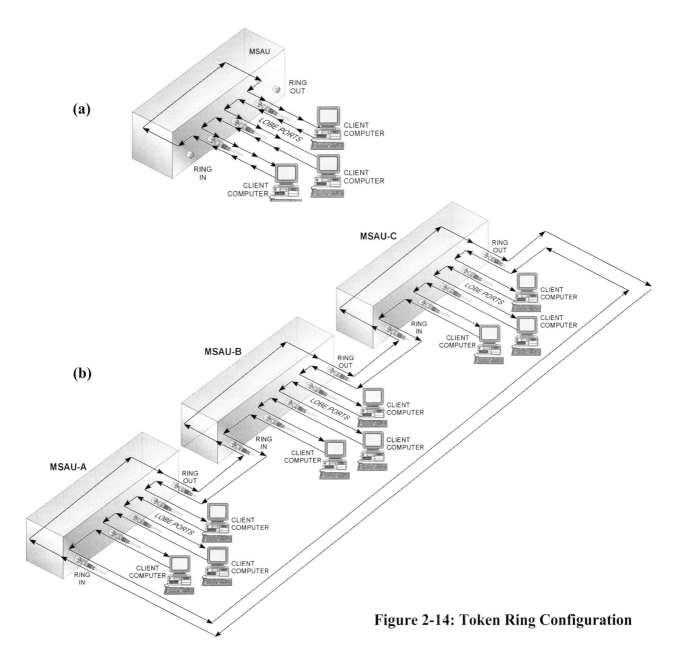

Figure 2-14: Token Ring Configuration

Ports on the MSAU are labeled Ring In, Ring Out, and Lobe. The lobe ports attach to nodes on the ring. The ring ports are only used to connect to other MSAUs, and can't be used to connect nodes to the ring. In Figure 2-14(a), there are no other MSAUs, so the ring ports simply loop signals back through the ring as shown. This occurs without any intervention from users or network administrators.

Figure 2-14(b) shows the same MSAU, but it's now connected to two other MSAUs. You can see that the ring ports are used to interconnect MSAUs, whereas lobe ports have nodes attached.

You should notice an outside ring that doesn't connect to any of the lobe ports. This is a secondary ring that's used if a node fails, causing a ring break. If that happened, the failed node would be wrapped out of the ring, and the secondary ring used in its place. You can see an example of ring-wrapping in Figure 2-15.

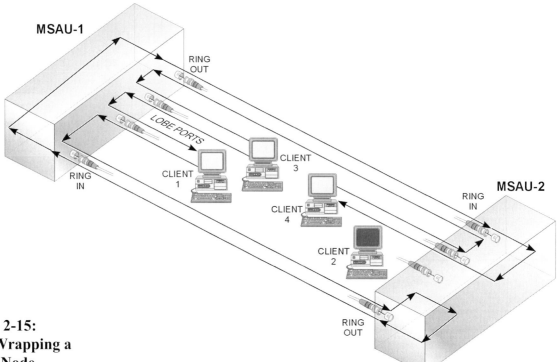

Figure 2-15:
Ring-Wrapping a
Failed Node

The outer ring is the secondary ring, and client node 2 has a failure. The problem may be in the cable connecting the node and MSAU2, or it may be in the client node. The MSAU detects the problem, and wraps the client out of the ring. Notice that in order for this to happen, data on the rings must be counterrotating.

Token Ring networks wrap a node from the network by using a process called beaconing. Every seven seconds, a test frame is sent around the ring (it starts with the first node to be powered-up) that includes the address of the sending node. The next node to receive the frame strips the address of the previous node from the frame and replaces it with its own; then sends it to the next node. If a node doesn't receive the frame within the seven-second time limit, it sends a beacon. The beacon contains the address of the sending node, the address of the upstream node that didn't send the test frame, and a beacon type. The beacon travels around the ring and if the node that didn't initially respond still doesn't respond, it's wrapped out of the ring.

downside

upside

On a Token Ring network, the cable is physically broken at the node. The data-in is said to enter the receiver on the **downside,** and exit via the transmitter on the **upside**. Once a station transmits, the token is returned to the idle state until it's received by the next station. The usual arrangement in a Token Ring is to have the sender's message rotate around the network, be removed by the receiver, and be regenerated around the loop until it arrives back at the original transmitter. Once it arrives, the transmitter checks the frame for errors, and if none are discovered, assumes it was received, error-free, by the receiving station.

The physical interconnections may take one of three forms:

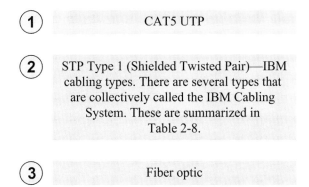

(1) CAT5 UTP

(2) STP Type 1 (Shielded Twisted Pair)—IBM cabling types. There are several types that are collectively called the IBM Cabling System. These are summarized in Table 2-8.

(3) Fiber optic

Table 2-8: IBM Cabling System

Type	AWG/Strand	Impedance	Shielding	Data Rate	Comments
1	22 AWG	150 Ω ±10%	Overall shield applied	16 Mbps	Between MAU and wall plate
2	22 AWG	150 Ω ±10%	Two pair shielded, then shielded together; additional four pair	16 Mbps	To carry data through walls; also carries 10BaseT
3	22/24 AWG	100 Ω ±10%	Minimum two twists/foot	16 Mbps	Token Ring UTP
5	62.5/125 μm	3.75 dB/km w/850 nm source 1.5 dB/km w/1300 nm source		100 Mbps	FDDI equivalent
6	26 AWG	150 Ω ±10%	Two pair twisted, then shielded	16 Mbps	From wall plate to station
9	26 AWG	150 Ω ±10%	Two pair twisted, then shielded	16 Mbps	From wall plate to station; accepts RJ-45 connector

UTP and STP cabling should not be mixed in the same ring network because they have different characteristic impedances and may cause the ring to crash. The IBM cables have the advantage of supporting up to 250 nodes on a single ring. UTP can support a maximum of 72 nodes. While IBM Type 1 cable supports more nodes, it's also more expensive, and not compatible with CAT5 UTP.

If you install a ring architecture, think carefully about what will happen to the ring in the future. Typically, UTP infrastructure—due to the small node limit—generates the creation of several small rings consisting of 50 to 70 users. The multiple MSAUs needed to interconnect the rings may offset the higher cost of the Type 1 cable. The frame format for Token Ring is shown in Figure 2-16.

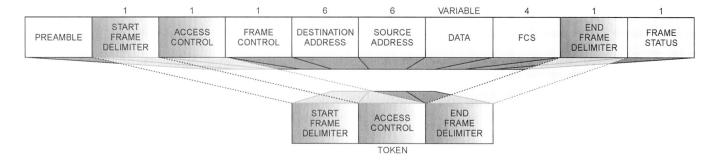

PREAMBLE	START FRAME DELIMITER	ACCESS CONTROL	FRAME CONTROL	DESTINATION ADDRESS	SOURCE ADDRESS	DATA	FCS	END FRAME DELIMITER	FRAME STATUS
	1	1	1	6	6	VARIABLE	4	1	1

START FRAME DELIMITER | **ACCESS CONTROL** | **END FRAME DELIMITER**

TOKEN

Figure 2-16: Token Ring Frame Format

It closely resembles the format for the token bus. The Start Frame Delimiter is one byte, and is used to alert nodes to the arrival of a token, a full frame of commands, or user data. The actual token is formed by the Start Frame Delimiter, Access Control, and End Frame Delimiter fields.

The Access Control field designates the frame as a Token or Command/Data frame. It also includes Priority and Reservation fields (used for demand priority scheduling) and a monitor bit. The monitor bit is examined to determine if a frame is endlessly circling the ring (which may happen if a node sends a frame that gets wrapped out before it returns, due to a failure).

A Token Ring frame is designated as a Data or Command frame. A Data frame contains node data, as well as information to upper-layer protocols. A Command frame contains no user data or upper-layer information. It's used only to carry control information for the ring.

The Frame Control field is used to indicate if the frame is data or command. IEEE 802.5 contains a source and a destination address, and as in Ethernet, these are six bytes each.

In Figure 2-16 you can see the portion of the frame that constitutes the token and which is the complete frame. When a station receives a token, it must first remove any messages addressed to it. It does so by examining the destination address field. Notice that the token will also be used to form the first two fields of the frame that's delivered to the node, along with the last byte if the token contains user data.

Since the transmission times of nodes can be predicted, Token Ring has a huge advantage over Ethernet. Token Ring has a huge advantage over CSMA/CD networks in that it's deterministic. This means that the nodes transmit at specific, predictable times. Since the transmission times of nodes can be predicted, so can the delivery times. Without contention on the network, there are no collisions. Ultimately, this has led to a general consensus that Token Ring networks offer a higher degree of reliability, and integrity, than Ethernet networks.

IEEE 802.11 WIRELESS

Wireless technologies have been utilized in networking for many years. But at the local area network level, their use has been sporadic. The reason for the sparse usage has been a lack of standards supporting wireless networking, and a system that offers compatibility with existing wiring infrastructures, particularly with IEEE 802.3 Ethernet.

The IEEE released an approved standard for wireless networking in the late 1990's, called IEEE 802.11. The standard specified a radio frequency (RF) carrier in the 2.4 GHz band, along with the use of infrared to carry data signals. The maximum data rate at the time was 2 Mbps. The equipment used with the original 802.11 standard was expensive. Due to data rates that were far less than standard 10 Mbps Ethernet, and the cost associated with wireless LANs, the market acceptance was lackluster.

In 1999, the IEEE approved an modification to the standard that is called IEEE 802.11b. The significance of the modification was that 802.11b called for maximum data rates of 11 Mbps, a fivefold increase over the original data rates, and on a par with standard Ethernet speeds. In the few years since the release of the original standard, equipment cost has decreased significantly. Consumers now have reasons to purchase and deploy wireless LANs and the demand for products that adhere to the IEEE 802.11b standard has been huge.

> **NOTE**
>
> IEEE 802.11b calls for maximum data rates of 11 Mbps.

In 2000, the IEEE approved the IEEE 802.11a standard. This standard offers even higher data rates, peaking at 54 Mbps. Commercial products began shipping for 802.11a late in 2001.

This section will focus on the IEEE standards 802.11b and 802.11a.

IEEE 802.11b

A wireless network is implemented with a wireless card installed into an expansion slot of a computer, and that communicates with an access point. The basic architecture is shown in Figure 2-17.

When node A in the figure has data to send to node B, the data is modulated onto a carrier falling in 2.4 GHz range, and sent to the access point. The access point (AP) has a function similar to a wired hub used with 10Base-T Ethernet networks. It receives signals from nodes and passes them through to the destination node.

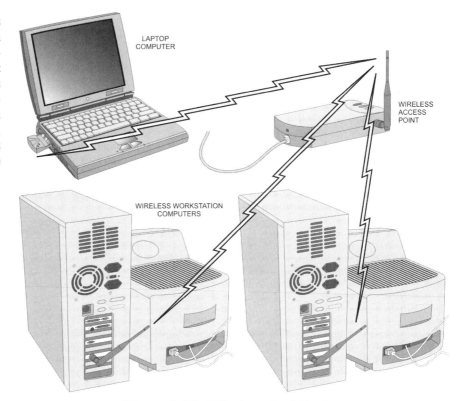

LAPTOP COMPUTER

WIRELESS ACCESS POINT

WIRELESS WORKSTATION COMPUTERS

Figure 2-17: Wireless Architecture

Most APs include an RJ-45 port that's used to connect the wireless network to a wired Ethernet LAN. In a typical implementation, the CAT-5 cable from the AP is connected to a wired hub port. Wired workstations communicate with wireless workstations via the AP.

The 802.11 standard allows three methods for stations to communicate with the AP:

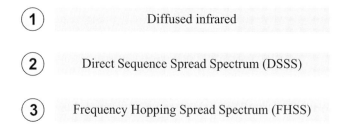

Diffused infrared data rates are 1 and 2 Mbps and the range between transmitter and receiver is ten meters. Unlike the radio frequencies used in DSSS and FHSS, infrared does not require a clear line-of-sight between communicating stations. In other words, it's said to be diffused. Infrared operates in the 850 nm to 950 nm range.

Due to range limitations and low data rates, diffused infrared has not been widely accepted in wireless local area networks (WLAN).

DSSS is the most widely deployed system used with commercial 802.11b products. Data rates currently peak at 11 Mbps and fall back to about 2 Mbps with increases in range to the AP. DSSS essentially uses amplitude modulation in generating a data signal from the wireless card. The data signal is first modulated with a pseudorandom noise signal (some type of phase shift keying, such as binary or quadrature PSK, is used). This produces a signal that has a random bit pattern that corresponds to the data bit. Then, the pseudo noise modulated signal is modulated (mixed) onto a carrier that falls in the 2.4 GHz range.

The resulting signal is a lower power pulse that is spread over a wide frequency range. To a receiver that doesn't contain the hardware to decode the modulated signal, it will appear as low power noise. But to the AP, or another wireless card, the received signal is demodulated by mixing the received carrier with the same pseudorandom noise signal originally used to modulate the carrier, producing the original amplitude modulated signal. Finally, a phase shift keying demodulator extracts the original data signal.

Note that 802.11b utilizes a double modulation scheme to produce the transmitted signal. The effect is that the transmitted signal is spread over a wide frequency range, and is, typically, transmitting at lower power levels than many noise sources. This means that, in the demodulation process, the original data is accurately detected using low power levels.

This doesn't mean that 802.11b products are immune from noise interference, though. The 2.4 GHz range is a crowded and unlicensed frequency range that is used to support microwave ovens and cellular phones.

Frequency Hopping Spread Spectrum supports data rates up to 11 Mbps. With increases in range from card to AP, the data rates fall back to about 2 Mbps. As with DSSS, FHSS operates in the 2.4 GHz range. The bandwidth consists of 79 sub-bands. Each of the sub-bands has a bandwidth of 1 MHz and data packets are required to traverse a minimum of 22 hops among the 79 sub-bands. The idea is that data packets are likely to be lost or garbled, but the number of minimum hops nearly guarantees that if this happens, the packet will be restored at another hop.

The essence of frequency hopping is a reliance on changing frequencies often. This results in a received signal that is low in distortion. FHSS also uses a pseudorandom noise generator to produce the transmitted signal. The generated signal contains a bit code that corresponds to a particular frequency pattern. The frequency pattern is used to tell the transmitter the precise interval frequencies that the signal is to be transmitted. At the receiver, the same pseudorandom noise is used to demodulate the signal and extract the original data bits.

Since a signal using FHSS is sent over multiple frequencies, the likelihood of the entire signal being distorted is low. This means that FHSS is far more immune to interference than DSSP products. Unfortunately, the practical range of FHSS is much lower than that of DSSS.

Data in a WLAN is sent using the access protocol Carrier Sense Multiple Access/ Collision Avoidance (CSMA/CA). Recall that Ethernet workstations access the network using Carrier Sense Multiple Access/ Collision Detection (CSMA/CD). Since the two network types use different network access protocols, they are not directly compatible. But more will be said about this later in this section.

> In a CSMA/CA network, stations wait before transmitting and listen to see if there is traffic on the network.

If there is, the station waits and tries again later. If no other stations are sending data, the transmitting station begins ending frames. The frame format used with IEEE 802.11b networks is shown in Figure 2-18.

Figure 2-18: IEEE 802.11b Frame Format

The Frame Control (FC) field is used to identify the type of frame being sent. As in some types of Ethernet frames, a wireless frame may contain user data, or it may be used to communicate network conditions with the AP.

The Duration Identification field is a secondary contention system unique to wireless systems. Wireless workstations may be several access points removed from one another; that is, a transmitting station may not be able to "see" the destination workstation because it is connected to a different AP (access points can be daisy-chained together in a WLAN). For this situation, a workstation can book an amount of time that it will have access to the network. The Duration ID field is used to specify the amount of time that the station will have the network. During this time, other stations will not use the network.

The Source and Destination Address fields contain the MAC addresses of the transmitting and receiving workstations. As with Ethernet network cards, 802.11 cards and access points have unique MAC addresses assigned at the time of manufacture.

The Sequence Number field contains a count of the frames sent to a single address. For example, if a station has five frames to send, it will include the number of frames to be sent with s sequential count of each frame as it's sent. If the receiving station receives a frame out of sequence, it will ask that the missing frame be retransmitted.

The Data field contains user data.

The CRC, or cyclic redundancy check, field contains a 32-bit composite of the frame that is used by the receiver for error checking.

The total frame length is about 1500 bytes, the same as CSMA/CD. With 28 bytes of frame overhead, the user data field can contain a maximum of 1472 bytes.

The IEEE 802.11b standard contains specifications for frame format, access methods, and radio frequency parameters. Once implemented, an 802.11b LAN is expected to perform to minimal standards of length between workstations and AP. At the maximum data rate of 11 Mbps, the minimum length is specified at 50 meters, or about 150 feet.

The further a workstation is moved away from an AP, the lower the data rate. The minimum data rate is 1 Mbps. The maximum distance at any data rate varies with the material that the radio waves must pass through between workstation and AP. Vendors will typically quote specifications for communication through an open-air environment; that is, a path with no walls or other obstructions. Commercial cards can transmit up to about a quarter mile at the lowest data rates in an open-air setting.

IEEE 802.11a

The IEEE 802.11a uses CSMA/CA for the network access protocol, and the frame format is the same as used with 802.11b. Where the two differ is data rates and methods used to modulate user data onto the carrier.

IEEE 802.11a uses a 5 GHz carrier (5.1 GHz to 5.85 GHz). The 802.11a frequency range is separated into eight, 20 MHz channels. Each of the 20 MHz channels consists of 52 narrow-band carriers that have a bandwidth of 300 kHz. Each of the 52 narrow-band channels can carry 125 kbps of data.

The 52 subcarriers in a 20 MHz channels are sent simultaneously, in parallel. The receiving device (another 802.11a card or an 802.11a access point) processes the data contained in each 52 MHz subchannel. Each channel contains a small part of the total data sent. Once all 52 channels have been processed by the receiver, the complete amount of data transmitted will be received.

Since the channel bandwidth is 20 MHz wide, a large amount of data can be sent using 802.11a. Currently, the standard specifies a maximum data rate of 54 Mbps.

IEEE 802.11a uses a multiplexing scheme called Orthogonal Frequency Division Multiplexing (OFDM) to send the data across the 52 subchannels. At the transmitting station, the total data to be sent is divided across all 52 channels, then transmitted at the same time.

Once the data has been assigned one of the 52 subcarrier frequencies, it's modulated onto the subcarrier. IEEE 802.11a uses 64-bit Quadrature Amplitude Modulation (64-QAM) as the modulation method. 64-QAM is a subset of phase shift keying in which a single waveform of the carrier is phase shifted 64 times to represent the 64 bits being modulated onto it.

The standard allows for data rates to scale according to range between the stations. The rates decrease in 6 Mbps increments down to 6 Mbps. Currently, expect the maximum range of 54 Mbps at no more than 150 feet.

There are several enhancements in the work for 802.11a. The first is a 108 Mbps option but it's limited to two workstations communicating without an access point. A second, called the 5 GHz Unified Protocol (5-UP), allows for dynamic assignment of the 20 MHz subcarriers. Adaptive multiplexers that have been on the market for many years use a similar approach that allows stations with a lot of data to send to grab a larger share of the available bandwidth for short periods.

IEEE 802.11b and 802.11a are not compatible. That is, an 802.11a station cannot send data to another workstation through an 802.11b access point. At the time of this writing, there were products nearing release that contained circuitry for both standards in a single access point. Essentially, the AP contains discrete antennas for both standards and separate modulation and detection hardware. The idea behind the combination product is similar to that used with AM/FM radios.

Table 2-9 compares features of IEEE 802.11b and 802.11a.

Features	IEEE 802.11b	IEEE 802.11a
Carrier Frequency	2.4 GHz-2.4835 GHz	5.15 GHz-5.825 GHz
Radio Technology/ Modulation Method	DSSS FHSS Infrared Numerous modulation methods including PSK, QAM	OFDM 64-QAM
Range	150 feet at highest data rate	150 feet at highest data rate
Data Rate	11 Mbps	54 Mbps
Output Power	About 100 mW for DSSS. 500 mW for FHSS	50 mW to 1 W at the highest frequency
Client Connection	PCI, ISA, PCMCIA typical. Most APs include RJ-45.	PCI, ISA, PCMCIA typical. Most APs include RJ-45.
Wired LAN Connection	Typical is RJ-45; some APs include DSL and cable modem.	RJ-45
Security	40-bit WEP	40-bit WEP

Table 2-9: A Features Comparison between IEEE 802.11b and IEEE 802.11a

IEEE 802.11 Security

As an option, 802.11 networks can be secured against unauthorized used of data. The IEEE felt that a potential drawback to implementing the standard would be concern for securing sensitive data. Note that a similar concern is not addressed in IEEE 802.3 for Ethernet, apparently because wired LANs are more difficult to tap for user data.

Two methods are used for security with the standard: authentication and encryption. Authentication refers to a scheme in which a workstation must prove that it is authorized to receive data. Encryption refers to obscuring the data so that a key is required to decipher the content.

The system used for authentication and encryption is called Wired Equivalent Privacy (WEP). WEP employs the RC4 Pseudo-Random Number Generator algorithm with a 40-bit key. The transmitting station uses the key to encipher the data, and the receiving station uses another key to decipher the data. Only stations that have been identified to receive the scrambled data may decipher it.

The key is set by the user, or whomever configures the wireless card. Typically, the key is entered using a series of hexadecimal numbers, or ASCII characters. Some vendors allow for additional security using 28-bit keys, but the IEEE standard specifies only 40-bit keys.

Wireless networks are actually quite secure without encryption. But it's important to realize that because transmissions are sent over the widest possible coverage (that resembles a large lobe emanating from the AP), an unauthorized user could receive wireless transmissions from the parking lot of a company if he knows only a minimal amount of information about the network.

WIRED AND WIRELESS LANS

A wireless LAN cannot directly connect to a wired LAN. Ethernet, IEEE 802.3, uses CSMA/CD as the network access protocol, while wireless uses CSMA/CA as the network access protocol. The two protocols are incompatible. But, as mentioned earlier, most commercial access points include a RJ-45 connector to connect the AP to a wired hub.

> **NOTE**
>
> Access protocols have to do with the rules and methodology used by the various hardware to allow each user access to the network.

In order to connect two networks that are using different network access protocols, a bridge is used. A bridge converts from one network access protocol to another—from 802.3 to 802.11, or from 802.5 to 802.3, for example.

Figure 2-19 shows a simplified bridge used in a WLAN. (For details on bridging methods, see Chapter 3.) When a frame from the Ethernet LAN is sent to the access point, all fields except for the source and destination addresses and the user data are stripped and replaced with CSMA/CA fields. The newly formatted frame is assigned a duration ID that contains a time and duration in which the frame will be sent to the destination address. The AP will store the frame until the correct time assigned to the frame.

When frames are sent from the WLAN to the Ethernet LAN, the headers are stripped as well. The source and destination MAC addresses are retained along with the user data. Now, the AP will hold the frame while it attempts to gain access to the 802.3 LAN through contention as described earlier in this chapter.

Most commercial access points include a bridge for connecting wireless and wired LANs. The technology is widely deployed in converting other protocols and doesn't add significant cost to the AP. Some APs go a step further and include hardware for connecting to a cable modem or DSL (Digital Subscriber Line) telephone connection. Optionally, you may also purchase APs that have routing capabilities so that more than one user at a time can connect to wide area networks such as the Internet.

Wireless networks overcome many problems that are inherent in wired LANs. The single most important feature they offer is mobility for users. This is an important consideration as many companies migrate from using desktop computers to laptop computers. For now, though, it appears that WLANs will find their greatest acceptance in homes and in smaller businesses. Table 2-10 lists several pros and cons of wired and wireless networks.

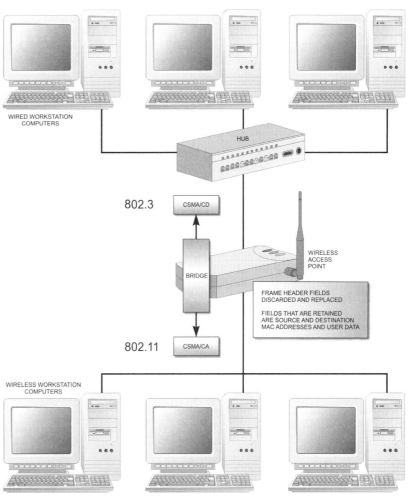

Figure 2-19: Bridging in Access Points

Features	Wired	Wireless
Cost	Low, except for complex hubs. (See Installation below.)	Higher than for wired NICs. Typical cost: $100 for wireless card, and $200 for the AP.
Data Rate	10 Mbps minimum; 1 Gbps maximum	11 Mbps to 54 Mbps; less at ranges over 150 feet. Some vendors include a 108 Mbps option.
Installation	Difficult and expensive	Easy and quick
Configuration	Easy among mixed vendors	Easy, but not all vendors interoperate
Security	None, other than difficult access to the cabling	40-bit encryption key; very secure. Without encryption turned-on, may be very insecure.
Reliability	Highly reliable for 10/100 Mbps NICs and hubs	Highly reliable for 802.11 NICs and APs; unknown for 802.11a
Range	150 feet for Ethernet	150 feet for maximum data rates, up to 1,500 (or more) feet for lower data rates

Table 2-10: Wired and Wireless Networks Compared

LOGICAL LINK CONTROL PROTOCOLS

The Logical Link Control describes the conventions a sender and receiver follow to ensure the data flow is orderly. They correspond to the IEEE 802.2 standards.

The LLC is a software interface that is situated between the software that controls network interface hardware, such as found on the **Network Interface Card (NIC)**, and the communication software running on a network, such as Windows NT/2000 or NetBIOS. The NIC is where the MAC controls—Ethernet, Token Ring—are found. LLC information will be encapsulated in a MAC frame, but the MAC function will remain unaware of the LLC, or any other layer information. However, once an exchange is initiated between nodes, the MAC frames its data, and then turns the frame over to the LLC, where the LLC information is placed in the MAC frame (in the Information field).

The LLC uses a software structure, called a **Service Access Point (SAP)**, that interfaces the Network layer and the MAC sublayer. The SAP is responsible for communicating the MAC frame to specific network communications software, such as NetWare, NetBIOS, etc. In this way, the communications software is made aware that a frame will be sent across the network, and the MAC layer will be made aware of the type of software running on the network. Table 2-11 lists several vendors and their assigned SAP values.

Vendors who want to be compliant to the Data Link layer of the OSI model (and most do at this level) must have an SAP value assigned to their Network-layer software. As you'll see shortly, the SAP is a formal field in the LLC frame.

Before examining the intricacies of the LLC, let's clarify some LLC terminology.

- *Type I LLC:* In a Type I LLC, frames from the MAC sublayer pass through the LLC SAP, and the only service they receive is to differentiate them for the particular communications software running at the Network layer.

- *Type II LLC:* Type II LLC also differentiates MAC frames for the Network-layer software, but the frames are also given sequence numbers so that the receiving node can track individual frames, and send back an acknowledgment that they were received. This creates a level of network reliability not found in a Type I network.

- *Connectionless Service:* A connectionless protocol doesn't track the sequence of frames or packets of frames. A connectionless service, at the Data Link layer, is Type I LLC. Connectionless frames may also be referred to as Datagrams, a carryover from IBM.

- *Connection-Oriented Service:* A connection-oriented protocol assigns sequence numbers to frames passed into the LLC, and tracks them at the receiving node. At the Data Link layer, it's the same as Type II LLC. Because the frames are tracked, connection-oriented protocols are also called reliable.

Network Interface Card (NIC)

Service Access Point (SAP)

┌─ TEST TIP ─────
Know the correct IEEE specification for the LLC sublayer.
└────────────────

SAP Value	Vendor
00	Null LSAP
02	Individual LLC Sublayer Management Function
03	Group LLC Sublayer Management Function
04	IBM SNA Path Control (individual)
05	IBM SNA Path Control (group)
06	ARPANET Internet Protocol (IP)
08	SNA
0C	SNA
0E	PROWAY (IEC955) Network Management & Initialization
18	Texas Instruments
42	IEEE 802.1 Bridge Spanning Tree Protocol
4E	EIA RS-511 Manufacturing Message Service
7E	ISO 8208 (X.25 over IEEE 802.2 Type 2 LLC)
80	Xerox Network Systems (XNS)
86	Nestar
8E	PROWAY (IEC 955) Active Station List Maintenance
98	ARPANET Address Resolution Protocol (ARP)
BC	Banyan VINES
AA	SubNetwork Access Protocol (SNAP)
E0	Novell NetWare
F0	IBM NetBIOS
F4	IBM LAN Management (individual)
F5	IBM LAN Management (group)
F8	IBM Remote Program Load (RPL)
FA	Ungermann-Bass
FE	ISO Network Layer Protocol
FF	Global LSAP

Table 2-11:
Vendor SAP Values

LLC Frame Format

The frame format for the LLC sublayer is shown in Figure 2-20. Keep in mind that the LLC frame will be embedded in the information (also called data) field of a MAC frame. Shortly, we'll look at frame exchanges at the LLC layer, but keep in mind it's assumed the LLC content is embedded in a MAC frame.

- *Information Field:* The Information Field contains user data as well as frames from any of the layers of the OSI Reference Model. In the OSI model, lower layer frames are encapsulated by upper layer frames. But the LLC sublayer is encapsulated by the MAC sublayer frame. The maximum size of this field is determined by the MAC protocol; 1,500 bytes for Ethernet.

- Destination Service Access Point contains the Network layer identifier used to differentiate between communication software types.

- *SSAP:* Source Service Access Point contains Network layer identifier used in differentiating the type of communication software.

**Figure 2-20:
LLC Sublayer Frame
Format**

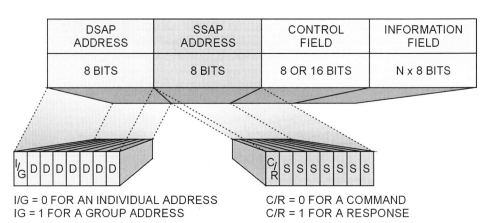

Notice in Figure 2-20 that a single SAP is listed for each of the network software vendors. But the LLC frame contains both a Source field and a Destination field, which implies different logical locations. The reason for this is that the same value is used in both the DSAP and SSAP fields. How, and why, would a destination and a source identifier be the same value? There are two ways to look at it.

First, consider the network from the viewpoint of a MAC frame. A user on the network has gained access to the network using a MAC protocol (such as Ethernet), placed data in the information frame, and is now ready to send that framed data to another user. The MAC frame contains the physical address of the destination user, but doesn't know how to get there. Fortunately, we have a Network layer protocol to get the frame to the physical address contained in the MAC frame.

Let's assume that the network protocol is using NetWare (Novell). The DSAP makes any necessary changes to the MAC frame so it can be sent across the Novell network. That is, the source/identity of the network software (NetWare) is specified by the SAP value.

Now, when a frame is returned from the distant user, the NIC card (in the local computer) needs to know what type of communication software was used to send the frame to the physical address assigned to it. Since it's a Novell network running NetWare at the Network layer, the destination node is informed about this by an SAP identifier for NetWare.

This may seem silly, but you have to understand the problem. The LLC sublayer, as with all other layers of the model, is supposed to be independent of subordinate layers, and the Network layer is supposed to be independent of the LLC sublayer. In other words, it's not the Network layer's responsibility to figure out how to tell the LLC what type of software it's running. It's responsible for getting frames to the right address. Therefore, the destination and source SAP values are the same in the LLC frame.

However, the LLC does need to know what type of MAC frame is being used. Technically, a standard LLC frame can be placed inside any type of MAC frame—Ethernet, Token Ring, etc. The type of frame is indicated in the Control field of the LLC. This field also tracks frames that are sent and received, as well as provides link administrative information to the LLC and Network layer.

It's important to note that recent network operating systems allow users to specify source and destination SAP values that are different. Windows NT/2000, for example, permits interconnectivity with Novell servers. This wasn't always the case. Users directly configure SAP values during configuration of network interface cards when the network operating system is specified.

The length of the Control field may be one or two bytes, depending on the size of the address fields. The longer the address, and the more frames sent without an acknowledgment, the longer the Control field needs to be. The 8- or 16-bit Control field is the heart of the LLC functions, so we need to take a detailed look at how it works. To do so, we'll focus on bit-oriented protocols that are most commonly used in LANs.

BIT-ORIENTED PROTOCOLS

Bit-oriented protocols have high efficiency and low overhead. SDLC (Synchronous Data Link Control), HDLC (High-Level Data Link Control), and LAPB (Link Access Protocol-Balanced) are bit-oriented protocols. Conversely, character-oriented protocols, such as IBM Binary Synchronous Communication (BCS), frame and send blocks of characters at a time.

With character-oriented protocols, transmitter and receiver synchronization is dependent upon synchronizing the characters. The character synchronization occurs for each character when asynchronous communication is used, and for blocks of characters in BSC, making it the more efficient protocol.

The bit-oriented protocols improve upon the efficiency of BSC as well as incorporate text transparency into the frame—that is, transparency is an integral part of bit protocols. Text transparency refers to including network-specific characters within the information field. For example, there's a specific bit pattern for "reject frame." Without text transparency, the receiving workstation will eject the frame that it's processing if the "reject frame" bit pattern is encountered. The BSC user has the option of not using text transparency, which reduces overhead, but at a cost of increasing errors.

In 1968, the CCITT (now the ITU) developed the bit protocol, High-Level Data Link Control (HDLC). Many dominant vendors of the time worked closely with CCITT in developing the protocol. The result has been the evolution of several protocols that are very similar to HDLC. In addition to HDLC, the following are the major bit protocols in use today. They're functionally the same as HDLC.

(1) Normal Response Mode (NRM): HDLC grew out of IBM's SDLC protocol, and NRM was, and still is, used in many point-to-point (PPP) topologies.

(2) Link Access Protocol (LAP): An early implementation, it's been replaced by LAPx series protocols.

(3) Link Access Protocol-Balanced (LAPB): LAPB is common in X.25 telecommunications networks, as well as local area networks.

(4) Link Access Protocol, ISDN D-Channel (LAPD): The HDLC-equivalent framing for ISDN and Frame Relay networks.

(5) Link Access Protocol for Modems (LAPM): Referenced in ITU's V.42 standard for error-correcting in modems.

(6) Synchronous Data Link Control (SDLC): IBM standardized Data Link protocols, and the CCITT used SDLC as the basis for HDLC.

We'll take a look at two implementations of the bit-level protocol HDLC: in the normal response mode, and LAPB, which is a peer-to-peer technique.

There are three types of LLC sublayer protocols; asynchronous, synchronous, and bit-oriented.

HDLC

High-Level Data Link Control (HDLC)

In 1979, the International Standards Organization formally adopted **High-Level Data Link Control (HDLC)** as the protocol for the Data Link layer of the OSI reference model. It should be considered the dominant Data Link protocol, and those protocols mentioned in the previous section should be considered as subsets of HDLC. In actual operation, the differences are slight.

As previously mentioned, HDLC is a full-duplex protocol, but it's not restricted to full-duplex channels. It was designed to accommodate a broad range of paths from sender to receiver, so that if a receiver is located at the end of a multipoint network, HDLC can still be used. This is true even for low-speed, broadcast (simplex) networks.

As will be shown shortly, HDLC provides for transparent text by incorporating it directly into the frame and does so with a single bit, which saves considerable overhead. This system of integrating text transparency makes HDLC a very efficient protocol.

HDLC has the capability of transmitting seven, and in some cases 128 frames without an acknowledgment. On a full-duplex channel, acknowledgments are often "piggybacked" onto data frames between transmitting stations. HDLC-formatted data travels considerably quicker than BSC on channels of the same bits-per-second rate.

The ISO has provided for two modes of HDLC operation. Stations on a network may be configured for a **Normal Response Mode (NRM)**, or an **Asynchronous Response Mode (ARM)**. The normal-mode stations are designated as **primary** or **secondary**. Within a network, only one primary is permitted, but there may be many secondaries. Before transmitting, the secondaries must first have permission from the primary, and in addition, they are forbidden to transmit to one another. The primary may transmit at any time to any, or all, of the secondaries. Each of the secondaries has a unique address that's provided for in the HDLC frame format. The address of the primary is implied. Since the secondaries may only transmit to the primary, their frame addresses are their own. In this way, the primary is able to determine which secondary data frame has been received.

In the asynchronous response mode, the primary/secondary designation is followed, but the secondaries may transmit to the primary without the express permission to do so. However they're still forbidden to exchange data among themselves. An alternative form of this mode is the **Asynchronous Mode-Balanced (AMB)**, which is commonly implemented as LAPB. A network configured in the balanced mode disregards the primary/secondary terminology. Stations on the network are **peers**, and may communicate with one another, as well as initiate and stop exchanges.

Of the three modes, the normal response mode is common in distributed networks where nodes are supplying collected data to a host. A data acquisition network, used in an industrial setting that monitors process control variables, may use NRM. Some older server-based LANs used the ARM mode. Most modern LANs use the LAPB version as well as many wide area protocols. Most business LANs use the LAPB version by default.

The frame format for HDLC is shown in Figure 2-21. Notice that the LLC frame has been singled out for clarity. HDLC is a layer 2 protocol, so it's inclusive of the MAC and LLC sublayers. The frame format shown in the figure is redundant with the earlier figure for an Ethernet frame, except it contains the LLC field, the Control field. It's worth mentioning that layer 2 is a logical level of the OSI model, so it doesn't specify physical network parameters, such as connector pin-outs, signal levels, data rates, and so on. These are found elsewhere, in the IEEE 802 standards, for example.

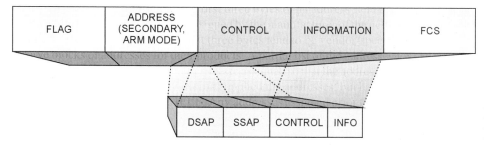

Figure 2-21: HDLC Frame Format

The frame is bound by flags with a fixed bit pattern of 01111110. This pattern tells the receiver that a data frame is to follow. The ending flag has the same pattern, and when consecutive frames are transmitted, the same bit pattern is used to signify the beginning of the next frame. This means that the Start and End fields of consecutive frames use the same bits. HDLC also contains an abort flag, which has the bit pattern 01111111. If for some reason, a sending or receiving station wanted to disconnect a link, it would send the abort flag, and the seven consecutive 1's would tell the receiving station to disconnect.

The next field in the frame is the Address field. In the balanced mode, the frame contains an address field for the source node as well as the destination node. It's one byte in length, and in the figure, only the address of the secondary station is shown. The length of the address can vary up to six bytes in length in the balanced mode, depending on the implementation. Ethernet, for example, permits a 6-byte address.

The Control field, which is actually a portion of the LLC sublayer, is also one byte long, and is the heart of HDLC, and the LLC in general. The Control field identifies the type of frame being transmitted. It contains a sequencing scheme so that the primary and secondaries can track those frames that were received error-free, and it includes a method of polling, used between stations, that identifies the last frame sent. The actual length of the Control field can vary up to two bytes. More will be said about the Control field shortly.

The Information field contains user data. The length of the field isn't specified; that's left to the communicating stations. While its length is indirectly a function of the Data Link layer, it is formally determined by the Transport layer. The reason for this is that error-free, end-to-end communication is partly determined by machine capabilities. The receiving station contains buffers that store data while it's being fetched into a computer. If the Information field is made too long, the buffers will overflow, and parts of the message will be lost. In practice then, the Information field has some predetermined length. Actual sizes may vary from less than a hundred bytes, to well over ten thousand bytes.

The **Frame Check Sequence (FCS)** field, also called the **Cyclic Redundancy Check (CRC)** field, is used for detecting errors. The field is two bytes in length, typically. However, it may also be longer. For a large frame of, say, 16 kB, a 32-bit CRC field is needed to ensure all errors are caught. The IEEE 802.3 standard for Ethernet stipulates a 4-byte CRC field.

At a minimum, an HDLC frame contains 32 bits between flags—8 in the address, 8 in the control field, and 16 in the Frame Check field. Any frame less than 32 bits between flags is considered invalid, and will produce a NAK (negative-acknowledgment) response from the LLC sublayer.

With 8 bits in the address field, 256 stations can be assigned unique addresses. If there are more than 256 stations, HDLC has an extended mode, which allows any number of stations to be addressed. The extended mode is identified with a logic 0 in the LSB (Least Significant Bit) of the Address field. The LSB is the first bit of the Address field to be transmitted. The number of address bits are usually extended by **octets**, or by 8 bits at a time. If the LSB of the address field is a 1, the frame will be in the basic format of 8 bits in the Address field. When the **extended addressing mode** is used, the Control field is also extended. An additional 8 bits are added to the basic length, to give a total Control field length of 16 bits. Note that when HDLC is incorporated in an Ethernet LAN, the address field will be extended to 6 bytes to incorporate MAC addresses.

There are three types of HDLC frames: **information**, **supervisory**, and **numbered frames**. These are identified by the bit configuration of the Control field, as shown in Figure 2-22. Information frames are used to carry user data from primary to secondary, or from secondary to primary, or, in the balanced mode, between any two stations. Supervisory frames are used to acknowledge correctly received frames, as well as to inform stations of various operating conditions such as a busy station, a station that's not busy, and to reject bad frames. **Unnumbered frames** contain special link functions, such as initiating the link between stations, disconnecting the link, setting the frame mode (normal, asynchronous, balanced synchronous), or tracking nonsequenced frames.

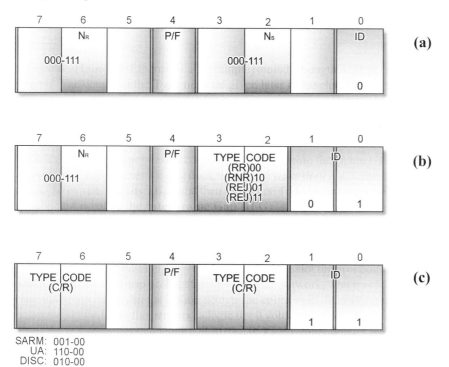

Figure 2-22: HDLC Control Fields

The Control field of the Information frame is shown in Figure 2-22(a). The LSB of the field is the frame identifier. A logic 0 in this bit identifies the frame type as Information. The receiver will expect user data to be contained in the frame. In bit place 4 is the P/F, or Poll/Final bit. The purpose of the P/F bit depends upon the usage. When a primary sends a frame to a secondary, and sets the P/F to 1, it's a poll to the secondary. Another way to say it is that if the P/F bit is set to Poll, the secondary must make a response. For example, if the primary were to ask the secondary if it has data to send, and the primary had set the P/F bit, the secondary would have to respond as to whether or not it had data to send.

If the primary sends data to the secondary and required an acknowledgment that the data was received, it would set the P/F bit. The secondary would then send a frame back to the primary to say it had received the frame. The foregoing illustrates the polling function of the P/F bit. But note that the terminology of "primary" and "secondary" means the same as source and receiver in the balanced mode.

The P/F bit is also used to indicate the final frame of data sent. For example, if a secondary had five data frames to send, it would transmit the first four frames with the P/F bit set to 0. In the fifth frame, the secondary would set the P/F to 1. This tells the primary that the fifth frame is the last frame to be transmitted from the secondary. In this case, the P/F bit tells the receiving station which frame is the final frame. In either a poll or final situation, a P/F bit set to a logic 0 is ignored.

number of frames
sent (NS)

number of frames
received (NR)

The NS and NR fields of the Information frame are used to maintain proper sequencing between primary and secondary stations. **NS** refers to the **number of frames sent**, and **NR** refers to the **number of frames received**. The HDLC system of frame sequencing ensures that no frames are lost between stations.

For example, if a primary has three frames to send to a secondary, it would sequentially number the frames sent in the NS field. The first frame to be sent would have a count of 000, the second frame would have a count of 001, and the third frame would have a count of 010. The count sequence permits the receiving secondary to check each frame. If a frame is lost, the primary will be able to tell because it won't be able to account for the frame in the sequential count. The NR field has a similar function, except it's sent to the transmitter from the receiver, telling it the number of frames received.

The 3-bit send and receive fields means that up to eight frames can be sent, until the field reaches the maximum count of 111. Once the maximum count is reached, the fields roll over to 000. HDLC allows for seven frames to be sent and received without an acknowledgment. A primary can send seven consecutive frames of data without the secondary responding. This represents a significant improvement over BSC, in which an acknowledgment is required after each frame of data.

The bit configuration for the Control field of a Supervisory frame is shown in Figure 2-22(b). Supervisory frames don't have Information fields. They're used to manage conditions on the link. The conditions of a primary or secondary encounter are contained in the Control field of the Supervisory frame. The first two bits of the Control field identify it as Supervisory by the 01 configuration.

As with information frames, a P/F bit is contained in the Supervisory Control field. The P/F bit is set to 1 when a Supervisory frame is used to ask a secondary if it has data to send. The secondary must respond to the command. Supervisory frames are also used to acknowledge receipt of data frames. If a secondary had sent four frames to the primary, the primary would acknowledge with the NR count equal to four. The frame would have the P/F bit set to 1 because, in this case, it would indicate the final frame sent from primary to secondary.

The Supervisory frame also contains a Type field in bit positions two and three. The type of Supervisory frame describes several conditions of the link between stations on the network. The **Receive Ready** (**RR**) is used when stations—usually the primary, or source of data—sends polls asking if there's any data to be sent, or to tell the destination node that it has data to send. It's a general indication that conditions on the network are normal. **Receive-Not-Ready** (**RNR**) is a busy response from a polled station. Most of the time, RNR is sent because the polled station's buffers are filled, and it's unable to accept new data. The polling station will continue to poll (using an RR Supervisory frame) until the busy condition is cleared. A **Reject** (**REJ**) is sent when a data error is found in the CRC field. When a problem is discovered by the receiving station, it ignores any frames received after the bad frame. It sends a REJ frame back to the transmitter with the NR count set to the last good frame that was received. For example, if the third frame received by a secondary contained an error, it would send an REJ frame, with the NR reading a count of two, back to the primary. This tells the primary that the first two frames were received successfully, so it retransmits beginning with the third frame.

Receive Ready (RR)

Receive-Not-Ready
(RNR)

Reject (REJ)

Sequence Reject
(SREJ)

Another type of Supervisory frame is the **Sequence Reject** (**SREJ**). If, after the third frame, a secondary received an Information frame with NS = 5, it would generate a SREJ to the primary. The SREJ would contain NR = 4. This tells the primary that the frames received after the third frame were out of sequence, and the primary would retransmit, beginning with the fourth frame. If this doesn't clear the problem, the secondary would respond with an REJ.

The Control field for Unnumbered frames is shown in Figure 2-22(c). An Unnumbered frame is used to start the link exchange, as well as to disconnect links. The first two bits of the field identify the frame as Unnumbered. The fifth bit is called a Poll/Final bit, and is used in the command/response methods of Information and Supervisory frames. If a station sends an Unnumbered frame with the P/F bit set to 1, a response is expected. As with Supervisory frames, there are several types of Unnumbered frames. The particular type of frame is given in a 5-bit **command/response code** (also called modifier function bits). For example, to initiate a link exchange, a series of Unnumbered frames are sent, back and forth, between two stations. The following text describes the procedure.

A station initiates the exchange by sending an Unnumbered Command frame (P/F = 1) to a receiver. The initiator contains a **Set Asynchronous-Response Mode (SARM)**. The SARM is a command asking another station to set up a link. The receiving station sends back an Unnumbered Acknowledgment (UA). At this point the link has been established. Supervisory frames will now be sent, with RR in the Type field, and Information frames containing the user data will be exchanged. If the initiator wishes to terminate the link, a **Disconnect (DISC)** Unnumbered frame is sent to the receiver. HDLC allows for up to 32 commands and 32 responses for Unnumbered frames. The type of frame depends on the network mode—asynchronous response mode, normal response mode, or asynchronous balanced mode.

The SARM and **Set Normal Response Mode (SNRM)** are from IBM's SDLC. As local and wide area networks proliferated, IBM extended the number of frames that could be transmitted, up to 128, without requiring an acknowledgment. This mode is called **Set Asynchronous Balanced Mode Extended (SABME)**, which is pronounced sa-bim-ee. The IEEE incorporated SABME directly into the 802.2 protocol, and it should be considered the standardized implementation of HDLC.

The Information field must be free to transmit any bit sequence in order to achieve data transparency. Recall that the header and trailer flags are 01111110. For HDLC to be truly transparent, it must be able to include in the Information field bit streams containing six consecutive 1's without a receiver interpreting the 1's as a trailing flag. HDLC uses a technique called **bit stuffing**, or **zero insertion**, as shown in Figure 2-23. When the sender finds six consecutive 1's in the Information field, a bit generator inserts a 0 after the fifth bit.

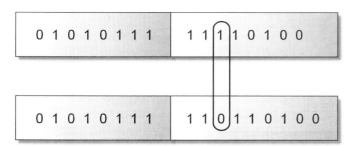

Figure 2-23: HDLC Text Transparency Using Character Stuffing

Bit-oriented protocols provide virtual communications using bit-stuffing techniques. At the receiver, the 0 is deleted. Bit stuffing ensures that any number of consecutive 1's greater than five will be a flag, or an error.

The last field is the **Frame Check Sequence (FCS)**. It's used to detect errors.

The HDLC Control field, DSAP, and SSAP all constitute the LLC sublayer information. The remainder of the HDLC frame comprises the MAC sublayer information, as described under the IEEE 802.3 section of this chapter. Together, the two form a Data Link frame.

Now, we're ready to look at data flow using HDLC. The first example shows HDLC in the normal response mode, and is illustrated in Figure 2-24.

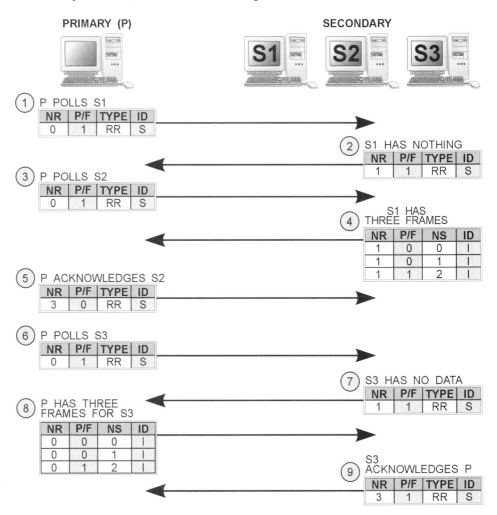

Figure 2-24: HDLC Data Flow Between Primary and Three Secondary Stations

A single primary (P) is communicating with three secondaries (S1, S2, S3). The Control field is the only portion of the frame shown, but you should assume that each exchange includes flags, address, FCS, and an Information field for Information frames. The Address field contains the address of the secondary station, and the primary address is implied. If a secondary sends data to the primary, the Address field is the address of the secondary. The devices in Figure 2-24, then, are operating in the normal response mode.

The data flow sequence is as follows:

(1) The primary polls S1, to determine if the station has data to send. The primary has transmitted a Supervisory frame—the I/D field would read 01. The NR field reads 0 because the primary has received no data from the secondary. The P/F bit is set to 1. Recall that when the P/F is set in a Supervisory frame from a primary, a polled secondary must respond. The Type field is set to RR. This means the primary is asking the secondary if it has data to send.

(2) S1 has no data, and replies to the primary demand for a response with a Supervisory frame. Notice the NR field is set to 1. This tells the receiver S1 received one frame of data. The Type field is set to RR, telling the primary it acknowledges the poll, and is ready to transmit data—but the P/F bit is set to 1, meaning this frame is the final frame from S1, and, by inference, S1 has no data to send.

(3) The primary polls S2. Again, a Supervisory frame is sent. The Control field is identical to the poll in step 1. Keep in mind, the Address field will differ since S2 has its own address.

(4) S2 has three Information frames to send. In each frame the NR field is set at 1, acknowledging receipt of the polling frame from step 3. In the first two frames, the P/F bit is off, but in the third frame, it's been turned on, telling the primary that the third frame will be the final frame sent. The secondary knows it will send three frames, and numbers the frames sequentially in the NS field. The frames are transmitted one after another. The primary doesn't acknowledge the transfer until it reads the P/F bit set in the last frame.

(5) The primary acknowledges receipt of the data by sending a supervisory frame to S2. The NR field reads a count of 3. This tells S2 that the receiver accepted three frames, and detected no errors. The P/F bit is turned off, because it has no function in an acknowledgment. The type of supervisory frame is RR.

(6) The primary polls S3.

(7) S3 has no data to send.

(8) The primary has three frames to send to S3 and transmits three information frames. Note that the NS field indicates the number of the frame sent, not the number of frames sent.

(9) S3 acknowledges the correct receipt of three frames by returning a Supervisory frame to the primary. Here, the NR field shows the actual number of frames received (3), not the number of the last frame received (2).

There's some variation in the actual implementation of HDLC. For example, a secondary reply to a primary poll may not update the NR field (Figure 2-24, step 2). In some cases, a primary will acknowledge receipt of secondary data in an Information field. If, in step 5, the primary had data to send to S2, it would send Information frames with the NR field set to 2. The set NR field would acknowledge that the primary had received two frames from S2.

An example of a data error is shown in Figure 2-25. In this example, the primary is communicating with a single secondary.

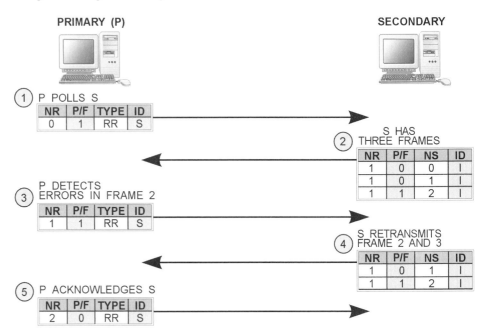

Figure 2-25: HDLC Error Control

(1) The primary sends a Supervisory frame to poll the secondary.

(2) The secondary sends three frames of data to the primary.

(3) The primary detects an error in the second frame during a frame sequence check. The primary doesn't stop the secondary from transmitting; it simply ignores any data received after the error frame. In the last frame, the P/F bit is turned on, and the secondary waits for an acknowledgment.

(4) The primary transmits a Supervisor RR frame with an NR count of 1. The secondary interprets the frame as a positive acknowledgment that the first frame was received, but not the second and third.

(5) The secondary retransmits frames 2 and 3. Frame 2 has NR = 1 to acknowledge the primary's step three frame. P/F = 0 since frame 2 isn't the last transmitted frame. NS = 1 since this is the second frame, and ID = I because it's an Information frame. The third frame has the P/F bit = 1 because it's the last frame, and the NS = 2, since it's the third frame.

(6) The primary sends an acknowledgment with the NR counter set to 2, indicating the last two frames were received correctly.

In order to avoid confusion, the number of frames transmitted without an acknowledgment is seven—the maximum count of the NR field. But keep in mind, HDLC allows up to 128 frames to be sent. Sending so many frames without an acknowledgment might not be a good idea. Suppose an early frame, perhaps the third, was corrupted. The receiver wouldn't get an acknowledgment that the remaining 125 frames had been ignored until after they were sent. HDLC may also use REJ rather than an RR, or an unnumbered frame may be used to convey link problems.

In the LAPB mode, the connection must first be set up before any data is sent. To do so, the source station sends an unnumbered SABME frame to the destination node. Table 2-12 shows the sequence as viewed from a protocol analyzer. In order to make it easier to follow events, the data has been placed in a tabular format. The setup occurs in the first four lines. The remaining lines show data exchanges between two nodes.

Table 2-12: HDLC LAPB Data Exchange

Line #	Source	Dest.	Sublayer	C/R	DSAP	SSAP	Type	P/F	NR	NS
1	Node_A	Node_B	LLC	C	FO	FO	SABME	P	------	------
2	Node_B	Node_A	LLC	R	FO	FO	UA	F	------	------
3	Node_A	Node_B	LLC	C	FO	FO	RR	P	O	------
4	Node_B	Node_A	LLC	R	FO	FO	RR	F	O	------
5	Node_A	Node_B	LLC	C	FO	FO	I	F	O	0
6	Node_A	Node_B	LLC	C	FO	FO	I	P	O	1
7	Node_B	Node_A	LLC	R	FO	FO	RR	F	2	------
8	Node_B	Node_A	LLC	C	FO	FO	I	P	2	0
9	Node_A	Node_B	LLC	R	FO	FO	RR	F	1	------
10	Node_A	Node_B	LLC	C	FO	FO	I	P	1	2
12	Node_B	Node_A	LLC	R	FO	FO	RR	F	3	------
13	Node_B	Node_A	LLC	C	FO	FO	I	P	3	1
14	Node_A	Node_B	LLC	R	FO	FO	RR	F	2	------
15	Node_A	Node_B	LLC	C	FO	FO	I	F	2	3
16	Node_A	Node_B	LLC	C	FO	FO	I	P	2	4
17	Node_B	Node_A	LLC	R	FO	FO	RR	F	5	------

A protocol analyzer will show specific layers of data, or all layers. You select the level of detail, typically from a list of menu options. In Table 2-12, the LLC sublayer has been selected. The DSAP and SSAP are FO, which is Novell NetWare. In other words, NetWare is running at the Network Layer during this transaction. Since these fields remain constant throughout the exchange, no more will be said about them.

① Node_A sends a SABME frame to Node_B. This sets up the link as LAPB. Node_A has sent a command (C) frame, which means it expects a response from the destination node. To reinforce this, the Poll (P) bit is set. Node_B must acknowledge the command from Node_A.

② Node_B sends back a response (R) in an Unnumbered Acknowledgment (UA) frame. Node_B, by sending the UA, is telling Node_A that it's not busy and that the link between the two of them is consistent—they're both using FO at the Network Layer. Although Node_A expects to see the P/F bit set to F, it's irrelevant. Node_B wouldn't set it to P because that would instruct Node_A to send back a response (R), which it couldn't do because it hadn't received a command (C) from Node_B.

③ Node_A sends a Receive Ready (RR) command (C) to Node_B, with the Number Receive (NR) field set to 0. It's telling Node_B that it is ready to send data, and that its NR field should be set to 0, because no frames have been sent yet.

④ Node_B responds (R) with a RR frame that has NR = 0. This is an acknowledgment that its NR field is indeed set to 0. This exchange is like synchronizing watches in the LLC sublayer.

At this point, the link has been set up, and the two stations can send data frames back and forth. The remaining lines do just that. But one station will send a couple of frames before getting an acknowledgment from the destination. Although it could send as many as 128, this isn't likely to occur except in very slow WANs, and LANs in which the server is overloaded. In fact, if a destination node doesn't send back an acknowledgment every four or five frames, you should suspect a problem. You'll want to know why it's taking so long for the destination to respond.

⑤ Node_A sends an Information frame to Node_B with C set. This frame contains user data in the Information field. Notice that the P/F bit is set to F. This means that Node_A doesn't expect an acknowledgment to this frame. Node_B could acknowledge it, anyway, although in this example it doesn't. NR = 0 means it has received no frames from Node_B. NS = 0 tells the destination the number of the frame that it's now sending. This is important because although Node_A is sending frame number 0, Node_B would indicate that it has received one frame.

⑥ Node_A sends another Information frame to Node_B. This time the P/F bit is set to P, so Node_B must return an acknowledgment. NR = 0 because Node_A still hasn't received any frames from B. NS = 1 because this is the number of the frame it's sending.

⑦ Node_B responds (R) with an RR frame. NR = 2 does because Node_B has received two frames.

(8) Node_B has some data of its own to send to A and does so by sending a command (C) in an information (I) frame with the poll (P) bit set. This is telling A that it expects an acknowledgment. NR = 2 because it has received two frames from A, and NS = 0 because the number of the frame it's sending is 0.

(9) Node_A responds (R) to the command with an RR frame, and has NR=1 since it received one frame from B.

(10) Node_A sends back some data in an Information frame. NR = 1 and NS = 2 because it's received one frame from B, and is sending frame number 2, which is the third frame it has sent.

(11) Node_B responds to the command with an RR frame that has NR = 3. Although the final (F) bit is set, it means nothing.

(12) Node_B now wants to send data. It does so in an Information frame with the P/F bit set to P, so it expects an immediate acknowledgment from A. NR=3 because it has still only received three frames from A, but NS=1 because the number of the frame it's sending is 1.

(13) Node_A acknowledges in an RR frame with NR = 2 since it has received two frames from B/.

(14) Node_A also takes an opportunity to send data in an information frame. With the P/F bit at F, it doesn't require an immediate acknowledgment. NR = 2 because it has received two frames, and NS = 3 because 3 is the number of the frame it's sending.

(15) Node_A, being a bit of a network hog, sends another frame. Notice that NR = 2 remains unchanged, but NS = 4 since this is frame number 4. It has the P bit set so B must acknowledge receipt.

(16) Node_B responds (R) as instructed in an RR frame. NR = 5 because it has received a total of five frames from Node_B.

This scenario could go on and on, but these data exchange steps should be enough to give you an idea about the activities occurring in the Data Link layer. You may have wondered how it was possible, not only for computers to find one another on a large network, but to ensure that the information sent actually got to the right computer. Reliability, as designed into the NS and NR fields, is an assumption in Data Link protocols. This extends to the IEEE 802.x protocols, because they use an identical logical implementation of HDLC. As mentioned earlier in this chapter, Data Link protocols are well documented and widely implemented—because they work, and work reliably.

HDLC offers the widest versatility of all bit-oriented protocols, because it imposes fewer restrictions on users. IBM's SDLC, which is very similar to HDLC, requires information fields to be a multiple of 8 bits in length. HDLC has no length limitations in the information field (but, practically, the length is set by the MAC sublayer access method—Token Ring, Ethernet, etc.). SDLC, on the other hand, contains many more commands/responses in unnumbered frames than does HDLC. For example, IBM has incorporated a test command that checks the integrity of a link. HDLC must depend upon the initial dialogue between stations to ensure that the link is workable. LLC Type I has a command called TEST. Technically, any command found in Type I is included in Type II. But note that it's not needed, since in LAPB, the link is tested when the two stations set up the initial ink. This is a Type II test.

The practice of bit stuffing—also used in SDLC—decreases the efficiency of HDLC. But, for the most part, the extra bits are worth the true transparency found in HDLC. Unfortunately, it complicates the hardware at each end of the link, since bit insertion and removal circuitry is required.

FIBER DISTRIBUTED DATA INTERFACE (FDDI)

An FDDI network transmits data at 100 Mbps on a ring, with a maximum distance of 100 km.

The expectation of network users over the last several years has changed from one of enormous amounts of computing power, to one of speed and volume. This is particularly true with the widespread use of available screen presentation software—Windows, Presentation Manager, large memory-intensive applications that accompany engineering applications, and multimedia programs. Computer users have come to expect the same high level of screen enhancements for all the work they do on computers. The problem with conventional LAN technologies is that they lack the bandwidth required to handle a large base of users who are exchanging graphics-intensive work.

A CSMA/CD, Ethernet LAN has a bandwidth of 10 Mbps, while a Token Ring network operates at 4, or 16 Mbps. Ethernet is available at 1,000 Mbps, but only with a contention access method. 100VG-AnyLAN operates on ring topologies, but isn't widely deployed. Although Token Ring only runs at 16 Mbps, the good thing about it is that node access can be made deterministic, an option not available with Ethernet. What's needed is a technology that offers the access advantages of Token Ring, and the speed of Ethernet.

The solution is the **Fiber Distributed Data Interface** (**FDDI**). FDDI is a 100 Mbps fiber-optic network that's specified in the standards of the American National Standards Institute (ANSI), as well as the ISO. This standard, as will be shown shortly, corresponds to the first two layers of the ISO Open System Interconnection (OSI) model for data communications.

FDDI networks can coexist with common mid-speed systems, such as Ethernet and Token Ring, and are, in fact, typically installed to interconnect other LANs.

> **NOTE**
>
> FDDI is the Fiber Distributed Data Interface protocol used for sending data at 100 Mbps over fiber-optic cable in LANs. The standard includes a set of protocols corresponding to the first two layers of the OSI model.

Before beginning a discussion of FDDI, it's important to distinguish it from a related system—the Synchronous Optical NETwork (SONET). SONET networks were developed primarily by the telecommunication carriers as a fiber optics–based system for interconnecting high-speed networks, with reasonable compatibility. It begins at speeds of 54.840 Mbps, and increases in increments to over 2.5 Gbps. SONET isn't acceptable for LANs, because it doesn't address Physical layer access methods. A SONET network, then, is applicable to wide area networks, while FDDI is associated with local area networks.

Specifically, FDDI is finding a larger range of user applications in the areas of real-time applications, distributed applications, client/server-based systems, and, as mentioned previously, graphics applications. Real-time applications include the process control industry, in which the mixture of volatile chemicals must be monitored continuously. Distributed applications include those tasks accomplished in tandem, among users with multiple systems. In a client/server system, the network connects the user to a database that contains the memory-resident programs holding print, scan, graphic, directory, and other network services. FDDI offers quick access to servers, so they can handle the many requests they receive.

In each of these examples, the user gains access to data, and it is routed on a shared network cable. The cabling is shared among many users, and must have the bandwidth necessary to accommodate the requests. Fiber-optic systems, when compared to twisted pair and coaxial cable, have very wide bandwidth and speed characteristics. As you'll see later in this section, FDDI is a versatile technology, allowing network administrators to use their existing twisted-pair cabling for transmitting 100 Mbps data from a fiber backbone.

FDDI is characterized by a dual-ring topology, as shown in Figure 2-26(a). The outside ring is known as the primary, or active ring, while the inside ring is called the secondary ring. Stations gain access to the active ring through a token-passing arrangement that allows equal network time for all nodes. If a node should fail, or lose power, the ring reroutes data around the station onto the secondary ring. In Figure 2-26(b), node 2 has failed. Notice that the failed station has been bypassed, taking it out of the network, while the other stations continue operating. When this happens, the network is said to have "wrapped" the failed node. A loopback route on the secondary ring creates a single, virtual ring.

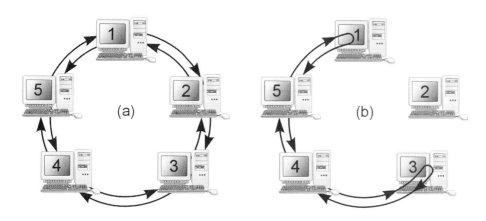

Figure 2-26:
FDDI Dual-Ring

In networks where the loading is exceeding the current technology of the departments, FDDI is used as a backbone for feeding other LANs. The LANs are connected to the fiber backbone in a star configuration, and are considered to be conventional local area networks connected to a FDDI network, as shown in Figure 2-27. Notice that the LANs are independent networks, connected to one another by the fiber backbone. The cable media in the LANs may be fiber, twisted pair, or coaxial cable.

An FDDI network transmits data at 100 Mbps on a ring with a maximum distance of 100 km. The distance between stations, called the link distance, is 2 km for multimode fiber, and 60 km for single-mode cable. The maximum distance may be extended to 200 km by utilizing both rings in the network, but doing so eliminates the fallback channel if there's a station fault. When both rings are used in a single ring, the maximum number of stations increases to 1,000.

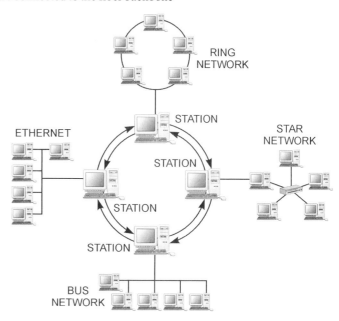

Figure 2-27: Backbone Connectivity For LANs

FDDI Protocol Stack

FDDI is patterned after the first two layers of the OSI model, and consists of four ANSI standards: the Physical Medium Dependent, Physical Layer Protocol, Media Access Control, and Station Management.

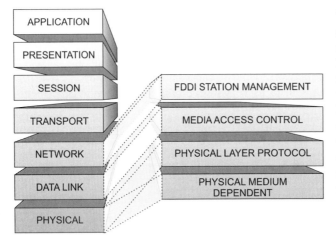

Figure 2-28: FDDI Protocol Stack

The standards are shown in Figure 2-28 along with the corresponding layers in the OSI model. The Physical Medium Dependent describes the type of optical interface, connectors, and characteristics of the cable. The Physical Layer Protocol discusses the encoding and decoding of data on the ring. Media Access Control provides for token transmission on the ring, framing of data, and symbol management. Station Management monitors the network for faults, recovery, and station configuration.

Physical Medium Dependent

The Physical Medium Dependent (PMD) layer contains specifications for cable and connector types, as well as the designation of receive and transport on the connectors. Devices attached to an FDDI ring are described by a single- or dual-ring attachment.

Devices attaching to both rings are called Class A devices, while those only attached to the active ring are called Class B devices. Normally, "device" is a generic term referring to the stations on the ring (computers, concentrators, bridges, or routers). Keep in mind that the usual topology used with FDDI is a dual ring of trees, with the trees branching off the ring as self-contained LANs. These LANs interface to the rings via a concentrator.

Figure 2-29 shows several devices attached to the ring, along with the correct class designation. The dual-attached station may represent a mainframe computer, or large file server, containing engineering drawings. The same is true of the single-attached station. On the right side of the ring are two concentrators, one dual-attached, while the other is single-attached. Typically, concentrators serve as an interface for conventional mid-speed LANs, providing data encoding and the necessary frame formatting.

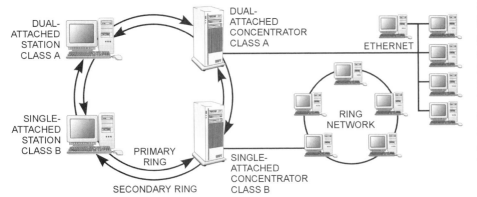

Figure 2-29: FDDI Device Classifications

Each device attachment includes a uniquely keyed connector. The connector types are illustrated in Figure 2-30, along with their respective pinouts.

Figure 2-31 is the physical connection for a dual-attached device.

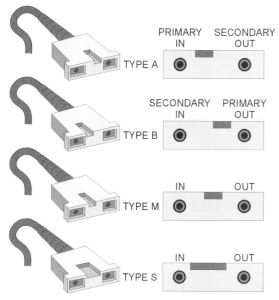

Figure 2-30: FDDI Connectors and Pinouts

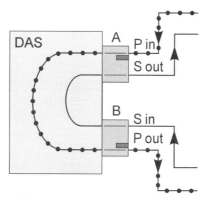

Figure 2-31: Connecting a Dual-Attached Station

The ANSI standard describes the characteristics for fiber-optic cabling used in the FDDI ring. The cables may be multimode, or single-mode. In multimode cable light enters the cable at various angles and reflects along the cable in many directions. In a single-mode cable, the light tends to travel in parallel lines for the length of the cable. Laser light is often single-mode, while the light emitted from LEDs is generally multimode.

A single-mode cable will have less dispersion of the light wave, and consequently, less distortion of data bits. Because there is less dispersion, light travels further along the single-mode cable than the multimode before repeaters are needed, although at a higher cost.

In addition to being single- and multimode, cable may be stepped-index or graded-index. A stepped-index cable refracts at the junction of the core and cladding in a sharp index, as shown in Figure 2-32.

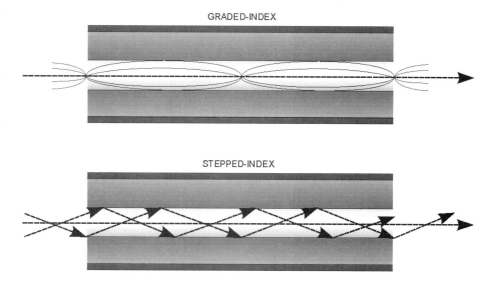

Figure 2-32: Indexed Fiber Cable

Graded-index cable includes layers of cladding material, with smaller refraction indexes relative to the distance from the core. The graded nature of the core results in the light waves traversing the cable with fewer refractions, and far less dispersion of the light. It is the choice fiber cable for handling high data rates. The precise specifications for multimode and single-mode cables are detailed in Table 2-13.

**Table 2-13:
Multimode and
Single-Mode Fiber
Specifications**

Multimode		
Nominal Core Diameter	**Cladding Diameter**	**Nominal Numerical Aperture**
50 microns	125 microns	0.20
50 microns	125 microns	0.21
50 microns	125 microns	0.22
62.5 microns	125 microns	0.275
85 microns	125 microns	0.26
100 microns	140 microns	0.29
Single-Mode		
Nominal Core Diameter	**Cladding Diameter**	**Nominal Numerical Aperture**
8 microns	125 microns	0.20

**Table 2-14:
CuDDI UL Ratings
for 24AWG
Twisted-Pair Cable**

In addition to standards for fiber cable, ANSI has a similar set of standards for transmitting 100 Mbps data over CAT5 UTP. The standard is referred to as the Copper Distributed Data Interface (CuDDI). Table 2-14 provides the CuDDI UL rating specifications for a 24 AWG twisted pair cable.

EIA/TIA Category	Underwriters Laboratories	Industry Standard Application	Attenuation @ 1 MHz dB/1,000 ft	Attenuation @ 4 MHz dB/1,000 ft	Attenuation @ 16 MHz dB/1,000 ft	NEXT dB @ 1,000 ft	Maximum Data Rate
	Level 1	Voice, RS232	Not Specified	Not Specified	Not Specified	Not Specified	Not Specified
Similar to IBM Type 3	Level 2	ISDN, 120 Kbps	8.0	Not Specified	Not Specified	Not Specified	Not Specified
Category 3	Level 3	LAN, 10Base-T	7.8	17	40	23	10 Mbps
Category 4	Level 4	Super, IEEE 802.5	6.5	13	27	38	16 Mbps
Category 5	Level 5	TPDDI	6.3	13	25	44	100 Mbps

Physical Layer Protocol

The Physical Layer Protocol is involved with clock rates, repeat functions, and symbol encoding and decoding. In order to achieve the high data rates that fiber is capable of, FDDI encodes the data into groups of symbols, using a modified version of Nonreturn to Zero (NRZ). Unipolar NRZ is used for FDDI, where a logic 1 is represented by a positive voltage, and a logic 0 is represented by 0 volts. In a light-based system, there are no voltages, so the encoding must be modified. Figure 2-33 shows an example of FDDI encoding.

Figure 2-33: FDDI Encoding Scheme

In an FDDI system, a bit is defined as a change of state in the light, such as the presence or absence of light. A node samples the light (every 8 ns) coming from another node. If the light has changed states, it's a logic 1. If the light hasn't changed states, it's a logic 0.

From sample 0 to sample 1, the light changes from off to on. This change of state is represented by a logic 1 bit. During the next three samples, the light doesn't change states (it remains on) so the state is encoded as three logic 0s. At sample 5, the node will detect that the light has changed states, so it encodes the change as a logic 1. The next transition doesn't occur until sample 11 is taken. The light goes from on to off, so this is encoded as a logic 1. This goes on and on with a logic 1 generated for each change in the status of the light. The NRZ-encoded data is then separated into 5-bit symbol groups. The symbol groups and their assigned functions, are listed in Table 2-15.

The reason for organizing the bits into groups of five is that the FDDI clock rate is set at 125 MHz—a multiple of five. The fifth bit in the symbol is used as a synchronizing bit, so that the receiver can properly track the symbols as they arrive. Once the symbol arrives at the receiver, the fifth bit is stripped from the group. This means that although the FDDI clock rate is 125 MHz, the actual data is transmitted at 80% of that rate, or 100 MHz, because the fifth bit is stripped from the symbol.

The Physical Layer Protocol also is responsible for ensuring that all of the attached stations serve as repeaters for frames that are intended for another station. This is accomplished by examining the station address in the data frame. If the frame contains an address other than the station possessing it, it is copied and sent to the next station. There may be times when the next station is busy, and unable to receive a frame that's being repeated. In this case, the station holds the frame in an elastic buffer, until the next station is free to receive the frame. An elastic buffer is simply an area of RAM set aside to handle overflow frames.

Table 2-15: FDDI NRZ Symbol Coding

Decimal	Binary	ASCII	Meaning
Line State Symbols			
00	00000	Q	Quiet
31	11111	I	Idle
04	00100	H	Halt
Starting Delimiter			
24	11000	J	1st of Seq SD Pair
17	10001	K	2nd of Seq SD Pair
Ending Delimiter			
13	01101	T	Terminates Data Stream
Control Indicator			
07	00111	R	Reset (Logical 0)
25	11001	S	Set (Logical 1)
Invalid Code Assignments			
01	00001	H or V	H = Halt
02	00010	H or V	V = Violation
03	00011	V	
05	00101	V	
06	00110	V	Used for consecutive code-bit zeros or duty cycle requirements
08	01000	H or V	
12	01100	V	
16	10000	H or V	

Media Access Control

With a maximum frame length of 9,000 symbols, an FDDI frame has a maximum bit length of 4 bits/symbol × 9,000 symbols = 36,000 bits, or 4,500 bytes.

The Media Access Control (MAC) layer marks the formal separation from hardware-oriented protocols to software-oriented protocols. The FDDI MAC is responsible for frame-formatting, error detection and transmission, as well as providing the ring token. The FDDI frame format is pictured in Figure 2-34. The data is frame-formatted before it's encoded.

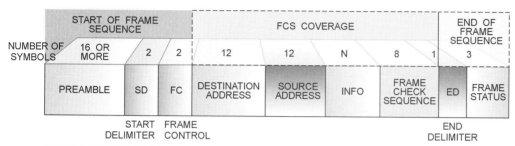

MAXIMUM FRAME LENGTH = 900 SYMBOLS (INCLUDING 4 SYMBOLS OF PREAMBLE)

Figure 2-34: FDDI Frame Format

The preamble is a minimum of four symbols, and may be many more. It's used to establish clock synchronization among all stations attached to the network. The start delimiter designates the end of the preamble. At the other end of the frame, the end delimiter denotes the end of the frame. The Frame Control field specifies the function of the frame. The frame may carry user data, or it may contain instructions to the stations concerning faults, configuration, token searches, etc.

The token, passed from station to station, consists of the preamble, start delimiter, frame control, and end delimiter. A station receiving the token can tell what's in the attached FDDI frame by examining the Frame Control fields. The frame may be one of the following:

- *LLC:* A code of 50h in the Frame Control field tells the station that the Info field has an LLC sublayer frame in it, as well as headers from the upper layers.

- *SMT:* The Frame Control field will have a code of 41h or 4Fh in it, if station management information is contained in the Info field.

- *MAC:* A frame with C2h or C3h in the Frame Control field contains MAC sublayer information, including user information.

The 48-bit destination and source Address fields are derived from MAC addresses. Figure 2-35 shows an example of an Ethernet address, along with the corresponding FDDI address. Note that the 48-bit FDDI address is an inverted version of the 48-bit Ethernet address. The inverted, or canonical, form is then separated into 12 4-bit symbols for the FDDI frame.

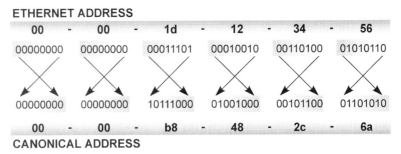

Figure 2-35: FDDI Addressing Scheme

Following the Address fields is the Information field, which contains the user data. Although there is no minimum limit to the Information field, the maximum size is dictated by the length of the frame. As mentioned, the frame length is not to exceed 9,000 symbols.

The Frame Check Sequence field performs error detection on a portion of the frame. It covers the source and destination addresses, and the Information field. The reason for not including the entire frame is that error detection slows the movement of frames through the network. FDDI contains several invalid symbols that may occur in the delimiter, or Frame Control fields, which will result in a rejection from a receiving station. This does not mean that some faulty frames will not arrive at the stations, but the chance occurrence is worth the increase in speed.

The final field is the Frame Status. The purpose of the Frame Status field is to provide the stations with management information concerning the frame they are handling. For example, a receiving station may recognize an invalid symbol code in the frame, and set the Frame Status to inform the next station that there is a problem with the frame. As you'll see shortly, this is important because all frames are transmitted through each station on the network, until they arrive back at the original sender. If the frame comes back with the error indicator set, the original sender knows there is a problem, and will send the frame again. Other uses of the Frame Status indicator are to note that the address in the frame is valid, or that the frame was successfully repeated to the next station, which is another way of saying that the station successfully copied the frame.

The Media Access Control layer also frame-formats the ring token. The token format is illustrated in Figure 2-36. It's an 84-bit frame consisting of sixteen symbols of preamble, a two-symbol start delimiter, two-symbol Frame Control field, and a one-symbol frame end delimiter. In the token frame, the Frame Control field carries a set or reset instruction. When set, the token is dedicated to a particular station, and when reset, it's available to the next station.

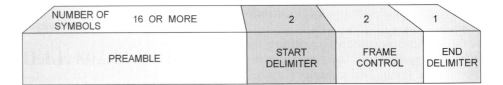

Figure 2-36: Token Frame Format

Once the data is frame-formatted, it is available for encoding and transmission over the network. Before the stations can gain access to the network, they must compete for the token. The process of gaining the token is called claiming and initialization.

The process begins with all stations issuing a claim frame. The claim frame contains a randomly generated number called a target token rotation-time value. The stations with the shorter rotation time values repeat the claim frame. Stations with a longer rotation time value are excused from the competition. The issuance of claim frames continues, with the time parameter set shorter and shorter, until ultimately, a station emerges with the shortest rotation time value. This is the station that wins the token.

The specific, winning target token rotation-time value is also the time that the token will complete a cycle around the ring. All losing stations will set their transmission times in accordance to the target rotation time. For example, if the value is one second, this means that the token will complete a trip around the ring in a second. Each station then knows the exact amount of time it has access to the token for transmitting or receiving data.

In addition to sending and receiving data frames, the stations connected to a ring network must also serve as repeaters for frames intended for other stations. You may wonder, if a station repeats frames, when does it have time to transmit? The repeater function is handled independently of the token. For example, assume that Station A is sending to Station C. Station A, possessing the token, transmits the frame to B. Since the frame is not addressed to B, it sends the frame on to station C. When Station A is finished transmitting, or the rotation time value expires, the token moves to Station B, which has already received the frame destined for Station C and sent it on. Now that it has the token, Station B transmits its own data.

Can a station that is repeating a frame send it at the same time that a station in possession of the token is transmitting? No. Only one station has access to the ring at any time. What happens to repeat frames while another station is transmitting? They are held in elastic buffers until the network is free. This occurs in the time between a frame being transmitted, and the expiration of the rotation timer.

Timing considerations don't always fall into place as neatly as just described. A station may use the entire time available to send a long frame, and the frame may be cut short due to the timer expiring. Then the token goes to the next station and it sends a frame. In the meantime, the elastic buffers of the stations are filling with frames to be repeated. In the worst case, the ring crashes. Usually, this situation does not occur because the frame lengths are limited to 9,000 symbols, and the rotation time is set slightly higher. This should allow time for repeating frames, as well as time for sending the maximum frame length.

Suppose Station A finishes transmitting a frame, and releases the token to Station B, but B does not receive the frame from A. Any station failing to receive a frame generates a beacon. A beacon is a Token frame the sender transmits to itself. If it does not receive its beacon, it declares a broken ring, and forces a wrap condition.

A ring wrap is shown in Figure 2-37, where the frame was lost between Station A and Station B. By wrapping around the cable between the two stations, the ring continues to operate using the counterrotating redundancy of the primary and secondary rings. It's important to mention that single-attached stations may be cut out of the ring if they are located in the section that has been eliminated.

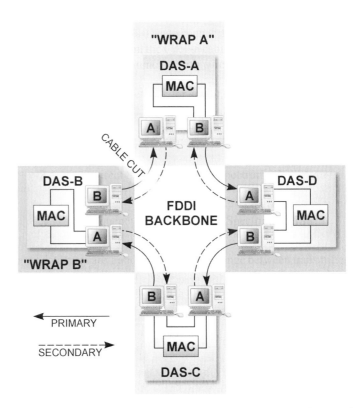

Figure 2-37: Ring Wrapping a Fault Condition

Symbol management, which refers to the generation and monitoring of network-control instructions, originates in the Media Access Control layer. The software examines data frames for invalid symbols and link conditions, and ensures the symbols generated are appropriate to a particular situation.

Station Management

The Station Management layer provides for individual station control of the FDDI system. Note that Station Management is not centralized in an FDDI network, but is delegated to each device attached to the ring. The stations are responsible for managing the lower layers, as well as coordinating events among all stations. In this respect, the devices are management peers on the network.

KEY POINTS REVIEW

This chapter has presented an extensive explanation of the IEEE 802 series of protocols.

- Access protocols have to do with the rules and methodology used by the various hardware to allow each user access to the network.

- The most widely used media-access protocols are CSMA/CD (Carrier-Sense Multiple Access/Collision Detection), CSMA/CA (Carrier-Sense Multiple Access/Collision Avoidance), token ring passing, and token bus.

- The IEEE 802 standards govern the Logical and Data Link layer specs of LANs.

- The lower sublevel of the OSI Data Link layer is Media Access Control, while the upper sublevel is called Logical Link Control.

- Systems management between the Physical OSI layer, the Logical Link sublayer, and the Media Access Control sublayer is described by IEEE 802.1.

- Logical-Link Control (LLC) is described by IEEE 802.2.

- Media Access Control is described by the IEEE 802.3 (CSMA/CD Ethernet), 802.4 (Token Bus), and 802.5 (Token Ring) standards.

- The two main access methods for LANs are contention and token passing.

- The 802.3 standard (CSMA/CD) was derived from an earlier data-communications effort called Ethernet undertaken jointly by the Xerox, Digital Equipment, and Intel companies.

- Ethernet networks are designed to detect the collisions that occur when two stations attempt to transmit on the data channel simultaneously.

- Once a collision is detected by a transmitting station, it sends a 32-bit jam signal to give the other transmitting station(s) time to detect the collision.

- After the jam is transmitted, a station will execute a backoff delay of some randomly selected time interval before trying to transmit again.

- Ethernet networks may operate at 10, 100, or 1,000 Mbps data rates, and use UTP, fiber-optic, or coaxial cable in the cabling infrastructure.

- A token-passing network passes an access signal, called a token, to each station, based upon a priority table contained in network software. This ensures that each station has time on the network.

- In a Token Ring network, the token is transferred to each station sequentially, in a loop architecture.

- FDDI is the Fiber Distributed Data Interface protocol used for sending data at 100 Mbps over fiber-optic cable in LANs. The standard includes a set of protocols corresponding to the first two layers of the OSI model.

At this point, review the objectives listed at the beginning of the chapter to be certain that you understand and can perform them. Afterward, answer the review questions that follow to verify your knowledge of the information.

REVIEW QUESTIONS

The following questions test your knowledge of the material presented in this chapter:

1. Fiber-optic connector types are specified in the _____ layer.

2. An FDDI symbol group contains _____ data bit(s) and _____ synchronizing bit(s).

3. What is the signaling rate, and cable type, for 100Base-FX?

4. Describe the process of contention access in a bus network.

5. According to the token recovery procedure for a token bus network, what happens to a station that loses the token?

6. In a Token Ring network, how does the transmitting station know if its message was received?

7. What is the length of addressing fields in the 802 series protocols?

8. What is the data rate of 1000Base-TX?

9. What is DSSS?

10. What is the maximum data rate of IEEE 802.11a?

11. If a collision is to occur on an IEEE 802.3 CSMA/CD network, it will occur within the first _____ bits of the frame.

12. What is the data rate of a 10Base-5 network?

13. What is the difference between CSMA/CD and CSMA/CA?

14. Describe how the LLC serves as an interface between the MAC sublayer and the Network layer.

15. In order to connect to a wired LAN, an IEEE 802.11 AP must incorporate a _____ .

EXAM QUESTIONS

1. In a contention-based LAN, the nodes gain access to the channel by
   _____.
   a. having access to a token
   b. competing for the channel
   c. receiving permission from a primary station
   d. requesting permission from a predecessor

2. A CSMA/CD frame ensures data is sent to the correct node by _____.
   a. including a source and a destination address
   b. including a Frame Control field
   c. including an Access Control field
   d. including a Frame Check Sequence field

3. The purpose of the Access Control field in a token ring frame is _____.
   a. as a start frame field
   b. to designate source and destination addresses
   c. to designate the frame as a token or command frame
   d. to carry user data

4. The maximum data rate of the FDDI standard is _____.
   a. 100 Mbps
   b. 20 Mbps
   c. 10 Mbps
   d. 2 Mbps

5. Typically, FDDI is used to _____.
   a. provide a wide area connection
   b. serve as a port to the Internet
   c. recover from network errors
   d. interconnect LANs

6. A 10Base-T network using CAT5 UTP may be a maximum length from hub
   port to node of _____.
   a. 25 m
   b. 50 m
   c. 100 m
   d. 200 m

7. The maximum data rate on an IEEE 802.11b network is _____.
   a. 11 Mbps
   b. 48 Mbps
   c. 54 Mbps
   d. 108 Mbps

8. What network access method is used for IEEE 802.3?
   a. CSMA/CD
   b. CSMA/CA
   c. LAPB
   d. HDLC

9. What is the media type used with 100Base-FX?
   a. UTP
   b. STP
   c. coaxial
   d. fiber optic

10. What is the purpose of SAP used in IEEE 802.2?
    a. It identifies the type of network software.
    b. It's the method used by nodes to access the network.
    c. It provides for error correction.
    d. It determines the MAC sublayer protocol.

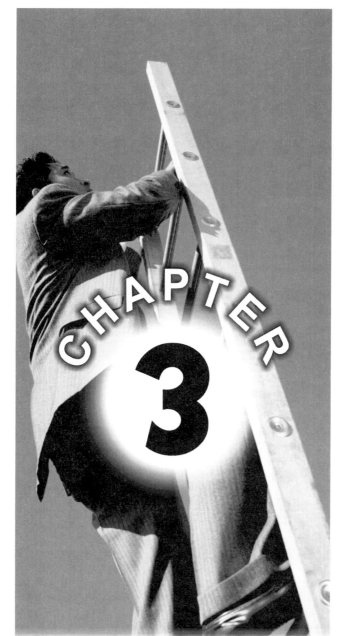

CHAPTER 3

NETWORKING HARDWARE

LEARNING
OBJECTIVES

LEARNING OBJECTIVES

Upon completion of this chapter and its related lab procedures, you will be able to perform the following tasks:

1. Identify the purpose, functions, and features of the following network components:

   - Network interface cards

   - Hub

   - Bridge

   - Router

   - Switch

   - Wireless access points

   - Gateway

   - CSU/DSU

   - Modems

   - ISDN adapters

NETWORKING HARDWARE

INTRODUCTION

The hardware commonly used with networks is described in this chapter. Along with wiring infrastructures, networking hardware is a much overlooked aspect of engineering a network. But it's imperative that a networking professional have a reasonable understanding of the range of hardware that is available along with the protocols used with the hardware, particularly the IEEE 802 series of protocols described in the previous chapter.

The Network+ Exam assumes a working knowledge of the basic purpose of the hardware described in this section, as well as the appropriate use of the hardware. For example, an Ethernet LAN can't use a wireless access point, and a CSU/DSU can't be used with ISDN.

It's impossible to design and implement a functioning network without understanding the capabilities of the hardware. This chapter provides an overview of common components. The next chapter, The **ISO OSI Reference Model**, places these same components in the context of a practical model for networking.

ISO OSI Reference Model

NIC

A **network interface card** (**NIC**), also called a network adapter, is a printed circuit card used to access the network resources. A NIC contains electronic circuitry that organizes data into unique frames so that the data can be sent, and received, on the network.

network interface card (NIC)

A NIC is specialized to the access protocol running on the network. The most common NICs are for Ethernet and Token Ring access protocols. Since the application for a NIC is specialized, you must know the access protocol running on the network before you install the NIC.

When you buy and install a NIC, you must know the type of network that it's to be installed in. Typically, the card specifications will list the IEEE protocols that the card supports. For example, a card will be compliant with IEEE 802.3, Ethernet, 10/100Base-T. Note that in the above example, if the card were placed in a machine to connect to a Token Ring network, the connection would fail.

┌─ **TEST TIP** ─┐
Know that NIC cards are access protocol specific.
└────────────┘

The NIC card serves several important functions in a network. It organizes data that's to be sent into the frames that were described in Chapter 2. Since no workstation can have unlimited access to a network, the frames are of a predictable length. Ethernet frames, for example, are about 1500 bytes. This includes the user data as well as any overhead such as MAC addresses, control fields, and error checking fields.

Error checking is done by the NIC. The NIC receives a frame and before transferring user data to the computer, the frame is checked for errors using the CRC field of the frame. If there's a problem, the frame will be rejected.

Through a rather complicated process (detailed in Chapter 5), the NIC will be the first decision point in determining where a frame of data will go once it leaves a computer. That is, the NIC decides whether the frame will be sent to another device on the local network, or to a remote network.

The NIC, in conjunction with the network access protocol, monitors conditions on the network. For example, it will track collisions on an Ethernet network, the number of frames lost, the number of bad frames, or the number of times that a frame had to be retransmitted.

A NIC slips into the expansion slot of a server or workstation. Data to be sent onto the network is transferred to the NIC on the parallel bus within the computer. The NIC converts the parallel data to serial data, packages the data into a frame, and sends it to the network.

When a NIC receives data from the network, it removes the **frame headers** (the portion of a frame that doesn't contain user data), and converts the received serial data to parallel.

Figure 3-1 illustrates the different bus styles used in the majority of NICs.

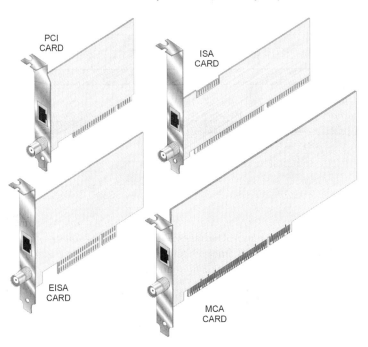

Figure 3-1: Common NIC Expansion Bus Types

Bus styles include:

- The **Peripheral Component Interconnect** (**PCI**) style is the most common bus style in use. It supports a 32-bit parallel bus. PCI NICs should be used in Pentium and Power PC-based computers, and later. It provides the fastest transfer rates of all bus styles.

- The **Extended Industry Standard Architecture (EISA)** style supports a 32-bit bus. Adapted from the earlier Industry Standard Architecture bus, it's backward compatible with the original ISA standard, meaning that an EISA NIC can also be used in computers with a 16-bit bus. While an EISA card transfers data along a bus the same size as a PCI card, it may not have the performance enhancements of PCI (such as RAM buffers or an onboard microprocessor).

- The **Industry Standard Architecture (ISA)** originally supported an 8-bit bus architecture. The bus was later extended to 16-bit. An ISA NIC will be found in older servers and workstations.

- The **Micro Channel Architecture bus** was developed by IBM. A Micro Channel Architecture bus will support a 16- or 32-bit bus. But since the bus is electrically different than the ISA standard, it can only be used in computers that use the Micro Channel Architecture bus, such as an IBM PS/2.

- The **Personal Computer Memory Card International Association (PCMCIA)** is a bus style used in all notebook computers and in some desktop computers.

The NIC that you install must use the same type of bus as the server or workstation that it's installed in. Most computers will support more than one bus, such as expansion slots for PCI or EISA.

The physical connector on a NIC may be one of two basic types. The first is an RJ-45 connector, which resembles an oversized telephone connector (an RJ-11 connector. "RJ" stands for registered jack.). RJ-45 connectors contain eight pins and connect to **unshielded twisted pair** (UTP) cabling.

The second type of NIC connector is a **BNC (British Naval Connector)**. A BNC connector is used with coaxial cable. A NIC may have a BNC connector, an RJ-45 connector, or both types of connectors.

A NIC is installed in a computer by slipping it into one of the expansion slots of the computer. Once installed, the card must be configured. There are a couple of ways to configure a NIC.

Most workstations running Windows operating systems, and some servers (Windows 2000, for example), support Microsoft's **Plug-and-Play** (**PnP**) functionality. A PnP-compliant device such as a NIC is automatically configured by the operating system. The idea is that you install the card, turn on power to the computer, and PnP handles the configuration details. The Plug and Play function may not always work if the device being installed only partially supports PnP operations. Some operating systems may not support PnP operations by default. For example, many non-Windows operating systems such as UNIX may not automatically configure hardware devices at all.

For a NIC that can't be configured with PnP, you must manually configure the card. There are two ways to do so. The first is accomplished using a software configuration. The second method requires you to manually position jumper or DIP switches.

Regardless of the method used to configure the NIC (or other adapters, such as modems), there are three settings that you should be aware of:

Interrupt Request (IRQ)

- **Interrupt Request (IRQ):** The IRQ is a signal sent to the system microprocessor indicating that a device requires the attention of the microprocessor. All peripherals in a computer (mouse, keyboard, CD-ROM) are assigned a unique IRQ so that the microprocessor will know which device it's communicating with. Any unused IRQ will work for a NIC, but IRQ 10 has become a de facto standard.

Base Input/Output (I/O) Port

- **Base Input/Output (I/O) Port:** The base I/O port is a hexadecimal number used by the system microprocessor to identify the destination of data sent to a peripheral device. Since the bus in a computer is shared by all peripherals, the base I/O port identifies where data is to be sent within the computer. The base I/O port for all devices must be unique. Common 32-bit base I/O ports are 0300 and 031F.

Base Memory Address

- **Base Memory Address:** The base memory address is a unique area of the computer RAM where data is temporarily stored. Since data moves very quickly on the computer parallel bus, it needs to be stored while the slower serial data is moved out of the NIC and onto the network wire. As with the IRQ and base I/O port, the base memory address must be unique for the NIC. A common base memory address is the hexadecimal address D8000.

┌─ TEST TIP ──────────────────────────

Be aware that when configuring a NIC, the IRQ, I/O port, and base memory address must not conflict with any other devices.

Data that's sent to a workstation (or server) is placed on the network by the NIC. In an Ethernet network, all data is placed on a common bus (not at the same time, though). To ensure that data placed on the bus is received by the correct workstation, each NIC has an address used to distinguish it from all other workstations. The address is called the **MAC** (**Media Access Control**), or physical address. The Media Access Control is a sublayer of the Data Link layer of the OSI Reference Model. (See Chapter 4 for an overview of the OSI Reference Model.)

MAC (Media Access Control)

MAC address

A **MAC address** is a 48-bit number expressed as six hexadecimal numbers. All devices (such as servers and workstations) that will be sending and receiving data frames have a MAC address. Each MAC address must be unique for each device on the network. An example of a MAC address is 00-60-08-71-C7-B2. The MAC address isn't user configurable; that is, the device ships from a manufacturer with the address "burned" into it.

Since all MAC addresses are unique, the address serves to uniquely identify all hardware that has access to the network resources. This is important to understand because it means that devices other than computers will also have a NIC if they connect directly to a network. Most devices described in the remainder of this chapter will have a MAC address.

IP address

A NIC card will also be assigned another address, called the **IP address**. IP, or Internet Protocol, is discussed in detail in Chapter 5. An IP address is a 32-bit number that's used to locate a device on a network, no matter where the device is located. Keep in mind that there are millions of devices with unique MAC addresses. Trying to pinpoint any one of them anywhere in the world would be a mind-numbing exercise. IP addresses—due to the manner in which the address is defined—allow hardware devices to be assigned to a particular network, and to a particular device. Once you know where the network is, all that's left is to resolve the part of the IP address that identifies the device to the actual MAC address.

Although an IP address isn't required on local area networks, all NIC cards support IP addressing. The reason is that in order to access the Internet, or to connect separate networks, an IP address is required.

Table 3-1 summarizes network interface cards.

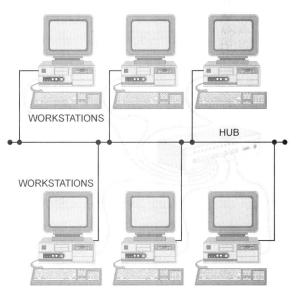

		Table 3-1: Summary of Network Interface Cards
Purpose	A hardware device used to access the network, package data into frames, check for errors, and to send and receive data.	
Functions	Organizes data into frames.	
	Checks received frames for errors.	
	Tracks the receipt of frames.	
	Are specific to network access protocols such as IEEE 802.3, 802.4, and 802.5. This dictates the particular method used to access the network.	
	Has a unique MAC address assigned by the manufacturer. The MAC address allows the device that the card is installed in to be distinguished from all other network devices.	
Features	NIC cards comply with one of several bus standards.	
	The network connection may be RJ-45, BNC, or both.	
	Many NICs, particularly Ethernet cards, support multiple data rates such as 10 or 100 Mbps.	
	All NICs support logical addressing such as IP addresses.	
	Most NIC cards are autoconfigured when installed into a computer with very little user intervention required.	

HUB

A **hub** is a device used to provide centralized access to the network. Hubs are used in a physical star topology, as shown in Figure 3-2. The network nodes connect to ports in the hub via a cable such as UTP or coaxial. One end of the cable plugs into the node NIC card while the other end plugs into a port on a hub.

The advantage of a hub is that it can be located at a central point in the network. The alternative to using a hub is to daisy-chain the nodes with cable segments. In a network in which the nodes aren't likely to change location, this is fine. But in a more dynamic setting, physical changes in location can create a wiring nightmare since each time a node is moved, the cable segment linking the node to its neighbors must be replaced. A hub simplifies changes since, if a node is moved, all that's needed is to run a cable from the new location to an available port on the hub.

Most local area networks use hubs in a star topology due to the relative ease of installation of connecting servers, workstations, and other devices.

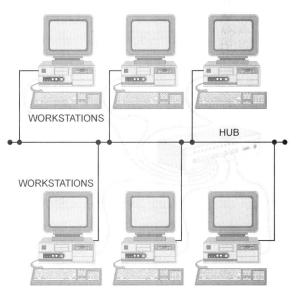

Figure 3-2: A Hub is Used in a Physical Star Topology

TEST TIP

Be prepared to identify a hub in a star topology.

passive

active

repeaters

physical topology

logical topology

Multistation Access Unit (MSAU or MAU)

stacking

crossover circuit

straight-through pinning

Hubs are classified as either **passive** or **active**. A passive hub is nothing more than a pass-through for data. A passive hub doesn't alter the data signal in any way; it receives its power from the connected computers. If a data signal becomes noisy, a passive hub will pass the noise along with the data signal. Typically, passive hubs are small and inexpensive. A passive hub for a small network may have as few as four ports.

An active hub operates under its own power supply. Data signals may be amplified in an active hub to restore signal losses, or to remove noise. Active hubs are also called **repeaters**. For larger networks, active hubs that have from 12 to 32 ports are common.

In addition to being placed in a **physical topology** such as a star, a hub participates in a logical topology. A **logical topology** refers to the specific method a server or workstation uses to access the network. Ethernet, for example, is a bus technology. A hub in an Ethernet network includes an internal bus that nodes compete for before they are able to use the network resources. The hub in an Ethernet LAN, then, uses a logical bus topology. But the physical topology of the network is a star.

A Token Ring network, on the other hand, may also be implemented in a physical star. The Token Ring "hub" is actually called a **Multistation Access Unit** (**MSAU** or **MAU**). Within the MSAU is a logical ring topology. Nodes are connected to each port in the hub ring. When a node is connected to the ring, it may send or receive data.

Hubs come in many varieties and offer many features. A passive hub may have as few as four ports, while an active hub could have 32 or more ports. For Ethernet and Token Ring, the hub connection will be an RJ-45 port or, less likely these days, a coaxial BNC connector.

Some hubs support remote configuration and management. This means that a network administrator can configure the hub from a remote workstation. The physical connection between the hub and remote workstation may be via CAT5 UTP or a serial or parallel cable connection. Configuration features may include data collection on any or all ports such as the number of frames sent and received through the port, password protection for the hub, or lockout of specified MAC addresses.

Some hubs can be connected together. This practice is called **stacking**. The advantage of stacking hubs is that it allows for expansion of the network at some future time. On an Ethernet network, there can be a maximum of 132 devices connected to each other. Stackable hubs allow for orderly growth if the network grows to this size.

The connection between hub and node on an Ethernet network is usually via RJ-45 connectors with CAT5 UTP cable. At each hub port, there is a "crossover" circuit. A **crossover circuit** is used to reverse the Tx and Rx pins of the RJ-45. The crossover is built into the hardware of the hub and is transparent to users. When connecting a hub port to node NIC, both ends of the CAT5 cable are pinned to the same connector pins on both ends of the cable. This is called **straight-through pinning**.

However, when connecting hubs together, a separate port is usually reserved for the connection. Typically, the port will be marked to designate it, frequently with an X. This means that a crossover cable is needed between the two hub ports that are to be connected. A crossover cable has the +/−Tx and +/−Rx pins reversed at each end of the connection.

Table 3-2 summarizes characteristics of hubs.

Purpose	A hub provides a centralized connection point for network access.	**Table 3-2: Characteristics of Hubs**
Functions	A hub is used in a physical star topology.	
	Ethernet hubs use a logical bus topology for network access.	
	Token Ring hubs use a logical ring topology for network access.	
	A passive hub receives power for nodes connected to it and serves only as a data pass-through.	
	An active hub has its own power source and may regenerate degraded data signals. Some active hubs also support remote management for configuring the hub.	
Features	Most hubs use RJ-45 connectors called ports.	
	The number of ports ranges from 4 to over 32 for each hub.	
	On larger hubs, at least one port may be used for stacking hubs. A crossover cable must be used when stacking hubs.	
	Remote management is an option on larger or more expensive hubs. Remote management allows for software configuration of the hub.	

BRIDGE

A **bridge** is primarily used to connect networks that use different network access protocols. For example, a bridge is used to connect users on an Ethernet LAN and users on a Token Ring LAN. Wireless access points that have an Ethernet port employ a bridge to connect the IEEE 802.11b users and the Ethernet users.

A bridge is also used to reduce network traffic by filtering data frames on a network. A frame is the unit of measure of data that's sent between nodes. Frames contain headers that specify source and destination addresses as well as a header for error checking. A bridge examines MAC addresses to determine whether the frame should be sent on to another portion of a network, or it should remain in the portion of the network where it originated.

For example, an Ethernet LAN may grow over the years to the point that it slows due to the large number of workstations sending and receiving data. Network traffic congestion can be reduced by separating workstations into groups, particularly groups that tend to exchange information frequently. The separated groups are called segments. A **segment** is a portion of a network in which any node on that portion of the network can sense whether any other node is transmitting data frames.

Bridges use two basic methods for bridging network segments. The bridging methods are called **transparent bridging** and **source-route bridging**.

In a transparent bridge, the bridge collects MAC addresses of all nodes on the network. It then compares the source and destination addresses of received frames to the addresses in its table. Based on the result of the comparison, the bridge will determine whether a frame is destined for the same segment it originated from, or it's to be forwarded to another segment. Transparent bridges are used with Ethernet LANs.

Figure 3-3 shows an example of transparent bridging. In the figure, an Ethernet LAN has been separated into two segments. The workstations will send frames that contain a source and destination MAC address (the MAC address that's burned into the NIC). When workstation A-1 sends a message to workstation A-2, the frame is first sent to the bridge. The bridge examines the destination address in the frame and compares it to the MAC addresses in its tables. Since the destination address is on the same segment as the source address in the frame, the bridge ignores the frame. If, however, A-1 sends a frame of data to workstation B-2 on segment B, the bridge will forward the frame to segment B.

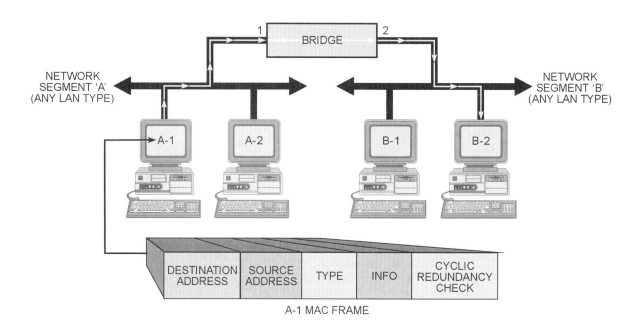

Figure 3-3: A Transparent Bridge Examines MAC Addresses of Data Frames

If a transparent bridge doesn't recognize the destination address of a frame, it broadcasts the frame to all segments except the segment that the frame originated from. (A **broadcast message** is a message sent to all nodes on a network.)

In a source-routing bridge, each workstation provides path information to the destination node. Used in Token Ring networks, a source-routing bridge only transfers the frame to the destination segment. The workstation does the majority of the work since it dictates to the bridge the route that the frame is to take.

An advantage of source-routing over transparent bridging is that frames may be transferred faster. The source-routing bridge will store the path information when it's delivered from the workstation and use that same path each time a frame arrives that's to be sent to the same destination address. Transparent bridges, on the other hand, examine each frame and compare the address to information in their address tables, which takes time and slows the network.

Since a bridge is a Data Link layer device, it can be used to connect networks with different access protocols. For example, a bridge may connect Token Ring and Ethernet segments. A **translation bridge** is used to connect segments that utilize different access protocols.

Figure 3-4 shows an example of a translation bridge. The network is composed of Ethernet, Token Bus and Token Ring segments. A workstation on the Ethernet segment sends a frame to the Token Ring segment. When the first bridge receives the frame, it examines the MAC address and determines the frame is to be sent on. Before sending the frame, it converts the frame headers from Ethernet to Token Bus. When bridge 2 receives the frame, it also examines the destination address, determines that the frame is destined for a workstation on the Token Ring segment, and converts the frame format from Token Bus to Token Ring. The frame is then placed on the Token Ring segment and delivered to the destination workstation.

> **TEST TIP**
>
> Be aware that the most common use of a bridge is for translation between access protocols.

A translation bridge is noted for interoperability among LAN access protocols. As shown in Figure 3-4, it's used to bridge data frames across different segment types such as Ethernet and Token Ring. Transparent and source-route bridging will only connect segments that use the same access protocols such as Ethernet or Token Ring—but not both in the same network.

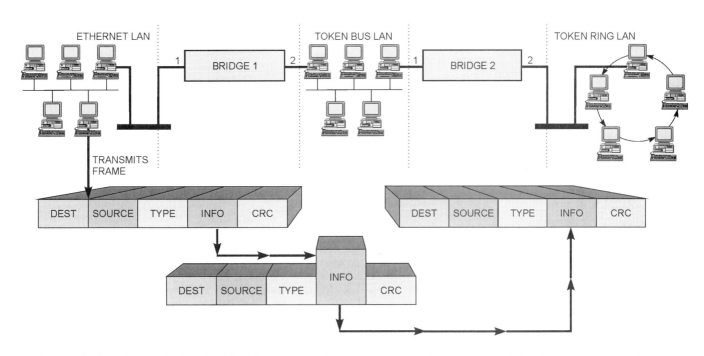

Figure 3-4: A Translation Bridge is Used to Connect Network Segments That Use Different Access Protocols

Table 3-3 summarizes characteristics of bridges.

Table 3-3:
Characteristics of
Bridges

Purpose	Bridges translate between different network access protocols such as Token Ring and Ethernet.
	Bridges segment large or congested networks that use the same network access protocol.
Functions	A transparent bridge stores MAC addresses of all nodes to determine whether a frame remains on the originating network or is passed to another network segment.
	A source-routing bridge passes the frames based on destination routes as supplied by the connected nodes.
	A translation bridge converts from one network access protocol to a different network access protocol.
Features	Bridge functions may be built into other devices such as bridge capabilities built into some wireless access points.
	Bridges offer a means for reducing congestion on networks.
	Bridges provide a means for connecting dissimilar networks.

ROUTER

router

A **router** is used to connect different networks and, occasionally, different network segments. A "network" in this context, refers to a group of nodes that share the same network portion of an IP address. If two groups of nodes don't have the same network portion of an IP address, they are located on different networks.

Routers operate at the Network layer of the OSI model. A router isn't concerned if the data it receives originated from a Token Ring LAN or an Ethernet LAN. The router is only concerned with getting the data to the correct destination network.

A router may be used to connect network segments by examining MAC addresses in a manner that's similar to a bridge. Both devices use MAC addresses at the Data Link layer to forward data. A router, however, goes a step further by also looking at IP addresses to locate remote networks. There are differences between the two devices as well. A bridge will forward any unknown destination MAC address. A router will discard an unknown MAC address. A bridge will forward broadcast messages to all network segments. A router will discard broadcast messages. A bridge will forward a message if the destination address is known, even if the frame is corrupted. A router will discard a corrupted frame.

In some situations, a router may be more effective than a bridge for linking segments on a network. For example, if several access protocols are used on portions of a network, the router can be used to decrease traffic congestion by filtering all broadcast messages as well as all corrupted frames.

To directly connect network workstations to the Internet, a router is used at the interface of the local network (where the workstations reside) and the Internet. The router will locate a remote network (such as a web site server) so that the workstation user can connect to the remote site and download the content of that site to the local workstation.

To successfully transfer data across networks, a router relies on logical addresses. The most common logical address used by routers is an IP (Internet Protocol) address. An IP address is a 32-bit address that's composed of a network portion and a host portion. The network portion of the address identifies the source or destination network, while the host portion of the address identifies the specific source or destination node on a network. (For details on IP addresses, see Chapter 5, Network Protocols.)

Figure 3-5 illustrates the method routers use to locate a node on a remote network. The router interconnects data packets across a network running TCP/IP. The network consists of an Ethernet, a Token Ring, and a Token Bus LAN. Notice that the router allows computers on all three LANs to communicate, regardless of the topology and access protocols. The LAN hardware used with the computers may be from diverse vendors, and operate at different bandwidths. The router, because it is basically concerned only with network addresses, is involved in a limited capacity at the Physical layer and the Data Link layer. This is the reason why the LAN hardware, cabling medium, and access protocols may all be different, but the networks can still communicate.

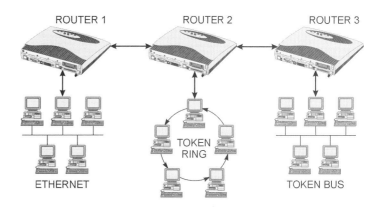

Assume that a workstation on the Ethernet LAN sends a message to a workstation on the remote Token Bus LAN. The table shown with the figure includes generic MAC addresses of the IP packets, along with generic IP addresses. The first two columns contain destination and source MAC addresses of the router and respective LAN nodes. Initially, the MAC source address is the address of the node on the Ethernet LAN, and the destination address is the MAC for router 1. When the frame arrives at the router, the physical addressing fields of the MAC frame are removed, leaving only the IP addresses, user data, and error checking (shown in the figure as **CRC**, which stands for **Cyclic Redundancy Check**) fields.

MAC DESTINATION	MAC SOURCE	IP SOURCE	IP DESTINATION	DATA	CRC
ROUTER 1	ETHERNET NODE	ETHERNET NODE	TOKEN BUS NODE	XXX	XXX
ROUTER 2	ROUTER 1	ETHERNET NODE	TOKEN BUS NODE	XXX	XXX
ROUTER 3	ROUTER 2	ETHERNET NODE	TOKEN BUS NODE	XXX	XXX

Figure 3-5: A Router Transfers Data Packets between Different Networks.

Notice that the IP addresses never change. This is because they are the only indication of where the frames are going as they move from router to router. At each router hop, the router will compare its list of MAC addresses to the destination IP address. If they aren't the same, it will reframe the MAC addresses and pass it on.

Since router 1 isn't the destination for the frame, router 1 reframes the message with new MAC address fields. Router 1 is now the source of the message and the destination address is the MAC address of router 2.

Router 2 compares its list of IP addresses to the destination IP address in the received frame. Since the destination IP address isn't located on the Token Bus network, router 3 reframes the message. Now the source MAC address will be the MAC address of router 2 and the destination MAC address will be the MAC address of router 3.

Router 3 will strip the MAC addresses and examine the destination IP address in the frame. It will compare the destination IP address with the list of IP addresses in its tables and correctly determine that the message is destined for the Token Ring network. The message will now be delivered to the node on the Token Ring network whose IP address matches the MAC address that the router has in its tables.

The process of locating specific nodes on a large network such as the Internet is a bit more involved. Typically, a user won't know the IP address of a remote node or network. However, the user will likely know the Internet domain name of the remote node, or the host name of the node. An Internet domain name is a name proceeding a suffix such as com, edu, or net. For example, the domain name of Microsoft is microsoft.com. Host names follow a similar convention. Before a router can begin to route a message to a remote network, it must know the IP address of the remote node. The process used to convert domain or host names to IP addresses is called the **Domain Name Service (DNS)**. For routers used to interconnect networks on the Internet, the process of resolving domain names to IP addresses must be performed before a message is sent to a router.

A router is used to connect network users to the Internet. Even if a home-based user connects to an ISP via a modem, the ISP will have routers installed at the intersection to the Internet. If the router isn't working properly, it's impossible to access the Internet. If the router is down, network users will not be able to access the Internet at all. But note that if the routers used at an ISP are down, a user will likely be able to connect to the ISP site, but won't be able to go beyond it.

One of two types of routers can be used to gather information about the networks the router is connected to. The first type of router is called a **static router**. A static router receives IP addressing information manually. That is, a network administrator will periodically update addressing tables in a static router. The update is required any time a node address changes.

The second type of router is called a **dynamic router**. A dynamic router learns addressing information automatically, without intervention from the network administrator. Dynamic routers broadcast the addressing information in their tables in the form of advertisements. For example, a dynamic router may send (or advertise) its list of IP addresses to adjacent routers once every thirty seconds. The adjacent routers compare this list with their list of IP addresses, and if there's a difference, update their table with the new information.

TEST TIP

Be aware that routers send and receive advertisements that automatically update the router database.

Router advertisements tend to increase network congestion. But the only alternative is to update addressing information manually. The time spent manually updating router tables far exceeds the disadvantage of increased router traffic due to advertisements.

Routers route data packets across the Internet by using routing protocols. The most common routing protocol used on the Internet is called **Border Gateway Protocol (BGP)**. BGP is run on routers that are installed at the interface of a local network to the Internet. BGP contains dynamic characteristics that make it an excellent choice for Internet applications. These include the use of a 30-second "keep-alive" message sent between routers that's used to detect failed routers, or routes that aren't operational. The efficiency of a router running BGP is very good since it initially receives a complete route table update when it's first connected to the Internet. After the initial update, changes in the router are incremental, which means that the information in the routing table reflects only changes—not a complete table update.

Other common routing protocols include **RIP (Routing Information Protocol)**, **OSPF (Open Shortest Path First)**, **IGRP (Interior Gateway Routing Protocol)**, and **EIGRP (Enhanced Interior Gateway Routing Protocol)**. The difference between these protocols and BGP is that they are "interior" routing protocols. An **interior routing protocol** is used to interconnect network segments, or networks on an intranet. An interior routing protocol isn't normally used at the interface of the local network and the Internet, whereas BGP runs data packets across the local network and Internet interface.

Table 3-4 summarizes characteristics of routers.

Translational bridges are known for their interoperability. This refers to the capability of the bridge to work in many LAN environments, and across the product lines of many vendors. Their intelligence stretches the very definition of a bridge. In fact, translational bridges are frequently called **brouters**.

A brouter (bridge/router) is used to interconnect LANs (it's MAC-protocol specific as opposed to a router, which isn't), and also contains routing capabilities that allow packets to be forwarded outside the subnet domain.

A bridge must work within the local environment, since it doesn't have the ability to route to a network address other than its own. A brouter collects and maintains IP and MAC addresses, and may be called upon to supply these from a transmitting node.

Table 3-4: Characteristics of Routers

Purpose	A router is used to locate different networks. It may also be used to control traffic on larger LANs.
Functions	It connects network segments by examining IP and MAC addresses.
	It connects different networks by examining the network portion of an IP address.
	It maintains tables of node IP addresses that are used to locate other network devices.
Features	A router that connects network segments employs an interior routing protocol such as IGRP.
	A router that connects different networks is likely to use BGP.
	Some routers support both router protocols.
	A router may be used in place of a bridge to reduce network broadcast messages or corrupt data packets.

brouters

SWITCH

A **switch** allows each connected node to be dynamically connected to any other node port. The connections established between ports in a switch are handled with software. The connection is a virtual circuit that is built up and torn down each time a node connects to a different port. In effect, a switch provides a direct and dedicated connection between two nodes.

Physically, a switch resembles a conventional hub. It has ports to which nodes are connected via the cabling infrastructure. In a conventional 10Base-T hub (such as 10 Mbps Ethernet), each node listens for traffic on the bus (located in the hub). When a message is sent from a workstation, it arrives at the hub and is placed on the bus. The message is then repeated to all nodes connected to the hub. If the destination MAC address matches the MAC address of one of the workstations, that workstation receives the message. All other workstations ignore the message. Notice that each time a frame is sent, the total bandwidth of the network (10 Mbps in a 10Base-T network) is divided among all nodes since each message is sent to all nodes.

A switch avoids dividing the available bandwidth by providing a direct connection between two ports. Rather than a logical bus or ring topology, a switch uses a logical mesh topology. A switch implements a logical mesh with a **backplane**. A backplane allows any port to be connected to any other port. During the time two ports are connected, data is sent at the full bandwidth that's available since no other nodes are connected to the two ports. The effect is a dramatic increase in the time required to send a packet from one node to another.

switch

backplane

Since a switch automatically connects two nodes, there's no reason that other nodes must wait to send or receive data. The connections occur between two nodes only. And, since the nodes are directly connected, a data message can be immediately forwarded onto the destination node, even before the complete frame has arrived at the switch. This process is called **cut-through**. A cut-through switch provides high speeds and throughput. Throughput, in the context of a switch, refers to the time required to process data at the switch. The less time the switch spends with the frame, the higher the throughput.

A switch may also process data using a method called **store-and-forward**. In a store-and-forward switch, the complete data message is received and buffered (stored) by the switch before it is sent to the destination node. Since the switch is in possession of the complete message, it may check the message for errors, provide filtering between network segments, or reframe the message so that it can be sent to a segment that uses a different access protocol than the source segment.

The advantage of a switch over conventional hubs is that each port offers the connected nodes the full bandwidth that's available on the network.

Table 3-5 summarizes characteristics of switches.

Table 3-5: Characteristics of Switches

Purpose	A switch uses a logical mesh topology to provide the full bandwidth of a network to connected nodes.
Functions	Similar in appearance to a hub, a switch's connections are via RJ-45 connectors and UTP cabling.
	A switch uses a logical connection to directly and dynamically connect two nodes.
	A switch offers much higher speed and throughput than a conventional hub.
Features	Some switches offer cut-through, which allows a message to be forwarded to the destination before the complete message is received.
	A store-and-forward switch receives the entire message before processing. Once received, the message may be further manipulated.

WIRELESS ACCESS POINTS

Wireless access points (AP), described in Chapter 12 as part of the IEEE 802.11 protocols, serve as a centralized network connection for nodes equipped with wireless cards. Functionally, an AP is equivalent to a wired hub.

A wireless AP contains two antennas—one to receive signals from nodes, and one to transmit signals to nodes. Depending on the IEEE 802.11 protocol, the band pass (range of frequencies) of the antenna will fall into the 2.4 GHz range, or the 5 GHz range. But due to the wide separation of the frequency band pass, there is not currently a commercially viable antenna that will handle both frequency ranges.

Most APs have vertical antennas that can be adjusted for the best reception and transmission, based upon the needs of users as well as physical obstructions. Recall that IEEE 802.11 range capabilities are limited by walls or other obstructions.

An AP may be configured using software provided by the vendor. Typically, the configuration is conducted by a computer with a connection to the AP via a USB or serial cable. The AP is the first component to be configured in a wireless LAN and requires numerous decisions to be made such as whether to use encryption, assignment of a name to the AP, or the assignment of an IP address.

TEST TIP

Know that if a user is too far from the AP, there will not be a wireless connection.

The vendor-supplied software will also, typically, collect statistical data on the network connection. The type of data collected varies but generally is related to the data rate at any particular time, the number of dropped and retransmitted frames, and the total number of bytes sent and received, and may include a listing of all connected computers.

There's no theoretical limit to how many computers can be connected to a single AP. The standard doesn't specify an upper limit. But most vendor literature sets the upper limit at about 64 machines. (A more practical upper limit is 10 to 15 computers.) Some experimentation is needed in an actual network since the speed is largely determined by the types of files sent through the AP. Files that are graphics-intensive (therefore, large) will slow the network down.

Many APs include a bridge that allows for connections to a wired 10/100Base-T Ethernet LAN. Recall that IEEE 802.11 uses CSMA/CA for the network access protocol, whereas Ethernet uses CSMA/CD. The AP will have an RJ-45 connector from which CAT5 cable is used to connect to a wired hub. To a user on the network, the AP will be transparent when viewing all computers connected.

Another trend with wireless APs is to include routing capabilities along with connections for cable modems and ISDN lines (both are described later in this chapter). For the home-based or small business user, a similarly equipped AP provides the majority of hardware needed for multi-user access to the Internet and e-mail.

A small number of vendors supply APs that can handle either 802.11b or 802.11a network traffic in the same enclosure. But note that the AP includes dedicated antennas for both frequency ranges, much like AM/FM radios have an antenna for AM and an antenna for FM. At this time, the standard does not provide for backward compatibility from 54 Mbps 802.11a to 11 Mbps 802.11b.

Table 3-6 summarizes characteristics of wireless access points.

Table 3-6: Characteristics of Wireless Access Points

Purpose	A wireless access point provides a single and centralized connection point for computers to communicate with wireless technology.
Functions	It provides for direct connections between any two devices to communicate.
	It utilizes the IEEE 802.11b/a standards.
	Dedicated antennas are required to handle data at either 802.11b or 802.11a.
	A wireless access point typically allows full-speed connections at 300 feet and maximum ranges (at lower data rates) up to about 1500 feet.
	It utilizes the CSMA/CA network access protocol.
Features	Commercial APs include a bridge for connection to wired networks.
	Configuration software provided by vendors allows the AP to be remotely managed.
	Some commercial APs include routing capabilities as well as connections for cable modems and ISDN lines.
	Some APs include both 802.11b and 802.11a hardware in the same enclosure, which allows both wireless NICs to communicate through the same AP.

GATEWAY

A **gateway** is a device used to convert from one incompatible protocol to another protocol. A gateway may operate at any layer of the OSI model, or at several layers of the model. For example, a gateway would be used to convert from TCP/IP to Novell SPX/IPX.

The processing power required to convert from one incompatible protocol to another is considerable. If possible, the conversion should be avoided. Instead, plan to use common protocols on a network. This will save time and money.

Table 3-7 summarizes characteristics of gateways.

**Table 3-7:
Characteristics of
Gateways**

Purpose	A gateway converts between two different network protocols.
Functions	Most commonly, a gateway converts between completely dissimilar network systems, including: • TCP/IP • SPX/IPX
Features	Extensive hardware and software are required for complete protocol conversions.

CSU/DSU

Digital telecommunications systems require an interface between the user premises and the high-speed digital connections. The most common high-speed digital telecommunication system is called the **T-carrier system**. T-carrier levels are designated as T-1, T-3, T4, etc., with each level corresponding to the speed of the line.

The interface used between the T-carrier line and the user premises is a hardware device called a **Channel Service Unit/ Digital Service Unit (CSU/DSU)**. The CSU/DSU provides a connection between the user premise and the telecommunication facilities. The CSU/DSU must be installed at the user premises. In a CSU/DSU, the Channel Unit recovers multiplexed data, while the Digital Unit removes encoding that was used to package the data.

The channel specifications are set up in the CSU/DSU. These include the channel rate (64 Kbps), frame type, number of channels (such as 24 for 1.544 Mbps T1 connection), and so forth.

> ┌─ TEST TIP ─────
> Know that a CSU/DSU is a device that's unique to T-carrier channels.

Figure 3-6 shows a typical T1 connection. In the figure, a LAN is using the connection to communicate with another LAN. Data from the LAN nodes is first sent to a router. The router switches the data into the CSU/DSU in a process that is essentially time-division multiplexing. The CSU/DSU then formats the data into T1 frames and sends it, through a V.35 cable, to the T-carrier facilities.

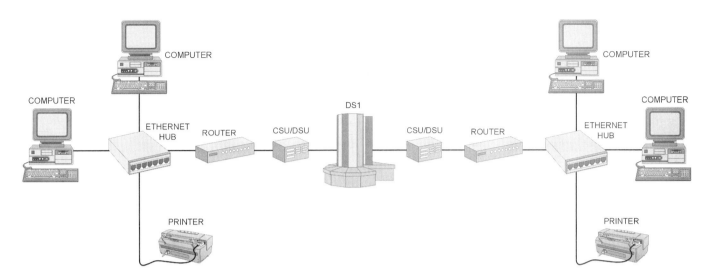

At the remote LAN, the CSU/DSU accepts T1 frames through another V.35 cable, strips the T1 encoding, and demultiplexes the frames. The router selects the correct LAN node based on the node addresses encapsulated in the LAN's data frames. Notice that in order to implement a T1 line, you must buy a CSU/DSU unit along with a router. This is why you need to do your homework before setting up a T1 line. Setting up and maintaining a router is formidable in itself.

Figure 3-6: Typical T1 Interconnection

MODEMS

A **modem** converts digital data into a format suitable for transmission over a long distance. It also accepts transmitted data and reconverts it back into digital data. The term "modem" is an acronym for modulator/demodulator. A modem is a vehicle for sending and receiving data. For the most part, a modem is needed to transmit and receive data when the communicating devices are separated by more than 50 feet. (This distance may be extended to 100 feet in environments relatively free of electrical noise.)

modem

By far, the single largest application of modems is to interface computers to the telephone network.

Modems always work in pairs, as shown in Figure 3-7. Typically, they handle data transfer over telephone lines. The phone lines were originally intended to pass analog voice signals within a bandwidth containing the fundamental frequencies of most voices. These frequencies occur in the range of 300 Hz to 3,300 Hz. This means that in order for a computer user to make use of the extensive telephone network, any data transmitted through it must be manipulated to fit the tight constraints of the phone system. The individual channels allocated by phone companies to subscribers have a bandwidth of 3,300 Hz – 300 Hz = 3,000 Hz.

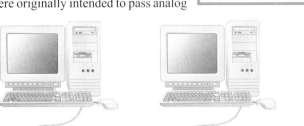

Figure 3-7: Modems Work in Pairs

In practice, the available bandwidth beyond the local loop extends to 4,000 Hz. Conditions in the voice channel have improved significantly over the past decade. For computers, this translates to extra bandwidth, so that the full 4 kHz channel width is routinely used to send data. The modem is used to modify data in such a way that it fits the bandwidth limitations of phone channels without degrading the original information.

A modem is a transceiver in that it has the ability to transmit as well as receive. As you'll recall, data traffic may take one of three forms: simplex, half duplex, and full duplex. Simplex is one-way-only communication. A television receiver is a simplex device since it receives, but can't transmit, information. Half-duplex traffic occurs in both directions between communicating devices; however, the two-way traffic cannot occur simultaneously. Citizen band radios are half-duplex devices. Full duplex means data is allowed to travel simultaneously between communicating stations. Telephones are common full-duplex devices. A modem can be configured to work as simplex, half duplex, or full duplex. In this chapter, all discussions on modems are centered around full-duplex transmissions.

Modem pairs must be compatible. In the case of modems, compatibility refers to speed (bps), frame format (**synchronous** or **asynchronous**), word length, parity, etc., as well as interface protocols. For the most part, modems in the United States use the EIA/TIA-232 interface standard for signaling conventions. When the modem is fitted into a PC's expansion slot, it will include a Universal Asynchronous Receiver-Transmitter (UART) parallel interface.

In Figure 3-7, modem A may accept data from the personal computer, and frame-format it as synchronous or asynchronous, determine the type of parity, and modulate a carrier for transmission over the phone lines. The data is then transmitted. At the receiving modem (modem B), the message frame is demodulated from the carrier, and parity is checked. The data is then converted into binary logic levels and passed into the receiving computer.

Once data leaves a modem, it's treated like a telephone call by the phone companies. In fact, to send a message through a modem, you must supply the phone number of the receiving modem. Circuitry within modems handles the telephone interface and operation.

A modem provides a computer user with a tremendous amount of access. Literally, a good modem makes the difference in working at an isolated PC and accessing the great, wide-open spaces of the Internet.

Nearly all of data communications utilize modems—from the single user at home with a PC, to internationally distributed networks of conglomerate corporations. In the past decade the price of modems has dropped so significantly that a good-quality, V.90 modem can be purchased for under $100. The World Wide Web is merely an amusing curiosity without a modem.

This section takes a thorough look at all aspects of modems. First, we'll start with modem standards, commonly called the V-Series, or "V-dot," standards.

V-Series Recommendations

The *V-Series Recommendations for modems* are published by the **International Telecommunication Union (ITU)**, formerly called **CCITT (Consultative Committee for International Telephony)**. The ITU, headquartered in Geneva, Switzerland, is "an international organization within which governments and the private sector coordinate global telecom networks and services." In short, the ITU is composed of representatives from industry and government, who try to hammer out a standard that will encourage interoperability between vendors and manufacturers.

Interoperability is the key word. It's intended to encourage competition without giving any single company a technological advantage due to the deep pockets of a few large vendors. It also provides a measure of flexibility for the user since the buyer isn't tied to one company's product line.

While the recommendations cover many aspects of telecommunications, at a minimum they will tell you the following information directly related to modems:

- The highest data rate of the modem

- The type of modulation used in a modem

- The communication method between modems (simplex, half duplex, full duplex)

- The telco connection between modems (point-to-point 2-wire, switched, etc.)

The ITU V-Series recommendations are important to networking personnel because they define attributes such as data rates, modulation methods, encoding methods, connections, and so on. As with other protocols, the V-Series doesn't attempt to dictate to manufacturers how to implement the recommendations, but instead specifies outcomes. Table 3-8 lists several ITU-Series Recommendations.

Table 3-8: ITU-Series Modem/Telephone Network Recommendations

Series A	Organization of the work of the ITU
Series G	Transmission systems, media, digital systems, and networks
Series I	Integrated Services Digital Networks (ISDN)
Series L	Construction, installation, and protection of outside cable and elements
Series P	Telephone transmission quality, telephone installations, and networks
Series V	Data communication over the telephone network
Series X	Data networks and open-system communication

Table 3-9 lists selected V-Series recommendations for data communications over the telephone network. Prior to acceptance of standards, the only broadly embraced guidelines were proprietary from AT&T. These were called the Bell Standards.

Table 3-9: V-Series Modem/Telephone Network Recommendations

V-Series	Bell Standards
V.2	Power levels for data transmission
V.17	2-wire fax modem with rates up to 14.4 Kbps
V.21	300 bps standard
V.22	1,200 bps standard for use on a point-to-point 2-wire leased line
V.22bis	2,400 bps FDM standard for use on point-to-point 2-wire leased lines
V.23	600/1,200 baud standard
V.24	Definitions for interchange circuits between DTE and DCE
V.25bis	Synchronous/asynchronous auto-dialing procedures on switched networks
V.26bis	2,400/1,200 bps standard
V.27bis	4,800/2,400 bps standard
V.29	9,600 bps standard for use on 4-wire leased lines
V.32bis	9,600 bps duplex standard for use on phone networks and leased lines
V.33	14.4 Kbps standard for use on 4-wire leased lines
V.34	33.6 Kbps standard for use on phone networks and leased point-to-point 2-wire lines
V.42bis	Data compression procedures for DTE using error-correction
V.90	56,000 bps (56 kbps) standard

As you can see, the Bell Standards only cover lower speed modems. The reason is that shortly after modems became accessible to the general public, AT&T embraced the standards published at that time by the CCITT.

Standards change frequently. Even older standards change over time, so you should check frequently with the ITU to make sure you remain current with the latest technological trends.

Operations Between Modems

A modem connects to the port (serial or parallel) of a computer on one side and the telephone line on the other side. The modem may be internal (meaning it connects to the parallel bus of the host computer), or it may be external (meaning it connects to the serial bus via a EIA/TIA-232 interface). Neither type has a particular advantage over the other, although external modems are slightly more expensive.

Historically, modems have been classified as analog or digital. The distinction is evident: An analog modem converts digital data from a computer to analog, in order to send it across the analog local loop to a central office, whereas a digital modem works exclusively in the **Public Switched Telephone Network** (**PSTN**) in which all data is digital (for the most part).

Figure 3-8(a) illustrates the use of a modem in a typical environment.

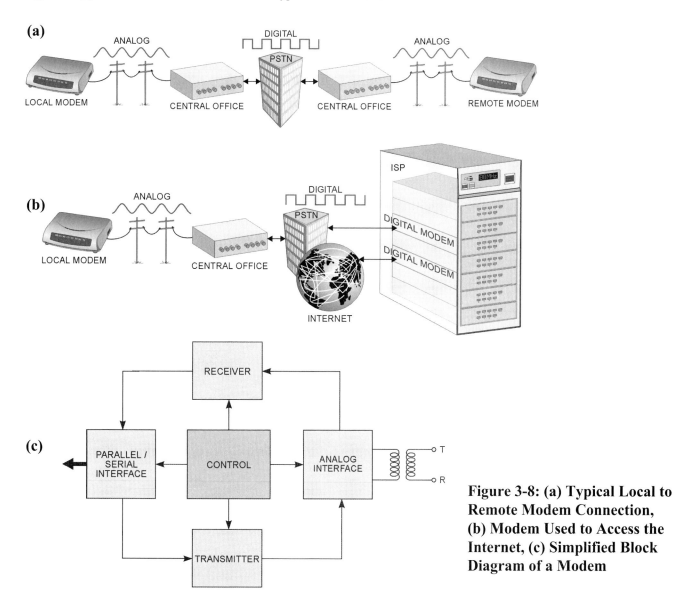

Figure 3-8: (a) Typical Local to Remote Modem Connection, (b) Modem Used to Access the Internet, (c) Simplified Block Diagram of a Modem

A source modem is sending data to a remote modem. Notice that the connection on both ends from the modem to the central office is an analog loop, but once the signal enters the PSTN it's converted to digital. Both modems must be capable of converting transmitted data from digital to analog, and received data from analog back to digital. In addition, the modems have a very narrow bandwidth to work within; a bandwidth that was designed for voice communications, and not data communications (text, video, graphics).

A local modem transmitting to a remote modem has to be able to manipulate data in a way that the remote modem will understand, or at least emulate the distant modem. Manipulating the data means matching the data rate abilities of the two, formatting data the same way with parity and stop/start bits, using the same modulators/ demodulators, and so on. In practice, modems have "fallback" capabilities. This means that when two modems attempt to connect, they negotiate specifics of the connection. The most common negotiating involves the speed of the connection. The fastest modems have multiple fallback data rates so that they will adjust to the fastest speed of a slower, remote modem.

Of course, we expect the remote modem to receive the data that is sent, so a modem will also anticipate noise and distortion characteristics of the link between them, and compensate for it with pre-equalization before it's transmitted.

Figure 3-8(b) illustrates a familiar scenario for a modem. This time, the modem is in a home and is used to access the Internet. Notice here that the modems used at the **Internet Service Provider** (**ISP**) are digital. The PSTN and the Internet are digital entities, so there's no need for an analog conversion; it only occurs on the downstream side from the telephone central office to the residence.

The analog-digital and digital-analog conversions in Figure 3-8(a) create noise in the form of quantization errors. (A quantization error is the difference that occurs between the actual analog amplitude of a signal, and the digitized level of the same signal.) There will always be some error when data signals are converted. But if the error is kept to a minimum, the effect won't be appreciable. However, if the error is allowed to become significant, often resulting from numerous and cumulative signal conversions, the result is an increase in bit error rates and slower data rates. In part (b) of the figure, also notice that the analog-to-digital and digital-to-analog conversions don't occur on the remote side, since the home-based user only accesses digital data. Consequently, the amount of quantization error is greatly reduced.

When analog data is converted in a modem to digital data, small signal amplitudes are represented by more bits than the large signals. This is done to normalize the amplitude difference and results in a relatively flat signal-to-noise ratio for all amplitudes. If this isn't done, then small signals may be obscured by noise that has the same or a greater amplitude. A low signal-to-noise ratio results in a high number of errors.

There is a relationship between errors and data rates on a telephone channel. Channel bandwidth and capacity are directly related. Since the voice channel is bandwidth-challenged, the capacity that data can be sent across it will be limited. What is the limit? It turns out to be about 35 kbps. For the scenario shown in Figure 3-8(a), data rates will be limited to V.34 speeds of 33.6 kbps.

For the situation shown in Figure 3-8(b), the user will still access the Internet at V.34 data rates, and will be able to receive data at much higher speeds. But we're getting ahead of ourselves. First, let's take a look at some broad capabilities of modems.

Modem Parameters

A block diagram of a simplified modem is shown in Figure 3-8(c). As shown, the modem has a telephone line connection, depicted as T and R. T and R stand for **tip** and **ring**, a carry-over term from the telephone industry. In a 4-wire telephone cable, ring is the red wire and tip is the green wire. (The other two wires in the four-wire package are routinely not used.) For access to the public network, these are the only wires needed. A signal received from the telephone line will be accepted by the analog interface and switched to the receive section. In the receiver, the carrier is demodulated and converted from analog to digital data. The digital data is sent to the parallel interface, where it is converted from serial to parallel data and sent to a computer along a parallel data bus.

Information to be transmitted is converted to serial data in the parallel interface. The transmitter section converts the logic levels to analog in one of several modulation methods. The modulated carrier is then coupled to the public telephone network by the analog device.

In Figure 3-8(c), the modem can either transmit or receive, but can't do so simultaneously; therefore, it's a half-duplex modem. All modems are actually full-duplex devices, so they send and receive at the same time. To do so, each requires a transmit carrier and a receive carrier. Modulation creates frequency changes centered around the carriers. The total amount of carrier change equates to the bandwidth of the transmit and receive channels.

How does the internal circuitry determine whether a signal is a legitimately received signal? A transmitting modem is designated as the originate modem and must transmit at a carrier frequency specified for various types of modems. The receiving modem is designated the answer modem. It responds to the originate modem at a specified frequency as well. For example, a modem that uses **Frequency-Shift Keying (FSK)** modulation transmits at 1,170 Hz in the originate mode, and the answer modem responds at 2,125 Hz. The answer and originate frequencies are fixed within modems and depend upon the data rate and type of modulation used. Of course, the answer modem may work in the originate mode, and the modem that was formally in the originate mode would now respond in the answer mode. A modem only responds to legitimate answer and originate frequencies.

A modem may operate in an originate or **answer mode**. The **originate mode** initiates the data exchange whereas the answer mode responds to an originate modem. Modems have specific originate and answer carrier frequencies.

Another general observation concerning the simple modem of Figure 3-8(c) relates to the actual hardware interface. On the tip and ring side, modems are equipped with a standard RJ-11 modular telephone jack. This is a female connector identical to the wall jacks used with ordinary telephones. The modem plugs directly into the wall jack via a cable with suitable male telephone jacks.

On the computer side, the modem connects to an EIA/ITU-232 serial port (for an external modem). EIA/ITU-232 signaling conventions are universally installed in commercial modems. The handshaking protocols associated with the interface are also common to modems. The interface is designed to be compatible with 16550 **UARTs (Universal Asynchronous Receiver Transmitter)**. These UARTs are designed to support high-speed modem connections at data rates up to 115,200 bps.

Before examining the functions and parameters of modems, one other aspect of Figure 3-8(c) is noteworthy: It doesn't contain a complex arrangement of the blocks of data flow. This is true of most modems. The demand for the product has been such that ICs are available to perform all functions of a modem with a minimum amount of support chips. This has the added feature of making high-quality, fast modems available to the general public at reasonable prices.

A modem may be packaged as an independent device that is situated near the computer, and is referred to as an external modem. It connects to the computer with an EIA/TIA-232 cable, and to the telephone network with a conventional telephone jack. **Stand-alone** modems have the advantage of being portable—they're easily moved for connection to other computers. In addition, they usually have status indicators that inform the operator of the status of the message transmission as well as providing information in the event there's a problem.

Another type of modem is the older **acoustically coupled** variety. A telephone handset rests on a cradle packaged with the modem. The modem monitors the line with tone-detection circuitry. When a distant modem wants to send data, the acoustical modem will decipher the incoming tones through the telephone-handset microphone. The disadvantage to these types of modems is the additional equipment that's needed—handset and cradle, and tone-detection circuits. Some people prefer acoustical modems since they usually double as a telephone.

The most common type of modem is an **internal modem**. It plugs directly into an available expansion slot of a computer, or it may be a part of the computer interface adapter. In either case, internal modems offer the advantage of savings on cable and connector costs, as well as a reduction in noise that may be induced into the cables. An internal modem truly makes a computer a mobile system.

Almost all modems are configured and used either with software that's running on the computer, or with software provided by the modem manufacturer. Windows operating systems, for example, all include a generic terminal emulator (HyperTerminal) that allows you to directly access the modem via a keyboard. Or, for accessing the Internet, the configuration and initialization of a modem is performed with software, as well.

What if a distant modem wants to send you a message but you're not there to answer a call? A modem normally has an **auto answer** feature that can respond to tone signals from push-button phones or pulses from rotary-dial telephone exchanges. The ability to respond to either type of call makes the modem compatible with nearly all the telephones and switching equipment in the United States. When the tone detectors in the modem detect a call, the originate modem is signaled that the connection has been successfully completed.

In addition to auto answer, most modems are equipped with **auto dialing**. The example given earlier of a call placed from the keyboard is an example of auto dialing. A modem may contain onboard **Random-Access Memory (RAM)** in which you can store telephone numbers and initiate the call with the system software at the keyboard.

Modems also contain all the necessary circuitry so that the modem has voice-call capabilities. That is, you use the same modem chip to place a voice call as you do a data call. And since it handles voice and data, why not graphics, as well? Most modems also have fax capabilities, but the data rate is currently limited to 14.4 kbps.

Hayes AT Command Set

The functionality of a modem is contained in the **Hayes command set**. These are software commands used to configure the modem. In Windows-based software, much of the configuration is implemented within dialog boxes. For example, when you click the modem icon in Control Panel, the Modem Properties box opens. Highlight your modem in the list, and click on the Properties button.

Another dialog box opens, which contains configuration data about your modem; COM port, speaker volume, word length, maximum speed, word length, number of stop bits, and so on. The information you see in these boxes is normally contained in the NVRAM (nonvolatile random access memory) chip on the modem card. AT commands allow you to access the NVRAM to see what you're currently using.

AT commands can tell you quite a bit about your modem. Unfortunately, not all modem manufacturers give you access to them, and those who do don't always make it easy. It takes a little experimenting. Be cautious when nosing around the AT commands, since any changes you make will affect how your modem works.

Table 3-10 shows a partial list of AT commands. While these are typical, they may differ from those used by your modem since each manufacturer implements the commands a little differently. The next section explains how to view the command set.

Command	Description
&$	Help
A/	Repeat Last Command
A>	Continuously Repeat Command
AT	Command Mode Preface
A	Answer Call
B0	V.xx Mode
B1	Bell Answer Sequence
D0	Dial Telephone Number
D$	Help Dial Commands
M0	Sound Off

Table 3-10: Sampling of Hayes AT Commands

Modulation in Modems

Modulation schemes—the methods used to place data onto a carrier frequency—are complex. Modems of nearly all types utilize some type of modulation method. This section provides detailed information on modulation methods used for modems. Note that modem modulation is not central to the Network+ Exam, but it is important in understanding the functionality of modems, and particularly in understanding how cable modems work.

Modulation is the process of superimposing data upon a carrier. Modulating a carrier may be necessary for a couple of reasons. The distance between communicating devices may be several thousand feet, causing the signal-to-noise ratio to drop below an acceptable level. When this happens, high error rates are likely to occur. For these longer distances (exceeding 100 feet), the data signal is modulated onto a carrier. The carrier is operated at a frequency that will sustain the energy losses in the cable, thus maintaining an acceptable signal-to-noise ratio.

If data is to be transmitted through the telephone network, modulation is a requirement. As mentioned earlier, the limited bandwidth (4 kHz) of a telephone voice channel is the primary reason for this requirement. In addition to this, a large segment of the telephone system is analog, whereas the data leaving the computer is digital. The digital data must be converted to analog to be transmitted into the telephone network and modulated onto a carrier in such a way that the intelligence of the original data is retained across the analog phone lines.

Modulation used with modems is a variation of AM, FM, and PM. Four types of modulation will be examined in this section: Frequency-Shift Keying (FSK), Phase-Shift Keying (PSK), Differential Phase-Shift Keying (DPSK), and Quadrature Amplitude Modulation (QAM). Keep in mind that when data leaves a modem and arrives at the Central Office of the telco, it will be subjected to other signal manipulations such as pulse amplitude modulation, encoding, and a wide range of multiplexing techniques.

A basic understanding of modulation remains important, even though modems can be purchased containing a single modem chip and only a few support components. The reason is that the type of modulation has a significant impact on how fast data can be exchanged between modems.

Frequency-Shift Keying (FSK)

Frequency-Shift Keying (FSK) is a modulation method in which the carrier frequency is shifted higher or lower to represent a logic 1 or 0. It's generally reserved for low-speed modems of 300 bps. As will be shown shortly, it utilizes an extravagant amount of the precious voice-channel bandwidth. On the positive side, FSK is easy to implement and demodulate.

Figure 3-9 shows digital data modulated onto a 1,170 Hz carrier. The carrier frequency is well within the voice-channel bandwidth. A logic 1 modulated onto the carrier shifts the carrier forward to 1,270 Hz, while a logic 0 shifts the carrier back to 1,070 Hz, for a nominal bandwidth of 200 Hz.

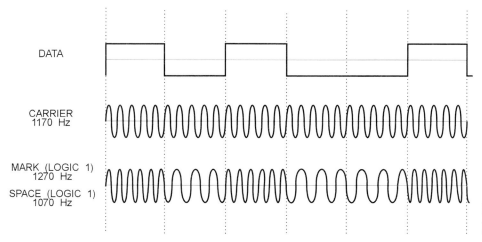

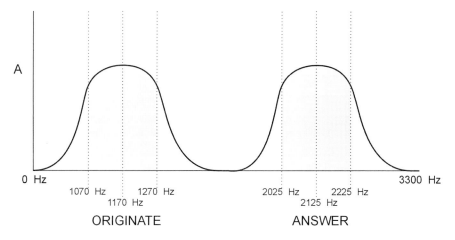

Figure 3-9: FSK Modulation

However, with each frequency change, harmonic sidebands will be generated at $2 \times$ bps $= 2 \times$ 300 bps $= 600$ Hz. This means that in order to superimpose a 300 bps square wave using FSK, 600 Hz of the voice channel must be reserved. Keep in mind that over a communications channel, two modems are used. The transmitting modem is called the **originate** or **calling modem** and the receiving modem is called the **answer modem**. There must be sufficient space in the voice channel to permit the modems to operate in either mode.

FSK represents bit changes by shifting the carrier higher and lower for logic 1's and 0's. FSK modems require plenty of bandwidth and are restricted to low speeds.

Figure 3-10 illustrates the bandwidth allocation for an FSK modem. The originate modem is centered at 1,170 Hz and the answer modem is centered at 2,125 Hz. A mark, logic 1, is shifted to 2,225 Hz in the answer mode and a logic 0 shifts the carrier back to 2,025 Hz.

Figure 3-10: Bandwidth Allocation for an FSK Modem

Due to **harmonics** contained in the 300 bps data, the effective bandwidth required in the answer mode is also 600 Hz. The large bandwidth requirement of FSK is the reason that the answer and originate carriers are located so far apart.

What if the data rate increased to 600 bps? The answer and originate modes would both require 1,200 Hz of bandwidth each, for a total of 2,400 Hz of the 4,000 Hz available in the voice channel. This leaves very little room and, in fact, approaches the maximum data rate at which information can be reliably transmitted. While FSK modems are unacceptable at higher data rates, the simplicity of FSK modulators and demodulators resulted in low-priced modems becoming available to many users and, in turn, spurred the development of higher speed modems that could be purchased at reasonable prices.

Phase-Shift Keying (PSK)

The concept of **Phase-Shift Keying (PSK)** is shown in Figure 3-11. For each change of logic level, the phase of the carrier is inverted 180 degrees. The receiver detects logic level changes only when it detects the phase inversion. PSK, as shown in the figure, suffers from the same bandwidth problems as FSK. Also, if a long string of logic 1's or 0's arrives at the receiver, synchronization between transmitter and receiver may be lost. To keep the receiver clocked to the transmitter, there should be a change of carrier frequency at the end of each bit, even if there's a logic level change.

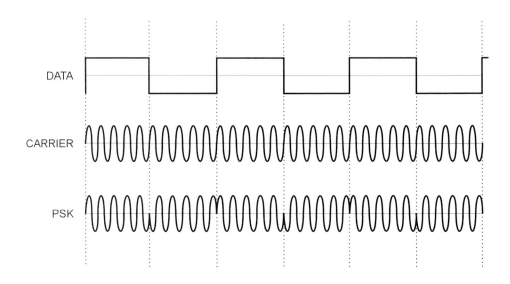

Figure 3-11: PSK Modulation

PSK represents logic 1's and 0's by inverting the phase of the carrier for each bit change.

Since the bandwidth of the voice channel restricts the data rate at which information can be transmitted, it's necessary to use more bits to express a change of the voice-channel carrier. FSK represented a single bit change by shifting the carrier. As we saw in Figure 3-10, four frequency changes (two each for answer and originate) were enough to consume a large amount of the bandwidth. An alternative to this technique is to have two or more bits produce a carrier change. In this way, the voice-channel bandwidth is more efficiently utilized. The process of having multiple bits, or symbols, produce a carrier change refers to **baud**. If a symbol contains two bits (a **dibit**) and modulates a 1,200 bps carrier, then the baud rate is:

$$
\text{Baud Rate} = bps/N_s
$$
$$
\text{Baud Rate} = 1200/2
$$
$$
\text{Baud Rate} = 600
$$

where N_s is the number of bits per symbol.

It's important to note that the term baud rate has been degraded within the industry through incorrect usage. It's often used synonymously, and incorrectly, with bps (bits per second). The two terms are equal only when the bits per symbol is one, as in FSK. Modem manufacturers specify data rates only in bps.

PSK readily lends itself to multiple bits per symbol. When the data phase modulates a carrier in such a way as to make more efficient use of the channel, it's referred to as differential phase-shift keying.

PSK is a marginal improvement over FSK. But, once it's modified to address the two problems described above, it delivers much superior results. The improved version of PSK is Differential Phase-Shift Keying (DPSK).

Differential Phase-Shift Keying (DPSK)

Differential Phase-Shift Keying (**DPSK**) represents data bits by phase shifting the carrier in increments that are smaller than available with FSK. This allows a greater number of bits per symbol.

DPSK is an extended version of the PSK described in the previous section. DPSK permits the symbol encoding to change the phase based upon the phase position of the previous symbol. Using this approach, there's no need to transmit a portion of the carrier to be used for phase demodulation at the receiver. The receiver will look for the signal to fall within predetermined boundaries. The assumption that the phase-modulated data will drift due to jitters and ringing makes DPSK more fault-tolerant than straight PSK.

DPSK derives its name from the fact that the information symbols are located at some phase-shifted point that is established by the first symbol of a word. The phase location of succeeding symbols will differ from the reference point based upon encoding. The truth table for 2-bit DPSK is shown in Figure 3-12(a). The phase shifts shown in the figure represent four phase positions, and are shown graphically in the constellation map of Figure 3-12(b).

A constellation map is nothing more than a vector representation of phase angles. Recall that signals have amplitudes and exist in time. When several points (representing signal amplitudes) are plotted (according to their phase relationship to the reference signal), the vectors look like a constellation of stars—hence, the name constellation map.

The truth table is that of a 2,400 bps, V.26 modem. Since four positions of the 360-degree constellation are used, it's usually called DQPSK, with "Q" referring to quaternary or **quadrature**, in deference to the four phase positions. You may also see it referred to in literature as 4-PSK, or simply QPSK. When PSK was introduced in the previous section, only two phase changes were described—so, it would aptly be called 2-PSK.

Dibit	Phase Shift	Alternate Phase Shift
00	0°	45°
01	90°	315°
11	180°	225°
10	270°	135°

(a)

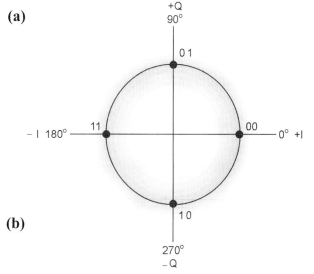

(b)

Figure 3-12: DPSK Truth Table and Constellation Map

Symbol rates of 4 and 8 are common with DPSK (referred to as 4-DPSK or QPSK, and 8-DPSK). Symbol rates beyond 8 bits per symbol are difficult, because phase jitters make the separation between symbols difficult to interpret. For 8-DPSK, there are 3 bits per symbol (tribits). The encoded bits are separated by 22.5 degrees, so phase jitters may cause the 3-bit symbol groupings to blur across the narrow separation, making demodulation at the receiver impossible. The maximum number of bits per symbol for DPSK is 16.

DPSK is used extensively in 1,200 bps and 2,400 bps modems. An examination of a typical modulator will help to clarify how the modulation method is implemented in the modem. A 4-PSK (QPSK, DQPSK) modulator is shown in Figure 3-13(a).

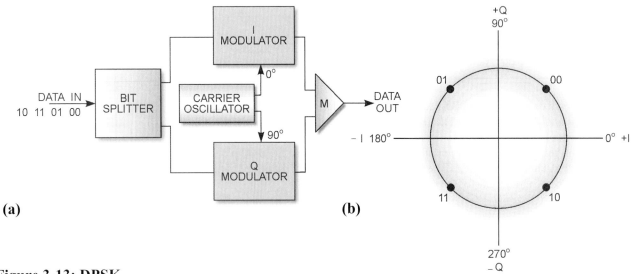

(a)

(b)

Figure 3-13: DPSK Modulator

Serial data is clocked into the bit splitter in dibit pairs. The first bit is designated the **Least Significant Bit** (**LSB**) and the second bit is the Most Significant Bit (MSB). A logic 0 from the bit splitter is a positive voltage and a logic 1 is a negative voltage. The bits are sent to a balanced modulator from the bit splitter.

A carrier is generated from a crystal oscillator and applied to both modulators. The carrier applied to the I modulator is in phase with the crystal oscillator. The carrier applied to the other modulator (the Q modulator, for quadrature or quaternary) is first shifted 90 degrees. The output of the I modulator will be in phase with the carrier, while the output of the Q modulator will be phase-shifted 90 degrees. The two modulator outputs are combined in the summing amplifier and their vector sum will be the output data.

Now, an 8-bit data word can be modulated. We'll select the bit pairs from the truth table of Figure 3-12(a): 00 01 11 10. The 00 dibit will be the first applied to the modulator. The bit to the right of each dibit is the Least Significant Bit (LSB) and will be applied to the Q modulator, while the left bit is the **Most Significant Bit** (**MSB**) and will be applied to the I modulator. Logic 0's are converted to positive voltages in the bit splitter. The I modulator output will be positive and is designated +I. The Q output is also positive, and is designated +Q. These two positive signals, separated by 90 degrees, are added vectorially in the summing amplifier to produce a positive voltage that's phase-separated by 45 degrees from the I carrier.

The position of the 00 dibit is plotted on the constellation map of Figure 3-13(b). Note that it's located at 45 degrees, between +I and +Q. This point will be the location from which all other phase shifts will be referenced.

The next dibit is 01. The logic 1 is the LSB. A logic 1 is converted to a negative voltage in the bit splitter. It's applied to the **Q modulator** and will be phase-shifted 90 degrees. The positive-voltage logic 0 is applied to the **I modulator**. The +I from the logic 0 and the –Q of the logic 1 are summed. Their position on the constellation map is a 90-degree phase shift from the 00 dibit reference.

The next dibit is 11. Logic 1's are converted to negative voltages and will appear at the summing amplifier as –I –Q. The truth table calls for a 180-degree phase shift, and the –I –Q location is 180 degrees from the reference set by 00 (the first dibit).

The last dibit is 10. The LSB is 0. It will be output from the Q modulator as +Q. The logic 1 will be output from the I modulator as –I. This is a 270-degree phase shift from the original 00 reference.

The disadvantage to the DPSK modulator just described is the 0-degree phase change for the 00 dibit. If a long string of 0's is transmitted, the carrier wouldn't be shifted. A communicating modem may lose synchronization. Alternate phase shifts are 45 degrees, 135 degrees, 225 degrees, and 315 degrees for 00, 01, 11, 10, respectively. Using the alternate change, the carrier will be shifted for each symbol, ensuring that the modems won't lose carrier synchronization.

DPSK solves both problems of FSK—the carrier synchronization is timed, and more bits are available. In fact, a 2,400 bps data rate with 2-bits-per-symbol modulation will propagate through the voice channel at a baud rate of 1,200, effectively doubling the utilization of the channel.

As mentioned earlier, 16 binary levels per symbol have successfully phase modulated a carrier. Unfortunately, each bit increase per symbol raises the noise and distortion levels at the receiver. This is due to phase jitter.

Phase jitter is the unavoidable delay in arrival times of the symbols created by harmonic distortion of the logic levels carried by the symbol. As the bits-per-symbol increase, so does the noise. The remedy is to increase the channel Signal-to-Noise Ratio (SNR). However, for each doubling of the bits-per-symbol, the SNR must be doubled. The additional circuitry and power consumption may not justify the higher baud rates.

Quadrature Amplitude Modulation (QAM)

A modulation technique that responds to the symbol limitations is **Quadrature Amplitude Modulation (QAM)**. QAM specifies amplitude as well as phase changes to modulate the carrier. A 4-bit-per-symbol constellation map of QAM is shown in Figure 3-14(a). In this arrangement, 16 symbol points, or locations, represent the carrier modulation scheme. In other words, Figure 3-14 illustrates the constellation of 16-point QAM. QAM transmitters are used to modulate data rates at 2,400 bps and higher. The 33.6 kbps modems use QAM on transmit and receive sides, while 56k modems use QAM only on the transmit side.

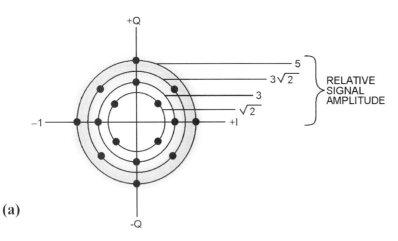

(a)

Q_1	ABSOLUTE PHASE		RELATIVE AMPLITUDE	Q_2	Q_3	Q_4	PHASE CHANGE
0	$0°$	$90°$	3	0	0	1	$0°$
1	$180°$	$270°$	5	0	0	0	$45°$
0	$45°$	$135°$	$\sqrt{2}$	0	1	0	$90°$
1	$225°$	$315°$	$3\sqrt{2}$	0	1	1	$135°$
				1	1	1	$180°$
				1	1	0	$225°$
				1	0	0	$270°$
				1	0	1	$315°$

(b)

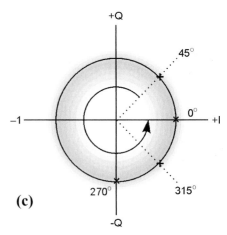

(c)

Figure 3-14: QAM Signal Amplitude and Phase Constellation, Truth Table, and Constellation Map for the Quad Bit 0101

QAM represents bit changes by varying the carrier amplitude as well as shifting the carrier phase. QAM is the most commonly used modulation method for higher speed modems.

Consider the advantage of using multiple bits per symbol. In Figure 3-14, a baud rate of 2,400 yields a bps rate of 2,400 baud × 4 bits-per-symbol = 9,600 bps. A 9,600 bps data rate can be transmitted at 2,400 baud through the voice channel using QAM. Now, if the symbol rate increased to 14 bits-per-symbol, the effective data rate will be 2,400 baud × 14 bits-per-symbol = 33,600 bps.

In addition to shifting the carrier phase, QAM makes use of the available power level spectrum within the voice channel. Since **Bit Error Rates** (**BERs**)—which are caused by noise—decrease with high signal-to-noise ratios, it's advantageous to transmit data at several factors above the 1 mW reference. QAM simply uses that available power to combine amplitude modulation with phase modulation.

The level of the amplitude is not as strictly constrained as it is within the commercial broadcast radio industry. Transmitted messages in data communications may vary over several decibel decades. Rather than prescribe specific power levels, QAM amplitude variations are described as the ratios between various amplitudes. In the example of Figure 3-14, the four amplitudes are referenced to the first quad bit.

The truth table of the QAM constellation map is shown in Figure 3-14(b). The first bit, or LSB, is designated as Q1. It serves to anchor the remaining three bits in the quad by serving as a base from which amplitude levels and phase changes for the quad are referenced. The four amplitude levels are shown as $\sqrt{2}$, 3, $3\sqrt{2}$, and 5.

These are relative amplitudes whose absolute value in watts, voltage, or current depends on the channel parameters. It's the job of the modem transmitter to establish power levels and scale the amplitude variations accordingly. The Q1 bit also establishes an absolute phase reference. The other three bits will be sourced to this reference to shift the carrier phase. The amount of phase change is determined by the combination of bits Q2, Q3, and Q4.

As an example, the quad bit 0101 will produce the constellation map of Figure 3-14(c). The 0 bit is the LSB. From the truth table, with Q1 equal to a logic 0, the absolute phase may be referenced at 0 degrees, 90 degrees, 45 degrees, and 315 degrees from the +I carrier. We'll select 45 degrees. At an absolute 45-degree phase angle, the amplitude of this quad will lie in the $\sqrt{2}$ plane. Now, the bit arrangement of Q2, Q3, and Q4 (which is 101) is found on the truth table. This bit arrangement produces a 315-degree phase change from the point established by Q1. It also lies in a concentric circle in the $\sqrt{2}$ amplitude plane as determined by Q1. The quad's bit positions are marked on the constellation map of Figure 3-14(c). Literally, then, when the carrier is phase-shifted 315 degrees, and the amplitude of the carrier is equal to $\sqrt{2}$ times the available channel power, the receiver will detect a 0101 bit stream.

A next set of quad bits will then be shifted into the transmitter in a manner similar to the DPSK transmitter discussed earlier. The transmitter assigns the new Q1 bit an absolute phase position and relative amplitude. The bit pattern of the next three bits would be examined to determine the amount of phase change required.

Single-amplitude QAM is also an option as well as 2-, 4-, 8-, and 16-bit symbols. If the single-amplitude option is selected, the operation is identical to DPSK.

What if, in the example of Figure 3-14(c), the next quad bit was identical to our example? The transmitter may select the same absolute phase and relative amplitude as before. If a long string of this bit pattern was transmitted, the transmitter could continue to send at the same phase change and amplitude. This is a potential problem for several reasons. One reason involves the level of transmitted power. If the modem transmits continuously at a relative amplitude of 5, it is delivering the maximum power level to the channel. Continuously transmitting at this level decreases the efficiency of the channel.

Another problem is that of intersymbol interference. Generally, the modem converts the digital levels to analog for transmission over the voice channel. The analog symbols resemble normally distributed sine waves. If all symbols are transmitted at similar power levels and at the same degree of phase shift, the symbols are sure to overlap and smear together. This blurring together of the symbols describes ISI.

A modem addresses the problems above in two ways. An **adaptive equalizer** is included in the modem to compensate for channel-induced ISI. To avoid the problem of repetitive selection of the same phase and amplitude (a common occurrence for long strings of 1's and 0's) the modulated data is scrambled. **Scrambling** is not done for any reason of security, but rather to ensure the signal power is consistent across the voice channel.

Modems routinely scramble data in order to reduce intersymbol interference as well as to evenly distribute the signal power.

The **scrambler** consists of a series of shift registers into which the symbols are clocked. At selected points on the shift registers are taps, as shown in Figure 3-15. The data is sampled at the taps and summed together using two exclusive-OR gates. The number of registers and the placement of taps are derived from the **generator polynomial** shown in the figure. The result is that the repetition described earlier is avoided, since the scrambler ensures a different bit arrangement due to the cyclical movement of data through the registers, and the redundant summing of the bits.

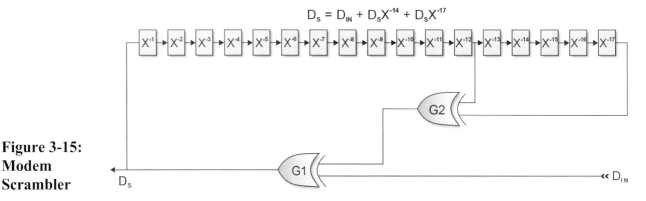

$$D_s = D_{IN} + D_s X^{-14} + D_s X^{-17}$$

Figure 3-15: Modem Scrambler

A **descrambler** in the receiving circuitry of the answer modem provides an inverse operation. Data scramblers are incorporated into all modern modems. They're an integral part of the initial exchange of bits between the transmit and receive modems, used to establish synchronization.

Table 3-11: Characteristics of Modems

Table 3-11 summarizes characteristics of modems.

Purpose	A modem is used to provide the interface between a computer and the telephone network.
Functions	It converts digital signals from a computer to analog signals.
	It converts analog signals from the telephone network to digital signals for a computer.
	It modulates data so that it can be placed on a carrier frequency that falls within the telephone line bandwidth.
	It scrambles modulated data to avoid interference.
	It conditions signal strength using equalization to compensate for line weaknesses.
	It provides for full-duplex operation.
	It negotiates data rates with remote modem.
Features	Modems may be analog or digital.
	Modems may be external, internal, or acoustical.
	Most modems provide for auto-answer.
	Most modems include fax operations.
	Most modems use the Hayes AT command set for functionality.
	Most computer operating systems include software programs that allow for easy setup, configuration, and initialization of modems.

CABLE MODEM

A **cable modem** uploads and downloads data using the existing cable television (CATV) wiring infrastructure. The wiring infrastructure consists of coaxial or, more likely, fiber-optic cabling. Since coaxial and fiber-optic cable have wider bandwidth capabilities than the wiring used in the analog telephone loop, data will travel at faster rates than over the CATV system.

Data rates can vary widely for a cable modem. The maximum rate is close to 36 Mbps, while typical rates will fall in the range of 300 kbps to about 10 Mbps.

A cable modem uses the wide bandwidth that's available on the CATV cable to transfer data at very high speeds. Typical applications include Internet access, distance learning, or medical diagnoses to rural areas. The obstacle to implementing access to computers is that the current system is primarily simplex in nature. That is, data travels in only one direction over the CATV cable. At the cable head-end, cable television is piped to homes and business via a point-to-multipoint configuration. The multipoint cables lead to boxes, which attach to television sets. A television receives information; but it doesn't transmit back any information, so there hasn't been much need to incorporate transceivers at the head-end that can send as well as receive data.

But in order to access and communicate with a distant network such as the Internet, full-duplex communication is a requirement. While there are a couple of methods to implement full-duplex operation with cable modems, Figure 3-16 shows the fastest method. A cable modem is placed at the user site. A CAT 5 UTP cable is connected between the cable modem and a NIC card in the computer. The NIC is a 10Base-T card at the subscriber site. The cable modem uses a BNC to attach the coaxial cable from the CATV plant to the cable modem.

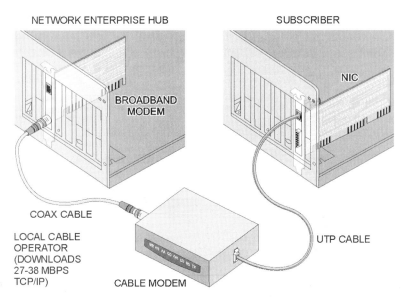

Figure 3-16: Cable Modems Use the Existing Cable Television Coaxial and Fiber-Optic Cabling Infrastructure for Transferring Data

A cable modem uses TCP/IP as the internetworking protocol. This is a requirement since the Internet identifies nodes with an IP address.

An alternative to the method shown in Figure 3-16 is to use a V.34 modem (33.6 kbps data rate) for uploads from the computer to the ISP. Downloads are received from the CATV cable as described above. But when data is sent to the ISP, it's transferred across the analog telephone network. This system alleviates the cable operator from installing expensive transceivers at the cable plant. The effect on the user is minimal since uploads mainly consist of mouse clicks on Internet sites.

The cable television network uses a bus topology. Each cable subscriber is attached to the bus with a segment of coaxial or fiber-optic cable. All subscribers share the bandwidth. Potentially, data rates used for Internet access will slow with the number of connected subscribers. While a cable modem may be able to receive data at 36 Mbps, don't expect downloads at this rate. Still, cable modems are very fast when compared to competing technologies. An analog V.90 modem downloads at rates slightly lower than 53 kbps, while an ISDN connection provides a maximum data rate of 128 kbps.

The standard currently governing cable modems is the **Data Over Cable Service Interface Specification (DOCSIS)**, which was established by the **Multimedia Cable Network Systems (MCNS)**, a consortium of cable companies. This is a consortium within the cable television industry that sets cable-based standards. The DOCSIS standard was approved by the ITU in March of 1998.

Pertinent specifications of the DOCSIS standard are:

Downstream

- *Modulation:* 64- and 256-QAM

- *Carrier Rate:* 6 MHz

- *Data Rate:* 27 or 36 Mbps

Upstream

- *Modulation:* QPSK or 16-QAM

- *Carrier:* Variable, 200 kHz to 3.2 MHz

- *Data Rate:* 320 kbps to 10 Mbps

Subscriber Interface

- 10Base-T

Network Interface

- 10Base-T

- 100Base-T

- ATM

- FDDI

A competing standard is the IEEE 802.14 (not approved at the time of this writing). The IEEE standard specifies ATM (Asynchronous Transfer Mode) at the user interface, rather than 10Base-T. (See Chapter 9 for details on ATM.) All data formatted to the ATM protocol is separated into 53-byte frames, or cells, as they're called. The cell size is fixed and predictable. Comparatively, an Ethernet frame is about 1,500 bytes, while an IP packet is about 64,000 bytes.

The huge advantage of using ATM is that the small cells can be passed through nearly any type of network on their way to a final destination. This makes ATM very routable across nearly all network types. Because of the almost guaranteed routability of ATM, it's used for multimedia applications such as video, voice, and graphics.

While cable operators have included ATM in the DOCSIS standard, don't expect to see it widely implemented for some time to come; the operators feel it adds an unnecessary level of complexity to the system and increases the time to market for cable modems. The IEEE would specifically require that subscribers interface to the operator using ATM.

The IEEE 802.14 standard is the better one because it looks to the future and anticipates bandwidth demands on the coaxial cable that the DOCSIS standard won't be able to address. Unfortunately, it also increases the cost of implementing cable modems.

If the user is accessing the cable operator through a network, there are more options available—100 Mbps Ethernet, FDDI (Fiber Distributed Data Interface, a fiber-optic standard that's discussed in Chapter 9) at 100 Mbps, or ATM. In this configuration, a single cable modem at the subscriber site is used to connect the network users (which can range in number from four to a maximum of sixteen). The cable modem connects to a hub via Cat 5 UTP cable.

Table 3-12 summarizes characteristics of cable modems.

Purpose	A cable modem provides high-speed network access, particularly to the Internet, over the CATV system.
Functions	A cable modem provides for very fast data downloads from the Internet; typical speeds are 300 kbps to 10 Mbps.
	For full-duplex cable systems, uploads are 300 kbps to about 10 Mbps.
	For simplex cable systems, uploads are sent via a V.34 analog modem through the telephone lines.
Features	A cable modem connection requires a 10Base-T NIC installed in the subscriber computer, the cable modem, and a CAT 5 UTP cable connecting the two.
	Multi-user access is permitted with a 10/100Base-T hub. Up to 16 users may share the same connection.
	The standard currently used to govern cable modems is DOCSIS; the IEEE standard is IEEE 802.14.

Table 3-12: Characteristics of Cable Modems

ISDN ADAPTER

Integrated Services Digital Network (ISDN) is a set of digital services that are available over telephone lines. ISDN is a complete digital solution from end-user to end-user. Since the connection is all digital, data rates can be much higher than on an analog telephone connection, as high as 128 kbps.

ISDN is an alternative to conventional telephone connections for Internet access or for wide area connections in a multi-user environment. ISDN competes with fractional T-1 and cable modems.

┌─ **TEST TIP** ─┐

Be aware that ISDN is a complete digital solution between users.

Users are charged a monthly fee to use ISDN. The equipment needed to interface and use the service is specialized and limited to ISDN technology. Due to geographical limits of ISDN, it may not be available in all areas, or if it is, may not be cost-effective. The end-user site must be within 18,000 feet (3.4 miles) of the local loop central office to receive an ISDN line. (A central office is a local telephone switching center. It's designated by the first three digits of a local, seven-digit telephone number.) The distance limitation may be exceeded if a wide-bandwidth repeater is installed. The cost of the repeater is passed on to customers and may offset cost advantages of ISDN over a competing technology.

As ISDN frame carries data in a **Bearer channel (B channel)** that has a 64 kbps bandwidth. On older telephone systems, B channels may drop to 56 kbps. A **Data channel (D channel)** carries supervisor and signaling information at 16 kbps (and sometimes at 64 kbps).

There are two types of ISDN connections, a **Basic Rate Interface (BRI)**, and a **Primary Rate Interface (PRI)**. A BRI connection is composed of two 64 kbps B channels and one 16 kbps D channel. It's normally referred to as BRI 2B+D. A PRI channel has 23 64 kbps B channels and one 64 kbps D channel. It's normally called PRI 23B+D.

Channel information in an ISDN line is sent one byte after another. For example, if two devices are connected to the line, the first device will send a byte of data, then the next device sends a byte, then the first device sends a byte. The bearer channels are then routinely multiplexed. A single facility may have many ISDN lines with the channels multiplexed onto a single channel. When B channels are multiplexed, the connection is described by including an H suffix. Typical transmission rates are:

- BRI H0 = 6 B channels (384 kbps)

- PRI H10 = 23 B channels (1472 kbps)

- PRI H11 = 24 B channels (1536 kbps)

- BRI+PRI H12 = 30 B channels (1929 kbps)

ISDN Interfaces

ISDN comes with its own equipment and interfaces that are needed to establish a physical connection. Refer to Figure 3-17 to place the definitions described below to their place in the physical layout.

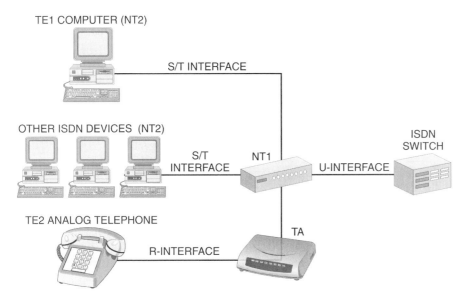

Figure 3-17: ISDN Reference Points

An ISDN connection is described using interface references.

ISDN Terminals

- *TE1:* Terminal Equipment Type 1. A subscriber-side device that is specialized for ISDN. This may include a computer connection or an ISDN telephone. These are shown in the figure as TE1 Computer and Other ISDN Devices.

- *TE2:* Terminal Equipment Type 2. Also a subscriber-side device but one that pre-dates the ISDN standard, such as the analog telephone shown in the figure.

Terminal Adapter (TA)

A terminal adapter is needed only to connect older style equipment to an ISDN line. The analog telephone is shown with a TA because it's not ISDN-ready. TAs are sometimes, incorrectly, called ISDN modems. A TA may be either a stand-alone device or a printed circuit board inside the TE2 device. If it's an external device, it connects to the TE2 via a standard physical interface such as EIA/TIA-232 or V.35.

Network Termination

- *(NT1) Network Termination Type 1:* An NT1 is a device at the ISDN switch side (in Europe—but at the customer site in North America) of the connection that performs a 2-wire to 4-wire conversion. Four physical wires are used at the subscriber side for full-duplex transmission. Two of the wires are used for transmit and two for receiving. Many ISDN devices have an NT1 built into them that makes installations easier and quicker.

- *(NT2) Network Termination Type 2:* An NT2 handles layer 2 and 3 ISDN protocols. Since these are included in all ISDN devices, they are shown in the figure in parentheses with TE1 devices.

Reference Interface

ISDN specifies several reference points that define logical interfaces between terminals and network termination points.

- **S Interface:** The reference point between subscriber-side ISDN equipment and NT2.

- **T Interface:** The reference point between NT1 and NT2. Notice in the figure that the S and T interface are shown on the same line. First, they're electrically identical; second, a S reference is inside the subscriber device.

- **R Interface:** The reference point between non-ISDN devices and a TA. The analog telephone has an R interface since it's not ISDN equipment.

- **U Interface:** The reference between the carrier switch and the ISDN device (NT1) at the subscriber site. Keep in mind, ISDN is intended to provide digital connections using a 2-wire local loop. The U interface refers to this 2-to-4 wire hybrid.

Figure 3-18 shows a typical application of ISDN. A small LAN is arranged in a star topology with a hub. One of the hub ports is connected to a router. The router contains an ISDN adapter. The adapter is likely to be a circuit card or module that plugs into the router and contains all electronics needed for the NT1 at the U interface. The NT1 contains an RJ-45 connector. UTP cable terminated with RJ-45 connectors (using straight-through pinning) is used to connect the NT1 U interface to an ISDN line terminated at a wall plate near the router.

The ISDN line connects to an ISDN switch at the central office. If the network in Figure 3-18 is to be used for Internet access, the connection will continue from the ISDN switch to an ISP. The ISP must also have an ISDN switch.

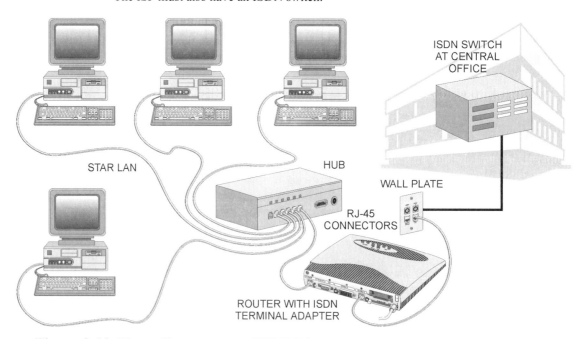

Figure 3-18: Users Connect to an ISDN Line Through a Hub that Connects to a Router that May Contain an ISDN Terminal Adapter

Table 3-13 summarizes characteristics of ISDN adapters.

Purpose	An ISDN adapter is used to provide a digital connection directly to the user telephone or data equipment.
Functions	It provides for 128 kbps or 64 kbps data connections.
	It allows for multi-user access through a single connection.
	It allows for simultaneous voice and data exchanges.
Features	ISDN equipment is specific to digital ISDN connections.
	Users have the full range of telephone and data features available over analog lines but at faster rates and with less noise and distortion.

Table 3-13: Characteristics of ISDN Adapters

KEY POINTS REVIEW

This chapter has presented an extensive exploration of the hardware commonly used with networks.

- A NIC is used to access the network, package data into frames, check for errors, and send and receive data.

- A hub provides a centralized connection point for wired network access.

- A bridge is used to translate between different network access protocols such as Token Ring and Ethernet; and to segment large or congested networks that use the same network access protocol.

- A router is used to locate different networks. It may also be used to control traffic on larger LANs.

- A switch uses a logical mesh topology to provide the full bandwidth of a network to connected nodes.

- A wireless access point provides a single and centralized connection point for computers to communicate with wireless technology.

- A gateway is used to convert between two different network protocols.

- A modem is used to provide the interface between a computer and the telephone network.

- A cable modem provides high-speed network access, particularly to the Internet, over the CATV system.

- An ISDN adapter is used to provide a digital connection directly to a user telephone or data equipment.

At this point, review the objectives listed at the beginning of the chapter to be certain that you understand and can perform them. Afterward, answer the review questions that follow to verify your knowledge of the information.

REVIEW QUESTIONS

The following questions test your knowledge of the material presented in this chapter:

1. Which networking device provides digital user-to-user voice and data connections?

2. To connect computers on a Token Ring network to computers on an Ethernet network, which networking hardware device is needed?

3. To achieve download data rates of 1 Mbps over the cable television infrastructure, which devices are needed?

4. In order to connect multiple users equipped with IEEE 802.11b cards, what is needed?

5. Which network device operates in a manner similar to a conventional hub but provides the full bandwidth of the channel to users?

6. What is needed to connect two 10Base-T hubs together?

7. What router protocol is commonly used to connect to the Internet?

8. To access the Internet over an analog telephone line, what hardware device is required?

9. Two large networks need to be connected together. The protocols running on the networks are not the same. To successfully connect users on both networks, what hardware device is needed?

10. To prevent a large number of network broadcasts from congesting a network, which network device should be used?

11. It's desired that wireless network users be able to access a server on a wired LAN. To do so, the AP must incorporate a(n) _____.

12. How do dynamic routers update their tables of addresses?

13. What is the maximum data rate of an ISDN line?

14. For nearly all analog modems, what is the name of the command set that controls functionality of the modem?

15. Which type of switch allows a data frame to be sent on to the destination before the frame has been fully received by the switch?

1. To provide connectivity between ten computers equipped with 10Base-T NICs, which of the following would be the best choice?
   a. hub
   b. router
   c. bridge
   d. gateway

2. On an Ethernet network, which of the following is responsible for packaging data into frames?
   a. modem
   b. ISDN adapter
   c. NIC
   d. bridge

3. What type of bridge converts from Token Ring to Ethernet?
   a. transparent
   b. translation
   c. source-routing
   d. cut-through

4. An ISDN connection is described as BRI 2B+D. How many 64 kbps channels does the connection have?
   a. 1
   b. 6
   c. 3
   d. 2

5. The hub used in a Token Ring network is called a _____.
   a. switch
   b. MSAU
   c. store-and-forward hub
   d. bus

6. To connect network users to the Internet, which of the following is required?
   a. router
   b. hub
   c. gateway
   d. bridge

7. As the distance between users and wireless AP increases, how are data rates through the AP affected?
   a. Data rates increase.
   b. Data rates remain unchanged.
   c. Data rates double with a doubling of distance.
   d. Data rates decrease.

8. What type of connector should a NIC have for use in a 10Base-T LAN?
   a. RJ-11
   b. BNC
   c. RJ-45
   d. V.34

9. An analog modem is communicating with another, slower, modem. Which of the following is to be expected?
a. The speed of the connection will be at the speed of the fastest modem.
b. The speed of the connection will be at the speed of the slowest modem.
c. Since the two modems are unmatched in speed, the connection will be terminated.
d. Due to the modem mismatch, an ISDN adapter must be used.

10. For an ISDN connection, the maximum distance from central office to end-user premises is _____.
a. 3,000 feet
b. 6,000 feet
c. 18,000 feet
d. 24,000 feet

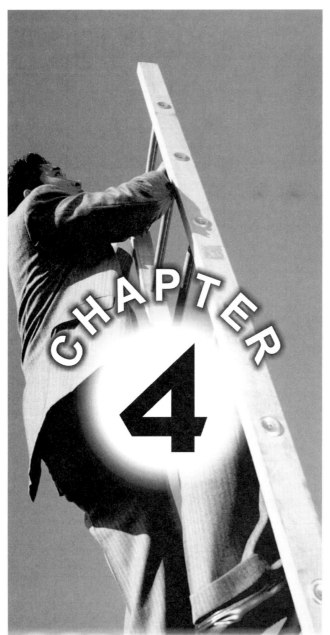

CHAPTER 4

ISO OSI REFERENCE MODEL

LEARNING
OBJECTIVES

LEARNING OBJECTIVES

Upon completion of this chapter and its related lab procedures, you will be able to perform the following tasks:

1. Define protocol.

2. Describe the hierarchical nature of the OSI Reference Model.

3. State the benefits of the OSI Reference Model.

4. Define the layers of the OSI model, and identify the protocols and functions that pertain to each layer.

5. Identify the OSI layers at which the following network components operate:

   - Hubs

   - Switches

   - Bridges

   - Routers

   - Network interface cards

6. Describe the functions of the MAC and LLC sublayers.

7. State specific applications that the MAC and LLC sublayers govern.

8. Define connectionless and connection-oriented protocols.

CHAPTER 7

ISO OSI REFERENCE MODEL

INTRODUCTION

Protocols are the rules governing the organization and transmission of data. In many cases, the rules are written as recommendations, or descriptions, of how data should be packaged and transmitted. Individual vendors are responsible for designing and building equipment that will actually implement a protocol. This has resulted in a multitude of "exceptions to the rule." Many of the standard protocols have roots in large computer and office automation companies. What has become a standard protocol was once a proprietary protocol belonging to a company. IBM's Synchronous Data Link Control (SDLC) is the forerunner of the standard protocol High-Level Data Link Control (HDLC). The Xerox/Intel/Digital Ethernet is the foundation of the IEEE Carrier Sense Multiple Access/Collision Detection (CSMA/CD) standard, Ethernet. IBM uses SDLC extensively, and many other vendors support HDLC. Both protocols are very similar, but they're not the same. The same holds true for Ethernet.

The **OSI ISO Reference Model for Data Communications** is the accepted tool used to measure and describe networking systems. A true understanding of the layers of the model is essential both in understanding internetworking, and in taking the Network+ Certification exam.

ISO OSI Reference Model for Data Communications

Within this chapter, the emphasis is placed upon protocol standards written by respected standards organizations. Even within these standards, many liberties by vendors are taken—and often encouraged—by standards organizations. In this way, precautions have been taken that won't make data communications inflexible to technological developments.

For the most part, the intent of a protocol is software-oriented. But, as we'll see shortly, this directly affects the actual movement of data. To have a clear understanding of data transfer, it's necessary to study the force driving the data—the data communication protocols.

PROTOCOL FUNCTIONS

Most of the information presented so far in this book has evolved from a wide-ranging set of rules that attempt to make the exchange of data between computers an orderly process. Those sets of rules are collectively called **protocols**.

protocols

A protocol is a set of rules that define the exchange of data between two or more devices on a network. A protocol is a logical concept. It does not consist of any physical devices, but describes how data can be exchanged between computers, or other devices of similar architectures.

There are many protocols in use today, and they are always expanding to respond to technological developments. As changes in the industry occur, the protocols themselves will change. But data communication protocols will always have three basic functions:

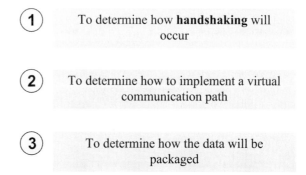

handshaking

1. To determine how **handshaking** will occur

2. To determine how to implement a virtual communication path

3. To determine how the data will be packaged

Handshaking is a broad term that refers to the initial communications between two devices on a network. A good example of handshaking is so-called well-known ports such as the port for HTTP (Hyper Text Transport Protocol) that's used for web access. The port is 80. HTTP signals are passed through port 80 because a set of communication dialogs have been defined for the port that sets up the initial contact between two devices. In other words, the devices utilize port 80 as a handshaking tool to learn a bit about one another's capabilities.

virtual communications path

A **virtual communications path** is a medium that appears to exist but actually doesn't. A long distance telephone call is a virtual communications path. A caller in Miami talking to someone in Los Angeles appears to be connected by a wire, but in reality there are central offices, switching centers, and perhaps microwave links between the two telephones. A protocol establishes the same illusion between computers. The protocol anticipates problems and directs that the data be prepared accordingly. In order to accomplish this, protocols establish procedures for error detection and correction.

A virtual communications path is established with the EIA/TIA-232 connector and the software conventions used with the connection. As far as the computer (or user) is concerned, there's a wire that lets data move from the PC to the printer when a print command is initiated. The protocol recognizes the differences between the PC and the printer, and realizes that problems may arise. Consequently, it requires that the communicating devices be informed of problems by including error detection. In this case, a parity bit is included.

Computers must know how to package the data before sending any data . Will they communicate a bit at a time, a character at a time, a hundred characters, or a hundred pages? The IEEE 802.x series of protocols are very much involved in defining how data is to be packaged into frames before it's sent across a network. In regard to frames and protocols in general, the main point to keep in mind is that the protocols must be compatible. For example, IEEE 802.1 devices cannot directly communicate with IEEE 802.5 devices.

Moving information to various places around the globe would be an impossibly confusing task without some sort of guidelines. The designers of data communications systems more or less follow a model developed by the International Standards Organization. The model is called the Open System Interconnection (OSI) reference model.

OPEN SYSTEM INTERCONNECTION MODEL

In 1975 the International Standards Organization began work on the **Open System Inter-connection (OSI)** Reference Model. Their work was completed three years later, in 1978. The final structure of the model is shown in Figure 4-1.

At first glance, it may seem like three years was a long time to develop a simple block diagram. But the organization had the very difficult job of deciding what constitutes a data communications system, and determining what its major functions would be. The OSI model provides designers and users of data communications a logical structure for defining protocols for a variety of network configurations.

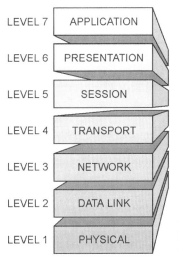

Figure 4-1: OSI Reference Model

The time was ripe for a widely respected organization to advance a model to which vendors could refer when developing data communications products. In 1974 IBM pioneered their own model, called **System Network Architecture (SNA)**. The purpose of SNA was to bring a sense of organization and compatibility to the IBM product line. The SNA model was proprietary to IBM, meaning it was designed for their current products, as well as those products still on the drawing board. And while SNA did (and does) provide a blueprint for IBM networks, it also had a significant impact on the product development of smaller, less influential data processing vendors. These smaller organizations were in business, in many cases, to fill product gaps of IBM. Their products tended to address a particular weakness of some aspect of the IBM line. Effectively, SNA placed IBM in a position to dictate to smaller companies the specifics of their products.

Other, larger vendors were quick to see the value of SNA. For example, **Digital Equipment Corporation (DEC)** and National Cash Register (NCR) produced their own models. In those days, networking was an emerging industry, and incredibly confusing due to a lack of standardization and compatibility among vendors. The danger to smaller companies and users was that the proprietary communication models would restrict the development of the industry to a few major players—based upon their past and present products, as well as their future plans. As you can probably surmise, what was good business for IBM, DEC, or NCR wasn't necessarily good for the data communications user.

The impact of computers in general was exceeding the corporate bounds of large companies, and to their credit, the major vendors were sensitive to the negative aspects of proprietary models. Their models would ultimately regulate growth, inhibit new developments, and restrict information access to a few of the key companies. The OSI model was intended to provide all vendors with a blueprint for networking.

> **NOTE**
>
> The OSI model describes the scope of data communications, and the various functions of a data communication system.

The OSI model specifies the functions of exchanging data over seven levels, or layers. It does not state how the functions are to be implemented. This is left to vendors. Within the functions are protocols describing the specifics of the functions. This is an important part of the model. If the vendors themselves are left to determine how to implement a protocol, then a reasonable sense of standardization will be achieved without sacrificing opportunities for developing and using new technologies. The idea here is similar to using 120Vac for households. The houses may be required to provide 120Vac at the outlets, but how the voltage is produced is determined by a vendor, the local electric company. If a new technology is developed, the electric company needs to have the flexibility to change the method used to produce the 120Vac.

The Rationale for the ISO Model

Why use a layered approach in a data communication model? Examine the simple network of Figure 4-2(a). A point-to-point network is illustrated. In a point-to-point topology, data is exchanged only between two devices at any one time. Imagine that the data exchange is taking place between two compatible computers. In order for the exchange to occur, there must be rules governing the program tasks to be done. These include procedures for how a dialogue is initiated and stopped, error detection, how acknowledgments that data has been received are made, etc. Before the program tasks can be done at all, there also has to be an agreement between the two computers about the electrical structure of the data, and how the two computers will be physically connected.

The user tasks and programs (software) can be lumped together as a single unit, and labeled layer 2. The electrical and mechanical specifications (hardware) can be organized under the label, layer 1. Notice that layer 2 describes the data and layer 1 transfers the data. Layer 1 will transfer any data—it doesn't matter if it's a computer instruction or a sentence in a report. Conversely, it's not the job of layer 2 to figure out the **amplitude** of a bit, but to make sure the proper number of bits are successfully received. The two layers are separate entities but are bound by the common purpose of transferring data.

amplitude

LAYER 2: USER TASKS AND PROGRAMS

LAYER1: ELECTRICAL AND MECHANICAL SPECIFICATIONS

LAYER 3: NETWORK
LAYER 2: DATA
LAYER 1: PHYSICAL

LAYER 4: TRANSPORT
LAYER 3: NETWORK
LAYER 2: DATA
LAYER 1: PHYSICAL

LAYER 6: PRESENTATION
LAYER 5: SESSION
LAYER 4: TRANSPORT
LAYER 3: NETWORK
LAYER 2: DATA
LAYER 1: PHYSICAL

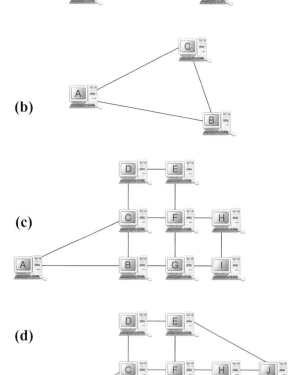

Figure 4-2: Developing a Layered Approach to Protocols

Now, imagine we decided to expand the simple network by adding another computer, as shown in Figure 4-2(b). The third computer (or node as it's commonly called) provides a new dimension. In the simple point-to-point network, a single layer was dedicated to all software tasks. The three-node network presents complications that require careful decisions to be made. If computer "A" sends a message to "B", how will it ensure it's not sent to "C" instead? And if "B" wants to acknowledge receipt of the message, what's to prevent the acknowledgment from being sent to "C" rather than "A"? Clearly, layer 2 will need to be subdivided. It will retain its original job of seeing that data moves through the network in an organized manner. However, the complexity of including the third computer will be attended to at the Network layer. This layer will assign each computer a unique address so as to avoid the confusion described above.

The Network layer may also establish the routes that data may take. For example, if a message is to be sent from "A" to "C", the Network layer could contain a fallback route of "A" to "B" to "C" in the event that the "A" to "C" link were to be disabled.

Many more nodes can now be added, since the third layer is involved with organizing the network as a whole, the second layer is responsible for describing the structure of the data, and the first layer specifies the electrical and mechanical specifications.

In Figure 4-2(c) more nodes have been added, bringing more options for selecting data routes. If node "A" sends data to node "I", there are quite a few paths the data can travel. And if all of the nodes were to transmit and receive at the same time, the number of wires connecting them would be unmanageable. Due to the sheer volume of available nodes and routes, an opportunity exists for expanding our network layer by providing a new layer with some additional functions. Since this new layer is concerned with transporting data across a complex network, it will be called the Transport layer.

The Transport layer has the primary purpose of seeing that the network operates efficiently. Efficiency in data communication means multiplexing and switching, so the Transport layer will ensure that the links between nodes can carry many messages by multiplexing the data. As the Network layer assigned each node a unique address within the network, the Transport layer will address the nodes, too. But in order to prevent the functions of the Transport layer from straying from the purpose of maintaining network efficiency, we'll assign the transport addresses with no thought as to where a node actually is in the network. In fact, we won't even be concerned if a specific node is in our network, or not!

The Transport layer is an elusive concept, but consider the possibilities by referring to Figure 4-3. Node "J" falls outside the network, but a user at "A" has decided to send data to it anyway. The fact that "J" isn't in the network is no problem to the transport layer. Since it's involved in end-to-end communication, it assigns "J" a transport address. Now that "J" has a transport address, will the data get there? It's the responsibility of the Network layer to determine a path to "J". If the Network layer determines there is no route, it will inform the Transport layer.

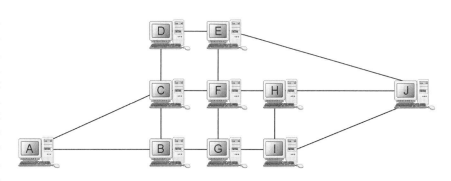

Figure 4-3: Node Arrangement Requiring a Six-Layer Approach

The Transport layer would be particularly helpful if "J" belonged to a network in another area, and the Network layer could route data through the long distance telephone network. If this were the case, our network would now have worldwide access.

In reality, all addressing is accomplished prior to the Transport layer in the actual OSI model as IP and MAC addresses. But the Transport layer retains the responsibility of transporting data between stations and ensuring a quality connection between the stations.

As the sophistication of our network grows, it may be time to determine particular features of the data exchange sessions among nodes. For example, will the sessions resemble the full-duplex convention of a telephone call? Will the nodes take turns sending data in a half-duplex mode? Or will some nodes be the recipients of broadcast data (as in simplex)? If the network contains many paths, or links, it may be multiplexed along different routes. A feature the session layer may incorporate would be a system of recovering when a link malfunctions. A node sending a long message to another node should have a way of recovering from a problem that pops up near the end of the message, without losing the complete message.

It may become necessary to also regulate communications among nodes, so that certain nodes are forbidden to engage in a communication session with other nodes. Or, certain nodes may be permitted to communicate only with an assigned host, and the host is permitted to communicate only through other hosts. Therefore, the Session layer establishes the conventions to be followed by the various nodes of the network.

Our simple network has grown and become sophisticated to the point that the original software layer has been divided several times. Throughout the growth, it's been assumed that all the nodes have been compatible in the way data is presented to the user. Now, we'll add two new computers, "K" and "L", in Figure 4-2(d). Let's suppose that these new computers are personal computers and they convert data into ASCII for displaying on CRTs, while all other computers in the network code data in EBCDIC. If computer "A" sends an EBCDIC encoded message to the PC at "K", how will "K" display it, since it handles only ASCII?

This new challenge hasn't previously been encountered in the network. All of the layers thus far have been involved in the management of the network itself, and little thought has been given to the presentation of the data messages. What if terminal "K" was located in a faraway country—like Korea? Or suppose this network was involved with national defense, and the data needed to be encrypted? Obviously, we need a layer that's involved in data interpretations, because data bits are coded in many ways, sometimes many times over.

This layer is called the Presentation layer, since it's involved in the manipulations needed to present data to the nodes in a manner each recognizes.

There is, of course, a final layer: the Application layer. Its name correctly implies the functions of this layer: What does our network do? What is its purpose? The applications of the network are user-defined, and determine the implementation of the lower layers. For example, the network may have one function—to transfer files back and forth between the nodes. If so, then a file transfer protocol will need to be defined at this level.

Once the application of the network is decided, then the Presentation layer can determine how data will be presented at each end node. The Session layer can decide the back-and-forth conventions to be followed in the communication dialogue, while the Transport layer sees that the end-to-end communication is done in an efficient manner. The Network layer determines the node-to-node route that data will take through the network, while the Data layer organizes the information into manageable units. Finally, the Physical layer actually transports the data.

Perhaps now you can see why it took several years to complete the OSI model. It's indeed difficult to determine what constitutes a sophisticated system, and then separate the system into logical areas. The layered approach was taken to allow both simple and complex networks an opportunity to implement standard protocols. It's common to have networks similar to Figure 4-2(b), but if the network is implemented with the OSI protocols it can be interfaced to a network like the one shown in Figure 4-2(d), using the same set of protocols.

Not all layers of the model are used, or even necessary, in all applications. If the personal computers hadn't been added to our network, the Presentation layer might not have been necessary. On the other hand, a future product may be developed that includes a new encoding scheme. The OSI model is versatile enough so that this development can be incorporated into the presentation layer without affecting any of the other layers.

Each layer is subordinate to the layer above it. Recall that the Transport layer in our network assigned the "J" node a logical address, and the Network layer had to determine a route over to "J". The higher, adjacent layer is referred to as a user. The Transport layer made use of the Network layer's ability to route the data. The lower adjacent layer is called a provider. The Network layer provides a route to the address specified by the Transport layer.

Peer-to-Peer Communication

The OSI model consists of seven levels: Application, Presentation, Session, Transport, Network, Data Link, and Physical.

The model provides for a **hierarchical relationship**, as discussed above within a network. But the model also provides a **peer-to-peer relationship** for end-users, as illustrated in Figure 4-4. From transmitter to receiver, data messages filter through successive layers of the model. In order to ensure consistent compliance to the model protocols, the end-users must have a way of communicating with each other.

The OSI model accomplishes this through logical connections in the application, Presentation, Session, and Transport layers. These layers are involved in end-to-end communication, designated by the dotted lines in Figure 4-4. The Network and Data Link connection is also logical, but these two layers include all points between the end stations. The Physical layer is the only level at which data is actually transmitted or received.

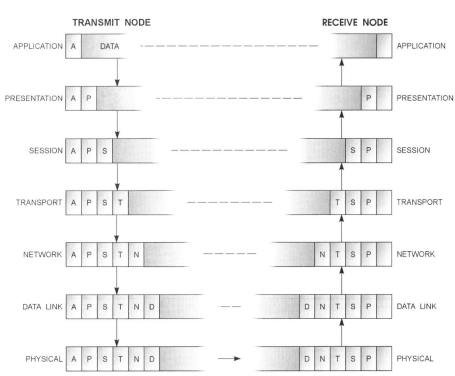

Figure 4-4: Peer-to-Peer Communication Within OSI Layers

How is a logical connection made? First of all, a logical connection doesn't actually exist in a physical sense. The only "real" connections are found at the Physical layer. The logical connections are facilitated through the communication software, and can be found in the **headers** preceding the data message. In Figure 4-4, a header is added to the message, at each level, down to the physical layer. A header isn't needed here, because the Physical layer isn't a logical connection. The receiving node successively strips the headers as the data percolates up through the layers of the model.

What is in the header? Adding headers at the various levels is similar to the telephone numbers dialed when you make a phone call. They precede your message and contain not only routing information, but information needed at telephone exchanges for processing the call. The same is true for the OSI model. A network header contains the route that data is to take through the network, but it may also contain a message to the network layer at the other end. For example, the Network layer is responsible for regulating the rate at which data moves through a network. Within the header there may be a message providing the receiving Network layer pertinent information regarding data rates. With the use of headers appended to the application message, a logical peer connection is made between each layer at both ends of the communication link.

While Figure 4-4 shows all layers being used, keep in mind that it's not always necessary or desirable to include them all. However, the standards committee sought to develop a model that would accommodate present and future developments. Without restricting new technologies, it also facilitates the implementation of the protocols for communications systems at all levels of complexity.

The benefits of the layered approach to the OSI model can be summarized as follows:

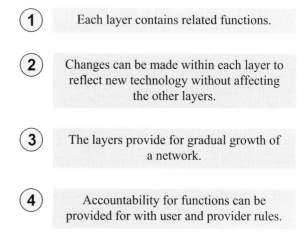

1. Each layer contains related functions.

2. Changes can be made within each layer to reflect new technology without affecting the other layers.

3. The layers provide for gradual growth of a network.

4. Accountability for functions can be provided for with user and provider rules.

The following sections provide a more detailed overview of the seven layers of the OSI model. It's important to understand that the model is incomplete, in particular in the upper layers. While the OSI has had broad acceptance in the industry, many vendors advertise their products as "look-alikes" or "similar to OSI." Before a look-alike is selected to implement the OSI protocols, it would be wise to thoroughly research the product under consideration.

In some cases, parts of the model have been abandoned entirely. Think of the OSI model as a set of guidelines for designing and understanding large and small networks.

APPLICATION LAYER

The **Application layer** provides support to those functions that are necessary to initiate the application.

This is the only level at which the user has direct contact with the model. The specific application functions that are used obviously depend upon the application itself, and are often part of its reason for existence.

The Application layer is implemented with user-specific software. Typical examples include e-mail of file transfer protocol (FTP).

It's the final check for ensuring the quality of the lower layers and does so by forming the proper environment to initiate the data transfer.

More and more, this level is being associated with software packages since they contain the components needed to use the software—and this is synonymous with application-level functions. For example, airline reservation software requires password IDs for security purposes. The sign-on procedure would be an application function since it's a procedure necessary to implement the application of making an airline reservation.

Functions of the Application layer are:

(1) To provide a facility for serving end-users

(2) To authenticate user IDs and passwords

(3) To provide for file requests or file transfers

(4) To provide for downline loading (transfer of data from remote host to remote terminal, and vice versa)

(5) To determine the quality of service from lower layers. If a problem occurs at a lower layer, the application should incorporate a means of notifying the user, such as an error message.

(6) To provide for remote job entry. A remote terminal would be given access to the application maintained in the host, which could be located thousands of miles away.

(7) To provide for utilizing user applications, such as off-the-shelf software for work processing, database management, and spreadsheet preparation.

Examples of specific Application layer protocols include:

- *DNS:* The Domain Name System (database system used to map host names, IP addresses, and e-mail routing)

- *FTP:* File transfer Protocol (transfers files by copying files from one system to another)

- *BootP:* Bootstrap Protocol (defines how to determine the IP of a diskless system when bootstrapped)

- *SNMP:* Simple Network Management Protocol (defines packet exchanges)

- *Telnet:* Telnet Protocol (provides access to differing nodes or host types)

- *SMTP:* Simple Mail Transfer Protocol (e-mail)

- *NFS:* Network File System (provides for file access to servers)

PRESENTATION LAYER

The **Presentation layer** is responsible for ensuring data is formatted for proper presentation to users.

At the Presentation layer, the syntax and format of information are determined. The Presentation layer ensures that data messages are received in a format that's understood. In order to accomplish this, the Presentation layer has to retain the content of a data message while modifying the **syntax** of the data for the end user.

In the earlier example, an EBCDIC message had to be converted to an ASCII message. A virtual terminal circuit must be in place to make such a conversion. A **virtual terminal circuit** describes how data is to be displayed on CRT screens despite coding differences.

The Presentation layer defines fields for **remote data entry** work such as may be found in an inventory system. The operator is required to enter quantities of various items and the Presentation layer describes where the data entry fields are located on the screen. Most database report fields that are viewed on a screen, including interactive screens such as shopping carts on e-commerce web sites, are Presentation layer entities,

The Presentation layer is also responsible for managing special events such as **data encryption** and **foreign language translation**.

The functions of the Presentation layer are:

1 To change data syntax in order to meet the needs of the source and destination of the message

2 To visually present and interpret data for user intervention or use

3 To provide for data compression, encryption, and coding

4 To inform the Session layer when to establish a session, as well as when to terminate the session

Protocols that are specific to the Presentation layer include:

- *ASCII:* American Standard Code For Information Interchange, a standardized code that assigns seven or eight bits to each alphanumeric character

- *EBCDIC:* Extended Binary Coded Decimal Interchange Code, an IBM code in which alphanumeric characters are represented by eight bits

- *Unicode:* A code that allows for translation from one language to another such as from English to Chinese

SESSION LAYER

The purpose of the **Session layer** is to set up a communication dialog that allows two devices to exchange data over a network.

One of the most common examples of a Session layer service involves well-known ports. A well-known port is a software process that begins the applications defined at the Application layer. For example, HTTP is the application used on the World Wide Web portion of the Internet. HTTP is specified at the Application layer, a web browser is defined in the Presentation layer, and the actual channel is set up between workstation and server at the Session layer. The port number reserved for HTTP is port 80. Port 80 is recognized by Internet servers as a request to launch the HTTP application. Any negotiating that must occur between workstation and server is accomplished in back-and-forth communication over the port. Once the details have been determined, HTTP can be started and the user's web browser will launch.

The decision of whether the nodes will engage in full duplex, half duplex, or simplex is made in this layer. In practice, the decision is somewhat imposed by the presentation layer, since code conversions, display formats, and remote job entry dictate the type of dialogue. The session layer, though, extends the choice. It may permit a half-duplex dialogue to be interrupted, or allow a simplex dialogue to operate as a full-duplex dialogue. For example, a remote terminal containing an inventory is actually maintained at the host. The display screen contains a list of items and their respective quantities. This is a simplex network in which the host is broadcasting data to the remote terminal. If a quantity change is needed, the operator enters the new quantity and when the ENTER key is pressed, the channel is then operating in a full-duplex mode: The CRT screen retains the display of the inventory even as the operator transmits the quantity updates back to the host.

checkpointing

The Session layer also manages a process called **checkpointing**. A checkpoint is inserted into data messages to allow the session to recover from network failures without losing the complete message. This saves time when large amounts of data have been transmitted and the connection fails near the end of the message.

synchronization

Since the mode of transmission is determined at this level, **synchronization** must also occur. Synchronizing headers are necessary so that complete messages are received. If the synchronization (which is often the checkpoint) is lost, the Session layer can determine that a problem exists. While direct error control isn't a function of the Session layer, it is nonetheless implied through checkpointing and synchronizing headers.

server message blocks (SMB)

requestor

redirector

Another example of a Session layer service involves **server message blocks** (**SMB**). Windows operating systems use SMB to maintain connections between devices (computers and servers, or computers and printers, for example) on a network. When a computer requests a file that resides on a server, the computer sends a **requestor** to the server. A requestor is a message sent to a server to request a service from the server—a file in this example. The server will respond with a **redirector**. A redirector is a software object that receives the request and sends the request to the originating computer. In other words, the redirector will send the file to the computer.

SMB occurs at the Session layer since it's a mechanism for setting up and maintaining the connection between server and workstation. But note that once the file is made available to the workstation, the appearance of the file on the workstation screen is handled by the Presentation layer.

As the Presentation layer is partly responsible for decisions made in the Session layer, the Transport layer is forced to map the Session layer decisions for each session. That is, the Transport layer will be required to know the mode of dialogue of each session.

NOTE

The Session layer manages the end-to-end dialogue prepared for in the Presentation layer.

The functions of the Session layer are:

(1) To start and stop data transfer

(2) To provide dialogue control via full duplex, half duplex, simplex, or a combination of these

(3) To open the channel in order to launch applications specified at the Application layer

(4) To provide for the recovery from network failure without losing the complete message

(5) To provide mapping functions to the Transport layer for each session. The Transport layer may then provide identical destinations via multiplexing for sessions whose address lay in similar routes.

Session layer protocols include the following:

- *NetBIOS:* Network Basic Input Output System, a Microsoft software interface that allows for networking

- *Winsock:* A socket is used to set up the connection between two network processes and to interface between protocols. Sockets use well-known ports as described in this section.

TRANSPORT LAYER

The **Transport layer** is concerned with end-to-end communication across the network.

Transport layer

virtual path

It is the last of the upper layers to be concerned with only end-users. It establishes a **virtual path**, from transmitter to receiver, by assigning end-users an address without regard to their position in the network. The end-user address is supplied to the Network layer, where the actual route to the address will be determined.

Since this layer is involved with making sure that data messages are accurately received, there's an implied quality-control function of the Transport layer. The original intent of the layer was to establish a virtual channel from user to user, but this has proved to be difficult. In addition, the specific protocols for the Transport layer were written in 1984, then revised in 1986. The explosion of computer networks since then took the standards organization by surprise, and the protocols were written after they were already needed in the industry. Without specific protocols, data communications users implemented what they had, which were Network, Data Link, and Physical layer protocols. This was unfortunate, because the Transport layer has very powerful capabilities. The 1986 revisions provided for choices that permitted many functions that were being handled by the network layer to be a formal component of the Transport layer.

These functions are called **classes of service**, and they allow data to be sent over a network with varying degrees of quality. They are, strictly speaking, Transport layer functions. However, as previously stated, network users implemented them in the Network layer as they were needed, at a time before the established protocols were specifically written.

The Transport layer also assigns end-user addresses in the header, appended to data messages. These end-user addresses are mapped onto machine addresses in the Network layer. The Transport layer doesn't care where the end user is, because the Network layer is left the job of finding the user. The implication of the network address is that networks are permitted to change in structure and topology without a consequent software change in this layer. Many networks require a **user password**, and a **user ID**, before access to the network is granted. This is an example of a transport address mapped onto a Network layer address.

Don't let Transport layer addressing confuse you, because it may or may not be used in a network. What is used though, almost universally, are Network and Data Link layer addresses. A Network layer address is a logical convention. An IP address is a Network layer link address. This is typically called the MAC address (from the MAC sublayer of the Data Link layer), and it specifies the physical location of a node.

The IP address, detailed in the next chapter, contains two components: a network address and a host address. The network address specifies the network where the destination machine is located, while the host address specifies that machine on the network. There may be hundreds of unique host addresses that use the same network address. Together, the complete address is called the IP address. Note that the network portion of the IP is actually a Transport layer function since the Transport layer is responsible for getting data between two end-points. But, as you'll see in the next section, the Network layer is responsible for establishing the actual route between the two end-points. Conventionally, then, the IP address is said to be a function of the Network layer. In practice, the network portion of the IP address is a transport function and it is implemented in the Network layer.

In establishing a virtual path between end-users, the Transport layer has been given the function of determining whether multiplexing is called for. This is done by evaluating each dialogue session established in the Session layer.

Data rate flow control is handled by the Transport layer. Data rates between networks may be much slower than within a network. The gateways connecting networks are composed of relays, and the switching time of the relays contribute to the time it takes data to arrive at the destination. The Transport layer regulates flow control by allocating data amounts. Data allocation is initiated by the transmitting station, and provided for in the Transport header. The sending station will send a message to the receiver asking it how much data should be sent. The receiver responds—through a transport header tacked-on to a message traveling back to the sender—by specifying the amount of data it can receive in a future time period.

The Transport layer provides for negotiation concerning flow rates. In the discussion of allocating data rates, the transmitter asked the receiver the amount of data it could handle. The negotiated function begins with the transmitter offering a data rate to the receiving station. The receiver may accept the offer, or it may send back a counter-offer. The counter-offer must be less than the original offer from the transmitter. In most transport level services, negotiations don't extend beyond the counter-offer. If the transmitter won't accept the counter, it disconnects the channel.

Data rates may be allocated by the receiver, or negotiated between the transmitter and receiver. In practice, negotiation is the more efficient of the two since the initial proposal may be acceptable, whereas allocation will always require the receiver to respond to the request from the transmitter. This means that, at a minimum, the allocation method will require three exchanges, while the negotiated method will require two exchanges.

Once the data rate is agreed upon, the transport layer has to ensure the data will be delivered at this rate. Consider, if the data rate of the transmitting station network is 10 Mbps and the data rate of the receiving station network is 1 Mbps, how will the Transport layer resolve the data rates? If messages are allowed to flow continuously from the high-speed network into the low-speed network, the receiving buffers of the slower network are sure to overflow, and much of the message will be lost. The answer lies in blocking messages into smaller units, and timing the release of the blocks through the network. Messages from the slow receiving end back to the high-speed transmitter can be **concatenated**.

concatenated

A concatenated network is one in which message blocks are transmitted over various links that may run in parallel. The effect is to speed the arrival time of the data. Once the messages are blocked, they're arranged in **packets** at the network layer. A data packet contains link addresses within a network, whereas the **data block** contains only the end-user address.

packets

data block

The functions of the Transport layer are:

(**1**) To assign **end-user addresses**

end-user addresses

(**2**) To regulate data flow using allocation or regulation

(**3**) To provide message blocking and concentration

(**4**) To evaluate the need for multiplexing

(**5**) To provide for the sequencing of blocked messages. This provides the receiver with a way of checking to see if all messages have been received.

(**6**) To provide for error detection and recovery. This is provided for in sequencing and service classes.

(**7**) To provide five classes of service intended to match the needs of the user to network characteristics

The five classes of service provided for in the Transport layer are:

Class 0

Class 0 fulfills the minimum requirements of the Transport layer: Message **block segmentation**, end-user addressing, error detection, **block sequencing**. If a problem occurs in the Network layer, the Transport layer has no method for recovering; consequently, the connection will be lost. The ability of a network to recover from problems is described in terms of being **robust**. A class 0 network is not very robust, since it can't recover from problems easily.

Class 1

Class 1 is somewhat more robust than class 0. Recovery from problems is accomplished by adding a sequencing header to each block of data. If a problem causes the transmission to be interrupted, the end receiver notifies the end transmitter about the last block received (identified by the **block sequence number**), and the transmitter resumes with the next block in the sequence.

Class 2

Class 2 is primarily concerned with flow control. It allows multiple Transport layers to be transmitted through a single channel. This is done by multiplexing the various layers. As in class 0, the class 2 has no provision for recovering if the network crashes.

Class 3

Class 3 is identical to class 2, except that a recovery capability is added. A class 3 Transport layer recovers from a problem by reestablishing the connection, and by adding sequencing headers, as in class 1.

Class 4

Class 4 is the same as class 3, except it's more tolerant to problems such as a lost data block, out-of-sequence blocks, or received blocks that are heavily distorted. Any of these problems can cause a network failure in the previous classes, but a class 4 includes the capability of resolving the problems and continuing the transmission. A class 4 Transport layer is the most robust of the five classes.

Examples of Transport layer protocols are:

- *TCP:* Transmission Control Protocol (used to establish a reliable connection between client and server)

- *UDP:* User Datagram Protocol (simple TCP implementation, without the reliability)

block segmentation

block sequencing

robust

block sequence number

TEST TIP

Be able to relate two or three protocols to each layer of the OSI model.

NETWORK LAYER

The **Network layer** determines the actual route the data will take across the network.

It implements the virtual path created in the Transport layer. As the Transport layer separates data into blocks, the Network layer organizes the blocks into **data packets**. The number of packets are negotiated by internetwork nodes. There may be from 1 to 4,095 packets, or more.

Routing to the correct network node occurs at the Network layer.

Routing techniques in the Network layer may be **fixed**, **stochastic**, or **adaptive**. A fixed route will be carefully mapped, and won't change. A stochastic route carries the promise of eventual delivery. These routes are usually selected for short messages, called datagrams, sent between two stations that frequently communicate. An adaptive route is a concatenated path, and it's based upon the performance of the network. The routes described above are de-termined by the class of service selected in the Transport layer. For example, Class 4 service would probably be sent along an adaptive route, since it contains capabilities for recovering from out-of-sequence data blocks.

The Network layer also implements link multiplexing when called for in the Transport layer. This marks a departure from the end-to-end functions of the higher levels. It's the first layer to become directly involved in the links connecting end-to-end users, serving as an interface. It must provide a virtual path to the upper layers across multimedia networks and various data rates, and incorporate means of detecting and recovering from errors if called for in the upper layers. Many of the details of these functions are delegated to the Data Link layer, but the Network layer implies the tasks to be conducted at the Data Link layer by its selection of routes, packetizing data, etc.

Since this layer is responsible for forwarding packets onto other stations, it includes a logical addressing scheme. The most common one is called **Internet Protocol** (**IP**), and it consists of a logical address that may be assigned to a node, or to an entire network. The address is logical, meaning that the location of a node with an assigned IP can be moved anywhere, or transferred to another node as needed. This frequently occurs with Internet service providers when they assign so-called "dynamic" IPs to their subscribers. Each time you log onto the Internet (logons occur at the transport layer), you're assigned a different IP, although your physical address remains unchanged.

Routing data packets across a network is the responsibility of the Network layer. To achieve this, we use routers. A router contains huge libraries of logical addresses, as well as the next "hop" needed to get to a logical address. The widespread use of routers has spawned many routing protocols, and these will be described later in this book.

It may be of some (possibly confusing) interest to you that the functionality of the Transport and Network layers was blurred for many years, and the confusion carries over to the present. The original intention of the Transport layer was to assign logical addressing, while the Network layer was to route data packets from a physical address, assigned at the Data Link layer, to the transport layer's logical address. Note that this is in contradiction to the functions of these two layers as described above. Remember, networking vendors needed the functions of the Transport layer before it was finalized, so they did the best with what they had—which was the Network layer. Consequently, many Transport layer functions were designed into equipment that, technically, operated at the Network layer.

By the time the Transport layer was finished, the need for it was in full swing. This is fortunate, because the Transport layer is the most useful of all the layers in the OSI model for wide area networking, such as Internet applications. At present, the accepted functions of these two layers are as previously described.

The functions of the Network layer are:

(1) To establish which routes the data will take

(2) To provide for multiplexing of data channels

(3) To separate data into packets

(4) To detect and recover from errors

(5) To establish, maintain, and terminate connections

Examples of Network layer protocols include:

- *IP:* Internet Protocol (used in conjunction with TCP, and UDP but has no reliability)

- *IGNP:* Internet Group Management Protocol (used to multicast hosts or routers)

- *BGP:* Border Gateway Protocol (used to communicate between systems with different underlying protocols, and routers)

- *RIP:* Routing Information Protocol (most widely implemented router protocol)

- *ARP:* Address Resolution protocol (allows mapping of 32-bit IP addresses to other types of addresses)

- *RARP:* Reverse Address Resolution Protocol (allows mapping between some other address type and 32-bit IPs)

- *OSPF:* Open Shortest Path First (a newer and better version of RIP)

- *ICMP:* Internet Control Message Protocol (communications network control information such as errors within an IP frame)

The most common hardware device associated with the Network layer is a router (and the router portion of brouters). A router is capable of interpreting IP addresses. In particular, a router examines the network portion of an IP in an attempt to determine where a packet of data is going. Generally speaking, routers don't rely directly on MAC addresses, although there will always be a reconciliation between an IP address and the MAC address when routers are looking for one another.

DATA LINK LAYER

> The purpose of the **Data Link layer** is to provide for the accurate exchange of data between two nodes.

A node refers to communication equipment that receives and/or transmits. A data message may be shifted through many nodes enroute to the destination, but the Data Link layer is concerned only with point-to-point communication between nodes. A final, Data Link layer will be appended to the message frame, along with a Start Of Frame (SOF) header (or, flag, as it's commonly called), an End Of Frame (EOF) header, and a field dedicated to detecting errors of the entire frame. This includes the headers from the various layers.

When discussing data communications protocols, the functions of the Data Link layer are most frequently described. One of the reasons for this is that this layer is heavily documented, and its protocols are widely adhered to within the industry. In fact, sublayers of the Data Link layer form the foundation for the majority of local area networks in place today.

Details of the sublayers were presented in Chapter 2 in regard to the IEEE 802.x series of protocols.

> The Data Link layer contains two major subdivisions: the **Media Access Control (MAC)** protocols, and the **Logical Link Control (LLC)** protocols.

> The MAC sublayer refers to techniques the workstation uses to gain access to a network or communication channel.

For example, in a Ethernet network, it's forbidden for two stations to have access to the network simultaneously. But how do the two stations "know" that their data is about to collide? The MAC protocols specify that a **disallowed voltage** (1.5V) will appear across the network if this occurs. Channel monitors will read the voltage, and both stations will wait awhile before trying again.

The MAC sublayer is a logical convention, but it's closely, and inseparably, involved in the Physical layer implementation. Since it is so closely involved in the physical attribute of data transfers, it's common to think of the MAC sublayer protocols as also encompassing the Physical layer.

The Logical Link Control sublayer describes conventions to be followed by the sender and the receiver to ensure that the link's communication is reliable and the data flow is orderly.

The LLC provides for a distinct interface to the Network layer.

The functions of the Data Link layer are:

(1) To provide for frame formatting

(2) To provide error detection and recovery

(3) To provide access methods for networks

(4) To provide for transmission between nodes

Examples of Data Link protocols include:

- *PPP:* Point-to-Point Protocol (an improved version of SLIP)

- *PPTP:* Point-to-Point Tunneling Protocol is a version of PPP that mandates encryption be used between nodes

- *IEEE 802.2:* IEEE protocol for the Logical Link Control sublayer

- *IEEE 802.x:* All other IEEE 802 protocols are partially Data Link layer protocols, and partially physical layer protocols.

- *SLIP:* Serial Line Internet Protocol (provides for serial encapsulation of IP frames)

- *CSLIP:* Compressed Serial Line Internet Protocol (an improved version of SLIP)

┌─ **TEST TIP** ─┐
Be aware of which ISO layers brouters work at.
└─────────────────┘

Common hardware associated with the Data Link layer includes NIC cards, adapters, hubs, switches, and bridges (and the bridge portion of brouters). The one common trait each of these devices has is that they rely on MAC addresses for their operation. A NIC card, for example, has MAC addresses embedded into it and is the device on a network that gives a computer a physical presence. A hub and a switch both have MAC addresses. The presence of the MAC addresses identifies them as network devices.

PHYSICAL LAYER

Physical layer

polarity

The purpose of the **Physical layer** is the actual transmission of data. It includes the physical connection of stations to the network, and the parameters of electrical signals such as the amplitude and **polarity** of data bits. The processes of full duplex, half duplex, and simplex are accounted for at this layer with the proper selection of channel media, and the formatting of data flow.

The OSI Physical layer is quite detailed in its description of the acceptable mechanical and electrical parameters. Unfortunately, the protocol hasn't been widely accepted in the United States. Instead, the standard implementation of the Physical layer has been the EIA/TIA-232 **Electronic Industries Association (EIA)** standard, as well as the common RJ-45 connector and cabling.

The functions of the Physical layer are:

(1) To transmit data between connections

(2) To provide electrical and mechanical parameters for data connections, and channel media

(3) To activate and deactivate physical connections

The Physical layer has been implemented with a combination of Data Link and Physical layer protocols, most notably the IEEE 802 series of protocols. The reason these are included as a Physical layer protocol—since they're typically referred to as Data Link protocols—is that they include many physical characteristics. The correct way to describe the IEEE protocols is as a combination of logical Data Link attributes and Physical layer attributes, since they cross the boundary between the MAC sublayer and the Physical layer.

Physical layer protocols are:

- *ISO 2110:* which defines the encapsulation of IP datagrams for Ethernet

- *IEEE 802.x:* which defines the structure of frames in an IEEE 802 network

Common hardware associated with the Physical layer includes connectors such as RJ-45, SC, and RJ-11; and cabling such as UTP, fiber optic, or coaxial. Network hubs operate at the Physical layer as well. Note that the common element between connectors and cabling is that these devices are directly involved in handling bits of data.

A connector cannot recognize a MAC address since it only recognizes data bits. A hub does not directly recognize data bits but it does recognize frames of data that are appropriately formatted with MAC addresses. A router doesn't directly recognize frames but it does recognize packets of frames that are appropriately formatted and addressed with an IP address.

OTHER DATA COMMUNICATION MODELS

The OSI Reference Model is a blueprint for data communications. It competes for acceptance with IBM's **System Network Architecture (SNA)**, and Digital Equipment Corporation's **Digital Network Architecture (DNA)**. Both are displayed, along with the OSI model, in Figure 4-5. IBM has indicated a gradual support for the OSI protocols. This won't be too difficult because the OSI and SNA are quite similar. Digital's DNA model is considerably different. It lends itself more to local area networks than to large distributed systems.

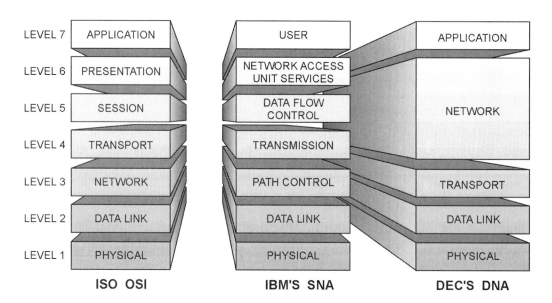

Figure 4-5: Comparison of OSI, SNA, and DNA Data Communication Reference Models

The Data Link protocols of DEC are full-duplex character-oriented protocols whose frame format is significantly different than HDLC or SDLC (framing methods used at the Data Link layer). There has been widespread support for the intent, if not the specific implementation, of the OSI model. But as far as DEC is concerned, it's not likely to grow since the company was bought by Compaq and Cabletron Systems, and now doesn't exist. Even if large vendors such as IBM never comply with all OSI requirements, its proprietary model still serves to present a logical framework for pursuing the broader issues of data communications systems.

In addition to the complete networking descriptions, such as the OSI model and IBM's SNA, there are many other widely used partial implementations. For the Internet, the TCP/IP protocol stack (described in Chapter 5) is frequently used to design, build, or describe an internetworking system. Microsoft has NetBIOS, a model that's proprietary to their operating systems, particularly network operating systems such as Windows NT/2000/XP. But generally speaking, even these models can be broadly mapped to the OSI model either in whole or in part.

gateway

The hardware device used to convert from one system of networking protocols to another system of protocols is a **gateway**. For example, to convert from the OSI model to the SNA model, a gateway is required.

KEY POINTS REVIEW

This chapter has presented an extensive exploration of the ISO OSI Reference Model.

- Protocols are the rules governing data communication.

- The three functions of a protocol are: to determine how handshaking will occur, to determine how a virtual communications path is implemented, and to determine how data will be packaged.

- The OSI model describes the scope of data communications, and the various functions of a data communication system.

- The OSI model consists of seven levels: Application, Presentation, Session, Transport, Network, Data Link, and Physical.

- The Application layer provides support to those functions that are necessary to initiate the application. Application examples include e-mail, FTP, and HTTP.

- The Presentation layer is responsible for ensuring data is formatted for proper presentation to users.

- The Session layer manages the end-to-end dialogue prepared for in the presentation layer.

- The Transport layer is concerned with end-to-end communication across the network.

- The Network layer determines the actual route the data will take across a network.

- The purpose of the Data Link layer is to provide for the accurate exchange of data between two nodes.

- The Data Link level contains two sublayers: Logical Link Control (LLC), and Media Access Control (MAC).

- The Logical Link Control sublayer describes the conventions that a sender and receiver follow to ensure the data flow is orderly.

- The Media Access Control level describes methods stations use to gain access to a communication channel.

At this point, review the objectives listed at the beginning of the chapter to be certain that you understand and can perform them. Afterward, answer the review questions that follow to verify your knowledge of the information.

REVIEW QUESTIONS

The following questions test your knowledge of the material presented in this chapter:

1. Define protocol.

2. What is the purpose of the OSI Reference Model?

3. Which OSI layer is responsible for ensuring that the syntax of the data is acceptable to the receiver and transmitter?

4. List several functions of the Data Link layer.

5. What is the purpose of the LLC sublayer?

6. What layer is a router associated with?

7. A web browser is best associated with which layer of the OSI model?

8. Which layer of the OSI model is e-mail associated with?

9. Why are the IEEE 802.x protocols associated with both the Data Link and Physical layers?

10. Which class of service in the Transport layer offers the best solution for recovering from errors?

11. State the seven layers of the OSI model.

12. What are several protocols that are used in the Application layer?

13. What do the five classes found in the Transport layer represent?

14. Why is the OSI model described as a hierarchical model?

15. What is needed to convert from the OSI model protocols to the IBM SNA model protocols?

1. A protocol is defined as _____.
    a. a hardware entity
    b. the transfer of data between dissimilar devices
    c. rules describing the exchange of data between similar devices
    d. rules for implementing network hardware

2. An example of virtual communication is _____.
    a. the telephone system
    b. the address bus in a PC
    c. CAT 5 UTP
    d. fiber-optic cable

3. In addition to a hierarchical relationship between layers of the OSI model, the layers also have a(n) _____ relationship.
    a. adversarial
    b. proportional
    c. unstable
    d. peer

4. Which layer of the OSI model would be responsible for ensuring that a message sent in Spanish is displayed in English at the receiving terminal?
    a. Application layer
    b. Presentation layer
    c. Transport layer
    d. Data Link layer

5. The purpose of the MAC sublayer is _____.
    a. to package data into frames
    b. to provide a virtual path across coaxial cable
    c. to describe how stations gain access to the network
    d. to assign logical addresses

6. A 10Base-T hub is associated with which layer of the OSI model?
    a. Session
    b. Physical
    c. Data Link
    d. Network

7. A RJ-45 connector is associated with which layer of the OSI model?
    a. Presentation
    b. Data Link
    c. Transport
    d. Physical

8. What is the purpose of the Network layer?
    a. to determine the route to the network destination
    b. to assign addresses to nodes
    c. to organize data into frames
    d. to initiate the dialog between end stations

9. What is the purpose of the Transport layer?
    a. end-to-end communication across the network
    b. formatting data for proper presentation
    c. specifying electrical and mechanical parameters
    d. assigning logical addresses

10. Which layer of the OSI model is a NIC card associated with?
    a. Physical
    b. Data Link
    c. Network
    d. Transport

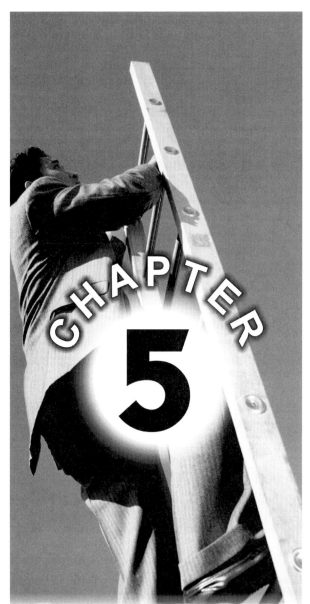

NETWORK PROTOCOLS

LEARNING
OBJECTIVES

LEARNING OBJECTIVES

Upon completion of this chapter and its related lab procedures, you will be able to perform the following tasks:

1. Associate IP with its functions.

2. Differentiate between the following network protocols in terms of routing, addressing schemes, interoperability, and naming conventions:

   - TCP/IP
   - NetBEUI
   - IPX/SPX
   - AppleTalk

3. Define the purpose, function, and/or use of the following protocols within TCP/IP:

   - IP
   - HTTPS
   - TCP
   - POP3/IMAP4
   - UDP
   - TELNET
   - FTP
   - ICMP
   - TFTP
   - ARP
   - SMTP
   - NTP
   - HTTP

4. Define the function of TCP/IP ports.

5. Identify well-known ports.

6. Identify IP address (IPv4 and IPv6) and their default subnet masks.

7. Identify the differences between public versus private networks.

8. Explain the fundamental concepts of TCP/IP addressing.

9. Describe the purpose of a socket in a TCP setup.

10. State the content and length of a TCP header.

11. State the content and length of a UDP header.

12. State the content and length of an IP header.

13. State the difference between classful and classless IP addresses.

14. Differentiate between internetwork address classes.

15. Given a network address, subnet address, and host address, create a subnet to include network, subnet, and host address.

16. Discuss the advantage of CIDR over classful IP addresses.

17. Given IPs and subnet addresses between two nodes, use the ANDed route determination algorithm to validate a local or remote route.

NETWORK PROTOCOLS

INTRODUCTION

This chapter discusses the concepts, technologies, standards, and services that comprise the operations that occur on a network—short of extending it to the wide area arena. To join networks, it's not enough to simply access the network media. Data packets must also be routed to the destination node, and transported with a reasonable degree of reliability in an environment that will detect, and deal with, errors (lost packets, garbled frames, etc.).

In this chapter, we examine the intricacies of the Network and Transport layers. These are realized using what's broadly called internetwork protocols, and specifically the TCP/IP suite of protocols.

The essentials of TCP and IP are discussed first. And since the IP addressing scheme has been overtaxed with the explosion of LANs and the Internet, we'll see how it's been expanded through a system of subnetting. Repeaters, bridges, routers, and gateways—the physical interconnect technologies—are described, along with methods for carrying data between LANs using different access methods. Several transport services, used to increase the performance of networks, are also examined.

NETWORK AND TRANSPORT LAYER PROTOCOLS

The **Network layer** is responsible for routing data frames from a source to a destination node. The Transport layer is responsible for ensuring there's an adequate and reliable connection between the two points. Typically, a frame of data may "hop" from one device to another (usually through routers) on its way to the destination node. The Network layer protocols ensure that a route can be found between the two communicating devices, then sends the packet on its way. At the Transport layer, once a route is selected, the two must maintain an open virtual circuit that is at once capable of detecting errors and providing for a reasonable degree of reliability between the two nodes.

Notice that the intentions of the Network and Transport layers differ. Consequently, there are protocols for both layers with the most common being the TCP/IP suite, the Transmission Control Protocol/ Internet Protocol. Broadly speaking, you can relate TCP and IP to the OSI model as follows: TCP operates at the Transport layer while IP operates at the Network layer. TCP/IP is an almost universally used protocol because it was designed to be vendor independent, capable of transporting data with no regard to the particular network a computer is attached to. This means that computers on an Ethernet LAN, a wide area network, or a point-to point connection between a PC and ISP, are viewed as equals by TCP/IP.

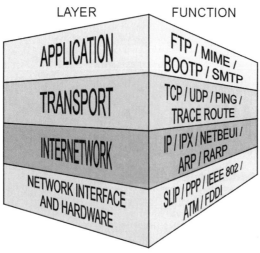

| LAYER | FUNCTION |

Figure 5-1: Model for Internetworking Protocols

Figure 5-1 shows a model for internetworking protocols. This model is a more accurate view of the functions of a suite of protocols that span internets. The word "internet" in this context refers not only to the Internet, but large networks—such as intranets—that may or may not access the Internet.

The model consists of four layers that describe the functionality of events at each. The complete model, as shown, is commonly called the TCP/IP protocol suite. At the **Application layer** are user functions, such as file transfers and Internet mail. The **Transport layer** contains protocols dealing with reliable (connection-oriented) end-to-end processes. TCP is the most widely used. UDP is the User Defined Protocol, and represents an unreliable (connectionless) implementation of TCP. Transport layer utilities include Ping, and Trace Route, which are used to troubleshoot the end-to-end connection.

The **Internetwork layer** includes protocols that frame data so it can be sent from node to node. This is a connectionless layer, so it doesn't assume responsibility for any packet sent. (TCP is the reliable half of the suite.) Neither does it provide flow control or error recovery. However, the protocols used at this layer may very well provide error detection, flow control, and so on—at least at this layer, but not above it. For example, HDLC provides for flow control, and error detection, as do all of the IEEE 802.3 standards. The Internetwork layer does, however, map a route to the destination node so it contains addressing information to that node. The Network Interface and Hardware layer is roughly analogous to the Data Link and Physical layers of the OSI model. As you can see from the wide variety of protocols supported at this layer, the TCP/IP suite can use nearly any Network layer interface.

> **NOTE**
>
> A **connection-oriented** protocol means that acknowledgements are sent from destination back to source node to let it know that a packet has been received. A **connectionless** protocol does not send acknowledgements. There is no way to be certain that a packet has been received with connectionless protocols.

A **Network layer** protocol in the OSI model (the Internetwork layer for the Internet model in Figure 5-1) is necessary because protocols for the Data Link and Physical layers don't contain routing mechanisms. Logical Link Control protocols from the Data Link layer lack the intricate header fields needed to transport data across different types of media and architecture. HDLC, the bit protocol from the LLC sublayer, is not routable. An Internetwork protocol is used to carry the LAN's media-access frame to another location.

What the lower two layers do offer is a physical MAC address. This is the address embedded in a NIC card. It's the address that specifically locates the machine, much as your house number on a street specifically locates you. You also have a zip code that's used to generally locate you. A zip code may cover many streets, or small towns, so it's a convenient way for the post office to broadly sort mail—separate it into piles according to zip codes, get each pile to the right zip code, than let local clerks separate it into actual addresses. The Network layer takes a similar approach in assigning logical addresses that are based on a network address and a machine address. A data packet can be sent to a network address, and it's up to that network to locate the logical machine address.

TCP/IP is a product of the Department of Defense. Bound by law to purchase from the lowest bidder that met the purchasing specifications, it inadvertently created a situation in which one branch of the military bought computers from IBM, another from Wang, and another from DEC. During a war, or other national emergency, the various branches are expected to communicate and support one another. However, it became apparent that they couldn't because the computer vendors were using proprietary internetworking protocols that simply weren't compatible.

In order to merge vendor incompatibilities, the TCP/IP protocol suite was instituted in 1981, although it had been around, in a different and limited format, since 1969. The military wanted to switch to an alternate communication route if communications were lost at any site due to enemy action, regardless of who supplied the site hardware. TCP/IP was first tested under battlefield conditions in the Gulf War with Iraq. The United States and allies did in fact destroy Iraq's known communication centers, but they were still able to communicate by switching to alternate sites, since they were running TCP/IP on their networked computer systems. While this was irritating to the United States and allies, it also proved the functionality of TCP/IP—it did exactly as it was designed to do.

Network layer protocols are abstract devices, existing only in software. As such, they offer a tremendous degree of flexibility because they are designed with little regard to the hardware used to implement them. Figure 5-2 illustrates the universal equality concept of TCP/IP. Several types of networks are connected together to form an internetwork. The Internet protocol, TCP/IP, transports messages from LAN to LAN. The size of a WAN is unimportant to the protocol; the network shown in Figure 5-2 may be found in an office building, or the four LANs may be distributed in different states, or countries.

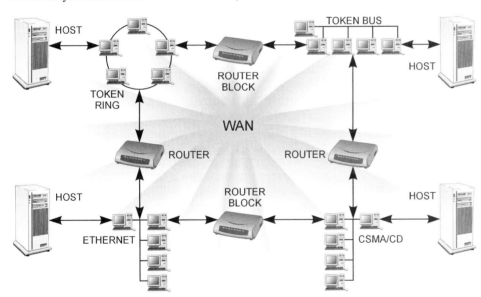

Figure 5-2: TCP/IP Treats All Networks Equally

It doesn't matter whether PCs are in the LANs, or they are composed of mainframe computers. As was previously mentioned, TCP/IP is not dependent on the machine type. As a practical point, though, some computers work better with it than do others.

A router provides an interconnection between networks using the same Network layer protocols. Notice in Figure 5-2 that the four LANs are connected by a router block. Routers and gateways are internetworking machines that provide a physical connection for implementing the Internet protocol.

Recall that a bridge doesn't function at the Internetworking layer; it focuses on data frames at the Data Link layer of the OSI model. It's concerned with the movement of data frames and, as such, is network protocol independent. What a bridge does do is to interconnect LANs—those that share the same network access protocol such as Ethernet or Token Ring.

A router provides interconnections between networks of similar network protocols, such as TCP/IP, or Xerox's XNS. Routers can send frames with or without the same network portion of an IP address.

Network interconnection machines connect networks, not other machines on a network. When the Ethernet LAN sends a message to the token-bus LAN, the bridge or router transports the message from network to network. When the message arrives at the destination LAN—the token-bus LAN—it's then routed to the correct computer.

How does the message "know" it's at the right machine, or at the right network? The answer lies in the complex addressing scheme used with IP. A 32-bit Address field in the header contains all the information necessary to get the message to the right place. It's the job of the interconnecting machines to interpret the header, and decide on a routing path for the message. All machines connected to a TCP/IP network are assigned unique addresses and are called hosts, including routers, bridges, gateways, PCs, programmable logic units (PLCs), and, perhaps, printers.

The LANs in Figure 5-2 show one host on each, but, in fact, there may be hundreds or thousands of hosts.

TCP is based upon reliable, **connection-oriented** delivery services. The system is reliable because there are end-to-end acknowledgments that the data was received. If it's lost, the sender or receiver will be informed of the loss. There are several mechanisms in TCP for guaranteeing delivery. One is a sliding window mechanism that tracks packets. Typically, data is divided into packets, and the packets are transmitted through the network. They may travel to the destination over different links, and arrive out of sequence. The receiver will acknowledge receipt of sequentially numbered packets. More on this later.

TEST TIP

Know the difference between connection-oriented and connectionless protocols.

IP, on the other hand, is unreliable, best-effort, *connectionless* delivery. It is a best-effort system, because error control is included for the header, though not for the data field. The error-detection field in the header is a sincere effort to deliver the information. The system is connectionless because there's no acknowledgment that an IP packet arrived.

TRANSMISSION CONTROL PROTOCOL (TCP)

An interconnected network is a system of interconnected terminals, or local networks, spread over a large area.

Transmission Control Protocol (TCP) is responsible for process-to-process communications between two interconnected devices. A process (identified by a port number) in this context refers to underlying applications such as file transfers, telnet, or e-mail. While, technically, any host running TCP/IP could perform a TCP setup, this more typically occurs between servers, or routers and servers. TCP provides software services for a common interface between the physical network and user applications. The services run independently of the physical topology, or media access, running at the Physical and Data Link layers. Since the physical parameters of the data that's transferred using TCP are transparent to it, TCP is able to interconnect networks of different physical attributes, so that the user perceives it to be a single interconnected network—what we call an internet.

TCP/IP is a widely-used, internetworking protocol that is nonproprietary. It is based on a 32-bit addressing scheme and is the IP used on the Internet. The TCP portion of the protocol provides a connection-oriented transport protocol with advanced error correction and recovery capabilities.

TCP uses a software abstract called a **socket** to communicate processes.

A socket is used as a programming interface to the communication protocol (TCP, for example). Once set up, a socket includes all addressing information between two communicating devices, the process that's to be called upon, and the transport protocol to be used. It's important to understand that we're backtracking a bit, because a socket is set up before any user data flows between the two devices.

Imagine two servers in an internetwork using TCP, and the local server wants to utilize the services of a remote server. The servers must set up a connection. The sequence, using sockets, is as follows:

- *Initiate:* Three parameters are initiated. The address family specifies the method of addressing used by the socket, such as UNIX. Type refers to the socket interface to be used. Specifically, type describes a connection-oriented (TCP) or connectionless (UDP) service, as well as direct connections to utilities that are run at a lower level, such as Ping. Protocol is the protocol that will be run between the stations such as TCP, IP, or UDP.

- *Bind:* Registers a port address to a socket. In order to do so, two pieces of information are needed: the local address and the local process. The address will be the port number, while processes refer to the functionality of the service such as file transfers or web access.

- *Listen:* The local station indicates the number of connection requests it can handle (it can deal with more than one at the same time). It also ensures that the address family, type, and protocol are consistent, by listening to the remote server's reply.

- *Accept:* The remote server accepts the connection by verifying its address, and indicating the process it will be providing.

- *Communicate:* Exchange between the two servers consists of read/write socket calls.

- *Close:* Once the socket is closed (which originates from a field of the TCP header) the connection ceases. At this time, no information related to the connection that may be stored in port buffers is retained.

The process that's to be performed in the communication between servers is identified by port. A port is a 16-bit number that refers incoming messages to an application that will process them. For example, when you connect to a server on the Internet, and the download of text and graphics begins, you're connected to an HTTP application (process) that's specified by a port number (80, in this example). The port is identified as both a source and a destination. The meaning varies with the context. When information is downloaded from the Internet, there may be many source ports that compose the specified web page. Each of these will be identified by a unique port number. However, all of the information will be sent to destination port number 80, for an HTTP process. To the client requesting the web page, the destination port will be 80, which is the requested process.

Both UDP and TCP use ports to identify a specific process. Many of the port numbers are standardized, and are referred to as **well-known ports**. Similarly, their associated applications are called "well-known services." Table 5-1 lists several well-known port numbers, and their provided services. These ports, from 0 through 1023, are assigned by the Internet Assigned Numbers Authority (IANA). Port numbers from 1024 through 65535 (called ephemeral ports) aren't assigned, and are frequently used in user-developed programs.

Table 5-1:
Well-Known Ports

Service	Well-Known Port Number
FTP	21, 20
Telnet	23
SMTP Mail	25
HTTP (WWW)	80
POP3 (Mail)	110
News	144
IRC	6667

┌─ TEST TIP ─────────
Memorize the well-known port numbers listed in Table 5-1.

So, a socket is used to set up a connection between two stations, and a port is the service the stations will be using. Once the socket is finished, an association between the two machines will be completed. The association represents a logical connection between the machines that's uniquely identified with the format shown in Figure 5-3.

Figure 5-3:
Socket Format

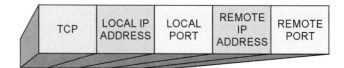

TCP is the framework that ensures data communications between the two machines. To do so, it must fulfill the following services:

- *Stream Data Transfer:* The application provides the connection with streams of data bytes, without concern for the number of bytes, or whether the communicating machines can accommodate the total number and rate of delivery. TCP will organize the byte stream into fragments, then pass them on to the IP to be, perhaps, further organized into datagrams. TCP will determine when the fragments are delivered to IP for transmission.

- *Reliability:* As a connection-oriented and reliable protocol, TCP will expect an acknowledgment from the receiving station for fragments that have been transmitted.

- *Flow Control:* As byte streams are delivered to TCP from the application, the receiver must tell the sender the number of bytes it can receive before its buffers overflow. This is done during acknowledgments.

- *Multiplexing:* As mentioned, TCP servers can handle more than one request at a time by assigning port numbers, and multiplexing the requests to well-known ports.

- *Logical Connections:* A logical connection is set up with sockets (for TCP) and ports (for both TCP and UDP).

- *Full-Duplex Operation:* Data moves in both directions at the same time during a TCP connection.

These are the fundamental services that TCP provides to the applications running on it. In order to do so, it uses a prescribed frame format to communicate the level of services to the layers in the protocol suite. The TCP frame is embedded in the Data field of an IP frame. The frame format for TCP is shown in Figure 5-4.

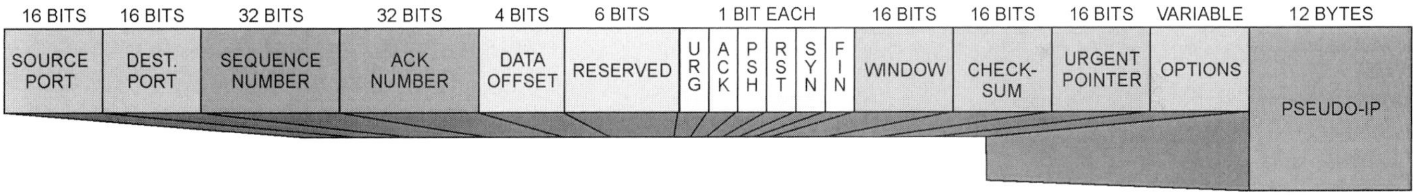

- *Source Port (16 bits):* The receiver uses its port number when replying.

- *Destination Port (16 bits):* The destination port.

- *Sequence Number (32 bits):* This field contains the sequence number of the first data byte in the segment. The next segment will contain the sequence number of the first data byte in its segment. At the receiver, the sequence numbers will be collected, and all must be accounted for to ensure that all data has been received.

- *Acknowledgment Number (32 bits):* This is the value of the next sequence number that the receiver expects to be sent. This fill is used during acknowledgments—when the ACK bit is set to 1.

- *Data Offset (4 bits):* This is the size of the header expressed as the number of 32-bit words. It's used to tell the receiver where the header ends and the Data field begins.

- *Reserved (6 bits):* Not used.

Figure 5-4: TCP Frame Format

- *URG (Urgent Pointer Field) (1 bit):* When set, it means that the data contained in the Urgent Pointer field is significant (it may mean nothing when the URG bit is 0).

- *ACK (Acknowledgment) (1 bit):* When set, it means that the Acknowledgment Number field has significant information.

- *PSH (Push) (1 bit):* When set, any data held in the buffers is sent.

- *RST (Reset) (1 bit):* Resets the connection.

- *SYN (Synchronization) (1 bit):* When set, this indicates that the Sequence Number field is significant, and that the frame received is one of a series of fragments.

- *FIN:* (Finish) (1 bit): When set, it marks the last fragment to be sent.

- *Window (16 bits):* The receiver returns this in an ACK to tell the sender the number of bytes it can accept.

- *Checksum (16 bits):* An error-detection algorithm that looks for bit errors on the TCP header, Data field, and a portion of the IP header (the Source and Destination IP addresses, Protocol, and Length fields).

- *Urgent Pointer (16 bits):* Specifies the first data octet following the urgent data. This indicates data in a buffer that must be sent immediately.

- *Options (variable size):* There are three options available in a TCP header. These are the End Of Option List, No operation, and Maximum Fragment Size, which is used to tell the sender the size of the largest fragment it can process.

- *Pseudo-IP (typically 12 bytes):* Includes the Source and Destination IP addresses, the protocol being used (UDP), and the length of the UDP datagram. This information is taken from the IP header.

NOTE

Once a socket is in place, TCP transmission occurs.

A final field may include padding that's used to fill the header size to a multiple of 32 bits. While a TCP fragment has a variable data field, it's normally constrained by protocols at the lower layers (IP, Ethernet, etc.). As mentioned, once a socket is in place, TCP transmission occurs. The TCP header and data are encapsulated in a lower layer frame, normally IP. IP, in turn, is encapsulated in a lower layer frame such as Ethernet or Token Ring.

TCP is an intensive protocol implementation and may not be needed under certain circumstances. IP may be run on a local network, without the benefits of TCP, if the network administrator determines that the network is reliable and efficient. However, if users on the network want to communicate outside the local environment, a Transport layer protocol is required. Still, TCP may represent overkill for some applications. IPX, the Network layer protocol used with Novell NetWare, offers benefits that IP doesn't, and is frequently run with UDP. Other applications that occur in real-time, such as interactive gaming, can't wait for acknowledgments. Once they arrived, they would be obsolete. For these applications, UDP offers alternative Transport layer access.

Most network operating systems support TCP/IP operations with a suite of protocols and utilities. These utilities include:

• IP	• FTP	• HTTP	• POP3/IMAP4
• TCP	• TFTP	• HTTPS	• TELNET
• UDP	• SMTP	• NTP	• ICMP
			• ARP

These protocols and utilities are covered in detail throughout the remainder of the chapter.

User Datagram Protocol (UDP)

User Datagram Protocol (**UDP**) is a streamlined implementation of TCP. In fact, in all cases where TCP is run, UDP is also run (though not utilized). UDP is a connectionless (un-reliable with no flow control or error recovery) mechanism supplied to the IP. A UDP datagram is encapsulated in the Data field of IP. Essentially, it provides a software interface between the IP and the application to be run. Applications include those run for TCP, such as mail, file transfer (TFTP), or Domain Name Server (DNS).

User Datagram Protocol (UDP)

UDP is a streamlined implementation of TCP.

UDP interfaces applications and the IP via port numbers, such as those shown in Table 5-1. UDP is the protocol specified in the header of an IP packet. Once invoked, it does nothing more than multiplex and demultiplex application processes at the designated ports. The header format for UDP is illustrated in Figure 5-5.

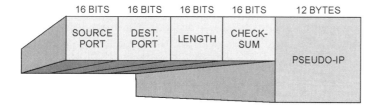

Figure 5-5: UDP Frame Format

The header is 20 bytes in length. Notice that all fields in UDP are a part of a TCP header. This is why UDP is always running when TCP is the specified protocol.

- *Source Port (16 bits):* The application process port at the sender

- *Destination Port (16 bits):* The application process port at the destination

- *Length (16 bits):* Total length of the UDP datagram, including the header

- *Checksum (16 bits):* Bit error detection algorithm that covers the UDP header, pseudo-IP header, and UDP Data field

- *Pseudo-IP (typically 12 bytes):* Includes the Source and Destination IP addresses, the protocol being used (UDP), and the length of the UDP datagram. This informa-tion is taken from the IP header.

As mentioned, UDP is a quick and streamlined Transport layer protocol. It's used in applica-tions where flow control and retransmission of lost packets either can't be done (real-time applications like live broadcasts), or when an upper layer protocol does it. As mentioned, NetWare IP uses UDP because it provides for flow control, error detection, etc.

INTERNET PROTOCOL

As mentioned before, Internet Protocol (IP) is a best-effort, unreliable, connectionless protocol. It depends on TCP to provide these attributes. IP is associated with the Network layer of the OSI model. In essence, it's the responsibility of IP to determine a path to any destination device that is also running IP. IP is not concerned with protocols running at the Data Link layer. IP can be used with Ethernet, Token Ring, wireless, or nearly any other network access protocol.

IP is a best-effort, unreliable, connectionless protocol.

32-bit addressing

IP uses a **32-bit addressing** scheme to locate devices on both large and small networks. Note that an IP address is a logical address. When a data packet is sent using IP, there will be a point at which the logical address must be associated with a physical machine. The method used for this association is to relate the logical IP address to the machine MAC address.

The most common version of IP is version 4. A more recent version, version 6, has been approved but is not widely deployed. IPv6 will be discussed after Ipv4 in this chapter.

IPv4

IP messages are sent in the form of a **datagram** (also called a **packet**), shown in Figure 5-6.

datagram

packet

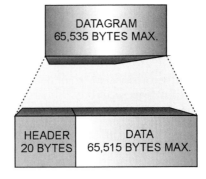

**Figure 5-6:
Datagram
Layout**

A datagram is the unit of measure for an IP transmission. A datagram has a maximum length of 65,535 bytes, including the header, although it could be much smaller. All datagrams contain source and destination addresses (these are the IP addresses). The datagram is patterned after the addressing methods used with physical networks: It consists of a header field and a data field, as pictured in Figure 5-7. The most common type of header is 20 bytes long. For a fully loaded datagram, the maximum Data field length is $65,535 - 20 = 65,515$ bytes. Enroute to the ultimate destination, datagrams are passed along from device to device, normally through a router or gateway. As it moves up to another layer, such as the Transport layer, TCP (or some other protocol) information is encapsulated within the Data field of the IP frame.

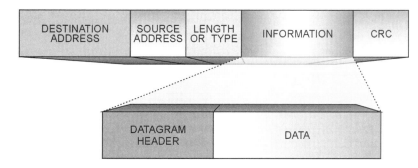

Figure 5-7: IP Packet Orientation Within a Datagram

The IP packet format is depicted in Figure 5-8. The VR/HL field contains the software version being used, and the header length. VR and HL both occupy 4 bits of the field. The software version is important because networks, and the machines connecting them, may be running an earlier version. They may not be able to process a datagram encoded in a more recent version, causing the datagram to be rejected. The current version of the IP is 4.

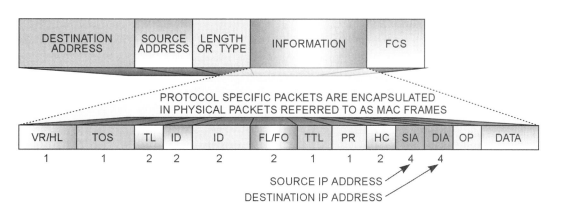

The 4-bit header states the length of the header in 32-bit words. For example, a header consisting of 20 bytes will show 5 in the HL field, which is equal to 20 bytes × 8 / 32 = 5. The IP allows for options in the Header field. Options extend the length of the field, and contain instructions for tracking the datagram across the system.

Figure 5-8: IP Packet Format

The 1-byte Type Of Service field, shown in Figure 5-9, describes how the datagram should be treated enroute to the destination. Bits 1, 2, and 3 of the field are called Precedence. Precedence is an indication of the significance of the datagram to the operation of the network. Datagrams that include control instructions, making the transport quicker or more reliable, are given precedence over datagrams containing word-processing files. The D, T, and R bits are indicators of the level of transport service needed for the datagram. D is low delay, T is high throughput, and R is high reliability. These bits provide help to the interconnecting machines as to the route that the datagram is to take. In most cases, a router has several options for routing datagrams passing through it, and will look at the DTR bits before arbitrarily selecting the route. Of course, not all routers or gateways support the Type Of Service field.

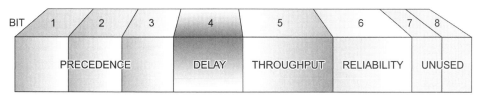

Figure 5-9: Type of Service Field

The 16-bit TL field states the total length of the datagram, measured in bytes. The total length includes the header and the data. As was previously mentioned, the total length may be a maximum of 65,535 bytes.

The next three fields, ID (Identification), FL (Flag), and FO (Fragmentation Offset), are all related to the fragmentation of a datagram. Fragmentation is the process of dividing the datagram so that the length is smaller. Fragmentation results when datagrams are separated to accommodate the frame lengths of networks through which they pass enroute to the destination. Remember that a wide area network is often a collection of LANs. An Ethernet LAN transmits frames with a maximum length of about 1,500 bytes. If a datagram is enroute to a destination, and has to pass through an Ethernet, the size of the datagram must be compatible with the frame-formatting requirements of the Ethernet, or 1,500 bytes. Because of this, datagrams are fragmented.

Once a datagram has been fragmented, it remains so until arriving at the destination, where it is reassembled. There is no guarantee that the fragmented packets will arrive at the receiver in the same sequence. The destination, then, must be able to tell which packets belong to which datagrams, which portion of the fragment has arrived, and which fragment is the last. The receiver can reassemble the fragments into the original datagram by using the information contained in the Fragmentation fields.

The 2-byte ID field is a unique number generated for each datagram transmitted over the network. As the datagram is fragmented, the header of the datagram is copied onto each fragment, including the ID field. Then, when the fragments arrive at the receiver, the receiver looks at the ID field and the source address of each packet to determine the constitution of the original datagram.

The Flag is a 3-bit field responsible for controlling fragmentation, and for identifying the last fragment of the datagram. The second bit is the control bit. When the control bit is set, it is an instruction to avoid fragmenting the datagram. A router that sees the bit set will not fragment the datagram, but if it is unable to send the message along without fragmentation, it will disable the datagram and send an error message back to the source station. The first bit, when turned off, identifies the last fragment. This will be the only fragment that has the bit turned off, and the receiver can now determine all fragments of the datagram.

It does so by examining the Total Length field of the fragment, and the Fragment Offset field. Fragment Offset is a 13-bit field containing a byte count equal to the numerical order of the fragmented datagram. For example, consider a 2,000-byte datagram fragmented into four 500-byte fragments. The first fragment contains an offset of 0, since it begins with the first byte in the field. The second fragment has an offset of 500, because it contains the second 500-byte fragment set. The offset in the third fragment reads 1,000 because it contains bytes 1,000 through 1,499 of the datagram. The last fragment will show 1,500 in the offset, and will also have the more-fragments bit in the Flag field turned off to indicate that this is the last fragment.

The Total Length field of the fragment shows only the length of the fragment, and not the total length of the datagram. However, the receiver can add the byte-count in the Total Length field to the offset, and determine the size of the datagram. For example, the fourth fragment in the above example will show a total length of 520 bytes (500 bytes in the data field + 20 bytes of header = 520). Subtracting the header bytes gives the size of the data field, 500 bytes. The offset in the fourth fragment reads 1,500. By adding the size of the data field (500 bytes) to the offset (1,500 bytes), the receiver will determine that the original datagram must be 2,000 bytes long (1,500 bytes offset + 500 bytes in the data field = 2,000 bytes).

The receiver collects all the fragments with identical IDs, and reassembles them according to the numerical byte-sequence contained in the Offset fields. It will know if any fragments are missing, because the total byte-count must be equal to 2,000.

Time-To-Live is a 1-byte field specifying the time, in seconds, that a datagram may remain on the network. Typically, it is set to 20 seconds. If the datagram is permitted to move indefinitely from link to link, it has probably become degraded (the destination address is lost or garbled, etc.), and will never arrive at the receiver. The Time-To-Live field in an IP header sets a limit on the time the network is allowed to deliver the datagram.

> The Time-To-Live field in an IP header sets a limit on the time the network is allowed to deliver the datagram.

The 1-byte Protocol field describes the protocol governing the datagram. The 16-bit checksum is an algorithm used to check for errors in the header. Note that the header checksum looks only at the header, since the Data field has its own error detection. The reason for separating the two is that only the headers are examined by interconnecting machines. They process information in the Data field as bit streams. Checking headers for errors saves time when the datagram is moving through the routers or gateways.

The Source and Destination fields contain addresses of the sender and receiver. An Internet address is assigned by the Network Information Center (NIC), and is a requirement for connecting to the Internet. However, many corporate WANs also use TCP/IP. These addresses may be of any format the network manager wants to devise, but if the WAN will, at some future date, be connected to the Internet, the proprietary addresses will have to be scrapped and exchanged for addresses assigned by the NIC. It would be wise to request addresses from the NIC for possible future connection to the Internet. The following discussion of addresses assumes that the datagram will be formatted for Internet transportation.

IP ADDRESSING

An IP address consists of 32 bits, so, $2^{32} = 4,294,967,296$ unique addresses. While four billion addresses is a lot, it is finite. A time will come when all four billion addresses have been used. Then what? When IP was first introduced and finalized in the early 80's, no one suspected that the Internet would be such a powerful and consuming force. At that time, 32 bits seemed like enough, especially since the Internet was for scientists, computer nerds, and soldiers. Who could have foreseen that our grandmothers would one day be web surfing?

In the early days, it seemed that large networks, populated with thousands of machines, would be the future. The potential of client-server systems was untapped, as well as the concept of managing network resources into clusters—or workgroups, as we call them. In the early 1980s, 16 kB of RAM was huge, and a 10 MB hard drive was prohibitively expensive. A 32-bit addressing scheme made sense, and has served us well, notwithstanding a significant number of critics who attack the system as inefficient and flawed. It's all of that, but only in the context of the huge number of users who require a logical address—a situation that no one could have foreseen.

Of course, things change. The current supply of IP addresses will be depleted in the next 30 years at the current demand rate. Actually, that's less of a problem than having four billion users attached to the Internet—we would have to redefine our notion of slow. But, assuming technology keeps a step ahead of Internet traffic, a time will come when not everyone will be able to use the Internet, because they won't be able to get an IP address (or a MAC address, for that matter).

The current IP is at version 4 (IPv.4), with the experimental version 5 (IPv.5) waiting in the wings. A change to the protocol has been approved for IP version 6 (also known as IP-next generation, IPng), which intends to address (pun intended) the limitations of IPv.4. We'll take a look at a couple of implementations of IPv.4, called classful and classless IP addressing.

Classful IP

IP address classes A, B, and C differentiate in the numbers of networks and host addresses being utilized by a specific organization. Class-A addresses are identified by a logic 0 in their bit-1 position. Class-B addresses are identified with logic 10 in the first two bit positions. A class-C address contains 110 in the first three bit positions, as shown in Figure 5-10.

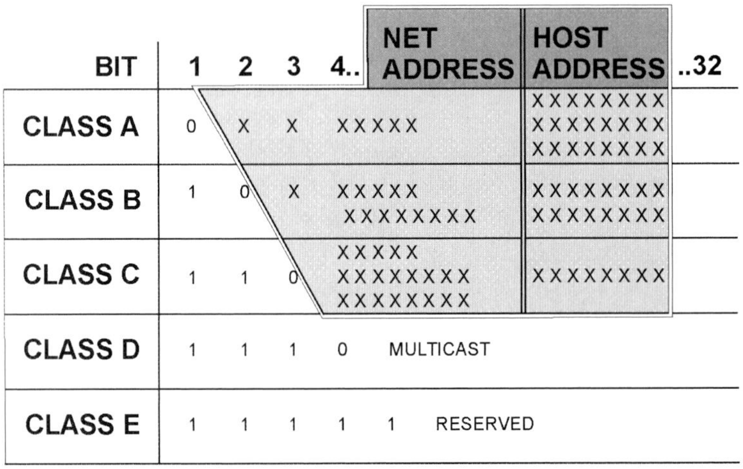

BIT	1	2	3	4..	NET ADDRESS	HOST ADDRESS	..32
CLASS A	0	X	X	X X X X X		X X X X X X X X X X X X X X X X X X X X X X X X	
CLASS B	1	0	X	X X X X X X X X X X X X X		X X X X X X X X X X X X X X X X	
CLASS C	1	1	0	X X X X X X X X X X X X X X X X X X X X X		X X X X X X X X	
CLASS D	1	1	1	0	MULTICAST		
CLASS E	1	1	1	1	1	RESERVED	

Figure 5-10: IP Address Classes

IP address classes A, B, and C differentiate in the numbers of networks and host addresses being utilized by a specific organization.

In terms of calculations, these are the high-order bits in the address. The idea behind address classes is that some large organizations will have a few large networks and many hosts. Some medium-size organizations will have equal numbers of hosts and networks, while small organizations will have many interconnected networks with a small number of hosts.

TEST TIP

Be able to determine the class of an IP address for a dotted decimal IP address.

Keep in mind, a host is any node (machine) that has an IP address and communicates on the interconnected network. A network refers to a physical network—a LAN or WAN. So, the address contains the general location of the receiver (the network address), and the specific location of the destination machine (the host address). Note that these are logical addresses, not physical addresses. Each host also has a physical address (the MAC address), which locates the machine on its network wire. As you can probably guess, there must be some type of system that will map logical and physical addresses. That system is called a routing protocol, and we'll take a look at it in a later section.

The Internet address system is separated into five classes that specify the numbers of networks and hosts. The address follows the Decimal Dotted Notation procedure for grouping the address.

The general structure of the IP classes is also shown in Figure 5-10. Each class separates the 32 bits into a **network** and a **host address**. As mentioned above, the sequence of higher order bits determines the class. Since these are reserved, they aren't available for addressing.

network

host address

class-A address

A **class-A address** can accommodate $2^{24} - 2 = 16,777,214$ hosts, with 24 bits in the host field. The reason 2 is subtracted is that 0.0.0.0 is reserved for the default network, and 127.0.0.1 is reserved for a loopback test. Datagrams can be sent to $2^7 - 2 = 126$ destination networks. At this time, all class-A addresses have been assigned.

The Host field of a **class-B address** has 16 bits; so it can respond to $2^{16} - 2 = 65,534$ host machines. The two highest order bits in the network field are set to 10, leaving 14 bits for the network address. Using 14 bits, 2^{14} (or 16,384) individual networks may be addressed.

class-B address

In the **class-C address**, the Network field is 24 bits long. The three highest-order bits are set to 110, leaving 21 bits for network addresses. This priovides a total of $2^{21} = 2,097,152$ network assignments. The host number contains 8 bits for $2^8 - 2 = 254$ host machines.

class-C address

By convention, the address fields of Figure 5-10 are separated into four 8-bit groups. The first byte of a class-A address contains the network number and the class bit, while the remaining three bytes contain the host address. The first two bytes of a class-B address are the network address, along with the 2-bit class identifier, and the last two bytes are the host number. The network number for a class-C address is in the first three bytes, along with the 3-bit class code, and the host address is in the last byte. This method for expressing TCP/IP addresses is called **Decimal Dotted Notation**.

Decimal Dotted Notation

The binary format for addresses described above is normally converted to base 10 numbers. For example, consider the class-B address:

	bit 32		**bit 1**
Binary (**Base₂**)	10000110.10001101.01001010.00010111		
Decimal (**Base₁₀**)	134 . 141 . 74 . 23		

The decimal notation is converted to base10 and the dots represent the byte separation. It is the base 10 number that's used when referring to an Internet address, but as you can see, it is a derivative of the binary machine code. In this example, host machine .74.23 is located on network 134.141.

As a matter of numerical interest, the leftmost byte, or number, of a class-A network is numbered 1 through 126. Class-B networks are numbered 128 through 191 and class-C networks are numbered 192 through 223.

A class-D address signifies a multicast, which is a method for sending data to all hosts or networks. There are two types of broadcasting on networks: *directed* and *limited* broadcasts. A **directed broadcast** is used to send data to all of the hosts specified by the network number. Any host portion of the address set to all 1's is a directed broadcast. A **limited broadcast** is used to contact all stations on the local network. A limited address contains thirty-two 1's in the address field. This type of broadcast is used when a host is first connected to the network. It sends the limited broadcast to all other hosts on its network, basically asking, "Do any hosts on the network know my address?" All hosts look up the new host's address and respond with the number. From that point on, the new host knows its address.

A final class of IP addresses is class E. Class-E addresses are reserved for experimental purposes.

IP includes several special addresses that are invalid. All 0's in the host or network fields are interpreted to mean this host, or this network, which is useful when two machines on the same local network are communicating. When a host does not know the number of the network it's attached to, it may send a message with all 0's in the network field, meaning "this network." Other hosts will respond to the request with the network number, and the host records it for future transmissions. Any IP address beginning with 127 is an invalid address, since 127 is used for loopback testing. A packet may be looped back to test the integrity of the links, or to measure throughput. When an interconnection machine receives the 127.0.0.1 network address, it sends it back to the source network without transmitting it onto the Internet. In fact, this is a local loopback and never arrives on the network wire.

Any IP address beginning with 127 is an invalid address.

IP Subnets

An **IP subnet** is used to separate the network portion from the host portion of an IP address.

This is necessary because a NIC card needs to determine whether a packet will be going to another station on the local network, or to a station on an entirely different network.

Another use of a subnet is to divide a single network address by segmenting the address. This means that the network and host portions of an IP address are separated in a manner that's nonstandard. The section on CIDR provides more detail on this process.

In class-B and class-C network addresses, the number of networks is somewhat restricted. Many organizations need to add more of their networks to the Internet, but there are not enough addresses to support the demand. The interim solution has been to create subnetworks. Subnets allow a site to divide the host portion of the address into two parts, which define more network address bits, and fewer host address bits. This allows an organization to deploy more networks without requesting additional IPs, and it reduces the number of routes on the Internet, which helps to control congestion.

Figure 5-11 shows a router connected to the Internet. The router services a number of separate networks. The router IP at the Internet interface is a class-B 134.141.0.0. All packets with this network address will be received by the router. The router will then determine the correct subnet based on the third octet of the address received from the Internet. Once at the subnet, the packet is sent on to the host identified by the fourth octet of the address.

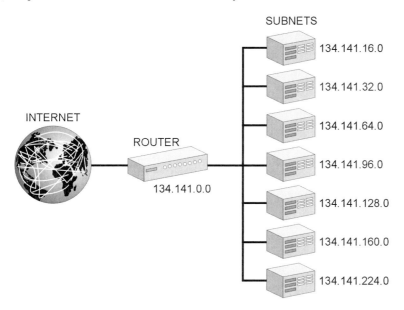

Figure 5-11: Subnetting a Network Address

For example, in the class-B address 134.141.16.23, the network address is 134.141. The host address is 16.23. A subnet is created by extending the network address to the third byte so that it becomes 134.141.X, with X = 0 to 254. Host address 23 will be located at one of these subnet addresses. The subnetwork is transparent to machines outside the subnet; they still communicate with host 23 by sending messages to network 134.141. Only at the local network is the subnet created.

Subnetworks are identified by a default **subnet network mask** (or natural mask), which is the decimal number 255. A series of "255" masks are used to indicate the boundaries of the subnetwork. Conventionally, in a classful system, the 255 corresponds to the network portion of an IP in the following manner:

- A class-A IP address with the first byte reserved for network addresses has a default subnet mask of 255.0.0.0.

- A class-B IP address has the first two bytes reserved for network addresses, so the default subnet mask would be 255.255.0.0.

- And a class-C IP address has a default subnet mask of 255.255.255.0 since the first three bytes are reserved for network addresses.

The decimal 255 is used to mask the network portion of an IP and only leave open the host portion.

subnet network mask

┌─ TEST TIP ─────
│ For a given IPv4 IP address,
│ be able to select the correct
│ subnet mask.
└──────────────

The default subnet masks as described are conventional for each class. However, a network manager is free to slice up the mask as needed—within limits, which we'll look at shortly.

Convention beside the point, any address followed by the 255 mask is identified as a host. Keep in mind that the idea of a subnet mask is to artificially create more network addresses. A class-B network uses 14 bits of the first two octets, leaving 65,534 host addresses. If you need only 3,000 host addresses, the remaining 62,534 hosts assignments will be wasted. And if you added a remote network, you would have to request another IP to address hosts on it. The classful system, as you can see, tends to create waste for class-A and class-B IPs.

When a mask is used, a router looks only at the bits constrained by the mask to determine which subnet a packet is addressed to. It follows that router communications must include the mask in the address header of packets it sends and receives. For example, in the class-B address above, the sequence would be:

134 . 141 . 16 . 23, then, 255 . 255 .255 .16.

> When a mask is used, a router looks only at the bits constrained by the mask to determine which subnet a packet is addressed to.

Now the message will be sent to host 23 on subnet 16 of network 134.141. The default mask covers the first two octets since these are the network address octets of a class-B IP. The mask in the third octet is used to mark the value of the subnet. The fourth octet, of course, is the value of the host address.

Let's look at another example using the network address 134.141.0.0. This is a class-B address, and we want to subnet it to network 96, host 21. This address, using subnetting, would use extended addressing, as shown in Figure 5-12.

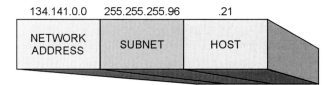

Figure 5-12: Extended Subnet Addressing

This complete address would be carried on the network, and passed between stations and routers or gateways. Outside the network, all packets would arrive addressed to 134.141.X.X. E-mail sent through the Internet, for example, would have no knowledge of the subnetting that occurs at the local level. Once the packet arrives at the class-B address, the router will add the subnet string and pass the packet on to the correct subnet address and host.

Notice that this class-B address without subnetting accounts for merely a single network address. However, with subnetting, it can create an additional 254 network addresses.

Admittedly, the number of hosts on each network has been drastically reduced (to 254 on each subnet network), but this isn't such a bad thing. Networks are routinely segmented into smaller sizes anyway for the purposes of better network management (higher throughput, less bandwidth demands, faster speeds, etc.).

Why have more network addresses that host addresses? First, there are more LANs than the addressing scheme can support. Second, a single host address may be used by more than one computer. The host machine may be a communications controller that does the protocol encoding, and has a dozen PCs, or terminals, connected to it. When a PC user signs onto the Internet, the address of the host—the communication controller—is used. The protocol is not concerned with the arrangement the controller has with the PCs and terminals, since it deals only with packets of data.

Classless IP (CIDR)

By 1992, the Internet Task Force determined that the supply of class-B addresses would be exhausted in the mid-nineties. As an interim solution, until IPv.6 solves the problems associated with 32-bit IP addresses, the **Classless Inter-Domain Routing (CIDR)**, pronounced "cider," was developed. CIDR is intended to accomplish two primary goals:

- To reduce the current reliance on a classful system.

- To support route aggregation where a single network address can be used to represent the addresses of thousands of hosts.

This has the benefit of reducing routing tables that point to network addresses (currently numbering about 30,000+ routes) and reducing the effect of route flapping. First, if a single address can be used to represent 1,000 routes, then the amount of route information that must be maintained in a router is reduced. Flapping refers to changes in route availability. If a router is taken offline, it's no longer available as a valid route, and a "flap" is then created in the routing tables of all other routers.

Conventional classes are eliminated with CIDR. CIDR routers use a network prefix to determine the line between network address and host address, rather than the first several bits of the address to specify a class. There are still 32 bits in the IP, but all of the bits are used for addressing. And instead of a predetermined dividing line between network and host, the network address may be arbitrarily chosen.

> CIDR is intended to accomplish two primary goals: to reduce the current reliance on a classful system; and to support route aggregation where a single network address can be used to represent the addresses of thousands of hosts.

Routers exchange addressing data on a network. If a packet uses a router as a hop to another location, and the router doesn't have the packet address in its router tables, it updates them with it. Whenever a node comes online, it's said to "advertise" its presence and in the process, router tables are updated with the address of the new host. A router that is located at the interface to a group of local networks and the Internet will advertise all new addresses.

When CIDR is used, the information exchanged between routers contains a mask that specifies the length of the network portion of an IP address. The mask, called a prefix-length, is a bit-count that begins with the leftmost bit of the address. For example, an address with 22 bits in the network portion of the address would be advertised with 22 bits in the length-prefix bit-count, and would be called a /22 address. The host address would occupy the last 10 bits of the address.

And a classful router won't understand the conventions used with CIDR, so it's common to use network prefixes that are multiples of the class arrangement. Table 5-2 shows commonly used CIDR addressing schemes. By using prefix multiples, host machines will interpret the addresses as if they were classful.

Table 5-2:
CIDR Addressing
Schemes

CIDR Prefix Length	Dotted Decimal	Number Individual Addresses
/13	255.248.0.0	512,000
/14	255.252.0.0	256,000
/15	255.254.0.0	128,000
/16	255.255.0.0	64,000
/17	255.255.128.0	32,000
/18	255.255.192.0	16,000
/19	255.255.224.0	8,000
/20	255.255.240.0	4,000
/21	255.255.248.0	2,000
/22	255.255.252.0	1,000
/23	255.255.254.0	512
/24	255.255.255.0	256
/25	255.255.255.128	128
/26	255.255.255.192	64
/27	255.255.255.224	32

Let's look at an example. Assume that an ISP has the class-B address 200.25.0.0. With 16 bits in the host, 65,536 addresses can be created. But the ISP wants to assign only 4,096 addresses, beginning at 200.25.16. This requires 12 bits in the host portion of the address, and is the same as 24 class-C addresses (4,096/256 = 24). Now, the block of 4,096 addresses can be divided by a power of two. This is typically accomplished by successively dividing the address by two, until the block is composed of a series of consecutively smaller blocks.

Address 200.25.16.0/20 is first divided by two so that now there will be two blocks with 2,048 addresses in each block. One of the blocks is retained and the other is set aside in order to subdivide. The first part of the process looks like this:

Original block: 200.25.16.0/20 11001000.00011001.00010000.00000000

First block: 200.25.16.0/21 11001000.00011001.00010000.00000000

Set-aside: 200.25.24.0/21 11001000.00011001.00011000.00000000

The original block of 4,096 address had been divided into two 2,048-address blocks. The underlined portion of the binary address represents the network portion of the address.

2,048 Set-aside: 200.25.24.0/21   11001000.00011001.00011000.00000000

Second block: 200.25.24.0/22   11001000.00011001.00011000.00000000

1,024 Set-aside: 200.25.28.0/22   11001000.00011001.00011100.00000000

The second block of 2,048 addresses is divided into two blocks of 1,024 addresses.

1024 Set-aside: 200.25.28/22 11001000.00011001.00011100.00000000

Third Block: 200.25.28.0/23   11001000.00011001.00011100.00000000

Fourth block: 200.25.30.0/23   11001000.00011001.00011110.00000000

By dividing the block of 1,024 address, two blocks of 512 addresses are created. From the single 200.25.0.0/16 address, the ISP has provided four unique blocks of address as in:

(1) Block 1: 2,048 addresses starting at 200.25.16.0/21
(or 8 class C addresses)

(2) Block 2: 1,024 addresses starting at 200.25.24.0/22
(or 4 class C addresses)

(3) Block 3: 512 addresses starting at 200.25.28.0/23
(or 2 class C addresses)

(4) Block 4: 512 addresses starting at 200.25.30.0/23
(or 2 class C addresses)

The blocks could have been further subdivided, but it's important to make sure that each block remains a multiple of 2 so that classful routers will interpret the address as classful.

The router-to-Internet interface in this example will advertise an address of 200.25.16.0/16. The /16 will be included in the network prefix. Since the routes to the four networks all occur through a single Internet port of the base router, traffic routes on the Internet have been reduced, or aggregated, since they occur offline from Internet routes. CIDR therefore, represents an interim strategy to aggregate Internet routes, as well as a means to inject flexibility into, and improve the efficiency of the present IPv4 scheme.

IPv6

IP version 6, also called **IP Next Generation (IPng)**, improves upon IPv4 by extending the address fields in the IP header from 32 bits to 128 bits. IPv6 is intended to represent an evolution of IP rather than an immediate and wholesale replacement for IPv4.

IP version 6, also called IP Next Generation (IPng), improves upon IPv4 by extending the address fields in the IP header from 32 bits to 128 bits.

The broad goals of IPv6 are:

- To provide for transition from IPv4
- Simplify the header fields of IP
- Provide for authentication and privacy
- To expand quality of service capabilities
- To expand routing capabilities
- To expand addressing capabilities
- To improve support for options

IPv6 was designed to interoperate side-by-side with 32-bit addressing of IPv4. That is, an IPv6 node can send packets over a network infrastructure that includes IPv4-only routers. Or, IPv4-only nodes can send packets over a network populated with routers that support IPv6. It was expected that IPv4 will be used for many years and that a complete transition to IPv6 may never be complete.

As you'll see shortly, the address field of IPv6 is four times as long as that of IPv4, but the header size of IPv6 is only twice as long. Some fields were eliminated while others were made optional.

One of the biggest weaknesses of TCP/IP is the lack of any security. What security there is has been imposed upon networks at the Application layer, generally with a software utility that encrypts a packet, or by implementing another protocol. IPv6 provides for authenticating the sender of a packet as well as encrypting the content of a packet. The immediate effect on the Internet will be reduction of denial-of-service attacks on web servers in which the attacker steals a legitimate IP address to launch the attack.

The address field in IPv6 anticipates that there will be certain global addresses assigned to routers and servers, particularly those connected to the Internet. When a message is sent to one of these devices, IPv6 will autoconfigure the address fields in the header.

As mentioned, the address field has been expanded to 128 bits. Within the address, certain bit patterns allow a packet to be directed to a single node or a group of nodes, or to be sent globally. This is radically different than with IPv4, which allows only target messages to a single node, or messages to be sent globally.

Quality of service is provided for in the IPv4 header but is rarely manipulated. Usually, the quality of service specifies that acknowledgements be sent back from the receiver. IPv6 has vastly expanded the quality options so that routers will better understand how to treat a received packet.

The options available with IPv6 may include instruction to the destination node, information concerning fragmentation of a packet, or information to routers that is examined at each hop the packet makes on its way to the destination. A router may not need to look at the options field at all. With IPv4, routers are required to examine any optional fields whether they affect the function of the router or not.

The header format for IPv6 is shown in Figure 5-13. The purpose of each field is:

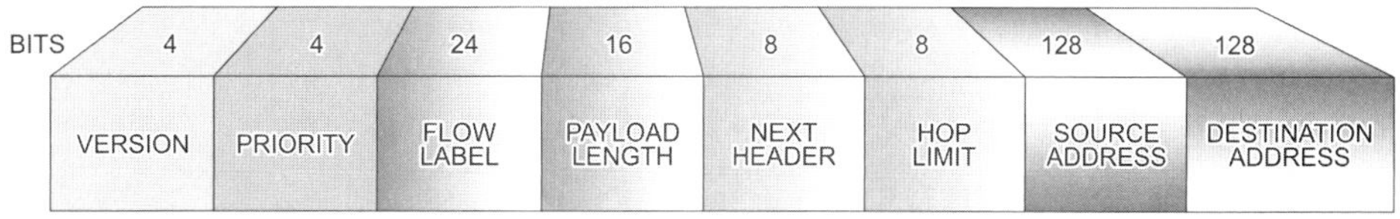

Figure 5-13:
IPv6 Header Format

- *Version:* 6

- *Priority:* This 4-bit field allows the source node of a packet to prioritize how to treat packets when the network is congested. Further, packets are divided between those that can be discarded and those that can't. Values 0 through 7 are designated for those packets that can't be discarded, such as HTTP requests or routing protocols. In this case, the packet may be delayed but not discarded. A value of 0 means that a packet has the lowest priority. Packets that can be discarded, such as streaming audio, are prioritized in the 8 through 15 range. For these packets, an audio message specified as high-fidelity would be a candidate for discarding while an audio packet with low fidelity would be specified with a 15 so that it would be least likely to be discarded.

- *Flow Label:* This field is used to communicate specific information on handling packets to routers. The flow label is a 24-bit, randomly generated number that flags the router to examine the header for special instructions. For example, the label may represent a specific route that the sender wants the packet to travel to the destination. A router may, in the future, cache the requirements and the flow label and treat future packets from the same source based upon the flow instructions without examining the instruction.

- *Payload Length:* Specifies the length of the packet in bytes following the IP header

- *Next Header:* Specifies the type of header immediately following the IP header

- *Hop Limit:* This 8-bit field is decremented by one at each router the packet passes through. If the counter reaches 0, it's discarded under the assumption that it's caught in a routing loop.

- *Source Address:* 128-bit address of the source node

- *Destination Address:* 128-bit address of the destination node

IPv6 allows an optional extension header to be placed between the IPv6 header and the transport layer header (TCP or UDP). Extensions available with IPv6 include fragmentation information, routing information, authentication, or destination options that are used by the destination node. Placing options outside the IP header means that routers won't examine them and improves on the efficiency of IPv4.

IPv6 allows for three types of addresses:

- *Unicast:* A unicast address specifies a single interface. IPv6 addresses are not node specific like IPv4. Instead, an IPv6 address is sent to a network interface. In the unicast address, the interface is a specific node.

- *Anycast:* An anycast address means that a message can be sent to more than one interface. For example, an anycast message may be sent to a group of routers or servers who have a common prefix address. In the typical case, the message will actually be received by the first interface, or the nearest interface.

- *Multicast:* A multicast address is the same as a broadcast used with IPv4. A broadcast is sent to a large number of nodes. In IPv6, a multicast is sent to a group of interfaces. The group can be defined to be node-specific, link-specific, site-specific, organizational-specific, or global, which means every machine connected to the Internet will receive the message (only routers are permitted to send global messages).

> NOTE
>
> IPv6 allows for three type of addresses: unicast, anycast, multicast.

Table 5-3: IPv6 Address Allocation

Allocation	Binary Prefix
Reserved for Testing	0000 0000
Reserved for NSAP Allocation	0000 0001
Reserved for IPX Allocation	0000 001
Provider-based Unicast Allocation	010
Link Local Addressing	1111 1110 10
Site Local Addressing	1111 1110 11
Multicast Addressing	1111 1111

The type of address is determined by the bit pattern at the beginning of the header. Table 5-3 lists the allocation of bits for the assigned addresses:

The NSAP is Network Service Access Point and is an Internet service provider. IPX is a protocol used with Novell NetWare networks, and combines a network address with the node MAC address. A Provider Unicast address refers to the address assigned to an Internet Service Provider, that is then assigned to subscribers of the ISP. This address is similar to the IP address currently assigned to each subscriber under IPv4. Since many ISP are ports to the Internet, they will have their own address. A Neutral Unicast address refers to a proprietary or private address such as those used on an intranet. A Link local address refers to an address specifying a node. It generally consists of a site local address and the 48-bit MAC address of the node. A site local address refers to a subnet of computers and is analogous to the network portion of an IPv4 address.

An anycast address may be assigned to more than one interface. It's not listed in the table because unicast address space is used for anycast addresses. The anycast address will specify more than one interface that is to receive the message. In order to distinguish the anycast message from a unicast message, the receiving nodes must be configured to receive anycast packets. The way this is done is through addressing in the packet. The address will likely describe the receivable nodes in terms of the topology they reside in. Since the nodes will have the same address stored, they will receive a message when it's sent.

Anycast messages are new and still experimental. Currently, it seems their greatest potential is for complex Internet routers.

IPv6 addresses are displayed a bit differently than IPv4 addresses. An IPv6 address is written using colon-hexadecimal form. A typical example of an IPv6 address is:

1080:BA56:1234:5678:8ABC:DEF1:74A2:89C1

Colons are used to separate eight groups of 16 bits represented in hexadecimal notation.

Since IPv6 addresses are so long, they may be abbreviated in one of two ways. Note that an address may contain long strings of 0's. To avoid confusion and errors when the address contains 0's it's permissible to show the 0's with a double colon as in:

1080:0:0:0:0:0:7435:BC67

1080::7453:BC67

Note that the compressed form of the address is easier to read. The double colon may only be used once when the address is compressed.

Another acceptable way to represent IPv6 addresses is similar to the notation used with CIDR. Recall that CIDR utilizes a convention in which the network portion of an address is indicated with a forward slash, as in 192.168.100.1/16. IPv6 makes use of this same convention when an address uses a fixed prefix. As an example:

1080:0:0:0:0:0:7435:BC67

If the first 96 bits represent the prefix, then the address may be written as:

1080:0:0:0:0:0:7435:BC67/96

Or, using compression, as:

1080::7453:BC67/96

IPv6 addressing schemes are compatible with IPv4 schemes. When a message that is IPv4-only is sent through a network infrastructure that uses IPv6, the IPv4 address is placed in the far-right bit space of the IPv6 address. For example:

IPv4 address is 192.168.100.1

may be placed in an IPv6 address as 1080:0:0:0:0:7435:192.168.100.1

Note that the higher order bits are in hexadecimal to total 96 bits, while the lower order bits are in dotted decimal to total 32 bits, for a total address length of 128 bits.

Conversely, if an IPv6 packet is sent through an IPv4-only infrastructure, the IPv6 header is encapsulated with an IPv4 header. The address in the above example would appear as:

IPv4	IPv6
192.168.100.1	1080:0:0:0:0:7435:192.168.100.1

Once the packet re-enters an IPv6 node, the IPv4 header at the beginning of the address will be stripped, leaving only the IPv6 header.

IPv6 is still in its infancy but appears to overcome the major obstacles and limitations of IPv4.

Private and Public Networks

Broadly speaking, a network may be described as a **public network**, or a **private network**. The terms refer to who can access the resources on a network. If anyone can access a network, it's a public network. An example of a public network is the Internet. But if access is limited, then only those with permission may access the network. An example of a private network is a corporate intranet. An easy method of controlling access is by assigning passwords, and this method is frequently used.

Another method used is by assigning public and private IP addresses. For example, a workstation that has been assigned the IP address 192.168.100.25 must be on a private network. Private IP addresses are rejected by routers on the Internet; hence, the workstation can't connect directly to the Internet—or directly utilize public interconnection facilities such as the long distance telephone carrier backbones.

If a workstation is assigned the IP address 200.50.125.34, it has been assigned a public IP address and, therefore, may be a part of a public network such as the Internet. All devices that directly connect to the Internet must have a public IP address.

For the purposes of the Network+ Exam, consider that a reference to public and private networks is a reference to using public and private IP addresses.

ADDRESS RESOLUTION PROTOCOL (ARP)

Address Resolution Protocol (ARP) is a TCP/IP protocol that maps the physical address of a node to the logical address. An IP address contains two addresses—a network address and a host address. The network address broadly describes where a node is located, and the host address specifically locates the node. Still, IP is a logical, and ephemeral, addressing scheme. The host potion of the IP address must be specifically linked to a machine. The technique used to make the link is to match the IP address to the MAC address of the machine NIC card. The technology used to make the link is ARP.

> Address Resolution Protocol (ARP) is a TCP/IP protocol that maps the physical address of a node to the logical address.

In addition to being a route determination protocol, ARP also includes attributes for using it as a tool for manually updating router tables. More is said about this aspect of ARP in Chapter 6.

An IP is a logical address used for locating a network. The host portion of the address has little value outside the local environment other than to specify the logical presence of a node on a LAN. If an address arrives at a router or gateway, the network and host portion will be compared to addresses in its table, and if a match is found, it will accept the packet.

Suppose the router is the base port to the Internet, and connects directly and indirectly to a thousand nodes on distributed LANs. How does it locate the node that matches the host address in the IP? If a node on the LAN wants to send a message to another node on the same LAN, how does the router know the recipient is on the same LAN? Or if the node wants to communicate with a node on a different LAN, how will the router know the difference?

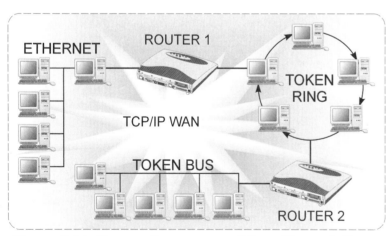

Figure 5-14: Routers Interconnect Many Network Types

First, a host must resolve the destination node's IP to a MAC address. It does so by using the Address Resolution Protocol (ARP). Let's look at a typical application of router IPs, shown in Figure 5-14. Two routers are being used to interconnect three LANs.

A router provides interconnections at the Network layer of the OSI model. As with a bridge, it looks closely at the data frames, and passes only those intended for other network segments, or those intended for entirely different networks. In this respect, the router is capable of conserving greater amounts of bandwidth than a bridge, because the bridge looks only as far as the MAC layer of level two. Bridges are "blind" to internetworking protocols; consequently, they're unable to filter between different networks.

A router is protocol-specific. It passes data packets between networks based upon routing information contained in the Network layer header.

Typically, the router will decide the best path for the packet to take, which may be the cheapest, or the one requiring the fewest hops between routers. This is a significant departure from a bridge, which maintains alternative paths for data frames. These fallback paths represent unused bandwidth, which must be maintained and paid for.

The primary disadvantage of a router is that the interconnect protocols must be the same. Examples of Internet protocols are TCP/IP, Novell's Internet Packet Exchange (IPX), Digital Equipment Corporation's DECnet, or the Xerox Network Service (XNS).

When used in a wide area network application, each router must be capable of supporting the specific Internet protocol being used, or be able to translate from one to another.

In Figure 5-14, the router interconnects data packets across a network running TCP/IP. The network consists of an Ethernet, a Token Ring, and a Token Bus LAN. Notice that the router allows computers on all three LANs to communicate, regardless of the topology and access protocols. The LAN hardware used with the computers may be from diverse vendors and operate at different bandwidths. The router, because it is basically concerned only with network addresses, is involved in a limited capacity at the Physical layer and the Data Link layer. This is why the LAN hardware, cabling medium, and access protocols may all be different, but yet the networks can still communicate.

The routing process for the three-LAN wide area network is shown in Figure 5-15. Assume that a PC on the Ethernet LAN sends a message to a PC on the remote Token Bus LAN. To the right are the MAC addresses of the IP packet, along with the IP addresses. The first two columns contain destination and source MAC addresses of the router, and the respective LAN nodes. Initially, the MAC source address is the address of the node on the Ethernet LAN, and the destination address is the MAC for router 1. When the frame arrives at the router, the physical addressing fields of the MAC frame are removed, leaving only the IP addresses, data (which includes upper layer headers such as TCP and IP), and CRC fields.

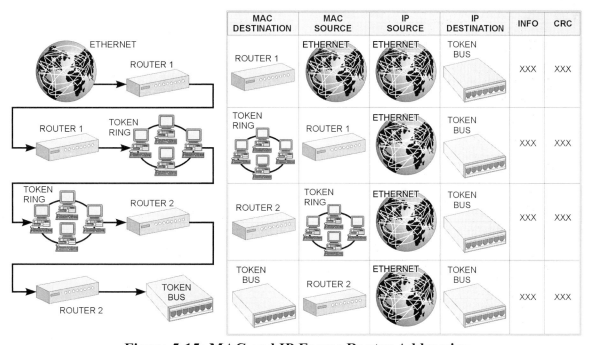

Figure 5-15: MAC and IP Frame Router Addressing

Notice that the IPs never change, because they are the only indication of where the frame is going as it moves from router to router. At each router hop, the router will compare its list of MAC addresses to the destination IP address. If no match exists, it will reframe the MAC addresses and pass the frame on.

Now router 1 reframes the message with new MAC address fields. Keep in mind that router 1 is now the source of the message, and the next destination is the Token Ring network. The ultimate destination PC is located on the Token Bus LAN, so the Token Ring LAN doesn't accept the message. Instead, it passes it on to the next router. Once again, the MAC address headers are stripped, and the data, IP address, and CRC fields reframed. This time, the source address is the Token Ring LAN, and the destination is router 2. Router 2 strips the MAC headers and reframes the message with the Token Bus LAN as the destination address, and router 2 as the source address. This is the final destination of the frame, so it doesn't go any further. The message is now delivered to the specific computer on the Token Bus network.

How does the message know where the computer is on the network? Recall that the OSI model is a peer-to-peer, hierarchical system. Each function of the upper layers of the model is appended to lower layer functions. This is reviewed in Figure 5-16. Headers from the upper layers of the model are encapsulated within the data field of the MAC frame. This is why the source and destination IPs don't change—they aren't affected by physical address changes.

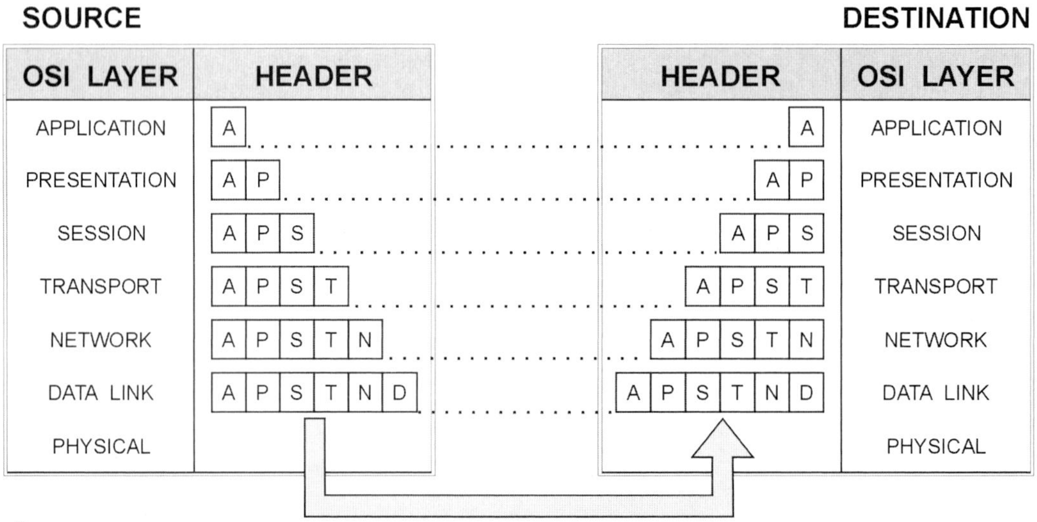

SOURCE   **DESTINATION**

Figure 5-16: Layers of the OSI Peer-to-Peer Relationship

Included in the information field are the 32-bit source and destination IP addresses. While the headers surrounding the Information field are stripped and reframed, the field itself remains intact, and is transmitted from network to network until the message arrives at the destination. Recall that it contains a specific network/host address, which is the destination network, as well as the logical address of the destination computer.

The physical and logical addresses now need to be resolved. That is, a mechanism is needed to allow a node to determine whether it can communicate directly to another node, or it requires the reframing services of a router in order to get a message to it. For example, if the Ethernet node sent a message to another node on its own LAN, it wouldn't have to use the router for stripping and appending the MAC layer addressing. It would simply send the message to the Ethernet destination. Only when the destination node is located on another network does the router have to be involved in determining the physical path.

Route Determination Logic (RDL)

First, a node has to decide if a destination is remote, or local. A local destination is defined as being within the same address space as the source. This includes any subnetted addresses. A remote destination is defined as being outside the network address space, including any subnetted addresses. This was the example just described. The destination was remote because the Ethernet node was unable to resolve the Token Ring IP address to its own network IP address.

> The process of determining whether a packet is to remain on the local network or is to be sent to another network is called **Route Determination Logic** (**RDL**).

Route Determination Logic uses the following algorithm:

(Destination IP AND Source Subnet Mask) = (Source IP AND Source IP Subnet Mask)

The AND in the equation indicates the logical AND operation. If the two operations result in the same value, it's assumed that both nodes reside on the same network, and the messages are sent directly. However, if the two values don't match, the destination is assumed to lie on a remote network, and the source node must utilize the look-up services of a router, or gateway, to determine the MAC address to place in its datagram.

Assume the existence of two networking nodes. Node 1, at IP 150.150.1.10, wants to send a message to Node 2, at IP 150.150.2.20, but doesn't know if it can do so directly. To find out, it performs route determination logic by first ANDing the IP of Node 1 with the subnet mask for Node 1, as shown in Table 5-4.

Decimal IP		150	150	1	10
Binary IP		10010110	10010110	00000001	00001010
Decimal Mask		255	255	0	0
Binary Mask		11111111	11111111	00000000	00000000
AND	Binary	10010110	10010110	00000000	00000000
Result	Decimal	150	150	0	0

Table 5-4: ANDing Node 1's IP and Subnet Mask

Next, the IP of Node 2 and the subnet mask of Node 1 are ANDed, as shown in Table 7-5.

Decimal IP		150	150	2	20
Binary IP		10010110	10010110	00000010	00010100
Decimal Mask		255	255	0	0
Binary Mask		11111111	11111111	00000000	00000000
AND	Binary	10010110	10010110	00000000	00000000
Result	Decimal	150	150	0	0

Table 5-5: ANDing Node 2's IP and Node 1's Subnet Mask

Since the ANDed results of both operations yield the same address, 150.150.0.0, Node 1 will assume they are on the same network, and send the message directly to Node 2. If they aren't the same, Node 1 will determine that Node 2 is on a remote network. It will first look up Node 2's MAC address in its address cache (located on the local server), and if it's found, ARP will cease, and Node 1 will add the Node 2 MAC address to its IP datagram and send the message directly to it. However, if the MAC address isn't in its cache, ARP continues, using one of several protocol implementations.

The ARP finds a specific network within a WAN, and dynamically maps logical addresses with physical addresses. This means that the router will match the Internet address contained in the Information field of the MAC header to the actual location of the computer. Implied in the protocol is the ability of the router to establish a path, perhaps composed of multiple links, to the destination network.

ARP Implementations

normal

proxy

reverse ARP

There are three types of ARP protocols: **normal**, **proxy**, and **reverse ARP**.

The three types are depicted in Figure 5-17. Station A wants to send data to B. To do so, A needs to know the local MAC address of B. The local MAC address is the actual address of the computer for station B. Remember, this is placed in the Information field of the Internet MAC frame. Station A sends an ARP, in the form of a MAC broadcast, requesting B's MAC address. Broadcasting on the Internet is a special address; the router must have broadcast capabilities to run ARP. The broadcast ARP is sent to all host networks on the Internet or wide area network.

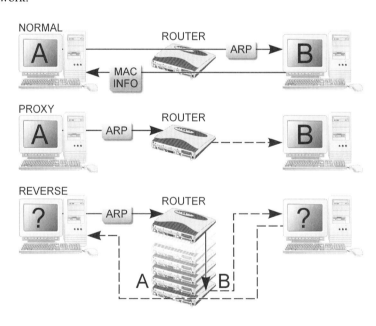

**Figure 5-17:
ARP Protocols**

When operating in the normal ARP mode, the router will forward the ARP through to station B, as shown in Figure 5-17. In response to the ARP, station B will send a frame back with its MAC information. The router forwards the B response, but with the router's MAC information added. This serves as an acknowledgment to station A that the B station has been located. A normal-type ARP guarantees the system that the destination will be available for message delivery.

In a proxy ARP, the router receives the ARP from station A. The router instead of station B responds to station A's ARP. In order to do so, the router has already mapped the logical, and physical, location of B. The advantage of a proxy ARP is that network traffic is reduced. The disadvantage is that there is no guarantee that station B will still be at the logical, and physical, location stored in the router map. By this time, it may have been moved and assigned a new address.

A third type of ARP is the Reverse Address Resolution Protocol (RARP). Once again, station A wants to transmit to station B, but the logical addresses of both A and B are unknown. This would mean that the two stations do not know their own Internet addresses. In such a situation, the router bridges the frames, passing them from router to router until the appropriate network accepts the broadcast and responds with the MAC containing the logical, and physical, address.

There are many academic and vendor proprietary routing protocols, but not all of them will route the common Internet protocols, such as TCP/IP. Due to the significant expense of routers, it is particularly important to evaluate the router against the specific parameters of the interconnected networks into which it will be installed.

A frequent question facing network administrators, when considering plans to expand a network or to interconnect remote networks is: Which is better, a bridge or a router?

A network using routers is more expensive, and specific to a given protocol. But a network using routers will utilize all of the communication paths. Since a network built with bridges does not process the Network layer protocols, it is cheaper, quicker, and supports multi-vendor equipment. However, a bridged system also includes stand-by links organized in a bridge topology, such as the Spanning Tree Algorithm Topology. While serving to reduce possible collisions, this arrangement also decreases the overall network efficiency.

Therefore, the final decision must be based on price/performance/functionality versus the actual communication costs.

FTP

FTP (File Transfer Protocol) is a means of downloading files to your computer or uploading them from your computer to an FTP site. Like e-mail, FTP retains a distinct structure, probably because it too was introduced early in the formation of the Internet. Probably the widest application of FTP is for downloading software or software enhancements. For example, many vendors have a download section at their web site. If you've bought a product from a vendor's web site in the past, you can use the site to download the latest revision of the software that's used in the product. Patches, upgrades, or fixes to problems are routinely posted at a company's download area.

> FTP (File Transfer Protocol) is a means of downloading files to your computer or uploading them from your computer to an FTP site

Older web browsers don't directly support FTP, but most include FTP software to initiate and control the download. Both Netscape and Internet Explorer allow you to download from a web site. For example, you can download the most current version of a software upgrade and save it to a file.

FTP is used for testing TCP/IP connections to determine accurate data rates across a wide area network. On a Windows 9x workstation, an FTP client is required, such as WS_FTP95. The usual method is to download a large (more than 100 kB) zipped file using the FTP client. Once the file has been downloaded, the number of bytes received divided by the duration time of the download provides an accurate data rate for the channel.

Note that downloading files using a web browser such as Netscape will introduce errors into data rate measurements since the browser is constantly updating graphical changes. Make sure the file is zipped, because modems routinely compress files—unless they've already been compressed.

FTP is assigned to well-known ports 20 or 21. When a web browser is configured on a workstation, the port is user configurable. You need to know the domain name of the FTP server you'll be using such as *ftp.server.com*. In a commercial network that connects users to the Internet, FTP access is typically filtered out; that is, it's not accessible to users without special permissions. The reason is that FTP offers no security. When enabled, it essentially becomes an open back door for intruders to enter the network.

Once you've requested and have been granted FTP access, you may find it's limited to only the remote FTP server that you requested. Most network administrators are very careful when approving requests for FTP access.

TFTP

Trivial File Transport Protocol (TFTP)

TFTP stands for **Trivial File Transport Protocol**. TFTP is a simplified version of FTP. TFTP provides no security in the form of password prompts. Essentially, it's even less secure than FTP.

> TFTP is a simplified version of FTP. TFTP provides no security in the form of password prompts.

The best use of TFTP is to utilize it with UDP for the purpose of initializing hardware on dedicated terminals of diskless workstations.

SMTP

Electronic mail (e-mail) is a staple of the Internet. E-mail is a quick and reliable method of sending messages. In addition to a basic text message, e-mail includes provisions for attaching nearly any file type to an message so that graphics, sound files, or video files can be easily sent to individualized recipients.

> The protocol that defines e-mail is called the **Simple Mail Transport Protocol**, or **SMTP**.

Before you can send or receive e-mail, you must have access to a server running the SMTP protocol. The client workstation connected to the mail server must have access to the e-mail server that runs SMTP.

Figure 5-18 shows a typical e-mail screen with headers completed. This is typical of most e-mail software. You're required to insert the recipient's e-mail address, and in some packages include a subject. The message text is entered in the body of the message and is in ASCII format.

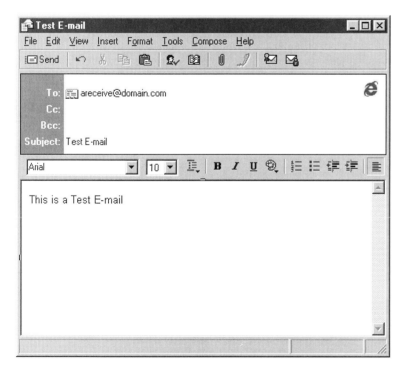

Figure 5-18: Typical E-mail Screen

Notice the format of the sender and receiver names. The user name comes before the @ symbol and usually represents the name of the individual or business holding the e-mail account. The domain names of the computer where the e-mail account is maintained are placed after the @ symbol. When an e-mail is sent, it's first uploaded into an e-mail server. (E-mail, as it's organized on most networks, follows a client-server arrangement with the sender acting as client and the receiver acting as server.) The local server will query domain name servers (DNS) to resolve the receiver's address. Once this is done, the server contacts the remote server that holds the receiver's account and notifies it of a message.

The two servers engage in a bit of handshaking that follows the following format:

(1) Sender sends TCP connection established, and the receiver responds with a receiver ready message.

(2) Sender sends a HELLO (Hello) command.

(3) Receiver responds with an acknowledgment that includes its domain name.

(4) Sender compares the received domain name to the name in the To: field of the message.

(5) Sender sends TCP connection established, and the receiver responds with a receiver ready message.

(6) The receiver responds with an OK.

(7) There may be more than one recipient of a message, and the sender will now notify the receiver of all recipients one by one. The receiver will determine that all receivers are valid and send back an OK.

(8) Sender sends a DATA command, which is used to tell the receiver that the body of the message will be sent next.

(9) Receiver responds with a start mail input.

(10) The sender sends the message line by line.

(11) The receiver sends an OK for each line received.

(12) Once all lines are sent, the sender sends a QUIT command to terminate the session.

(13) The receiver responds with a service closing transmission channel command.

The receiver may have messages of its own to send and if it does, the roles of the two servers will swap and the forging (beginning with step 5) will be repeated.

If you had a constant connection to the Internet, SMTP would be all that's needed to send and receive e-mail. If you can't send e-mail, the first place to look is to see if you have a valid connection to a server that runs SMTP.

But most of us don't have a continuous connection, even when the connection is through a network; there are times when we disconnect from the Internet. If, during one of those times, an e-mail is received, we wouldn't be able to receive it because our end of the SMTP handshaking process would be turned off.

To overcome this disadvantage, SMTP includes a protocol that allows e-mail to be held at a SMTP server and downloaded to a client at some other time. The protocol is called POP3.

NOTE

If you can't send e-mail, the first place to look is to see if you have a valid connection to a server that runs SMTP.

POP3 AND IMAP4

The protocol used to handle e-mail reception is called **Post Office Protocol v.3**, or POP3. (There are earlier versions of POP but they aren't compatible with version 3, and shouldn't be used.)

POP3 mimics the SMTP end of an e-mail dialogue and stores the received message until you ask to retrieve it. POP3 is a client-side protocol that must be installed on the workstation in order for e-mail to be downloaded to the client. That way, your e-mail is automatic and continues to be received when you're not around to handle it yourself, or when you're not connected to the Internet.

A client e-mail package such as Eudora, Lotus Notes cc:mail, or Microsoft Outlook Express contains a POP3 e-mail client that conforms to the SMTP protocol.

A drawback of the POP3 protocol is that it's best suited when e-mail is accessed from one computer. If you use a notebook computer, you can take your computer wherever you go. But if you are in a situation where you use different computers, your e-mail is likely to be spread around several machines.

To overcome this disadvantage, the **Internet Access Message Protocol** (**IMAP**, currently at version 4) was developed at Stanford University.

IMAP4 allows you to download e-mail at any time using any machine.

Post Office Protocol v.3 (POP3)

Internet Access Message Protocol (IMAP)

The intent of IMAP4 is to:

- Be compatible with Internet messaging standards such as MIME
- Allow message access and management from more than one computer
- Provide for support to concurrent access to shared mailboxes
- Allow the type of server file format to be transparent to the client software

In short, IMAP4 allows you to download e-mail at any time using any machine. Typically, use of IMAP4 is limited to Internet e-mail such as Hot Mail accounts. Gradually, the standard is expected to be widely deployed on desktop operating systems.

HTTP

HTTP, or **Hypertext Transfer Protocol**, is a client-server protocol used to send and receive files on the Internet.

A client is any network workstation that sends a request to a web server. A client may be a stand-alone computer connected to the Internet through an ISP, or it may be a workstation on a network that is connected to the Internet through an ISP. Nearly any file type can be sent using HTTP. Most Internet applications on the World Wide Web use HTTP.

HTTP consists of a request-response process. This means that a client will initiate a request to a server for files contained at the server, and the server will respond to the request by sending the files. Let's look at an example.

Before the client can send a request, it must be running the HTTP protocol. HTTP is packaged will all web browsers and is the default protocol with browsers such as Internet Explorer and Netscape. When HTTP is initiated from a workstation, the HTTP application is started at a remote server. HTTP applications are stipulated in the protocol by specifying the well-known port number 80.

From the client side, the user interaction with HTTP is straightforward. In the address windows of the browser, HTTP is entered along with the domain name of the server and, optionally, the path to the requested resource. A typical client-side request may appear in the web browser address window as:

http://internet.com/file.htm

When the user enters the request, the domain name is resolved to an IP address and the site *internet.com* is found.

At the *internet.com* site, the HTTP server will respond to the request. Depending on the HTTP server software, the response may vary somewhat, but the following server response steps are accurate for most web servers:

- *Authorization Translation:* The server will verify that the request is from an authorized source if necessary. For public Internet sites, a password and username aren't required, so this step is skipped. But for many intranet sites, a valid username and password are required before access is granted. If the site is password-protected, the server will check the username and password to determine whether they are valid before processing the request.

- *Name Translation:* The server translates the requested resource into a local file path. The resource is called a Uniform Resource Identifier (URI) and consists of the portion of a URL following the domain name. For example, when a user enters *www.internet.com/file.htm*, file.htm is the URI.

- *Path check:* Once the URI is converted into a local path, the server will check that the requested resource is valid, and that the requestor (the client-side user) is authorized to receive the file. This step is necessary because documents on an HTTP server are extensively linked. The URI file.htm may actually consist of many linked files, all of which will be returned to the client computer. Before sending the file, the server will ensure that the user is authorized for all of the files. The user may be authorized to receive some of the files, but not all of them, in which case the server will send only those files that the user is authorized to receive.

- *Object Type:* The server will next determine the type of file that's to be sent using MIME, which is Multi-Purpose Internet Mail Encoding. MIME is a protocol used to standardize file extensions so that if a web server has a file called file.htm, the client computer will know that the file will be displayed using HTML. Or, if a file is called file.jpg, the client web browser will know to display the file as a graphic using the JPG standard.

- *Response:* The server will send the requested file to the client computer.

- *Log:* Once the file is sent, the server will record the transaction in a log file. Web server logs may be as simple as a brief entry that notes the time of the transaction, the outcome of the request, and the size of the request. Or they may be extensively logged to track usernames, record any errors that were generated, or the amount of time that the server was occupied while responding to the request.

A web server may not be able to respond to a client request. The requestor may not be authorized to receive the resource, the server may not be able to translate the request to a local file path, or the path to the requested file may not be valid. If any steps of the response process fail, the server should still send a response back to the client indicating that the request couldn't be completed.

HTTPS

HTTPS is a secure version of HTTP.

HTTPS is a subset of HTTP and stands for **Hypertext Transfer Protocol Secure**. Except for the initial setup of the connection to a server, HTTP files are sent in a manner that's exactly as described in the HTTP section.

The difference lies in the initial setup between the client workstation and the server. HTTPS uses a protocol called Secure Socket Layer (SSL). SSL was invented so that credit card purchases made over the Internet would be safe and without fraud. SSL is detailed in Chapter 7. Essentially, SSL requires that both sides of a connection be authenticated (that is, they are who they say they are), and that data be encrypted and decrypted.

HTTPS, which has been assigned the well-known port 443, initiates a secure process during the Session layer handshaking of TCP. When the 443 SSL process is started, authentication occurs by examining certificates that each side possesses (when credit cards are used). If the certificates are deemed to be valid and haven't been tampered with, the 443 socket is opened.

Hypertext Transfer
Protocol Secure
(HTTPS)

TEST TIP

Know that HTTPS is the secure version of HTTP.

Once the socket is open, data will begin moving back and forth between the two stations along with the HTTP requests. The data will be encrypted when it leaves a sending station, then decrypted when it arrives at the receiving station.

HTTPS is a very secure protocol and is widely used on the Internet.

TELNET

Telnet is a service that allows you to "telephone-net" into another computer so that you can utilize its resources.

Telnet includes a command-line interface similar to a DOS-based system. Most web browsers do not include a client for Telnet access. Most operating systems include a utility that allows you to launch Telnet from a DOS shell (for Windows) by entering telnet at the command prompt. For other operating systems, a terminal emulator may be needed along with a telnet client. A terminal emulator is a software package that allows a terminal to mimic another terminal type.

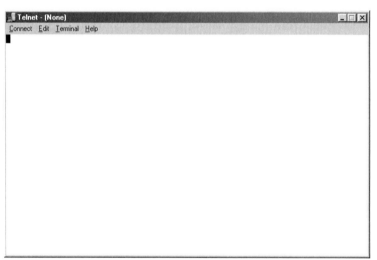

Figure 5-19: Telnet Screen

Figure 5-19 shows a Telnet screen launched from a Windows 98 workstation. With the Telnet service running, you can now connect to a Telnet host. The host can be specified by choosing Remote System from the Connect drop-down menu. Figure 5-20 shows the host name dialog box.

Telnet allows a user at a remote computer to connect to a remote server. The computer doesn't have to be running the same operating system as the remote server. This is an ideal situation for a PC-to-mainframe connection since the PC will have a radically different operating system than the mainframe.

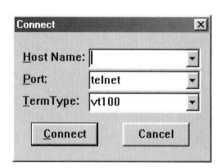

Figure 5-20: Telnet Host Dialog Box

ICMP

ICMP, or **Internet Control Message Protocol**, is a TCP/IP protocol used to deliver network operation messages.

Internet Control
Message Protocol
(ICMP)

This includes the announcement of errors on the network, of congestion that would slow delivery of messages, of timeouts when the TTL filed in an IP packet expires, and for troubleshooting.

The Ping utility, used to test for connectivity to remote devices, is an ICMP message.

ICMP messages are identified by type. Table 5-6 lists a sample of types and their explanation.

Type	Type Name
0	Echo Reply
3	Destination Unreachable
5	Redirect
11	Time Exceeded
37	Domain Name Request

Table 5-6: ICMP Types

NTP

NTP, or **Network Time Protocol**, is a TCP/IP protocol used to synchronize the clocks of servers that use or are connected to the Internet.

Network Time
Protocol (NTP)

NTP attempts to establish a reference time that all computers will use. Currently, the protocol is accurate to within a nanosecond.

The correct time is important, particularly for e-commerce web sites. Imagine a scenario in which a customer makes a purchase with a credit card on a commercial site, but due to time differences, the purchase was paid for before the purchase was made.

NTP makes use of a number of top-level NTP servers. The NTP servers are sources of time and are used as a reference from which other servers determine the correct time. In the event that there are differences in the time between servers, NTP will combine the time from several servers and determine the best estimate of the time. As mentioned, NTP is very accurate. It can even determine the correct time if a server is taken down for some reason. The correct time can be recreated using past estimates and accounting for the time that the server is down.

NTP is supported by most versions of UNIX, Windows 2000 and XP, and Windows 4.0 as a downloaded plug-in.

IPX/SPX

IPX/SPX (Internetwork Packet Exchange/ Sequence Packet Exchange) is a proprietary networking protocol developed by Novell for their NetWare network operating system.

The IPX/SPX suite of protocols serves the same function as TCP/IP—it permits data packets to be reliably sent across networks.

SPX is responsible for initiating connections between nodes and guaranteeing the delivery of packets. When a node wants to connect to another, a socket is set up between the two devices using SPX. Since SPX provides for reliable, guaranteed delivery of packets, it requires that the destination node send acknowledgements for packets received. Optionally, up to eight packets may be sent from a source before an acknowledgement is expected. SPX provides sequencing numbers to strings of packets so that the destination node can interpret the packets in the correct order. If any packets in the sequence are missing, the source node will not receive an acknowledgement that the packet was received and will resend the missing packet.

IPX is responsible for determining a route to the destination station, and carries logical addresses. Like IP, IPX is a connectionless, unreliable protocol that relies on a Transport layer protocol for reliability and to open sessions between devices. IPX uses the Novell Transport layer protocol **SPX (Sequenced Packet Exchange)**. Together, the two protocols are called the IPX/SPX suite of protocols.

IPX packets can be routed when associated with SPX.

The header format for an IPX packet is shown in Figure 5-21.

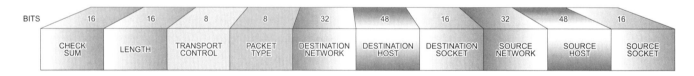

Figure 5-21: IPX Header Format

The purpose of the header fields are as follows:

- *Checksum:* 16-bit field used for error checking. By default, this is a dummy checksum that is set to hexadecimal FFFF.

- *Packet Length:* Specifies the length of the complete IPX packet in bytes

- *Transport Control:* This field is a counter that shows the number of routers that the packet has passed through. When the count reaches 16, the packet is discarded under the assumption that the router believes the packet to be lost in a route loop.

- *Packet type:* The upper layer protocol services. Typically, this is special.

- *Destination Network, Node, Socket:* The destination address of the receiving device

- *Source Network, Node, Socket:* The address of the device that is the source of the packet

- *Upper-layer Information:* Data intended for upper-layer protocols

The address fielding of an IPX header is a total of 80 bits and includes a network address and a node address. The address is subdivided as:

Network address: 32 bits

Node address: 48 bits

> The address fielding an IPX header is a total of 80 bits and includes a network address and a node address.

When used in an intranet (with no connection to the Internet), the network address is assigned by the network administrator. The node address is usually the MAC address on the device's NIC card. A typical IPX address may appear as:

000000B6:00-06-80-11-CA

Note that the usual convention when writing an IPX address is to separate the network address from the node address by a colon. All IPX addresses must be unique on the network. This is the reason that MAC addresses are usually used for the node address. The network address can be any unique address assigned by the network administrator. One technique used in many NetWare networks is to convert an assigned IP address to its hexadecimal equivalent and use this number as the network address. This practice ensures that the network addresses will also be unique.

IPX is frequently sent on a TCP/IP network and delivered to another network that uses IPX. The way that this is done is to encapsulate the IPX header in an IP frame. The IP frame will have 32-bit source and destination addresses (for IPv4) and will be treated as any other IP packet.

Once the frame arrives at the destination node, the IP headers are stripped and the frame operated upon in the NetWare network using the IPV network and node addresses.

APPLETALK

> **AppleTalk** is the networking protocol used with Apple Macintosh operating systems.

AppleTalk

All Macintosh computers ship with AppleTalk. Unlike IP or IPX, AppleTalk provides far more user-type services such as naming of network devices, and file and printer sharing. AppleTalk is a complete suite of networking protocols and consists of the following:

- *DDP:* The Datagram Delivery Protocol is a Network layer protocol that is analogous to IP.

- *ADSP:* AppleTalk Data Stream Protocol is a Session layer-type protocol that is responsible for end-to-end dialog between stations. It shares characteristics of TCP.

- *ATP:* The AppleTalk Transaction Protocol is used to transport instructions and packets over the network. It shares characteristics of TCP.

- *NBP:* The Name Binding Protocol is a protocol that maps computer (or server) names to AppleTalk addresses.

The basic AppleTalk address is 24 bits long and consists of a network number and a node ID. An example of the address is:

10.8

Where 10 is the decimal value of the network number, and 8 is the decimal value of the node ID. Notice that the syntax used with AppleTalk is to use a decimal point to separate the network number and the node number. All physical devices connected to an AppleTalk network have an address similar to the example shown.

> The basic AppleTalk address is 24 bits long and consists of a network number and a node ID.

AppleTalk devices may also be named in the same manner that computers and servers on a Windows-based network are named using NetBIOS names. As with Windows, the naming convention used with AppleTalk is for the convenience of humans; all devices still must have a network number and node ID.

AppleTalk is fully routable between different networks. Like IPX, the AppleTalk frames must be encapsulated into an IP frame.

NETBEUI

> **NetBEUI, NetBIOS Extended User Interface**, is a Network layer protocol used on all Windows platforms.

NetBEUI originates from NetBIOS, the communication software developed by IBM that lets computers communicate on a network. For the most part, NetBEUI contains Session and Application layer functions but fails to provide for the addressing needed at the Network layer.

NetBEUI addresses are in the form of "computer names." NetBEUI was added to the NetBIOS software specifically to provide an addressing mechanism that would be easy to set up and run efficiently on small to medium size LANs. It has performed very well over the years and, for small Windows networks, is preferable over more intense network protocols such as TCP/IP.

Early consumer versions of the Windows operating system did not recognize or use DNS domain names. Instead, they employed a proprietary NetBIOS naming convention that worked with Microsoft networks. This naming system allowed names of 15 characters or less and could not handle any spaces or special characters. When Microsoft began actively pursuing Internet connectivity, it added DNS services to its operating systems.

With NetBEUI, devices on a network are assigned names. Transparent to users on the network, the computer name is mapped to the MAC address of the unit. All names must be unique on a NetBEUI LAN, as all MAC addresses are unique.

NetBEUI constantly searches for new computers that have been added to or taken off the network. It does so by sending broadcast packets across the network. All nodes on a NetBEUI LAN broadcast frequent messages, as well as reply to messages directed to them. The extensive use of broadcast messages with NetBEUI has a tendency to slow down network traffic. This is the primary reason why NetBEUI is size limited and is recommended for small to medium LANs.

Unlike TCP/IP, IPX, and AppleTalk, NetBEUI is not a routable protocol. This means that a packet from a NetBEUI LAN can't be sent through a router to another LAN. The simple name addressing scheme prevents the packets from being routed.

There is one exception to this—a virtual private network (VPN) allows NetBEUI packets to be sent over the Internet once they are encapsulated in an IP header. But for the purposes of the Network+ Exam, consider NetBEUI to be a nonroutable protocol.

> **TEST TIP**
> For all protocols in the chapter associated with the Network layer, be able to state which ones can be routed, and which ones cannot be routed.

> **TEST TIP**
> Remember that NetBIOS commonly uses names made up of 15 characters or less and cannot contain any special characters.

KEY POINTS REVIEW

This chapter has presented an extensive exploration of network protocols.

- An interconnected network is a system of interconnected terminals, or local networks, spread over large area.

- TCP/IP is a widely used, internetworking protocol that is nonproprietary. It is based on a 32-bit addressing scheme, and is the IP used on the Internet.

- TCP uses a software abstract called a socket to communicate processes.

- A port is the service that stations will be using once a socket is set up. Ports are numbered and are referred to as well-known ports.

- Fragmentation results when datagrams are separated to accommodate the frame lengths of networks through which they pass enoute to the destination.

- UDP is a streamlined implementation of TCP.

- IP is a best-effort, unreliable, connectionless protocol.

- The Time-To-Live field in an IP header sets a limit on the time the network is allowed to deliver the datagram.

- IP address classes A, B, and C differentiate in the numbers of networks and host addresses being utilized by a specific organization.

- As a matter of numerical interest, the leftmost byte, or number, of a class-A network is numbered 1 through 126. Class-B networks are numbered 128 through 191, and class-C networks are numbered 192 through 223.

- The Internet address system is separated into five classes that specify the numbers of networks and hosts. The address follows the Decimal Dotted Notation procedure for grouping addresses.

- Any IP address beginning with 127 is an invalid address.

- An IP subnet is used to separate the network portion from the host portion of an IP address.

- The decimal 255 is used to mask the network portion of an IP and only leave open the host portion.

- A class-A IP address has a default subnet mask of 255.0.0.0.

- A class-B IP address has a default subnet mask of 255.255.0.0.

- A class-C IP address has a default subnet mask of 255.255.255.0.

- CIDR is intended to accomplish two primary goals: To reduce the current reliance on a classful system and to support route aggregation where a single network address can be used to represent the addresses of thousands of hosts.

- IP version 6, also called IP Next Generation (IPng), improves upon IPv4 by extending the address fields in the IP header from 32 bits to 128 bits.

- IPv6 allows for three type of address: unicast, anycast, and multicast.

- Address Resolution Protocol (ARP) is a TCP/IP protocol that maps the physical address of a node to the logical address.

- The process of determining whether a packet is to remain on the local network, or is to be sent to another network is called Route Determination Logic (RDL).

- Advance Resolution Protocol is a router protocol that maps the physical address of a node to the logical address.

- There are three types of ARP protocols: normal, proxy, and reverse ARP.

- FTP (File Transfer Protocol) is a means of downloading files to your computer or uploading them from your computer to an FTP site

- TFTP is a simplified version of FTP. TFTP provides no security in the form of password prompts.

- The protocol that defines e-mail is called the Simple Mail Transport Protocol, or SMTP.

- The protocol used to handle e-mail reception is called Post Office Protocol v.3, or POP3.

- IMAP4 allows you to download e-mail at any time using any machine.

- HTTP, or Hypertext Transfer Protocol, is a client-server protocol used to send and receive files on the Internet.

- HTTPS is a secure version of HTTP.

- Telnet is a service that allows you to "telephone-net" into another computer so that you can utilize its resources.

- ICMP, or Internet Control Message Protocol, is a TCP/IP protocol used to deliver network operation messages.

- NTP, or Network Time Protocol, is a TCP/IP protocol used to synchronize the clocks of servers that use or are connected to the Internet.

- IPX/SPX (Internetwork Packet Exchange/ Sequence Packet Exchange) is a proprietary networking protocol developed by Novell for their NetWare network operating system.

- SPX is responsible for initiating connections between nodes and guaranteeing the delivery of packets.

- IPX is responsible for determining a route to the destination station, and carries logical addresses.

- The address fielding of an IPX header is a total of 80 bits and includes a network address and a node address.

- AppleTalk is the networking protocol used with Apple Macintosh operating systems.

- The basic AppleTalk address is 24 bits long and consists of a network number and a node ID.

- NetBEUI, NetBIOS Extended User Interface, is a Network layer protocol used on all Windows platforms.

- NetBEUI addresses are in the form of "computer names."

At this point, review the objectives listed at the beginning of the chapter to be certain that you understand and can perform them. Afterward, answer the review questions that follow to verify your knowledge of the information.

REVIEW QUESTIONS

The following questions test your knowledge of the material presented in this chapter:

1. What is a socket?

2. What is a well-known port?

3. What is UDP?

4. Why is IP described as unreliable?

5. The length of an IPv4 address field is _____ bits.

6. What is the purpose of the TTL field in an IP header?

7. An IPv4 address that has 23 for the leftmost byte is a class ____ address.

8. What is the IP address 127.0.0.1 used for?

9. What is the purpose of a subnet?

10. What is the default subnet mask for a class-B IP address?

11. How does a router determine whether a message is destined for a location outside the local network?

12. How many bits are in the address field of an IPv6 header?

13. What is an IPv6 unicast address?

14. Describe the procedure for locating a destination node by using the broadcast ARP.

15. How many bits are in each address field of an IPX header?

EXAM QUESTIONS

1. The time-to-live field in the TCP/IP header is used to _____.
   a. specify the time that a datagram may remain on the network
   b. specify the time of data bits
   c. specify the time before each network reconfiguration
   d. specify the end of a frame

2. Convert the following Class-B TCP/IP address to a base ten number:
   10000110.10001101.01001010.00010111
   a. 23.74.141.134
   b. 74.134.23.141
   c. 134.141.74.23
   d. 141.23.134.74

3. How is a subnetwork identified using TCP/IP?
   a. by the binary number 10101010
   b. by the decimal number 255.255.255
   c. by the decimal number 127.127
   d. by the binary number 1010.101010

4. When a router uses a normal ARP _____.
   a. the destination station responds to the arp
   b. the router defaults to a bridge
   c. the router provides the destination address to the requestor
   d. a request for a station's address is sent to all network hosts

5. Which of the following network addresses represent an IPv6 address:
   a. 10.234.100.1
   b. 45:A5:92:C2:65:AD
   c. 000000B6:00-06-80-11-CA
   d. 1080::7453:BC67

6. Which of the following is the correct subnet mask to use for an IPv4 Class-C IP address:
   a. 255
   b. 255.255
   c. 255.255.255
   d. 255.255.255.255

7. Which of the following includes authentication and encryption for transferring files over the Internet?
   a. TFTP
   b. HTTPS
   c. Telnet
   d. ICMP

8. Which of the following is commonly used to deliver messages to nodes concerning the operation of the network?
   a. FTP
   b. ICMP
   c. ARP
   d. NTP

9. The protocol used to synchronize time on computers connected to the Internet is _____.
   a. SMTP
   b. POP3
   c. IMAP4
   d. NTP

10. What is the well-known port number used for FTP?
    a. 21
    b. 80
    c. 445
    d. 34

CHAPTER

6

TCP/IP UTILITIES

LEARNING
OBJECTIVES

Upon completion of this chapter and its related lab procedures, you will be able to perform the following tasks:

1. Given a troubleshooting scenario, select the appropriate TCP/IP utility from among the following:

   - Tracert

   - Ping

   - ARP

   - Netstat

   - Nbstat

   - Ipconfig

   - WinIPcfg

   - Nslookup

CHAPTER 8

TCP/IP UTILITIES

INTRODUCTION

TCP/IP comes equipped with a variety of tools that can be used to provide a considerable amount of information about your computer, its place in a network, and other devices you're connected to. You might not have access to all the utilities mentioned in this section. Which ones you can access depends on the utilities that were bundled in your network or desktop operating system. The most common tools are discussed, along with instructions for using them.

The utility commands are entered from a DOS shell using a command prompt. You can determine which utilities are installed on a Windows 9x or Windows NT/2000 station by looking in the Program files. Many of these tools are used primarily for checking wide area connections—that is, connections to the Internet or between intranets.

To use a tool from a Windows client, navigate the *Start/Programs/Accessories/Command Prompt* path. At the C: prompt (or its equivalent), enter the command as described in this chapter for the desired tool.

ADDRESS RESOLUTION PROTOCOL (ARP)

> **Address Resolution Protocol (ARP)** is a tool used to map IP addresses to physical MAC addresses.

Address Resolution Protocol (ARP)

Not only is it a tool available for use in troubleshooting, ARP is routinely used between routers to resolve addresses (see Chapter 5 for in-depth information on the route determination capabilities of ARP). At the LAN and client level, the resolution maps are contained in clients or servers and include physical and logical addresses for machines.

ARP is a useful tool for examining the contents of ARP caches on either the client or server station.

To use ARP, type:

arp

Your screen will show the commands available for use with ARP, as shown in Figure 6-1.

Figure 6-1: Commands Available with the ARP Utility

At the command prompt, enter:

arp -a

You should see information similar to that shown in Figure 6-2. Notice that multiple listings are shown. These detail all the computer's connections.

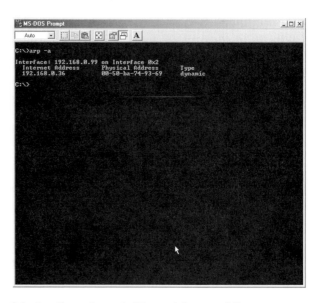

Figure 6-2: Results of the arp -a Command

The meanings of the headings shown in Figure 6-2 are as follows:

- *Interface* is the IP of the machine running the ARP utility.

- *Internet Address* is the address of a server that the machine is connected to.

- *Physical Address* is the Data Link layer physical MAC address of the local machine.

- *Type* is the type of connection from local machine to server. It may be dynamic or static.

In addition to querying the ARP cache, you may add entries to it with the -s command or delete entries from it with the -d command. (The reference to "commands" used with these utilities is somewhat misleading. UNIX calls them "switches.")

IPCONFIG AND WINIPCFG

Ipconfig is a utility that provides addressing information for the workstation where the utility is entered.

At the command prompt, enter:

ipconfig /all

As you can see in Figure 6-3, you can easily determine a workstation's physical MAC address, IP address, and subnet mask by using this utility. In addition, all other adapter cards to which the workstation is currently connected are listed.

Ethernet adapter	:
Description	: Compex RL2000 PCI Ethernet Adapter
Physical Address	: 00-80-48-C5-2A-BE
DHCP Enabled	: No
IP Address	: 192.168.20.2
Subnet Mask	: 255.255.255.0
Default Gateway	:
Primary WINS Server	:
Secondary WINS Server	:
Lease Obtained	:
Lease Expires	:

Figure 6-3: Sample of the TCP/IP Utility Ipconfig

For a quick overview of the configuration, enter:

Ipconfig

┌─ TEST TIP ─────────────────
│ Know that to learn the MAC address of a
│ workstation, ipconfig is used.
└────────────────────────────

This returns the same information as just described but in abbreviated form. Figure 6-4 shows an example of the results from entering ipconfig.

Figure 6-4: The Ipconfig Utility

Winipcfg is used to determine addressing information on a Windows 95 workstation.

Figure 6-5: Winipcfg Utility

At the command prompt of the Windows 95 workstation, enter:

winipcfg

An example of winipcfg is shown in Figure 6-5. The information that is returned is similar to the information returned when entering ipconfig.

While Windows 9x and Windows 2000 use the ipconfig command to view the configuration of the network (including the IP adddresses), the UNIX and Linux platforms use the ifconfig utility for this purpose. Likewise, NetWare uses the config command to obtain information about network addresses.

NBTSTAT

The **nbtstat** utility (NetBIOS over a TCP connection) is used with Windows machines to provide NetBIOS name information about the remote connection.

When entered, it shows information about workstation NetBIOS names and their corresponding IP addresses. In addition, nbtstat can be used to determine the status of a remote connection—whether it's active or not.

From the system prompt, type:

nbtstat

The screen will fill with commands available with the tool.

At the command prompt, type:

nbtstat -n

This command is used to show the NetBIOS name of the workstation where the command is entered. Notice in Figure 6-6 that it also includes the workstation's IP address.

C:\WINDOWS>nbtstat -n
Node IP Address: [192.168.20.2] Scope Id: [ ]

NetBIOS Local Name Table

Name	Type	Status
NET_PLUS	Unique	Registered
WORKGROUP	Group	Registered
NET_PLUS	Unique	Registered
NET_PLUS	Unique	Registered
WORKGROUP <1E>	Group	Registered
WORKGROUP	Unique	Registered
MSBROWSE	Group	Registered
JRATLIFF	Unique	Registered

Figure 6-6: The TCP/IP Utility Nbtstat –n

Using the -c switch with the nbstat command will display all the addresses that have been resolved by the system. This will enable you to view the list of NetBIOS names and their associated IP addresses that have been resolved.

TEST TIP

Know which command can be used to view listings of NetBIOS names that have been resolved by the system.

NETSTAT

Netstat is a tool used to display all current Network layer connections.

Netstat

This means you'll see TCP/IP or UDP protocols that are active at the time the tool is used. Netstat lists the network connections. To display a list of all the options available with the netstat command, type the following at the command prompt:

Netstat /?

TEST TIP

Be aware that Route and Netstat can be used to view the routing tables in Windows systems.

From the list, you can see that using an -r switch will display a listing of the contents of the routing table for all the connections on the server that your machine is connected to. The Route command can also be used to perform this function. (It also shows which connections are active at the time the utility is run.) At the command prompt, type:

netstat -r

TEST TIP

Know that the -r switch is used with netstat to display all connections.

Another interesting application of netstat is to view statistics related to the interface of your machine to the network. At the command prompt, type:

netstat -e

You will see the number of bytes received and transmitted, the type of packets, and, of particular interest, the number of errors generated. An example of netstat -e is shown in Figure 6-7.

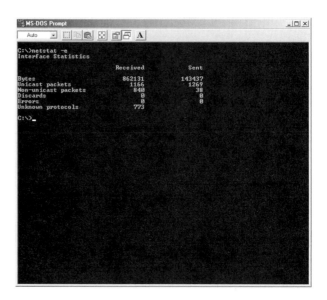

**Figure 6-7:
Netstat Provides
Statistical Information**

For example, suppose you suspect that a client has a faulty network interface card. Using netstat -e, you can find out how many errors occurred at the client.

Adding a number to the end of the netstat -e command is optional. For example, adding 5 to the end of the command will update the listing every 5 seconds.

PING

Ping is used to check connectivity between two networked devices.

Ping sends an echo packet to a specified address; the packet is returned to your machine if the specified address is active. If the address isn't active, you receive a message stating that the transaction has timed out. The effect of the ping tool is similar to measuring continuity with an ohm meter. It checks to see if two network devices are connected.

To initiate ping, enter:

ping

The screen will list all the commands used with the tool. At the command prompt, type:

ping xxx.xxx.xxx.xxx

where xxx.xxx.xxx.xxx is the IP address of the server you're connected to. As you can see from the reply, the connection from your machine to the server is working. Now try pinging an IP address that is unknown to your network. At the command prompt, type:

ping 123.456.789.123

After a short wait, you should receive the following message:

Request timed out.

This means that the packet couldn't find a destination at the specified address and after a while it was discarded. The notation TTL stands for Time To Live and is a field in the IP header. It's an instruction to any devices receiving the packet to discard it if the time specified in the field is exceeded.

Now, connect to the Internet and ping 192.31.7.130. Your screen will look similar to Figure 6-8.

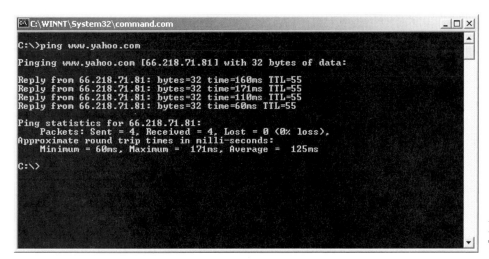

Figure 6-8:
The Ping Utility

Adding a -t switch to the Ping command will cause the system to send continuous ping requests to a remote system.

TRACERT

Tracert allows you to see the path to a remote IP address.

When an IP address is specified, tracert lists the number of hops to the destination, along with the IP addresses of each router along the way. You can specify the number of hops to the destination to determine the most efficient route. It's also a good tool to use to determine whether a problem lies at the remote address or within the route to the destination.

For example, suppose that you ping a remote server but don't receive a response. The question then becomes: Is the problem at the destination, or at one of the routers along the way? The way to pinpoint the problem is to connect to the router that is at the end of the list, and then try to connect to the destination from there. If you can't, the problem most likely lies at that router.

To initiate tracert, type:

tracert

The screen will show all the tracert commands. Now, while connected to the Internet, type:

tracert -h 192.31.7.130

This will show the path to the Cisco site. Your screen will show the number of hops to the site from your location, along with the time from hop to hop. An example is shown in Figure 6-9.

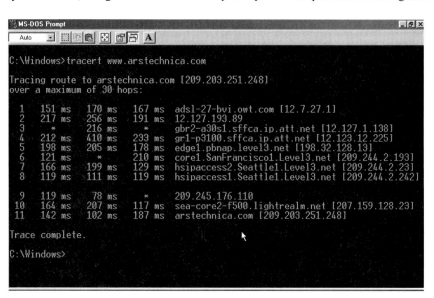

**Figure 6-9:
The Tracert Utility**

Tracert is more appropriate in a wide area environment. You can try using it while connected to the Internet by specifying well-known IP addresses, such as the address for Microsoft or Netscape.

NSLOOKUP

Nslookup

Nslookup is used to determine the name or IP address of domain name servers.

As a troubleshooting tool, nslookup is of value for determining the IP address for host names, or for remote servers on the Internet.

Typically, nslookup is used in combination with other TCP/IP utilities. For example, you may need to ping a server but only know the host name of the server. You enter the host name, and the IP address will be returned. Then, using the IP address, you can ping the server.

Figure 6-10 shows an example of using nslookup from the command prompt. When the domain name *cisco.com* was entered, the IP address for the site was returned.

**Figure 6-10:
The Nslookup Utility**

KEY POINTS REVIEW

An overview of TCP/IP utilities has been presented in this chapter.

- ARP is a tool used to map IP addresses to physical MAC addresses.

- Ipconfig is a utility that provides addressing information for the workstation where the utility is entered.

- Winipconfg is used to determine addressing information on a Windows 95 workstation.

- The nbtstat utility (NetBIOS over a TCP connection) is used with Windows machines to provide NetBIOS name information about the remote connection.

- Netstat is a tool used to display all current Network-layer connections.

- Ping is used to check connectivity between two networked devices.

- Tracert allows you to see the path to a remote IP address.

- Nslookup is used to determine the name or IP address of DNS servers that a workstation is connected to.

At this point, review the objectives listed at the beginning of the chapter to be certain that you understand and can perform them. Afterward, answer the review questions that follow to verify your knowledge of the information.

REVIEW QUESTIONS

The following questions test your knowledge of the material presented in this chapter:

1. What is the purpose of ARP?

2. What is the purpose of ipconfig?

3. What is the purpose of winipcfg?

4. What is the purpose of nbstat?

5. What is the purpose of netstat?

6. What is the purpose of ping?

7. What is the purpose of tracert?

8. What is the purpose of nslookup?

9. To show the IP addresses of all routers between a client workstation and remote server, which diagnostic tool should be used?

10. On a Windows client computer, what screen is used to enter TCP/IP utilities?

11. When the command netstat -r is entered, what information will be returned?

12. When the command nbtstat -n is entered, what information is returned?

13. When the command ipconfig /all is entered, what information is returned?

14. To add entries to an ARP cache, what command should be entered at the command prompt?

15. When a ping to an IP address is successful, what will the screen return?

EXAM QUESTIONS

1. Which of the following diagnostic tools is the best choice to use for displaying the IP address of a workstation?
   a. ipconfig
   b. tracert
   c. winipcfg
   d. ARP

2. Which of the following utilities returns the number of errors generated during a connection?
   a. ipconfig
   b. ping
   c. netstat
   d. telnet 6

3. Which of the following utilities would you use to determine the number of hops to a specific destination?
   a. ping
   b. netstat
   c. tracert
   d. nbtstat

4. Which utility is used to test for connectivity between networked devices?
   a. tracert
   b. ping
   c. nslookup
   d. netstat C

5. To learn addressing information about a Windows 95 workstation, which utility should be entered?
   a. ARP
   b. tracert
   c. ping
   d. winipcfg

6. A user is having trouble connecting to a DNS server. Which TCP/IP utility can be used to determine the IP address of the DNS servers that the user's workstation is connected to?
   a. nslookup
   b. netstat
   c. nbstat
   d. winipcfg

7. To learn the content of a client or server routing cache, which utility should be used?
   a. tracert
   b. ARP
   c. ipconfig
   d. netstat

8. A user needs to know the names of other computers connected to the user's workstation. Which TCP/IP utility should be used?
   a. netstat
   b. nbstat
   c. tracert
   d. nslookup

9. When the command netstat -e 10 is entered at the command prompt, what will be returned?
   a. the IP address of the attached workstation
   b. the time to a remote server that is updated every ten seconds
   c. A remote computer is tested for connectivity ten times.
   d. a listing of statistical information about the connected interface that is updated every ten seconds

10. To determine the time to a remote server located at 192.168.10.30, what TCP/IP utility should be entered?
    a. ping 192.168.10.30
    b. tracert 192.168.10.30
    c. tracert -n 192.168.10.30
    d. nslookup -s 192.168.10.30

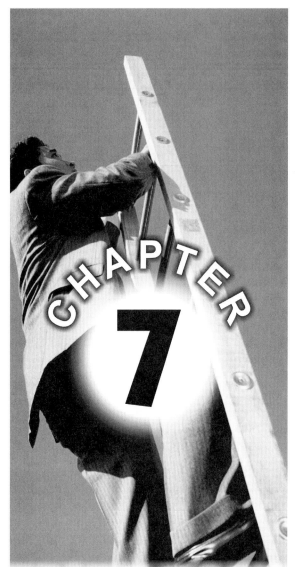

CHAPTER
7

REMOTE ACCESS
AND SECURITY
PROTOCOLS

LEARNING
OBJECTIVES

Upon completion of this chapter and its related lab procedures, you will be able to perform the following tasks:

1. Define the function of the following remote access protocols and services:

    - RAS
    - PPP
    - PPTP
    - SLIP
    - ICA

2. Identify the following security protocols and describe their purpose and function:

    - IPsec
    - L2TP
    - SSL
    - Kerberos

CHAPTER 7

REMOTE ACCESS AND SECURITY PROTOCOLS

INTRODUCTION

Networks are global, providing millions of stand-alone computers access to large and powerful servers on the Internet, as well as access to corporate servers.

A seamless connection to these servers is provided by remote access services, or RAS.

This chapter describes protocols related to RAS. The protocols and conventions used in setting up and maintaining a connection between a computer and a remote server are described first. Next, specific protocols related to securing a remote access connection are described.

Fortunately, newer computer operating systems do most of the setup and configuration work for us. Generally, the autoconfigurations work well—until there's a problem. The Network+ exam recognizes that in order to troubleshoot a RAS connection, you need a sense of how the connection works.

Let's get started.

REMOTE ACCESS SERVICE

Remote Access Service (RAS) refers to the techniques and practices employed in connecting a client computer to the services of a remote server.

Figure 7-1 depicts the essential requirements needed for a RAS connection.

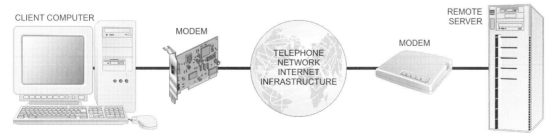

Figure 7-1: Remote Access Service

A client is any device that will be using the services of the server—a desktop or notebook computer, a handheld device, an e-mail client, etc. The figure shows the client connecting through a modem to the telephone network. Rather than a telephone network, the client could be wireless and connect via satellite, or the connection could be through a cable modem over broadband coaxial cable. Regardless, there must be some infrastructure through which the client will connect to the remote server.

The client is required to have certain software installed to set up, maintain, and transfer data over the connection. The software techniques used with RAS connections are covered in the remaining sections of this chapter.

The modem is necessary to convert digital data from the client to analog data for transmission over the local loop portion of the telephone network. The local loop is the section of the telephone connection from the client to the local switching office.

At the server end is the remote server that connects (in the figure) to the telephone system with the help of a modem. Like the client, the server will have appropriate software installed that permits it to use the infrastructure as well as to respond to requests from remote clients.

A RAS connection requires several components:

- A client with connection software installed.

- A network infrastructure. This may be the telephone system for dial-up connections, coaxial cable used with cable modems, or the atmosphere for wireless connections.

- A server computer with server software configured for using the connection to remote clients.

In addition to basic services described above, a RAS connection is likely to:

- Specify remote access protocols

- Specify network protocols

- Provide for authentication and encryption

- Manage access to the remote server

Remote access protocols refer to the protocols used to set up, maintain, and transfer data across the remote connection. The most common RAS protocols that handle these tasks are PPP, PPTP, and SLIP. All three are detailed in the following sections. Remote access protocols are Data Link layer protocols, and as such, are suitable only for connections between two points—the client and server.

Network protocols are needed to create the illusion of a virtual path between client and remote server. Since, once data leaves a client modem, it could travel in numerous directions, the RAS protocols such as PPP need additional information. Network protocols—TCP/IP or IPX/SPX—provide the upper layer connectivity and reliability between client and server.

Authentication and encryption may or may not be needed. But on all RAS software on client computers, it's available as an option. **Authentication** is the process of determining whether someone who requests access is really who they say they are. Authentication is implemented in a variety of ways with the most common being the use of passwords. If you know the password, you must be who you say you are. **Encryption** is the process of coding information so that the meaning of messages is obscured. There are specific encryption techniques (described later in this chapter), as well as specific protocols that incorporate encryption techniques (also described in this chapter).

Authentication

Encryption

Access to the resources of a server is accomplished at the server end of the connection. This includes permissions to read or modify files on the server, use of specific software on the server, permissions to send and receive e-mail, or permission to utilize the server for Internet access.

In some cases, the RAS server may be the entry point to a company intranet, and the server must determine how to get you to other clients or servers on the intranet. Authentication is handled by the server, and once a client is authenticated, the level of access as well as the amount of access is handled by the server.

Typically, a portion of the management function of the RAS server is to account for all requests made for access, including client requests that were denied. This provides statistical data for network administrators that is helpful in evaluating attempts to breach the security of a network.

Remote access services are normally available for use with client operating systems upon demand of the user. The software tools are usually available and all that's needed is for the client user to install and set up any required hardware (modem, ISDN adapter, cable modem, etc.). On the other end, RAS capabilities are installed as a service available with network operating systems. Network operating systems include Windows NT or 2000, Novell NetWare, UNIX, or Linux.

POINT-TO-POINT PROTOCOL (PPP)

Point-to-Point Protocol (PPP)

The **Point-to-Point Protocol** (**PPP**) is a communication protocol used to send data across serial communication links.

PPP is the most widely used wide-area protocol for accessing Internet service providers via a dial-up connection through the telephone network. Today, it's employed almost universally in stand-alone Internet connections using an ISP, but this wasn't always the case. In the early and late 1980s, most of the connections to the Internet were through LANs (with Ethernet being the most common) or public switched networks (using the X.25 standard). As access to the Internet boomed, the need for resolving IP addresses directly to a desktop computer took on a greater sense of urgency.

Enter PPP. Almost all personal computers support serial, point-to-point communication via EIA/TIA-232 interfaces. Unfortunately, there wasn't a standard that allowed for IP addresses to be assigned directly to remote computers over telephone connections.

PPP is a very versatile RAS protocol that offers users the following services:

- Assigns and manages IP addresses

- Communicates in either asynchronous (using start and stop bits) and synchronous (HDLC using acknowledgements)

- Can be configured to run more than one Network layer protocol simultaneously. These include IP, IPX, DECnet, and AppleTalk.

- Includes link configuration, quality testing, and error detection

PPP runs transparently across any Physical layer interface. Typically, these include EIA/TIA-232, V.35, EIA/TIA-422, or EIA/TIA-423, as well as a telephone RJ-11 connector. Data rates between the two end points of the link aren't addressed in the protocol. That's left to the physical implementation of the interface. The protocol does require that the link be full-duplex, and use either asynchronous or synchronous operation.

Beyond the physical characteristics of the protocol, PPP specifies three components that comprise the protocol:

- The PPP Link Layer Protocol

- The PPP Link Control Protocol

- The PPP Network Control Protocol

Link Layer Protocol

The **Link Layer Protocol** is based on the structure, frame format, and operation of HDLC (High-Level Data Link Control). Its purpose is to frame data and provide for error control. The frame format of a PPP frame is shown in Figure 7-2. While the format is slightly different than HDLC, its operation is quite similar.

**Figure 7-2:
PPP Frame Format**

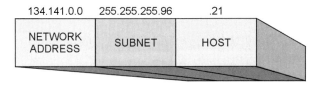

The fields in the frame are:

- *Flag:* Two of the fields in a PPP frame consist of 1-byte flags (01111110) that are used to mark the beginning or end of the frame.

- *ADDRESS:* A 1-byte address, containing the bit sequence 11111111, is the standard broadcast address used in HDLC. Since addressing between two points on a link isn't a problem, the actual address is implied by sending frames in the wire between connected nodes.

- *Control:* A 1-byte control field contains the sequence 00000011. This signifies user data in an unsequenced (LLC, Type 1) frame.

- *Protocol:* The 2-byte protocol field identifies the upper-layer protocol encapsulated in the PPP frame (TCP/IP, IPS/SPX). The data field contains user data, as well as encapsulated upper-layer frames. By default, the data field is set for a maximum length of 1,500 bytes, but other values are permitted as long as both ends of the connection consent to the larger size.

- *Frame Check Sequence:* Error detection is handled by the 2-byte frame check sequence field. Also, by consent of the communicating stations, this field may be extended to 4-bytes for improved quality of service between the two points.

Link Control Protocol

The **Link Control Protocol** is responsible for setting up, configuring, maintaining, and terminating the connection. During establishment and configuration, the Maximum Receive Unit (MRU) is specified. The MRU is the maximum length of the data field in the PPP frame. The quality of the link is tested to determine whether it's sufficient for communication to occur between the two nodes. Negotiation for Network layer protocols is handled by the Link Control Protocol. Network protocols can be set up and taken down at any time during the communication, and may be run simultaneously. However, both ends of the link have to agree on what protocols will be used.

The **Network Control Protocol** is concerned with negotiating the dynamic allocation of IP addresses. Depending on the Network layer protocol specified in the protocol field of the PPP frame, this layer will respond differently.

PPP has another advantage in that it can, as an option, employ authentication protocols. The purpose of an authentication protocol is to provide a level of security by ensuring that the node requesting a PPP connection is valid.

There are two types of authentication protocols commonly used with PPP:

- **Password Authentication Protocol (PAP):** This client is authenticated by sending a user name, and password, to the server. The server compares the name and password to its database, and if it's a match, opens the connection.

- **Challenge Handshake Authentication Protocol (CHAP):** The server generates a random string of bits and sends them, along with its host name, to the client. The client uses the host name to look up a cipher key, encrypts the random string, and sends it back to the host. The host uses the same key to decrypt the random string. If it matches the original random string sent to the client, the connection is opened.

TEST TIP

From a list of acronyms, be able to select RAS protocols as presented in this chapter.

POINT-TO-POINT TUNNELING PROTOCOL (PPTP)

Point-to-Point Tunneling Protocol (PPTP) is a protocol used to securely transport PPP packets over a TCP/IP network such as the Internet.

This makes it an ideal choice for mobile users, or telecommuters, who need access to a remote server, but lack a direct connection for dialing into the server. With PPTP, the user dials into the ISP using a local telephone number, then encapsulates the PPP packet in a TCP/IP frame addressed to the IP of the remote server.

Once the packet arrives at the server the TCP/IP headers are stripped, and the PPP packet, which may be carrying TCP/IP data, or NetBEUI, or IPX packets, is reformatted for the remote server. When responding to the remote client, the server follows a similar approach. For example, if the remote server is a Windows 2000 machine, it may encapsulate NetBEUI packets in the PPTP packet, and send them onto the Internet in a TCP/IP packet. At the receiving end, the TCP/IP headers are discarded, and the encapsulated NetBEUI frame is downloaded into the client machine.

PPTP offers a distinct advantage over PPP:

- It requires that data be encrypted (with PPP, encryption is an option) using either PAP or CHAP.

The result is a very secure connection between the client and a remote server that doesn't require the use of expensive dedicated lines between client and server. In effect, a PPTP connection is a secure virtual private network, since it uses the Internet as the communication medium.

Figure 7-3 shows a personal computer connected to the analog telephone system through a modem, and then to the Internet Service Provider. This is a typical application for either PPP or PPTP. Note that although the RAS connection shows PPTP, addressing, routing, and reliability are handled by TCP/IP.

**Figure 7-3:
PC-to-Internet
Connection**

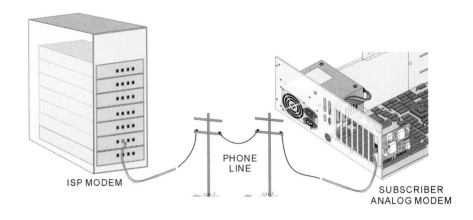

ISP MODEM

PHONE
LINE

SUBSCRIBER
ANALOG MODEM

SERIAL LINE INTERNET PROTOCOL (SLIP)

Serial Line Internet Protocol (SLIP) is the forerunner to PPP.

It has the same function; to connect nodes in a point-to-point configuration. However, SLIP has some disadvantages when compared to PPP.

SLIP can only transport TCP/IP.

PPP not only can transport multi-Network layer protocols, but it can do them simultaneously. For the user connecting to the Internet from a modem through the telephone system, this doesn't mean much because they will probably be using TCP/IP anyway.

The configuration of a PPP link is automated in the Link Control Protocol. All you have to do is provide the telephone number of the ISP, and PPP takes over from there. With SLIP, many configuration parameters are set up manually. The most important is the IP address. An IP used in a SLIP connection is static; it must be given to you by the ISP and they must give you the IP of the remote server. You enter these when setting up the connections. Other parameters may also need to be set up manually, such as the MRU and Maximum Transmission Unit (MTU), which is the maximum size of a PPP frame.

User authentication can be troublesome in SLIP connections. You have to rely on the ISP for providing a login and password prompt. However, if this differs significantly from the requirements of your computer (operating system, BIOS, etc.), it may not work. To get it to work requires that you make changes to INI login scripts, or create one yourself.

PPP, as mentioned above, verifies clients using either PAP or CHAP. These are standardized options for PPP, and routinely included with PPP software.

To summarize SLIP services:

- SLIP uses static assigned IP addresses, while PPP uses dynamically assigned IP addresses.

- SLIP lacks the autoconfiguration capabilities of PPP, which means you may have to do some of the configuration manually.

- SLIP only encapsulates TCP/IP in the data field, which means it won't route Novell (IPX) or Apple (AppleTalk) Network layer protocols.

INDEPENDENT COMPUTER ARCHITECTURE (ICA)

ICA, or **Independent Computer Architecture**, is a server-based technology that allows applications to be run from a remote server and appear on a client screen as if actually running on the screen.

Independent
Computer
Architecture (ICA)

The intent of ICA is to extend business applications in a manner that's low-cost, predictable, and secure.

ICA consists of three components:

- A server component

- A client component

- A network communication protocol component

The server component consists of software (licensed from Citrix Corp.) that is installed on servers. From the software component, users gain access to applications running on the server. The client component is a small software client (around 300 kbytes). The client software is typically a free download and allows the user to access the ICA server software.

ICA networking communication protocols are the protocols running on the connection between client and server. ICA is protocol-independent. It will run on TCP/IP, IPX/SPX, NetBEUI, ISDN, PPP, Frame Relay, or ATM.

In addition to being network communication protocol–independent, ICA is also hardware-independent. It runs on Intel-based microprocessor machines (Windows) as well as Motorola-based machines (Macintosh).

With hardware independence comes operating system independence. ICA clients may be installed on computers, personal data assistants (PDAs), and wireless devices running any Windows client operating systems such as Windows 2000 or Windows XP, UNIX, Java applications, Windows CE, or Linux.

Services available with ICA include:

- It's communication protocol–independent.

- ICA is hardware-independent.

- ICA is operating system-independent.

- Applications run on servers and not on clients.

ICA brings extremely high efficiencies to remote connections. The server software separates the application that's to be performed (such as a file transfer or the launch of a programming script) from the user interface. All applications run on the server. However, the interface for an application runs on the client machine in a web browser. To the user, it appears as if the application is running on the client computer. The only time that data is transferred in appreciable amounts is when the user interacts with the interface, such as when clicking on hyper-linked text. The linked file isn't actually transferred to the user; rather, the mouse click associated with choosing the link is transferred to the server; then, the server display changes to the files connected to the link.

Note that in a typical HTTP connection over a PPP dial-up connection, the linked file would be downloaded to the client machine. The maximum amount of channel bandwidth would be needed and cause the corresponding download to be slow. Since this activity doesn't occur with ICA, very small bandwidths are needed for remote access. Typically, ICA requires about 5–10 kbps of bandwidth.

Several applications in which ICA would be beneficial include:

- *Branch Offices:* For a company with many offices located over a wide area, ICA is ideal since the branch offices can be populated with low-cost hardware and utilize the resident features of ICA server software.

- *Cross Platforms:* For a company with a mixture of hardware and operating systems, ICA provides for a standardized client that is independent of the client hardware and software.

- *Contract Applications:* ICA allows applications to be contracted to clients and used on a pay-per-use basis. For example, a company may have a sporadic need for expensive software. Rather than buying the software, the company could rent it and run desired applications over an ICA connection.

ICA is a considerable departure from the RAS protocols discussed earlier in this chapter. PPP is a technology that allows two computers to connect together, for example. ICA, on the other hand, allows a client computer to connect to a server and utilize the services of the server in a manner that's low-cost, secure, and efficient.

RAS SECURITY PROTOCOLS

Currently, four security-driven protocols are used with RAS accounts:

- *PPTP:* Point-to-Point Tunneling Protocol

- *L2F:* Layer 2 Forwarding

- *L2TP:* Layer 2 Tunneling Protocol

- *IPsec:* IP Security

When implemented, these are usually discussed in the context of a **virtual private network** (VPN). A VPN is any secure network over the Internet that appears to users as a direct, point-to-point connection. Of course, it's not a direct connection since data leaving a remote client computer may take multiple paths along the route to the remote server. But what differentiates a VPN is that it, typically, can carry nearly any Network layer protocol to the ultimate destination. This includes nonroutable protocols such as NetBEUI.

PPTP

The PPTP protocol was described earlier in this chapter. PPTP has been widely used since Microsoft included it on Windows NT 4.0, included a Windows 95 patch for PPTP, and included it as part of the Windows 98 operating system. Since PPTP, like PPP, relies on link information at layer 2 of the OSI Reference Model, it can be used to transport nearly any network protocol across the Internet. For example, a PPTP connection will transport IPX, NetBEUI, or AppleTalk packets to a remote server.

Compared to other VPN protocols described in this section, PPP has a huge disadvantage in that it can carry only one channel for each connection. This means that only a single user can connect to the Internet using PPP. Small networks often employ PPP for multiple users by installing Internet server software that allows more than one user access, but the time that each user connects is divided by all users. If more than one user is connected at the same time, download speeds drop significantly since the server manages connection on a round-robin basis.

PPTP encapsulates the data to be sent along with standard PPP headers. The PPTP protocol headers include fields for authenticating end-point connections (users, or a client machine and a server) and for encrypting the data.

Recall the salient characteristics of PPTP:

- It allows non-TCP/IP frames to be sent through the Internet.

- It requires that data be encrypted (with PPP, encryption is an option) using either PAP or CHAP.

L2F

The **L2F protocol** was developed by Cisco. It shares many of the strengths of PPTP but also addresses some PPTP weaknesses. L2F uses PPP to authenticate end-point connections. This means that a client-to-network connection will have PPP installed and use PPP to connect to a local ISP. The ISP will then employ L2F to create a tunnel to the remote server.

L2F is a layer 2 protocol, so it can carry network protocols other than IP such as IPX or NetBEUI. Unlike PPTP (and PPP), L2F may be used in about any type of network environment other than IP. Since Network layer protocols aren't recognized by L2F, it can be deployed on ATM networks or Frame Relay networks. (See Chapter 9 for more information on ATM and Frame Relay.)

> **NOTE**
>
> L2F uses PPP to authenticate end-point connections. L2F is a layer 2 protocols so it can carry network protocols other than IP.

L2F can establish more than one connection in the tunnel established between the end-points. In other word, L2F is a **multilink protocol**. This means that an ISP using L2F can select the best routes to send data packets so that they are likely to arrive at the server faster than if the connection used PPTP.

The characteristics of L2F are:

- It uses PPP to authenticate end-point connections.

- It may be used in about any type of network environment, in addition to IP, such as ATM networks or Frame Relay.

- It is a multilink protocol.

L2TP

The **L2TP protocol** uses PPP to provide dial-up authentication access. It's currently being developed by the Internet Engineering Task Force (IETF) as a future replacement for PPTP and L2F. Like its predecessors, L2TP can carry packets from non-IP networks. The tunneling mechanism used with L2TP is based on the multiple-connection tunnel used with L2F. However, a tunnel protocol is being defined for technologies other than IP-based networks (such as the Internet) that includes X.25, Frame Relay, and ATM.

PPTP, L2F, and L2TP are essentially authentication protocols that are used to encapsulate data messages, and do not directly incorporate data encryption. Typically, the encryption scheme is a public key cipher that's bundled with modern web browsers. Note that SLIP does not provide authentication since it doesn't support encryption. However, the final version of L2TP is expected to incorporate the encryption methods that are stock with IPsec.

L2PT provides the following:

- It uses PPP to provide dial-up authentication access.

- It utilizes multiple-connection properties like PPP.

- It can carry technologies other than IP packets such as ATM and Frame Relay.

IPsec

IP security (IPsec) was developed in conjunction with the next version of IP, IP version 6. Since IPv6 is compatible with IPv4, it's being used to provide authentication and encryption for IPv4-based networks.

A data packet (using IPv4) that's subjected to IPsec may be authenticated, encrypted, or both authenticated and encrypted. The two processes are separated at the Transport and Network layers so that only the Transport layer header (TCP or UDP) or the Network layer packet may be authenticated, encrypted, or both. Note that the other security protocols described use PPP for authentication.

The first process is called the Transport mode and provides basic authentication and encryption. The second process is called Tunneling mode and provides the highest level of security. IPsec supports multiple tunnels over a single connection. In order to do so, IPsec must be supported by the PPP multilink protocol (PPP-MP) protocol. This refers to the ability to transfer a stream of packets over different routes. The packets, upon arrival at the destination, are reassembled according to the sequence numbers in the PPP header control field.

IPsec is a layer 3 protocol. It can only be used with IP packets; consequently, it won't carry IPX or NetBEUI packets. In a typical implementation, a workstation user will send data destined to a remote network and use the Internet as the VPN infrastructure. At the local router interface to the ISP connection, the packet is fitted with authentication and encryption headers, encrypted, then sent to the ISP over a PPP connection. The ISP encapsulates the packet with source and destination IP addresses that are drawn from a pool of packets that have been specified for the VPN. The packet is then sent to the remote network where the packet headers are stripped and the data decrypted. Note that the ISP server must be set up in a PPP-MP configuration in order to track multiple connections back to the local network.

Since the source and destination IP addresses are drawn from a pool of addresses, the source of the packet is protected from intruders on the Internet.

IPsec provides for numerous encryption schemes. The list at this time is as follows:

> Private Key, DES, Triple DES
> Public Key, RSA
> Hash Key message digests
> Digital Certificates

Common features of IPsec include:

- It incorporates the authentication and encryption features of IPv6 for use over IPv4 networks.

- It is used only on IP-based networks—not IPX or NetBEUI networks.

- It is used on authentication and encryption at either the TCP or IP header, or both.

It's important to understand that a secure protocol such as those described in this section are intended to protect user data and to ensure that the person (or machine) using the network is authorized to do so. None of the protocols described will stop an unauthorized intruder or prevent an unauthorized person from capturing data packets. Keeping out intruders is the function of proxies and firewalls—also discussed in Chapter 13.

SECURE SOCKET LAYER PROTOCOL

The **Secure Socket Layer** (**SSL**) protocol is used to authenticate users or e-commerce servers on the Internet, and to encrypt/ decrypt messages (particularly credit card purchases) using public key encryption.

In addition, SSL encrypts data between the Internet browser and Internet server.

The protocol consists of a digital certificate that the e-commerce site must possess before a web browser will be able to authenticate the site. The digital certificate is issued by a **Certificate Authority (CA)**. The role of the CA in the SSL session is to authenticate the holder of a certificate (such as an e-commerce server), and to provide a digital signature that will reveal if the certificate has been compromised.

CA certificates are pre-installed in all modern web browsers. The browser uses the CA to authenticate a web server.

Examples of CAs include:

- VeriSign

- Thawte

- Microsoft

- ATT

- GTE

- InternetMCI

The digital certificate used in a public key transaction is used to authenticate the web site, typically an e-commerce site that accepts credit card orders. The reason that the site must be authenticated is that it's not too difficult to copy a complete web site, then post the site using a domain name that's very similar to the "real" site. For example, it easy to mistake the site **micrsoft.com**, for **microsoft.com**. A purchaser may be lured to the first site, make a purchase, and never receive the purchased item.

The certificate will typically include the following information:

- The name of the holder of the certificate. If the certificate is to be used on a web site, the URL of the site will be listed.

- The name of the CA that issued the certificate

- The date that the certificate became valid

- The date that the certificate will expire

- A digital signature

The digital signature (a hexadecimal number) is used to indicate if the certificate has been modified in any way. If a certificate has been stolen for use on a bogus e-commerce site, then the thief must modify the certificate so that the bogus site can present the certificate to a web browser. But when the certificate is modified, the signature will change. A change in the signature will create a change in the keys used in the encryption process. Since the keys will change, the key held by the bogus site won't be able to decrypt information encrypted by the browser.

A digital signature may also be called a **hash secret**. A hash secret, or hash key, is generated by producing a number that's based on the content of the certificate. The key is encrypted with the remaining contents of the certificate during the initial setup of a SSL session and is sent to a browser. The browser runs the hash function to produce the original digital signature. The message is then decrypted with the public key. If the digital signature that's decrypted matches the digital signature in the browser's database, then the browser knows that the server is authentic.

---TEST TIP---

Be able to select the URL that is using SSL from a list of URLs.

A connection to a certificate server that uses SSL will use a URL that begins with https://. For example, a site called **https://buy.now.com** is a secure site in which messages between the browser and server will be encrypted. The browser will indicate that the connection is secure by displaying a locked padlock, or key, near the bottom corner of the browser.

KERBEROS

Kerberos is an authentication scheme used to identify parties engaged in electronic communication.

Authentication is the process of identifying two parties engaged in communication across an open network such as the Internet. One of the earliest authentication systems, Kerberos was developed at the Massachusetts Institute of Technology. Kerberos authenticates the parties by embedding a key (assigned to each of the parties) in the messages that are exchanged. When a message is sent, the key in the message is compared to the key assigned to the sender. If the two match, then the receiving party will know that the message was sent by a trusted party. Since both parties use the same key, and both parties know the key, the key is a private key.

Figure 7-4 shows the simplicity of Kerberos. The sender sends a request to exchange data with a receiver by including a message key in the request. The receiver compares the sender's message key with its key. Since the two keys are identical, the receiver returns a message indicating that the sender has been authenticated. Message packets will now be exchanged between the two parties.

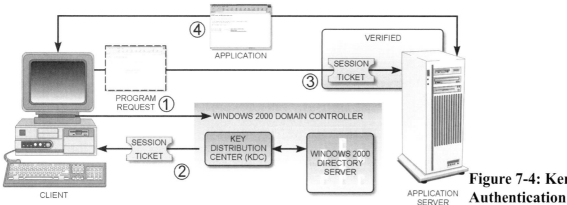

Figure 7-4: Kerberos Authentication

Other authentication systems require usernames and passwords. A form that requires a user to enter a username and password is an authentication system. If you know the correct username and password, the system assumes that you are who you say you are. Password systems have weaknesses. The most apparent weakness is that passwords are compromised by writing them down, or by allowing others to see them when they're entered.

Features of Kerberos include:

- It's an authentication tool.

- It uses a private key for encryption.

KEY POINTS REVIEW

This chapter has presented an extensive exploration of RAS and security protocols.

- Remote Access Service (RAS) refers to the techniques and practices employed in connecting a client computer to the services of a remote server.

- The services available with remote access service include:

  - It specifies remote access protocols.

  - It specifies network protocols.

  - It provides for authentication and encryption.

  - It manages access to the remote server.

  - It sets up and maintains connections between client and server.

- The Point-to-Point Protocol (PPP) is a communication protocol used to send data across serial communication links.

- Services available with PPP include:

  - It assigns and manages IP addresses.

  - It communicates in either asynchronous (using start and stop bits) or synchronous (HDLC using acknowledgements).

  - It can be configured to run more than one Network layer protocol simultaneously. These include IP, IPX, DECnet, and AppleTalk.

  - It includes link configuration, quality testing, and error detection

- PPP is a three-layer protocol consisting of:

  - The PPP Link Layer Protocol

  - The PPP Link Control Protocol

  - The PPP Network Control Protocol

- Common authentication schemes used with PPP or PPTP are PAP CHAP.

- PPTP is a protocol used to securely transport PPP packets over a TCP/IP network such as the Internet.

  - Services offered with PPTP include:

    - It allows non-TCP/IP frames to be sent through the Internet.

    - It requires that data be encrypted (with PPP, encryption is an option) using either PAP or CHAP.

  - Serial Line Internet Protocol (SLIP) is the forerunner to PPP.

- SLIP services include:

  - SLIP uses static assigned IP addresses, whereas PPP uses dynamically assigned IP addresses.

  - SLIP lacks the autoconfiguration capabilities of PPP, which means you may have to do some of the configuration manually.

  - SLIP only encapsulates TCP/IP in the data field, which means it won't route Novell (IPX) or Apple (AppleTalk) Network layer protocols.

- ICA, or Independent Computer Architecture, is a server-based technology that allows applications to be run from a remote server and appear on a client screen as if they were actually running on the screen.

- Services available with ICA include:

  - It's communication protocol–independent.

  - ICA is hardware-independent.

  - ICA is operating system–independent.

  - Applications run on servers and not on clients.

- L2F uses PPP to authenticate end-point connections.

- L2F is a layer 2 protocol, so it can carry network protocols other than IP.

- The characteristics of L2F are:

  - It uses PPP to authenticate end-point connections.

  - It may be used in about any type of network environment, in addition to IP, such as ATM networks or Frame Relay.

  - It is a multilink protocol.

- The L2TP protocol uses PPP to provide dial-up authentication access.

- L2PT provides the following:

  - It uses PPP to provide dial-up authentication access.

  - It utilizes multiple-connection properties like PPP.

  - It can carry technologies other than IP packets, such as ATM and Frame Relay.

- IPsec is used to provide authentication and encryption for IPv4-based networks.

- Common features of IPsec include:

  - It incorporates the authentication and encryption features of IPv6 for use over IPv4 networks.

  - It is used only on IP-based networks—not IPX or NetBEUI networks.

  - It is used on authentication and encryption at either the TCP or IP header, or both.

- The Secure Socket Layer (SSL) protocol is used to authenticate users or e-commerce servers on the Internet, and to encrypt/ decrypt messages using public key encryption.

- The role of the CA in the SSL session is to authenticate the holder of a certificate (such as an e-commerce server), and to provide a digital signature that will reveal if the certificate has been compromised.

- Kerberos is an authentication scheme used to identify parties engaged in electronic communication.

- Features of Kerberos include:

    - It's an authentication tool.

    - It uses a private key for encryption.

At this point, review the objectives listed at the beginning of the chapter to be certain that you understand and can perform them. Afterward, answer the review questions that follow to verify your knowledge of the information.

REVIEW QUESTIONS

The following questions test your knowledge of the material presented in this chapter:

1. How do PPP and SLIP differ?

2. How does PTPP improve upon PPP?

3. List two of the services provided by RAS.

4. What is authentication in regard to RAS security?

5. What is the purpose of the PPP Link Layer Protocol?

6. What is CHAP?

7. A SLIP RAS connection on an IPX/SPX network has failed. What are possible reasons for the failure?

8. How do the channel bandwidth requirements of ICA compare to those needed for PPP?

9. List two positive characteristics of ICA.

10. What is a VPN?

11. How are users authenticated using L2F?

12. Of the security protocols described in this chapter, which support multiple links?

13. What is the primary difference between L2F and L2TP?

14. Which Network layer protocol is IPsec used with?

15. When an HTTP application over the Internet employs SSL, what application is used?

264   CHAPTER 7

1. Which of the following best describes RAS?
    a. the hardware and software necessary for remote devices to exchange data
    b. the communication software needed to connect to a remote server
    c. the hardware needed to access an Internet service provider
    d. the modem used in a computer

2. Which of the following are used for authentication with PPP?
    a. DEC
    b. TCP
    c. L2F
    d. CHAP

3. Which of the following can use only static assigned IP addresses?
    a. PPP
    b. PPTP
    c. SLIP
    d. ICA

4. Which of the following RAS technologies has applications run on remote servers, rather than on the connected client?
    a. ICA
    b. PPP
    c. SLIP
    d. PPTP

5. What is the purpose of the CA used in SSL?
    a. encryption
    b. authentication
    c. encapsulation
    d. decryption

6. What type of encryption key is used with Kerberos?
    a. public
    b. open
    c. private
    d. closed

7. What is the purpose of including a digital signature with a SSL CA?
    a. to encrypt messages
    b. to hold public encryption keys
    c. to provide a tunnel for data channels
    d. to reveal if the certificate has been compromised

8. What is PAP?
    a. an authentication tool
    b. an encryption tool
    c. a troubleshooting tool
    d. a monitoring tool

9. Which of the following does not rely on PPP for authentication?
    a. L2F
    b. L2TP
    c. IPsec
    d. PPTP

10. Which layer of the PPP protocol is responsible for negotiating IP addresses?
    a. Link Control Protocol
    b. Network Control Protocol
    c. Link Layer Protocol
    d. Frame Format

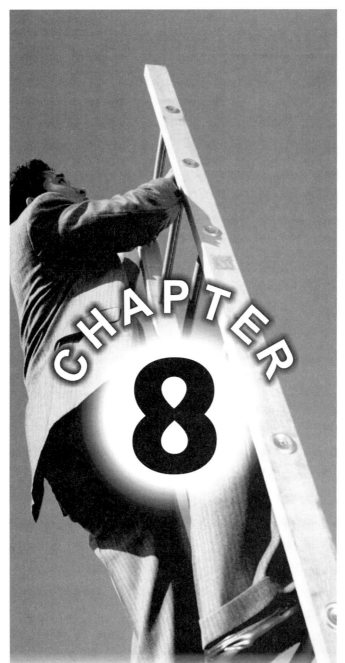

8

NETWORK SERVICES

LEARNING
OBJECTIVES

LEARNING OBJECTIVES

Upon completion of this chapter and its related lab procedures, you will be able to perform the following tasks:

1. Identify the purpose of the following network services:

    - DHCP

    - BootP

    - DNS

    - NAT

    - WINS

    - SNMP

CHAPTER 8

NETWORK SERVICES

INTRODUCTION

Network services, in the parlance of the Network+ exam, revolve around naming devices attached to networks, and then reconciling the names to IP addresses, as well as software management tools. This chapter provides an overview of the most common services. It's important to separate the purpose of each of the services because although some of them are similar in their functions, each is unique.

Most of the network services described in this chapter may be applied to local—private—networks, or to the Internet. Because services such as DNS and DHCP, among others, are so widely deployed to Internet applications, the chapter begins with an overview of the Internet—how it began, the different areas of the Internet, and why the protocols discussed in this chapter are relevant and important.

THE INTERNET

The Internet is a network of networks. It began in the United States in 1969, when four universities—UCLA, UCSB, Stanford Research Institute, and the University of Utah—became four interconnected nodes without a defined exit point. The four sites used different computers to transfer files, and later, e-mail. The interconnection of the four sites originated as a research project funded by the Defense Advance Research Projects Agency (DARPA).

DARPA was studying the architecture and protocols of interconnect technology as a defense strategy. The Department of Defense wanted a method of connecting computers, built by different vendors, that allowed them to communicate with each other. That way, if a communication link was lost during battle, an alternative path could be used through another computer system. Developments from 1969 to the present have accelerated the development of interconnect technology at a break-neck pace.

> The Internet is a network of networks.

Early protocols, from the beginnings of the Internet, evolved into what would become the present-day TCP/IP suite of interconnect protocols by 1974. These protocols were tested across a wide area network known as ARPANET.

ARPANET was a very successful internetworking system, connecting several large research universities, government research centers, as well as a few vendors (notably IBM). As the system grew, the Department of Defense decreed that all users on the Internet employ TCP/IP protocols as an interim strategy, prior to the full development of the ISO OSI Reference Model. At the same time, the ARPANET was split into two groups, due to the size and complexity of the network. The two groups were called the ARPANET, used for additional research in internetworking; and MILNET, used for military applications of the technology.

Researchers at the University of California at Berkeley pioneered many aspects of TCP/IP. It became the official wide-area protocol for the Internet in 1982, which, incidentally, was the year the name "Internet" became an official noun.

These scientists used computers with an early version of the UNIX operating system, and in particular, the UNIX utilities that made it simple for users to implement TCP/IP applications. In essence, the quasi standard of internetworking protocols, TCP/IP, had UNIX as a base for its implementation.

This is why TCP/IP does not work as well with DOS-based PCs as with UNIX machines. DOS was intended for stand-alone computers, whereas internetworking was designed into UNIX PCs.

In 1985, the National Science Foundation funded access to its six regional research centers, in the United States, through the ARPANET system. The NSF extended its interest in internetworking by building a long-haul backbone network, operating on a T-1 line at 1.544 Mbps, that made access easier. At this point, all of the supercomputers, owned by the NSF, were accessible through ARPANET. In the same year, the NSF partly funded a series of regional networks connecting university research centers to its high-speed backbone, which allowed scientists access to the large computers of the NSF.

The NSF, as the major source of funding and support for the Internet, changed the name of the ARPANET backbone, and regional centers, to NSFNET. The NSF was technically the Internet, and access was limited to organizations performing research or educational pursuits—which generally means large universities. But in 1991, the NSF lifted the no-commercial restrictions from the Internet, and in 1995, the NSFNET reverted to its original status as a research network. The World Wide Web was introduced in 1991, and in 1995, it passed more traffic than any other Internet service.

These days, you pay a nominal fee to access the Internet, and agree (that is, your access service provider agrees) to pass packets intended for other portions of the vast system. Typically, a single-PC subscriber in a residence pays about $20 a month for an Internet connection. All you need is a PC, a modem, and the correct protocols (TCP/IP) to start the transaction.

No one owns the Internet—no government, private business, or individual. No one regulates it, either. The closest entity to a regulator is The Internet Society, which is tasked to develop the architecture of the Internet. In recent years, however, many governments around the world have tried to bring it under some type of centralized control (with varying amounts of success), but that control has remained elusive, mostly because the Internet spans national and geographical boundaries. What's legal in this country may be illegal in another country; and if the questionable item originates in this country, how can another country forbid its inclusion on the Internet without first changing the laws of this country?

There's some consensus as to what's illegal—child pornography and credit card fraud, for example. In the United States, it's generally recognized that if you conduct an illegal transaction on the Internet in this country, it doesn't matter where it originates. The ethical and legal debates surrounding the Internet rage daily, with little chance that they'll be sorted out any time soon.

No one knows for sure how many computers are connected to the Internet. Certainly, the number is in the millions. Through subnetting of host computer addresses, the number of computers and users has spiraled beyond the point of reasonable tracking. A list of domain addresses (as in *www.microsoft.com*, for example) can be assembled, but that doesn't take into account the hundreds or thousands of PCs subnetted to a single host address.

Virtually all large universities, and private and public research centers, are connected. Most businesses have an Internet presence. Thousands more users have access to portions of the Internet—from its large databases, to e-mail, to the World Wide Web, and to all of the services that are available.

World Wide Web (WWW)

What services are available? The **World Wide Web** (**WWW**), Gopher, FTP (File Transfer Protocol), Telnet, and e-mail, to name a few. In addition, there are dozens of subsets, including Internet Relay Chat (IRC, also called Chat), mail lists, live video, Voice-over-Internet, etc. The list grows daily.

The WWW is the graphical area of the Internet and is where most of us spend our time surfing. It requires a graphical interface such as Internet Explorer or Netscape Navigator. With the point-and-click capabilities of web browsers (first popularized by Mosaic), we're free from having to know any of the specialized syntax used with the Internet.

The web, much like the graphical interface pioneered by Apple, brought the Internet to all of us. Rapidly (in less than five years), the web has been extended to include all services on the Internet. The browser hides the initiation behind our requests, so that from a web site, we can start an e-mail program, and it runs transparently under the browser; or files may be downloaded using FTP from another web site.

> The World Wide Web is the graphical area of the Internet. Other services available from the Internet include file transfers, telnet, and e-mail.

Gopher

However, the other Internet services remain. For example, **Gopher**, a giant database of topics, originally consisted of a series of menus that compiled information on the Internet.

The most famous gopher was at the University of Minnesota, and you can still go there today to sample the feel of it. Beginning at a top-level menu, you could descend for what seemed like forever, moving from one heading to the next. Search tools were available, and the most widely used one was called Archie. Much of the information originally contained at the gopher sites has now been converted to web sites.

Telnet is a service that allows you to "telephone-net" into another computer. The original idea was that if you were in Atlanta, and needed access to information stored on a computer in Dallas, you could telnet into it. The information was presented on your terminal screen, just as if you were sitting in Dallas at a terminal connected directly to the Dallas computer. Telnet remains, but its application is specialized and limited. Originally, you could visit the Library of Congress by telnetting to their site. Now, you go via the web. Many of the applications invoked using telnet are now handled by servers in a LAN or WAN. Telnet is still a valuable tool, but its use tends to be specialized for companies, or educational institutions, in which users are working at diskless terminals, or stand-alone PCs, and need access to resources on a large computer.

E-mail remains intact. It's a separate entity from the web, and uses a completely different protocol architecture than most of the Internet. Why? The reason is historical. The first e-mail standard was written in 1977 (RFC 733), well before TCP/IP was adopted. File transfers were common in those days, when users, who were primarily academics and researchers, needed a way to discuss their work. E-mail was, and is, a simple method of communicating electronically. It was patterned after the postal system (that is, snail-mail that takes days to get from one address to another), except it's much faster. It uses simple text messages that typically are less than 1 kbyte in length. With most e-mail software, you can customize your message to include carbon copies, attachments, or links to web sites.

FTP (File Transfer Protocol) is a means of downloading files to your computer, or uploading them from your computer to an FTP site. Like e-mail, FTP retains a distinct structure, probably because it too was introduced early in the formation of the Internet. The widest application of FTP is for downloading software, or software enhancements. For example, many vendors maintain download sections at their web sites. If you've bought products from these vendors in the past, you can use these sites to download the latest software revisions used in their products. Patches, upgrades, or fixes to problems are routinely posted at a vendor's download area.

For many of us, the Internet is an up-to-date and easily-accessible technical reference library. For business, it's a way to get messages out in a very cost-effective manner, since the Internet—on a cost-per-user basis—is cheap. E-commerce has proved to be a very efficient method for delivering products to consumers via credit card transactions. We visit web sites to learn about products, as well as the technology surrounding the products. Many sites include tutorials, written by experts in their fields, that are free from editorial constraints, such as length and complexity, that too often stifle the print media. But, if you're patient and you follow links to cross-reference facts, you'll forgive writings that aren't clear and are often rambling or occasionally wrong, because these are the creators of the Internet, a vast and sprawling interconnection of diverse networks.

It's an unfortunate occurrence that some web sites are now protecting specialized information that not long ago was freely available in company white papers, but is now only available to verifiable, or paying, customers. The Internet, founded on the concept of free exchange of ideas and practices, exists due to the pursuit, by certain academic pioneers, of an unregulated communication medium that has changed the world in the last decade. But too often, the papers that are made available on the modern Internet have a strong marketing slant, so that they tend to read more like an advertisement than an instructional concept paper. This is a trend that we should resist. Those who use the Internet as a reference tend to revisit those sites that provide the Internet community with factual, unbiased information. This should also be your approach, while staying away from sites that only want to take money from you.

Bulletin boards are also widely used on the Internet, with more than 2,000 topics currently available. The official name of the Internet bulletin boards is **USENET**. USENET topics are categorized under seven newsgroups: computers, science, recreational, social, USENET news, miscellaneous, and talk. USENET articles are written by Internet users, covering thousands of subjects. Table 8-1 is a partial listing of topics.

> **NOTE**
>
> USENET is the official name of the Internet bulletin boards.

Artificial Intelligence
Neural Networks
IBM PCs and Compatible Programs
Cognitive Engineering
Data Communications
Computer Graphics
Employment, Careers
Legalities and Ethics of the Law
Reviews of Star Trek Books, Films, etc.
Antiques
Poems
Food, Cooking, and Recipes
Medicine
Travel

Table 8-1: Examples of USENET Topics

Huge databases, covering topics as diverse as computer networking to recipes for broccoli, are available for viewing, and in some cases, for downloading onto your PC.

Table 8-2: Example Databases

Table 8-2 lists several popular databases.

DATABASE	INFORMATION	ACCESS
History	American history topics	Telnet: **ukanaix.cc.ukans.edu** Login: **history**
Dartmouth College Library Online System	Info on titles, authors, and publications	Telnet: **library.dartmouth.edu**
Freenet	News from USA Today, Sports, etc.	Telnet: **freenet-in-{a,b,c}.cwru.edu**
Health Sciences Libraries Consortium	Listings of PC and MAC programs used in health sciences education	Telnet: **shrwyw.hslc.org** Login: **cbl**
Internet Resource Guide	Internet resources and how to access	Mail: **info-server@nnsc.nsf.net**
Launchpad	Access to many library systems across the country. Searches and downloads.	Telnet: **launchpad.unc.edu** Login: **launch**
Library of Congress	Records of millions of publications	Telnet: **locis.loc.gov**
Music Server	Music archives, guitar TAB files, lyrics, MIDI files, and mailing lists	Anonymous FTP: **ftp.uwp.edu** Path: **/pub/music**
NASA News	Info on current spacecraft and projects	Finger: **nasanews@space.mit.edu**
PC Magazine	Programs and source code for many PC Magazine utility programs	Anonymous FTP: **ftp.cco.caltech.edu** Path: **/pub/ibmpc/pcmag**
People on the Internet	Services to search for, and find, someone on the Internet	Gopher: **yaleinfo.yale.edu** Choose: **People on the Internet**
Searching the Internet	Tools to search the Internet for any specific resource. Uses Archie, Hytelnet, Veronica, Wais, and the WWW.	Gopher: **yaleinfo.yale.edu** Choose: **Internet Resources | Searching the Internet with...**
Social Security Administration	SSA info, and how to obtain information on others for genealogical purposes	Anonymous FTP: **oak.oakland.edu** Path: **/pub/misc/ss-info**
Virtual Reality	Articles about single-user virtual reality, with Interactive Fiction archive access	Anonymous FTP: **ftp.u.washington.edu** Path: **/public/VirtualReality**

Internet chat

Internet chat is similar to e-mail, except it's interactive and instantaneous.

It's the written equivalent to speaking. Terminal conversations are generally topic-oriented, and by using the list command, a user can view descriptions of the current topics, or channels, as they are referred to.

So how does it work? How is it possible to use a local telephone number to access sites all around the world, without paying long distance charges for the access? Let's take a look at the broad protocols used to decipher Internet and network addresses, and resolve the trip details that users make.

DOMAIN NAME SYSTEM (DNS)

The **Domain Name System**, or **DNS**, is the service that translates computer and server names referred to as **Fully-Qualified Domain Names (FQDN)** to IP addresses.

The DNS is most prevalent on the Internet and identifies the name of web sites. For example, the FQDN of the Cisco web site is *www.cisco.com*. This is the address of the Cisco site. But the name has little value outside convenience for humans. The unique qualifier for the site is the IP address assigned to the Cisco web server. DNS is the system that allows us to use names for servers, and transparently converts the names to unique IP addresses.

Let's get some terminology out of the way before delving into how DNS works. Figure 8-1 shows the Microsoft web site using the Internet Explorer web browser from Microsoft. We're told we're at this site by the address in the Address field:

http://www.microsoft.com

So, the web address for Microsoft is *www.microsoft.com*. Microsoft also has an IP address. But which is easier to remember—a name, or a number? For most people, the name-version of the address is the least challenging. But machines connected to the Internet only understand numbers—binary numbers, at that. We use naming conventions because they're easier for us to remember and track, but a machine must be able to convert from the name that's entered in an address box to a numerical address.

TEST TIP

Know that DNS resolves FQDNs to IP addresses.

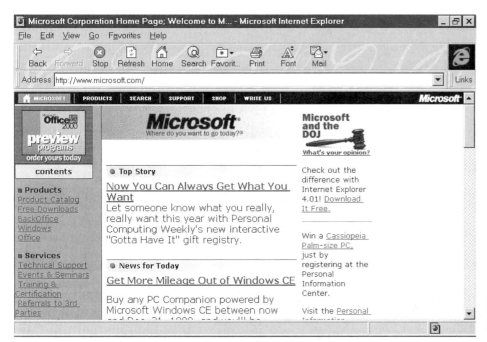

**Figure 8-1:
Microsoft Web Site**

A web address, called a URL (Universal Resource Locator), follows the Domain Name System convention. A DNS must be mapped to an IP address, since the two can't be derived from each other. Note that the name as well as the IP address must be unique to all devices connected to the network.

Name abbreviations, which correspond to the decimal address, are separated by decimal points into a series of zones. Table 8-3 lists the top-level zone codes and their meanings. Domain names are unique on the Internet. The organization that assigns them is called InterNIC (*www.internic.org/*). If you want to set up a web site using a domain name for your company, you'd request the name from an authorized InterNIC vendor such as Network Solutions, pay a small fee, and within a couple of days, it's done. Your domain name, which is also your web site address, would then be added to the name servers on the Internet.

Table 8-3: Top-Level Zone Codes

ZONE	DESCRIPTION
com	Commercial Business
edu	Educational Institution
gov	Government Agency
int	International Organization
mil	Military Site
net	Networking Organization
org	Miscellaneous Non-Profit Organization

DNS is a hierarchical system that begins with root name servers, as shown in Figure 8-2.

There are about a dozen root servers, and these servers represent the single periods in domain names. A root server knows where top-level domain name servers are located. For example, if the address you're trying to reach is a .com address, the root server will direct you to a top-level server for .com. There are top-level DNS servers for .org, .net, .edu, and so on. Each top-level DNS server has authority for a domain.

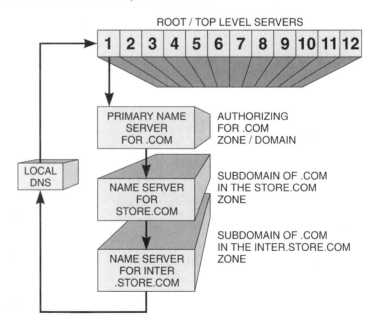

Figure 8-2: DNS Server Hierarchy

The authority for a domain is frequently delegated to a subdomain. The DNS server of a subdomain has authority for a zone residing at the subdomain. A subdomain may be further subdivided into more intricate DNS servers that have authority for narrow zones within that subdomain.

Let's look at a fictional example, using the pseudo-Internet name of **internet.store.com**. Let's further pretend that the name originates from a retail company called Store, and that it has divisions for Internet products, telecommunications products, and consumer electronics products. The address is read from right to left, and is interpreted as:

- *com*—specifies the domain as a commercial site

- *store*—represents a subdomain of the .com zone/domain. Some companies use this convention to physically and logically separate their Internet sites. This is often the case with large companies that have a diverse product offering. Note that store.com may also be an equally valid address but will always be associated with internet.store.com.

- *internet*—Describes the name of the company of the commercial site, or, in this example, a division within the company; the Internet division of the company called Store. This is usually an abbreviation of the actual company name, university, government agency, etc. When domain names are selected, most companies try to use a name that represents their actual business, without being too long (it can contain up to 48 characters).

┌─ **TEST TIP** ─┐

Know that a domain name is interpreted from right to left.

So, for the Internet address *internet.store.com*, a subdomain "internet" is in the subdomain "store", which is in the .com domain. Typically, a web site address is written in lower-case letters because, at one time, the UNIX-based routers and servers on the Internet could only understand lower case. That's not the situation today, but if your request for an address is passed along to an older machine, it may not be able to correctly interpret an address containing capital letters.

Now, let's see what would happen if the above fictional address were entered in the address field of a web browser. The sequence of events is as follows:

(1) The local DNS server (the DNS server that your computer is assigned to) would first look to see if it has the domain name in its memory cache. We'll assume it doesn't.

(2) The local DNS server will query a root DNS server for a match to internet.store.com. Functional DNS servers, such as the local DNS to which our example computer is attached, contain a static list of IP addresses for all root DNS servers.

(3) The root server will refer your DNS to a list of primary .com (domain) servers.

(4) Your DNS will select one of the .com servers, and ask it for the address of internet.store.com.

(5) The .com domain DNS server will refer you to a list of store.com subdomain servers (if there are any).

6 Your DNS server will query one of the store.com subdomain DNS servers for internet.store.com.

7 The store.com subdomain servers may refer you to a list of subdomain DNS servers for internet.store.com. Or, if there are no additional subdomains, it will return the IP address of internet.store.com.

Once the IP address of internet.store.com is located by querying through the DNS server hierarchy, your local DNS server will cache all of the information it returns. The next time you enter *internet.store.com*, the local DNS server will match the domain name to the correct IP address, because it is stored in its cache. This reduces the amount of traffic routed through the root and top-level DNS servers (which, in the United States, are the same server).

Notice in Figure 8-2 that DNS servers may be classified as a **zone** or a **domain**. A zone refers to the range of addresses that a DNS server is responsible for. A domain is the name of the address. Depending on the context, these terms could mean the same thing. The top-level server is responsible for the .com zone, and all domain names within the zone. This holds true, unless authority for a domain name has been delegated to a subdomain zone. Internet.com is a subdomain of the .com zone, and this DNS server is responsible for addresses in the internet.com zone.

When you set up an Internet connection, you have the option of selecting the IP address of a Primary DNS and a Secondary DNS. These are two physically different servers that should be located on separate networks. When you apply for the authority of domain names, your server IP address is added to the list of domain servers. If your DNS crashes and you don't have a secondary DNS, then requests for IP addresses to domain names on your server will be returned unanswered—it will appear as if the sites maintained in your DNS server don't exist. So, the usual practice is to have a secondary DNS.

A DNS server is responsible for resolving domain names to IP addresses. For web-based applications, the domain name is refaced with the application to be invoked during the session, as in:

http://www.microsoft.com

When you access the Internet, you invoke an application on a port at the Internet interface. HTTP is a "well-known" port, at port number 80. HTTP stands for Hypertext Transfer Protocol, and is the protocol used to launch an Internet session using HTML, which stands for Hypertext Markup Language. Then, to get to a web site, you first specify the application port (port 80) using HTTP. The colon and forward slashes used with a domain name are UNIX conventions used to separate commands, interfaces, or server files and directories.

Next, you specify the address (or **Universal Resource Locator**, **URL**, as it's sometimes called) as in *www.microsoft.com/*. The DNS will then begin searching for an IP address that matches the domain name microsoft.com. The last / character isn't required, but it's a good idea to include it, because some DNS servers search all microsoft.com addresses, eliminating those with /extensions before returning a result. Some web browsers place the slash by default when you press the ENTER key. If yours doesn't, go ahead and include the forward slash because it speeds up the name-to-IP resolution, and gets you to a site faster.

The *www* tells the HTTP port that this site is a World Wide Web site—and not an FTP, Gopher, or telnet site. What happens if you don't include it? It depends. At worst, the DNS won't find a match, and at best, it'll default to www. HTTP launches HTML, which can be run on an FTP or a Gopher site, as well as a web site, so you should specify which service you want the DNS to search. For example, if you wanted to go to the Microsoft FTP site, you'd enter the address as:

ftp://ftp.microsoft.com/

DNS is essential to navigating the Internet, and may be used extensively on private networks as well. The most common problem confronting users is failure to specify the IP address of the first local or remote DNS server that a computer will query when resolving domain names to IP addresses. If a DNS server is specified, the browser has no indication of where to go to retrieve the IP address of the desired site. To a user, it appears as if they can't connect to the Internet.

BOOT PROTOCOL (BOOTP)

> **BootP (Boot Protocol)** allows a diskless client to boot from a remote server in order to determine its IP address.

A diskless client means that the client may not have the standard hard drive featured in computers. Instead, the client, such as a router, switch, or sophisticated hub, has nonvolatile RAM (random access memory) that is used to load a file that will boot the client.

Once the client boots, it can discover its own IP address by querying a remote server.

Figure 8-3 illustrates the process of a client determining its IP address. When the client boots, it sends a broadcast message called BOOTREQUEST. The server, which also supports BootP, sends a message called BOOTREPLY back to the client. The reply will contain the client IP address, the IP address of the remote server, as well as IP addresses of required routers.

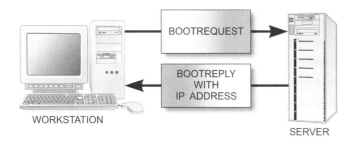

Figure 8-3: IP Address Determination

BootP has been the most common method used to assign IP addresses to remote clients. It alleviated increasing the complexity of a client hardware for assigning a static IP. Essentially, then, BootP is a method for dynamically assigning IP addresses.

BootP uses a command-line interface and is best suited to UNIX environments. With the preponderance of NetWare and Windows, an opportunity was presented to make the interface easier while expanding the options of BootP. The resulting improvement is called DHCP and is presented in the next section.

DYNAMIC HOST CONFIGURATION PROTOCOL (DHCP)

Dynamic Host Configuration Protocol, or **DHCP**, is the protocol used for dynamically assigning IP addresses to remote clients. It's used on many local networks, and used almost exclusively by ISPs when assigning IP addresses to computers connecting to the Internet.

> **NOTE**
> DHCP is used to dynamically assign IP addresses to domain names.

A dynamic IP assignment means that each time you initiate the connection through your ISP, you'll be given a different IP address. During your Internet session, this will be your IP, and the address to which a remote server downloads files to your computer.

> **TEST TIP**
> Know the difference between DHCP, DNS, and WINS.

When a computer running a DHCP client is booted, it requests an IP from the DHCP server at the ISP. The ISP has been assigned a block of IP address, and enters this range of addresses when the DHCP parameters are first set up. The DHCP server will assign the IP for a "lease period" that's determined by the network administrator. With an ISP, this may be for the duration of an Internet session, or it may be for a specific time, say three hours. At that time, your IP address expires and you lose access to the Internet.

Normally, a DHCP server assigns IP addresses at boot-up of the client computer, and continues the lease until the client logs off a network—either a LAN connection or an Internet connection. Windows NT 3.5 and up, as well as Windows 9x, Me, 2000, and XP, have built-in support for DHCP. Figure 8-4 indicates that the IP addresses for the Internet connection shown are assigned (dynamically) by the ISP. When possible, you should use DHCP for assigning user IP addresses. The advantages of DHCP include:

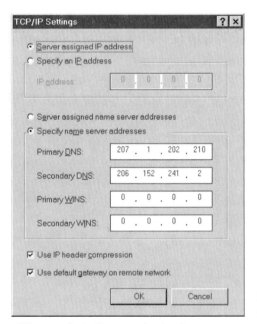

Figure 8-4: Dynamic Assignment of IP Addresses

- It allows the management of IP addresses to be centralized. While some may argue that this isn't an advantage, you have to remember that IP addresses are getting less and less available. If you have a user that signs onto the Internet once in the morning to send and receive e-mail, then dedicating an IP address to a single, one-hour daily application is very inefficient.

- An IP address is a Network layer function and must be mapped to a physical MAC-layer address. With DHCP you can move a client computer without having to reassign the IP address, since it will receive a different IP when it reboots.

- DHCP works side by side with static IP addresses—those addresses that are permanently assigned to a network node such as a router or server. This involves a bit of manual intervention, since the block of dynamic IP addresses (called the DHCP scope) needs to be kept separate from the static IP addresses.

Keep in mind that an IP address may also be permanently assigned to a network-connected device. In this scenario, the client is said to have a static IP. A static IP address is assigned to only one client. If there's a need to make a significant change with the client—such as an upgrade to the operating system or a new NIC card—the client will need to be reconfigured for the static IP address parameters.

If you have a stand-alone modem connected to an ISP from your home, you connect to the ISP using the point-to-point (PPP) protocol. Because it's a point-to-point connection, you don't need a physical MAC-layer address, since your location is implied. There's only you at one end of the connection, and the ISP at the other. The ISP may permanently assign you an IP address, and you use this number when setting up the connection.

WINDOWS INTERNET NAMING SERVICE (WINS)

Windows Internet Naming Service (WINS)

Windows Internet Naming Service, **WINS**, is responsible for reconciling Microsoft NetBIOS names to IP addresses.

Servers running TCP/IP may also run WINS with Windows NT or 2000. WINS contains a lookup table to resolve computer names to IP addresses. Notice the similarity to the DNS service in which a site is given a name and corresponding IP address. WINS extends to NetBIOS at the Session layer of the OSI model, allowing computer names to be expressed as:

   *computername**sharename**path*

This is a standard Microsoft convention called Universal Naming Convention (UNC) that's followed with Windows NT. Note that the syntax begins with two backslashes, followed by the computer name, a single backslash, then the name of a file, directory, etc. With WINS, you can extend this same convenience to all computers using NT. The advantage is that it relieves you of manually entering NetBIOS and IP addresses for name resolution (this can be done manually in the LMHOST map) and then manually changing the map tables when there's a change.

With NetBIOS, a client running NT must broadcast a request for a destination IP. Broadcasts increase traffic on the network, and may in fact be rejected, since not all routers will pass NetBIOS names. If the destination is on a different LAN, this may happen. With WINS, this situation doesn't occur, since a single table lookup is all that's needed to resolve the computer name to an IP address.

> **TEST TIP**
>
> Be able to select the path to a file that uses UNC.

SIMPLE NETWORK MANAGEMENT PROTOCOL (SNMP)

SNMP (Simple Network Management Protocol)

SNMP, or **Simple Network Management Protocol**, is used to manage networks.

The protocol is referred to as "simple" because it takes a small amount of code to implement. Among the management tasks that SNMP can handle are:

- Event notification
- Accessing hardware

- Accessing software

- Implementing software changes

Event notification refers to problem reporting on a network. A client, for example, may use SNMP to report a number of lost data packets that exceed some predetermined threshold. Events with SNMP are usually referred to as **traps**.

Accessing hardware and software means that SNMP may be used to learn about remote hardware or software. Once the hardware or software is understood, the proper protocols can be used on a network.

Software changes include firmware changes delivered to remote clients, or the installation of new protocols.

The physical architecture of SNMP relies upon two components: the Network management system (NMS), and the agent. The structure is shown in Figure 8-5. The NMS is the software used to manage remote clients. The **agent** is the client that is being managed by NMS. An agent may be any physical device on a network but is commonly associated with routers, switches, hubs, or wireless access points.

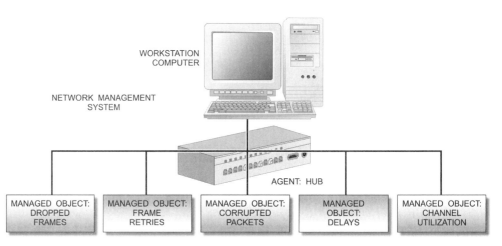

Figure 8-5: Physical Structure of SNMP

The agents contain **managed objects**. A managed object is any parameter on the network that's to be managed. Examples include hardware information of a specific device such as the fact that a particular hub is 10Base-T. Or, an object may refer to a specific statistic such as the number of packets dropped during a session.

All defined objects are arranged in a management information base (MIB). A MIB defines the object that's to be managed by either the agent or the NMS. Note that a MIB is not a database-implementation such as Access or SQL. Rather, a MIB consists only of particulars of the objects to be managed. A MIB can reside in any database since it is database-independent.

Information is exchanged between agent and NMS devices using messages called protocol data units, or PDUs. A PDU is formal frame of data used to send SNMP messages. It includes overhead fields and a data field that identifies the object. SNMP follows a command and response format in which the NMS sends a command to the agent in the guise of a PDU and the agent responds with the requested information, also in the form of a PDU.

Related to SNMP is RMON, which stands for Remote Monitoring. RMON uses expanded MIBs to report a broader range of network data with an emphasis on trouble information.

NETWORK ADDRESS TRANSLATION (NAT)

NAT, or **network address translation**, is a protocol that allows for a private IP address to be converted to a public IP address.

The purpose of NAT is to conserve IPv4 address assignments by encouraging the use of private IP addresses on a LAN, while still allowing the LAN nodes Internet access. In order to access the Internet, the private IP address used by the LAN nodes must be replaced with a public IP address. NAT is the protocol used to make the switch in IP addresses.

Figure 8-6 shows how a typical application of NAT is implemented. Three computers—labeled A, B and C—are connected to a hub. One of the hub ports connects to a router. The router connects to an ISP on the Internet. Note that computer A has been assigned a private IP address and a unique port number. In this example, the port number is not a well-known port (port numbers up to 1023), but an ephemeral port (port numbers from 1024 up to 65,535). Recall that ephemeral ports are not pre-assigned to a specific application.

When a networked computer using TCP/IP starts, the computer is assigned a port number above 1023 for the session. The port number should uniquely distinguish the machine from other computers on the network (although there are no reasonable safeguards to prevent two machines from using the same port number if they start up at the same time).

In the figure, computer A has the IP address of 10.100.20.10, which is a private IP address. The port number being used is 1025. Suppose the user of the computer A launches HTTP (well-known port number 80) in a browser to go to a web site. If the web site is located at 200.1.1.1, then the address space of the IP packet will be:

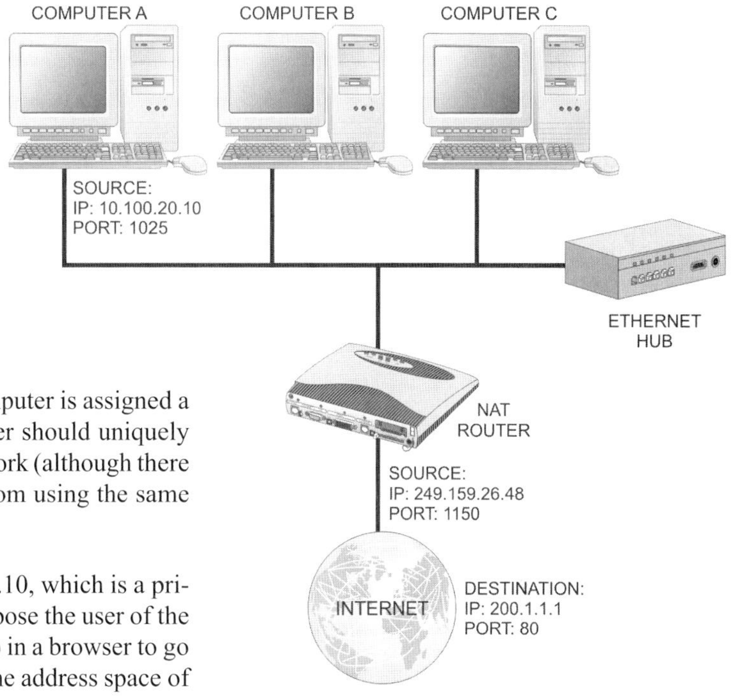

COMPUTER A   COMPUTER B   COMPUTER C

SOURCE:
IP: 10.100.20.10
PORT: 1025

ETHERNET HUB

NAT ROUTER

SOURCE:
IP: 249.159.26.48
PORT: 1150

INTERNET

DESTINATION:
IP: 200.1.1.1
PORT: 80

Figure 8-6: NAT Implementation

      Source address and port number:
      10.100.20.10   1025

      Destination address and port number:
      200.1.1.1   80

Since the destination address is off the LAN, the packet will be accepted by the router. Because the router supports NAT, it will strip the private source address and replace it with a public address. If the public address assigned to the router is 249.159.26.48, the address space of the packet sent from computer A will now be:

      Source address and port number:
      249.159.26.48   1025

      Destination address and port number:
      200.1.1.1   80

As you can see, the private IP address was stripped and replaced with a valid public IP address. In addition, the router replaced the port number generated by computer C and replaced it with one of its own port numbers.

The router, upon initially receiving the packet from computer C, will add an entry to its NAT tables that contains the computer C private IP address, the port number generated by the computer, and the port number it generated. The router will refer to the map when the remote web server sends a reply back to computer C.

When the reply arrives, the router will match the port number in the destination field of IP to the port number generated by computer C. Once the match is made, the destination IP and port number will be stripped from the received packet and replaced with the private IP address and port number for computer C.

The advantage of NAT is that it saves on using valuable public IP addresses. The NAT protocol is widely deployed and is particularly helpful for smaller businesses and home-based networks.

In the Windows NT/2000 Server operating systems there is a service called **Internet Connection Sharing (ICS)** that is very similar to the NAT in that it enables many different computers to share a single connection to the Internet. While NAT is designed to handle Internet traffic for large organizations, ICS is intended for use in small businesses and home use.

— TEST TIP —

Know what ICS is, what it is used for and, and what types of operating systems support it.

KEY POINTS REVIEW

An overview of network services has been presented in this chapter.

- The Internet is a network of networks.

- The World Wide Web is the graphical area of the Internet. Other services available from the Internet include file transfers, telnet, and e-mail.

- The official name of the Internet bulletin boards is USENET.

- Internet chat, similar to e-mail, is interactive and instantaneous.

- The Domain Name System, or DNS, is the service that translates computer and server names to IP addresses.

- DNS is a hierarchical system that begins with root name servers.

- BootP (Boot Protocol) allows a diskless client to boot from a remote server in order to determine its IP address.

- Dynamic Host Configuration Protocol, or DHCP, is the protocol used for dynamically assigning IP addresses to remote clients.

- Windows Internet Naming Service, WINS, is responsible for resolving Microsoft NetBIOS names to IP addresses.

- SNMP, or Simple Network Management Protocol, is used to manage networks.

- NAT, or network address translation, is a protocol that allows for a private IP address to be converted to a public IP address.

At this point, review the objectives listed at the beginning of the chapter to be certain that you understand and can perform them. Afterward, answer the review questions that follow to verify your knowledge of the information.

REVIEW QUESTIONS

The following questions test your knowledge of the material presented in this chapter:

1. What is the Internet?

2. What is gopher?

3. Which area of the Internet is noted for extensive multimedia?

4. What is the purpose of DNS?

5. For the domain name *doc.help.com*, list the sequence used by DNS servers in deciphering the name.

6. What is a root DNS server?

7. What is a domain DNS server?

8. What is a zone name?

9. What is the purpose of BootP?

10. Write a definition of DHCP.

11. How is WINS used in networks?

12. List three services available with SNMP.

13. What advantage does NAT offer?

14. What is UNC?

15. For the server name *server*, a directory called *directory,* and a file called *file*, express the path to *file* using UNC.

EXAM QUESTIONS

1. Which network service converts domain names to IP addresses?
   a. DNS
   b. WINS
   c. SNMP
   d. DHCP

2. Which network service allows a diskless client to boot in order to learn its IP address?
   a. Telnet
   b. NAT
   c. BootP
   d. WINS

3. Which network service should be used to learn about network problems?
   a. USENET
   b. SNMP
   c. NetBIOS
   d. DNS

4. Which network service allows private IP addresses to be converted to public IP addresses?
   a. FTP
   b. WINS
   c. DHCP
   d. NAT

5. Which network service is used to dynamically assign IP addresses to clients?
   a. SNMP
   b. DHCP
   c. Gopher
   d. STMP

6. What is maintained on root name servers?
   a. the location of domain servers
   b. all registered domain names
   c. all assigned IP addresses
   d. the location of all local DNS servers

7. Which network service is used to convert NetBIOS computer names to IP addresses?
   a. DNS
   b. BootP
   c. WINS
   d. DHCP

8. Which of the following best represents UNC?
   a. www.internet.com
   b. http://www.internet.com
   c. //server/internet/doc
   d. //server/internet.doc

9. Which network service replaces the port number generated by a client and replaces it with another port number?
   a. WINS
   b. DNS
   c. DHCP
   d. NAT

10. Which network service uses managed objects to refer to a parameter that's being managed?
    a. SNMP
    b. Telnet
    c. NAT
    d. BootP

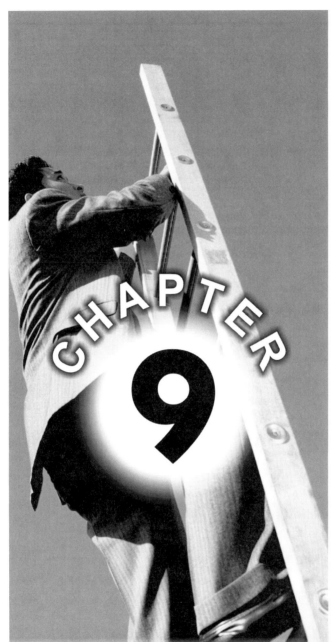

CHAPTER 9

WAN TECHNOLOGIES

LEARNING
OBJECTIVES

LEARNING OBJECTIVES

Upon completion of this chapter and its related lab procedures, you will be able to perform the following tasks:

1. Identify the basic characteristics of the following WAN technologies:

   - ISDN

   - FDDI

   - ATM

   - Frame Relay

   - SONET

   - T-Carrier

   - Optical Carrier

WAN TECHNOLOGIES

INTRODUCTION

A wide area network covers a large geographical area. How large? Well, larger than a campus setting or a town. Normally we think of a WAN as interconnecting networks spread around a country or around the world. The Internet is a WAN. A network linking San Francisco, Miami, and New York is a WAN.

Slowly, then, a new definition of a WAN has begun to emerge. A WAN is a network of interconnected networks, and they may cover about any size geographical area. We're beginning to associate the phrase "wide area" with a lot of nodes, rather than a big landmass area. Still, the geographical description remains valid, as well. In fact, as far as the Network+ exam is concerned, consider a WAN to be any network that covers an area larger than a city.

In this chapter, think of a WAN most appropriately as the Internet, a true network of networks. We don't know how big the Internet is, since it's autonomous from governments and private industry. But, certainly, it connects many networks.

There are numerous ways to access wide area networks, and we'll take a look at several of them along with a couple of technologies that have been around for many years, and show no signs of going away.

CIRCUIT AND PACKET SWITCHING

Circuit and packet switching refer to the path that data or voice communications makes through the local and long distance telephone systems. There are two primary technologies in use: *circuit switching* and *packet switching*. Generally, data communications is associated with packet switching, while voice communications are associated with circuit switching.

Before discussing the technologies, let's summarize a few definitions:

- **Circuit Switching** A circuit-switched network is one in which a path is set up and maintained between two devices for the duration of the transmission.

- **Packet Switching** A packet-switched network is one in which data may travel across many paths between two devices.

Virtual Circuit

Connection-oriented

Connectionless

Frequency Division
Multiple Access
(FDMA)

Time Division
Multiple Access
(TDMA)

- **Virtual Circuit** A virtual circuit (also called a permanent virtual circuit) refers to a specified amount of bandwidth that's guaranteed for the duration of a transmission between two devices. Packet switched networks use virtual circuits.

- **Connection-oriented** A connection-oriented network, when applied to wide area networks (WANs), refers to the guarantee of a transmission path or bandwidth. A virtual circuit is an example of a connection-oriented network. The most common connection-oriented protocol is TCP.

- **Connectionless** A connectionless network is one in which there is no guarantee of a path between two end-devices, or that the bandwidth will be available for the two devices to communicate. This type of connection is often called "best-effort." Connectionless protocols such as UDP (User Defined Protocol) and HTTP (Hyper-Text Transfer Protocol) use a best-effort strategy for sending data packets.

- **Frequency Division Multiple Access (FDMA)** FDMA is a multiplexing technique in which the channel bandwidth is divided into discrete units that are permanently made available to all users. Broadcast AM, FM, and television are examples of FDMA.

- **Time Division Multiple Access (TDMA)** TDMA is a multiplexing technique in which the full channel bandwidth is available to each user for specific time periods. All of the bandwidth technology types described in this section use TDMA.

Circuit Switching

Circuit switching consists of a dedicated channel between devices on each end of a connection.

The most common application of circuit switching is found in the twisted pair telephone network, also called the Public Switched Telephone Network (PSTN). Circuit switching is ideally suited for voice communications because the dedicated circuit allows voice communication to be delivered in real-time, in a sequential manner.

When a voice is converted to electronic format, it's represented by a series of bits that are grouped into some larger grouping—such as a byte. Each group of bits is transmitted through the dedicated channel one after the other. On the receiving end, the bits are converted back into audio in the same order that they were received.

In a packet switched network, the groups of bits—organized into frames, packets, or cells—may not be received in the same order they were sent. Consequently, the bits must be reordered into the original sequence before being processed as data. As you can see, the reordering process creates delays that users find unacceptable in voice communications.

Typically, circuit switching data rates mimic those found with dial-up connections—53 kbps maximum. Since a dedicated channel is created between the end connections, circuit switching is connection-oriented. A long as the connection is maintained, all of the switching equipment between the ends remains dedicated, ensuring that information is not lost.

A circuit-switched communication carries one channel, such as a single telephone call on each circuit. When data is transmitted through the channel, there will be times when the line is idle, like the time between key strokes on a keyboard. Even though no information is being sent, the channel remains and represents wasted bandwidth.

In addition to land-based PSTN systems, all cellular communication uses circuit switching.

For a detailed examination of the telephone system refer to the Electronic Reference Shelf—"The Telephone System" located on the CD that accompanies this book.

Table 9-1 summarizes characteristics of circuit switching.

Application	Voice communication
Data Rate	53 kbps
Switching Technique	Circuit switching
Connection Type	Connection-oriented
Data Unit Length	Variable
Media	Primarily twisted pair
Capacity	1 channel

Table 9-1: Circuit Switching Summary

Packet Switching

> Packet switching is an end-to-end digital technology that is primarily used for data communications.

Typically, packet switching is involved in transmitting data over a large geographical area, usually in a WAN. This could be from city to city, country to country, or continent to continent. A WAN typically connects Data Terminal Equipment (DTE) in one area to a DTE in another area. A DTE is just about any programmable device—a computer, a network of computers, a front-end processor, or controller. The DTE gains access to the WAN through Data-Communication (circuit terminating) Equipment (DCE). The most common DCE is a modem.

The ideal WAN limits itself to protocols describing the DTE/DCE relationship as one of simultaneous transmitter and receiver. The communication medium between the transmitting and receiving DTE/DCEs would be a transparent connection. In the terminology of WANs, transparency is referred to as a virtual connection, and is depicted in Figure 9-1.

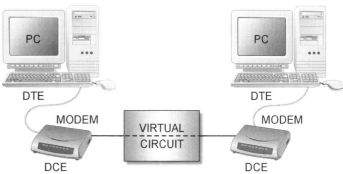

Figure 9-1: WAN Virtual Connection

ITU X.25 Recommendation

The medium appears to the user as a single wire connecting the transmitter and receiver. The WAN described above is implemented using the packet-switching technique, and data is said to travel over a packet-switching network. The most widely deployed protocol used for packet switching is the ITU X.25 standard. Although most media could be used to carry X.25 traffic, copper twisted pair wiring predominates.

X.25 packet switching is an older transport protocol used in WANs, and is modeled after the public telephone system. Based on LAPB protocols, it's a reliable, but slow, technology.

The concept of packet switching is embodied in the recommendation of ITU X.25. X.25 is an interface standard that describes the connection of DTEs and DCEs to public switching networks. Essentially, the recommendation is a technology limited to the ports of the DTE, and the ports of the DCE. It is a time-tested technology that's been used successfully since the 1970s. Within the past twenty years, increased data rates, and advances in the physical medium (fiber optics in particular), have caused vendors to question the performance of X.25. Indeed, new techniques will eventually replace conventional packet switching, primarily because X.25 data travels in 64 kbps frames called packets.

The objective of X.25 is to provide a complete communications system for data transfer. The recommendation is modeled after the public telephone system. The DTE is equivalent to the phone subscriber, and the DCE is equivalent to the central office. Considering the complexities of making a long distance telephone call, the system is relatively easy to use. X.25 has been designed to provide the same relative ease to users who need to send and receive data.

Messages to be sent through a packet network are broken into pieces (packets), and appropriate flags, headers, control, and error-checking fields added. Since the data is held in discrete packets, the packets may be sent along different paths to the ultimate destination. As such, X.25 packet switching is a connectionless protocol.

The X.25 protocol adopted a layered approach to data flow that parallels the OSI reference model. As you can see in Figure 9-2, the first three layers of the OSI and the X.25 are the same.

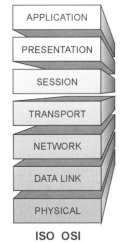
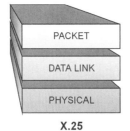

Figure 9-2: ITU X.25 Recommendation

At level 1, the X.25 interface specifications are contained in the X.21 recommendations. X.21 describes physical, electrical, and functional characteristics of level 1. The recommendation specifies a 15-pin synchronous interface that's widely used in Europe, but hasn't gained much of a following in the U.S., due to the prevalence of EIA/TIA-232. The ITU has approved an interface functionally equivalent to EIA/TIA-232 in the X.21 bis recommendation. (The word "bis" is a Swiss term for alternate.)

The Data Link level (level 2) describes the procedures used by the DTE and DCE for synchronization, control, and error detection. X.25 uses a subset of HDLC, Link-Access Procedure-Balanced (LAPB). For X.25 networks, the Normal Response Mode (NRM) of LAPB is used. In the NRM, a station was designated as either primary or secondary. A secondary station cannot transmit without receiving permission from the primary. The LAPB protocol is operated in the Asynchronous Balanced Mode (ABM). In this mode, a separate primary and secondary aren't recognized. Each station on the network can initiate a transmission, or terminate the connection.

You shouldn't be misled by the "asynchronous" in asynchronous balanced mode. Data flow through an X.25 network is synchronous; "asynchronous" describes the autonomy of the stations. Each station can transmit a packet of data onto the network whenever it chooses to do so. The Data Link frame format for X.25 is very similar to HDLC, as you'll see shortly.

Level 3, the Packet level (also called the Network level since this level has nearly the same function as the Network layer in the OSI model), describes the format of packets and includes a Control field header that governs packet exchanges between DTE and DCE, as well as information for routing between devices on the network.

The user has several services available on a packet-switched network. The network may provide the user with a virtual circuit. A **virtual circuit** is a logical connection through the network. The stations at either end may disconnect the connection at any time. This is quite similar to a subscriber telephone call. The packet network establishes the route of least delay, and maintains it while the transmission takes place. An alternative (and more expensive) service is a **permanent virtual circuit**. Stations at either end of the network are assigned a permanent address, and can communicate at any time without the station dialog inherent in establishing a connection. While more expensive, a permanent virtual connection is quicker because the stations do not have to validate addresses.

A user with a virtual circuit is billed for the time that the connection is in place, and the number of packets that are sent. A permanent virtual circuit user is charged a flat, monthly fee. Packet switching has many other options available to users that are similar to the options offered to telephone subscribers. Reverse charges allow a transmitter to bill the receiver for packets sent to it. Local-charge prevention prohibits reverse, or third-party, charges. Call redirection, similar to call-forwarding, allows the network to redirect data.

X.25 Packet Frame Format

The frame format for packet networks is shown in Figure 9-3. The actual packet is the network-level header field and the user data field. The rest of the frame is similar to HDLC. The beginning flag synchronizes the DTE and DCE, and is 8 bits wide, with a value of 01111110. The end flag signals the end of the frame, and also has a bit pattern of 01111110.

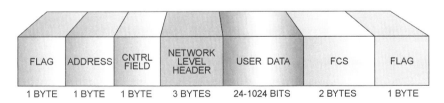

FLAG	ADDRESS	CNTRL FIELD	NETWORK LEVEL HEADER	USER DATA	FCS	FLAG
1 BYTE	1 BYTE	1 BYTE	3 BYTES	24-1024 BITS	2 BYTES	1 BYTE

Figure 9-3: X.25 Frame Format

The one-byte address identifies the DTE and DCE. It is a fixed bit pattern, whose assignment to the DTE and DCE depends upon the usage. The address follows the command/response scheme used with unnumbered frames in HDLC. In the case of X.25, the process is simpler since all exchanges are point-to-point between the DCE and DTE.

Since only two devices are involved, the address will only be one of two values: 10000000, or 11000000. When a station (DTE or DCE) sends a command, the address specifies the receiver (DTE or DCE). When a station makes a response, the address specifies the station responding. The specific command or response is contained in the Control field.

The LAPB command address assignments are:

(1) 10000000, when the DTE sends a command to the DCE. The address is specifying the DCE.

(2) 1100000, when the DCE sends a command to the DTE. Now, the address specifies the DTE.

The LAPB response address assignments are:

(1) 11000000, when the DTE responds to a command from the DCE. The address specifies the DTE.

(2) 10000000, when the DCE responds to a command from the DTE. The address specifies the DCE.

An example of the command/response is illustrated in Figure 9-4.

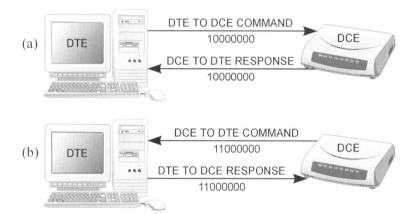

Figure 9-4: Command/Response Assignments of LAPB Protocol

In Figure 9-4(a), the DTE is sending a command to the DCE. The DTE might be sending a Receive Ready (RR) in the Control field, asking the DCE if it can receive data.

The DCE makes an appropriate response to the DTE command. In Figure 9-4(b), the roles have reversed. Now the DCE is sending a command to the DTE, and the DTE replies with an appropriate response.

The Control field has basically the same function in LAPB as it did in HDLC. The Control field serves as the data link header. As in HDLC, there are three types of Control fields: *Information*, *Supervisory*, and *Unnumbered*. The Information field controls the transfer of user data. The Supervisory field manages control of the link between DTE and DCE. The Unnumbered field deals with specialized network management functions.

Table 9-2 summarizes the structure of the three types of Control fields. Note that it is very similar to HDLC for Information and Supervisory fields. The Unnumbered field has commands and responses unique to LAPB. Set Synchronous Response Mode (SARM) is a request by a station to set up the synch for data transfer. The proper response to a SARM is an Unnumbered Acknowledgment (UA). The link initiator then sends a Set Synchronous Balance Mode (SABM), which sets the receive and send counters in the stations to zero. These counters track the sequencing of data packets. Again, the appropriate response is UA. A Command Reject (CMDR) is sent in response to a frame that was received carrying a prohibited command. For example, if a RR frame is sent before the SARM, the response would be CMDR. A Frame Reject (FRMR) would be sent in similar circumstances.

Table 9-2: X.25 Control Fields

Format	Commands	Responses
Information Transfer	I (information)	
Supervisory	RR (receive ready) RNR (receive not ready) REJ (reject)	RR (receive ready) RNR (receive not ready) REJ (reject)
Unnumbered	SARM (set asynchronous response mode)	DM (disconnect mode)
	SABM (set asynchronous balanced mode)	
	DISC (disconnect)	UA (unnumbered acknowledgment)
		CMDR (command reject) FRMR (frame reject)

The Number Sent (NS) and Number Received (NR) in the Information field are used to ensure proper sequencing between DTE and DCE. Both NS and NR have 3-bit parameters. A station can send seven packet frames before being sent a response from the receiver. A response is sent using a Supervisory frame, which specifies only a NR field. If seven packets are sent to the DCE, it will send a Supervisory frame with RR set, and the NR = 1. Why? The NS from the transmitting station holds the number of frames sent. The NR field in the Information frame is set to the number it expects to receive in the Supervisory frame from the receiver.

Figure 9-5 demonstrates the sequencing.

In Figure 9-5(a), the DTE is transmitting the seventh packet (NS = 111). The NR field is incremented by one, to 001. The DCE acknowledges it has received the seventh packet by returning to the DTE the number of the next packet it expects to receive.

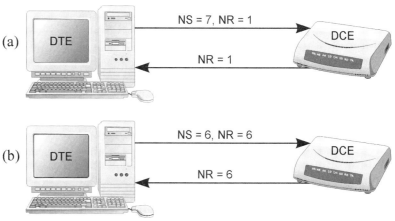

Figure 9-5: Packet Sequencing Procedure

A similar situation is shown in Figure 9-5(b). The DTE is sending packet 5. It expects a supervisory return response from the DCE, with NR = 6. The DCE would know a response is expected because the last DTE frame would have the P/F bit set. The DCE received the 5 packets because it sends NR = 6, meaning it expects the next packet from the DTE to be numbered 6. If, in Figure 9-5(b), the DCE had sent NR = 5, the DTE would realize the sixth packet had been lost, because its own NR is set at 6. In this manner, the DTE and DCE check the sequence of packets sent and received.

The User data field is a minimum of 24 bits long, and a maximum of 1,024. The actual packet is sent in the User data field, along with the Network-level header data. The network header is generally 24 bits (3 bytes), and comprises the minimum bit length. Much of the exchange between DTE and DCE consists of commands and responses carried by Supervisory frames. Supervisory frames do not carry user data.

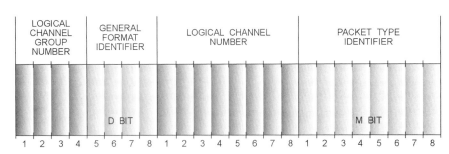

Figure 9-6: Network-Level Header Field

Figure 9-6 illustrates the Network-level Header field. The field is responsible for packet format, and for directing an orderly data flow between the DTE and DCE. The header is considered to be part of the packet.

The logical channel group identifies the group of which the channel is a part. The X.25 gateway connecting the DEC to a packet network contains 16 group channels. Each group channel contains 256 logical channels. As an example, a header may be group channel 7, and logical channel 150. A group, then, can contain up to 4096 channels. A single gateway supports 40 simultaneous full-duplex channels.

The General Format Identifier (GFI) describes the overall header format. For example, 0001 is the data packet format. Other bit patterns describe diagnostics, flow control (RR RNR, reset indications), and connection setups (call request, call accepted, or incoming call). X.25 networks installed since 1984 have a D-bit option in the general format identifier. D-bit = 1 when the calling station requests delivery confirmation from the called station.

The Packet Type Identifier (PTI) describes the function of the packet. The general format identifier may indicate that the packet is a call setup packet. For example, the DCE may send an incoming call to the DTE. The bit pattern for incoming calls is 00001011. Whereas the format identifier is a general indicator of the packet's function, the packet type identifier is a specific indicator of the function. The M-bit contained in the Packet-Type field stands for more data. When this bit is set to 1, additional packets have been transmitted, and should be considered a part of a unit. If the M-bit is turned off, there are no more packets.

The users of packet networks find them to be an advantage for short, bursty traffic. An exchange of small files among field offices several times a day wouldn't cost-justify a dedicated phone line between the users. The packet network would usually be cheaper than public phone lines. Packet networks route the packets dynamically—intelligent nodes in the network select the path offering the least amount of congestion. Efficiency is maximized, while the costs of using the network are thereby kept at a minimum. As mentioned earlier, packet networks also have the advantage of offering a variety of services to data-communication users that are similar to services offered to phone subscribers.

Table 9-3 summarizes characteristics of X.25 packet switching.

Application	Data
Data Rate	56/64 kbps
Switching Technique	Packet/ packet
Connection Type	Connectionless
Data Unit Length	Variable (up to 1024 bits)
Media	Primarily twisted pair
Capacity	Up to 4096 channels

Table 9-3: Summary of X.25 Characteristics

FIBER DISTRIBUTED DATA INTERFACE (FDDI)

The **Fiber Distributed Data Interface** (**FDDI**) standard was described in detail in Chapter 2. In this section, we'll review the main attributes of the standard.

FDDI uses fiber-optic media to deliver data packets at speeds up to 100 Mbps. In a WAN environment, FDDI is typically used as a backbone to interconnect LANs. A backbone is a common data pathway, and serves a single high-speed route for data.

FDDI is configured on a ring topology. The ring will have two data paths, one for data and one for redundancy in case the primary ring breaks. LANs may be physically connected to the ring and a bridge will perform Data Link layer protocol conversions if necessary.

Since FDDI is a Data Link layer protocol, it does not have the ability to route data packets; consequently, it must be used in conjunction with an upper-layer protocol that provides for routing. TCP/IP is the most common network protocol used on FDDI networks.

A FDDI packet has a maximum length of 36,000 bits. Physical nodes use an inverted form of their MAC address for node identification on a FDDI network. When combined with TCP/IP, any FDDI node can be logically located with IP, and physically located with the inverted MAC address.

The characteristics of FDDI are summarized in Table 9-4.

Table 9-4: FDDI Characteristics

Application	Data communication
Data Rate	100 Mbps
Switching Technique	N/A
Connection Type	Connectionless (FDDI relies on TCP for connection-oriented reliability)
Data Unit Length	36,000 bits
Media	Fiber optic
Capacity	1 channel without multiplexing

FRAME RELAY

Frame Relay is a packet-switched technology with a variable-length data field that was designed for the Integrated Services Digital Network (ISDN, described in a later section of this chapter). It uses a statistical multiplexer for sending messages from many sources over a Permanent Virtual Circuit (PVC) to the destination. Note that with a multiplexer, source stations are using the same channel link to the destination. A Frame Relay network is illustrated in Figure 9-7.

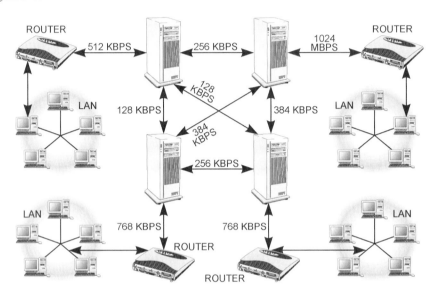

Figure 9-7: Frame-Relay Network

Frame Relay is a packet-switched technology with a variable-length data field.

Frame Relay is a variable-bandwidth, packet-switched technology that utilizes Data Link layer concepts to send data faster than X.25.

In Figure 9-7, four LANs are connected in a WAN using Frame Relay switching. The LANs communicate over a permanent virtual circuit, typically across twisted pair wiring. This is set up and maintained by a common carrier, such as AT&T, MCI, etc. The LAN manager specifies which nodes on the LANs will be communicating, and this determines the size and number of PVCs. The Frame Relay switch stores the PVC, and will use it when the nodes transmit. But note that it's up to the long distance carrier to implement some type of switching technology between Frame Relay interfaces. Frame Relay is called a connection-oriented technology, but via the permanent virtual circuit set up between interfaces.

The LANs gain access to the PVC at the carrier Point Of Presence (POP). The POP is the physical connection at which the carrier assumes control of the data.

The carriers offer PVCs at varying data rates. The data rate corresponds to channel bandwidth. The LAN user specifies the PVC rates, based upon a best-estimate of node usage. From this estimate, a Committed Information Rate (CIR) is derived. The CIR is the sum of the PVC bandwidths for each LAN. The user specifies the CIR bandwidth, and the Frame Relay switch multiplexes the LAN nodes onto the assigned PVCs.

The advantage of Frame Relay networks is that bandwidth is made variable, and can be matched to the bandwidth needs of the user. This may range from 4 kbps to a full T1 1.544 Mbps link.

Frame Relay networks work particularly well with mildly bursty data, such as the intermittent keystrokes associated with order entries. They are capable of exceeding the CIR for brief periods, because the switch incorporates a statistical multiplexer. Statistical multiplexers contain buffer pools that allow the data rate to exceed the aggregate rate for short periods.

The reason that Frame Relay transports data so much faster than X.25 is that it only uses the first two layers of the OSI protocol model, the Physical and Data Link layers. The significance of this is that the Network layer functions are not available to Frame Relay networks. This translates into higher throughput, which results in higher speeds.

The data-link protocol used by Frame Relay is the Link-Access Procedure-D (LAPD). LAPD was originally designed for ISDN systems, and provides for multiple logical links over the same channel. LAPD is similar to HDLC, but with fewer header fields.

Frame Relay transports data at higher rates than X.25, and it is usually implemented at a lower cost than leased lines. Like X.25, users are offered variable amounts of bandwidth. The weakness of Frame Relay is that it is restricted to data transmissions. In addition, Frame Relay packets are prone to being lost, when statistical multiplexer buffers approach the overflow point. Due to the flow-control capabilities of multiplexers, data from the LAN nodes is slowed down to avoid losing the packets; this has tended to cast some doubt on the superior data-rate attributes of Frame Relay.

Table 9-5 summarizes characteristics of Frame Relay.

Application	Data communication
Data Rate	4 kbps and up
Switching Technique	N/A
Connection Type	Connection-oriented
Data Unit Length	Variable
Media	Primarily twisted pair
Capacity	Multiple channels at the interface to the carrier network.

Table 9-5: Frame Relay Characteristics

ASYNCHRONOUS TRANSFER MODE (ATM)

Asynchronous Transfer Mode (ATM) is a cell relay standard that uses 53-byte cells for transporting text, voice, video, music, or graphic messages.

ATM was developed by AT&T in 1980 as a technique for transmitting voice and data in a packet format. In 1988, the ITU (CCITT) selected ATM as a standard to use with Broadband ISDN (BISDN). ATM is the standard that describes cell relay technology.

The strength of ATM, and the reason many believe it will be the transport service of the future for both WANs and LANs, is its ability to support large-bandwidth connections that are scalable to the user's needs. Bandwidth scalability refers to a channel that is bandwidth-flexible, such as Frame Relay and X.25. ATM is also noted for providing bit-level service. Bit-level service refers to transmissions at the Data Link level; ATM uses only the first two levels of the OSI model.

The ability of a protocol to address individual bits is important to transmitting video. Not only does video require large-bandwidth channels, but the channels must also be of a high quality. This is because the user is much more sensitive to video phase distortion than noise distortion. That is, our eyes are more sensitive to phase distortion than are our ears.

ATM is the only network service standard capable of carrying voice, data, and video. As Table 9-6 shows, the bandwidth needs of these three classes of data differ considerably. LANs are usually designed for a fixed amount of bandwidth, and the only way to increase the bandwidth is to change to another type of LAN, such as FDDI. However, this may be wasteful if users are only occasionally sending voice or video.

Table 9-6: Bandwidth Requirements for Information Transfer

Object	Basic	Compression	Compressed
1-page Business Letter	5 kbits	4:1	1.3 kbits
20-page Document with Graphics	40 Mbits	4:1	10 Mbits
Voice	64 kbps	8:1	8 kbits
1-page FAX	1 Mbits	14:1	75 kbits
24-bit Computer Image	800 Mbits	100:1	8 Mbits
Full Motion Video (NTSC)	45 Mbps	50:1	1 Mbps
Full Motion Video (HDTV)	150 Mbps	50:1	3 Mbps

Table 9-7: BISDN Model

Upper Layer Services and Applications	
ATM Adaption Layer	Convergence sublayer
	Segmentation and reassembly
ATM Layer	Cell formatting
Physical Layer	Transmission convergence
	Physical medium

Originally, ATM was defined as part of the broadband ISDN model by the ITU, as shown in Table 9-7. Three ATM layers are defined in the BISDN model: the Physical layer, the ATM layer, and the ATM Adaption layer, which replace the first three layers of the OSI model. Note that a network layer is not described. This allows ATM cells to be switched more rapidly than conventional packet switching, since the header will not include routing protocols. This can be accomplished directly with internetworking protocols (TCP/IP).

The Physical layer describes how the ATM cells are transported, and includes the physical interface, channel media, and data rates. Unlike other technologies, ATM can be operated over many physical layers and through many physical interfaces. Currently, ATM transports cells through user interfaces (such as a connection to a LAN) at the following data rates:

1. 100 Mbps multimode fiber optic

2. 155 Mbps multimode fiber optic

3. 155 Mbps OC3 SONET

4. 45 Mbps DS3 (T3) WAN interface

The DS3 interface is targeted to telecommunications carriers, which typically use coaxial or fiber cable, and twisted-pair connections to LANs. The 100 Mbps fiber connection is targeted to LANs, and specifically to FDDI LANs running twisted-pair cables. The SONET specification reflects the status of current technology, and will no doubt include the higher rates, such as OC-24 (1.2 Gbps) and OC-48 (2.5 Gbps) as the need arises.

Due to the small size of ATM cells, they can also be routed through 10 Mbps Ethernet networks, or Token Ring networks. The implication is that there is no set data rate at which ATM must be run.

The ATM layer of the model describes the cell format of ATM. ATM uses small fixed-size cells, 53 bytes long. The header occupies 5 bytes, and the information field is 48 bytes. The cell format of ATM is pictured in Figure 9-8. The General Flow Control (GFC) field provides a method for multiple workstations to use the same interface. ATM cells are statistically multiplexed. The GFC indicates to the multiplexer that more than one station is feeding a single port, and it needs to be aware that the time slot given to the port will contain data from multiple users.

The three Virtual Path Identifier (VPI) and two Virtual Channel Identifier (VCI) fields serve as an addressing mechanism, used by the ATM switches. A virtual channel represents a guaranteed link from source switch to destination switch. Each port on an ATM switch, which is connected to a user station, has a virtual channel to a destination switch. This is illustrated in Figure 9-9.

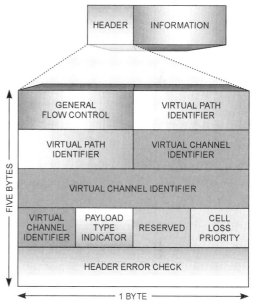

Figure 9-8: ATM Cell Header Format

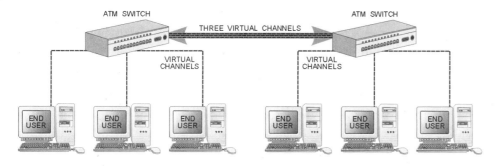

Figure 9-9: ATM Virtual Channels and Virtual Paths

Users on one LAN site are connected to users on another through a virtual path. A virtual path is a single cable carrying a number of virtual channels. The VCI, or VPI, indicates the addresses of ATM switches. Once the cell arrives at the destination switch, connection tables are used to send it to the ultimate user destination. Using virtual switch addresses allows ATM to be independent of Network-layer routing protocols.

The Payload Type Indicator (PTI) identifies the contents of the Information field—user data, management, or control signals. The Cell Loss Priority (CLP) contains instructions for dropping cells if the channel becomes congested, and the network is on the verge of crashing. Error detection, and correction, of single-bit errors is accomplished in the Header Error Check (HEC) field.

Nearly ten percent of an ATM cell is reserved for the header. This constitutes a considerable amount of relative overhead, and is considered a significant weakness.

The ATM Adaption layer prepares higher layer data, such as Switched Multi-Megabit Data (SMDS), for conversion to cells. SMDS is a cell-based transmission service that provides for a wide variety of access speeds, up to a maximum bandwidth of 45 Mbps, with destination addressing. It is connectionless. Being cell-based, it has been widely associated with complex ATM networks.

Table 9-8: Classes of the ATM Adaption Layer

Since ATM supports several different types of applications, the CCITT developed classes of ATM adaption layers to respond to the varying characteristics of the applications. The classes are summarized in Table 9-8.

Type	Service	Application	Control
1	Constant Bit-Rate Support		Connection-oriented
2	Variable Bit-Rate Support	Video	Connection-oriented
3	Variable Bit-Rate Support	Frame Relay	Connection-oriented
4	Variable Bit-Rate Support	SMDS	Connectionless
5	Variable Bit-Rate Support	Simple and Efficient Adaption Layer (SEAL)	Connection-oriented or connectionless

ATM is regarded as the base of network technology for the future. The reason for this is its capability to process multimedia data over any physical network. This means ATM is compatible with all LAN and WAN technologies. Futurists speculate that ATM networks will simultaneously provide users with voice, data, and video services on a workstation, and run on upgraded physical nets, such as Ethernet or token ring.

Characteristics of ATM are summarized in Table 9-9.

Application	Voice, data, and video communication
Data Rate	Variable connectionless
Switching Technique	N/A
Connection Type	Connectionless
Data Unit Length	53-byte cell
Media	Twisted pair and fiber optic
Capacity	1 channel

**Table 9-9:
ATM Characteristics**

DIGITAL T-CARRIER

T-Carrier is a digital transmission technology widely used in WANs and carried over long distance common carrier networks.

T-Carrier

The most common T-Carrier group is the T1. A T1 facility multiplexes 24 voice channels. Each channel is transmitted at 64 kbps for a total T1 data rate of 1.544 Mbps.

The T-Carrier digital technology has been around for over thirty years. In that time, it has evolved from a trunk-to-trunk transmission method to a fully-implemented solution. This means that there are no analog portions from source to destination for digital signals that originate in a computer. The effect is a very reliable low-distortion link. Data is transmitted at either 56 kbps or 64 kbps, in both directions, as opposed to rates in which there is an analog portion. In the case of the analog local loop, the upstream rate is fixed at a maximum of 35 kbps, while the downstream rate (using V.90 modems) is 53 kbps maximum.

A T-Carrier system multiplexes digital data using time division multiplexing (TDM) techniques. The T-Carrier digital hierarchy is pictured in Figure 9-10.

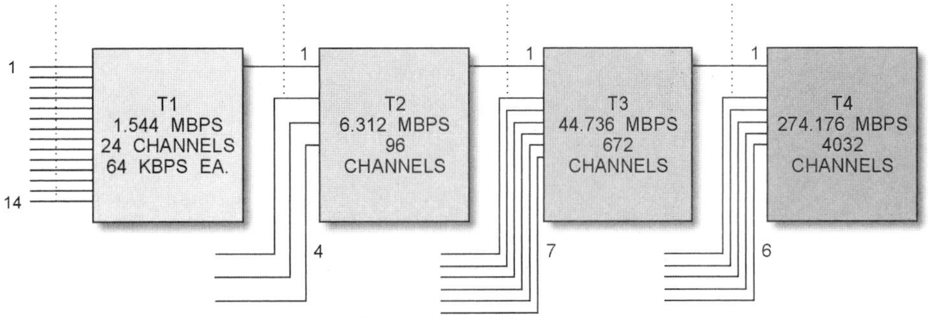

The popular T1 transmission facility combines 24 voice channels. When an analog signal is converted to PCM (pulse code modulation), it's sampled 8,000 times a second, since the highest frequency of the voice channel is 4,000 Hz. A PCM signal contains eight bits in the code. The data rate of a PCM-encoded signal in the T-Carrier system will then be 8 bits × 8,000 samples = 64 kbps. Each of the 24 PCM-encoded voice channels has a bps rate equal to 64 kbps. The data rate of the T1 system supports the channels at 1.544 Mbps. Within the T1 system, the channel signals are referred to as DS0, for digital service. A T1 channel is often called DS1.

**Figure 9-10:
T-Carrier Digital
Hierarchy**

For more in-depth information about pulse code modulation (PCM) refer to the Electronic Reference Shelf—"The Telephone System" located on the CD that accompanies this book.

A T1 multiplexer may transmit data from the twenty-four channels by alternating bits from each channel, in which case it would be utilizing bit-interleaved TDM. Or, it may alternately transmit 8-bit samples from each chord, and then be utilizing word-interleaved TDM.

DS and Tx are often used synonymously, but this isn't technically correct. DS refers to the physical digital signal, while T (for Transmission) refers to the type of carrier.

A T2 carrier contains 96 PCM channels (DS-2 signals) at 6.312 Mbps. Seven T2 facilities are multiplexed at the T3 facility to produce the 672-channel DS-3 signal. Six T3 groups are multiplexed to form the 274.176 Mbps T4 carrier. The T4 facility produces 4032 voice channels.

Table 9-10 presents the hierarchy in a table format.

**Table 9-10:
T-Carrier Digital
Hierarchy**

T-Carrier	Digital Signal	Linespeed	T1 Multiple	Channel Capacity
	DS0	64 kbps	1/24 of a T1	1 channel
T1	DS1	1.544 Mbps	1 T1	24 channels
T1C	D1C	3.152 Mbps	2 T1's	48 channels
T2	DS2	6.312 Mbps	4 T1's	96 channels
T3	DS3	44.736 Mbps	28 T1's	672 channels
T3C	DS3C	89.472 Mbps	56 T1's	1,344 channels
T4	DS4	274.176 Mbps	168 T1's	4,032 channels

Notice that there are subdivisions at T1C and T3C, due to advances in channel bank technology. A channel bank is the terminating equipment used to format each channel. As the technology improved over the years, more channels could be framed within a channel bank, which filled some wide gaps from T1 to T2, and from T3 to T4. In practice, T1 and T3 are the normal carrier implementations.

T-Carriers are replacing most analog systems. In some places, the only remaining analog portion of the telephone system is the subscriber loop. Soon, the analog loop signals will be converted to digital as well. At this time, there are thousands of T1 facilities.

A large corporation may lease T-Carrier facilities from the common carrier, or install their own. The corporation is given direct access to the facility from a local network, called a Private Branch Exchange (PBX), so that data from computer equipment need not go through the analog local loops. The result is a high-speed, all-digital path to a remote location. With a T1 connection, you pay based on distance, unlike Frame Relay where you pay a flat rate each month. A corporation with a large amount of data traffic can lease the facility for about the same cost per channel as an unconditioned voice-grade channel. Dedicated T1 facilities have made sense only to users with high volumes of data traffic. But what about a medium or small corporation?

Until recently, there was little cost justification to a small company in leasing a 24-channel T1 facility. If the company's average channel use was only half the capability of the facility, it would be paying for a large amount of unused bandwidth. The common carriers now recognize that many potential customers were shut out of leasing a T-Carrier system because they had to lease the entire 24-channel bandwidth. To open up these markets, the common carriers have created Fractional T1 (FT1).

Now, a small- or medium-size company can lease portions of a T1 facility as their needs require. The significance of FT1 is that digital communication is now available to nearly any size corporation, and is particularly beneficial to organizations with hundreds of regional offices—of which no single one transmits enough information to utilize a full T1 facility, but collectively, may use many facilities.

Installing T1 requires some careful thought, and a fundamental understanding of the technology. This is particularly true when you consider that there are alternatives such as Frame Relay and X.25. Later in this chapter, you'll see how to implement a T1 line and to weigh the pros and cons of committing an organization to T-Carrier.

T-Carrier Frame Format

A T1 frame consists of twenty-four PCM-encoded 8-bit channels carried in the frame. A single framing bit precedes the 192 data bits to give a total frame length of 193 bits. The frame is sampled 8,000 times each second, or once every 125 ms (1/8,000 = 125 ms). Since there are 193 bits in the frame, the time of each bit is 125/193 = .647 ms. This translates to a data rate of 1.544 Mbps.

The framing bit serves as a marker to identify the beginning of the frame. As the frame is transferred through various switching facilities, and at the final receiver, it allows the equipment to synchronize to small differences in bit times so that the frame won't be lost.

All T-carriers other than T-1 frame the channels differently, and treat a T1 frame as nothing more than a series of bits. This is why a T1C carrier with 48 channels transmits at 3.153 Mbps rather than the expected 2 × 1.544 Mbps.

T-Carrier framing has been through numerous changes. With each change, more data was sent faster. The changes are the direct results of chip technology and channel bank advances. There are five different channel banks in the system, and they are referred to as D1, D2, D3, D4, and DCT (Digital Carrier Trunk), which is only used between T-Carrier facilities, and therefore, is not available to subscribers.

The channel banks are the equipment responsible for combining the channels at the T-Carrier facility. The channel banks for T1 use a D4 (digital) bank. They're responsible for gating the 24 channels into the facility, companding (compression at the transmitter), PCM-encoding, and interleaving onto the T1 channel. A simplified block diagram of the D4 channel bank is pictured in Figure 9-11.

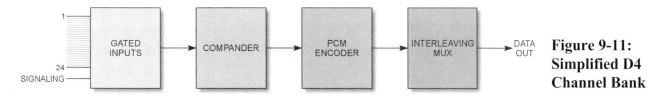

Figure 9-11: Simplified D4 Channel Bank

The original D1 banks (DIA, B, and C) sampled 8-bit voice channels at 8,000 times a second. However, one of the eight bits was used for signaling information such as on-hook, off-hook, etc. This left seven bits to actually carry the voice information, and resulted in a voice signaling rate of 56 kbps. This is why, if you live in an area that uses older channel banks, the telco can only provide you with 56 kbps on a T1 line.

With signaling data being sent every eighth bit, the frames were synchronized by alternating 1's and 0's in the 193rd bit position. The receiver synchronized to this bit sequence by searching for the pattern across all frames received. The idea was that it was unlikely that random data would ever produce this bit pattern at each 193rd bit time. This is the way it worked until the frames were transmitted, and the system locked up each time a 1 kHz test tone was sent through the network. It produced alternating 1's and 0's every 193 bits. The tone has since been changed to 1,004 Hz.

D1 channel banks may still be used around the country, but it's difficult to send data through them because of the 7-bit user data restriction, unless a modified codec is used at the source. Instead, you're more likely to encounter channel banks that use all eight bits for data.

This was implemented in the next channel-bank iteration called D2. A D2 bank has 96 channels packaged into the bank, while a D1 has 72. D3 and D4 banks have 144 channels in the same bank. Channel density increased for each bay of channel banks, but so did the amount of user data, from 56 kbps to 64 kbps.

In a D1 channel bank, losing a bit in each channel for signaling couldn't be detected in voice communications, but when digital data was sent through the same system, the results were disastrous. Starting with D2, all eight bits of the sample were reserved for user data. Well, not quite all; the system still needed to transfer signaling information, but it turned out that it wasn't necessary to send it with each channel. Instead, it was sent every sixth frame—and this led to the use of superframes.

Table 9-11 shows the frame format for a D4 channel bank, called a superframe. A superframe contains twelve T1 frames. Each frame has 193 bits. Except for the sixth and twelfth frames, all eight bits contain user data. In the sixth and twelfth frames, one bit is designated for carrying signaling information that contains the status of the connection.

Table 9-11:
Superframe Format

Frame Number	Terminal Sync Bit	Superframe Sync Bit	Information Bits	Signaling Bit
1	1	-	1 through 8	-
2	-	0	1 through 8	-
3	0	-	1 through 8	-
4	-	1	1 through 8	-
5	1	-	1 through 8	-
6	-	1	1 through 7	8
7	0	-	1 through 8	-
8	-	1	1 through 8	-
9	1	-	1 through 8	-
10	-	1	1 through 8	-
11	0	-	1 through 8	-
12	-	0	1 through 8	8

The 193rd bit in each frame is still used for frame synchronization. Beginning with D2, synchronization was divided between terminal framing and superframe synchronization. Terminal synchronization is used by the terminal equipment at the ends of the link to ensure channel synchronization, while superframe synchronization ensures the full twelve T1 frames are tracked through each switching facility along the route to the destination.

Each synchronization technique uses a specific 6-bit code that's interleaved within the superframe. The bit codes are as follows:

Terminal: 101010
Superframe: 001110

Once the two codes are interleaved at bit position 193 in each of the T1 frames, they generate the following 12-bit code:

100011011100

As you can see in Table 9-11, the terminal synchronization bits are placed in each of the odd numbered frames, while the superframe synchronization bits are placed in each of the even numbered frames.

With this code, the transmit and receive stations will know if a frame is lost and will be able to correctly track channel data within ± two frames. Keep in mind that in a superframe, twelve 12-channel T1 frames (144 total channels) are being transmitted.

A superframe contains twelve T1 frames. The extended superframe contains twenty-four 12-channel T1 frames.

T-Carrier frame formats were enlarged with AT&T's Extended Superframe Format (ESF). The format is illustrated in Table 9-12.

The ESF contains twenty four 12-channel T1 frames (288 total channels). Bit 193 is multiplexed to serve three distinct purposes:

- The Fe bit provides frame synchronization at every fourth frame using the bit pattern 001011. Fe serves the same purpose as the S and T bits in the D4 format.

- The Data Link (DL) bit carries line performance information at every other frame.

- The CRC-6 is a 6-bit cyclic redundancy check that inspects all 4,632 bits of the frame for errors.

Signaling data is retained at every sixth frame as it is for a D4 superframe. The data rate for both D4 and ESF approaches 64 kbps. Due to the sixth frame signaling bits (sometimes called "robbed bit," or 7 5/6 coding, since 5 of 6 frames contain eight user bits and one frame contains seven user bits) the data rate (user information rate) will never reach a full 64 kbps.

If you install a T1 connection today, expect to use D4 channel banks. Your data will be sent using the D4 superframe, or maybe the Extended Superframe Format. With ESF, more information will be sent more quickly, since fewer overhead bits will be sent.

Frame Number	Fe Bit	Data Link Bit	CRC-6	Information Bits	Signaling Bit
1	-	m	-	1 through 8	-
2	-	-	C1	1 through 8	-
3	-	m	-	1 through 8	-
4	0	-	-	1 through 8	-
5	-	m	-	1 through 8	-
6	-	-	C2	1 through 7	8
7	-	m	-	1 through 8	-
8	0	-	-	1 through 8	-
9	-	m	-	1 through 8	-
10	-	-	C3	1 through 8	-
11	-	m	-	1 through 8	-
12	1	-	-	1 through 7	8
13	-	m	-	1 through 8	-
14	-	-	C4	1 through 8	-
15	-	m	-	1 through 8	-
16	0	-	-	1 through 8	-
17	-	m	-	1 through 8	-
18	-	-	C5	1 through 7	8
19	-	m	-	1 through 8	-
20	1	-	-	1 through 8	-
21	-	m	-	1 through 8	-
22	-	-	C6	1 through 8	-
23	-	m	-	1 through 8	-
24	1	-	-	1 through 7	8

Table 9-12: Extended Superframe Format

T-Carrier Signals and Connectors

A DS1 pulse has a positive amplitude of 3.0 volts, and a line rate of 1.544 Mbps.

Each T-Carrier DS pulse is defined for the carrier type. The specifications for a DS4 will be different than for a DS1, for example. Since most T-Carrier signaling occurs at the fundamental T1 level for end-users, this section will be limited to DS1 signal characteristics and connector types. Table 9-13 lists the criteria for DS1 pulses that are imposed on T1 lines.

Table 9-13: DS1 Signal Characteristics

PARAMETER	VALUE
Line Rate	1.544 MHz ± 75 Hz
Cable Length	6,000 Feet
Signal Amplitude	+ Voltage: 3V, ± .3V
Attenuation at Receiver	1.5 to 22.5 dB

The line rate is at the expected 1.544 Mbps. The cable length is limited to 6,000 feet with losses at the receiver falling between 15 and 22.5 dB. T1 uses solid 24AWG UTP, Category 2 cabling, that has a characteristic impedance of $100\,\Omega$.

T1 uses Alternate Mark Inversion (AMI) as the coding scheme. Logic 1's are alternately inverted, while logic 0's are 0V. The original AT&T specification (contained in publication 62411) states that the positive voltage will be $3.0V \pm .3V$. The negative voltage is stated in absolute values; that is without a – sign. Instead, the specification says that the negative alternation of the AMI code will be within .2V of the positive alternation, but will not be less than 2.7V or more than 3.3V.

There are two connectors used with T1 lines. The AT&T specification calls for a subminiature female connector with the pinout shown in Table 9-14. As you can see, the connector appears to represent a bit of overkill, since most of the pins aren't used. They were originally intended for future applications, when connecting remote LANs via T1.

The American National Standards Institute (ANSI) has published a T1 specification using a CAT2-compliant RJ-48 connector with only four wire pairs. The pinout of the ANSI connector is depicted in Table 9-15.

Table 9-14: AT&T T1 Connector Pinout

Pin	Signal
1	Send Data (tip)
2	Reserved for Network
3	Receive Data (tip)
4	Reserved for Network
5	Not Defined
6	Not Defined
7	Not Defined
8	Not Defined
9	Send Data (ring)
10	No Connection
11	Receive Data (ring)
12	No Connection
13	No Connection
14	No Connection
15	No Connection

Table 9-15: ANSI T1 Connector Pinout

Pin	Signal
1	Transmit (ring)
2	Not Used
3	Not Used
4	Receive (ring)
5	Receive (tip)
6	Not Used
7	Not Used
8	Transmit (tip)

T-Carrier Multiplexing

Earlier, it was stated that the T-Carriers use time-division multiplexing at the switching facilities. There are two formats the carriers use with TDM—word interleaving and bit interleaving. Word interleaving is illustrated in Figure 9-12(a).

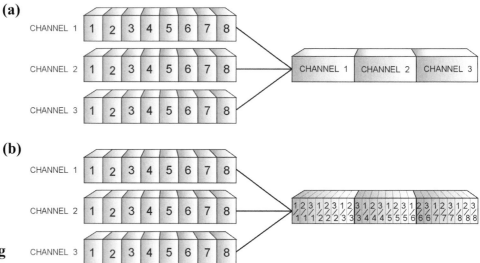

Figure 9-12: Word and Bit Interleaving

On the left, three 8-bit channels are shown. These are time-division multiplexed as complete 8-bit words, one after the other. Typically, this is the method used at T1 facilities. If you have a full T1 line available at your location, this is how the data from users who access the connection will be treated. Once the data leaves your site, it will be multiplexed across trunk lines at the higher levels. The approach at these levels is a bit different.

Figure 9-12(b) shows bit interleaving. Instead of complete words being interleaved, bits from the channel are alternately transmitted. The figure shows the leftmost bit as channel 1, bit 1 (1/1). In the next bit position, channel 2, bit 1 (2/1) is sent. Channel 3, bit 1, is next to be transmitted. Since there are only three channels in Figure 9-12, the rotation starts back at channel 1. Now, bit 2 of channel 1 is interleaved (1/2). The process continues with each channel taking a turn at placing a bit on the line, until all eight bits of each channel are sent.

Bit interleaving is done at the upper levels of the T-Carrier hierarchy, because data traffic is complex to the point that the high-speed facilities are concerned only with switching streams of bits. A T1 carrier, on the other hand, can attach address identifiers so that common frames can be directed to a particular location.

Table 9-16 summarizes T–carrier characteristics.

Table 9-16: Summary of T-Carrier Characteristics

Application	Voice, data, and video communication
Data Rate	DS0 Channel: 64 kbps T1: 1.544 Mbps, T1c: 3.152 Mbps, T2: 6.312 Mbps, T3: 44.736 Mbps, T3c: 44.736 Mbps, T4: 274.176 Mbps E1: 2.048 Mbps
Switching Technique	Circuit/ frame
Connection Type	Connection-oriented
Data Unit Length	193 bits
Media	Primarily twisted pair
Capacity	24 to 4032 channels

Europe and some other parts of the world outside North America have adopted a multiplexed digital carrier system that is a bit different from the T-Carrier system. In Europe, the system is referred to as **E-carrier**.

The basic signaling rate is a DS0 signal that's transmitted at 64 kbps. The signal is developed using a modified form of PCM-encoding (PCM is Pulse Code Modulation, a digital technique for superimposing data onto a stream of square waves) that allows a DS0 signal to have better noise immunity at small signal levels. (The T-Carrier system provides better noise immunity for idle channels, or channels in which data or voice is sent intermittently.)

The basic E-carrier frame, called an E1, contains 30 64 kbps channels. The frame contains 256 bits.

The European carrier hierarchy is shown in Table 9-17.

**Table 9-17:
European Carrier
Hierarchy**

E-carrier	Digital Signal	Line Speed	Channel Capacity
	DS0	64 Kbps	1 Channel
E1	DS1	2.048 Mbps	20 Channel
E2	DS2	8.448 Mbps	120 Channel
E3	DS3	34.368 Mbps	480 Channel
E4	DS4	139.268 Mbps	1920 Channel
E5	DS5	565.148 Mbps	7680 Channel

SONET

> The Synchronous Optical Network is the fiber-optic alternative to digital carrier systems.

SONET (Synchronous Optical NETwork) is the optical-based transmission standard for telecommunications. Data in a SONET network is transmitted through fiber-optic cables and may consist of voice, data, graphics, or video.

SONET networks provide the following services:

- Reduction in copper-based equipment costs and increased reliability.

- Frame lengths of sufficient size to carry management information about the link and the payload carried in the frame.

- The establishment of accepted standards, which permit networks to be built that are vendor-independent.

- The ability to format lower speed frames, such as DS1, and multiplex these using a synchronous structure.

- The creation of an architecture that promotes future development at varying transmission rates.

Only within the past ten years has SONET been deployed to any extent. Prior to this, there were only competing and proprietary implementations. However, with the deregulation of the telecommunications industry in 1982, it became advantageous for common carriers to develop a single standard (begun in 1984) that would transparently pass optical signals from one company to another. The benefit to those carriers was that it increased traffic through their networks, thereby increasing their revenues.

Today, SONET is widely embraced. It is the optical cousin to the T-Carrier system, but one that runs much faster and with considerably more flexibility.

SONET Signals

The basic SONET signal is called STS1. It propagates at 51.84 Mbps through an OC1 channel.

SONET was designed to carry multiple optical signals by byte-interleaving the frames. At the lowest level is the Synchronous Transport Signal-1 (STS1), which has a frame length of 6,480 bits and operates at 51.84 Mbps. STS signals are transported by an Optical Carrier (OC) that corresponds to the bit rate of the STS. Therefore, STS1 will be transmitted through an OC1 channel.

What if three STS signals (STS3) need to be transmitted? They will be carried through a channel with a bandwidth of 3×51.84 Mbps = 155.520 Mbps, or through an OC3 channel.

Table 9-18: SONET Data Rates

SONET Signal	Data Rate
OC-1	51.840 Mbps
OC-3	155.52 Mbps
OC-9	466.560 Mbps
OC-12	622.080 Mbps
OC-18	933.120 Mbps
OC-24	1244.160 Mbps
OC-36	1866.240 Mbps
OC-48	2488.320 Mbps

Notice that in the SONET channel hierarchy, succeeding levels are direct multiples of the base STS-1 rate. In a T-Carrier system, this wasn't the case because above T1 the channels used bit stuffing (a method used to offset timing differences) for synchronization. The OC carrier rates for the SONET standard are listed in Table 9-18, which illustrates the SONET signaling hierarchy.

At the lowest level of STS1, an OC1 channel can accommodate a T3 line. And at OC192, 192 T3 lines can be carried through the channel. This is due to the very high bandwidth capability of fiber-optic cables. Since the signals are multiplexed, they are carried on a single fiber-optic cable.

All data on a SONET network is synchronized to a master atomic clock that resides at the OC3, or higher, level. An OC1 channel, for example, is synchronized, but a SONET requirement is that the synch pulse must originate at OC3 or above.

A T1 line is asynchronous. Each terminal provides its own means of clocking bits—by tracking the 193rd bit position. As you may expect, when a T1 frame is sent through several terminals on its way to a destination node, the timing will vary somewhat due to minor differences in equipment tolerances, environmental changes, and so forth. And, since each terminal is providing its own clocking pulse, the clocks can be expected to be off by some amount. This means that a T1 signal probably won't ever be exactly 1.544 Mbps, but could vary above or below that amount by a couple of hundred bps. When the T1 signal is multiplexed to T3, the errors propagate so that a 44.736 Mbps T3 rate may be off by as much as 2,000 bits. These tolerances are provided for and corrected in the T-Carrier system by stuffing extra bits in a frame that is off-frequency. That's why a T3 line isn't some direct multiple of a T1 line. The extra bits cause it to operate at a different data rate and even then, this rate can't be precisely nailed down. SONET doesn't have this problem, since all frames are synchronized to stable master clocks.

SONET Frame Format

A SONET frame has a length of 810 bytes.

The frame format for SONET is shown in Figure 9-13. The frame consists of 27 bytes of transport overhead, and 783 bytes of payload, called the Synchronous Payload Envelope (SPE). The SPE is further subdivided into the STS path and the actual payload.

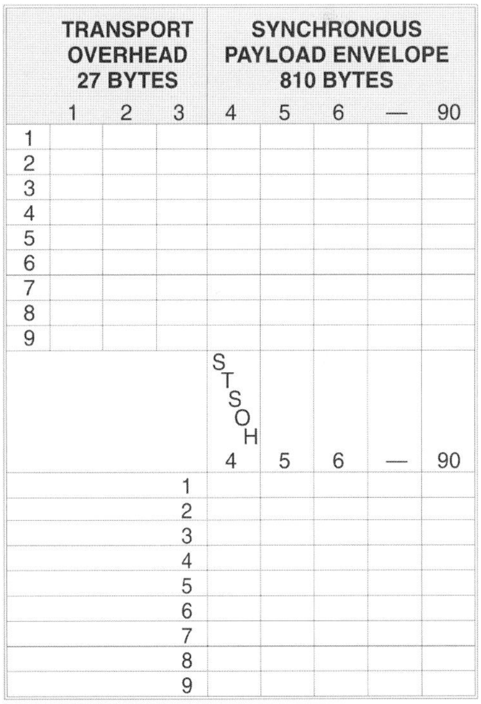

SONET frames are byte-interleaved through a SONET network, so it's convenient to depict the frame as a series of bytes that occupy rows and columns. The frame consists of nine rows and ninety columns. With nine bytes in each column, there are 9 bytes × 90 columns = 810 bytes in the frame. With 810 bytes in the frame, there are 8 bits/ byte × 810 bytes = 6480 bits in the frame. 8000 frames are transmitted/second, so 8000 frames × 6480 bits/ frame = 51,840,000 bps, or 51.840 Mbps.

The transport overhead occupies the first three columns of the frame, and contains information pertinent to source-to-destination communication. This includes framing bytes to mark the beginning of the frame, low-level error-checking, a 192 kbps channel for Operations, Administration, Maintenance, and Provisioning (OAM&P) messages, pointers used to indicate the location of the first byte of the STS1 in the SPE, and alarm and defect signaling.

As mentioned, the SPE is subdivided into STS (Synchronous Transport Signals) path overhead (PO) and the actual payload of the frame. The STS path overhead consists of nine bytes that occupy the first column of the SPE. The path overhead provides performance information concerning the SPE, labels the contents of the SPE, provides status information of the SPE back to the originating terminal, and transmits a signal ahead to the receiving terminal that's intended to ensure the connection continues. This means that in a full-duplex line, the transmitting node should always be aware of any problems with the frame it transmitted, and the frame will always know in advance of problems with the receiving destination. This is one reason that SONET is extremely reliable as compared to the WAN protocol TCP/IP, which transmits on a best-guess effort that a data packet will actually arrive at its destination. (In practice, it's the IP portion of the protocol suite that sends using "best-guess." Best-guess means that the receiving node doesn't return an acknowledgment that a packet was received.)

Figure 9-13: SONET Frame Format

TEST TIP

Be sure to remember that SONET uses fiber-optic cable for the transmission media.

The STS path overhead also contains a byte called the Virtual Tributary (VT) Multi-frame Indicator Byte. The byte contains an indicator to so-called tributary payloads. A tributary payload consists of non-SONET information such as a T1 frame. Although all of these payloads are referred to as VTs, this is not a correct title for all such payloads. SONET will encapsulate a T-Carrier frame within the SPE as a virtual SONET tributary by modifying the T-Carrier data rate. It does so by converting the electrical signal to optical, synchronously clocking T1 data at a basic rate of 1.728 Mbps and then single-step multiplexing this rate thirty times until it's at the OC1 rate of 51.84 Mbps.

Once the DS signals are clocked into the SONET network, they can be multiplexed to any of the higher OC levels. Because they are encapsulated within the STS frame, they need to be labeled and tracked. This is what the VT Multi-frame Indicator Byte does. Since they're easily identified within the SPE, they can be dropped at any point and converted back to the original DS rate by demultiplexing the SONET rates.

SONET Network Elements and Configuration

There are several physical elements in a SONET network that are unique to the technology and so they come with their own terminology. Before reviewing common SONET topologies, you need to have a basic idea of the types of SONET elements, or the physical devices used in a SONET network.

A terminating multiplexer is a concentrator placed at the entrance of a SONET network and is shown in Figure 9-14.

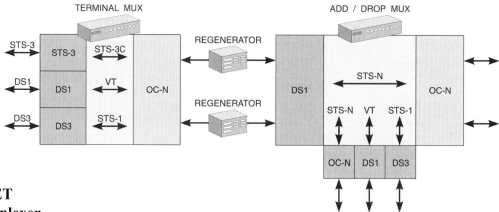

Figure 9-14: SONET Terminating Multiplexer

It's used to multiplex various STS signals up to a higher OC level, as well as to convert DS signals to VT and above levels. Notice that several inputs consisting of SONET and T-Carrier signals are applied to the input ports of the multiplexer. The T-Carriers are converted to VT rates, then multiplexed to the basic STS-1 rate, and finally multiplexed to the OC rate at the port output. This figure shows two ports at the output, but one is for transmit and the other is for receive (a full-duplex connection).

Optical signals lose signal strength with distance. Regenerators are inserted in-line with the fiber cable, and serve the same purpose as a repeater in a copper-based network—they restore the amplitude and shape of the signal.

An add/drop multiplexer is used to multiplex various inputs into an OC channel. Notice that it's inserted in-line with the OC channel. A typical application of an add/drop multiplexer is the convergence of T-Carriers from many areas. These are coupled onto the OC channel at the add/drop. Existing traffic on the OC channel isn't affected by the new data, since it's treated as multiplexed frames that are added to the new, converted frames.

The add/ drop will also demultiplex VT frames within the STS frame, and convert them back to their original T-Carrier frequency. Then, they are routed out of the SONET network and back to a T-Carrier line.

There are three basic configurations used with SONET:

- Point-to-Point

- Hub (Star)

- Ring

All are illustrated in Figure 9-15, although the ring architecture is the most widely deployed.

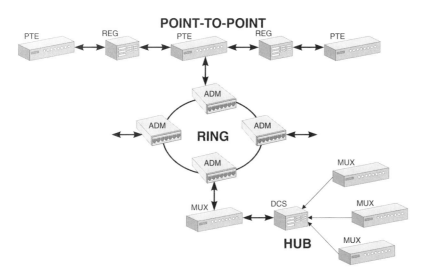

Figure 9-15: SONET Configuration

A point-to-point topology uses terminating multiplexers at each end, and one or more regenerators between them. Typically, this arrangement is used to link DS signals across long distances, thereby boosting the data rate of the DS signals while retaining asynchronous compatibility at both ends of the optical link.

In a hub or star network, a broadband cross-connect is installed as the hub. The cross-connect is used to switch SONET and T-Carrier data rates. In the figure, all signals entering and exiting the hub are SONET optical. The blocks labeled MUX are actually add/drop units used to convert the T-Carrier tributaries and STS frames to a common OC rate. The DCS hub then becomes a high-speed optical switch. Since all information in this segment of the network flows through it, the hub is in a perfect position to manage all aspects of the network, from changing logical port connections to monitoring and reporting performance data.

In the ring topology, add/drop multiplexers serve as an interface to the SONET network. The ADM converts all inputs to a common ring speed and couples them onto the network. Rings have the advantage of survivability by including redundant, fallback rings that will wrap around a cut fiber cable. This allows the ring to operate even when the primary transmission path is broken. Typically, the fallback, or secondary, ring is geographically separate from the primary ring, so that if the primary is lost due to a thunderstorm, earthquake, etc., the secondary isn't likely to be broken by the same event.

The characteristics of SONET are summarized in Table 9-19.

Table 9-19: SONET Characteristics

Application	Voice, data, and video communication
Data Rate	51.84 Mbps
Connection Type	Connection-oriented
Data Unit Length	6480 bits
Media	Fiber optic
Capacity	In excess of 48

INTEGRATED SERVICES DIGITAL NETWORK

Integrated Services Digital Network (ISDN)

Integrated Services Digital Network (ISDN) is a set of digital services available to users over telephone lines.

It's an alternative to conventional telephone connections for Internet access or for wide area connections in a multi-user environment. ISDN modems compete with fractional T1, cable modems, and, to a lesser degree, Frame Relay.

ISDN is a complete digital solution from end-user to end-user. The significance of this is that voice, text, graphics, video, music, and other material is routinely sent across an ISDN connection at very fast data rates. Because the connection is all digital, data rates can be much higher than an analog telephone connection. With V.90 modems, a user can expect download rates of about 48 kbps, but with ISDN, 128 kbps are typical. (Note that kilo (k), when used with ISDN, is actually 1,000—not the 1,024 that you may associate with powers of 2.)

Users are charged a tariff to use ISDN. The equipment needed to interface and use the services is specialized, and limited to ISDN technology. Due to the geographical limits of ISDN, it may not be available in all areas, or if it is, it may not be cost-effective if your facility is located too far from a central office. Currently, you must be within 18,000 feet (3.4 miles) of the CO to receive an ISDN line. The length may be extended if a wide-bandwidth repeater is installed, but this cost is passed on to customers, and may very well offset cost advantages of ISDN over a competing technology.

ISDN Terminology

As ISDN frame carries data in a Bearer channel (B channel) that has a 64 kbps bandwidth. On older telephone systems, B channels may drop to 56 kbps. A Data channel (D channel) carries supervisor and signaling information at 16 kbps (and sometimes at 64 kbps).

There are two types of ISDN connections, a Basic Rate Interface (BRI) and a Primary Rate Interface (PRI). A BRI connection is composed of two 64 kbps B channels, and one 16 kbps D channel. It's normally referred to as BRI 2B+D. A PRI channel has 23 64 kbps B channels and one 64 kbps D channel. It's normally called PRI 23B+D.

Channel information in an ISDN line is byte-multiplexed, so it's common to aggregate (interleave) the B channels. When this is done, the connection is described by including an H suffix. Typical aggregate rates are:

- H0 = 6 B channels (384 kbps)

- H10 = 23 B channels (1,472 kbps)

- H11 = 24 B channels (1,536 kbps)

- H12 = 30 B channels (1,929 kbps)

ISDN Interfaces

As mentioned, ISDN comes with its own equipment and interfaces that are needed to establish a physical connection. Refer to Figure 9-16 to place the definitions described below to their place in the physical layout.

ISDN Terminals

- *TE1:* Terminal Equipment Type 1. A subscriber-side device that is specialized for ISDN. This may include a computer connection or an ISDN telephone. These are both shown, and labeled as TE1.

- *TE2:* Terminal Equipment Type 2. Also a subscriber-side device, but one that pre-dates the ISDN standard, such as the analog telephone shown.

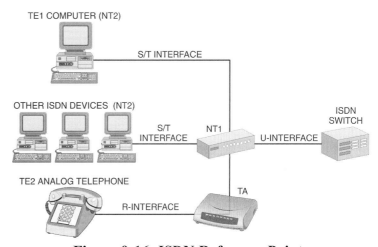

Figure 9-16: ISDN Reference Points

Terminal Adapter (TA)

- A terminal adapter is needed only to connect older style equipment to an ISDN line. The analog telephone is shown with a TA because it's not ISDN-ready. TAs are sometimes, incorrectly, called ISDN modems. A TA may be either a stand-alone device, or a printed circuit board inside the TE2 device. If it's an external device, it connects to the TE2 via a standard physical interface such as EIA/TIA-232 or V.35.

Network Termination

- *(NT1) Network Termination Type 1:* An NT1 is a device at the ISDN switch side (in Europe—but at the customer side in North America) of the connection that performs a 2-wire to 4-wire conversion. Four physical wires are used at the subscriber side for full-duplex transmission. Two of the wires are used for transmit, and two for receiving. Many ISDN devices have an NT1 built into them, which makes installation easier and quicker.

- *(NT2) Network Termination Type 2:* An NT2 handles layer 2 and 3 ISDN protocols. Since these are included in all ISDN devices, they are shown in parentheses with the TE1 devices.

Reference Interface

ISDN specifies several reference points that define the logical interfaces between terminals and network termination points.

- *S Interface:* The reference point between subscriber-side ISDN equipment and NT2.

- *T Interface:* The reference point between NT1 and NT2. Notice that the S and T interfaces are shown on the same line. First, they're electrically identical; second, a S reference is inside the subscriber device.

- *R Interface:* The reference point between non-ISDN devices and a TA. The analog telephone has an R interface since it's not ISDN equipment.

- *U Interface:* The reference between the carrier switch and the ISDN device (NT1) at the subscriber side. Keep in mind, ISDN is intended to provide digital connections using the existing 2-wire local loop. The U interface refers to this 2-to-4 wire hybrid.

ISDN Layer Protocol

ISDN provides digital services, at up to 128 kbps, directly to the desktop for computers, fax, or telephones.

The ISDN standard (ITU I and G-series documents) is composed of three protocol layers—the Physical layer, Data Link layer, and the Network layer. They are roughly analogous to the first three layers of the OSI model, and use many of the same conventions and practices.

The Physical layer is responsible for frame formatting ISDN data, establishing data rates and signal levels. An ISDN frame consists of 2 bytes of the first B channel (B1), 2 bytes of the second B channel (B2), 4 bits from the D channel (D), 10 bits for link maintenance (L), and 2 bits for synchronization (F), for a total frame length of 48 bits. This is shown in Figure 9-17.

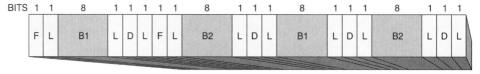

Figure 9-17: ISDN Physical Layer Frame

TOTAL FRAME LENGTH = 48 BITS   DATA = 36 BITS   OVERHEAD = 12 BITS
F = SYNCHRONIZATION   L = ADJUST AVERAGE BIT VALUE   B1, B2, D = USER DATA AND SIGNALING

At the U interface, ISDN frames are combined into a single unit that contains five 48-bit frames. This gives a total length of 240 bits. This is the size of the frame that's sent from the ISDN switch to the NT1 at the subscriber side. Bit times on an ISDN line are 6.25 μs, for a total bandwidth of 160 kbps. This bandwidth is divided as follows:

- Overhead: 16 kbps
- D channel: 16 kbps
- 2 64 bps B channels: 128 bps

Data is sent in a superframe consisting of eight 240-byte frames for a total of 1,920 bits. The Data Link layer uses the LAPD implementation of HDLC. The frame format is shown in Figure 9-18.

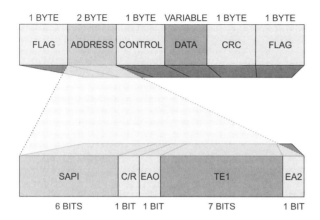

Figure 9-18: LAPD Frame Used with ISDN

The Flag and Control fields are identical to those used in HDLC with Supervisory, Information, and Unnumbered frames. The Address field—which may be extended to 2 bytes—differs from HDLC. The C/R field designates the frame as command or response. The EA fields (extended addressing 1 and 2) are used to signify whether the address field is 1 or 2 bytes in length. If EA1 is set, the length is 1 byte. The TEI field (Terminal Endpoint Identifier) is used to specify a single terminal (0–6310), or multiple terminals (64–12610). A third TEI for broadcast messages is set when the field is configured for 12710. The six-bit SAPI (Service Access Point Identifier) identifies the point where layer 2 LAPD provides services to layer 3.

The Network layer is used to specify the type of signaling that will be used on an ISDN line. It may be circuit-switched, packet-switched, or user-to-user. It addition, the setup, maintenance, and termination of the session are handled by the Network layer. The process is very similar to that used with X.25.

An ISDN line is more expensive than an analog telephone line connection (as used by the plain old telephone system, or POTS), but cheaper than a T1 line. It can accommodate multiple users (up to seven devices on the subscriber side), whereas a POTS line can handle only one. A T1 connection, of course, can multiplex many users. As mentioned earlier, ISDN is much faster than an analog connection, but far slower than either T1 or cable modem access. In some organizations, Frame Relay is an acceptable intermediary between an analog or ISDN connection, and a T1 connection. With Frame Relay, multiple users are supported and data rates are high, but toll charges can easily make it an expensive choice.

Table 9-20 summarizes characteristics of ISDN.

Application	Voice, data, and video communication
Data Rate	64 kbps
Connection Type	Connection-oriented
Data Unit Length	240 bits
Media	Twisted pair
Capacity	Up to 30 channels

Table 9-20: ISDN Characteristics

KEY POINTS REVIEW

An overview of network services has been presented in this chapter.

- Circuit switching consists of a dedicated channel between devices on each end of a connection.

- Packet switching is an end-to-end digital technology that is primarily used for data communications.

- X.25 is a connectionless protocol that uses packet switching to transfer data at 56 kbps or 64 kbps.

- FDDI is the Fiber Distributed Data Interface protocol used for sending data at 100 Mbps over fiber-optic cable in LANs.

- Frame Relay is a variable-bandwidth packet-switched technology used to transport data.

- Asynchronous Transfer Mode is a cell relay standard that uses 53-byte cells for transporting text, voice, video, music, or graphic messages.

- The T-Carrier system is composed of a DS0 signal that has a 64 kbps data rate. Twenty-four DS0 signals are combined into a T1 frame. The data rate of T1 is 1.544 Mbps.

- A T3 line contains 672 DS0 channels and has a data rate of 44.732 Mbps.

- The European equivalent of the North American T-carrier system uses an E1 line at a data rate of 2.084 Mbps, and an E3 line at a data rate of 34.368 Mbps.

- The Synchronous Optical Network (SONET) uses fiber-optic cable to transfer data. Examples of SONET data rates are OC1 at 51.840 Mbps, and OC12 at 622.080 Mbps.

- ISDN is a complete digital solution from end-user to end-user over digital telephone lines. An ISDN line requires an ISDN adapter at the subscriber side in order to access the line.

At this point, review the objectives listed at the beginning of the chapter to be certain that you understand and can perform them. Afterward, answer the review questions that follow to verify your knowledge of the information.

REVIEW QUESTIONS

The following questions test your knowledge of the material presented in this chapter:

1. What is the data rate of FDDI?

2. How many DS0 signals are in a T1 frame?

3. Why is X.25 a connectionless protocol?

4. What is the length of an ATM cell?

5. Which type of switching uses a dedicated channel between end connections?

6. What is the data rate of X.25 packet-switching networks?

7. Describe the bandwidth characteristics of Frame Relay.

8. What is the data rate of a T-1 connection?

9. What is the lowest speed of a SONET channel?

10. What is the media type used with FDDI?

11. What is the cell length for ATM?

12. What is the minimum data rate of ISDN?

13. What is the channel capacity of an X.25 network?

14. What type of information can be sent over an ATM connection?

15. What is the minimum frame size used for a T-1 line?

EXAM QUESTIONS

1. The maximum data rate of the FDDI standard is:
   a. 100 Mbps
   b. 20 Mbps
   c. 10 Mbps
   d. 2 Mbps

2. The data rate of an E3 line is:
   a. 1.544 Mbps
   b. 34.368 Mbps
   c. 44.736 Mbps
   d. 155.52 Mbps

3. What is the data rate of a DS0 signal?
   a. 128 kbps
   b. 4,000 kbps
   c. 64 kbps
   d. 256 kbps

4. Which of the following is a variable-bandwidth technology?
   a. T1
   b. ATM
   c. E3
   d. Frame Relay

5. Which of the following technologies would be the best choice for a network that sends and receives multimedia data? (Select all that apply.)
   a. ATM
   b. X.25
   c. Frame Relay
   d. T1

6. To provide the fastest data rates, which of the following should be used?
   a. OC3
   b. T1
   c. DS0
   d. E1

7. Which of the following is connectionless?
   a. circuit switching
   b. ISDN
   c. X.25 packet switching
   d. Frame Relay

8. What is the maximum capacity of T-Carrier lines?
   a. 12
   b. 4032
   c. 256
   d. 128

9. What media type is used with ISDN?
   a. fiber optic
   b. radio waves
   c. twisted pair
   d. coaxial cable

10. What size is a SONET frame?
    a. 6480 bits
    b. 4032 bits
    c. 193 bits
    d. 1500 bits

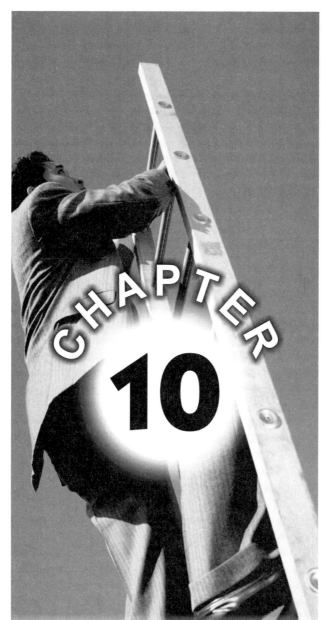

CHAPTER

10

OPERATING SYSTEMS

LEARNING
OBJECTIVES

LEARNING OBJECTIVES

U pon completion of this chapter and its related lab procedures, you will be able to perform the following tasks:

1. Identify the main purpose of subnetting and default gateways,

2. Identify the basic capabilities of the following server operating systems:

   - UNIX/Linux
   - NetWare
   - Windows
   - Macintosh

3. Identify the basic capabilities of the following clients:

   - UNIX/Linux
   - NetWare
   - Windows
   - Macintosh

4. Given a remote scenario, configure the connection.

5. Given a network configuration, select the appropriate NIC and network configuration settings.

6. Given specific parameters, configure a client to connect to the following servers:

   - UNIX/Linux
   - NetWare
   - Windows
   - Macintosh

7. Given a scenario, predict the impact of modifying, adding, or removing network services on network resources and users.

8. Identify the main characteristics of VLANs.

CHAPTER 10

OPERATING SYSTEMS

INTRODUCTION

This chapter offers a broad overview of operating system software and specific configuration settings. Certainly, Windows operating systems dominate client computers in business. On the server side, Windows NT, 2000, and XP are widely installed. But so are many UNIX servers and, increasingly, Linux servers.

The only way to be truly proficient with any software is to use it. You are strongly encouraged to spend time on Windows (at least version NT 4.0) and Linux.

The Network+ Exam requires that you be proficient in configuring and troubleshooting TCP/IP parameters on client computers. Included in this chapter are step-by-step instructions for configuring the most common networking protocols on a Windows workstation. As with operating systems, you must perform these configurations in order to truly have a grasp of what is needed.

Apple Macintosh information has been given its own section in this chapter. The version of Macintosh at the time of this writing was MAC X. Apple has always shared a structure similar to UNIX, but the graphical interface has often obscured this fact. A basic overview of Macintosh OS is presented and you should, if possible, spend time getting to know the OS before taking the exam.

OPERATING SYSTEM FUNDAMENTALS

Before looking at characteristics of specific network operating systems, you need to understand a few fundamental terms. In discussing network operating systems, we are primarily interested in client-server networks, also referred to as server-based networks.

A **server** is a centralized computer that provides network management processes to the network, and possibly applications and files to clients on the network. A **client** is a network user's computer that has access to applications and files on the server.

server

client

Although we are primarily interested in server-based networks, an alternative arrangement is a peer-to-peer network. In a peer-to-peer network, no central server manages processes and makes shared data and tools available to workstations. Rather, the workstations share data and tools with each other, and each one must perform some management and routing tasks. Peer-to-peer networks are not topologically defined. That is, they aren't described as a star, ring, or bus topology.

Traditionally, a network operating system (NOS) has been used as a means to share file and print services.

However, the role of a NOS has changed and now can be considered to provide, at a minimum, the following services:

- Directory services
- Application services
- File and print services
- Internet services

Directory services

Directory services refers to methods used to organize and control network resources. These include the organization of servers and the tools they provide to users and administrators. Examples of the tools include methods of backing up data, the level of control offered to users for protecting individual files and directories, the type of protocols that can be run on a network, and so on. Directory services are a central function of the NOS, and thus are also responsible, indirectly, for file and print services, application services, and Internet services.

Print and file services

Print and file services are the bread and butter of client-server networks. In fact, the economics of printers was a driving force behind the popularity of client-server networks. Because printers rarely are used nonstop by any one user, buying one for every user doesn't make good economic sense. Placing print services on a server is a way for many users to share one or more printers. (Because fewer are needed, the printers can be of higher quality and more reliable as well.) Similarly, a server has more tools available for managing files than a stand-alone operating system. The same tools could be installed on all user workstations, but not without considerable expense and time.

application service
Internet services

An **application service** refers to programs used by people on a network, such as word processing, spreadsheets, or other software that users routinely call upon to perform their jobs.

Internet services are an increasingly important part of a NOS, not only for access to the Internet, but for access to corporate intranets. As more and more business is conducted across interconnected networks, the tools and reliability of a NOS are becoming increasingly important for Internet applications.

Users are assigned to groups in many network operating systems. The network administrator assigns rights and permissions for users and groups. A right is a physical activity users perform, such as logging on to a particular computer or sending a document to a printer. A permission refers to data manipulation that users can perform, such as file access or read and write access. In short, a right involves a physical activity; whereas a permission is a data activity.

The Network+ exam emphasizes broad characteristics of Windows NT/2000/XP, Novell NetWare, and UNIX/Linux operating systems. In the following sections, you'll examine the main attributes of each.

WINDOWS

Windows NT is a follow-up to Windows for Workgroups 3.11. Someone at Microsoft must have a made a long list of shortcomings of the other NOSes and addressed them in NT. The system is hugely popular for several reasons. It's easy to set up and use. It works with other popular NOSes. It was specifically made for powerful network servers that have several microprocessors. It supports hard drives larger than 2 gigabytes. It permits you to run Windows 9x on clients, or you can install the NT client instead.

Since the NT iteration, Microsoft has released Windows 2000 and Windows XP server operating systems. Both of these are, fundamentally, improvements on the original NT system. Both 2000 and XP offer client versions of the operating system, although a network implementation may consist of clients running numerous versions of Windows such as 9x, Me, 2000, NT, or XP.

In a pure installation, a Windows server uses the Windows network operating system for both server and client operations. The workstations utilize Windows Workstation software; the server utilizes Windows Server software. The result is a self-contained operating system, and in particular, a system designed for business applications. It's equally at home in a small, local network or a large, globally distributed network.

Windows NT was designed for 32-bit applications; consequently, it won't support the 16-bit device drivers found in older PCs. This has allowed a considerable amount of flexibility for Microsoft designers because they don't have to worry about backward-compatibility issues. The server and workstation versions of Windows NT are modular components added to the basic operating system, making the package complete and enabling it to run across a common source code.

Windows NT/2000/XP is relatively easy to install; a basic installation can be performed in two hours.

Domains and Workgroups

All client computers on a Windows network participate in either a **domain** or a **workgroup**.

> A workgroup is a set of computers that can share access to each other's files and applications.

domain

workgroup

Each computer in the workgroup maintains a list of user accounts describing passwords and access rights. The user account information must be set up in each workstation in the workgroup. Members of a workgroup utilize the same network protocol and share the same workgroup name.

Administering a workgroup is difficult if the users move frequently from one workgroup to another. The difficulty arises because all user account information resides in each computer. If a change is made in workgroup membership, the user account information on each computer in the workgroup must be changed as well. However, for a small network in which user changes aren't likely to occur frequently, workgroups can be a very good organizational tool.

> A domain, in the strictest and most simplistic sense, is a collection of client computers that are administered by a server.

A single Windows server can be installed on a small network and client computers can be assigned to the domain name given to the server. Then, from the single server, a network administrator can organize the complete network simply by referencing the domain name.

Logging on to a domain gives you access to the client machines that are part of the domain. File and directory sharing are important functions of a NOS, and NT/2000/XP is no exception. However, just because you can access a machine doesn't mean you can access its contents. One of the jobs of a network administrator is to determine who has access to what.

After the choice between workgroup and domain is made, it's difficult to change, so choose wisely. Normally, the best choice when using Windows is to choose a domain, because it allows for central administration of the network resources. When a workgroup is used, some administrative tasks are performed at the workstation.

Network Protocols

Windows NT/2000/XP supports a wide array of protocols. (A protocol consists of the rules that data must follow while traversing the network.) Table 10-1 lists the major protocols supported. In addition, the Point-To-Point Tunneling Protocol (PPTP) is available for secure remote connections that use the Internet as the communication medium between remote users and an NT server.

Table 10-1: Network Protocols Supported by Windows Operating Systems

Protocol	Description
NetBEUI	NetBIOS Extended User Interface, a non-routable Microsoft protocol developed by IBM.
NWLink	A Microsoft version of Novell IPX/SPX (Internet Packet Exchange/Sequenced Packet Exchange); a routable protocol.
TCP/IP	Transmission Control Protocol/Internet Protocol, a routable protocol used in most wide area networks. Noted for its reliability. TCP/IP is the best protocol for larger or interconnected networks, and is the default protocol for Intel-based servers.
AppleTalk	The network protocol used by Macintosh computers. Windows NT allows Macintosh users to share MAC-files in NT server space and to share printers.
Remote Access	Remote access includes dial-up services such as SLIP (Serial Line Internet Protocol), PPP (Point-to-Point Protocol), ISDN, and PPTP (Point-to-Point Tunneling Protocol).

File Structures

Windows supports two file structures, FAT and NTFS.

FAT is short for File Allocation Table and is the type of file system used with DOS, Win 3.x, Win 9x/2000/XP, and OS/2. Because there is such a huge base of installed operating systems that employ FAT, you may feel compelled to set up the hard disk on an NT server with it. FAT is a 16-bit structure that, in earlier versions, restricted hard drive partitions to 2 gigabytes. A 32-bit version of FAT was made available by Microsoft so that the 2 gigabyte hard drive partition barrier could be overcome.

NTFS (NT File System) originated with the HPFS file structure that Microsoft and IBM developed for the OS/2 operating system. It's the recommended choice for Windows NT. NTFS is recommended over FAT because NTFS is the more secure of the two, and NTFS is not limited by the 2 GB partition limit of FAT. NTFS also utilizes the disk space far more efficiently than FAT.

You have the option of installing both FAT and NTFS in separate partitions. If, after the software is installed, you decide to convert all partitions to NTFS, NT permits this. However, to convert from NTFS to FAT requires reformatting disk partitions and reinstalling NT—in effect, there's no practical way of doing it.

NTFS is more efficient than FAT for larger file sizes. In effect, it supports unlimited partition sizes and attempts to restore good data and remove bad data in the event of a power loss. As mentioned, the security features of NTFS are superior to those of FAT. File and directory level security enable you to specify the access permissions to individual files and directories.

NOVELL NETWARE

As networks grew from several computers that needed a more efficient way to share files and printing, no other network operating system has evolved to meet the need like **Novell NetWare**. Although Windows NT may eclipse NetWare in the years ahead, NetWare is a testament to the versatility of software developers who have the ability to meet the demands of the marketplace year after year. Currently, NetWare is at Version 6.0. This is the most robust implementation that Novell has marketed to date.

There's a great deal of interoperability between NetWare and Windows NT. Although the two remain competitors, don't expect either to disappear anytime soon. Novell remains the dominant network operating system. There are still thousands of older versions of it running on small LANs and for many of the administrators of those LANs, it meets their needs and they have no reason to change.

Network Protocols

Table 10-2 lists network protocols supported by NetWare. See the section "Networking Protocols" later in this chapter for more information.

Table 10-2: NetWare Network Protocols

Protocol	Description
IPX/SPX	Novell's proprietary network protocol.
TCP/IP	A routable protocol and the most widely deployed for large and interconnected networks.
AppleTalk	Enables Macintosh clients to share files and printing on a NetWare server.
Source Route Bridging	Proprietary Novell routing protocol for connecting Token Ring networks.
NetWare Link	Novell's remote access protocols supported by NetWare include PPP, ATM (Asynchronous Transfer Mode), X.25 packet switching protocol, and Frame Relay.

Novell Directory Service

The basis of the Novell directory and file organization scheme is the **Novell Directory Service**, or **NDS**.

NDS is based on the ITU (formerly known as CCITT) standard X.500.

The Novell directory structure begins with a root. A root is the primary object from which the tree is built. This is normally followed by a name of a company or a department within a company. The root branches to organizations. For example, there may be organization headings for sales, accounting, production, and so forth. These could also be organized by cities, states, or whatever makes sense for a company. Branching from the organization level are organizational units. These may refer to individuals within a department, or cities within a state. Figure 10-1 shows an example of the NDS directory structure.

Notice that the NDS structure begins with root and branches to the organization level MARCRAFT_INC_CORP. From MARCRAFT_INC_CORP, there are two organizational units, ACCOUNTING and SALES. Each of these in turn contains two organizational units. Branching with NDS can continue as long as necessary, but Novell ships with a default structure that they recommend for networks with fewer than 1,000 objects. For most applications, you shouldn't have to spend an excessive amount of time designing the organizational structure.

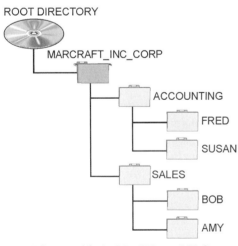

Figure 10-1: NetWare NDS Structure

The Novell file system consists of volumes and partitions. A partition is used to separate operating systems. For instance, a hard drive can be separated into two partitions with one containing NetWare and the other containing DOS. Up to four partitions can be placed on a single disk.

A volume is used to subdivide partitions into smaller units. With four allowable partitions on each disk, you can have up to eight volumes on a disk. Whereas a partition is limited to a single disk, a volume can span multiple disks. A volume is organized into logical groupings, such as user directories for various departments (for example, sales, production, and so on). A volume can also be created to contain application software available across the network.

Partitions and volumes are managed by two types of file services: Novell Storage Services (NSS), which first became available on version 5.0, and NetWare File System (NFS), which is the file service used on earlier versions of NetWare but is also available on version 5.0 and later.

With either service, directories and files are stored in volumes as just described. You specify which objects can access other objects along with the level of access: read only, read/write, or print. With NSS, space on all server hard drives is efficiently utilized. NSS collects all free space, as well as any space not used by a volume, and pools it. From this pool, you can create additional volumes and will always know how much actual hard drive space you have available.

UNIX

UNIX has been around for thirty years. It began as an experiment, commissioned by the U.S. government, to find a way of keeping military information systems running in the event of an attack. Keep in mind that an information system at that time consisted of a large mainframe computer with terminals connected to it. All the data resided in the mainframe, and although the computer had an endless number of security precautions installed, if a nuclear warhead were dropped anywhere in the vicinity of the computer, it would be destroyed along with all its data.

The problem was compounded by the many different mainframe computers in use, and the fact that very few of them were compatible with one other. In 1969 four computers successfully exchanged data using what would eventually become the TCP/IP protocol suite for internetworking. Although the information exchange was a huge stride forward, it lacked a critically important element—a network operating system. Back to the drawing board went the engineers and academics to create an operating system specifically designed for internetworking. They called it UNIX.

The UNIX operating system is portable. That is, it is adaptable to different situations, particularly machine types and file structures. Windows 95 isn't a portable operating system because it can't run on a Macintosh computer. Table 10-3 lists some of the more common UNIX flavors on the market. The differences are subtle, and all versions have strengths as outlined in the following sections.

Table 10-3: Common UNIX Flavors

UNIX Derivative	Proprietary Development Protocol
A/UX	Developed by Apple Computer and designed to run on MAC-II systems.
AIX	Developed by IBM and rigidly follows standards established by the federal government, such as POSIX.
BSD	Developed at the University of California at Berkeley. Variants are called BSD/OS, BSDI, FreeBSD, OpenBSD, and NetBSD. The latter runs on many PC-based operating systems.
Digital UNIX	64-bit UNIX that is extremely reliable and robust. Used on many large enterprise networks.
HP-UX	A Hewlett-Packard version that was designed for workstation use and includes HP-Vue, a proprietary GUI.
IRIX	Silicon Graphics, Inc. version used primarily for sophisticated graphics in two and three dimensions.
SunOS and Solaris	Developed by Sun Microsystems, Inc. SunOS runs on RISC-based processors; whereas Solaris runs on both Intel processors. Used extensively by ISPs because it can withstand sustained hits of resource-intensive requests, such as video, music, and graphics.
UNIXWare	Currently owned by SCO (Santa Cruz Operation); designed to run on Pentium and x86 processors.
Linux	Developed by Dutch programmer Linus Torvalds, Linux has been subsequently strengthened by many programmers. Due to the large number of hardware devices it supports, it's becoming a favorite for servers.

The strengths of UNIX are considerable:

- It supports 32- or 64-bit applications.

- It's multiuser. (A small Intel-based server, for example, can support several hundred users.)

- It comes with a complete TCP/IP suite for servers and clients.

- Its hierarchical file system is capable of multitasking. (Multitasking means that more than one operation, or task, can be addressed at the same time by the operating system.)

- It supports logical partitions. (A logical partition means that a physical hard drive has been separated into two or more logical drives.)

- It's the NOS most widely used with the Internet.

- Many versions of UNIX are free, or very inexpensive, when downloaded from the Internet.

Note that Windows NT and NetWare support only 32-bit applications. Because UNIX's 64-bit capability has far superior performance applications, such as graphics and mathematical computations, it is invariably preferred over either NT or NetWare for such applications. It's a true multiuser system. When UNIX users log in to the system, they can run any application. On an NT network, a user can run any client/server application. This is why Windows 9x or DOS applications can be stored on an NTFS server but not run on one. Unlike NT and NetWare, all commercial versions of UNIX ship with a complete package of TCP/IP.

UNIX is nonproprietary and therefore not bound to address quirky aspects of a proprietary network operating system. Being nonproprietary, UNIX tends to use widely understood and implemented protocols. In contrast, NT and NetWare use some proprietary protocols that may not be compatible across networks. For example, UNIX uses the globally implemented TCP/IP as its networking protocol. In contrast, both NT and NetWare use proprietary networking protocols, NetBEUI and IPX, respectively, which poses some challenges for interconnectivity of networks. Details and tradeoffs of the networking protocols of these three NOSes are discussed in more detail in the section "Networking Protocols" later in this chapter.

Directory Structure

The directory structure used with UNIX resembles a tree cluster similar to that of a DOS system.

Figure 10-2 illustrates a typical example. At the top-level is the root, indicated by the "/" symbol. Directories that branch from the root are called subdirectories. Subdirectories can have subdirectories as well. In the figure, the subdirectories /bill, /mary, and /bob are subdirectories of /home, which is a subdirectory of /. When written on a command line, the /notes directory appears as follows:

/home/mary/notes

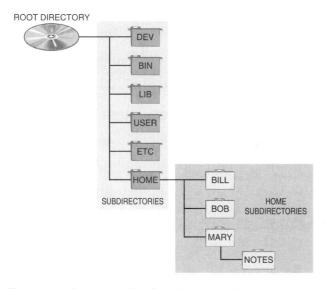

**Figure 10-2:
Directory Structure of
UNIX**

The preceding file structure is an example of an absolute path. Another way to specify files is to use a relative path. A relative path is specified at the time of login and starts at a specified filename. By specifying a relative path, the user logs on directly to their personal directory. For example, a relative path may appear as follows:

/mary/notes

Otherwise, the user Mary would be required to execute the proper UNIX commands that place her in the appropriate directory from the /home directory.

Files on a UNIX system are organized into user, groups, and all other users. This convention is helpful in applying security to files and directories. Mary, in the example, may want to give permission to other users in her group so that they'll be able to read her notes. If so, she can specify the level of access. Alternatively, she may want to specify that other group members can read and write to her notes.

LINUX

Linux is a subset of UNIX.

It's best described as a work-alike UNIX operating system that runs very well on client computers. Linux servers are becoming increasingly common as time has shown the OS to be stable and reliable.

Linux was developed by Linus Torvalds. The software was a cheap alternative to expensive, distributed versions of UNIX. Unlike UNIX, Linux can be obtained for free. But distributed versions of UNIX, which include support and various utilities, are generally more attractive since most required software components are included in the purchased package. Linux may be downloaded for free, or purchased from distributors such as Red Hat or Caldera.

For networking, Linux includes a complete set of TCP/IP protocols. A network administrator may configure clients using specific Linux command-line instructions, or by using a graphical user interface (GUI). As with any client computer, be prepared for the configuration by determining IP addresses, subnet masks, host name, along with IP addresses assigned to specialized services such as a DNS server or gateway.

Linux works across a large range of hardware including:

- Intel 386, 486, Pentium III, Pentium IV

- Motorola 69xxx based systems

- SARC, MIPS

The file system that is native to Linux is Network File System (NFS). In addition to some concerns about the security of NFS, NFS may be difficult to use with Windows clients. For this reason, many network administrators include SAMBA on Linux servers. SAMBA is a program that allows a Linux server to appear to be a Windows server to clients running Windows operating systems.

The command-line interface options are extensive for Linux, as they are for UNIX. The best way to get a feel for using Linux is to download a free version of it, or purchase a supported version from a distributor and experiment with it.

NETWORK CLIENTS

As noted earlier, network software has both a server and a client component. In this section, we look at the client software that is compatible with and optimal for Windows NT, Novell NetWare, and UNIX.

Since most operating systems on client computers use Windows, this section emphasizes the steps used with Windows to configure network settings. To Microsoft's credit, the TCP/IP screens on their various operating systems are little changed through the various iterations of the software (9x, Me, 2000, and XP).

Windows and NetWare Clients

Microsoft is noted for client operating systems. Virtually all the Microsoft operating systems run on a NetWare network as well as on an NT/2000/XP network. Both Microsoft and Novell support implementations of UNIX, generally with the TCP/IP protocol suite. In the case where different types of clients reside on a network, the universal solution is to install TCP/IP for those clients that don't natively support it (early versions of Windows for Workgroups, for example).

The major client operating systems supported by Windows and NetWare include the following:

- Windows NT Workstation
- Windows 9x, Me, 2000, XP
- Windows for Workgroups 3.1x
- Windows 3.1+

- MS-DOS clients
- OS/2 clients
- Apple Macintosh clients
- UNIX workstations

Windows NT/2000/XP Workstation

Not surprisingly, NT/2000/XP Server works seamlessly with its partner, Windows NT/2000/XP Workstation. The workstation versions use the same graphical interface as the server version and at first glance are difficult to distinguish from Server and the client OS.

Windows workstation operating systems are all designed to work in any of the following environments:

- As a stand-alone workstation
- As a member of a workgroup in a peer-to-peer network
- As a client in a Windows NT domain
- As a Novell NetWare client
- As a UNIX client

Windows 9x

As the predominant client operating system, Windows 9x (which includes Windows 95 and 98) is more likely to be found in a Windows server-based LAN. As with Windows Server and Workstation, it supports 32-bit networking protocols.

The operating systems can be used in any of the following environments:

- As a stand-alone workstation

- As a member of a workgroup in a peer-to-peer network

- As a client in a Windows NT domain

- As a Novell NetWare client

- As a UNIX client

UNIX Clients

A UNIX workstation communicates using TCP/IP. Client access to servers is best when the server also has UNIX installed. But a UNIX client isn't prohibited from accessing a NetWare or Windows NT server because both of these operating systems support TCP/IP.

Another interesting UNIX-related product is Linux, created by a Dutch programmer (Linus Torvalds) who was trying to improve the MINIX UNIX flavor that he was using (Linus and UNIX; hence, the name Linux). Linux is unique in that programmers around the world took an interest in it and developed hardware drivers for many devices. Soon, the volume of platforms that Linux was able to cross became quite extensive. Now, less than ten years after Torvalds first released his version of Linux—free of charge on the Internet—it's being used in many commercial applications as an alternative for Windows NT and Novell NetWare. Microsoft clients can be connected to Linux servers and the user typically has no idea that the client is not running on an NT server.

NETWORKING PROTOCOLS

The previous section on network operating systems overviewed the networking protocols supported by Windows NT/2000/XP, NetWare, and UNIX, respectively. In this section, we look more closely at the protocols. The three networking protocols that are predominant in the local area network level are:

- IPX
- IP
- NetBEUI

IPX, which stands for Internetwork Packet Exchange, is a proprietary networking protocol used by Novell.

It's the default network protocol for all NetWare networks, as well as for Windows NT networks.

IPX is a routable protocol, meaning it can be used to send packets of data between different networks. IPX includes a proprietary Novell addressing scheme that can be routed among many, but not all, types of networks. That is, the addressing used with IPX is nonstandard, so the data contained in the addressed packet isn't accepted by machines that aren't running Novell software.

IP, which stands for Internet Protocol, is a nonproprietary networking protocol.

Like IPX, IP can be routed. Unlike IPX, IP is supported by nearly all networking software. If IP is used to send a packet of data to another network, it's almost certain to be accepted because the destination machine almost certainly is running IP.

IP is normally associated with the protocol TCP to form the TCP/IP protocol suite. IP can run on networks of all sizes, from a small network with ten computers, to the millions of computers connected to the Internet.

NetBEUI, which stands for NetBIOS (Network Basic Input/Output System) Extended User Interface, is a network protocol originally developed by Microsoft and IBM. NetBEUI uses computer names as the logical addressing scheme for locating nodes on a network.

Because that system of addressing does not guarantee a unique address for every machine (a computer name can be duplicated from one network to the next), NetBEUI isn't routable. For example, you can't use it to send a message across the Internet to a distant network. (IP or IPX must be used.)

However, because the addressing scheme is very simple, NetBEUI is a fast network protocol. It's typically used in smaller networks that aren't connected to other networks. Windows 9x operating systems include NetBEUI as does Windows NT. It requires little in the way of setup and maintenance on network computers.

TCP/IP CLIENT CONFIGURATION

This section describes specifics of configuring clients for networking with TCP/IP. Under the Windows OS, the configuration screens are fairly consistent from Windows 95 through Windows XP.

Setting up TCP/IP in a client machine requires some initial planning. Here's some information you'll typically need:

- IP addresses for server and/or client, and the default gateway

- IP address of the domain name server (DNS), if it will be used

- Whether to use Windows Internet Naming Service (WINS)

- Whether to use dynamic host configuration protocol (DHCP) in the network

- Whether to use an IP proxy

- The host name and, if used, the Internet domain name

The following sections explain each of these choices in more detail. They also provide examples of the TCP/IP configuration process for a Windows 95 or 98 client. Most of these choices are pertinent for other types of clients as well.

Domain Name Service (DNS)

Domain Name Service or **System**, or **DNS**, is the service that translates Internet domain names—such as *www.microsoft.com*—into IP addresses.

This service is needed because humans find it easier to assign and remember verbal identifiers, but machines on the Internet recognize each other by numerical identifiers—IP addresses. DNS is the service that resolves these two systems of identification.

The decimal points in a verbal domain name separate the name into zones.

Table 10-4: Top-level Zone Codes

Zone Code	Description
com	Commercial business
edu	Educational institution
gov	Government agency
int	International organization
mil	Military
net	Networking organization
org	Nonprofit organization

Table 10-4 lists the top-level zone codes and their meanings.

DNS is a hierarchical system that begins with root name servers. There are about a dozen root servers. A root server knows where top-level domain name servers are located. In North America, a root server and a top-level server are the same. In other countries, the two are separate and distinct machines. For example, if the address you're trying to reach is a .com address, the root server will direct you to a top-level server for .com. There are top-level DNS servers for .org, .net, .edu, and so on. Each top-level DNS server has authority for a domain.

The authority for a domain is frequently delegated to a subdomain. The DNS server of a subdomain has authority for a zone residing at the subdomain. A subdomain may be further subdivided into more intricate DNS servers that have authority for narrow zones within that subdomain.

Let's look at an example, using the fictional Internet domain name *inter.store.com*. The name originates from a retail company called Store that has divisions for Internet, telecommunications, and consumer electronics products. The address is read by DNS servers from right to left, and it's interpreted like this:

1. *com* specifies the user as a commercial site.

2. *store* represents a subdomain of the .com zone/ domain. Subdomains can be used to physically and logically separate components of an Internet sites. For example, a company with a diverse product offering might create subdomains on a single Internet site for each product line. In this example, the address *store.com* might also be an equally valid address, but it will always be associated with *inter.store.com*. In other words, two domain names might point to the same IP address. Entering either of these domain names in a web browser will take you to the same address.

3. *inter* describes the name of the company of the commercial site, or, in this example, a division within a company—the Internet division of the company called Store. This is usually an abbreviation of the actual company name, university, government agency, and so on.

Figure 10-3 summarizes the DNS hierarchy.

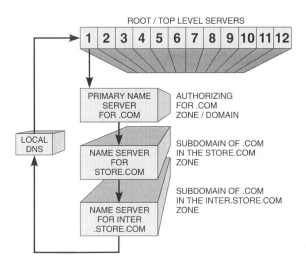

**Figure 10-3:
DNS Hierarchy**

So, for the Internet address *inter.store.com*, the subdomain *inter* is in the subdomain *store*, which is in the *.com* domain. Typically, a web site address is written in lowercase letters, because at one time UNIX-based routers and servers on the Internet could understand only lowercase. That's not the case today, but if your request for an address is passed along to an older machine, it might not be able to correctly interpret an address using capital letters.

Now, let's see what would happen if our fictional address were entered into a web browser. The sequence of events is as follows:

1. The local DNS server (the DNS server that your client computer is assigned to) looks to see if it has the domain name in its memory cache. We'll assume it doesn't.

2. The local DNS server queries a root DNS server for a match to *inter.store.com*. All functional DNS servers, including the local DNS, contain a static list of the IP addresses of all root DNS servers.

3. The root server refers your DNS to a list of primary .com (domain) servers.

4. Your DNS selects one of the .com servers and asks it for the address of *inter.store.com*.

5. The .com domain DNS server refers you to a list of *store.com* subdomain servers (if any exist).

6. Your DNS server queries one of the *store.com* subdomain DNS servers for *inter.store.com*.

7. The *store.com* subdomain server might refer you to a list of subdomain DNS servers for *inter.store.com*. Or, if there are no additional subdomains, it returns the IP address of *inter.store.com*.

Once the IP of *inter.store.com* is located by querying through the DNS server hierarchy, your local DNS server caches all the information it returns. The next time you enter *inter.store.com*, your DNS will match the domain name to the correct IP address, because it has it stored in its cache. This reduces traffic routed through root and top-level DNS servers (which, in the United States, are the same server).

Notice in Figure 10-3 that a DNS server may be identified by a zone or domain. A zone is the range of addresses that a DNS server is responsible for. For example, a server may be responsible for all .com zones or for only specific .com zones. A domain is the name of the address. For example, *store.com* is a domain. Depending on the context, a zone and a domain could be the same thing. The top-level server is responsible for the .com zone and all domain names within the zone, unless authority for a domain name has been delegated to a subdomain zone. *inter.store.com* is a subdomain of the .com zone, and this DNS server is responsible for addresses in the store.com zone. This would include *inter.store.com* as well as any other domain with a prefix to *store.com*.

If you want a TCP/IP client to be able to access Internet domains, such as web sites, you must specify a local DNS server when you configure the client. As mentioned earlier, this local DNS server is the first source the client will consult when trying to access an Internet domain.

In fact, you have the option of selecting both a primary DNS and a secondary DNS. These are two physically different servers that should be located on separate networks. That way, if your primary DNS server crashes or is busy, the secondary one can fulfill the client's request. If you have only one DNS server specified, and it crashes, client requests for IP addresses for domain names will be returned unanswered—it will appear as if the sites maintained in your DNS server don't exist. The usual practice is to have a secondary DNS server and to configure each client with the addresses of both the primary and secondary server.

When you access the Internet, you invoke an application on a port at the Internet interface. HTTP is a well-known port and is at port 80. HTTP, which stands for HyperText Transfer Protocol, is the protocol used to launch an Internet session using HTML, which stands for HyperText Markup Language. To get to a web site, you first specify the application port (port 80) by typing *http://*. The colon and slashes are UNIX conventions used to separate commands, interfaces, or server files and directories.

Next, you specify the address (Universal Resource Locator, or URL, as it is sometimes called), such as *www.microsoft.com/*. DNS will then begin searching for an IP address that matches the domain name *microsoft.com*. The last / isn't required, but it's a good idea because some DNS servers search all *microsoft.com* addresses, eliminating those with / extensions before returning a result. Some web browsers include the slash by default when you press the ENTER key. If your browser doesn't, include the slash, because it speeds up the name-to-IP resolution and takes you to a site faster.

The www tells the HTTP port that this site is a World Wide Web site—and not an FTP, Gopher, or telnet site. What happens if you don't include it? It depends. Specifying www in the domain name might be a requirement of the site you're trying to reach. In other words, when you include it in the domain name, it will map to a specific IP address during the DNS search. On the other hand, www isn't always a requirement. For example, a valid domain name is *mail.company.com*. An equally valid domain entry is *www.mail.company.com*.

These two domain names might point to the same IP address, or they might point to two entirely different IP addresses.

The following shows how to set up DNS on a Windows workstation:

1. Click on the *Start* button and choose *Settings*. Select *Control Panel* and double-click the *Network* icon.

2. From the *Configuration* tab of the *Network* dialog box, highlight TCP/IP for the installed network adapter and click on the *Properties* button.

3. Select the *DNS Configuration* tab in the *TCP/IP Properties* dialog box, as shown in Figure 10-4.

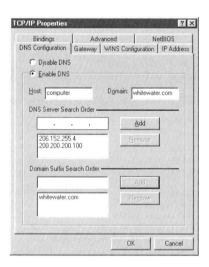

Figure 10-4: DNS Configuration Tab

4. Click on *Enable DNS* to indicate that the client will use DNS.

5. Enter the host name of the client computer. This name is used to identify the client machine in a network.

6. Enter the domain name of the system the client computer is connected to. Domain in this case refers to the Internet domain name, not a Windows NT domain. In the figure, the client (computer) is in the domain *whitewater.com*. The client's address, then, is *computer.whitewater.com*.

7. In the *DNS Server Search Order* field, enter the IP address of the DNS server. The *DNS Server Search Order* field allows you to specify more than one DNS server (one DNS IP address is required) for resolving names. The figure shows two DNS entries. The second will be used if the first is busy or disabled.

8. Optionally, you can enter the domain that you want the DNS server to search first in the *Domain Suffix Search Order* field. This field is used to specify which domain name is to be searched first for this client computer. Notice that Figure 10-4 specifies the domain that the client is in as the first domain to search.

9. Click on *OK* and restart the computer.

Assigning a Static IP Address

Every client that connects to the Internet needs an IP address so that it can receive data addressed to it from other networks or domains. For example, if you want to download data from a web site, the remote server you're connecting to has to have your computer's IP address in order to send the files. There are a couple of ways to configure an IP address for a TCP/IP client.

One way is to assign a permanent, or static, IP address to your computer. The following shows how to do this.

1. Click on the *Start* button and choose *Settings*. Select *Control Panel* and double-click the *Network* icon.

2. From the *Configuration* tab of the *Network* dialog box, highlight TCP/IP for the installed network adapter card. Click on the *Properties* button.

3. Select the *IP Address* tab in the *TCP/IP Properties* dialog box, as shown in Figure 10-5.

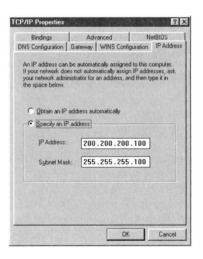

Figure 10-5:
IP Address Tab

4. Click on *Specify an IP address field*.

5. In the *IP Address* field, enter the assigned IP address for the workstation.

6. In the *Subnet Mask* field, enter the subnet mask for the network (if one is used).

7. Click on *OK* and restart the computer.

Static IP addresses are seldom used on stand-alone workstations. Instead, a list of available IP addresses is kept on the server, and the server distributes the addresses to clients on an as-needed basis.

If you have a workstation connected to an ISP from your home, you connect to the ISP using Point-to-Point Protocol (PPP). Because it's a point-to-point connection, you don't need a physical MAC-layer address; your location is implied because there's only you at one end and the ISP at the other. The ISP might assign you a permanent IP. You would use this number when setting up the connection.

Typically, IP addresses are assigned to workstations as temporary addresses, particularly when an ISP is involved. Routers or managed hubs are usually assigned static IP addresses. When a static IP address is assigned—to a workstation, router, web server, and so on—you use this number when configuring the device.

These days, however, it's rare to have an IP address assigned to a workstation. Typically, IP addresses are "loaned" on a temporary basis. The most common method for assigning temporary IP addresses is to use Dynamic Host Configuration Protocol.

Dynamic Host Configuration Protocol (DHCP)

A common method used to dynamically assign IP addresses to clients is **DHCP**, **Dynamic Host Configuration Protocol**.

Dynamic Host Configuration Protocol (DHCP)

A dynamic IP assignment means that each time a client initiates a connection to the Internet, it will be given a different IP address. For the duration of the Internet session, this will be the client's IP address—the address to which a remote server sends files for downloading to the client.

When a computer running a DHCP client is booted, it requests an IP address from the DHCP server at an Internet Service Provider (ISP) or a local server running DHCP.

The DHCP server has been assigned a block of IP addresses. IP addresses are assigned to clients as needed from this block. When you set up DHCP, you enter the start and end range of IP addresses that you've specified for dynamic assignment. The DHCP server will assign the IP address for a "lease period" that's determined by the network administrator. With an ISP, the lease period may be for the duration of an Internet session, or for a specific amount of time—say, three hours. At that time, your IP address expires and you lose access to the Internet. If DHCP is running on a network, the lease typically is guaranteed for a number of days or as little as several hours. The default lease is for three days.

Normally, a DHCP server assigns IPs at the boot-up of the client computer and continues the lease until the client logs off a network—either a LAN connection or an Internet connection. Windows NT 3.5 and later, as well as Windows 9x and later client operating systems, have built-in support for DHCP.

The following shows you how to configure DHCP for a Windows client.

1. Click on the *Start* button and choose *Settings*. Select *Control Panel* and double-click the *Network* icon.

2. From the *Configuration* tab of the *Network* dialog box, highlight TCP/IP for the installed network adapter card. Click on the *Properties* button.

3. Choose the *IP Address* tab from the *TCP/IP Properties* dialog box, as shown in Figure 10-6.

4. Click on the field labeled *Obtain an IP address automatically.*

5. Click on the *OK* button and restart the computer.

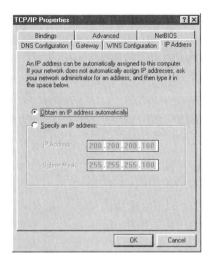

Figure 10-6:
IP Address Tab

When the workstation restarts, it will query the server for an IP address. The server will have been set up to assign IP addresses using DHCP and will assign the workstation an IP address. Notice that each time the workstation accesses the network, it might receive a different IP address.

Review the configuration steps required for assigning a static IP and the steps required for assigning a temporary IP. From an administrative point, temporary IP address assignments save network managers time and effort.

When possible, use DHCP to assign user IP addresses. Here are the advantages of DHCP:

- It allows the management of IP addresses to be centralized. Although some people might argue that this isn't an advantage, you have to remember that the pool of available IP addresses is diminishing. If you have a user who signs onto the Internet just once in the morning to send and receive e-mail, dedicating a static IP to this client is an inefficient use of a limited resource.

- IP addressing is a Network-layer function and must be mapped to a physical MAC-layer address. With DHCP you can move a client computer to a different network without having to reassign the IP address; the client will receive a different IP after it reboots.

- DHCP works side-by-side with static IP addresses. This involves a bit of manual intervention since the block of dynamic IP addresses (called the DHCP scope) needs to be kept separate from the static IP addresses. Some network devices, such as software-managed hubs, routers, and bridges, must be assigned a static IP address. DHCP allows both types of IP addresses to be administered from a single server.

Windows Internet Naming Service (WINS)

A server running TCP/IP may also run WINS with Windows.

Windows Internet Naming Service (WINS) contains a look-up table used to resolve computer names to IP addresses.

Notice the similarity to the DNS service, in which a site is given a name and a corresponding IP address. DNS is used to resolve Internet domain names to IP addresses.

WINS extends to NetBIOS at the Session layer of the OSI model. It allows computer names to be expressed as *\\computername\sharename\path*.

This is a standard Microsoft practice, called the Universal Naming Convention (UNC), that's followed with Windows or NetWare running NetBIOS over IPX. With WINS, you can extend this same convenience to all computers accessing NT/2000/XP or NetWare servers, or any other shared resource on a network.

The alternative to using WINS is doing the computer-name-to-IP-address resolution manually. This is done with a text file called HOSTS or LMHOSTS. HOSTS is used with Windows workstations for basic name-to-IP mapping. Each time a change occurs on the network, the file must be updated manually.

LMHOSTS, also available on Windows 9x and later workstations, performs computer-name-to-IP-address resolution as well. However, it's specified for use with a Windows NT network. If WINS isn't enabled on an NT/2000/XP network, you use LMHOSTS to manually edit changes.

LMHOSTS includes more options than HOSTS in recognition of the more powerful capabilities of Windows NT. A peculiarity of an LMHOSTS entry is that each command entry is preceded with the # symbol. For example, when you associate an entry with a specific domain name, the entry appears as:

      #DOM: domain name

The use of the # symbol is peculiar because the same symbol is used to comment out lines in the file. Commented-out lines consist of notes to the reader of the file. The notes are commented out so that they won't affect the functionality of command entries in the file.

If WINS isn't enabled on a server-based network, each workstation must send a broadcast requesting the IP address of the device (another workstation or a server) that they are connecting to. Broadcasts increase traffic on the network and may in fact be rejected since not all routers will pass NetBIOS names. If the destination is on a different LAN, this may happen.

With WINS, this situation doesn't occur since a single table lookup is all that's needed to resolve the computer name to an IP address.

The following shows you how to configure WINS on a Windows client.

1. Click on the *Start* button and select *Settings*. Choose *Control Panel* and double-click the *Network* icon.

2. In the *Network* dialog box, select the *Configuration* tab. Highlight TCP/IP for the installed network adapter card, and click on the *Properties* button.

3. Select the *WINS Configuration* tab, shown in Figure 10-7.

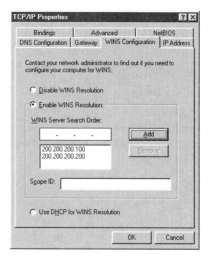

Figure 10-7: WINS Configuration Tab

4. Click on the field labeled *Enable WINS Resolution*.

5. Specify the IP address of a primary WINS server. This is the server that will resolve computer names to IP addresses. If a second WINS server is used, enter its IP in the *Secondary WINS Server* field.

6. The Scope ID defines a group of computers that recognize a registered NetBIOS name. Computers with the same Scope ID will be able to hear each other's NetBIOS "traffic" or messages. This is an optional field. The Scope ID is normally set at the server, not at the client.

7. Click on the *OK* button and restart the computer.

IP Default Gateway Setup

If the client will be accessing the Internet, it will need to go through a default gateway.

> In TCP/IP internetworking, the term gateway refers to a router, and sometimes another server, but is not a device that performs upper-layer protocol conversions.

The IP address of the default gateway must be specified at client configuration.

The following shows you how to configure an IP default gateway.

1. Click on the *Start* button and choose *Settings*. Select *Control Panel* and double-click the *Network* icon.

2. From the *Configuration* tab of the *Network* dialog box, highlight TCP/IP for the installed network adapter card. Click on the *Properties* button.

3. Select the *Gateway* tab in the *TCP/IP Properties* dialog box, shown in Figure 10-8.

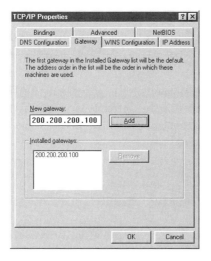

Figure 10-8:
Gateway Tab

4. In the *New gateway* field, enter the IP address of the router that the client will use to access the Internet.

5. Click on the *Add* button.

6. The IP address will appear in the *Installed gateways* field. If more than one gateway will be specified, enter each IP as just described. The first IP entered will become the default gateway. This means that when the client accesses the router, the first IP to be entered will be the first gateway that's tried. However, if this default gateway is busy, the client will move to the next IP on the list.

7. Click on the *OK* button and restart the computer.

On a network, it's critical that all devices be configured with both an IP address and a default subnet mask.

> The default subnet mask is used to determine whether an IP pack remains on the local network, or should be sent (via a router) to another network.

Using the pretext of a default gateway IP address, you may be able to see the value of subnetting. Suppose that a client computer has been given the network IP address of 10.200.20.15 using DHCP with a subnet mask of 255.0.0.0. Further, assume that the default gateway IP address is 192.168.150.5, with a subnet mask of 255.255.0.0. The network cards for the client and the gateway will examine the headers of all received packet IP addresses. The network cards will sum together the portion of the IP address identified by the subnet mask—192.168 for the client, and 10 for the gateway. If the sums are of equal value, the network cards of any device on the network will consider accepting the packet (the remainder of the IP address will specifically target the correct machine). But if they are not of equal value, the network card will reject the packet because the origination computer is on a different network.

In the above scenario, any IP packet that has 10 for the network portion of the IP address will be accepted by any other network device that has been assigned the same IP address that begins with 10. Those same network devices will reject an IP packet that begins with 192.168. A router/ gateway, however, will accept the packet.

In short, the default subnet mask is used to specify whether IP packets are intended for the local network, or should be sent on to another network.

PROXY IP

A proxy IP address is used at a network's interface to the Internet. All data going from the network to the Internet is given the same IP address. To an outsider, a proxy appears as if all data originates from the same node, which is typically a router.

The purpose of a proxy is to prevent an outsider from learning IP addresses of workstations and servers with the network. Since the outsider doesn't know the IP address of any devices on the network, the physical location of the device can't be learned, either. Recall that the Address Resolution Protocol is used to resolve IP addresses to MAC addresses.

If an intruder learns a server's MAC address, the specific location of the server can be identified, and the contents of the server may then be compromised.

A **proxy IP** is also called a **firewall**.

proxy IP

firewall

APPLE

Apple

Apple has historically been noted for innovative designs and technology. The company has not pursued ultra-fast microprocessor speeds but has instead focused on user needs. With the release of its newest operating system, MAC OS X, Apple truly enters the mainstream in terms of networking capabilities.

MAC OS X is a UNIX-based operating system but packaged with the GUI interface that Macintosh users have loved for years. There is a server version of OS X, as well as a stand-alone client version of the operating system.

MAC OS X Server is a cross-platform server that supports the following clients:

- Macintosh
- Windows
- UNIX
- Linux

No additional software is needed to utilize a Macintosh server in a networking environment that includes multiple-vendor operating systems. The server software ships with many features that include:

- *SAMBA:* SAMBA is file and print sharing software that makes a server appear as a Windows server to a client running a Windows operating system.

- *Apache:* A web server that is frequently installed on UNIX servers.

- *DNS:* DNS is used to resolve domain names to IP addresses.

- *DHCP:* DHCP is used to dynamically assign IP addresses to client network adapters.

- *TCP/IP:* Apple recommends that TCP/IP be run on Apple networks in order to ensure interoperability in networking.

- *SSL:* Secure Socket Layer is security software that provides encryption and authentication between clients and server.

- *POP and IMAP*: E-mail server software

- *RAID:* RAID is used for data disk redundancy and improved performance of hard drives.

- *NFS:* Network File System is the file and print sharing software that is native to UNIX systems.

- *AFP:* Apple File Protocol is the network protocol designed specifically for Macintosh computers. It does not interoperate with other operating systems.

With the release of MAC OS X, Macintosh clients have considerable versatility in the networking arena. A Macintosh client can be connected to any of the following servers:

- UNIX
- MAC OS X Server
- Windows
- NetWare
- Linux

The support for any of the above connections is built into the operating systems, so additional software and the consequent configuration is not required. A Macintosh system uses a "Connect to" dialog box for making the connection. All that's needed is to enter the name of the server and MAC OS X institutes the correct protocol handshaking to determine how to handle the transfer and connection. Note that, to the user, the multiple vendor servers appear no different.

CONFIGURATION PROBLEMS

When changes are made to a network client configuration, the client user will not be able to utilize the network resources appropriately. In this section, we'll take a look at the effects of making configuration changes to DHCP, DNS, and WINS.

Recall that DHCP is used to dynamically assign an IP address from a network server to a network client. The alternative to using DHCP is using a static IP address. A static IP address is permanently assigned to the client workstation.

Consider the effects of changing DHCP settings at either the client or the server:

- If the client is given a static IP address when the server is using DHCP to assign IP addresses, it's possible that two clients may try to use the same IP address. When this happens, one of the clients may be rejected from using the network.

- If a client is configured for a dynamic IP address, and the server has not been configured for DHCP, the client will never receive an IP address and, therefore, not be given access to the network.

DNS is used to resolve IP addresses with an Internet domain name. DNS settings typically affect access to a web browser or the Internet. A client may be configured with a static DNS IP address, or it may receive the IP address dynamically using DHCP.

Consider the effects of making changes to DNS settings:

- If the server is not configured for dynamically assigning the DNS IP address, and a static DNS IP address has not been assigned to the client, the client will not be able to access the Internet from a web browser when a domain name is entered.

- If the client is assigned a static DNS IP address, but the IP address of the DNS server has changed, the client will not be able to access the Internet.

- If the server uses DHCP to dynamically assign the DNS IP address, but the client has been assigned a static DNS IP address, Internet access could be denied if the static address is invalid. If the client does connect using the static IP address, response times may slow since the client can only use the DNS server that it's been assigned to.

WINS (Windows Internet Naming Service) is used to resolve NetBIOS computer names to IP addresses. The effects of making WINS changes include:

- If a network uses NETBEUI as the network protocol, WINS must be enabled on all clients. If WINS, and the IP associated with the WINS server, is not specified, Windows will have no way to resolve the name of a computer to the IP address assigned to that computer.

- If a network runs NETBEUI and TCP/IP simultaneously, ARP (Address Resolution Protocol), which resolves IP addresses to MAC hardware addresses, will allow IP packets to be sent appropriately.

- But if all clients and servers on a network are running TCP/IP, and a single client IP address is removed and NetBEUI enabled, that client may still be able to connect to other clients using WINS but will likely not be able to access another network such as the Internet.

For troubleshooting configuration scenarios on the Network+ exam, do spend some time on a network of several computers. Make changes to DHCP, DNS, and WINS and document the effects of the changes. But make sure that you have a solid understanding of the purposes of each of the three before doing so.

REMOTE CONNECTIVITY CONFIGURATION

In a Windows OS setting, the operating system may already have drivers for the modem you're installing. Then again, it may not. If the system doesn't have them, make sure you have a companion disk for your modem, so that you can install them yourself. Even better, check the chipset used with your modem. Make sure it's manufactured by a company you recognize and that has a web site, so you can download drivers and upgrades to the software.

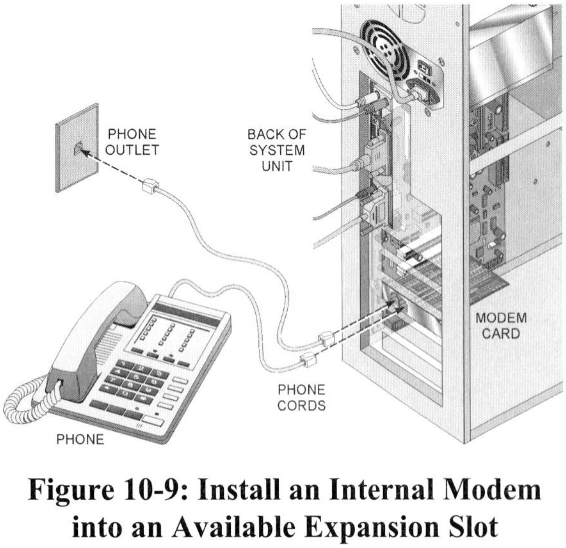

Typically, installation and configuration for a modem is easy. When it doesn't work, however, you may reach a point where you want to just sit down and gnash your teeth. Two areas commonly cause problems—interrupt and port setting conflicts. We'll take a look at these after setting up a modem that installs the way it's supposed to.

Figure 10-9 shows a modem being installed into an available expansion slot of a PC. The printed circuit board may have components that are sensitive to electrostatic discharge (ESD), so be sure to handle the board by the edges. Ideally, you should purchase and use an ESD wrist strap, connecting it to an actual earth ground such as a water pipe.

Figure 10-9: Install an Internal Modem into an Available Expansion Slot

To install the modem, exit all programs and shut the system down. Turn the power off to the computer. Remove the chassis cover. Locate an available expansion slot, and firmly press the board into the slot.

Internal modems are installed in an available expansion slot of a personal computer, and software is installed using the PC or network operating system software.

Once the modem is securely installed into an expansion slot, replace the chassis cover and turn the computer on.

Before installing the modem, review the following hardware resources. The information is necessary for installing modems, network interface cards, sound card, etc. The key point to hardware resources is that they must be unique for each device. If not, a conflict will disable the device.

- *IRQ:* Interrupt Request is a setting, assigned to each device in a computer, that's used to get the attention of the microprocessor. All devices must be assigned unique IRQs so the processor will be able to tell which device it's servicing. Common IRQs are shown in Table 10-5.

IRQ	DEVICE
0	System Timer
1	Keyboard
2	Secondary IRQ controller, or video adapter
3	Unassigned (may be specified for COM2 or COM4)
4	Serial Ports COM1 and COM3
5	Unassigned (may be used for LPT2 or sound card)
6	Floppy Disk Controller
7	Parallel Port LPT1
8	Real-time Clock
9	Unassigned (may be used for redirected IRQ2, sound card, or third IRQ controller)
10	Unassigned (may be used for primary SCSI controller)
11	Unassigned (may be used for secondary SCSI controller)
12	PS2 Mouse
13	Math Coprocessor (if used)
14	Primary Hard Drive Controller
15	Unassigned (may be used for secondary hard drive controller)

Table 10-5: Interrupt Requests and Corresponding Devices

Table 10-6: Common I/O Assignments

I/O PORT	DEVICE
200	Game Port
230	Bus Mouse
300	NIC Card
310	NIC Card
270	LPT3
3F8	COM1
2F8	COM2
278	LPT2
378	LPT1
3C0	EGA/VGA Video Adapter
3D0	CGA Video Adapter
3F0	Floppy Disk Controller

- *Base I/O Port:* The hexadecimal address that a microprocessor in a computer uses to communicate with a device in a computer. Base I/O assignments must be unique. Common I/O assignments are shown in Table 10-6.

- *Base Memory Address:* Buffer area in a computer's RAM memory where data coming in on a computer's parallel bus is stored while being converted to serial data to be transmitted from a serial port.

- *DMA:* A Direct Memory Address controller is used to transfer data in the NIC (Network Interface card) buffers directly into system memory. This relieves the microprocessor from devoting time and resources to the task.

For peripheral devices installed in a computer (NIC card, modem, sound card, etc.), the IRQ, DMA, and Base I/O must be unique. If not, there will be a resource conflict. To resolve the conflict, assign unique parameters to each device.

As Windows boots, it may detect the presence of the modem and generate a message saying that it's found new hardware, asking you if you want to install it. Click on YES, and if it doesn't initially find the modem, do the following to get to the configuration boxes:

1. Click on the *Start* button in the lower-left corner of your screen.

2. Highlight *Settings* in the *Start* menu selections, and click on *Control Panel*.

3. Click on the *Modem* icon. The *Modem Properties* box, shown in Figure 10-10, will open.

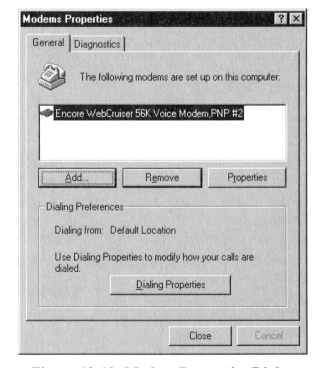

Figure 10-10: Modem Properties Dialog Box

4. Click on the *Add* button, and the *Install New Modem* box, pictured in Figure 10-11, will open.

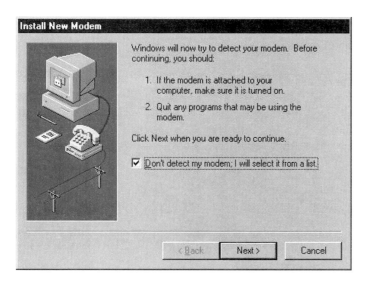

Figure 10-11: Install New Modem Dialog Box

You have two options here: let Windows detect your modem, or select it from a list. Leave the field unchecked and see if it will correctly detect it. This may save you time, but if your modem is relatively new and has drivers that weren't installed with Windows, you'll have to install them yourself from the disk.

5. Check the field labeled *Don't detect my modem; I will select it from a list*.

The dialog box will change to Figure 10-12. Now, you'll need to scan through the list to see if your modem is listed. If it is not, click on the *Back* button and remove the check from the "Don't detect my modem; I will select it from a list" box, and let Windows try to detect it. If it doesn't, go back to the screen shown in Figure 10-12, and click on the *Have Disk* button. A box will open telling you to place the disk in drive A and click on the *OK* button. The installation files will be on the disk, and you should follow the instructions as they open.

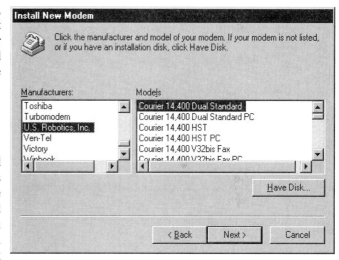

Figure 10-12: Select the Modem from the List

Once the drivers are installed, or Windows accepts your selection from the list of modems, a box will open, shown in Figure 10-13, prompting you to select one of the serial COM ports for your modem. For example, COM1 or COM3 would normally default to Interrupt Request (IRQ) 4, and be used for a serial mouse.

6. Choose *COM2*. Along with COM4, it will normally default to IRQ3.

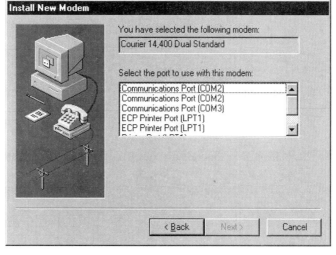

Figure 10-13: Select the COM Port Settings

The software will now complete the installation and you're almost finished. A final step is to make sure the modem works.

The quickest way to do this is to communicate with another modem; however, the most common method is to log on the Internet. If you're not yet hooked-up to cyberspace, all's not lost. You can use Windows' diagnostics by doing the following:

7. From Control Panel, click on the *Modems* icon. The *Modem Properties* dialog box will open.

8. Click on the tab labeled *Diagnostics*. A dialog box will open, listing all com ports. Highlight the port that your modem is on; then click on *More Info*.

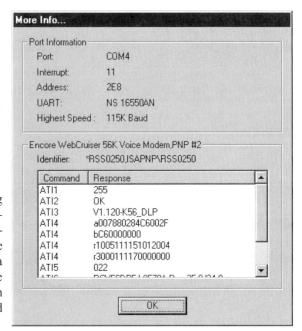

You'll receive a message telling you that Windows is communicating with the modem. In a couple of minutes, the results of the diagnostic test will be shown in a dialog box called *More Info*. The box will display information about your modem, as depicted in Figure 10-14.

Of particular interest are the commands listed at the bottom of the box. These are Hayes AT

Figure 10-14: Modem Diagnostics Test Results

commands for your modems. The AT commands control the functionality of modems. Notice that next to each command is an assortment of information that was generated. This means that the modem passed the diagnostic test since the computer software can communicate with the modem hardware.

Windows diagnostics for modems isn't a full test since it doesn't test the ability of the modem to send and receive files to a distant modem. But it sometimes detects discrepancies such as port and IRQ conflicts as well as faulty seating of the modem card.

If a modem doesn't respond, it's time to get serious. The next section is devoted to troubleshooting modem problems.

Modem Troubleshooting

Earlier it was said that problems with modem installations result from COM port and IRQ conflicts. A modem may appear to install and configure properly, as well as to be working when the diagnostics are run. Yet, when you connect a phone line to the modem, it may neither send nor receive.

You may think that Windows should warn you if you blew the installation. Typically, though, the only hints you get are when you try to dial out, and receive messages such as "No dial tone" or "Can't detect modem". This will seem strange, since the modem was detected when you installed it. How could there now be a problem?

Actually, the telephone line connection is the real acid test for a modem, and Windows can't test this function until you actually attempt to dial out. When you do, and the modem doesn't work, you get those cryptic messages. Now what?

Let's take a closer look at the COM port and IRQ settings. By the time you install a modem, many other subsystems have already been installed in the computer (mouse, floppy drive, hard drive, CD-ROM, etc.). There's a good chance that the port and interrupt you assigned to your modem is being used by another device. So you must find an unused port and IRQ for the modem.

This accomplished differently in different operating systems:

1. a. For a Windows client OS, click on the *System* icon in the Control Panel.
   b. Click on the *Device Manager* tab. Highlight the *Computer* icon at the top of the list of devices.
   c. Click on the *Properties* button. A listing of IRQs and their assigned devices will be displayed.

2. For Windows NT/2000/XP, click on *Run*. Type *WINMSD*. A similar listing will be displayed.

3. For Windows 3.x, exit Windows and at the DOS prompt, type *MSD*. Again, look for the IRQ/COM port listing.

The box will display all IRQs in your system and the devices they're assigned to. Look for the COM ports. For Plug-and-Play devices, Windows will attempt to assign COM2, IRQ3 to your modem. That's fine as long as these selections are not being used by another device. However, if you're getting conflicts, that's probably the case.

Usually, you can assign COM4 to the modem along with an unused IRQ. However, you should be somewhat cautious about choosing COM4. Video cards typically use some of the memory locations assigned to COM4, and because of this, many modem manufacturers don't recommend using this port.

Any unused IRQ will work. However, check your modem literature, and if possible, use an IRQ between 1 and 7. Many serial devices, including modems, won't work at interrupts above 7. If the modem documentation doesn't say one way or the other, all you can do is try assigning one of the higher IRQs.

A common problem during installation is conflicts between COM ports and interrupt requests (IRQs).

COM port and interrupt settings are configured on the hardware as well as the computer software, unless you have a Plug-and-Play modem. If so, all assignments are handled through software. If it's not Plug-and-Play, you'll have to manually change switch settings on the modem. These are usually black shunt switches that slide over vertical pins, or they may consist of ganged DIP switches. The settings for IRQ and COM ports will either be marked directly on the modem card, or the documentation will instruct you about how to set them.

To change the software settings, do the following:

1. For Windows, click on the *System* icon in Control Panel.

2. Click on the *Device Manager* tab. Highlight the device you want to change.

3. Double-click and/or click on the *Properties* button. A *Properties* dialog box will open.

4. Select the *Resources* tab. If the field marked "Use Automatic Settings" is checked, remove the check.

5. Highlight the resource you want to change (IRQ for modems) and click on the *Change Settings* button.

6. An *Edit* box will open. Change the IRQ setting and click on *OK*.

7. For Windows 3.x, double-click the *Ports* icon in the Control Panel.

8. Highlight the port used with your modem, then click on *Settings*, and then *Advanced*.

9. Select the IRQ you want to use for your modem.

COM port and interrupt conflicts are resolved by making sure the settings on the modem card (for non–Plug-and-Play devices) match those set up in the software. Once that's done, re-solve any other conflicts by checking to see if the port and IRQ you're using is being used by another device. Windows will tell you at the Resources tab in Device Manager if there's a conflict. If so, you must make a change.

VIRTUAL LOCAL AREA NETWORKS

Increasingly, the cost of communicating globally with voice and data has some companies scurrying for alternatives. The most promising technology to date for reining in data and telecommunications costs is a **virtual local area network (VLAN)**. A **virtual private network (VPN)** is a popular type of VLAN that uses special security and encryption techniques to provide secure and private connections across a public network such as the Internet.

A VLAN requires dedicated equipment on each end of the connection that allows messages entering the Internet to be encrypted, as well as for authenticating users. The equipment may be software- or hardware-based, or a combination of the two.

Typically, a VLAN allows remote users—such as telecommuters working from home, employees who travel extensively, or users at companies with many branch locations—access to corporate servers without using dedicated leased lines or expensive 800 dial-up connections. The per-use cost is the flat fee paid to an Internet service provider (ISP) each month.

Companies that implement a VLAN usually reap considerable savings from eliminating the bulk of long-distance toll charges. But there are other benefits as well. The majority of equipment that handles the VLAN must be located at a point of presence to the Internet. This refers to a port directly connected to the Internet backbone and is purchased from an ISP. In exchange for setting up the VLAN, the ISP will agree to—at least—minimal support for users connecting to the VLAN.

Note that with a VLAN, remote access servers and the banks of modems required to handle multiple callers in the field can be eliminated. This reduces the network complexity, costs, and support for a company.

By using the Internet as the transfer medium, other costly and complex technologies may be replaced. A good example is the electronic data interchange (EDI) used by many organizations for placing orders and sending invoices to distant suppliers. EDI requires the use of third-party contractors to handle the data exchanges and requires time and persistence to set up and maintain. A VPN can completely replace an EDI system since exchanges can use any type of data file—such as a simple Word document—for sending a purchase order. The information is protected since all VPN data is encrypted.

Another benefit to implementing a VLAN is scalability. If the network needs of a company grow, a VLAN can grow incrementally simply by installing the VLAN hardware or software on the user's computer. With a traditional wide area network, hardware and software are purchased in advance of actual needs with the assumption that an organization will grow to need the additional capability.

Increased efficiency is normally realized with VLANs. Leased lines and 800 toll-free dial-up accounts are notoriously slow when compared to broadband technologies like DSL and cable modems. For a remote worker with access to a cable modem, voice, data, and video are all possible over the VLAN. Streaming video over a dial-up connection is nearly impossible from many parts of the USA and other parts of the world.

As mentioned, a VPN provides a tunnel through the Internet that allows users—or networks—at either end to securely communicate. The ISP selected for the VPN must be able to support it. Therefore, not all ISPs meet the bill, and you should shop around when researching ISPs.

The ISP will handle the interface for the remote user to the Internet. All packets sent over the Internet will use a secure layer 3 protocol such as IP Secure Protocol (IPsec) or L2TP (Layer Two Tunneling Protocol).

The most common VPN protocol over the Internet is IPsec. IPsec allows about any type of packet to be encapsulated into the IP packet. These include NetBEUI frames, IPX, or AppleTalk. L2TP is a combination of the L2F (Layer Two Forwarding protocol) and the Point-to-Point Tunneling Protocol (PPTP). L2TP allows for any routable protocol to be encapsulated and transported to the remote destination. Routable protocols include IP, IPX, and AppleTalk.

When a user working from home wants to use the VPN, a connection to a local ISP is initiated. The connection may be over a dial-up connection, via a DSL line, or through a cable modem. Data is sent from the user using encrypted PPP from the remote user's workstation to the ISP. The ISP will then encapsulate the packets using IPsec or L2TP and handle the authentication with the destination site.

From a setup and maintenance standpoint, a VLAN makes a lot of sense. The remote user may have software installed that handles the VLAN connection to the ISP, or it may include a hardware network adapter or modem. Since authentication is required to verify that those who access the VLAN are authorized to do so, software or hardware (and usually a combination of the two) is required at both ends of the connection.

KEY POINTS REVIEW

An overview of operating systems and configuration has been presented in this chapter.

- A server is a centralized computer that provides network management processes to the network, and possibly applications and files to clients on the network.

- A client is a network user's computer that has access to applications and files on the server.

- A network operating system (NOS) is used as a means to share file and print services.

- A workgroup is a set of computers that can share access to each other's files and applications.

- A domain is a collection of client computers that are administered by a server.

- Windows supports two file structures, FAT and NTFS.

- The basis of the Novell directory and file organization scheme is the Novell Directory Service, or NDS.

- The directory structure used with UNIX resembles a tree cluster.

- Linux is a subset of UNIX.

- IPX, which stands for Internetwork Packet Exchange, is a proprietary networking protocol used by Novell.

- NetBEUI, which stands for NetBIOS (Network Basic Input/Output System) Extended User Interface, is a network protocol originally developed by Microsoft and IBM.

- IP, which stands for Internet Protocol, is a nonproprietary networking protocol.

- Domain Name Service, or DNS, is the service that translates Internet domain names into IP addresses.

- A common method used to dynamically assign IP addresses to clients is DHCP, Dynamic Host Configuration Protocol.

- WINS contains a look-up table used to resolve computer names to IP addresses.

- In TCP/IP internetworking, the term gateway refers to a router, and sometimes another server, but is not a device that performs upper-layer protocol conversions.

- The default subnet mask is used to specify whether IP packets are intended for the local network, or should be sent on to another network.

The following questions test your knowledge of the material presented in this chapter:

1. What parameters are needed to specify DNS for a client workstation?

2. Write a definition of a server.

3. What is the basis of the Novell file and directory service?

4. Which network operating system is IPX associated with?

5. What is the purpose of WINS?

6. What is the purpose of DNS?

7. What is the purpose of NetBEUI?

8. Why is a subnet mask required when configuring network parameters on a client computer?

9. Consider this scenario: A client connected to a DHCP server has the IP address setting set to "Dynamic". No WINS or DNS server IP is specified. The client is unable to connect to the Internet. What is the likely reason?

10. What is the basis of the Apple MAC OS X operating system?

11. Describe the difference between static and dynamic IP addresses.

12. List three network protocols supported by Windows N/2000/XP.

13. What is LMHOST?

14. What is the purpose of DHCP?

15. What is used to specify whether IP packets are intended for the local network, or should be sent on to another network?

EXAM QUESTIONS

1. To view a listing of IRQs assigned to a Windows workstation from the System Information window, what should be entered at the command prompt?
   a. REGEDIT
   b. PING
   c. Ipconfig
   d. WINMSD

2. In order to receive an IP address from a DHCP server, which of the following must be performed at the client?
   a. Enter a DNS number.
   b. Check the box labeled Specify an IP address.
   c. Check the field labeled Obtain an IP address automatically.
   d. Enable WINS.

3. What is the directory service of an operating system?
   a. methods used to organize and control network resources
   b. a way for many users to share one or more printers
   c. programs used by people on a network
   d. tools used to access the Internet

4. What is a workgroup?
   a. a set of computers sharing files from a server
   b. a set of computers that can share access to each other's files and applications
   c. the DHCP function built into Windows operating systems
   d. a group of network administrators

5. Which network protocol runs on UNIX systems?
   a. NetBEUI
   b. TCP/IP
   c. NetWare
   d. Windows

6. Which of the following is a routable protocol?
   a. NetBIOS
   b. NetBEUI
   c. DNS
   d. IPX

7. Which of the following is a nonroutable network protocol available with Windows operating systems?
   a. NetBEUI
   b. IPX
   c. TCP
   d. IP

8. Which of the following is used to resolve Internet domain names to IP addresses?
   a. WINS
   b. LMHOST
   c. DNS
   d. DHCP

9. To receive an IP address automatically, a workstation _____.
   a. must be manually configured by a network administrator
   b. must have a NIC in which the MAC is replaced with an IP address
   c. must be connected to a DHCP server
   d. must have WINS installed

10. Which of the following is used for computer-name-to-IP-address resolution manually?
    a. WINS
    b. DNS
    c. DHCP
    d. LMHOSTS

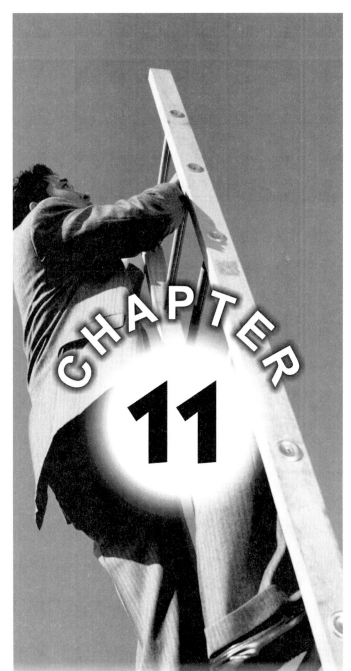

CHAPTER

11

NETWORK SYSTEMS

LEARNING
OBJECTIVES

LEARNING OBJECTIVES

Upon completion of this chapter and its related lab procedures, you will be able to perform the following tasks:

1. State three fundamental components of a network communications system.

2. State several applications of networking.

3. Prepare a brief definition of protocols.

4. Prepare a brief definition of the Open Systems Interconnect (OSI) model.

5. Define baseband and broadband.

6. Briefly describe three common network access methods.

7. Prepare a brief definition of baud and bit rate.

8. Prepare a brief definition of bandwidth.

9. State three common modulation methods used in networking.

10. Briefly describe characteristics of the Baudot, ACSII, and EBCDIC codes.

11. Prepare a brief definition of synchronous and asynchronous communication.

12. Identify the basic attributes, purpose, and function of simplex, half-duplex, and full-duplex transmission systems.

13. State three encoding schemes and describe the differences between them.

NETWORK SYSTEMS

INTRODUCTION

There's "all that information out there, and no way to get it." Truly, we are living in the information age. Hordes of salesmen want information describing our age, sex, income, and preference for toothpaste, shoes, socks, and soap. Engineers, scientists, and technicians search through manufacturer's product literature for the newest devices. Law enforcement officers would like to know if the driver they are pulling over for speeding has a history of shooting policemen. And perhaps we would like to have access to a million-volume library of electronics books, preferably from our home or office. Or maybe you are planning a flower garden and would like to know the plants that do well in direct sunlight, those that prefer shady areas, and those that like a little of both. Possibly you're planning to mix a few chemicals together in the hope of curing the common cold. But you're not sure if the mixture will result in the comfort of millions of people, or the destruction of all life on the planet.

All of that information is indeed out there, but getting to it is a bit of a problem. Information access has improved significantly in the past decade. Advances in communications products, greater standardization, and the proliferation of personal computers have thrust the data communications industry to the forefront of information processing. The widespread use and acceptance of the Internet is transforming the way we live and work. Although the reliability of network systems has improved tremendously, many snags and glitches remain.

However, we've made considerable progress from the first telegraph line from Baltimore to Washington, D.C. in 1884. Today, billions of dollars are transferred electronically all around the world. The composition of planets millions of miles away can be determined. A telephone conversation spanning the globe takes mere seconds to connect. By accessing corporate intranets, more of us are working at home.

Accomplishments in electronic communications over the past century have been phenomenal. The fundamental nature of the problem has not changed—that is, to get information from one point to another—but the methods and techniques of moving information have radically changed. The emphasis of data transfer these days is on efficiency, accuracy, quantity, and transparency. The basic function of a communications system is to transfer data. If, in order to transfer the data, a large amount of extra baggage must be carried, then efficiency suffers. And of course, the receiver expects to receive an exact replica of the data that was transmitted, so our tolerance for errors is extremely low. The search continues for transmission techniques that minimize, detect, or correct errors that occur on the way to the receiver.

A large portion of data is transmitted through long distance telephone facilities. These are the same facilities we use when making a long distance call. The long distance carriers bill data communications users the same way telephone companies bill their customers: by the amount of time their facilities are used in processing the call. If we could somehow quadruple our rate of speech, our phone bills would be cut by a fourth. Data communications users do just that. The idea is that the larger the amount of data transmitted in a unit of time, the cheaper will be the charge for using the facilities of long distance carriers.

The designers of networking systems have one rather strange aspect inherent in the job: They develop incredibly complex techniques for achieving the system characteristics described above, and then mask all of their work so that it appears to the everyday user as if it doesn't exist. Their goal is to make data transfers transparent to users. In turn, the users can concentrate on initiating the transfer at one end, and receiving data at the other end. All the things occurring in between appear invisible, or nonexistent, to them.

In this chapter, we'll begin to penetrate the transparency that cloaks data communications. Basic concepts are introduced, common terms are defined, and equipment fundamental to the industry is described. Some of the more common standards and protocols are introduced along with characteristics common to the many areas comprising data communications.

SYSTEM COMPONENTS

A communications system consists of three fundamental components: a sender, a message, and a receiver.

Figure 11-1 illustrates a familiar communication system, a telephone call. The caller is the sender, voices contain the message, and the individual answering the call is the receiver. All communication—written, oral, microwave, television, printed, or by telephone—consists of these components. We usually think of data communications as involving the exchange of data between computers. The phone system is a convenient pathway for carrying the exchange of data between computers. It would be valid to substitute computers for the telephones in Figure 11-1.

When data is exchanged between computers the sender is generally referred to as the **transmitter** and the computer accepting data is called the **receiver**.

As in the case of a telephone call, the assignment of transmitter and receiver to specific computers is relative; it depends on which computer is sending and which is receiving at any given time. As in telephone calls, the roles of computers reverse frequently from transmitter to receiver and vice versa. In the interest of simplification and coherency, the transmitting device in this book should be considered the transmitter, and the device on the other end considered the receiver.

Figure 11-1: Components of a Basic Communications System

Nearly every business has a need for data communications in one form or another. For the most part, the communication medium (all hardware and software between transmitter and receiver) used by businesses that are separated by distance is the local and long distance telephone network.

For data communication within a business, the medium used to transfer data may be one of several types. The most common is a wire-based system with unshielded twisted pair cabling being predominant. Coaxial cable may also be used. Increasingly, wireless systems—which use the atmosphere as the communication medium—are becoming common.

The reason the phone system has taken on a dominant role in data communications is because telephone wires are in nearly every home and office. The existing wire is a logical choice to use in linking computers together since it's already installed. The major drawback to using the telephone system is that it is intended to carry voice communication and not data. This has presented unique challenges to designers of data communications and has resulted in unique responses to the challenges.

A communication system proves its value most readily for a company with offices or stores scattered about the country. Consider a large, general merchandise retailer with 100 stores in twenty states. Each store may maintain 10,000 different items for sale. In order for the store to continue making money, it must restock the items it has sold. A network could be implemented using point-of-sale terminals. These are the checkout registers that use a bar code scanner or a stock number the cashier enters into the register at the time of checkout. Most point-of-sale terminals track the inventory of a store. The registers are linked to a computer—either at the store or at a centralized remote site—and when an item is sold, an inventory adjustment is made to the data maintained in the computer memory. Perhaps a report is automatically generated listing all items whose quantity in the store is below a specific level. The store manager then knows it's time to re-order that item.

Data communications readily lends itself to industrial plants. The communication system may monitor a hazardous or toxic process and send information about the process to employees who are at a safe distance. The system could also be used when portions of the process have been split, or distributed, among different areas of the plant. The system would monitor the progress of the processing and provide operators with status reports.

The financial community has made extensive use of data communications. Stock, bond, or currency traders need to know exactly what is happening in market exchanges around the world. If they receive dated or inaccurate information, their clients may lose thousands of dollars. The banking industry evaluates loan applications from reports maintained by credit bureaus. High-volume banks usually maintain an onsite terminal linked to credit bureau computers. The bank requests a report from the credit bureau. The bureau pulls the report from a large database and sends it to the bank, where it is printed on a local printer. The data travels back and forth on telephone lines.

More and more, computer users are discovering that access to a database provides them with a key to "all that information out there."

A database is generally contained in the memory of a large computer, and typically specializes in a specific subject.

For example, there are databases specializing in stock trading on the New York Stock Exchange, databases for lawyers providing the results of court decisions, and databases for the chemical industry describing sources for raw materials or new breakthroughs.

A company that maintains a database is called an **information service**. The company sells access to its database. Generally, all that's needed to gain access is a computer, a modem, and a password. You buy the password from the information service and are usually billed for the time you use their database.

By far, the most common use of network communications is day-to-day business. File sharing, e-mail, data entry, Internet, and database applications are routine uses of a business network. Indeed, networking in business in now ingrained into corporate cultures to the point that computer networking is an important strategic aim of successful companies.

A data communications network typically consists of a number of computers tied together in such a way that data can be exchanged among them. Many options are available for connecting computers together, and the bulk of this book is dedicated to describing them.

Generally, networks can be described as **wide area networks (WANs)** or **local area networks (LANs)**. The distinction between the two is not obvious.

TEST TIP

Know the difference between a LAN and a WAN.

A LAN consists of computers linked together in a room, a building, or a metropolitan area, whereas a WAN consists of computers connected together over a large geographical area; that is, areas falling outside a specific metropolitan area.

As a point of interest, networks that cover a city are sometimes referred to as metropolitan area networks (MAN). However, this text will describe networks in general as either WANs or LANs. Table 11-1 lists common networks according to geographical coverage.

**Table 11-1:
Geographical Coverage
of Networks**

Network	Coverage
Local Area Network (LAN)	A LAN covers a room or rooms within a building.
Campus Area Network (CAN)	A CAN covers several buildings in close proximity.
Metropolitan Area Network (MAN)	A MAN covers buildings within a city.
Wide Area Network (WAN)	A WAN covers a large area outside of a city, and may include global coverage.

Networks are such an important part of data communications that the next section explains the various methods used to classify and describe them.

As a general rule, a data communication system is applied in those situations in which it will make a positive financial impact on an organization. This means the system will assist the organization in earning more money, or will improve the efficiency of the way business is conducted. At a minimum, an organization with timely information has the means to make better-informed decisions affecting its markets, products, and employees.

PROTOCOLS

Protocols are the rules used with data communications.

Protocols

There are many protocols, and more are being developed each day to address new technologies.

The tendency of many data processing and networking vendors has been to carefully safeguard the technical details of their products. They do this so their competitors do not duplicate their products. But the computer industry has grown to the point of touching the lives of nearly everyone. Access to data files may mean life or death to an accident victim who is unable to tell a doctor about the medicines he is currently taking, or is allergic to. Timely access to information is a concern to the national defense. These situations, and many more like them, cross the boundaries of corporate competitiveness and the desire to protect trade secrets.

> **NOTE**
>
> The intention of protocols is to bring a sense of standardization to data communications.

Several highly respected standards organizations as well as several large data processing vendors recognize the implications of computer products on our daily lives, and have sought to bring a sense of order to the industry. Many of the standard protocols in use today were once proprietary products of large computer vendors. The process of standardizing data communications is an ongoing process. Standards change as technology changes. Many protocols have built-in flexibility that allows for changes without affecting other protocols.

A basic blueprint that describes the function of protocols for data communications is the **Open System Interconnection (OSI)** Reference Model.

Open System Interconnection (OSI)

It was published in 1978 by the International Standards Organization, and is shown in Figure 11-2. The OSI model takes a layered approach to a communication system in a manner similar to the layers of an onion. At the heart of an onion lies the innermost, or lowest layer, so the lowest layer of the OSI model concentrates on the most basic concepts of data transfer. The succeeding layers deal with progressively higher-order concepts until the final, or outermost layer, which involves the interaction of a user with the data communications system.

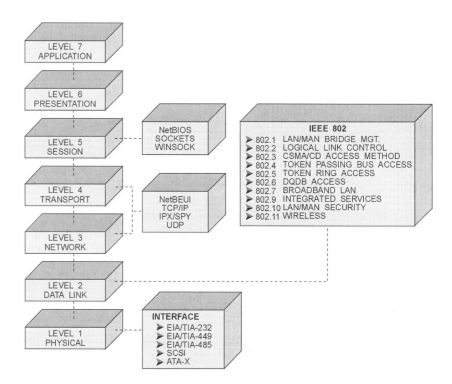

Figure 11-2: OSI Reference Model

While the OSI model was described in detail in Chapter 4, this material is fundamental to understanding protocols. Therefore, the following points briefly describe the function of each layer of the model in terms of protocols:

- **Physical Layer:** The Physical layer deals with electrical and mechanical aspects of networking. The size and type of cable connectors, the type of cabling, and the frequency, amplitude, and shape of data signals are discussed in Physical layer protocols.

- **Data Link Layer:** The Data Link layer is involved in standardizing the packaging of data (called frames or packets) that's exchanged between computers on a network. Ethernet and Token Ring are examples of Data Link layer protocols.

- **Network Layer:** The Network layer protocols define how different networks can communicate with one another. Examples of Network layer protocols are the Internet Protocol (IP) and Microsoft's NetBEUI.

- **Transport Layer:** The Transport layer is responsible for ensuring that data sent between networks actually arrives, and is the same data that was sent. Transmission Control Protocol (TCP) is the most common Transport layer protocol.

- **Session Layer:** The Session layer has the responsibility for managing dialogue between communication stations. A common Session layer duty involves communicating with ports for an Internet connection such as port 80 for the HTTP protocol.

- **Application Layer:** The Application layer stipulates the many purposes of the network. E-mail, HTTP Web access on the Internet, and file transfers using the FTP protocol are examples of Application layer protocols. There are many more and the ensuing chapters discuss the most common in detail.

- **Presentation Layer:** The Presentation layer ensures that data messages are received in a format that's understood. In order to accomplish this, the Presentation layer has to retain the content of a data message while modifying the syntax of the data for the end user. In addition, this layer defines fields for remote entry work such as may be found in an inventory system. It is also responsible for managing special events such as data encryption or foreign language translation.

The OSI model is one of many data communications models. Throughout this book, you'll have an opportunity to study other models. Various layers of the OSI model are widely quoted in equipment specifications, and it is central to the Network + exam. Figure 11-2 lists common protocols along with their association to the model.

Closely related to the model are protocols that delineate the layers. At the Physical layer are interface standards such as EIA/TIA-232, formerly known as RS-232C.

Protocols used to connect networks, or to send data across large networks are defined at the Network and Transport layers, with the most common being TCP/IP.

Keep in mind that a standard isn't a protocol. A standard explains how to implement a protocol, whereas the protocol describes outcomes.

Although understanding the ISO model in terms of protocols is important, this information does not specify how to implement them. That is for vendors to decide. Portions of the model are incomplete, particularly at the upper levels. Data communications designers and vendors have, for the most part, accepted the lower levels, and a concerted effort has been made to be faithful to the standards. However, the vendor determines the protocol implementation, and the temptation to protect the product from duplication is never absent. This often results in little modifications made here and there, to the point that it would be wise to thoroughly examine any claims of compatibility and quotes of adherence to specific protocols.

NETWORKS

> A **network** consists of hardware and software designed to direct and control data traffic.

network

Why bother with a network? The single most important reason is that it simplifies data transfer. Figure 11-3 shows five computers connected to one another without the benefit of a network. In order for the computers to exchange data, each must have a wire connected to the other. In the worst case, as shown in the illustration, each computer has output wires connected to each of the other computers as well as input wires from the other computers. The total number of wires linking the five computers together is twenty.

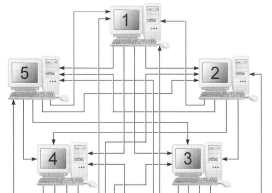

Figure 11-3: Connection Problems Linking Computers

In Figure 11-4, the same five computers have been linked in a network. Now, data transfer can take place with the use of only five wires. From a troubleshooting standpoint, it would be much easier to track down a wiring problem in Figure 11-4 than in Figure 11-3. If the system itself is simplified, then it is reasonable to assume that it will be more reliable.

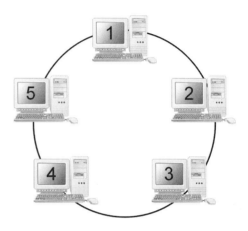

**Figure 11-4:
Connecting With a**

Five computers connected together is a small network. A local area network in an office building may tie together hundreds or thousands of computers. If Figure 11-3 looks like a wiring nightmare, you can imagine the difficulty of maintaining connections for a thousand computers.

A network has many characteristics. The description or classification of a network is often rooted in the characteristics having the greatest importance to the user. For example, the most important aspect may be the physical arrangement, or **topology**, of the network. To another network user, the primary concern may be the transmission medium selected—twisted pair wiring, coaxial cable, or fiber-optic cable. The different characteristics affect the performance of a network. In and of themselves, each media type has characteristics that offer performance, cost, or functional benefits. When considered collectively, the overall characteristics define the level at which the network will operate.

The operational level of the network is dictated by the application. To achieve the desired application the network must possess characteristics that, when used in conjunction with each other, will produce the desired result.

The physical arrangement of a network, called the network topology, is frequently used to describe a network. With the widespread proliferation of the Internet, and the common use of large interconnecting networks, topology has become somewhat difficult to nail down. But topology remains an integral characteristic of a network that indicates certain performance characteristics.

topology

Method of Transmission

Networks are sometimes described by the method used to transmit data. Generally, two alternatives are available: **baseband** and **broadband**. Baseband networks employ digital signaling to communicate packets of data. The data is transmitted directly to the network medium, normally twisted pair wiring or coaxial cable.

A baseband network uses digital signaling to send packets and typically allows only one data channel at a time.

Broadband networks use analog signaling and typically carry more than one data channel simultaneously.

When a computer receives a packet of data, it removes the user information contained in the packet, and processes it for the user. Baseband networks cover a small area—a room or building. Because of the short distances involved, the data is transmitted without the need for a carrier frequency.

Most local area networks use baseband signaling. Ethernet, for example, uses baseband.

Broadband networks are used when distances between computers—or other communicating devices—cover a wide area such as throughout a city, and beyond. Cable runs that are long—from building to building or from one part of a city to another—cover a sufficient distance that the data requires a carrier to transport it over long distances; thus, some type of modulation scheme is normally used with broadband networks.

Cable television systems, for example, use broadband for Internet connections via cable modems. Likewise, ISDN and DSL connections employ the analog telephone system to transmit information.

Broadband networks cover a broad range of frequencies. The frequency range may be divided hundreds of times so that hundreds of users can use the network channel simultaneously. This is the case in a cable system using cable modems. Baseband networks, on the other hand, cover a very narrow range of frequencies so that, normally, only one user at a time has access to the network channel. Ethernet, since it is a baseband technology, allows only one user at a time to access the channel.

Physical Connection Medium

The medium refers to the physical path taken by data.

A network can use a wide variety of **connection media**. The medium refers to the physical path taken by data. Typical media include copper wire, fiber-optic cable, microwaves, infrared, and radio waves.

Copper wire includes twisted wire pairs.

It is composed of 22- or 24-gauge copper wire twisted together like a braid. The wire is twisted together to eliminate common noise voltages that may be induced into the wire. Another copper wire medium in common use is coaxial cable. Coaxial cable has a single insulated copper wire enclosed with a copper braid. Enclosing the braid is the outer insulation. Historically, coaxial cable has been used in broadband applications, particularly in the cable television industry, as well as in many earlier computer networks.

In recent years, twisted pair cabling has advanced to where it competes equally with coax in a network environment. In fact, there's little justification in using coax for an Ethernet LAN with the availability of wide bandwidth (Category 5) twisted pair cabling.

A fiber-optic cable consists of a thin strand of glass or plastic cable surrounded by a jacket.

The data to be transmitted is converted from electrical energy to light energy and transmitted through the cable.

Fiber-optic cable is the choice medium for ground-based communication systems in which data integrity and speed are the most important considerations.

Fiber-optic cable has significantly lower losses than copper wire, and is immune from external electrical interference (lightning, motors, generators, microwaves) that creates much of the distortion found in copper-based systems. Fiber-optic cable offers one of the highest data speeds of all communication media.

Microwaves offer another alternative for transmission media.

Satellites use microwaves for relaying data from transmitter to receiver.

In recent years, satellite systems have experienced a surge of growth due to improvements in ground-based antennas and a decrease in the relative costs of utilizing satellites. Long distance telephone companies frequently employ microwave systems in their trunk lines, along with traditional land-based microwave.

trunk line

A **trunk line** is a major artery capable of carrying thousands of calls. The telephone companies modulate the many calls onto the carrier using sophisticated multiplexing techniques. Multiplexing is the process of combining many data signals onto a single channel.

Wireless networks offer another approach using microwave-based media.

A wireless network—either local or in a wide area—offers the greatest flexibility of all media types.

Wireless technology uses the atmosphere as the transmission medium.

More and more, the need to have networked computers be mobile is becoming increasingly important. Often, a copper or fiber connection isn't available where the need is; so organizations are turning to wireless technology as a temporary as well as a permanent infrastructure solution. Due to significant reductions in the cost of wireless technology, home users, as well as small offices, are finding wireless to be an attractive alternative to traditional copper-based wiring.

Access Control

A network user has to decide how the computers connected to the network will gain access to it. Three methods are generally used to control access: **collision detection**, **collision avoidance**, and **token-based**. In a network that uses collision detection, computers with data to send simply send it. Once the data is sent, if nothing happens, the computer continues to transmit. However, two computers may decide to send data packets at the same time. If they do, there will be a collision. In the event of a collision, both computers cease to transmit and they try again after a randomly selected delay. Ethernet uses collision detection as the means used by computers to gain access to the network.

Collision avoidance relies on computers first checking the network to determine whether another computer is transmitting data packets. If the network is in use, the computer waits and tries again later. In a collision avoidance scenario, there will never be collisions. Wireless networks (using the IEEE 802.11b protocol) use collision avoidance to gain access to the network.

Collision detection and collision avoidance share a disadvantage in that there's no guarantee that a computer will get access to the network. Token-based networks overcome this disadvantage. In a token-based system, a software token is passed from one computer to the next on the network. The computer that possesses the token is given access to the network and will send data packets if it has packets to send. The token contains a timer. Once the timer expires, the computer stops transmitting. The token is then passed to the next station on the network and it transmits packets. Token Ring networks are the most common network type to use a token-based access method.

The advantage of a token-based access scheme is that all computer stations are guaranteed access to the network. The disadvantage of using tokens is that it creates delays if not properly managed.

Network access methods are at the root of Data Link layer protocols. The IEEE 802.x series of local area network protocols describe access methods used for each protocol type. The IEEE 802.x protocols were described in detail in Chapter 2.

collision detection

collision avoidance

token-based

BAUD AND BIT RATE

baud rate

bits per second
(bps) rate

symbol

The speed at which data is transmitted is quoted in much of the technical literature as either the **baud rate** or **bits per second (bps) rate**. Baud rate describes the number of data symbols transmitted per second.

A **symbol** is a small group of bits into which data is organized at the time of modulation.

In other words, a symbol may contain one, or many bits of data. The number of transitions made from a logical 1 to a logical 0, and vice versa, within a second characterizes a symbol. The transition rate is called the baud of the channel.

Baud is an indication of the amount of information transmitted, while bps is the amount of total data transmitted.

The bits per second rate is the amount of data bits transmitted within a second. Notice that due to the practice of imposing more than one data bit onto each line transition, the number of transmitted data bits (the bps) will be higher than the rate of line transitions (the baud).

The use of symbols effectively increases the number of bits transmitted in the allotted bandwidth of a communication channel. A data communications symbol can contain 16 or more data bits. The specific number of bits contained in the symbol is determined by the method used to modulate the carrier.

Baud rate is calculated by:

$$\text{Baud} = bps/N$$

where *bps* is bits per second, and *N* is the number of bits per symbol.

For example, a Bell 201 modem has a specified data rate of 2400 bps. The number of bits per symbol is 8. The baud rate is equal to:

$$\text{Baud} = 2400 \text{ bps}/8 = 300$$

The **bit rate**, or bits per second, describes the number of discrete binary bits transmitted per second. It is a true measure of data rate. The bit rate is calculated by:

$$bps = 1/T$$

where T is the bit time in seconds.

For example, if the time of a single bit is measured and found to be 10 milliseconds (ms), then:

$$bps = 1/.01 = 100$$

Baud is a unitless quantity, and therefore can't be quantified. It has little meaning in evaluating the performance of a network, or the components comprising a network. Its value lies in the concept that many of the data bits that are sent over a network contain no user data. Therefore, in order to gain insight as to how much information is sent using a particular modulation scheme, we sometimes focus on baud rather than bps.

Increasingly, data communications literature uses baud and bps interchangeably. This usage is incorrect. The two are only equal at lower data rates of less than about 1200 bps.

All modems are classified by their bps rate.

Multiplexing schemes, in which a single channel may be divided to allow multiple users access, are devised around the bps rate of a channel. The digital systems of long distance carriers are specified by bps.

DATA TRANSMISSION

Information in a data communication system is transmitted in digital or analog formats. Analog data is common in many parts of the telephone system, although most regional and long distance carriers are aggressively replacing their analog systems with digital systems. The principal reason for the change to digital is that it is easier to generate, is compatible with the structure of data in computer systems, and noise and distortion are easier to remove from digital signals.

An analog signal uses many discrete values to represent a physical process (a voice, for example).

It's difficult, if not impossible, to remove some types of distortion in an analog signal without simultaneously degrading the signal. Analog-to-digital, and digital-to-analog integrated circuits have advanced to the point that an analog signal can be converted to digital, transmitted through a digital communication system, and converted back to analog at the receiver with nearly perfect clarity. Still, many segments of analog communications remain. Wireless networks as well as satellite communication systems use analog data when communicating.

When a user connects to the Internet using a dial-up telephone connection, an analog modem is used because nearly all subscriber loops are an analog connection.

> The subscriber loop is the circuit from a residential or office telephone to the local central office. The first three digits of a local telephone number designate a central office.

A computer user wishing to connect to the Internet utilizes the same loop circuit through a modem. The problem is that these circuits were designed for analog signals, and in particular, voice signals.

Figure 11-5 depicts the subscriber loop voice channel. The frequency response of the channel is 300 Hz-3300 Hz for a bandwidth of 3 kHz (3300 − 300 = 3000). All data transmitted through this channel must have a bandwidth no greater than 3 kHz.

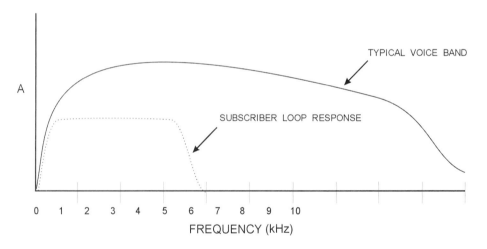

Figure 11-5: Frequency Response of Voice Channel

> **Bandwidth** (BW) is a particularly important aspect of data because it is a measure of the amount of actual data being transmitted.

And the amount of transmitted data is related to channel capacity. Channel capacity, measured in bits per second, is directly proportional to bandwidth.

This means that a channel with large BW can carry large amounts of information; a channel with a narrow BW can carry small amounts of information. The local subscriber loop has a narrow BW. The problem is compounded if a digital square wave is applied to a subscriber loop. Square waves, as we will see in Chapter 12, require far greater BW than does an analog signal. In order to achieve the benefits of digital data communications systems, designers have resorted to considerable subterfuge in developing modulation and multiplexing techniques that allow an analog system to behave as a digital system.

Compromise is the key criterion in bandwidth considerations. The greater the bandwidth, the more data can be transmitted in a given time. The costs of transmitting the data will also be cheaper; however, equipment costs are greater for large bandwidth systems than for narrower bandwidth systems.

MODULATION METHODS

Data may be modulated onto a carrier for several reasons. The frequency of the data may not be the same as that of an assigned, or allotted, channel. Wireless networks are assigned a frequency in the 2.4 GHz range. Data in a wireless network is sent at 11 Mbps. To be transmitted, the 11 Mbps data is modulated onto a 2.4 GHz carrier frequency. The FM radio-frequency range is from 88 MHz to 108 MHz. Obviously, that is out of the audible range. In the telephone voice channel, the carrier must be between 300 Hz and 3,300 Hz.

It is usual to have Mbps data rates modulating a 1,200 Hz carrier because the data frequency falls far outside the voice channel. In a microwave system, high carrier frequencies keep antennas down to manageable sizes. The use of a carrier is essential with some types of multiplexing techniques. A carrier with a broad bandwidth can be used to carry several thousand data signals by sharing the bandwidth.

Fundamentally, **modulation** is the process of superimposing data on a carrier.

modulation

Once the modulated carrier is transmitted, the data is detected at the receiving end. Detection, or demodulation, is the process of recovering data from the modulated carrier. There are three basic modulation methods: **amplitude modulation** (**AM**), **frequency modulation** (**FM**), and **phase modulation** (**PM**). In practice, it is very common to use various combinations of the three or to use a variation of one of the three basic methods. Furthermore, there is digital modulation and analog modulation. Nearly all variations of analog modulation can be traced back to AM, FM, or PM. Some digital modulation methods—pulse width modulation, for example—resemble FM since a digital carrier is modulated by varying the width of square waves. Other digital modulation techniques involve varying the amplitude of square waves in a manner similar to AM.

amplitude modulation (AM)

frequency modulation (FM)

phase modulation (PM)

Specific modulation methods are discussed in appropriate areas of the text. The following discussion describes the fundamentals of AM, FM, and PM.

Amplitude Modulation

Amplitude modulation is produced by simultaneously applying a carrier and data to any nonlinear device.

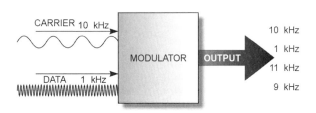

Figure 11-6: Producing Amplitude Modulation

As shown in Figure 11-6, this results in a 10 kHz carrier, the original 1 kHz data signal, the sum of the carrier and data (11 kHz), and the difference of the carrier and data (9 kHz). The sum frequency is called the upper sideband and the difference frequency is called the lower sideband.

In a conventional AM transmitter, the 1 kHz original data signal is filtered out. The carrier, upper sideband, and lower sideband are the transmitted frequencies. Each of these waveforms is depicted in Figure 11-7 in the time domain, as seen on an oscilloscope.

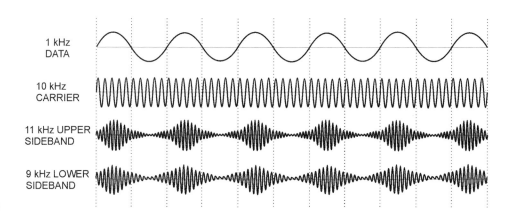

Figure 11-7: AM Modulation Envelope

There are several points to consider with the waveforms. First, notice the transmitted carrier contains no data; it is the same as when it was input to the modulator. In conventional AM, the carrier can contain up to 40% of the transmitted power. This is power containing no data. The carrier is used at the receiver to assist in recovering the original data. In some AM systems, the carrier is suppressed and not sent at all. This results in an improvement in the power efficiency.

Another interesting observation of the waveforms in Figure 11-7 involves the sidebands. The upper and lower sidebands are identical in all aspects except frequency. As mentioned earlier, it is the sidebands that contain the effects of the original data.

If one sideband were suppressed at the transmitter and the other transmitted, it would make little difference because they share the same characteristics.

Single-sideband (SSB) systems operate on the principle of suppressing one sideband and transmitting the other. The peculiar shape of the sidebands is called the **modulation envelope**.

The effect of the 1 kHz data signal can be seen by tracing the modulation envelope. The outline of the modulation envelope—either the positive or negative alternations of the sideband; they are identical—corresponds to the 1 kHz data. The amplitude of the modulation envelope is directly proportional to the amplitude of the data. The rate of amplitude changes is directly proportional to the frequency of the data. Note that the sidebands contain only the effect of the data frequency and amplitude variations; the data itself is lost.

AM is a simple and low-cost method of modulation. Conventional AM detectors are simple and easy to implement at the receiver. AM modulation requires a conservative amount of bandwidth. The bandwidth is equal to the difference of the upper and lower sidebands.

A major drawback to AM is its poor power efficiency. With the carrier requiring 40% of the transmitted power, the other 60% divides between the two sidebands. Since the sidebands are identical, the efficiency is calculated by $30/100 = 30\%$. Another drawback to AM is the difficulty in removing any noise picked up on the way to the receiver. With analog AM it is sometimes impossible to eliminate noise. In a digital AM system in which square waves are transmitted, greater successes are achieved in reducing noise.

Frequency Modulation

Frequency modulation (FM) is produced by varying the frequency of the carrier.

Frequency modulation (FM)

FM is illustrated in Figure 11-8.

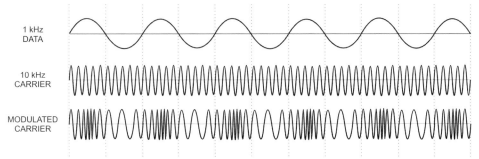

Figure 11-8: Frequency Modulation

On the positive alternation of the 1 kHz data, the frequency of the carrier increases. The amount of frequency increase is proportional to the amplitude of the data signal—the frequency of the carrier will be at its greatest at the peak value of the carrier. The negative alternation of the data causes the carrier frequency to decrease. As with the positive alternation, the greatest amount of frequency change occurs at the peak negative alternation.

The amount of frequency change, or deviation, is directly proportional to the amplitude of the data signal.

How quickly the carrier frequency changes is determined by the frequency of the data signal. In Figure 11-8, the carrier frequency is deviating at a 1 kHz rate. If the data frequency increases to 2 kHz, the rate of the carrier deviations will also increase to 2 kHz.

The deviation of the carrier above and below the center frequency does not readily lend itself to the bandwidth of the FM signal. In calculating BW for an AM signal, the lower sideband was subtracted from the upper sideband. Bandwidth calculations for FM are not quite as straightforward because the carrier, as it deviates above and below the center frequency, generates an infinite number of sidebands. The intelligence contained in the modulating signal is contained in the sum of all the sidebands. As a practical matter, those sidebands containing less than 1% of the total voltage of the waveform are considered negligible and can be deleted from bandwidth considerations. As a general rule, the sidebands are repetitively duplicated at diminishing voltage levels for a distance above and below the carrier. The distance between those sidebands that contain more than 1% of the waveform voltage comprises the bandwidth. Just how much is that? A method of calculating the bandwidth known as **Carson's rule** recognizes all sidebands containing 96% of the total radiated power.

Using this rule, bandwidth is calculated by:

$$BW = 2(\Delta F_c + F_m)$$

where F_c is the deviation produced by the modulating signal, and F_m is the frequency of the modulating signal.

Let's assume that a 1 kHz data signal produces a deviation of the FM carrier of 1 kHz. This is consistent with the sideband placement of the earlier example used for AM, and will provide a reference for comparing AM and FM. The bandwidth of the FM signal is:

$$BW = 2(\Delta F_c + F_m)$$
$$BW = 2(1 \text{ kHz} + 1 \text{ kHz})$$
$$BW = 2(2 \text{ kHz})$$
$$BW = 4 \text{ kHz}$$

This is twice the bandwidth of an equivalent AM signal. Reducing the amplitude of the modulation could reduce the FM bandwidth, but the sideband energy would be reduced as well. Although larger bandwidths increase channel capacities, the bandwidths available are usually sharply defined, which makes bandwidth considerations a high priority.

Using our example of a 1 kHz data signal, the BW from a conventional AM transmitter is 2 kHz. A 100 kHz communication channel can accommodate 50 AM transmissions (100 kHz/2 kHz = 50). The same 100 kHz channel can contain only 25 FM transmissions with a 4 kHz bandwidth (100 kHz/4 kHz = 25).

The wide bandwidth requirements of FM are somewhat offset by the superior noise-rejection qualities of FM. Since an FM signal contains no amplitude variations, passing the signal through a limiter can eliminate noise. A limiter clips the positive and negative alternations of the signal, thereby eliminating most of the noise.

Another advantage of FM is the distribution of radiated power. Less than 10% of the radiated power is contained in the carrier. The rest of the power is contained in the sidebands, of which there are many in FM. Low power consumption by the carrier makes FM one of the most widely used modulation schemes for broadband.

Phase Modulation

Phase modulation (PM) is a form of FM. Occasionally, it is referred to as indirect FM.

Phase modulation
(PM)

Summing together a carrier frequency, generated by a crystal oscillator, with the data signal produces phase modulation. The resulting signal is phase-distorted. The amount of distortion is proportional to the amplitude of the data signal, and the rate at which the phase shifts occur is proportional to the frequency of the data signal.

Phase-modulated systems are extremely stable, since a crystal generates the carrier. They find widespread use in data communications because of their stability and very narrow bandwidth. The bandwidth is comparable to AM.

A PM system shares the same noise-rejection qualities and power-efficiency advantages of FM.

Figure 11-9 illustrates PM using square waves, as would be found in a digital communications system.

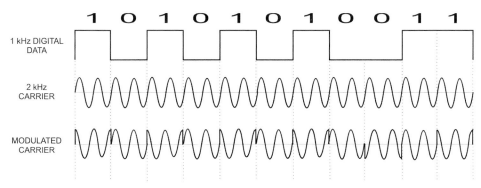

Figure 11-9: Phase Modulation

At the positive alternation of the 1 kHz data signal, the 2 kHz carrier phase is shifted 90 degrees ahead of the unmodulated carrier. The negative alternation of the data signal shifts the carrier phase to lag the unmodulated carrier by 90 degrees. In practice, the actual phase shift (leading or lagging) is conducted in reference to the position of the previous phase shift. For example, when the square waves in Figure 11-9 have two positive alternations in succession, the modulated carrier shifts forward 90 degrees for each alternation.

TERMINAL CODES

The control functions include arithmetic symbols, spaces, grammar characters, as well as codes that are used to process or transfer data. A code is a method of expression that data processing equipment can understand. Terminal codes are expressed in the language of computers (binary 1's and 0's).

The most common terminal codes are Baudot, the American Standard Code for Information Interchange (ASCII), and the Extended Binary Coded Decimal Interchange Code (EBCDIC).

> **Terminal codes** consist of binary numbers representing alphanumeric characters and special control functions.

Baudot

The **Baudot code** is an older code that was developed to permit teletypewriters to operate at high speeds. Originally, it was intended to be used by Morse code operators.

The idea was twofold: the operators needed a code that was standard in the length of the dots and dashes, and machines could assist in transferring the code if it were standardized. The Baudot code was never fully accepted by operators because they found it too difficult to standardize the length, or on/off characteristics, of the code.

There are many varieties of Baudot code, but the most common are 5-bit codes. The maximum number of characters represented by a 5-bit code is:

$$\text{max characters} = 2^B$$

where B is the length of the code.

$$\text{max characters} = 2^5$$
$$= 32$$

The Baudot code can represent 32 characters. If you consider 26 letters in the alphabet, 10 numbers (0-9), and codes for space, comma, period, etc., you can see the major disadvantage of Baudot. The code length restricts the flexibility of communications. It is a slow code that does not incorporate error-detection mechanisms. This makes it inappropriate for most modern communication equipment. The standardized Baudot code is shown in Figure 11-10.

Start	1 (LSB)	2	3	4	5 (MSB)	Stop	No Shift	Shift — U.S.A Teletype Commercial Keyboard
	●	●				●	A	—
	●			●	●	●	B	?
		●	●	●		●	C	:
	●			●		●	D	$
	●					●	E	3
	●		●	●		●	F	!
		●		●	●	●	G	&
			●		●	●	H	#
		●	●			●	I	8
	●	●		●		●	J	Bell
	●	●	●	●		●	K	(
		●			●	●	L	)
			●	●	●	●	M	.
			●	●		●	N	,
				●	●	●	O	9
		●	●		●	●	P	0
	●	●	●			●	Q	1
		●		●		●	R	4
	●		●			●	S	'
					●	●	T	5
	●	●	●			●	U	7
		●	●	●	●	●	V	;
	●	●			●	●	W	2
	●		●	●	●	●	X	/
	●		●		●	●	Y	6
	●				●	●	Z	"
						●	Blank	
	●	●	●	●	●	●	Letters shift	↓
	●	●		●	●	●	Figures shift	↑
			●			●	Space	▥
				●		●	Carriage return	<
		●				●	Line feed	≡

Figure 11-10: Standardized Baudot Code

EBCDIC

In 1962, IBM developed **EBCDIC** to overcome the deficiencies of Baudot codes. It is a true binary-based code, widely used in IBM machines. EBCDIC assigns 8 bits for each alphanumeric character and each of the control functions. An 8-bit code can produce 256 unique characters. Unfortunately, nearly half of the characters are unassigned. This represents a lot of waste, while at the same time it permits quite a bit of flexibility. The EBCDIC code is shown in Figure 11-11.

		MSD														
LSD		0 0000	1 0001	2 0010	3 0011	4 0100	5 0101	6 0110	7 0111	8 1000	9 1001	A 1010	B 1011	C 1100	D 1101	E 1110	F 1111
0	0000	NUL	DLE			SPACE	&	−									0
1	0001	SOH	DC1					/		a	j			A	J		1
2	0010	STX	DC2		SYN					b	k	s		B	K	S	2
3	0011	ETX	DC3							c	l	t		C	L	T	3
4	0100		RES	BYP						d	m	u		D	M	U	4
5	0101	HT	NL	LF	DC4					e	n	v		E	N	V	5
6	0110		BS	EOB						f	o	w		F	O	W	6
7	0111	DEL			EOT					g	p	x		G	P	X	7
8	1001		CAN							h	q	y		H	Q	Y	8
9	1001		EM							i	r	z		I	R	Z	9
A	1010					¢	!		:								
B	1011	VT				.	$	,	#	{	}						
C	1100	FF	FLS			<	*	%	@								
D	1101	CR	GS	ENQ	NAK	(	)	—	'					[		]	
E	1110	SO	RDS	ACK		+	;	>	=								
F	1111	SI	US	BEL	SUB	|	⌐	?	"								

Figure 11-11: EBCDIC Code

ASCII

ASCII was first published in its present form in 1967. ASCII is a 7-bit code. It is capable of producing 128 unique characters. Certain versions of ASCII use 8-bit character lengths. ASCII is the most widely used information code in the world today, because it was designed specifically for data-processing equipment. There are no unassigned ASCII characters. The ASCII code is shown in Figure 11-12.

As an example, consider the letter "A". The code for this letter is 41_{16}. The most significant digit (MSD) is 4_{16}, while the least significant digit (LSD) is 1_{16}.

The codes presented in this section—**terminal codes**—are a category of a far larger group called **information codes**.

		MSD							
		0 000	1 001	2 010	3 011	4 100	5 101	6 110	7 111
0	0000	NUL	DLE	SPACE	0	@	P	`	p
1	0001	SOH	DC1	!	1	A	Q	a	q
2	0010	STX	DC2	"	2	B	R	b	r
3	0011	ETX	DC3	#	3	C	S	c	s
4	0100	EOT	DC4	$	4	D	T	d	t
5	0101	ENQ	NAK	%	5	E	U	e	u
6	0110	ACK	SYN	&	6	F	V	f	v
7	0111	BEL	ETB	'	7	G	W	g	w
8	1000	BS	CAN	(	8	H	X	h	x
9	1001	HT	EM	)	9	I	Y	i	y
A	1010	LF	SUB	*	:	J	Z	j	z
B	1011	VT	ESC	+	;	K	[	k	{
C	1100	FF	FS	,	<	L	\	l	|
D	1101	CR	GS	–	=	M	]	m	}
E	1110	SO	RS	.	>	N	^	n	~
F	1111	SI	US	/	?	O	—	o	DEL

LSD is labeled on the left side of the table.

Information codes have a variety of applications, but share the common intent of manipulating data without changing the original meaning of the data.

**Figure 11-12:
ASCII Code**

Some information codes, such as **Manchester** and **Nonreturn to Zero**, are used to change the structure of an ASCII-coded word so that it can be transmitted with a minimum of errors. Other information codes, such as the **Cyclic Redundancy Check (CRC)**, are used for error-detection. Still others are used to correct errors, such as **Hamming codes**.

In all of the examples above, it is common to refer to the process of manipulating data bits as simply coding. As in the example of coding an ASCII word, the coding process may occur many times over, for a variety of applications, and to address the many problems that are encountered when transmitting data streams.

One of the challenges in transmitting data is for the receiver to determine that a character is being received. The receiver also needs a method of determining the start of a character and the end of a character. The problem is addressed at the transmitter by framing data words.

ASYNCHRONOUS AND SYNCHRONOUS DATA

Framing refers to methods of transmitting data that identify the start and stop of a character, or of long strings of characters. The two common methods of framing are called **asynchronous** and **synchronous**.

Asynchronous

Asynchronous transmission is characterized by keeping a communication channel in a steady-state condition until transmission occurs. Once it begins, each character is separated by start and stop bits (or equivalent characters).

The steady-state condition is referred to as a **mark**, and is represented by a logic 1.

When the line makes the transition from the binary 1 to binary 0, this is referred to as a **space**, and the receiver will decipher the transition as the start of a data stream.

The receiver will know the data stream is completed by detecting a **stop bit**.

Once the data has been sent, the line returns to the mark condition until more data are transmitted.

The format for asynchronous transmission is illustrated in Figure 11-13. The ASCII letter "T" is being transmitted. Prior to sending the letter, the line is in the mark state.

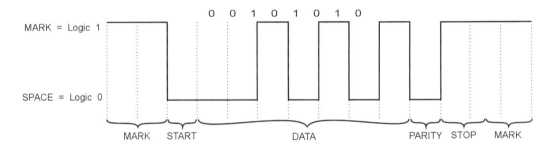

Figure 11-13: Asynchronous Data Format

The line makes the transition from high to low, or space, with the **start bit**.

Immediately following the start bit is the data. The stop bit, which may be 1, 1.5, or 2 bits long, tells the receiver the transmission is ended. The line will remain in the mark condition until more data is transmitted.

The **parity bit** is used for error detection.

Asynchronous transmission is fairly easy and inexpensive to implement. The major disadvantage is the time taken to transmit start and stop bits that contain no data. Many personal computers utilize asynchronous communications.

Synchronous

Synchronous literally means that the transmitter and receiver are synchronized. It improves upon asynchronous techniques by greatly reducing the bit space used for start and stop instructions.

Synchronous transmission is characterized by one character immediately following another without the inclusion of start/stop bits.

In addition, each bit contains a synch pulse. Typically, the synch pulse is inserted by shifting the phase of each bit of data. The synch pulse tells the receiver the exact time a bit occurs.

To appreciate the value of synchronization, imagine a message transmitted 2,000 miles over long distance telephone networks. By the time it arrives at the receiving end, it may be heavily distorted by propagation delays and noise. The receiver may begin extracting data too early or too late, thereby garbling the transmission. The problem is compounded at high data rates when bit times are short. When both the receiver and transmitter are synchronized, errors are less likely to occur. Each end will know if data is lost, because the synchronization pulse will also be lost.

The synchronous format is shown in Figure 11-14. The word "TWO" is being transmitted in ASCII. The line is held in the mark state until the start bit (or flag) occurs. The characters are sent and the transmission is terminated with a stop flag, at which time the line returns to the idle condition.

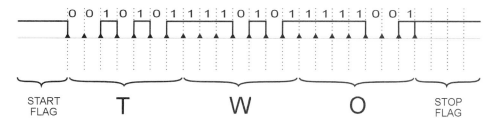

Figure 11-14: Synchronous Data Format

The carrier provides the synchronizing information. The synch pulse is depicted in Figure 11-14 by carets at each data bit. A common method of synchronization is achieved by shifting the relative phase of each bit for mark and space conditions, with a mark being a 90-degree shift forward, and a space represented by a 90-degree lagging shift. The shift is relative to the preceding bit. For example, the first two bits of the ASCII T are 0's.

As the two logic 0's occur, the carrier shifts back by 90 degrees, once for each logic 0. The third bit is a logic 1, so the carrier is shifted forward 90 degrees. If a long stream of binary 1's is transmitted (a mark state), the carrier will shift forward 90 degrees for each logic 1.

The receiver detects each 90-degree phase shift as a data bit. In this way, the receiver and the transmitter are synchronized.

Synchronous transmission is common at higher data rates, when long blocks of information are transmitted.

The advantage of synchronous over asynchronous is that communicating nodes can start and stop based on bit sequences, rather than driving the communication line high or low to represent the start or stop bits. When a receiver detects an agreed-upon sequence (usually, 10101010), it begins decoding the remaining bits based upon their bit position following the sequence. Hundreds of bits may be decoded before the actual user data is decoded, but the receiver will still pick it out because each received bit synchronizes it.

DATA FLOW STRUCTURE

Earlier, it was stated that a communications system consists of the sender, the message, and the receiver. Implicit in the description is that there exists a medium in which the data will flow. The medium can consist of copper wire, fiber optics, or the atmosphere (for microwaves). In a data communication system, the medium is structured in accordance with the direction of data flow. The flow of data can be structured in one of three different ways: simplex, half duplex, and full duplex.

Simplex

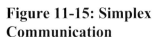

Simplex communication is one-way communication.

A simplex system is shown in Figure 11-15.

Figure 11-15: Simplex Communication

Data flows from the transmitter to the receiver, but not from the receiver to the transmitter. Examples of a simplex system are the terminals found in airports that list flight arrivals and departures.

Half Duplex

A **half-duplex** system allows data to flow from the transmitter to the receiver, and from the receiver to the transmitter, but only in one direction at a time.

In the half-duplex system of Figure 11-16, a computer is transmitting a message to another computer. Once the message has been received, the second computer sends back an acknowledgment that the message was received. Note that the terms transmitter and receiver are relative to the direction the data is traveling.

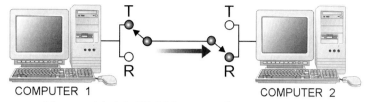

Figure 11-16: Half-Duplex Communication

The top of the figure shows the computer on the left serving as a transmitter, but when the computer on the right sends a reply, it serves as a receiver.

Full Duplex

Full-duplex systems permit data to flow in both directions simultaneously.

The most common full-duplex system is the telephone service. Conversations on the telephone can take place with both parties talking at the same time.

Full-duplex operation requires additional wiring and greater circuit complexity than simplex and half duplex. A full-duplex system is shown in Figure 11-17.

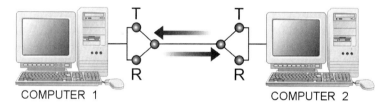

Figure 11-17: Full-Duplex Communication

Once again, a computer is sending a message to another computer. In the half-duplex system, the first computer waited for an acknowledgment from the second computer. In full duplex, the first computer could continue to transmit rather than wait for the line to become free. As with half duplex, equipment on both ends of the communication link assumes the dual role of transmitter and receiver.

Full-duplex is typically associated with high-speed communication between nodes. Half-duplex is used when speed is not a priority, but costs are. Simplex is primarily used to supply a peripheral with information, or to collect information from a peripheral.

ENCODING

Encoding

Encoding is the process of physically manipulating data. ASCII and EBCDIC are common examples of encoding. An alphanumeric character is encoded in a format that can be processed by a machine—the format used with much of networking is binary.

The ASCII character may be further encoded to allow for compensation of phase differences and the effects of reactive components (such as capacitive or inductive components) in a channel. Physical electronic devices cause these effects, or they may be caused by the physical arrangement of the network wiring infrastructure.

Undesired signal phase shifts and delays will garble data packets to the point that the original information contained in the packet can't be recovered. In most devices, such as modems and network cards, there is circuitry that compensates for phase problems through the use of equalization circuits.

Another type of troubling distortion is called dc shift. DC shift is a condition in which there is a gradually increasing line voltage caused by channel reactance. It happens because of the charge and discharge of the line capacitance and inductance, and is especially a problem when long strings of 0's or 1's are transmitted. If several thousand logic 0's are transmitted, the average line voltage will charge in accordance to the charging rate of the distributed line capacitance, and eventually settle at a steady-state, or dc, value.

A long series of 0's may be transmitted, but the receiver could interpret them as logic 1's due to the dc component. For this reason, the logic levels (the amount of voltage assigned to a logic 1 and a logic 0) of EIA/TIA-232 should be spaced as far apart as possible.

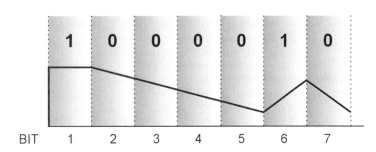

Figure 11-18: ASCII Character "A" Distorted by dc Level Shift

Figure 11-18 shows the letter "A" being transmitted in ASCII. The dc shift has been greatly exaggerated to illustrate the confusion the distortion can cause at the receiver. Notice there is not an immediate transition from the logic 1 at bit 1 to the logic 0 at bit 2. The receiver may very well interpret bit 2 as a logic 1 rather than a logic 0. The reactance is nearly discharged at bit 5, but bit 6 is a logic 1. The data rate here is much faster than the channel is capable of responding to, and a logic 1 at bit 6 does not quite develop before the channel is driven to a low at bit 7. The receiver will likely garble the original message due to the distortion of dc shift.

In many communication systems, the receiver and transmitter maintain proper clock timing through a clock synchronization pulse. Ordinarily, this synch pulse is the edge of the data bits. If the synch pulse is lost to the receiver, it can signal to the transmitter to send the data again. But if a portion of the transmitted message contains several thousand 0's, there will not be a bit edge for the receiver to lock on to for an extended period of time. The receiver will signal the transmitter that it has lost the data, the transmitter will send it again, and the receiver will once again lose the data on the long run of logic 0's. As you can see, this network would effectively crash.

Data bits are encoded to alleviate the dc shift and phase distortion problems just described. Most encoding schemes are structured to continuously alternate the bits so that the channel will not charge to a dc value. In many data systems, the type of equipment used prohibits dc voltages. For example, a channel may be coupled to the receiver by a transformer that has been installed as an impedance matching device. The transformer will not pass a dc voltage, and any dc values contained in the transmission will be blocked from the receiver. In a system containing ac-only components—like a transformer—data encoding is a necessity.

Codes that eliminate ISI and dc drift are Nonreturn to Zero, Manchester, and Alternate Mark Inversion. Each will be described in the following sections.

Nonreturn to Zero (NRZ)

Nonreturn to Zero (NRZ) encoding may be unipolar or bipolar, as shown in Figure 11-19.

Nonreturn to Zero (NRZ)

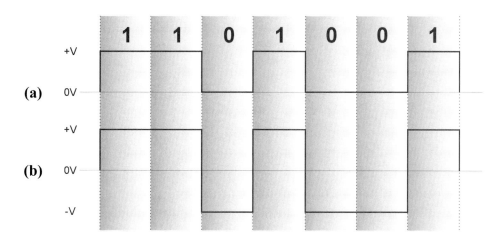

Figure 11-19: Unipolar and Bipolar NRZ Encoding

Unipolar NRZ, shown in Figure 11-19(a), is the type of encoding found in situations where transmission runs are short and there is little noise to interfere with the data bits. A good example would be inside a computer when square waves are transmitted between integrated circuits or PC boards. Data encoded with unipolar NRZ assigns a positive dc voltage to logic 1's and 0 volts to logic 1's. Within a computer, the logic 1's are generally +5 V and the logic 0's are 0V. This type of encoding does very little in addressing phase problems and dc shift. In fact, if unipolar NRZ is coupled through a transformer, the data will, at a minimum, be heavily distorted.

If a long string of logic 0's or 1's is transmitted through a long transmission line, the line will gradually charge to the average value of the dc. Also, timing synchronization will be lost between long bit runs of logic 1's and 0's.

Bipolar NRZ, shown in Figure 11-19(b), offers better performance. Logic 1's are assigned a positive voltage while a negative voltage represents logic 0's. If a data transmission contained an equal number of logic 1's and 0's, the average line voltage would be 0 V, and there would not be any dc shift. But the probability of adjacent bits being the same (a logic 1 followed by another logic 1) is much greater than having the bits consistently alternating between 1 and 0. If a long string of 1's or 0's is transmitted, bipolar NRZ will generate a dc shift as well as lose clock timing between the transmitter and receiver. These problems are the same as was found with unipolar NRZ, but because of the opposite polarity voltages used with bipolar NRZ, it consumes 50% less power than unipolar NRZ.

NRZ gets its name from the fact that the line voltage does not go to 0V between adjacent bits. Notice that the two logic-1 bits at the left hold the line in the high state. This can cause trouble in asynchronous channels because the line is held in the mark, or positive voltage, state during the time between transmissions. Since the line will charge to the average value of the voltage, it may not immediately respond to a logic 0 when it is transmitted.

Manchester II

Manchester II, or biphase, encoding is a popular encoding scheme since it eliminates the loss of clock signals as well as dc shift. Manchester II is shown in Figure 11-20.

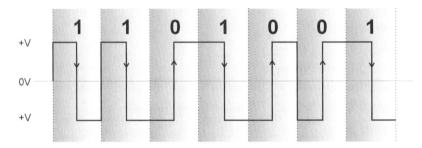

Figure 11-20:
Manchester II Encoding

The logic bits are represented by the transition occurring in the middle of a bit; logic 0 is represented by a low-to-high transition occurring in the middle of the bit. As you can see, there will never be a gradual increase in the line voltage because the voltage changes with each bit. In an asynchronous line, when the channel is held in the mark condition between transmissions, the channel voltage will continuously alternate as in an ac signal. The predictable alternations provide a ready-made clock signal for maintaining synchronization between the receiver and transmitter. Since the encoded data has the characteristics of an ac voltage, it will not be blocked or garbled by ac devices like transformers.

While Manchester II solves the problems of dc shift and loss of clock signals, it does so at the price of requiring twice as much bandwidth as does NRZ. The wider bandwidth is needed because +V and –V, or two states, represent each bit, whereas an NRZ bit is either +V or –V, but not both. The mid-bit transitions of Manchester II encoding effectively double the signaling rate, which necessitates doubling the bandwidth.

Alternate Mark Inversion (AMI)

Alternate Mark Inversion (AMI) is an encoding technique popular with long-distance digital telephone systems. It is illustrated in Figure 11-21. Logic 0's are represented by 0V while alternating the line voltage between +V and –V represents logic 1. AMI prevents dc shift due to the alternation from +V and –V for the 1 bits. Loss of timing between the receiver and the transmitter can occur for long 0-bit runs, but not for extended transmissions of logic 1's.

Alternate Mark Inversion (AMI)

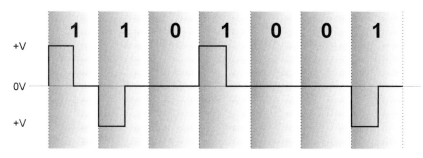

Figure 11-21: Alternate Mark Inversion Encoding

AMI is actually a variation of NRZ, except that the line voltage is permitted to return to 0V for logic 0's. It improves upon the clock-timing performance of NRZ as well as drastically reducing dc shift. Notice that the logic 1 pulses are only half as wide as the prescribed bit times. By reducing the transmitted 0, the duty cycle of AMI is 50%. This means that the data is transmitted using 50% less energy, which results in a significant power savings. The long distance carriers find AMI attractive because all the power consumed in the telephone system is provided (or purchased) by the long distance company. AMI saves money for these companies while simultaneously eliminating or reducing dc shift and timing problems.

KEY POINTS REVIEW

This chapter has presented an extensive exploration of the fundamentals of data communications.

- Protocols are the rules used with data communications.

- A network consists of hardware and software designed to direct and control data traffic.

- A baseband network uses digital signaling to send packets and typically allows only one data channel at a time.

- Broadband networks use analog signaling and typically carry more than one data channel simultaneously.

- Copper wire includes twisted wire pairs.

- Fiber-optic cable has significantly lower losses than copper wire, and is immune from external electrical interference (lightning, motors, generators, microwaves) that creates much of the distortion found in copper-based systems.

- Satellites use microwaves for relaying data from transmitter to receiver.

- Wireless technology uses the atmosphere as the transmission medium.

- The speed at which data is transmitted is quoted as the baud rate or bits per second (bps). Baud rate describes the number of data symbols transmitted per second.

- A symbol is a small group of bits into which data is organized at the time of modulation.

- Baud is an indication of the amount of information transmitted, while bps is the amount of total data transmitted.

- An analog signal uses many discrete values to represent a physical process (a voice, for example).

- The subscriber loop is the circuit from a residential or office telephone to the local central office, which is designated by the first three digits of a local telephone number.

- Bandwidth (BW) is a particularly important aspect of data because it is a measure of the amount of actual data being transmitted.

- Fundamentally, modulation is the process of superimposing data on a carrier.

- Amplitude modulation is produced by simultaneously applying a carrier and data to any nonlinear device.

- Frequency modulation (FM) is produced by varying the frequency of the carrier.

- Phase modulation (PM) is a form of FM. Occasionally, it is referred to as indirect FM.

- Terminal codes consist of binary numbers representing alphanumeric characters and special control functions.

- Framing refers to methods of transmitting data that identify the start and stop of a character, or of long strings of characters. The two common methods of framing are called asynchronous and synchronous.

- Simplex communication is one-way communication.

- A half-duplex system allows data to flow from the transmitter to the receiver, and from the receiver to the transmitter, but only in one direction at a time.

- Full-duplex systems permit data to flow in both directions simultaneously.

- Full duplex is high-speed communication. Half duplex is used when speed is not a priority, but costs are. Simplex is primarily used to supply a peripheral with information, or to collect information from a peripheral.

At this point, review the objectives listed at the beginning of the chapter to be certain that you understand and can perform them. Afterward, answer the review questions that follow to verify your knowledge of the information.

REVIEW QUESTIONS

The following questions test your knowledge of the material presented in this chapter:

1. In terms of geography, describe the difference between a local and a wide area network.

2. In a network using collision detection, how do computers gain access to the network?

3. Calculate the bits per second rate for a bit time of .1 ms.

4. Calculate baud for a modem transmitting at 14.4 kbps in which the number of bits per symbol is 4.

5. Describe the relationship between bandwidth and the amount of information that a data communication channel can carry.

6. Write a brief definition of simplex, half duplex, and full duplex.

7. What is the advantage to specifying a broad range for logic levels for an electrical interface?

8. Briefly describe the term "access method" as it relates to networking.

9. In a network that uses a token, how do computers gain access to the network?

10. Which layer of the OSI model describes electrical and mechanical parameters?

11. Which type of transmission employs start and stop bits between ASCII characters?

12. What is dc shift?

13. What type of data flow is used when data is sent in one direction only?

14. What type of data flow is required between computers that change files?

15. How are the amplitude and frequency of a data signal represented in a carrier using AM?

EXAM QUESTIONS

1. Which type of access method is used in an Ethernet network?
   a. Token Ring
   b. satellite
   c. collision detection
   d. collision avoidance

2. Which of the following is an example of a terminal code?
   a. ASCII
   b. SCSI
   c. FDDI
   d. IEEE

3. A communications system consists of a sender, a receiver, and a _____.
   a. modem
   b. message
   c. transmitter
   d. protocol

4. Which of the following is more likely to use broadband to transfer data?
   a. cable
   b. LAN
   c. Token Ring
   d. Ethernet

5. A type of communications media that's immune to electrical interference is _____.
   a. twisted pairs
   b. coaxial
   c. fiber optics
   d. microwaves

6. Which type of encoding scheme eliminates dc shift for long runs of both logic 1 and logic 0s?
   a. Manchester II
   b. AMI
   c. unipolar NRZ
   d. bipolar NRZ

7. An asynchronous data frame is characterized by _____.
   a. a start bit and stop bits
   b. a start bit and no stop bits
   c. no start or stop bits
   d. FM modulation

8. Data bits in asynchronous network are synchronized by:
   a. counting each bit
   b. measuring the bit times
   c. inverting the logic levels
   d. shifting the bit phase to represent 1's and 0's

9. A network channel has a data rate of 1200 bps and a baud of 300. How fast will data packets be transmitted over the channel?
   a. 300 bps
   b. 1200 bps
   c. 400 bps
   d. 3600 bps

10. Two users are exchanging messages on a network. First one user sends a message, then the other waits until the message is received before replying. What type of data flow structure does this describe?
   a. simplex
   b. half duplex
   c. full duplex
   d. ASCII

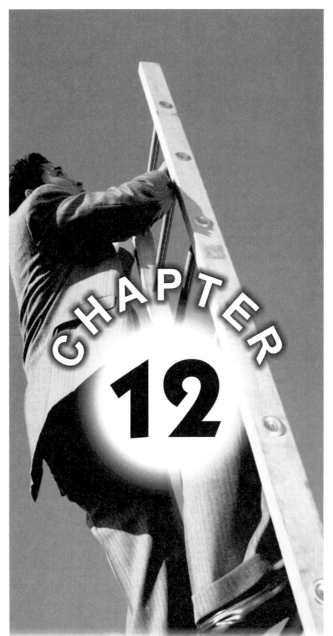

CHAPTER 12

NETWORK MEDIA LOSSES

LEARNING
OBJECTIVES

LEARNING OBJECTIVES

Upon completion of this chapter and its related lab procedures, you will be able to perform the following tasks:

1. Describe the relationship between line reactance and signal loss.

2. Define the following characteristics related to cable: distributed reactance, characteristic impedance, ISI, and equalization.

3. Explain the purpose of a terminator, and the problems encountered through improper use of a terminator.

4. Describe how equalization decreases ISI.

5. Describe how the resistance of a wire affects signal integrity.

6. Define atmospheric noise, impulse noise, frequency noise, and crosstalk. Give an example of each.

7. Calculate the signal-to-noise ratio of a communication channel.

8. Calculate the noise factor of a communication channel.

9. Describe common problems with fiber-optic cable that cause signal losses.

NETWORK MEDIA LOSSES

INTRODUCTION

Imagine that you are planning a family vacation to a resort area located 2,000 miles away. On the date of departure you and the family are packed and ready to go, except...you don't have a map, money, car, or reservations of any sort. In short, you're totally unprepared for any problems that may arise, the first one being getting out of the driveway. It's a little far-fetched to imagine ourselves in that situation, but it isn't too far off from what a data stream encounters upon leaving the transmitter. The data in a communication system faces many obstacles from the moment it's transmitted to the time it arrives at the destination. The fact that data moves in any organized manner at all is an accomplishment.

In fact, data networking is a very reliable, fault-tolerant segment of the communications industry. One of the reasons for its high reliability is that many of the obstacles facing data transmission have been identified and techniques selected to address the problems. Often, the techniques chosen are implemented before the data is transmitted. For example, if a transmission channel is found to attenuate the higher frequency components of a channel, those frequencies may be overamplified before the data is transmitted. The amplified frequencies will be attenuated on the way to the receiver, but because they've been overamplified, they will arrive at the receiver with the same amplitude as the lower frequencies. This is the basic concept of line equalizers.

In many cases the success rate of data arriving intact at the receiver is a function of media and environments. **ElectroMagnetic Interference (EMI)** is radio-frequency noise transmitted through the atmosphere. The source of EMI can be motors, generators, radio stations, lightening, or high-frequency electronic circuits. EMI causes problems when it cuts through a metallic conductor and a voltage is induced into the wire. For example, the EMI caused by lightning has an average period of 1 ms. If data is transmitted through a channel at 1 Mbps, then the lightning will distort, or destroy, 1,000 bits of data, or about 125 bytes. In many cases, steps can be taken to recover the data or to prevent the interference from distorting the information. Selecting the proper media for transmitting data goes a long way in preventing problems.

Electromagnetic Interference (EMI)

Fiber optics has been hailed as the transmission media totally immune from EMI interference—and it is. Fiber-optic cable can be run side-by-side with industrial-grade motors and not be affected by radiated noise. However, fiber remains an expensive option when compared to alternative, copper-based media. In addition, there are problems created during the installation of fiber cable that affect signal integrity. Care must be taken, and this chapter describes some of the typical pitfalls.

The types of problems encountered by data signals are analyzed in this chapter. In many cases, the problems are a natural symptom of the characteristics of the channel. Occasionally, system designers have utilized channel problems in such a way as to assist data transmission. For example, the principle of equalization, which is the process of overemphasizing the weak component of a signal, has been modified and used in data concentrators. With the use of concentrators the amount of data transmitted can be reduced 75% without any loss of the original information.

ELECTRICAL PROPERTIES OF CABLE

Twisted-pair wire and coaxial cable are more commonly used than fiber-optic cable. The wide base of installed copper media virtually guarantees it will not be superseded by optical systems in the near future. Indeed, in some cases, fiber is a very awkward media choice. In a bus configuration, it's difficult to install a fiber system because of the station taps to the bus. Twisted pair is the preferred medium in architectures where multiple data paths exist.

But whereas fiber-optic system performance is unaffected by frequency changes, copper wire is greatly affected. The effect of increasing frequency through copper produces the greatest disadvantages to the media. For either twisted pair or coaxial cable, the performance drops with increases in frequency. The maximum frequency limit of voice-grade twisted-pair wiring is about 1 MHz; for UTP CAT 5 it's 100 MHz (or far greater, as with Gigabit Ethernet, but special encoding techniques are needed); for thicknet or thinnet coaxial cable, it's 10 MHz; and for cable television coaxial cable the maximum rates are in the hundreds of megahertz. For the most part, copper media is limited at the upper frequency range because of the distributed capacitance and inductance of the wire runs. The reactive effects distort binary data to the point that a receiver will not be able to interpret the data. The following sections explore the nature of distributed reactance, its effects on data, and methods used to avoid some of the effects.

> **NOTE**
>
> The effect of capacitance and inductance in the wire channel is that signal integrity decreases with increases in signal frequency.

Distributed Reactance Losses

Parallel conductors, separated by an insulator, represent a capacitor. Coaxial cables are wrapped in a sheath, but inside, the solid center wire is separated from the braided conductor by a **polyurethane** insulator. The wires act like capacitor plates across the entire cable length. Twisted pairs are separated from one another by the insulating jacket. Similar to coax, the wire pairs represent capacitor plates, and the insulation represents a capacitor **dielectric**.

As a current moves through coaxial and twisted pairs, magnetic lines of force radiate from the wires and a voltage is induced into the other wire. As the lines of force cut into the conductors, the existing current in the wires opposes the change and the wires exhibit inductive properties.

polyurethane

dielectric

characteristic impedance

low-pass filter

> Copper cables contain a **characteristic impedance** of series inductance and parallel capacitance, which gives the cable the properties of a **low-pass filter**.

An equivalent circuit of a two-conductor cable is shown in Figure 12-1.

L1 and L2 represent the inductance of each wire, while C represents the capacitance exhibited by the cable. In actual practice, each wire length contains a series resistance and a parallel conductance. The series resistance consists of the actual resistance of the wire and the parallel conductance is the leakage of energy through the insulating material. These two factors have a negligible effect on the data signal and for this reason have not been included in the illustration.

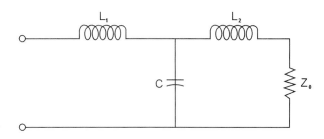

Figure 12-1: Equivalent Two-Conductor Cable Circuit

The circuit of Figure 12-1 also contains Z_o, which is the characteristic impedance of the cable. The characteristic impedance of a transmission line is the value of pure resistance with which the line must be terminated in order to transfer the maximum amount of energy to a load. An improperly terminated line results in reflected waves, or the amount of energy not coupled to the load, and they travel back through the line producing constructive as well as destructive effects on the line signal. Once a long transmission line is terminated properly, the energy propagating through the line is transferred to the load—the receiver—and reflected waves cease to degrade the data signal.

Use Table 12-1 as a guide for selecting various terminating resistances.

Table 12-1: Terminating Resistance Guide

Cable Terminations		
Cable Type	**Termination**	**Cable Technology**
RG-58A/U Thinnet	50 Ω ± 10%	Ethernet, 10Base-2
Thicknet Ethernet	50 Ω ± 10%	Ethernet, 10Base-5
RG-59/U	50 Ω ± 10%	CATV, ARCNET
RG62/U	93 Ω ± 10%	ARCNET, IBM Networks
Unshielded Twisted Pair	100–120 Ω	Ethernet, 10Base-T, 100Base-TX
Shielded Twisted Pair	150 Ω ± 10%	Token Ring

> ┌─ NOTE ─
> To prevent undesired signal reflections and to ensure that the maximum signal strength is transferred to the receiver, unused ends of copper-based cabling must be terminated with a resistance equaling the characteristic impedance of the cable.

Characteristic impedance is not dependent upon cable length; in fact, it depends only upon the effective capacitance and inductance of a particular cable. These values are found in manufacturers' data sheets. Characteristic impedance can be approximated by:

$$Z_o = \sqrt{L/C}$$

For example, a common coaxial cable is RG-58. It has a capacitance of 29.5 pF/ft and an inductance of 73 nH/ft. For any length of RG-58, the characteristic impedance is:

$$Z_o = \sqrt{\frac{73 \times 10^{-9}}{29.5 \times 10^{-12}}}$$

$$Z_o = 49.745 \text{ ohms}$$

This means that the RG-58 cable will behave as any circuit with a capacitor, an inductance, and a 50-ohm load. It will exhibit the same phase-shifts and time constants as any resistive-capacitive-inductive circuit.

Notice that Figure 12-1 is essentially a low-pass filter. As the applied frequency increases, the reactance of C decreases, resulting in less voltage being developed across Z_o. At some frequency, the impedance voltage drop will be 70% of the applied voltage. This represents the half-power point, or –3 dB loss, and defines the upper frequency limit of the cable.

One other observation can be made of Figure 12-1. At higher frequencies, or data rates, the impedance will integrate the data signals. The extent of integration is determined by the time constant (TC) of the circuit; in particular, that of the capacitor and characteristic impedance. When the width of the signal—a square wave—is equal to the time constant, there is little integration. But when the width of the data signal is much shorter, integration is severe and the data signal is heavily distorted.

Don't leave unused copper cables dangling in the air. Terminate them properly.

It's important to make a distinction between how frequency affects signal loss, and how the resistance of copper cable affects signal loss. Losses due to frequency changes, as mentioned above, are the result of line inductance and capacitance. Resistance has a negligible impact when the frequency changes. However, the resistance of the wiring dissipates electrical energy in the form of heat. The higher the resistance, the greater the signal energy loss. Resistance is directly proportional to the length of the wire.

What this means is that there will be a maximum distance that workstations on a network can be located away from one another. For example, in an Ethernet LAN using CAT 5 UTP cable, the maximum distance is about 150 feet. If the workstations are separated by more than 150 feet, the signal loss due to resistance of the wire may decrease the amount of signal amplitude to the point that data bits will be garbled. As you saw in Chapter 2, all LAN protocols specify maximum distances that nodes may be located from one another.

INTERSYMBOL INTERFERENCE

The reactive components of cables cause **Intersymbol Interference (ISI)**.

The combined effects of distributed inductance and capacitance and the characteristic impedance causes the ISI type of distortion. ISI is produced by a long charge or discharge of reactive components. The effect on a data signal is illustrated in Figure 12-2.

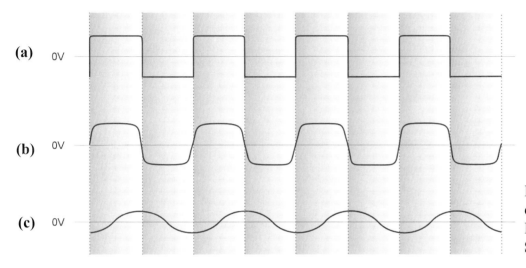

(a) 0V

(b) 0V

(c) 0V

Figure 12-2: Effects of Intersymbol Interference on Data Signals

In Figure 12-2(a), the corners of the square wave are slightly rounded. A binary signal propagating through a properly terminated line may arrive at the receiver with this mild amount of distortion. Circuitry at the receiver can return the signal to its original condition of sharp, clean edges. In Figure 12-2(b), the square wave has rounded corners and has also been **phase shifted**.

Recall that a capacitor and inductor produce voltage and current phase shifts. In most transmission lines, the phase angle characteristics of the capacitor predominate, causing the line current to lead line voltage by some amount of time. The line-induced phase shifts can cause problems in a system in which the data is phase modulating a carrier.

In many cases, the receiver will have difficulty discerning where a data bit begins and ends. As components of the square wave shift, some harmonic frequencies will travel faster through the line than others, but will arrive at the receiver with similar amplitudes. The delays cause the bits to run together. The worst case appears to the receiver, as shown in Figure 12-2(c). Here, the cumulative effects of ISI have severely degraded the data bits of Figure 12-2(a) so that a receiver will be unable to differentiate a logic 1 from a logic 0. Not only have the bits been shifted in time but the bit-per-second rate is high compared to the reactive time constants, so that the inductor and capacitor do not have time to discharge before the next data bit occurs.

ISI is the blurring together of data bits.

It's most noticeable in narrow bandwidth channels, as in telephone networks, and increases with data rates.

In a digital system, the distortion an individual bit receives (since the wave shape is easily restored) is not as important as is the specific segregation of logic 1's and 0's. ISI blurs the segregation between bits. A square wave requires a considerable amount of bandwidth. If the bandwidth is limited to begin with, maintaining distinct logic levels is even more difficult. If, in Figure 12-2(c), the receiver interpreted a logic 0 as 0-volts dc, it would decipher this data stream as continuous logic 1's.

The amount of ISI can be determined by evaluating the eye pattern of data bits with an oscilloscope. The scope is set to trigger on the edge of each bit with the time base adjusted so that one bit is displayed on the scope screen. A normal eye pattern appears as in Figure 12-3(a). By having the scope trigger on each data bit, a series of bits are superimposed on each other. If the internal scope trigger won't do this, use an external trigger taken from the data bits. The pattern shown in the figure shows four bits. Notice that the corners of the bits are slightly rounded, and all of the bits are of similar amplitudes. In this transmission channel, the bandwidth is adequate for the data rate since the square-wave corners are not severely rounded, indicating that the higher frequency harmonics have not been attenuated.

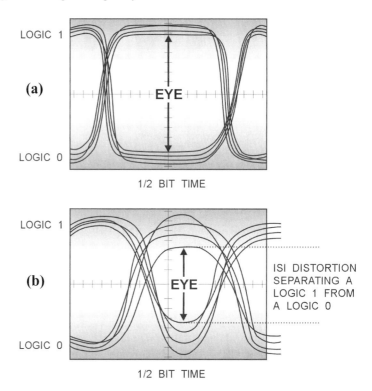

Figure 12-3: Evaluating the Eye Pattern with an Oscilloscope for ISI Distortion

You should also notice that all the frequency components have maintained their proper phase position as indicated by their relationships to the trigger. Because the scope triggers at the start of the data bit, some portion of the bit waveform would be delayed from the other portions if the bit components had been phase shifted.

Figure 12-3(b) shows a bit stream with ISI. The eye pattern has partially closed. This tells us that some frequencies have been attenuated. The rounded corners indicate that the bandwidth of the circuit is not adequate for the BPS of the bit stream. The narrowness of the eye tells the difference between a logic 1 and a logic 0. If the eye in this figure were to close much further, the receiver probably wouldn't be able to distinguish the binary 1 from a 0. Notice that in Figure 12-3(b), a phase shift is indicated since the bits are offset from the half-bit time. This time is simply one-half of the pulse width of the bit. In the example, many components of the bit stream have been delayed due to phase distortion, or jitter.

A receiver also evaluates eye patterns by evaluating a sample data stream that is sent ahead of the data. The eye pattern tells the receiver how the cable, or channel, characteristics will affect data bits. The sampling of data bits is called a training period. Once the receiver determines how the bits will be affected, it can take measures to compensate for the ISI. The compensation on the part of the receiver is called equalization.

Once a network is up and running, it's the responsibility of the network administrator to determine how well it's running. All network operating systems (Windows NT/ 2000/ XP, or Novell NetWare, for example) include network management software that can be used for indirectly evaluating network performance. The types of errors generated by ISI will cause data packets to be re-sent on a network. The number of re-sends is a measured metric of network management software. While it doesn't necessarily reveal the root cause of the problem, the metric is quite useful in indicating that something is wrong.

EQUALIZATION

ISI can be compensated for by equalizing the data stream.

> An equalizer separates signal frequencies through filtering and incorporates phase shifts to counter the effects of the channel.

Equalization of data signals can be understood by comparing it with the audio equalization used with audio equipment. The equalizer is placed at the receiver and has a series of slide switches that are associated with various audio frequencies. The listener can adjust the switches so that the higher frequencies are attenuated and the lower frequencies overamplified. The result will be more bass. An audio equalizer gives the listener a much greater degree of control to compensate for any weaknesses perceived in the audio.

A data equalizer follows a similar approach, except that the compensation is based upon an analysis of data after it has been transmitted through a communication channel. A data equalizer is capable of examining each symbol, or bit group, for ISI.

An equalizer's greatest strength is its ability to correct phase jitters and frequency attenuation. A block diagram of an equalizer is shown in Figure 12-4. The equalizer consists of filters D1, D2, D3; amplifiers A1, A2, A3; and a summing amplifier. Filter D1 is designed to shift a frequency forward by 10 ms, D2 incorporates no forward or delay shifts, and D3 produces a 10 ms delay to frequencies falling within its narrow band-pass range.

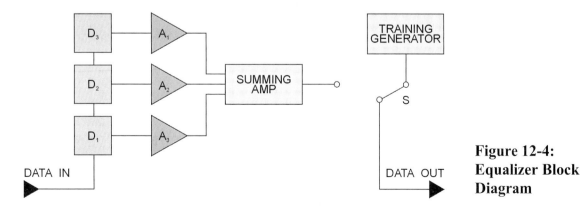

Figure 12-4: Equalizer Block Diagram

As an example of how the equalizer works, two frequency components from a data signal have been identified by the receiver as phase distorted by the channel. One frequency has been phase shifted forward by 10 ms and another is phase delayed, also by 10 ms. The equalizer samples the data and extracts a portion that has not been phase distorted to use as a reference. The reference is applied to filter D2. The frequency that was shifted forward is applied to D3. The D3 filter will delay this component 10 ms. The frequency that was delayed is applied to D1, and D1 shifts it forward 10 ms. The three signals are equally amplified and summed together in the summing amplifier. The output of the summing circuit should be a reasonable version of the original data.

The data equalizer described above is placed at the receiver and generally is a part of a modem circuitry as well as intelligent repeaters and hubs. Figure 12-4 contains a training generator. The training generator in a modem either transmits or receives a data stream of alternating 1's and 0's. The receiver analyzes the bits during a training period (about 10 ms for a 2,400 bps modem) to determine phase distortion and logic-level noise in a way similar to examining eye patterns with an oscilloscope.

Once the training period is ended, logic circuits in the equalizer activate the appropriate filtering action and any data received is equalized accordingly. Unfortunately, if line conditions change during the middle of a transmission, as is frequently the case, the equalizer will not respond to the change. It is left up to error-detection circuits in the receiver to identify problems resulting from spontaneous changes.

The foregoing described equalization at the receiver. If a system designer knows what distortion will occur in a channel, measures can be taken at the transmitter to compensate. The process of compensation at the transmitter is called pre-equalization. For example, if it was determined that a channel consistently delays a specific frequency range, these frequencies can be phase shifted forward at the transmitter. In this way, they will arrive at the receiver in phase with other frequencies. Pre-equalization at the transmitter and equalization at the receiver are common functions of high-speed modems.

A more sophisticated method of equalizing data is the use of an adaptive equalizer. An adaptive equalizer constantly samples and evaluates data for ISI. If a change occurs in the data transmission, the adaptive equalizer compensates for it. This overcomes the disadvantage of the equalizers discussed earlier, where, once the transmission begins, spontaneous problems are not compensated for.

An adaptive equalizer constantly samples and evaluates data for ISI.

Adaptive equalization adds expense and complexity to a data communication system. A signal that has been conditioned with an adaptive equalizer is also difficult to evaluate from a troubleshooting standpoint, because it may have very little resemblance to the square waves associated with digital logic. In satellite systems, signals have a tendency to either fade or arrive at the receiver as an echo. The adaptive equalizer will identify fading or echoes as they happen and will generate the appropriate phase shifts.

NOISE AND DISTORTION

Noise can be defined as any interference that causes a signal to deviate from its normal structure. This deviation from normal is commonly called distortion. Intersymbol interference is distortion that can disable an entire network. The effects of noise (distortion) on individual data bits, data frames, as well as on the complete network, is of vital concern. At a minimum, an error is generated, and in the worst case the network may become inoperable.

In the sections to follow, various types of noise are discussed along with techniques for measuring noise and distortion. In many cases, distortion is measured with respect to reference levels of power, voltage, or current, and described as a decibel that is above or below the reference. For this reason, decibels will be reviewed before describing the various types of noise affecting data signals.

Atmospheric Noise

Atmospheric noise

Atmospheric noise results from lightning, solar activity, and stellar radiation.

The static that results from lightning during thunderstorms is classified as atmospheric noise. It distorts radio and television signals for a few milliseconds, and is a nuisance in these situations, but usually doesn't disrupt the entire communication system. In data communications, a few milliseconds can represent hundreds of data bits, which could include several sentences of text.

Microwave communications forms the basis of satellite systems, and is used extensively in the telephone industry. A bolt of lightning releases vast amounts of energy into the surrounding atmosphere, and the energy radiates from the lightning source. As the radiated energy cuts any material capable of conducting electricity, a voltage is induced into the conductor, and the resulting current obliterates any signals that happen to be traveling through the conductor at the time.

In addition to lightning, sunspot activity creates atmospheric noise. On the sun, a sunspot is an explosion that releases a tremendous amount of energy that travels through the solar system, striking the Earth, and creating noise in a way similar to lightning strikes. Sunspots are cyclical, occurring about every 11 years, and can therefore be anticipated. Lightning is unpredictable, and the best way of dealing with it is prevention: Shielding of transmission lines is the usual remedy, as well as the extensive use of an Uninterruptible Power Supply (UPS) to support the system with battery power when the ac line voltage is down.

Fortunately, most solar noise is attenuated by the Earth's atmosphere and doesn't reach the surface. Since satellites don't have the benefit of the atmosphere to shield them, they're the most susceptible to sunspot noise, and to a barrage of noise emanating from the distant stars.

Within a building, noise in the atmosphere can affect signal integrity. The source of the noise can be difficult to trace. Fluorescent lighting, air conditioning, and heating blowers can be particularly troublesome. This is true for wired as well as wireless networks. The usual remedy for noise within a building is to either move the networking wires and equipment away from the noise source, or shield the source of noise.

Impulse Noise

Impulse noise

Impulse noise is sporadic and of short duration, usually caused by periodic use of electromechanical equipment or from a glitch that occasionally appears.

Mechanical switches, motors, generators, and engine ignition systems all contribute to the distortion of data bits, and are collectively called "impulse noise." It's generally of short duration and in close proximity to the affected data system.

The most troublesome aspect of impulse noise is locating the source of it. The source could be a few feet away or it could be hundreds of feet. It may be a mobile source, such as a portable generator or motor, or a device that's rarely activated, such as a flood pump. The simplest solution for impulse noise is to avoid installing networking equipment near devices that may radiate interfering noise. Impulse noise is of very short duration but capable of the highest intensity levels. It will jam data signals completely, but usually for less than a microsecond.

> **NOTE**
>
> Impulse noise is usually caused by electromechanical equipment.

Frequency Noise

Frequency noise

Frequency noise originates from 60 Hz wire, system clocks, or carrier frequencies.

Frequency noise is of a constant time but of variable amplitude. The most common type of frequency noise is the 60 Hz radiated from fluorescent lights and the associated wiring.

Recall from earlier discussions on the electrical characteristics of cables that they act as lowpass filters. The cable's distributed capacitance offers a high capacitive reactance to lower frequencies, making those frequencies available at the load. Realizing the problems of 60 Hz and 120 Hz (from full-wave rectification in power supplies), data communication systems are designed to have a lower cutoff frequency, above 200 Hz. For example, audio frequencies below 300 Hz are blocked from telephone channels to avoid 60 Hz interference.

Within digital communication equipment, system clock frequencies can also distort data signals. The solution in this situation involves the careful placement of clock generators in the equipment, and avoiding paralleling the clock printed-circuit board runs with data signal runs. Another solution involves frequency separation between the clock and data signal.

Crosstalk

Crosstalk is the electromagnetic induction (transmitted noise) that results from un-shielded cables laying in parallel.

Each cable acts as a transmitter and a receiver to/from the cable next to it. The earlier example of the clock signal interfering with data signals illustrates the problem of crosstalk. You may have been talking on the telephone and have heard another conversation. Crosstalk is a frequent problem in the telephone system because hundreds of cables may run in parallel. The energy from a cable radiates and cuts across adjacent cables, inducing a signal into them. While crosstalk in a telephone conversation is annoying, it generally doesn't prevent you from continuing your own conversation. But crosstalk between data signals can blur the distinction between logic levels and introduce a considerable error component into data.

Shielding is the common solution to crosstalk. Each cable can be shielded, as is the case with coaxial cable, or a bundle of cable may be shielded. The unfortunate effect of shielding is that it raises costs and consumes space. Due to the costs involved in shielding, other alternatives have been examined. For example, category 5 UTP has all but eliminated crosstalk of parallel network cables. However, these same data lines may induce a signal into voice cables if run side-by-side with them. This is why it's not a good idea to connect unused network UTP to voice circuits such as telephone extensions. The next section describes an effective method for obscuring noise.

NOISE ANALYSIS

It's one thing to have noise present in a communication system, and another to determine the extent of the problem resulting from noise. In many situations, the noise induced into communication channels can be prevented through shielding, changing the physical positions of interacting signals, conditioning a channel, or with the use of equalizers. Or, the noise can be ignored. Ignoring the noise, or taking no action, is a common technique and, certainly, the cheapest remedy. Ignoring noise is effective when the desired signal is much stronger than the offending noise. Two common methods are used to analyze the strength of the desired signal relative to the noise: Signal-to-Noise Ratio (SNR) and Noise Factor (NF). Both calculations provide an indication of the relative signal strength. If the signal is large compared to the noise, the noise is often ignored.

How large the difference can be varies with the application. Table 12-2 lists several acceptable SNRs. For any application, SNRs will decrease with bandwidth, source impedance, lack of shielding, increases in temperature, and increasing data rates.

Table 12-2: Typical SNRs of Communication Channels

Channel	Signal-to-Noise Ratio
Digital Communication	40 dB
Voice Telephone Channel	35 dB
Video Channel	50 dB
Microwave Systems	10 dB

Noise and distortion are expressed in decibels. The decibel results from the ratio of an actual value to a reference value. Reference values for data communications are 1 mW and 6 mW.

An analysis of noise can be made by calculating the signal-to-noise ratio.

The signal-to-noise ratio is a measure of the desired signal power relative to the noise signal power at the same point in a circuit. It's expressed mathematically as:

$$SNR = P_s/P_n$$

where P_s = the power of the desired signal and P_n = the power of the noise. It's often expressed in decibels as:

$$SNR = 10 \log (P_s/P_n)$$

For example, if the SNR is to be determined at the output of a transmitter, and the signal level is 2 mW and the noise is .5 mW, the SNR is:

$$SNR = 2 \text{ mW}/.5 \text{ mW}$$
$$SNR = 4$$

or, as a decibel:

$$SNR = 10 \log (P_s/P_n)$$
$$SNR = 10 \log (2 \text{ mW}/.5 \text{ mW})$$
$$SNR = 10 \log (4)$$
$$SNR = 10 (.602) \text{ dB}$$
$$SNR = 6 \text{ dB}$$

The SNR defines the amount of noise found in a signal at a given point—as at the transmitter output in the example above—but it doesn't give an indication of how much noise is picked up from the transmitter to receiver; that is, the amount of noise acquired across a cable run.

Noise factor (NF) is another method of analyzing noise, and is a more useful calculation for analyzing the noise characteristics of a system or device. It's the ratio of signal-to-noise at the system's input to the signal-to-noise at its output.

Noise factor is calculated as:

$$NF = 10 \log ((S_i/N_i)/(S_o/N_o))$$

where S_i/N_i is the signal-to-noise ratio at the input, and S_o/N_o is the signal-to-noise ratio at the output.

For example, suppose the NF of a transmission line is to be calculated. The signal level at the transmitter is 22 mW and the noise level is 1 mW. At the receiver, the signal level has dropped to 18.5 mW and the noise has increased to 2.25 mW.

$$NF = 10 \log ((S_i/N_i)/(S_o/N_o))$$
$$NF = 10 \log ((22 \text{ mW}/1 \text{ mW})/(18.5 \text{ mW}/2.25 \text{ mW}))$$
$$NF = 10 \log (22/8.22)$$
$$NF = 10 \log (2.676)$$
$$NF = 10 (.427) \text{ dB}$$
$$NF = 4.27 \text{ dB}$$

The SNR and NF are important to data communications because each provides an indication of the performance of the communications system. Specifically, they provide general information about the number of errors likely to be generated by the noise. The greater the S/N or NF, the fewer errors will occur. Why? Figure 12-5(a) shows a data stream with no noise, and 3-5(b) the same data shows distorted with large-amplitude noise.

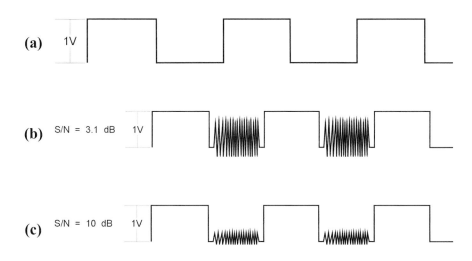

Figure 12-5: Noise and Distortion Contribute to Data Errors

The amplitude of the noise may be of sufficient amplitude that the receiver will interpret it as a logic 1 rather than a logic 0. In Figure 12-5(c), the level of noise is drastically reduced. At this level, the receiver will appropriately ignore it and interpret it as a logic 0.

Earlier, it was stated that noise is sometimes ignored. If the volume of noise is small compared to the signal strength, then ignoring it offers a realistic solution. An SNR of 40 dB in a digital data communication system will introduce about 5 errors for each one million bits. Most error-detection schemes will detect errors occurring at that rate, so an attempt to decrease the noise further may be a questionable exercise for most applications.

FIBER CABLE LOSSES

Although fiber cable has many advantages over copper wire, it's not without its drawbacks. As mentioned earlier, light disperses with distance causing a gradual loss in signal strength.

Varying angles of incidence cause rays to arrive at the receiver out of phase, causing modal dispersion. Losses due to dispersion and scattering are also dependent on the wavelength of the source light. At wavelengths of 1.3 λ and 1.5 λ, light travels at a relatively constant speed with low losses (about 2 dB/km). These wavelengths are called zero-dispersion wavelengths and are used in commercial long distance fiber-optic networks.

Connection losses contribute to signal degradation. Connection losses result from fiber splices, the interface of light source to fiber, and of fiber to light detector. The actual amount of signal attenuation is measured with a photometer. Gallium-arsenide LEDs (light-emitting diodes) are common light sources, but the light ends of these are rounded. Optical connectors are available that will focus the beam from the LED end to direct it into the fiber core. This helps to reduce modal dispersion but it decreases the amount of available light by about one-third. The decrease in light is a connection loss. Note that copper systems don't have this problem.

Misaligned connections also limit the amount of available light. Even when the alignment is perfect, the light coupling won't be 100% because the rays will reflect and refract at a splice or connection junction. Numerical Aperture (NA) losses are a result of connection mismatches as well. NA loss occurs when the critical angle of light emitted from a cable is different than the critical angle of the receiving cable. NA is a published specification of fiber cable and should be low (less than .5). The lower the NA, the tighter the critical angle, and more light will likely couple within the critical angle of the receiving cable.

> **NOTE**
>
> Losses in fiber-optic cable can usually be attributed to misaligned connectors, improper splices, and severe bends in the cable run.

Spectral dispersion causes losses in a fiber cable because some wavelengths travel faster along the cable length than others. By using laser energy, spectral dispersion is eliminated since only one wavelength is transmitted. However, when lasers aren't available (LEDs will likely be used), a broad spectrum of light will be sourced into the cable. At the receiving end, a data bit will appear to be stretched because not all wavelengths are arriving at the same time. This effect is similar to modal dispersion. Recall that a laser generates collimated light. This means that all the light is traveling in the same direction, and if you imagine the light as a series of single rays, they would travel in a nearly parallel manner.

When injected into a perfectly straight fiber cable, the rays travel as axial beams through the cable, neither reflecting nor refracting. In a bent cable, the axial rays will strike the core/cladding interface and reflect along the remaining distance to the receiver. Some of the energy will refract into the cladding and be lost. A bind in a fiber-optic cable will produce losses and signal attenuation. This is true of all optical cable types, so cable runs should be kept as straight as possible. Use wire ties liberally to bundle cable groups, and then anchor the bundle to supports in ceilings or walls. This will reduce sagging in the cable.

DECIBELS

decibel (dB)

A **decibel (dB)** describes the exponential way in which the ear responds to sound. Over the years, dBs have become a standard for evaluating the signal quality of electronic waveforms in general, and, in particular, the gain or loss of signal strength.

You may recall that dBs (a dB is a tenth of a bel) are derived from converting an electronic relationship to a logarithmic relationship. Logarithms simplify the arithmetic involved with exponents. In fact, a common logarithm (log) is the exponent of any base 10 number. The following illustrates examples of **common logs**:

common logs

$$10^4 = 10,000 = \text{a log of } 4$$
$$10^3 = 1,000 = \text{a log of } 3$$
$$10^2 = 100 = \text{a log of } 2$$
$$10^1 = 10 = \text{a log of } 1$$
$$10^0 = 1 = \text{a log of } 0$$
$$10^{-1} = .1 = \text{a log of } -1$$
$$10^{-2} = .01 = \text{a log of } -2$$
$$10^{-3} = .001 = \text{a log of } -3$$
$$10^{-4} = .0001 = \text{a log of } -4$$

Common logs have the number 10 as a base. A common log, then, represents the number of times that the number 10 has been multiplied by itself, along with any fractional amounts of 10. For example, the log of $144 = 2.15836$. The log represents the number of times 10 must be multiplied by itself to equal 144. Common logs are integrated with decibels in the following formula:

$$dB = 10 \log (P_o/P_i)$$

where P_o = power out and P_i = power in. The following examples show how dBs are used.

Example 1

An amplifier has an input power of 10 mW (milliwatts) and a power out of 20 mW. Calculate the **gain** in decibels.

$$dB = 10 \log (P_o/P_i)$$
$$dB = 10 \log (20 \text{ mW}/10 \text{ mW})$$
$$dB = 10 \log (2)$$
$$dB = 10 (.3)$$
$$dB = 3$$

Example 2

The power received through a transmission line is .25 mW. Using decibels, evaluate the performance of the line if the power at the transmitter is 1 mW.

$$dB = 10 \log (P_o/P_i)$$
$$dB = 10 \log (.25 \text{ mW}/1 \text{ mW})$$
$$dB = 10 (-.6)$$
$$dB = -6$$

Notice in the first example, the power from input to output doubled for a gain of 3 dB. With each doubling of the power, the dB gain will increase by a factor of 3. So, if $P_o = 40$ mW in example 1, the dB gain will be 6.

In the second example, the power at the receiver was less than the power transmitted. A **loss** of signal strength is indicated by a negative dB. It is sometimes difficult, as in example 2, to determine what is P_o and what is P_i. If you are unsure, it is usually helpful to draw a rough sketch of the problem and label it according to what is given. As dBs increase by three for each doubling of the power, they also decrease by three each time the power is halved, as in example 2. The amount of received power is one-fourth of the transmitted power; consequently, -6 dB represents the loss of signal strength. Signals for a particular frequency are often compared to a **reference level**. One milliwatt (mW) is a common audio and telephone industry reference. For example, a telephone transmission channel may exhibit a 6-dB loss. What is the value of the signal strength?

$$dB = 10 \log (P_o/P_i)$$
$$-6 \, dB = 10 \log (x/1 \text{ mW})$$
$$-.6 \, dB = \log (x/1 \text{ mW})$$
$$.25 = x/1 \text{ mW}$$
$$.25 \text{ mW} = x = P_o$$

When solving for one of the unknown power levels, begin with the basic decibel formula, fill in the given values, and solve for the unknown. The following examples should help to clarify the use of decibels.

Example 3

A **power amplifier** has 5 dB gain referenced to 6 mW. What is the output power?

$$dB = 10 \log (P_o/P_i)$$
$$5\ dB = 10 \log (P_o/6\ mW)$$
$$.5\ dB = \log (P_o/6\ mW)$$
$$\text{Inverse } \log .5 = P_o/6\ mW$$
$$3.16 = P_o/6\ mW$$
$$18.96\ mW = P_o$$

Example 4

A data signal is permitted no more than 1 dB of **attenuation**, or loss, from transmitter to receiver. You measure the transmitter power at 24.2 mW and the power received at 19.5 mW. Is this an acceptable amount of attenuation?

$$dB = 10 \log (P_o/P_i)$$
$$dB = 10 \log (19.5\ mW/24.2\ mW)$$
$$dB = 10 \log (.806)$$
$$dB = 10 (-.0936)$$
$$dB = -.936$$

The signal loss in this example is acceptable.

Decibels are used to express the ratio of many values. But a dB is significant only when referenced to some agreed-upon value. For example, it is meaningless to say a twisted-pair cable has 4 dB of loss.

If it is understood the loss is referenced to 1 mW, then the –4 dB is of practical value, because an indication is given of the severity of the loss. If a reference hasn't been agreed upon, then –4 dB could represent a loss from 100 W or from 10 mW. A 10 mW loss would cause very few problems in a twisted-pair line, but a 100 W loss would mean the line isn't functioning.

In a local network, power loss is a symptom, not a root cause of problems. If the power level of a data stream has degraded, and all segment lengths are within specification, the problem isn't likely to be the cable. Look for faulty transceivers in the network interface cards (NIC), hub malfunctions, or power supply problems in the nodes.

KEY POINTS REVIEW

- Copper cables contain a characteristic impedance of series inductance and parallel capacitance, which gives the cable the properties of a low-pass filter.

- The effect of capacitance and inductance in the wire channel is that signal integrity decreases with increases in signal frequency.

- The reactive components of cables cause intersymbol interference (ISI).

- ISI is the blurring together of data bits. It's most noticeable in narrow-bandwidth channels and increases with data rates.

- ISI can be compensated for by equalizing the data stream. An equalizer separates signal frequencies through filtering and incorporates phase shifts to counter the effects of the channel.

- Noise and distortion are expressed in decibels. The decibel results from the ratio of an actual value to a reference value. Reference values for data communications are 1 mW and 6 mW.

- Atmospheric noise results from lightning, solar activity, and stellar radiation.

- Impulse noise is sporadic and of short duration, usually caused by electromechanical equipment.

- Frequency noise originates from 60 Hz wire, system clocks, or carrier frequencies.

- Crosstalk is the electromagnetic induction that results from cables lying in parallel.

- An analysis of noise can be made by calculating the signal-to-noise ratio.

- Noise factor is another method of analyzing noise. It's the ratio of the signal-to-noise at the input of a system, to the signal-to-noise at the output of a system.

- Losses in fiber-optic cable can usually be attributed to misaligned connectors, improper splices, and severe bends in the cable run.

At this point, review the objectives listed at the beginning of the chapter to be certain that you understand and can perform them. Afterward, answer the review questions that follow to verify your knowledge of the information.

REVIEW QUESTIONS

The following questions test your knowledge of the material presented in this chapter:

1. What is intersymbol interference?

2. Calculate the noise factor of a channel with an SNR at the input of 14.3 mW, and an SNR at the output of 21.5 mW.

3. Describe how increase in frequency though copper wire runs affects data signals.

4. How is ISI compensated for in a data channel?

5. What is atmospheric noise? Give an example.

6. What is impulse noise? Give an example.

7. What is frequency noise? Give an example.

8. What is crosstalk?

9. How can crosstalk be avoided?

10. How do long copper wire runs affect signal integrity?

11. What are three common causes of losses in fiber-optic cables?

12. What is modal dispersion?

13. What is the characteristic impedance of a data channel?

14. Describe the process of adaptive equalization.

15. When is it appropriate to use pre-equalization?

EXAM QUESTIONS

1. As seen on an oscilloscope, a digital signal that's been transmitted through a channel with insufficient bandwidth will appear _____.
   a. sawtooth
   b. rectangular
   c. rounded at the corners
   d. with sharp, ninety-degree corners

2. In order to transfer the maximum amount of energy in a cable to the load, the load have a resistance equal to the _____ of the cable.
   a. capacitive reactance
   b. inductive reactance
   c. resistance
   d. characteristic impedance

3. The type of noise caused by unshielded cables lying in parallel is called
_____.
   a. atmospheric
   b. impulse
   c. crosstalk
   d. frequency

4. Determine the SNR of a system in which the signal out of a transmitter is 3.5 mW and the noise level is 20 μW.
   a. 7.52 dB
   b. 22.4 dB
   c. 41.7 dB
   d. 68.2 dB

5. The proper termination for an RG-58A network cable is _____.
   a. 50 ohms
   b. 93 ohms
   c. 100-120 ohms
   d. 150 ohms

6. Which of the following results in signals arriving out of phase in a fiber-optic cable?
   a. large number of incident angles
   b. incorrect line resistance
   c. large capacitive effects
   d. large inductive effects

7. What is EMI?
   a. a measure of the speed of fiber cable
   b. the effect of twisting wire pairs
   c. distortion caused by noise signals transmitted through the atmosphere
   d. a measure of the noise versus signal level of a data packet

8. Which of the following is most likely to generate impulse noise?
   a. cellular telephones
   b. a motor
   c. a fluorescent light
   d. crosstalk

9. Which of the following is most likely to generate frequency noise?
   a. cellular telephones
   b. a motor
   c. a fluorescent light
   d. crosstalk

10. Due to the reactive effects of twisted pair and coaxial cabling, how is a data signal affected with an increase in frequency, or bps rate?
   a. Signal integrity will decrease.
   b. Signal integrity will increase.
   c. Line resistance will increase.
   d. Line resistance will decrease.

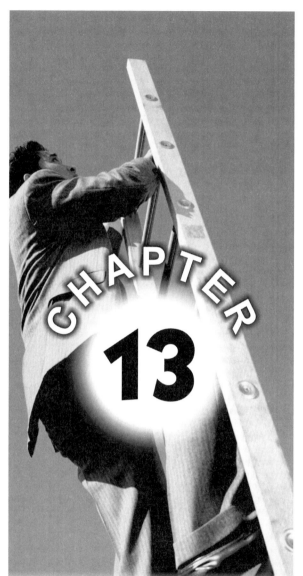

NETWORK PROTECTION

LEARNING
OBJECTIVES

Upon completion of this chapter and its related lab procedures, you will be able to perform the following tasks:

1. Identify the main characteristics of attached storage.

2. Identify the purpose and characteristics of fault tolerance.

3. Identify the purpose and characteristics of disaster recovery.

4. Identify the purpose, benefits, and characteristics of using a firewall.

5. Identify the purpose, benefits, and characteristics of using a proxy.

NETWORK PROTECTION

On a network, the server has the primary responsibility for controlling network operations and managing data flow on the network. In addition, a server may have been assigned a myriad array of other duties such as:

- Managing network user accounts

- Making application software available to users

- Managing Internet and e-mail accounts

- Providing storage space for users

- Providing a home or application database software

- Generating reports about the network

These are only a few examples of duties that a server could be configured to perform. For many network users, if a server is lost, there will be grave consequences. The most immediate consequence is, typically, that they are no longer able to access the network. Another grave consequence is loss of data.

Data loss is an extremely important consideration to users and companies. If financial, sales, inventory, and statistical data that resides on a server is lost, a company may never be able to re-create the lost data. Due to the seriousness of maintaining data integrity, this chapter begins with an overview of hardware that is essential to servers. While not intended to be an in-depth discussion of server hardware, the section should, nonetheless, set the stage for the remaining sections—all of which revolve around being prepared for the disastrous loss of network hardware.

We'll take a thorough look at several techniques used to protect network resources through the remainder of the chapter.

SERVER HARDWARE

Many characteristics of a server influence how well it performs, as well as represent vulnerabilities to network users. Several of the primary hardware characteristics that need to be monitored for server performance include:

- Microprocessor speed
- Peripheral interface
- RAM memory
- Cache
- Size and specifications of the hard drive
- Operating system
- Fault tolerance

Microprocessors exceeding 2 GHz are becoming the norm. These are fast microprocessors, and a server can't be fast enough. Why? As microprocessors become faster, users demand they be installed in their machines to handle complex software routines. These same routines may be installed on the server, and made available to multiple users simultaneously. Not only is the software complex, but each user expects to use it as if no one else was. The computing power needed to make a network appear to be transparent is considerable. Expect the speed and performance characteristics of microprocessors to increase continually.

> Servers may contain several microprocessors to handle requests quickly and transparently.

Servers may contain several microprocessors to handle requests quickly and transparently. You can set up a standard PC as a file server, and in a lightly loaded network containing a small number of clients, it will work fine. But if the network grows, the server can only respond to requests as fast as its microprocessors can process them. Buy a server, rather than a PC with server software installed in it, and make sure the server includes provisions for multiple processors.

There are two basic types of microprocessors:

- Complex Instruction Set Computing (CISC) microprocessors
- Reduced Instruction Set Computing (RISC) microprocessors

Of the two, CISC designs are the most widely used, since all Intel processors use this type of architecture. RISC is quicker and more efficient because less hardware is utilized to execute commands.

Which is better? There's far more software support for CISC than for RISC; so, even though RISC will perform better, this advantage is offset by the lack of software compatibility available for it. Until the full benefits of RISC can be exploited, use a CISC-based processor.

Note that motherboards containing the microprocessor will ship with ZIF sockets, which allow easy extraction and insertion of microprocessor integrated circuits. This is important because it allows the component to be replaced with a newer microprocessor while still retaining the original motherboard for as long as possible.

RAM (random access memory) memory is where most of the "application" part of application software is temporarily stored. When equipping a server, buy the fastest and largest amounts of RAM. RAM has a tremendous effect on the performance of servers and clients alike.

The **system cache** is a buffer, which stores data going to and from the microprocessor.

The microprocessor runs at a rate that may be tenfold higher than the network, or the internal bus of the computer the microprocessor is installed in. The buffer holds data temporarily when the processor is finished with it, and until the bus becomes available to send it to its destinations. It's a misconception to think that a 1 GHz computer is swapping files at that rate; the microprocessor is running at a high data rate, but data exchanges between the microprocessor and memory or I/O devices are limited to the speed of the system bus.

The server will interface to numerous peripherals besides the clients and hub. Web-access modems, tape backups, CD-ROM, a printer, or other devices linking a LAN to other networks may all be connected to the server. It's important than these peripherals don't interfere with the server's primary job of handling file transfers and managing the network.

The preferred interface for servers is the **Small Computer Systems Interface** (**SCSI**—pronounced "scuzzy").

With a SCSI interface card installed in a server, all devices can operate independently since the interface circuitry will queue requests, then service them when it's most efficient for the device to deliver the service.

Not all system board-connected devices transfer data at the same rate. Some are faster than others.

An Ultra-SCSI interface allows for speeds up to 320 Mbps. The connected devices can interface with the microprocessor at a speed that's closer to their native capabilities, rather than at a system-dictated speed. Another reason for using SCSI is that a device needn't shut down when the processor is communicating with another device.

A single SCSI card in a PCI slot allows simultaneous operation of up to 60 devices (using Ultra-SCSI with 15 devices on each of the four channels).

When purchasing server hardware, include a SCSI interface card, and then buy peripherals that are SCSI-compatible. The cabling is more complex with SCSI (devices external to the server are connected in a daisy chain manner using a cable that may have up to 68 pins), but other than making the connections, the rest is configurable from the card software or hardware via jumpers or switches. Figure 13-1 depicts two 50-pin SCSI connector pinouts, and Figure 13-2 shows the 50-pin Mini-Micro SCSI-2 connector pinout and the 68-pin Wide SCSI-3 primary connector pinout. In addition, a common, though nonstandard connector is DB-25 SCSI.

DB-50P SCSI RIBBON CABLE

Pin	Description	Pin	Description
1	Ground	2	Data 0
3	Ground	4	Data 1
5	Ground	6	Data 2
7	Ground	8	Data 3
9	Ground	10	Data 4
11	Ground	12	Data 5
13	Ground	14	Data 6
15	Ground	16	Data 7
17	Ground	18	Data Parity (Odd)
19	Ground	20	Ground
21	Ground	22	Ground
23	Ground	24	Ground
25	No Connection	26	No Connection
27	Ground	28	Ground
29	Ground	30	Ground
31	Ground	32	Attention
33	Ground	34	Ground
35	Ground	36	Busy
37	Ground	38	ACK
39	Ground	40	Reset
41	Ground	42	Message
43	Ground	44	Select
45	Ground	46	C/D
47	Ground	48	Request
49	Ground	50	I/O

2 ... 1
KEY
50 ... 49
MALE

"CENTRONICS" 50-PIN

Pin	Description	Pin	Description
26	-DB (0)	1	GND
27	-DB (1)	2	GND
28	-DB (2)	3	GND
29	-DB (3)	4	GND
30	-DB (4)	5	GND
31	-DB (5)	6	GND
32	-DB (6)	7	GND
33	-DB (7)	8	GND
34	-DB (8)	9	GND
35	GND	10	GND
36	GND	11	GND
37	RST	12	RST
38	TERMPWR	13	OPEN
39	RST	14	RST
40	GND	15	GND
41	-ATN	16	GND
42	GND	17	GND
43	BSY	18	GND
44	-ACK	19	GND
45	-RST	20	GND
46	-MSG	21	GND
47	-SEL	22	GND
48	-C/D	23	GND
49	-REQ	24	GND
50	-I/O	25	GND

26 ... 1
50 MALE 25

DB-50SA (OLD STYLE SUN SCSI)

Pin	Description	Pin	Description	Pin	Description
1	GND	18	GND	34	-DB (0)
2	-DB (0)	19	-DB (2)	35	GND
3	GND	20	GND	36	-DB (3)
4	-DB (4)	21	-DB (5)	37	GND
5	GND	22	GND	38	-DB (6)
6	-DB (7)	23	-DB (P)	39	GND
7	GND	24	GND	40	GND
8	GND	25	RST	41	RST
9	OPEN	26	RST	41	RST
10	RST	27	GND	42	TERMPWR
11	GND	28	GND	43	GND
12	GND	29	BSY	44	-ATN
13	GND	30	GND	45	GND
14	-RST	31	-MSG	46	-ACK
15	GND	32	GND	47	GND
16	-C/D	33	-REQ	48	-SEL
17	GND			49	GND
				50	-I/O

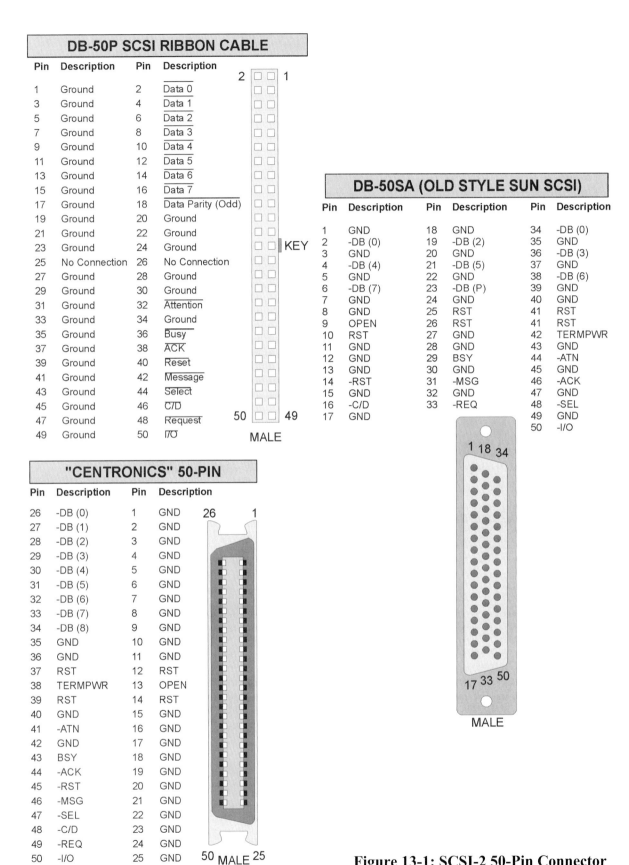

1 18 34
17 33 50
MALE

Figure 13-1: SCSI-2 50-Pin Connector Pinouts

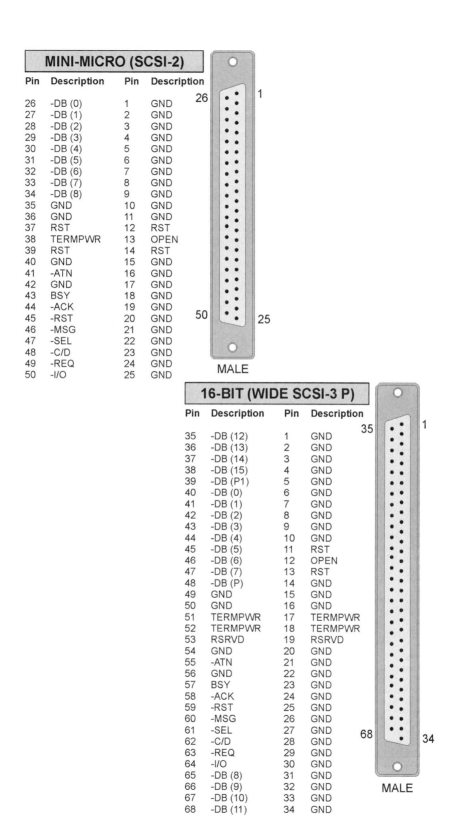

MINI-MICRO (SCSI-2)

Pin	Description	Pin	Description
26	-DB (0)	1	GND
27	-DB (1)	2	GND
28	-DB (2)	3	GND
29	-DB (3)	4	GND
30	-DB (4)	5	GND
31	-DB (5)	6	GND
32	-DB (6)	7	GND
33	-DB (7)	8	GND
34	-DB (8)	9	GND
35	GND	10	GND
36	GND	11	GND
37	RST	12	RST
38	TERMPWR	13	OPEN
39	RST	14	RST
40	GND	15	GND
41	-ATN	16	GND
42	GND	17	GND
43	BSY	18	GND
44	-ACK	19	GND
45	-RST	20	GND
46	-MSG	21	GND
47	-SEL	22	GND
48	-C/D	23	GND
49	-REQ	24	GND
50	-I/O	25	GND

MALE

16-BIT (WIDE SCSI-3 P)

Pin	Description	Pin	Description
35	-DB (12)	1	GND
36	-DB (13)	2	GND
37	-DB (14)	3	GND
38	-DB (15)	4	GND
39	-DB (P1)	5	GND
40	-DB (0)	6	GND
41	-DB (1)	7	GND
42	-DB (2)	8	GND
43	-DB (3)	9	GND
44	-DB (4)	10	GND
45	-DB (5)	11	RST
46	-DB (6)	12	OPEN
47	-DB (7)	13	RST
48	-DB (P)	14	GND
49	GND	15	GND
50	GND	16	GND
51	TERMPWR	17	TERMPWR
52	TERMPWR	18	TERMPWR
53	RSRVD	19	RSRVD
54	GND	20	GND
55	-ATN	21	GND
56	GND	22	GND
57	BSY	23	GND
58	-ACK	24	GND
59	-RST	25	GND
60	-MSG	26	GND
61	-SEL	27	GND
62	-C/D	28	GND
63	-REQ	29	GND
64	-I/O	30	GND
65	-DB (8)	31	GND
66	-DB (9)	32	GND
67	-DB (10)	33	GND
68	-DB (11)	34	GND

MALE

Figure 13-2: SCSI-2, 50-Pin Mini-Micro Pinout, and 68-Pin SCSI-3 Primary Connector Pinout

A hard drive is where user files, and in many cases, all application software will be stored. There are two important considerations, then, for a server hard drive. It should be big and fast! It's impossible to separate a discussion of hard drives and interface technology, since the two are intrinsically linked. Most hard drives are the IDE type, which stands for Integrated Device Electronics. An IDE hard drive is the same as an Advanced Technology Attachment (ATA) hard drive, although ATA is actually a reference to the type of bus attachments used in a computer. This text will use the terms IDE and ATA synonymously.

An improvement to IDE is EIDE. EIDE competes head-on with SCSI as a means of transferring data, with EIDE specifically referring to fixed disks (hard drives, tape drives, and CD-ROM) while SCSI includes all attached devices. Currently, EIDE hard drives transfer data to and from the drive (or drives, since the IDE/ATA standard supports more than two hard drives) at a maximum burst rate of 100 Mbps for ATA100-compliant hard drives. Compare this to the maximum data rate of a SCSI interface burst rate of 200 Mbps.

Currently, IDE hard drives transfer data to and from the drive at a maximum of 33 Mbps for ATA3-compliant hard drives. Compare this to the maximum data rate of a SCSI interface of 200 Mbps. The interface used with fixed disks—there may be more than one in a server—is critical to getting data to and from the disk. A SCSI interface competes with the microprocessor for speed, so data movement outside the drive isn't a problem. Getting it off the disk is the bottleneck.

The hard drive seeks the requested file, and the time it takes to do so slows the system down considerably. One way to offset the delay (known as latency in a hard drive) is to provide the disk with a large cache to store data, while the hard drive mechanics fetch and store files. Hard drives have built-in caches, but choose a drive with as much as you can get.

Hard drive sizes exceeding 40 gigabytes are readily available. How much do you actually need? Enough to meet your current as well as future demands. A quick way to determine size is to make a best-guess estimate of your current storage (add up the disk space used on all stand-alones), and multiply that total by 1.5. The future is difficult to predict, but keep in mind that new software releases can be counted on to hog memory. That's the case for purchasing a server that has room to add-on hard drives. You may not need the space now, or want to budget money for additional hard drives, but when the time comes, you'll have room to do so.

It has become increasingly common to connect non-computer devices to networks. These devices include network-ready printers and **Network Attached Storage** (**NAS**) devices. NAS devices connect directly to the network media as opposed to **Direct Attached Storage** (**DAS**) devices that connect to a host device such as a server. In a specialized type of storage network called a **Storage Area Network** (**SAN**), the entire network is basically made up of dedicated storage devices. The file system access protocols typically used in NAS systems include the Server Message Block (SMB) and Network File System (NFS) protocols.

An operating system (OS) controls and directs the operation of a computer system. Windows NT/2000/XP and UNIX have become popular operating systems because they combine operations of the computer hardware and network hardware—a combination that's hard to beat. But it's certainly not the only one available. Other operating systems are MS-DOS, OS/2, Windows 3.x, Windows 95, Windows 98, MAC OS, Linux, and NetWare.

Operating systems run beneath and, ideally, independent of networking software. It doesn't make a lot of sense to scrap all stand-alones when designing a network because their OS is UNIX, or Apple. Granted, some OS's are far more supported than others, but you must be sensitive to the needs of users, and determine whether a new operating system is a good idea when they must also learn conventions associated with a networking environment.

FAULT MANAGEMENT

Fault management is intended to detect problems, offer diagnostics, maintain a record of the problems, and, in some cases, correct the problems.

Companies can experience considerable losses if their networks aren't running smoothly.

The banking industry is heavily dependent on data communications in credit card departments, automated tellers, and for loan processing. Organizations, with far-flung offices that are electronically connected, may simply grind to a standstill if their network goes down.

Looking for problems in a network can be more frustrating than in many industries. The reason is that networks are designed to be transparent to users, and this characteristic, which makes them so desirable to laymen, is the same characteristic that can hide problems. That is, data communications inherently obscures the technical information needed by technicians. This is the huge advantage of using network analysis software that shows you the underlying activity in a network.

The ideal network is available to users 100% of the time services are requested. In reality, 98% availability is the average. The network manager addresses the 2% of the time that users are idle because of network problems.

Fault management is usually the first line of defense for managers, because it's preventive. Problem trends may be developing in the network, and the user may not be aware of anything amiss. For example, throughput may gradually decline, and the only symptom noticed by the user is that "the network seems slow today."

Fault management software may accomplish many of the troubleshooting tasks on a network. It's the intent of the software to do this without human intervention, which includes fixing problems in such a way as to keep the network running. For the most part, problems are fixed by reconfiguring. If a modem is disabled, data will be routed to another modem; or if a switch is stuck, the data traffic is sent via another switch, and so on. The only true solution to automated fault correction is redundancy. This isn't practical in most situations, since, to be fault-tolerant, a component will need to be duplicated—computers, printers, cabling, servers, etc.

If the fault management function can't fix a problem, the network manager is usually provided with recommendations of possible causes. But when that doesn't work, it's time to get the hands dirty. The next section describes the first line of fault management—security.

DATA SECURITY

Physical, **logical**, **procedural**, and **personnel security** must all be analyzed for weaknesses, and appropriate precautions taken to strengthen any found.

Errors often result from unintended events, such as electrical and mechanical failures, channel distortions, atmospheric disturbances, and so forth. In the following sections, data integrity will be analyzed from a different point of view—the protection of data communications from willful interception of data. While extensive networking of computer systems has had tremendous advantages, it's also highlighted the issue of privacy and security of personal data, corporate competitiveness, and governmental considerations. Prior to the widespread use of networks, security was primarily an issue associated with national defense and security of the government.

Within the past decade, telecommunications and LANs have facilitated information transfer to the point that ethical questions vie with the benefits of networking. Not only do we, as private individuals, wonder who has access to our personal information, but large corporations have similar concerns.

In the past, security was limited to the physical aspects of computers and the personnel working with them. Computers were housed in a central location, and access to the location could be controlled with door keys, badges, or sign-in logs. The personnel working with the computers—technicians, programmers, supervisors—were cleared through background checks. These practices remain an important part of data security, but the physical environment has been extensively altered.

There are a multitude of stories about computer hackers, sitting at home with their PCs and modems, gaining access to sensitive government facilities, financial institutions, or credit bureaus. Who hasn't heard about the hacker who diverts thousands of dollars from electronic fund networks to his own bank account? Security, once the domain of the government, is an issue that's become increasingly important to us due to the accessibility that computer networks have provided.

Figure 13-3 shows the Department of Defense computer network vulnerabilities chart, which profiles potential weaknesses of data-communication systems. These weaknesses may be divided into four categories: physical, logical, procedural, and personnel. The following sections provide characteristics and suggestions for addressing the vulnerabilities, as well as planning for faults that are likely to occur. The ultimate security process for computer data is to mask the content of the message through encryption, which will be described in later sections.

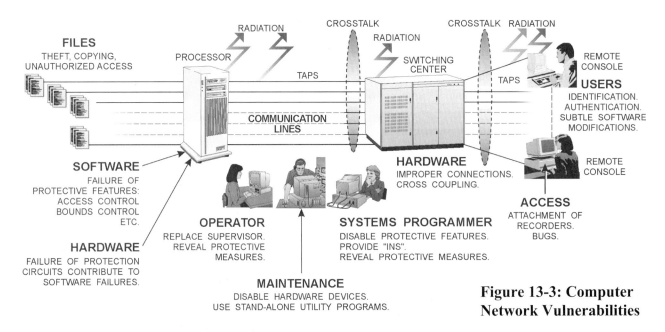

Figure 13-3: Computer Network Vulnerabilities

Physical

The physical element of data security involves computer hardware, the facility or office that houses the data, cable runs, and data printouts (hardcopy).

Information can be ingeniously encrypted, masked, or hidden in electronic files, but efforts to hide the information will be futile if a technically competent "snoop" encounters little difficulty getting to the data.

The first place to begin in analyzing physical security is with the obvious: How difficult is it to gain unauthorized access to the hardware? Hardware, in this context, includes remote terminals, communication controllers, multiplexers, servers, client PCs, printers, and cable runs. Many remote terminals, or client workstations, contain a key lockout that, when locked, disables the keyboard. Since remote terminals are usually scattered throughout many offices, it's important that users lock the terminal at the end of the day, and take the key with them—rather than tossing it into a desk drawer.

Remote terminals are cabled to a communications controller, which serves as an entry/exit port to a modem and the long-distance telephone network. Controllers are sophisticated devices that may be used for verifying user passwords, multiplexing, data compression, error control, or frame formatting. Typically, users in a large network are assigned various levels of access to the network. Each remote terminal is wired to a port on the controller. A savvy user can manipulate access via the ports, if it's known which port carries the data flowing from a user with the desired access. If access to a controller isn't limited, locking out keyboards is like swatting flies with a toothpick.

In a PC-based LAN, the server, typically, is the port to the outside, or WAN, connection. A router connects directly to the server, and whereas the router is a physical firewall, the server contains software firewall protection. If an intruder manages to get through the server, he/she then has access to the system resources.

If cable ports are vulnerable, cable runs beg for hackers. All that's required to tap a twisted-pair cable is to strip away a small amount of insulation from both wires and attach suitable recording equipment. Coax cable is more resistant to taps, but generally carries higher frequencies, which produce an increase in radiated energy. In effect, coax cable is a data transmitter, and a very sensitive receiver can capture and store the radiated data. The most secure cable medium is fiber-optic cable. Tapping a fiber cable without interrupting the data flow is very difficult, and since light doesn't contain the electromagnetic radiation of copper wire, there's no stray energy to capture.

From a security standpoint, it makes sense to install fiber cable, but, economically, it may not be feasible. The best solution for safeguarding wire runs is to control access to them. Locate the wiring harness in a locked cabinet, or room, that's separate from the breaker box of the building facilities. Efforts should be made to run cables down walls rather than allowing them to dangle, fully exposed, from ceilings. Avoid placing the cables in the same run as electrical wires, or telephone cable, where anyone with a belt full of tools may be able to gain access.

At sites in which CPUs, hard drives, or tape backups are kept, physical access should be controlled. The memory of a large computer is where the "gold" of the data is kept, and only those with a reason to be in the room should be there. Frequently, personnel records, financial data, medical histories, marketing strategies, or defense data reside in the computer memory. The computer-room traffic can be controlled with sign-in logs, ID badges issued to authorized employees and guests, or by ensuring that any doors to the room lock each time they're closed. Entry to the room can be restricted to those with a key.

Physical security planning should also include emergency situations, such as floods, earthquakes, power failures, and fire. Locating a million-dollar computer next to the hundred-year-old boiler is asking for trouble. If it doesn't blow up and incinerate the computer, it may very well float it into the next state when it starts to leak. Small wastebasket fires can quickly escalate into infernos if there's not a fire extinguisher nearby. The most effective means of dealing with earthquakes is to house a computer in a reinforced facility. And for those small jarring earthquakes, anchoring servers will protect much of the computer memory data.

Printouts, modem telephone numbers, written records of passwords and user IDs, or step-by-step instructions of how to utilize the network are all potential problems of physical security. The employment of properly trained personnel is the best course of action for preventing information from falling into the wrong hands, and periodic security audits will ensure that careless mistakes are kept to a minimum.

Data thieves need not be human beings. Water, for example, may take out your server and destroy all of its data. Environmental factors need the same level of attention as other forms of security. Some areas are prone to earthquakes, others tornadoes, some hurricanes, while other areas get hit with flooding. If your network resides in an area with less-than-reliable electrical service, you could have a server crash each time the electricity drops out.

Consider where you locate critical network components such as servers, routers, hubs, and bridges. If they are located too close to large industrial motors or generators, you'll have problems with Electro-Magnetic Interference (EMI). Place them in a basement, and their performance may erode due to excessive moisture. Put these devices in an attic, and the heat will cause them to slow down, and perhaps overheat and fail.

In a typical installation, critical components are located in a wiring closet. Access to the room is controlled, so that physical security is in place. Since the devices that run the network are located in the same room, maintenance and upgrades are easier to perform.

Choose the location of a wiring closet carefully. Make sure there's enough room to make changes on the equipment, that it's well lit, that it's air conditioned in the summer, and heated in the winter. It should be adequately removed from any devices that may cause EMI problems. In addition to motors and generators, put radios, cellular and cordless telephones, and satellite links on the list of items to keep away from. Table 13-1 lists several potential problem areas to consider when placing networking equipment.

Table 13-1: Location of Network Equipment

Physical Device	Action to Take
Servers, routers, hubs, bridges, gateways	Place in a secured wiring closet
Cabling—UTP, STP, coaxial	Run at right angles at crossovers, check for taps, coax may transmit data
Wiring closet	Ventilate with climate control, keep well-lit, secure door, floor, and walls, dehumidify, and locate away from EMI sources
Storage devices (disk/tape drives and media)	Secure in locked vault

Consider a case where users complain about the server taking a long time to respond. From a client computer, you log on as the administrator and check for problems, but none are identified on any of the server troubleshooting tools. The server is working, but it's working slow. What environmental factors may be causing the problem?

Depending on the time of year, the first consideration would be heat. If the wiring closet has become too hot, the server will slow. Another factor that could cause this is locating the equipment in a well-ventilated room, but not permitting the ventilation to cool the equipment. At least several inches of free space are needed for fan-cooled hubs and servers. If these units are backed up to a wall, the units will eventually overheat.

What if users complain that at certain times of the day, they lose data, or the server won't respond? After a while, the problem goes away, and everything appears normal. If heat or humidity were the cause, the problem wouldn't predictably disappear. Due to latency times, if a server became too hot, and then cooled as the air conditioning kicked in, it would require some time to cool. A more likely place to look is for sources of EMI. Radios contain an oscillator that, while capable of delivering low amounts of radiated power, is a source of EMI. It could be that portable generators used to run pumps, or other equipment, are programmed to turn on at specific times, and these are causing the problem.

Other pieces of network equipment can cause problems. A wireless LAN may interfere with cable-based clients, and the server, if the carrier isn't properly focused. For best results, use wireless systems that have infrared or laser (optical) carriers. Digital transmission facilities such as T-Carriers operate at high data rates, and, if located too close to other equipment or wiring harnesses, could cause EMI interference.

Once you've protected the system against theft, interference, and environmental factors, it's time to localize the protection of data. There are two ways of doing so: Provide redundant mass storage devices, and back up the data outside the workstation and server.

Logical

Logical security techniques involve defending the vulnerabilities of the network software.

Almost all network users gain access to a network by entering a password and/or user ID at a sign-on screen. User IDs can be of any length, with four to eight characters being the most common. The ID is usually assigned to the user, and consists of alphanumeric characters. The user password may be assigned, or the user may have the option of creating an original password.

User sign-on screens provide the first level of logical security. The practice of assigning user IDs (usually by network managers or security officers in information systems departments) ensures that a central authority retains control of the individuals offered network access, as well as a record of all individuals on the network. When users are given the option of changing their password, access security is increased. The most effective sign-on screens won't echo passwords back when the user types them in. But, if the password is compromised, the user may be the first to know, and can correct the problem immediately by changing passwords. The obvious should be avoided when selecting passwords, such as first or last names of users, job titles, birth dates, or the names of the user's children. Network administrators should make a practice of reviewing passwords.

A security policy should include keeping user names and passwords at or below eight characters so as to avoid errors when entering, and also to reduce the likelihood of the user forgetting them. Since most password encryption schemes are case-sensitive, the password should include a mix of upper- and lowercase letters as well as numerals and special characters. Consider the following examples of passwords:

- password

- barney

- aMN8dt$

- aBcDeF

The third password, aMN8dt$, is the most secure since it's not likely that an unauthorized user will attempt it as a random try to crack into the network. The last password, aBcDeF, is next best since it includes upper- and lowercase letters. However, it doesn't include numbers or special characters. The first two passwords will eventually be discovered. A password called password is often the default used during installations. A password called barney is often the name of the user or one of his children.

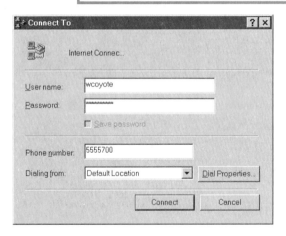

**Figure 13-4:
Example of User
Sign-On Screen**

Passwords and user IDs may be stored in various locations. A LAN without a file server contains both in the system software and each time the software is initiated, sign-on screens for all active PCs will be invoked. If the LAN has a file server, passwords and IDs are maintained at the file server. Figure 13-4 shows a typical example of a user sign-on screen.

To gain access to network resources, a user will be required to enter the following:

- **Username:** WCOYOTE

- **Password:** roadrunner. Note that passwords are encrypted and, in this example, will echo back as **********

For new users, the password is some default word used by all new users such as newuser. At the next logon, the user is prompted to enter a new password, then enter it again to confirm the selection. This is done to provide a measure of security for the user. However, in all network software, this is an option established by the network administrator.

Usernames identify users on the network and should be unique. The password allows the user access to network resources. As previously mentioned, network access is set up and maintained at the server. A login account is created for each user that specifies resources they are permitted to access. Note that "resources" in this context refers to any physical and logical objects on a network. These can include access to printers, files, and directories, to other servers, as well as access to modify access privileges.

Users should be given the option of changing passwords whenever they want. If this isn't possible, establish a policy that forces them to do so at least once a month. Normally, a notice pops up when the monthly time limit approaches, say 10 to 15 days before. The user then has two weeks to make the change. If they don't, they'll be prohibited from logging on when the password expires. This is a good system because it incorporates randomness into password changes. If all users change passwords on the same day at the same time, it won't be too difficult for a hacker to be in the right place at that specific time to catch the new password. Randomness makes it far more difficult for this to happen.

In a typical scenario, group accounts are defined by the network administrator. These accounts describe the rights that a user has been given on the system. Examples of rights include System Shutdown or Local Logon.

Once a group account has been set up, a user may be assigned to it. Essentially, groups are a tool that eases the management of user accounts. There will be users who perform similar tasks on a workstation, and utilize similar network services. A group account provides you with the flexibility to create a specific account, and then assign individuals to it.

In wide area networks, sign-on data is usually contained at ports to the WAN or, for diskless workstations, may reside at a communication controller. As was mentioned in the section on physical security, servers are susceptible to invasion by the technically informed. In fact, if a user (hacker) can defeat the controller sign-on requirement, a direct connection will result to the host CPU. A server is only moderately more complex than a PC, so defeating the device has a similar level of complexity.

Some distributed networks leave control of network access to a large mainframe host. Since the host may be located hundreds, or thousands, of miles from the remote terminal user, user passwords and IDs are quite secure. Unfortunately, this practice also requires that a considerable amount of memory be allotted for logons, when local servers are quite capable of handling the same job.

As mentioned, passwords provide the first level of security to the network. But users are notorious for writing them down and storing them in an unlocked desk drawer in an unlocked office. How can the network know that the person entering the correct password is the person who actually owns the password?

A technique for authenticating users is the callback system. As soon as the sign-on is completed, the remote host disconnects the link and calls the telephone number of the modem connecting the user's terminal to the network. The user must actually be at that number to receive the call. This prevents an unauthorized user from installing a terminal emulator in a home PC and accessing the remote host through a modem.

The host callback is generally a screen change. The user may be prompted to enter a common code, or, as is frequently the case, told to simply press the ENTER key on the keyboard. Pressing the ENTER key is equivalent to answering the callback.

Once access is granted to a network, several levels of security should be available. Broadly speaking, the levels are called browse, update, and unauthorized access. A browse function means the user has access to files and may read the information contained in them. The user is generally permitted to print the files as well (although printer access is another security option). While the files may be read (browsed), adding or deleting information isn't allowed at this level. In order to make changes, the user must be given update authority. Now, information can be written to and read from the file. The unauthorized access level forbids the user entry to a file.

When assigning individual user access, there are two terms to understand—rights and profiles. Rights refer to the authorized permission to perform specific actions on the network. Profiles are the configuration settings made for each user. For example, a profile may be created that places a user in a group. This group has been given certain rights to perform specific actions on the network.

A network administrator may also determine network policies. A policy includes system configurations that affect all users. An example of a policy is one built around passwords and logons.

For example, the following lists policies that may be applied to logons with server operating systems:

- *Maximum Password Age* sets the length of time that a password is used before expiring. At that time, the user must select a new password.

- *Minimum Password Age* sets the minimum amount of time a password can be used before the user selects another. This is intended to prevent a user from selecting the same password over and over.

- *Minimum Password Length* is the number of characters that a password must contain.

- *Password Uniqueness* is used to maintain a history of passwords. The administrator may specify that with each forced password selection, NT will remember previous passwords. This prevents the user from using the same password over and over.

- *Account Logout/No Account Logout* is used to specify what happens when a password is forgotten, or an authorized user attempts to sign on multiple times using another's user name. There are two options. First, nothing happens if the administrator checks the No Account Logout box. If the Account Logout box is checked, then a series of dialog boxes opens to set the parameters for the logout.

Policies may be applied to groups, as in the above example, or to individuals. An example of this is a policy for making registry changes to remote client computers. Since a registry change contains configuration settings for the client, the complete client system is affected.

Security levels are assigned by network managers or operators. The basis for permitting browse or update, or for denying access to specific files should be the nature of the tasks that the user is required to perform at the terminal. If, in the normal course of his/her job, the user needs access to a file, but lacks the need for changing data contained in the file, the browse access should be permitted, and the update denied.

The logical security safeguards mean little if the physical security of the network is ignored. Writing down modem phone numbers and passwords, or allowing the use, by others, of passwords defeats the intent of logical security.

Procedural

Procedural, in the context of data security, refers to established and documented practices for data security.

Clearly defined policies and procedures governing data security are essential. Employees with legitimate needs for accessing the network should have a clear understanding of data safeguards, and written procedures can help to clarify many gray areas. Regulations associated with security should be written clearly, in layman terms, and made readily available to network users. Responsibility for maintaining the procedures should be centralized at local sites so that when a crisis occurs, the procedures followed are current.

In many cases, a local network manager, or operator, doubles as security manager. It's important that the security responsibilities are handled by an individual with the authority and technical knowledge to adequately oversee data security.

Typical duties of security or network managers involve issuing updates affecting the network to concerned users, eliminating access authorization when employees leave or are transferred, conducting inspections to see if the procedures are being followed, and network training.

While network managers generally decide the appropriate level of access of users, it's normal procedure to include a one-over-one signature system when adding new users or providing update authorities. The signature system helps to avoid situations in which network managers show favoritism or abuse their authority.

Hardware upgrades and software updates should be proceduralized so they can be installed without adversely affecting other areas on a network. For example, a software patch may be released that addresses a weakness in the original software. The patch may be beneficial to some users but not all and may, in fact, cause some performance losses when installed. For those who need it, the loss in performance is compensated by the benefits of the patch. But for those who don't need it, the patch simply causes problems.

The same is true for newer versions of a software package released from the vendor. A procedure should be in place that requires the software to be installed and tested before upgrading all clients and servers. The bugs that the upgrade addresses may not be appropriate or needed, and, consequently, will only disrupt an otherwise functioning system.

Visit the download area of a vendor web site. You're likely to find fixes, patches, or upgrades for hardware or software. These all mean the same thing: an interim solution for bugs that have been discovered either during beta testing or after the product was formally released. The patch will have a file that describes the bug. This is known as test documentation because it typically contains the following information:

- Description of the bug, or known weakness

- The problem the patch or upgrade is designed to remedy

- A listing of any known conflict that may arise when the patch is installed

- Download and installation directions. These normally are achieved with the download.

- Revision control that follows the dotted decimal revision system of the product

    For example, a software package at the time you buy it may be at revision level 1.2. The next scheduled release of the package may be advertised as 1.3. In the meantime, bug fixes, patches, and interim upgrades may be at revision 1.2.1, 1.2.1a, etc.

Before installing an upgrade or patch, read the vendor literature related to it. There are good reasons to do this. The patch may not address your application, it may cause conflicts with other applications in your network, or, the cost of installing the upgrade may not be worth the benefit.

Similarly, a network operation needs to have a documented computer virus policy or procedure. For example, assume you choose an antivirus package and install it on all servers. Should it also be installed on the client machines? Print servers? Hubs and routers? Know the hardware on the network and be able to determine the appropriate solutions for protecting the hardware.

Personnel

The personnel using a network are the greatest threat to network security.

A recent study of large network users illustrated the perceived versus actual security threats to a network. The users perceived that hackers and viruses were their greatest security threat, but upon examining the realities of security problems, they found that users' curiosity about the network and programming errors were the culprits in 90% of the security glitches. The people working with, and around, the network caused the majority of the problems.

Many issues discussed in the previous sections directly involve network personnel. Network managers must restrict access to the network functions and hardware based upon a "job-needed" basis. If an individual doesn't need access to a particular file, access should be denied. In installations where very sensitive information is stored and exchanged, background checks are in order. Information affecting national security should only be shared by personnel with the proper security clearance.

Unfortunately, it is the personnel who have been cleared, received access to a network, and utilize the network on a regular basis, that are in the best position to misappropriate data, or inflict real damage to the network operation. Therefore, the importance of security should be continually emphasized. Remember, it's been shown that the curiosity of users is mainly responsible for security problems. In many cases, the guilty user is simply trying to "beat the system." While there are no guarantees for ensuring the integrity of network personnel, proper training, clear procedures, common sense physical safeguards, and software obstacles contribute in discouraging the negative aspects of curiosity.

USER- AND SHARE-LEVEL SECURITY

user-level

share-level

At its base level, security can be classified as either a **user-level** or a **share-level** model. Or, it may contain elements of both. A good networking practice involves an awareness of both types, then selecting one or both for the system.

User-level security allows an individual, or defined groups of users attempting to access network resources, to be validated against account information stored at the server.

Typically, user-level security, then, is associated with server-based LANs.

In order to initiate user-level security, the user of a workstation must specify it using the Access Control folder in the Network dialog box. The Access Control tab is shown in Figure 13-5. In the figure, user-level security has been selected. The user (or group of users) will be validated against the server domain name domain.

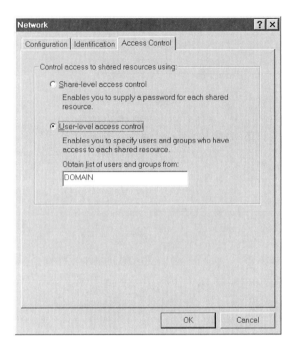

Figure 13-5: The Access Control Dialog Box Located in the Network Folder

User-level security involves individually authenticating each user who accesses the network. This is universally done with a user ID and a password. In some networks—the Internet, for example—this may be all that's needed to validate users. In a small LAN, or a departmental network, this may be all that's needed. If, for instance, five users in an engineering department are concurrently working on a product design, they will need access to each other's work. A simple way to do so is to password-protect the network, then permit authenticated users access to all of the information on it.

In a typical scenario, group accounts are defined by the network administrator. These accounts describe rights a user has been given on the system. Examples of rights include System Shutdown or Local Logon. Once a group account has been set up, a user may be assigned to it. Essentially, groups are a tool that eases the management of user accounts. From an administrative perspective, they save time over setting security for each user (which is how it must be done with share-level access). The option to use group accounts is set at the workstation by specifying user-level access.

TEST TIP

Be able to determine if share- or user-level security is specified given a description.

There will be users who perform similar tasks on a workstation and utilize similar network services. A group account provides you with the flexibility to create one account, then assign individuals to it.

Figure 13-6 shows the top-level screen for user properties. In the figure, a directory (or file, since the process is identical) has been selected to be shared. In Figure 13-7, the share options can be seen in the bottom-right corner of the dialog box and are as follows:

- *No Access*—This prevents any other users from either reading or modifying the contents of the directory.

- *Read*—Allows other users to read but not modify the contents of the directory or file

- *Change*—Allows other users to modify the content of the file

- *Full Control*—Allows other users to read as well as modify the file content

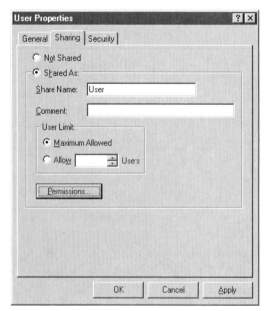

Figure 13-6: Share Tab of User Properties on a Windows NT Server

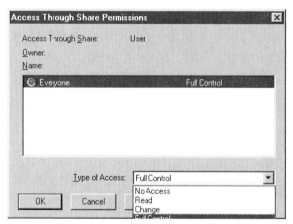

Figure 13-7: Access Permissions for the User Directory

The screen shot shown in Figure 13-6 is from the group user accounts of Windows NT. Once user-level access is specified on the workstations, group rights are set up at this screen. Then, in order to access a particular resource, the workstation first defaults to the server for password authentication. Once the server authenticates the user password, the workstation checks for additional restrictions at the local workstation (share-level access).

In wide area networks, sign-on data is usually contained at ports to the WAN, or, for diskless workstations, may reside at a communication controller. Servers are susceptible to invasion by the technically informed. In fact, if a user (hacker) can defeat the controller or server sign-on requirement, a direct connection to the host resources will result. A server is only moderately more complex than a PC, so that the skills needed in defeating the device have a similar level of complexity.

Some distributed networks leave control of network access to a large mainframe host or centralized server. Since the host may be located hundreds or thousands of miles from the remote terminal user, user passwords and IDs are quite secure. Unfortunately, this practice also requires that a considerable amount of memory be allotted for logons when local servers are quite capable of handling the same job.

In a variation of this, the user has complete authority to establish access to his account. This system is employed in a UNIX network but isn't as readily found in NetWare or NT. (Although users have the option, it becomes obscured in rights and policies controlled by the administrator.)

> Share-level security involves password-protecting each shared resource on a workstation.

It's typically associated with workgroup or peer-to-peer LANs, but can also be applied to server-based networks.

Share-level access provides a range of security direct to the user that user-level access doesn't. Unless you have a compelling reason for a specialized user-level account, you'll probably be grouped with those who have needs similar to your own. The depth of the access is assigned to you; whereas with share-level access you determine the depth of security.

Once a user has access to the network, a decision may need to be made that limits their access. For example, should all employees have access to payroll records? While some think this is a good idea, the fact is, it's likely to cause a considerable amount of consternation.

Figure 13-8 is an example of a Windows dialog box for setting share-level security on a folder. Three security options are available:

- *Read-only* allows a user with the read-only password to view the folder contents, but not modify them.

- *Full access* allows a user with the full-access password to read as well as modify the contents of the folder.

- *Depends on password* allows you to enter both read-only and full-access passwords. Users with one or the other password can access the file.

You may have information in a personal home directory that you simply don't want to share with every employee in the company, and it may not be appropriate to do so. This is the case for share-level access and it's not a hard one to make. All network operating systems use some type of shared access.

Passwords provide the first level of security to the network. But users are notorious for writing them down and storing them in an unlocked desk drawer in an unlocked office. How can the network be sure that the person entering the correct password is the person who owns the password?

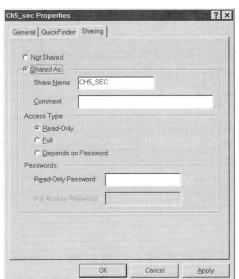

**Figure 13-8:
Share-level Security
Set Up on a Folder**

A technique for authenticating users is the **call-back system**. In a call-back system, as soon as the sign-on is completed the remote host disconnects the link and calls the telephone number of the modem connecting the user's terminal to the network. The user must actually be at that number to receive the call. This prevents an unauthorized user from installing a terminal emulator in a home PC and accessing the remote host through a modem.

In a call-back system, as soon as the sign-on is completed the remote host disconnects the link and calls the telephone number of the modem connecting the user's terminal to the network.

The host call-back is generally a screen change. The user may be prompted to enter a common code or, as is frequently the case, told to simply press the ENTER key on the keyboard. Pressing the ENTER key is equivalent to answering the call-back.

REDUNDANT ARRAY OF INEXPENSIVE DISKS (RAID)

Redundant Array of Inexpensive Disks (RAID) is a system of fault tolerance that may also be used to increase performance in systems that have multiple hard drives.

Methods used for fault tolerance may involve mirroring a disk, or striping multiple disks with data parity.

The standard used for network fault tolerance is the Redundant Array of Inexpensive Disks, or RAID. Originally developed at the University of California at Berkeley, RAID was first published as a white paper in 1987. In addition to providing against hardware losses, RAID may increase the performance of a hard drive by distributing read and write operations over multiple disks.

RAID is applied to fixed disks, or hard drives, and references to either of these terms in this chapter shouldn't be applied to other types of mass storage devices such as CD-ROMs, zip drives, floppy drives, optical drives, etc.

There are five levels associated with RAID, but they aren't all a measure of how well the data is protected. Rather, they describe how data is distributed among two or more fixed disks, and how data redundancy is achieved. In a PC LAN environment, however, RAID levels 1 and 5 are the most commonly employed.

RAID is implemented through a combination of hardware and software. A Windows server, for example, is software-equipped, right out of the box, for RAID 1 and 5. To implement it however, requires additional hardware.

We'll take a look at the particulars of each level, as well as define some common RAID terminology along the way.

RAID 0

RAID 0 incorporates no redundancy, and therefore, isn't actually a RAID element. What it does do is significantly increase the read/write performance of server hard drives. Figure 13-9 illustrates a RAID 0 implementation.

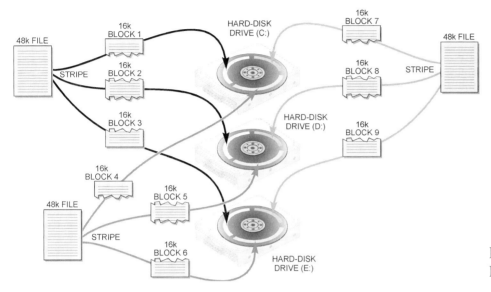

Figure 13-9: RAID 0 Implementation

RAID 0 incorporates no redundancy.

Shown are three hard drives, with the file data being striped to their fixed disks. Striping means that a block of data is separated and alternately written to sectors on each of the three disks. For example, suppose a 48 kB file is written to the disks. RAID 0 will write 16 kB to the first drive, 16 kB to the second drive, and 16 kB to the third drive. In other words, data blocks are striped across the fixed disks.

The date is written serially to each drive, which actually has a negligible effect on the time required to save a file. What does affect the performance of RAID 0 is the size of blocks. If the size is too small, then the commands associated with the write action, along with additional SCSI commands, may be excessive. This is configurable, and you may need to experiment with it a bit. A good starting point for minimum block sizes is 16 kB.

As mentioned, RAID 0 doesn't provide for redundancy; therefore, it has no fault tolerance attributes. RAID 0 provides improved throughput without parity. Parity is used with the other levels as a means for regenerating data, if it's lost on any of the fixed disks. If a fixed disk is lost in a RAID 0 system, all data is lost, and there is no means of recovering it; that is, it has no parity for data recovery.

When the block sizes are optimized, RAID 0 provides for improved throughput, particularly for read requests that occur in parallel—even if they are serially read afterwards.

Some RAID systems use a technique called sector-sparing, also referred to as hot-fixing. With sector-sparing, the disk controller and RAID software will detect a bad sector on a hard drive. When data is written to the bad sector, it will then be moved to a good sector.

> **TEST TIP**
> Know the purpose of RAID.

RAID 1

RAID 1 copies all of the data on one hard drive to another hard drive called a mirror drive.

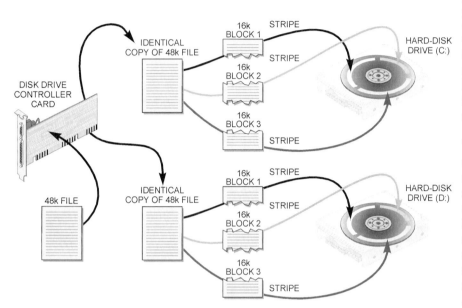

Figure 13-10 shows an example of RAID 1, in which data on a primary disk is copied to a mirror disk. Mirroring is a RAID term meaning simply that all data written to one hard drive is simultaneously written to a backup—or mirror—hard drive.

The advantage of RAID 1 is that if data on the primary drive is lost, it can still be recovered from the mirror drive. As far as a server is concerned, there's no difference between the two disks. The largest disadvantage of RAID 1 is the cost of duplicate disks. During write operations, the system slows moderately, since data is written to two disks instead of one. However, during read operations, system performance may improve because data can be read from both disks.

Figure 13-10: RAID 1 Copies Data to a Mirror Disk

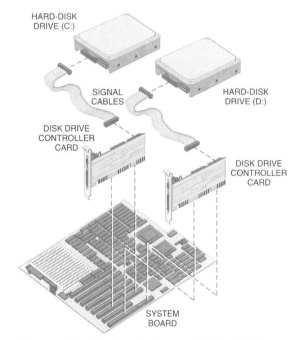

Whether the performance will improve or not depends on how RAID 1 is implemented. One implementation method is called round-robin scheduling. The server alternates between the two drives for read operations. The idea is that as a read operation completes on one drive, it can be immediately started on the next drive. The limiting factor of a hard drive is the mechanical action involved in moving the drive heads from sector to sector on a disk. This is called seek time, and currently averages about 9 ms on most hard drives.

In Figure 13-10, if the disk controller is lost, both hard drives are inaccessible. However, you should be able to replace the controller electronics, and be back in business shortly, unless the failing controller takes the drives with it when it goes. A technique for avoiding this possibility is to duplex RAID 1 by using separate disk controllers for each fixed disk. Duplexing refers to the practice of using a separate disk controller for each fixed disk. Figure 13-11 shows how the hardware is connected. As you can see, duplexing eliminates the disk controller as a single point of failure.

Figure 13-11: Duplexing with RAID 1

RAID 2

> RAID 2 uses fault tolerance to distribute data across multiple disk drives, at the bit level, using striping.

It's a proprietary technique (from Thinking Machines, Inc.) that utilizes disk striping with parity. Parity is an error-detection technique. The parity data is stored on redundant drives, and can be used to regenerate lost data if one of the primary drives fail.

The disadvantage of RAID 2 is the large number of dedicated parity drives that are required. It's typically used in applications where large amounts of data must be written or read from the drives. In a PC LAN, the reads and writes tend to be bursty and varied in size, with small file sizes being common. The overhead associated with frequent, and small, file transfers means RAID 2 isn't a good choice in this application. Instead, it's typically used for applications such as large audio or video files.

RAID 3

> RAID 3 is similar to RAID 2 in that a dedicated parity drive is used to duplicate data.

The difference is that data is stripped in bytes rather than bits, thus reducing the number of redundant drives required. Figure 13-12 shows how data is stored on a mirror disk using parity. Notice that the parity drive will be accessed during each write operation to the disks.

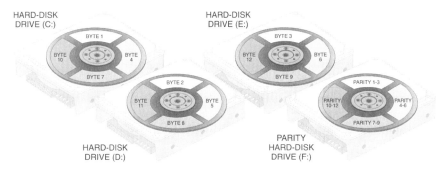

Figure 13-12: RAID 3 with a Parity Disk

This has a tendency to create queues for write operations, and slows down the performance of a server. During a read operation, performance improves, since the disks can be accessed at the same time, and the parity drive isn't needed.

Like RAID 2, RAID 3 is used for large file transfers. It's an improvement because the cost and overhead of the parity disk are reduced.

RAID 4

RAID 4 extends the concept of RAID 2 and 3 by striping disks with blocks of data rather than bits or bytes.

If a block size is set to 18 kB, then a read operation may require accessing a single disk, rather than multiple disks, as in the other two implementations. However, it still requires a dedicated parity drive, and during a write operation, performance will slow as the data is stored on one or more primary disks, and then written to the parity drive.

RAID 5

RAID 5 stripes both file and parity data across all disk drives.

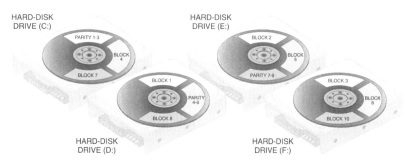

Figure 13-13: RAID 5 File and Parity Striping

As shown in Figure 13-13, a dedicated parity drive isn't used. For each stripe, a parity stripe is allotted to one of the disks.

RAID 2 through 4 require one or more dedicated parity drives. For disk reads, this has no effect on server performance, but for write operations, the server slows down, since data is duplicated on the parity drive. RAID 5 overcomes this by striping data to all drives, allowing parallel reads and writes, and speeding up the performance during write operations.

RAID 5 is the most common fault-tolerance method used in PC LANs. It makes for a more efficient system than RAID 1, since dedicated mirror disks aren't needed. If a primary disk fails, the server will re-create the lost data from parity stripes on the other disks. If this occurs, read operations will slow considerably, since the server must regenerate data in the parity stripe for the lost drive. Because the parity striping technique requires at least one other drive to retrieve data when one of the drives fails, a minimum of three physical drives are required to implement a RAID 5 solution.

SERVER AND WORKSTATION BACKUP

Servers and workstations employ data backups in the event of a disaster that may destroy crucial data.

The most common method used to back up data is tape. A tape backup system is used to back up the data stored on fixed disks. This is especially true for data you simply cannot do without. Not only is tape used to secure this class of information, it's also used to store data that, although not immediately needed on a server, still needs to be retained.

Several methods are used to back up server data on tape, and none of them are particularly satisfactory. The most common is a quarter-inch cartridge drive that uses a disk controller in the server. The network operating system routinely contains utility programs that are used to back up data from a hard drive.

What's needed is a strategy for backing up the data. At best, you can expect data transfer rates, from the disk to tape, to average about 100 MB a minute. If a 10 GB hard drive is backed up to tape, the complete transaction will require many hours to complete, and many tapes will need to be changed. Sometimes a full backup is needed—perhaps once a week—but it should be augmented with more efficient planning.

Once the backup hardware is determined, you need to decide on a system for backing up data from the server. Files stored on a server include a bit called the archive bit. File creation and modification will set the archive to 1 bit. This is used to tell the backup software the file is to be backed up. The state of the archive bit—set or not set—determines the backup strategy, unless a strategy is selected that ignores the bit.

Backup practices include the following techniques:

- **Normal backup**, also called a full backup, means that all data on a hard drive is backed up, regardless of the state of the archive bit. A backup strategy begins with a normal backup. The archive bit is reset back to 0 after the normal backup.

- **Incremental backup** occurs only on files that have changed since the last backup. It sets the archive bit back to 0.

- **Differential backup** occurs for all files that have changed since the last full backup. The archive bit is not reset after the differential backup.

Let's suppose you want to back up the server data once a day. That way, at worst, you'll only lose a single day of information if an earthquake wipes out the server. You could instruct the server to perform a complete backup, or you could back up only those files that have changed since the last backup. There are several variations to an incremental backup as described above, but they revolve around a similar theme. For example, a differential backup is similar to an incremental, except that the selected files are not marked. Similarly, when performing a daily copy, files that have changed on a specific day are backed up, but not marked as such. You should choose a time when server use is light for complete backups, and only back up changed files on a daily basis.

Many organizations implement a **Grandfather, Father, Son (GFS)** backup rotation system. These systems incorporate daily, weekly, and monthly backups into a rotation shedule. This provides three levels of incremental backup for system and data protection.

There is no RAID implementation that will allow you to restore fixed-disk data if the hard drives are destroyed by fire, flooding, earthquakes, theft, and so on. Server backups are simply good business practice, as well as common sense. The cost of the tape drive and the initial system setup is minimal compared to unrecoverable data.

In addition to tape backup systems, some files and directories are replicated. File and directory replication means that specified elements are stored on another computer. The other computer may be another server, or a workstation. Replication is typically used to duplicate logon scripts, system policy files, or large databases. A database is replicated when it's frequently accessed by many users. Once it resides on more than one machine, access times speed up, because if one server is busy, a user will be off-loaded to the replicated database.

Normal backup

Incremental backup

differential backup

TEST TIP

Know the difference between the different backup strategies.

Grandfather, Father, Son (GFS)

TEST TIP

Remember what a GFS rotation is.

In the usual situation, folders are replicated from one server to another. The machine that copies the folder to another machine is referred to as the export server, while the machine that receives the copy is called the import server. Folder replication, in addition to copying a file, automatically updates the copy when changes are made to the original. The frequency of the updates is configurable. For example, Windows NT defaults to 5 minutes, but can be set as low as 1 minute between updates.

If a second server isn't available, a workstation may be used for importing folders. The workstation is notified of updates in the same manner as when replication occurs between servers, but typically, a workstation can only import folder replications. It would not be used to export folders to other machines. The reason is that the workstation software can't support the management functions needed to administer updates.

Since workstations may be used to import and not export folders from servers, they still need a means of backing up their data. How this is done depends on a broad backup strategy designed for each LAN—or applied to all LANs consistently. The simplest strategy is to assign user directories on a server and back up the contents as part of the scheduled server tape backup.

Another method used for workstation backups involves removable media. Removable media refers to floppy disks, tape backups, or recordable CD devices called CD-Rs. Floppy disks, and to a lesser extent, CD backups, aren't a feasible solution for server backups due to the volume of material on a server versus the volume on a workstation.

Establish standard operating procedures for workstation and server backups. Most organizations defer responsibility for server data away from the client. This means that if you place data on the server, it will be backed up, and you needn't worry about it. Any folders on the workstation are the responsibility of the user. These may be backed up using floppy disk, tape, zip drives, or CD-R, as already mentioned.

PACKET FILTERS

A packet filter is set up to eliminate traffic that is inbound from the Internet to a network workstation, as well as to filter traffic that's bound from a network workstation to the Internet.

The filter is specific to fields in a TCP/IP packet and may include any of the following:

- Protocols such as IP, UDP, FTP, and Telnet

- Source IP address from the host where the packet originated

- Destination IP address for the host where the packet is to be sent

- Source port number such as 20 or 21 for FTP

- Destination port number such as 20 or 21 for FTP

In most cases, packet filtering is accomplished with a router. The specific vendor of the packet filter router will determine which of the filters listed above will be included in the router.

The packet filter setup on a firewall is sometimes configured in an across-the-board manner to filter certain fields. For example, telnet may be eliminated for all network users. If, however, there are specialized users who routinely participate in telnet sessions, the telnet restriction may be lifted through the use of access control lists.

A packet filter set on an IP address is used to screen known sources of trouble. Many organizations use destination IP address packet filters to block employees from accessing web sites that aren't appropriate to their business. At the same time, a block may be placed on all source IP addresses. Only source IP addresses that are known or trusted will be exempted from the filter. For example, a virtual private network (VPN) that uses the Internet for connecting networks may block IP addresses except for those that have been assigned by a DHCP server. Similarly, an extranet may block all IP addresses except those that originate from a trusted business partner or authorized employee.

In a similar manner, all TCP/IP port numbers may be filtered except those that are reserved for well-known ports (which range from 0 to 1023). This has the advantage of blocking an intruder using a port number that's disguised to appear legitimate when it's only intended to capture information about the connected client on the network. Block port filtering can cause problems when a company or ISP uses an unreserved well-known port number (numbers above 1023) for a specialized application. In a situation such as this, the port number must be exempted using access lists.

Access control lists may be employed in a firewall for directing exemptions to packet filters. For example, a file could be placed on the firewall called telnet_access. Listed in the file would be usernames that are permitted to establish a telnet connection to a remote site. The firewall will compare any packet with telnet in the header to the list of approved usernames, and if there's a match, open the connection to the remote telnet site. If there's not a match, the connection will be rejected.

FTP access is controlled in a similar way. In a large network, there may be a specific FTP server that accommodates all file uploads and downloads. But since FTP, like e-mail, is a source of viruses, a packet filter may be set so that uploads to the FTP server from the Internet are rejected. The filter is set so that the *put command* entered during the FTP session is rejected. However, Internet users connected to the FTP server may download files using the *get command* since it won't be filtered.

> **TEST TIP**
>
> Know that a packet filter may operate on both IP addresses and port numbers.

Table 13-2 shows an example of packet filtering that is focused on TCP port numbers.

Table 13-2: Packet Filtering

Line No.	Source IP Address	Destination IP Address	Source Port	Destination Port	Action
1	*	192.168.20.10	*	80	Accept
2	*	192.168.50.15	*	25	Accept
3	*	192.168.20.20	*	21	Accept
4	*	192.168.20.20	*	20	Accept
5	172.16.20.1	192.168.50.10	80	80	Reject

Line 1 of the packet filter is set so that all IP addresses (indicated with the *) will be admitted to a server located at 192.168.20.10. The server will accept any source port number, but will only be listening at port number 80, which is the TCP well-known port number for HTTP (the World Wide Web). The server will accept all web connections.

Line 2 of the packet filter is set so that all traffic destined for port number 25 will be sent to 192.168.50.15. Well-known port number 25 is for SMTP, the e-mail protocol used on the Internet. The e-mail server is located at IP address 192.168.50.15 and all incoming mail will be sent to this server.

Line number 3 is also set so that all source IP addresses will be accepted by a server located at 192.168.20.20 on well-known port number 20, which is the port number for FTP. The server will accept all FTP requests.

Line 4 is identical to the action described for Line 3 except the FTP server will be listening at port number 20 instead of port 21. Port numbers 20 and 21 are standardized for FTP use.

Line 5 of the packet filter is used to reject requests from the source IP address 172.16.20.1 on port 80. Notice that the incoming request is specified for the HTTP or web server. This line of the filter is used to block connections to the web site located at 172.16.20.1.

PROXY

proxy server

A **proxy server** is used to prevent network workstation IP addresses from being advertised on the Internet.

If a potential intruder captures a valid IP address, the intruder can use the address for several types of attacks that can cripple a network. (See the Intruder Detection section later in this chapter for more information about service attacks.)

In addition to preventing network IP addresses from being advertised to the Internet community, a proxy is useful in reverse situations. That is, it may be physically positioned so that the proxy is the only access point to a network. Since all inbound traffic must first pass through the proxy, the proxy can be used to filter packets as described above.

There are several other advantages to using a proxy:

- It serves as single device for gathering logging information from packets entering or exiting a network. Since only the proxy server (or servers since an e-mail server is essentially a proxy server for e-mail users) is involved in logging Internet traffic, other network machines, such as network servers, will not have to dedicate resources for capturing and maintaining the logs. The logs may capture source and destination IP addresses, domain name information, and so on.

- It can reduce packet-filtering schemes. Keep in mind that router packet filters can become complex if there are many users on a network and many customized packet filters. With a proxy server, a router can be installed that passes all traffic to and from the Internet without regard to filtering since the proxy will handle all packet filters. This improves the performance of the router.

- It can be used to authenticate inbound Internet traffic. For example, if an FTP file loaded with a virus is directed to the network, the proxy will first determine if an authorized FTP session has been opened with a network workstation or server. An authorized FTP session means that the user connected to the FTP server is authorized to do so, and the proxy will not interfere with the user's access. If the connection is not authorized, the FTP connection will be rejected by the proxy.

Typically, a proxy server is located at the interface to the Internet and may be used as a stand-alone security precaution, or in conjunction with a firewall. To provide the highest level of security, a proxy server should be used with a firewall, as described in the next section.

FIREWALLS

A firewall is software or hardware that's specifically used to thwart intruders from entering a network.

In some cases, a firewall may also be used to deny users access to specified host addresses, such as certain web sites.

There are numerous ways to physically install a firewall at the interface between the Internet and a network. Numerous software solutions are also available that will combine the firewall function with other features such as proxy server, packet filtering, and Network Address Translation (NAT) operations. In this section, four configurations will be described: Packet Filter, Dual-Homed, Choke-Gate, and Screened Subnet.

A **packet filter firewall** is pictured in Figure 13-14. The firewall is typically a router that supports packet filtering.

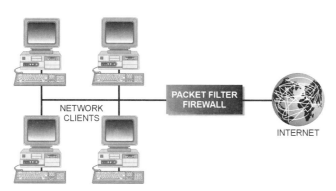

NETWORK CLIENTS
PACKET FILTER FIREWALL
INTERNET

Figure 13-14: Packet Filter Firewall

A packet-filter firewall is most common in smaller networks in which the information stored on the network is not security-sensitive. The firewall is normally installed at the point where the network interfaces to the Internet. All network users accessing the Internet must pass through the firewall before being connected to the Internet. Filters that may be configured on the firewall include any combination of filters previously described.

For traffic inbound from the Internet, the firewall may be configured to prevent any Internet application such as FTP uploads or e-mail. In addition, the firewall may reject all packets that are broadcast to all workstations connected to the Internet. This prevents the network workstations from being a target or unwitting accomplice in attacks against the network.

A **dual-homed firewall** is shown in Figure 13-15. A dual-homed firewall consists of a router and a proxy server that are contained in the same machine. The router is used as a single access point to and from the Internet. The proxy server is used to set all packet filters. Since a proxy server is essentially a computer, it can be software configured more efficiently than a router for setting filters. In addition, the proxy can be set up to capture traffic information for logging purposes.

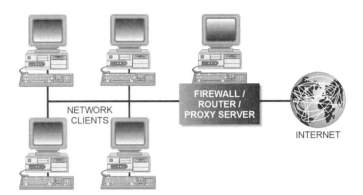

**Figure 13-15:
Dual-homed Firewall**

Note that in a dual-homed firewall, the router is used to specifically route data packets to and from the Internet, and the proxy is used to manipulate and control the data packets. The proxy is typically configured for filtering on usernames or user groups and will replace the source IP address of all out-bound traffic with a proxy IP address.

The advantage of a dual-homed firewall is that a single machine is used to route packets and to set filters. Since both functions are being handled by the same device, dual-homed firewalls run somewhat slower that other types.

A **choke-gate firewall**, shown in Figure 13-16, improves on the performance of a dual-homed firewall. A choke-gate firewall consists of a dedicated router and a dedicated firewall. The router is connected at the interface of the Internet. The proxy is connected to the internal side of the network. The router is responsible for handling packet flow to and from the network with no regard to filtering. Since the router is configured only for routing, it performs better than a firewall that combines the functions of a router and proxy server.

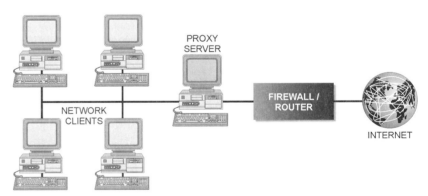

**Figure 13-16:
Choke-gate Firewall**

The proxy server performs all packet filtering. In addition, the proxy will replace workstation IP addresses with a proxy IP address and may also authenticate users via a password for connecting to the Internet. The proxy will typically log Internet-related activities such as the number of times that a user connects to the Internet, the length of the connection, and the sites that a user visited.

A choke-gate firewall adds another level of security for network users. Since the firewall consists of two devices that must be cleared, an intruder must pass through both devices before being admitted to a network.

A **screened-subnet firewall** is pictured in Figure 13-17. A screened-subnet firewall consists of a single router and multiple proxy servers. The proxy servers are normally dedicated to specific Internet applications such as e-mail, web, or FTP. All traffic destined for the network will enter through the router. In some cases, the router may be configured to deny all traffic having certain characteristics, such as a packet with the FTP put command. This will prevent all file uploads to the network FTP clients or servers.

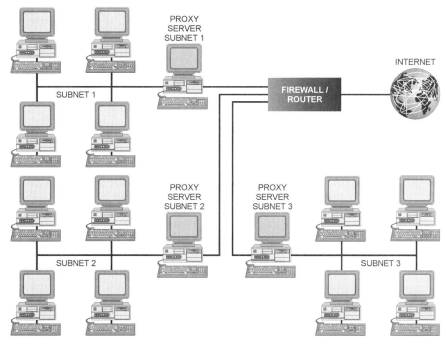

**Figure 13-17:
Screened-subnet Firewall**

The proxy servers are specified for functions such as e-mail or the web. For example, one of the proxy servers may be configured with packet filtering so that it only accepts the SMTP protocol; hence, the proxy server is actually a dedicated e-mail server. Another server may be configured with packet filtering so that it only accepts the HTTP protocol; hence, it's a web server.

A screened subnet is appropriate for larger networks where there are many users. Since numerous proxy servers are used in the firewall, a screened-subnet offers the highest level of security. The major disadvantages of a screened-subnet firewall are the additional expense of the proxy servers and the level of complexity required to configure packet filtering on the dedicated servers.

ANTIVIRUS SOFTWARE

Antivirus software is designed to detect computer viruses that may cripple servers or workstations.

The software may also repair known viruses so that they are not a threat to the computer.

Along the same lines as patches and upgrades, the efficient operation of a network mandates a documented computer virus policy or procedure. As an example, suppose you choose an antivirus package and install it on all servers. Should it also be installed on the client machines? Print servers? Will it work on all of these devices?

Consider a network in which you get a call from a user who tells you they think their workstation was infected with a virus from the server. Impossible, you think, because both client and server have antivirus software installed. You have a look anyway and, sure enough, it appears the client is infected with a virus. How is it possible when the virus software detects and cleans viruses?

This could be because a new virus has been released since you installed the detection software. If you choose McAfee or Norton antivirus solutions, you also buy periodic updates that are released when a new virus is found. The quickest way to install the updates is to download them from the vendor web site. You should receive notice when the updates are available, or you can check their web sites for the latest signatures.

The procedure you put in place needs to address updating installed virus software. Will you do it over the network, via disk at each workstation, or have users do it themselves? No matter which method you choose, document it, enforce it, and stick with it, particularly for workstations because these are likely to be the source of a virus. Many companies forbid employees to install any unauthorized software on a workstation.

This can get tricky for employees who routinely work at home and carry their work back and forth on a disk. Consider offering a virus scan to these individuals and requiring its use.

When selecting an antivirus software package, be aware that two types are available: **memory resident antivirus software** and **on-demand scanner antivirus software**. The following describes the differences between the two types:

- *Memory-resident virus scanners:* These scanners generally detect viruses, but can't correct them. They scan only selected files and remain active at all times that a computer is turned on.

- *On-demand virus scanners:* These scanners correct as well as detect viruses; they scan all files on a disk and must be manually activated or scheduled.

A commercial antivirus software package (such as McAfee Shield or Norton Antivirus) enables you to configure for either type, or a combination of both types.

A virus leaves a **signature** when it infects a computer. A virus signature is some detectable trace that indicates the presence of the virus. Normally, a virus is detected by comparing normal changes (those initiated by a user or the operating system) to data on a hard drive that appears to be unexpected (the change can't be accounted for by changes the user would have made or the operating system would routinely make).

Antivirus software should be installed on all servers as well as all workstations on the network. At least once a month, the vendor should be queried for the latest version of their software. This ensures that the coverage of the viruses the software detects remains up to date.

ALTERNATIVE POWER SUPPLIES

An alternative power supply is essentially a battery backup that maintains power to servers and other critical network devices in the event that the main power fails or fluctuates.

A power failure means a complete loss of power, also called a blackout. If this occurs without an alternative power supply, a network is down, and all data changed since the last backup may be lost. At a minimum, some data is lost. How critical the information on a network is at any given time determines whether this data loss is a concern.

Network equipment can also be affected by a brownout. A brownout occurs when a high-current device, such as a large motor, first starts. In the first several seconds, it draws a large amount of current from the power main, thereby temporarily starving other devices connected to the main. You've probably seen this as a brief dimming of lights when an air conditioning unit turns on.

The opposite of a brownout is a surge. When a device that draws a high current from the power main turns-off, there's a brief delay before the line current drops. The high current on the line is a surge current that can damage power supplies in PCs, servers, or other equipment, such as routers and hubs.

Another type of power fluctuation to be aware of is a transient spike. A spike is induced onto a main voltage line for numerous reasons—lightning or large generators and motors can cause the line voltage to spike for a brief time. Because a spike is of short duration, it contains a small amount of accompanying current and can usually be suppressed with switching power supplies in servers and PCs.

An alternative power supply should be able to address a complete power loss, as well as any of the fluctuations in power just described. An alternative power supply can be one of two types:

- Standby Power Supply (SPS)
- Uninterruptible Power Supply (UPS)

An SPS switches to a battery when power is lost. Figure 13-18 shows a block diagram of a server connected to an SPS. As long as power is available from the power mains, the relay gates power to the power supply of the server.

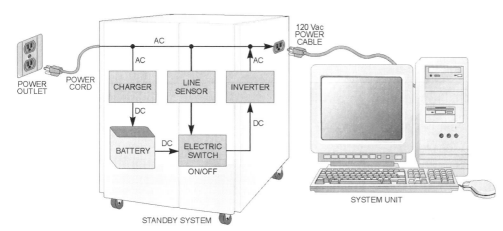

Figure 13-18: Server and SPS

But if the main supply fails, the relay switches to the battery backup. Notice that AC power is also supplied to an AC-to-DC rectifier. The rectified DC keeps the battery charged when it's not being used. But when power fails, the charged DC current from the battery is converted back to AC current in the DC-to-AC converter. With the relay switched, the converted AC current is then the source for the server.

The advantage of an SPS is that it's relatively inexpensive. A minor disadvantage is the time required to switch over to the battery backup. In newer models, this time is typically less than 5 ms. Note that a full cycle of 60 Hz current requires 16 ms to complete, so the SPS switches well within a single cycle time. The power supplies in servers and PCs have large filter capacitors that generally continue to supply the server during the brief switch-over time.

An Uninterruptible Power Supply, while also switching to a battery, avoids the switch-over time that could be a trouble spot for networks using an SPS. Figure 13-19 shows a system using a UPS that continually supplies server power if the main power is lost. Because a UPS is placed in series with the main power, there is no switch-over latency time. The UPS continues to supply power to the server without interruption.

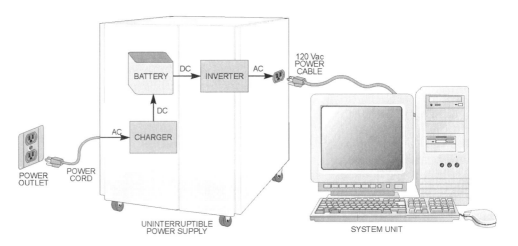

Figure 13-19: Continuous Power with SPS

The main AC current is first converted to DC current in the rectifier to keep the battery charged. The DC current from the battery is then converted back to AC and is the power source for the server. Notice that, as far as the server is concerned, all power originates from the battery.

A UPS is more expensive than an SPS, but it's generally considered to be more reliable than an SPS for continuously maintaining power to a network.

KEY POINTS REVIEW

An overview of network services has been presented in this chapter.

- Servers may contain several microprocessors to handle requests quickly and transparently.

- There are two basic types of microprocessors:

  - Complex Instruction Set Computing (CISC) microprocessors

  - Reduced Instruction Set Computing (RISC) microprocessors

- The system cache is a buffer, which stores data going to and from the microprocessor.

- The preferred interface for servers is the Small Computer Systems Interface.

- Fault management is intended to detect problems, offer diagnostics, maintain a record of the problems, and, in some cases, correct the problems.

- Physical, logical, procedural, and personnel security must all be analyzed for weaknesses, and appropriate precautions taken to strengthen any found.

- The physical element of data security involves computer hardware, the facility or office that houses the data, cable runs, and data printouts (hardcopy).

- Logical security techniques involve defending the vulnerabilities of the network software.

- Procedural, in the context of data security, refers to established and documented practices for data security.

- The personnel using a network are the greatest threat to network security.

- User-level security allows an individual, or defined groups of users attempting to access network resources, to be validated against account information stored at the server.

- Share-level security involves password-protecting each shared resource on a workstation.

- In a call-back system, as soon as the sign-on is completed the remote host disconnects the link and calls the telephone number of the modem connecting the user's terminal to the network.

- Redundant Array of Inexpensive Disks (RAID) is a system of fault tolerance that may also be used to increase performance in systems that have multiple hard drives.

- RAID 0 incorporates no redundancy.

- RAID 1 copies all of the data on one hard drive to another hard drive called a mirror drive.

- RAID 2 uses fault tolerance to distribute data across multiple disk drives, at the bit level, using striping.

- RAID 3 is similar to RAID 2 in that a dedicated parity drive is used to duplicate data.

- RAID 4 extends the concept of RAID 2 and 3 by striping disks with blocks of data rather than bits or bytes.

- RAID 5 stripes both file and parity data across all disk drives.

- Servers and workstations employ data backups in the event of a disaster that may destroy crucial data.

- Normal backup, also called a full backup, means that all data on a hard drive is backed up, regardless of the state of the archive bit.

- Incremental backup occurs only on files that have changed since the last full backup. A change to a file will set the archive bit to one, thus flagging it for the backup.

- A differential backup occurs for all files that have changed since the last full backup, regardless of whether they changed since the last differential backup. The archive bit is set to 1 when the file is modified and not reset after the backup.

- A packet filter is set up to eliminate traffic that is inbound from the Internet to a network workstation, as well as to filter traffic that's bound from a network workstation to the Internet.

- A proxy server is used to prevent network workstation IP addresses from being advertised on the Internet.

- A firewall is software or hardware that's specifically used to thwart intruders from entering a network.

- Antivirus software is designed to detect computer viruses that may cripple servers or workstations.

- An alternative power supply is essentially a battery backup that maintains power to servers and other critical network devices in the event that the main power fails or fluctuates.

- A standby power supply switches to a battery when power is lost.

- An Uninterruptible Power Supply, while also switching to a battery, avoids the switch-over time that could be a trouble spot for networks using an SPS.

At this point, review the objectives listed at the beginning of the chapter to be certain that you understand and can perform them. Afterward, answer the review questions that follow to verify your knowledge of the information.

REVIEW QUESTIONS

The following questions test your knowledge of the material presented in this chapter:

1. Define mirroring, and explain how it's used in fault tolerance.

2. Define striping, and explain how it relates to fault tolerance.

3. List several environmental factors that may affect a network's performance.

4. Describe the difference between CISC and RISC microprocessors.

5. Define fault management.

6. What do physical elements of network security encompass?

7. What do logical elements of network security encompass?

8. What do procedural elements of network security encompass?

9. What do personnel elements of security encompass?

10. Compare share-level security to user-level security.

11. What is RAID?

12. Which RAID level stripes both file and parity data across all disk drives?

13. Describe an incremental backup.

14. Describe a differential backup.

15. What is a packet filter?

EXAM QUESTIONS

1. What is the advantage of a UPS over an SPS?
   a. A UPS doesn't use a battery.
   b. A UPS avoids switching delays that an SPS has.
   c. A UPS derives power from a server.
   d. A UPS allows servers to operate indefinitely without power.

2. A backup strategy in which only files that have changed are backed up describes a(n) _____ backup.
   a. incremental
   b. differential
   c. full
   d. normal

3. Which RAID level contains no provisions for fault tolerance?
   a. RAID 4
   b. RAID 5
   c. RAID 1
   d. RAID 0

4. What is the purpose of a proxy server?
   a. to prevent network workstation IP addresses from being advertised on the Internet
   b. to filter unwanted packets from entering a network
   c. to dynamically assign IP addresses to client computers
   d. to track the Internet sites that users visit on the Internet

5. Which of the following is specifically intended to prevent unwanted visitors from entering a network from the Internet?
   a. proxy
   b. cache
   c. firewall
   d. RAID

6. What is the type of security implemented in which server accounts are stored and maintained on a server?
   a. procedural
   b. physical
   c. user-level
   d. share-level

7. When connecting a tape backup unit to a server, what is the preferred electrical interface between the server and the backup unit?
    a. differential
    b. SCSI
    c. incremental
    d. UPS

8. Of the following, which is the most secure password?
    a. password
    b. Password
    c. PassWord
    d. PaSsw8rD

9. Which of the following offers the greatest security threat to networks?
    a. hackers
    b. employees
    c. relatives of employees
    d. customers

10. What is the purpose of a packet filter?
    a. to eliminate certain packets based upon IP address or port number
    b. to reduce the size of incoming IP packets
    c. to increase network efficiencies by eliminating data packets
    d. to remove packets that are corrupt

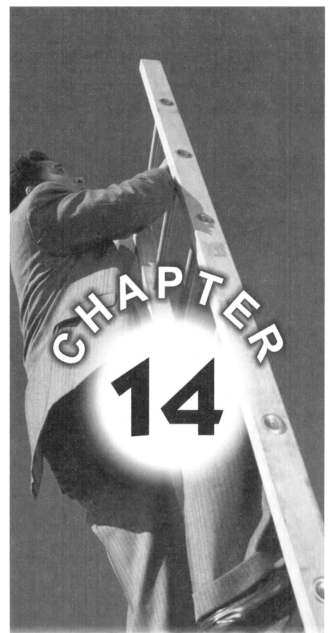

TROUBLESHOOTING STRATEGIES

LEARNING
OBJECTIVES

LEARNING OBJECTIVES

Upon completion of this chapter and its related lab procedures, you will be able to perform the following tasks:

1. Given a network problem scenario, select an appropriate course of action based on a general troubleshooting strategy. This strategy includes the following steps:

    a. Establish the symptoms.
    b. Identify the affected area.
    c. Establish what has changed.
    d. Select the most probable cause.
    e. Implement the solution.
    f. Test the result.
    g. Recognize the potential effects of the solution.
    h. Document the solution.

2. Given a troubleshooting scenario involving a small office/home office network failure (e.g., DSL, cable, home satellite, wireless, POTs), identify the cause of the failure.

3. Given a troubleshooting scenario involving a remote connectivity problem (e.g., authentication failure, protocol configuration, physical connectivity), identify the cause of the problem.

4. Given a wiring task, select the appropriate tool (e.g., wire crimper, media tester/ certifier, punch down tool, tone generator, optical tester, etc.).

5. Given a network scenario, interpret visual indicators (e.g., link lights, collision lights, etc.) to determine the nature of the problem.

6. Given a troubleshooting scenario involving a network with a particular physical topology (e.g., bus, star/hierarchical, mesh, ring, and wireless) and including a network diagram, identify the network area affected and the cause of the problem.

7. Given a network troubleshooting scenario involving a wiring/ infrastructure problem, identify the cause of the problem (e.g., bad media, interference, network hardware).

CHAPTER 11

TROUBLESHOOTING STRATEGIES

INTRODUCTION

Troubleshooting networks can be time consuming and difficult. CompTIA has offered a set of guidelines intended to streamline network troubleshooting procedures. While you may not agree with the steps presented in this chapter, or with the sequence in which the steps are presented, it's important for the purposes of the exam to adjust your troubleshooting approach.

This chapter is a basic overview of troubleshooting processes. Note that it builds upon concepts presented in the earlier chapters. Take some time after reading the chapter to review earlier concepts such as characteristics of cabling media, software influences on connectivity (DNS or DHCP settings, for example), and TCP/IP troubleshooting utilities such as ping or ipconfig.

STRATEGY FOR TROUBLESHOOTING

When a network problem is discovered, one of the most difficult first steps is trying to decide the extent of the problem. Consider a 1,000-node network using many hubs, routers, Internet connections, printers, and so on. Before applying a specific troubleshooting methodology, get a feel for how broad the problem is. In this section, you're offered a general set of guidelines to narrow the scope of problems.

An initial step in troubleshooting a problem that has come to your attention is to decide the extent of the problem. Does it affect the entire network, a single LAN, or a single user? Is it a problem that, at the moment is localized, but will eventually affect all users (such as a virus)? Is the problem associated with specific activities such as logons, printing, or file sharing?

To determine the extent of network problem, work through the following four steps:

1. Determine whether the entire network is affected.

2. Localize the extent of the problem to an area of the network.

3. Attempt to duplicate the problem.

4. Apply proven troubleshooting techniques.

First, determine whether the entire network is affected by the problem. The best way to do this is to compare the problem call with any other problem calls you have received from network users. If users on different segments are complaining of the same problem, you have a good indication that the problem is network-wide. Also, depending on your resources, you may be able to access problem logs on the affected network and gather information.

A network-wide problem is a rather broad statement. If the problem is indeed network-wide, you next need to decide whether it encompasses the network on a WAN level, a LAN level, a workgroups level, or on one of the components at the LAN level, such as server or workstation. After you determine that the problem exists across the network, you can work from the WAN level to the workstations level to determine the extent of the problem. The second step is used to narrow the extent of the problem.

In the second step, you localize the problem to specific areas of the network. Begin at the WAN level. Perhaps the LAN is interconnected to another LAN by a router. Check to see whether the connected LAN is experiencing similar problems. If an interconnected LAN is not affected by the problem, you can assume that the problem has been localized to a specific LAN and isn't affecting the WAN. However, if the connected LAN shows similar symptoms of the problem, you can assume the problem is WAN-wide. Your efforts can now focus on interconnection devices, such as routers, gateways, or switching hubs.

If the problem appears to affect only a LAN, check to see whether all of the LAN is affected. For example, some LANs contain several workgroups. A problem may be localized to a single workgroup. If so, the remaining workstations in the LAN can be ignored so you can focus on the workgroup setting. Now, you can examine each of the workstations in the workgroup to determine which may be causing the problem.

If, however, all workgroups are similarly affected, you can assume the entire LAN is affected. Any of the components of the LAN could be a source of the problem. This includes workstations, hubs, bridges, or servers. Typically, when a problem appears across all components in a LAN, a server is the likely culprit.

Notice that in the first two steps, you're attempting to establish the boundaries of the problem.

The third step is not always possible. It depends on the equipment at your disposal. The idea is to determine whether you can duplicate a problem by placing a suspect machine in a known good setting. For example, assume a router is the suspect. You would remove it and place it in a mock network to see whether the problem surfaces after all other devices are eliminated as potential problems. If you replicate the problem under these conditions, you know the router is bad, and you can replace it with a good one.

The last step says you should apply standard troubleshooting techniques. This occurs when you've isolated the problem to a specific network device. Notice that the four steps for identifying the extent of the problem bring you to the brink of troubleshooting, but you haven't actually begun troubleshooting yet. You still need to specify the nature of the problem, as discussed in the next section.

SYSTEMATIC APPROACH TO TROUBLESHOOTING

Table 14-1: CompTIA Troubleshooting Approach

CompTIA cites an approach to troubleshooting network problems for the Network+ competencies. The approach is shown in Table 14-1. For the purposes of taking the exam, you should become familiar with the steps in this approach.

The process outlined in Table 14-1 calls on many of the practices and concepts previously described in this book. Essentially, the strategy requires a careful analysis of a problem in which you draw upon knowledge of networking and experiences with previous problems.

Step 1	Establish the symptoms.
Step 2	Identify the affected area.
Step 3	Establish what has changed.
Step 4	Select the most probable cause.
Step 5	Implement the solution.
Step 6	Test the result.
Step 7	Recognize the potential effects of the solution.
Step 8	Document the solution.

The first step in the troubleshooting approach is to clearly and specifically describe the symptoms. For example, a user may say that the "network is running slow." But, to a network administrator, the phrase is meaningless. What is needed is an objective method to use in describing a problem such as "the network normally has a data throughput of 4 Mbytes/second, but over the last two weeks the throughput is averaging 3 Mbytes/second."

Before a network behavior can be classified as a problem, it must be described in relative terms. Is the network slow? What is normal? A problem is a deviation from the normal condition. If the normal response time is one second, and you notice the time leaps to five seconds, there's a problem. Five seconds is a deviation from the normal, one-second response time. In other words, step 1 is a directive to describe the symptoms (issues) surrounding the problem.

The second step, identify the affected area, refers to isolating the parts of the network with symptoms as opposed to parts that aren't affected. One way to do this is to re-create the symptoms that you developed in step 1. Typically, step 2 is easiest to perform when a problem is confined to a local environment—either a client, server, or software running on a LAN. For example, suppose a workstation user is unable to access a local server. You can remove the NIC in the workstation and place it in a second workstation. If the second workstation is unable to access the server, the problem has been re-created. The problem duplication approach assumes you have the minimal resources to duplicate the problem in an environment that's either identical or very similar to the one in question.

A problem can be duplicated very simply and inexpensively. For example, by switching ports on a hub, workstation connectivity can be checked as well as the operation of the hub port. In other situations, the expense of a suspect device may prevent duplicating the problem. Consider an enterprise hub that costs many thousands of dollars. A company may not have the resources that permit buying an extra hub for troubleshooting purposes. Even if it did, it may not be practical to remove the hub and place it in another network to see whether the same problem occurs.

Large networking vendors offer customers a support program that includes creating a duplicate network that's used for troubleshooting customer problems. By re-creating the symptoms of the problem on the duplicate network, the vendor can offer solutions to the actual problem. This is particularly beneficial for networks that can't go off-line for troubleshooting, such as hospitals and the military. The customer typically pays a hefty fee for problem duplication facilities at the vendor site.

In step 3, establish what has changed by comparing historical statistical data, or by comparing hardware and software records. For example, if a patch has been applied to the network software that addresses a previous problem, it may be that the patch has created a new problem. Or, if all NIC cards have ben upgraded from 10 Mbps to 100 Mbps, the problem is likely to be related to the hardware upgrade.

In step 4, you select the most probable cause by formulating a problem statement that matches the symptoms, areas affected, and network changes, as described previously. For example, if the original symptom related to a slow network, and the symptoms surfaced after a NIC upgrade from 10 Mbps to 100 Mbps; then the most probable cause of the problem is that the NIC cards aren't functioning properly. Based upon the information gathered in the first three steps, step 4 is the best educated guess as to a solution that will clear the problem.

In step 5, you implement the solution. You won't know for sure whether the hypothesis you formulated in step 4 is correct until you try the correction. Notice that implementing a correction can be time consuming for you and, at times, disruptive to network users. Because implementing the correction may affect the operation of the network, it's important that you stop and review the steps leading up to it. If you're wrong, you'll have to retrace the steps, formulate another correction, and then create disruptions once again as the correction is implemented.

In step 6, the correction is tested by checking to see whether the original symptoms of the problem have disappeared. If the 100 Mbps NICs are replaced because they slow the network, then the new cards need to be tested to make sure that they actually fixed the problem. This sounds like common sense—and it is—but it's surprising how many obvious fixes don't really fix the original problem

In step 7, you are to recognize the potential effects of the solution. This is important because it should provide a means of objectively measuring how good the solution is. To continue with the NIC problem, assume that once the cards are replaced, all works as it should during a test. But when the potential affects are analyzed, you determine that the NIC you plan to install doesn't have the correct drivers for the majority of operating systems installed. Now, although the slow data rate problem can be addressed, you have a driver problem.

Step 8 involves documenting the problem and the solution to the problem. Problem documentation makes good sense because if you have to deal with a similar problem in the future, you will have a reference that details steps that may solve it. In many companies, documenting problems and the resolution to the problems is a requirement. Not only is the information helpful for troubleshooting similar problems, but it can be used for gathering statistical data related to the time the network is available to users as well as the time the network resources are utilized.

Let's apply the approach to an example scenario. A user complains that she can't access or share files with other members of a workgroup. Let's work through the problem step by step using the ComTIA troubleshooting approach.

- **Step1:** *Establish the Symptoms.* After spending some time at the user's workstation, you verify that the problem affects file shares with other users; otherwise, her workstation appears to function properly. This completes step 1.

- **Step 2:** *Identify the Affected Area.* Your understanding of technology and of the interaction of the components of the workstation and the network is critical to isolating a problem. For example, it's very unlikely that a CD-ROM in the workstation affects file shares in the workstation. The CD-ROM and other unlikely causes can be rejected. The workstation operating system, Network-layer protocol, or the hard drive are all good candidates as the culprit. You can isolate the problem by checking similar network functions, such as printing. If all network-related functions aren't working properly, it's a good bet that the problem can be isolated to network configuration problems.

In addition, you should limit the range of the problem. That is, are any other workstations affected? We'll assume that all other workstations are sharing files without problems.

- **Step 3:** *Establish What Has Changed.* This involves sound thinking and, ideally, a well documented workstation. For example, most companies keep detailed records of hardware and software configurations for all computers. The documentation is used to compare actual configurations so that changes can be determined. We'll assume that the workstation is configured for static IP addressing, but all IP addresses are in fact assigned by a server using DHCP. A check of the workstation documentation will reveal that the NIC card TCP/IP settings should be set so that the IP address is assigned.

- **Step 4:** *Select the most Probable Cause.* You must state the correction very clearly in a manner that addresses the symptoms, range of the problem, and changes made. For example you might state, "This workstation is unable to share files with other workgroup members because the TCP/IP settings have been changed from a dynamic IP assignment to a static IP assignment. Since there is no static IP address assigned to the workstation, the user is unable to access the network in order to share files."

- **Step 5:** *Implement the Solution.* In this scenario, you set up the correct TCP/IP settings on the workstation so that the workstation IP address is assigned by the server.

- **Step 6:** *Test the Result.* After the network settings are configured, the workstation is checked to see whether files can now be shared. Notice that the test directly addresses the original problem. The workstation user was unable to share files; the correction is designed to eliminate this problem, and the workstation is tested specifically to determine whether files can now be shared.

- **Step 7:** *Recognize the Potential Effects of the Solution.* In the scenario described, there are relative few effects to consider. However, this step remains valid since one of the effects is that the server needs to have enough IP addresses so that the reconfigured workstation, as well as all other workstations on the network, will receive IP addresses.

- **Step 8:** *Document the Solution.* Carefully document the original problem and the resolution to the problem. Consider including any false starts you made. For example, in step 3, you might have isolated the problem to a faulty NIC card. But when a new card didn't correct the problem, you should note in the documentation that before replacing NIC cards, you should check the TCP/IP settings. Documenting false starts can save you time later, or can save time and effort for other technicians working on similar problems.

OPERATOR PROBLEMS VERSUS SYSTEM PROBLEMS

At times, a network problem may not be a network problem at all. It may be due to the user operating the system. Recall that the typical user doesn't know what's going on under the hood of the network. An error message that pops up on a monitor means to the user that there's a network problem.

If you're the one who supports network users, you first talk with them over the telephone. You might be located in the same building with the user or a thousand miles away. In the latter case, it's silly to jump on an airplane without first eliminating the user as the actual source of the problem. But keep in mind, tact is essential in these situations because the user's perception is that the network is at fault.

Table 14-2 lists a simple problem escalation protocol specified by CompTIA that should determine whether the user is the problem. First, have another operator perform the same steps as the first operator, but on a different machine. This second machine must be functionally the same as the first and the task must be the same. If the second operator can perform the task, the problem is localized with the first operator.

Table 14-2: Operator Versus System Problem Analysis

Step 1	Have a second operator perform the same task on an equivalent workstation.
Step 2	Have a second operator perform the same task on the original operator's workstation.
Step 3	Determine whether operators are following standard operating procedures.

Next have the second operator who successfully performed the task on another machine do the same task on the first machine. If the task can now be completed, it's time to do a bit of training with the first operator. If, however, the second operator can't perform the task on the first machine, you can be confident that the problem isn't with the operator (unless neither operator is following standard operating procedures for the task they're performing).

Ask whether the user knows the standard operating procedure for the task. If the network is properly documented, such a procedure will exist in a form the user can access. Have the operator read the procedure while performing it at the workstation. Note each step as it's being read. Have the operator echo the steps as he or she performs them. This serves two purposes: It enables you to listen for discrepancies in the procedure, and it enables you to determine whether the operator is misinterpreting a good procedure.

Imagine a situation in which you get a call and the operator complains that he can't save files to his personal directory on the server. You ascertain that all other network functions seem to be working and suspect the operator is entering incorrect information.

According to the steps outlined in Table 14-2, your next step is to have a second operator try saving a file to the server directory on an equivalent machine. Let's assume the operator was successful. What is the next step? Have the second operator try saving the file to the user's directory from the original workstation. We'll assume the operator was successful. You must now speak with the original operator and work step-by-step through the procedure to determine where the problem lies.

If the second operator wasn't able to save a file, then what? Tell him step-by-step what to do. Hopefully, the steps you cite are from a standard operating procedure (SOP). If this works, make sure the operators receive a copy of the SOP. If it doesn't work, the problem lies with the system and not with the operator.

Networks can be complicated. It's unreasonable to expect those who use them to be as knowledgeable as those who maintain them. Expect operator errors and plan on a systematic approach for isolating them from actual network problems. When the problem has been resolved, be sure to follow up in a couple of days to make sure the user isn't having more problems—because the problem could be intermittent—and document the resolution in a log. The information can be valuable source material for future user training.

SOHO NETWORK FAILURES

A SOHO (Small Office/ Home Office) may be a ready source of problems because a small business is not likely to have trained networking staff. Typically, a small business will contract to an IT company for computer and network support. Let's look a typical problems that a SOHO may experience.

Workstation hardware: Normally, hardware problems occur due to failure of a device such as a modem that no longer connects or a hard drive that has died. But if the hardware devices aren't bad, the next place to look is software drivers that are causing problems. Newer editions of Windows allow unsigned drivers to be installed but if the install is during the initial boot of a new machine, the user will receive ominous pop-up warnings from Microsoft recommending that the drivers not be installed. If the user continues with the installation, there could in fact be problems from the drivers.

- *Workstation Software:* Assuming that the installed software is tested to be compatible with the installed operating system, the most common problem here is a bad configuration. If a SOHO employee has decided to make changes in an effort to fix a problem, it is imperative that a document exist with the original settings so that the machine can be returned to the original configuration.

- *Remote Access:* Remote access refers to connecting to the Internet, a remote e-mail server, or a remote server on another network. For a SOHO, access will typically be via a cable modem, DSL line, the analog telephone network (called POTS, for Plain Old Telephone System), or possibly a satellite provider.

To test remote access, initiate the connection. This will verify the systems. Once you determine that the connection can't be made, check the software settings. If the workstations are configured properly, and all physical connections appear to be in place, it's time to call the remote access provider to determine whether the problem is outside the SOHO.

REMOTE CONNECTIVITY PROBLEMS

Remote connectivity problems refer to the full range of problems that may occur when trying to connect to a device that's located in another location. For example, a user may dial-in to a company server from home in order to check e-mail or to work with a file on a company server.

Physical problems related to remote connectivity refer to the hardware and cabling infrastructure needed to make the connection. For example, if a user can't connect using a dial-up modem, the first thing to check is to make sure that the phone cord from the modem to the phone line is connected.

> **NOTE**
>
> Remote connectivity problems typically involve physical, configuration, or authentication problems.

Physical problems can be frustrating since they may involve other parties. For example, a DSL line requires support from the phone company for troubleshooting. But the phone company can't be responsible for wiring within a building—the owner of the building needs to check and ensure that the cabling is suitable for DSL.

Protocol configurations are the most common cause of problems. For example, if a remote workstation is assigned an IP address using DHCP, a static IP address may be required to access a proxy server for e-mail or Internet access. The best bet in troubleshooting configuration problems is to establish a standard set of parameters; then write the parameters down.

Authentication refers to determining the identity of a user attempting remote access. Normally, authentication is implemented using user names and passwords. It's quite usual for users to forget passwords. If the level of authentication is taken beyond passwords, the process can be complicated. For example, some companies institute call-backs when a user attempts to connect to a remote server. A call-back requires that the connection be broken, and the server call back the number used to initially dial in. Once the user machine answers the call, the user name and password are entered. A problem with call-backs is that they may not work if the user is in a hotel in which in-coming calls are routed through switches.

PHYSICAL AND LOGICAL TROUBLE INDICATORS

Troubleshooting, in addition to using a systematic approach, requires using as many indicators as you can. Trouble indicators may be as simple as checking a power-on light, and as complex as interpreting software protocol analyzers. A printer, for example, won't print if it's not turned on, no matter how many times it's reconfigured.

Table 14-3 lists specific indicators that you should be aware of as a source of troubleshooting information. Sometimes called "dummy lights," these simple indicators can be a ready source of information for quickly resolving a problem. They can also become an uncomfortable reflection of your troubleshooting abilities if you overlook them.

1.	Link lights on NIC cards and hubs
2.	Power lights on workstations, printers, servers, hubs, tape back-ups, etc.
3.	Error displays such as error messages concerning printers or connections to a server or remote device
4.	Error logs and displays such as Event Viewer, or graphical displays such as Network Monitor
5.	Implement the solution

Table 14-3: Physical and Logical Trouble Indicators

Nearly all hardware devices have some type of light to indicate basic functions.

Check for applied power by looking for a power light. If it's not lit, check to see if power is applied; that is, is the device plugged in? If it's working from an Uninterruptible Power Supply (UPS, which is a battery), is the UPS fully charged? Blown fuses can be a source of power failure in boards that are mounted in a chassis. Most of these will also have some type of basic power indicator, usually an LED mounted somewhere on the board. The chassis may be operating, but a crucial board isn't because a fuse is blown. Take the time to make a thorough visual inspection when lack of power appears to be the culprit.

Link lights provide visual information about the connection and operational status of different network devices such as NICs, routers, and hubs. They can also provide a basic unit of information as to whether the device is performing it primary function. As with power supply problems, make a thorough visual inspection, particularly when the device is working under a loaded condition. Only then can you determine whether the lights are working properly.

Error messages that appear on a monitor may be communicated to you by an operator. An error message may or may not have any significance. Windows products are notorious for generating numbered error messages, and so-called "catastrophic errors." The error that's generated on a screen may only have significance to the native source code of the application software, and may mean nothing to a troubleshooter in the field. In other cases, it may lead directly to the source of a problem. Collect vendor error codes, document instances when they occur, and record the actions taken to clear the code. Eventually, you'll create a log that's useful in mapping error codes to a problem resolution.

An error log provides historical data about the performance of a network. An error log is set up to "trap" certain events on a network such as collisions, delays, processor usage, interrupt times, etc. You have quite a few options in how you view and analyze the information in an error log. A minimum threshold may be set so that normal conditions are exempted from the log.

For example, an Ethernet LAN is expected to experience collisions. From past history, you may have determined that 100 collisions each day is normal, so the threshold would be set for collisions exceeding 100. You may then further define the log to capture collisions that exceed 100 during a specific time-frame, say from 7:00 AM until 9:00 AM.

Most error logs place the data in a text file, so that it can be readily imported into most off-the-shelf software packages such as Word or Excel.

Closely related to error logs are performance monitors and protocol analyzers. Windows NT has a Performance Monitor and a Network Monitor. Performance Monitor is used to track attributes on client stations or a server, while Network Monitor tracks attributes across the network. Network Monitor can also display many attributes of an IP packet. In addition, it can be used to chart the network's statistical data, such as bandwidth usage, error rates, number of broadcast messages, and so on.

TEST TIP

Be aware that link lights provide instant feedback about connectivity and device operation.

PHYSICAL TOPOLOGY PROBLEMS

> Physical and logical connectivity refers to the hardware, cabling, connectors, and protocols running on a network.

After ascertaining whether the problem is local or across the network, determine whether the problem lies with physical connections or with logical (software) settings and configuration. A quick visual inspection of cabling may correct the problem. Compare the installed devices against the network floor plan to ensure equipment hasn't been changed without the proper approvals. After the physical connections have been ruled out, the easiest test is to ping. Try pinging several clients using 127.0.0.1 (or localhost), which is the local loopback test. Ping the local server as well as other clients on the LAN. Ping routers and default gateways. A ping to the default gateway IP address can eliminate many possible problems because if it works, the client, hub, and local server are probably all communicating properly.

Ping is also useful for testing by computer domain names. It's possible that an IP ping works, whereas a name ping doesn't. In the latter case, the physical and logical connections are okay, but the WINS or DNS isn't configured properly.

Physical problems with the network media can be difficult because the connectors are hidden and the equipment is often stored in an out-of-sight location, preferably one that's secured. But the good aspect of a physical problem (if there is one) is that it normally shows up during the installation of the network. Assuming the network equipment is working, physical media problems are one of the most common problems.

After a problem has been located in the physical media, it's time to fix it. A break in UTP cabling can be repaired with a solder splice. CAT 5 UTP uses eight wires that connect to an RJ-45 connector. The pinout for this connector can also be found in Chapter 2 — *IEEE 802.x Protocols*.

Coaxial cable may be thinnet or thicknet, and each interfaces to the network media using connection techniques.

Fiber-optic cabling uses only fiber connectors. There is considerable variety in the connectors available but you'll find some standardization in FDDI. The important point about fiber cables is that the connections must be clean and aligned so no loss of signal occurs at the connection. Because fiber cable isn't copper-based, it's the only cabling medium that's resistant to EMI (electro-magnetic interference).

EMI can be a problem with any copper-based wiring infrastructure. EMI can degrade or destroy long runs of digital data. Since a receiving node will reject garbled packets, the source node must resend the packets, which will cause network throughput to suffer and the network to slow down. The interference is caused by electromagnetic radiation emanating from electrical equipment.

Recall that topology refers to the physical architecture of a network, such as a star or ring configuration. The key to analyzing topology problems is in understanding characteristics such as limitations and strengths of the various topologies. Refer to Chapter 1 — *Network Topologies and Media* for a review of topologies.

Let's look at a couple of examples of topology problems along with typical problems. Figure 14-1 shows a typical network.

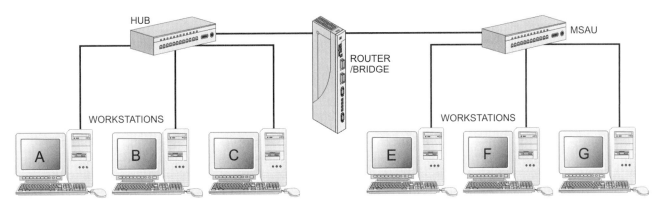

This figure shows two networks connected by a router and bridge. Why is a bridge needed? Notice the types of hubs used in the figure. The one on the left is a 10Base-T Ethernet hub, and the one on the right is a Token Ring MSAU hub. The labeling of the hubs is the give-away. In order for the two networks to communicate, a bridge is needed between the Ethernet and Token Ring protocols.

Figure 14-1: Network Diagram

Why is a router needed? The assumption is that the two networks are running TCP/IP and the router is used to translate between different network addresses between the two networks.

Now that the types of networks are identified, you can determine the speed of the network. A 10Base-T network operates at 10 Mbps, while the Token Ring network is operating at 16 Mbps. In addition, you can generally guess at the network media—CAT 5 cable on both networks, although the Token Ring LAN may be using shielded twisted pairs.

Several things can happen to this network that have the infrastructure as the root cause:

- Clients may not be able to access the network due to cabling or NIC problems.

- Either hub may go down. But note that before swapping out a hub that appears to be lost, you need to ping across the network so that connectivity through the hub can be measured.

Imagine that a user equipped with a notebook computer and wireless card is now added to the network. Use the same logic to approach infrastructure problems—check for connectivity across the wireless link using ping, or by using software utilities that ship with the card.

TEST EQUIPMENT

A wide range of test equipment is available to network technicians to troubleshoot network problems.

These range from low-cost **breakout boxes**, to expensive **protocol simulators**. Although this section highlights data-communications–specific test equipment, you shouldn't assume that the familiar multimeters and oscilloscopes aren't equally important.

breakout boxes

protocol simulators

loopback tests

You should remember the TCP/IP utilities described in Chapter 6. Ping, as you may recall, is a versatile tool used to perform **loopback tests**. These tests will verify your access to a particular piece of equipment, such as a server or router.

Bit-Error Rate Testers (BERTs)

The breakout box is one of the most common troubleshooting tools available, used for loopback tests, clock tracing, and signal monitoring. The instrument is connected in-line with cabling, in a serial fashion, in the same way that an ammeter is connected.

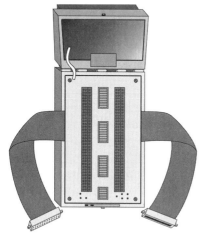

Figure 14-2: Breakout Box

Breakout boxes are available for nearly all interface types, and are often used to switch wire connections for test purposes. A commercial breakout box is shown in Figure 14-2.

Bit-Error Rate Testers (BERTs) check for individual bit degradation. A test signal is transmitted through the network, and when it returns, the bits are checked for integrity. BERTs are useful in noisy environments, where electromagnetic radiation is suspected of inducing unwanted voltages into network cabling. They track bit rates, message block errors, and errors that occur on positive or negative transitions. A BERT is pictured in Figure 14-3.

A bit-error rate tester is used to check for signal degradation in individual bits, messages, and continuous data streams.

Figure 14-3: BERT

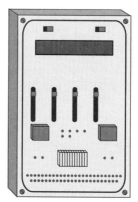

Cabling problems are nightmares for network managers. If the physical network plant isn't carefully documented, showing each cable and device connection, endless hours can be spent tracing wires around a room, or through a wiring harness. A detailed schematic of the network plant, along with a cable tester, will significantly reduce the amount of time spent troubleshooting cable malfunctions.

Cable testers

Cable testers are intended for checking continuity, opens, and shorts in network cabling.

Cable testers can be purchased that test twisted pair or coaxial. They can check each connection on a cable, and determine if the connection is open, continuous, or shorted. Depending on the type of tester, it may also check loop resistance, sheath continuity, insertion loss, or line impedance. The status of the cable is displayed by LEDs on most cable testers. Figure 14-4 is a picture of a cable tester.

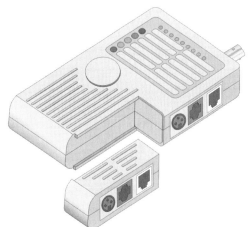

Figure 14-4: Cable Tester

Some cable testers are called **tone generators** because the indicate wire pairs in an 8-pair UTP by issuing a tone, or with an audible indicating the wire by number. A typical application is a large run of CAT5 cabling that may include hundreds of wire-pairs. A tone generator can be set so that it will emit a tone when a pair is located. This process is called **tone locating**, or "fox-and-hound."

tone generators

tone locating

Another very useful cable tester uses time-domain reflectometry (TDR). A TDR is used to locate cable breaks by working from only one end of a suspect cable. The principle behind the technology is to send a short pulse with a very fast rise-time through one end of the connection. At a cable break, the pulse will reflect due to a mismatch in impedance created by the break. When the reflected pulse is received back by the TDR, it converts the time between sending the pulse and the time to receive the echo to inches (or feet, meters, etc.). The accuracy of TDR is very good—within a half inch over several feet of wire to within a thousand feet over 50,000 feet of wire. As you may suspect, accuracy decreases for longer cable runs.

> Data and protocol analyzers identify protocol types, transmission speed, and the size of messages.

Data analyzers and **protocol analyzers** are sophisticated diagnostic tools, appropriate for networks in which data may be flowing in a variety of formats. For example, they may be helpful in large networks where a group of LANs are interconnected by a WAN. A data analyzer generally identifies transmission speed, type of protocol, and the number of bits in each character. A protocol analyzer identifies, and decodes, the network protocol. Protocol analyzers are available to identify most common protocols—SDLC, HDLC, X.25, BSC, and Ethernet. The analyzer decodes the protocol into easy-to-understand mnemonics. The mnemonics are displayed on a CRT. Some protocol analyzers allow the operator to display the decoded protocol in ASCII, EBCDIC, or hex. A data analyzer is pictured in Figure 14-5.

Data analyzers

protocol analyzers

While protocol analyzers may be a physical piece of test equipment, they're frequently software entities. Network Monitor and Performance Monitor, both used with Windows NT, are examples. They have the advantage of displaying network-related information in both real-time (as it occurs) and in recorded-time (in a log file to be viewed at a later date).

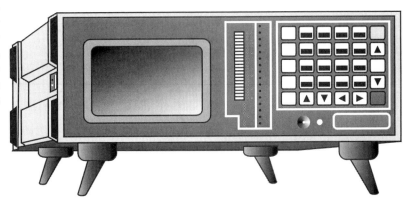

Figure 14-5: Data Analyzer

You shouldn't underestimate the value of an old standby troubleshooting tool—the oscilloscope. While a protocol analyzer shows data in binary or hexadecimal, an oscilloscope cab be used to check the integrity of the data against noise. For example, the scope can be used to view spikes on a data stream that couldn't be viewed with many protocol analyzers.

A **crossover cable** is used to directly connect two workstations.

A crossover cable may be necessary to troubleshoot NICs or hub ports. A crossover allows you to directly connect two stations, without a hub. Figure 14-6 shows an illustration of a crossover cable. Notice that pairs must remain consistent—RX+ and TX+ as a connection, for example. A crossover is merely a means of connecting the proper transmit pins of one NIC card to the corresponding receive pins of another NIC card, and vice versa.

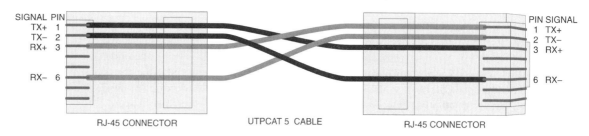

Figure 14-6: Crossover Cable

If two clients are connected together without a crossover, they will invariable collide when they both attempt to transmit at the same time. One may eventually gain access, but it won't last, because the other station will simply try again. Eventually, the link will crash.

A crossover cable is needed to connect two personal computers or two hubs. A connection from a NIC card in a PC to a hub port doesn't need a crossover since the crossover is made internally in the hub. For this connection, use straight-through pinning (pin 1 on one end of the cable connected to pin 1 on the other end of the cable, etc.).

In the absence of markings on a hub port, it's usually safe to assume that the crossover is handled by the hub. **However, check the hub documentation to make sure.** One or more ports are often switchable so you can use the internal crossover, or remove it to connect hubs together. The markings are as follows:

- *MDI: Media Dependent Interface*, allows you to use the port for connecting the hub to another hub using crossover pinning. Straight-through pinning can be used if the other hub performs the crossover function.

- *MDI-X: Media Independent Interface-Crossover*, when engaged, allows you to use the port for connecting to a NIC card in a PC (or similar device) using straight-through pinning. The hub performs the crossover function.

A punchdown is used to press connectors into a punchdown box. The punchdown box is typically used as an interconnection in a room that connects back to a hub in a secure closet. A punchdown provides straight-through pinning and is a convenience for centralizing connections in a room or small area.

A crimper tool is used to attach connectors to cable. The connectors are typically RJ-45 for network connections, and RJ-11 for telephone connections. A crimper may strip insulation from the wires and affix the connector, or it may be a simpler tool that only attaches the connector to the wire.

PERFORMANCE MANAGEMENT

Performance management is a means of objectively qualifying the performance of a network. When users complain, for example, that the network is slow, a tool is needed to define what "slow" means. The concepts presented in this section should lend some insight into how to do so.

> The performance management function is responsible for collecting analytical and empirical data for analyzing the integrity and efficiency of the network.

The purpose of performance management is to analyze the network's operational effectiveness. Generally, this involves evaluating the degree of network utilization, delays that messages encounter enroute to the destination, and the **throughput** of the network. Throughput describes the actual amount of data transmitted in a stated period of time.

Measurements are meaningless without agreed-upon evaluation criteria. For example, throughput is measured in bits for LANs, but in data packets or frames for WANs. Before analyzing the performance of the network, the evaluation criteria must be developed. Once this is done, there must be agreement on the point, or threshold, at which the performance information is considered to be significant. The utilization of a network is measured by considering the ratio of how much time a network is actually used to the time that services are available to users. It's stated as a percentage. One LAN may have a utilization rate of 50%, but another may have a 75% utilization rate. Network managers must determine the **thresholds of performance** parameters, as well as establish the specifics of the evaluation criteria. These are set by default in the software, and are user-selectable.

Once the evaluation thresholds have been set, performance information and statistics are collected in a database, which contains current and historical information. Current statistics advise the operators of problems that are occurring, or are about to occur. Once the thresholds are exceeded, the fault-management functions take over in dealing with the problem.

The historical database is maintained so that long-term trends can be analyzed. If, over a period of months, it appears as if the waiting time of transmitted messages is high compared to the total number of messages (system < response time), then network operators can fine-tune the network so that users will spend less time waiting for the services to be completed. The initialization for modifying network components (which is the job of the configuration function) is begun in performance management. The example given earlier of improving the system response rate is a case in point. The performance data has revealed a need to improve the rate, and informs the configuration function. The configuration management implements the needed changes.

The performance management features supported by network management vendors varies a great deal. **Trend analysis** based upon current and historical data is common. User-selectable thresholds, and evaluation parameters, are generally available. Some vendors supply reports of system anomalies. For example, such a report might mention short-term but recurring events, such as an increase in collisions when many users are using the same service. Reports available from the performance database are organized in units of time in most of the software—daily, weekly, monthly, etc.

The realization of performance requirements is a practice in predictability. The common technique for predicting network performance, and then measuring the performance, is based on performance models. A model is a method of analyzing the behavior of a network, and all network management tools make use of it. There are three primary network models used in evaluating performance: analytical models, simulation models, and empirical models. The analytical approach emphasizes average values in a system. Simulation models are developed on desktop PCs. The network is created in the PC, and analyzed without actually constructing the network. An empirical model is developed by analyzing events as they actually occur.

Simulation models

- **Simulation models** are typically of use in the design stage of a network. The network can be studied to see how it performs under varying loads, topology changes, hardware additions, and so forth. Simulations can also be helpful in evaluating long-term trends.

Analytical models

- **Analytical models** for studying network performance are commonly incorporated into network management software, and maintained in the database as a performance function. They form the base for historical data.

empirical model

- An **empirical model** is the ultimate in accuracy, since data is extracted from the system as it occurs. In performance management, the techniques of empirical modeling are applied in creating a database of current data.

The majority of data available to network managers is compiled by using the analytical and empirical methods. As mentioned earlier, network performance functions are clustered around network utilization, delays, and throughput. The following sections delineate common types of data available in these three areas. Keep in mind that the information has, at its source, a modeling approach, and as such, is suggesting intelligent and informed guesses.

Network Utilization

Network utilization should be concerned with the degree by which the network is being used. The common-sense reason is to determine whether the system is capable of delivering the services expected of it. Or, the network may be endowed with services that are seldom used, and hence, not needed.

Response time

Utilization, workload, and response times are interrelated. If all network components (computers, printers, modems, etc.) are engaged, the utilization will be high. Since the components are being used, the network services are in high demand. When the load on a network increases, response time is slower. **Response time** refers to the time it takes to complete a service.

Response time from a user's view is quite subjective. However, if there's a consensus that the network is "slow" during times of heavy use, the network manager will be expected to do something about it.

Network utilization is the ratio of the time a network is used to the total time it's available, or:

$$U = TB/T$$

where U = utilization expressed as a percentage, TB = the time that the network is busy, and T = the total time that the network is available.

If a LAN is available for use eight hours a day, and it's used six hours a day, the utilization is found by:

$$U = 6/8 = 75\%$$

Network availability is the amount of time the network services are available to users.

Closely related to utilization is the amount of time the network services are available. Availability considers components or services that aren't available and provides the network manager with insight to the time spent on network maintenance. Availability is found by:

$$A = (T - TD)/T$$

where A = availability expressed as a percentage, TD = time the network is down, and T = the total time that is available to use the network.

As an example, consider a LAN that's available for 10 hours, but a file server is taken down for maintenance for 1 hour. The time the network is available is found by:

$$A = (10 - 1)/10 = 90\%$$

This tells the network operator that on this particular day the network was available for 90% of the day. If this data is collected daily, a pattern will eventually emerge in which the manager can develop network reliability reports.

If, in the above example, a single PC were to fail for an hour in addition to the file server, is the network "down" for the hour it took to fix the PC? The answer is considered to be yes, because without the PC, the network is unable to provide the full range of services it was intended to provide. The availability is now determined as:

$$A = (10 - 2)/10 = 80\%$$

Network utilization is an indication of the demands for the network's services, and network availability describes the amount of time users can receive access to the network's services. But how does a network manager know if the users are receiving the full benefit of the services? One way is to track the **system service time**.

System service time is the average amount of time a message spends in the system enroute to its destination. It is calculated by:

$$S = B/C$$

where S = system service time, B = busy time, and C = the number of completed messages.

Imagine a LAN in which data is transmitted at 1 kbps. Ideally, a message could be sent in 1 ms (T = 1/bps = 1/1000 = 1 ms). In reality, the message contains overhead characters, network devices require time to add and strip the overhead, search files, and so forth. Let's assume that these miscellaneous tasks require 2 ms, so the total amount of time the network is busy is 1 ms + 2 ms = 3 ms. Now, we'll calculate the system service time.

$$S = 3 \text{ ms}/1000$$
$$S = .3 \text{ ms}$$

If the service time is calculated for the ideal LAN, it's:

$$S = 1 \text{ ms}/1000$$
$$S = .1 \text{ ms}$$

Not surprisingly, the amount of time a message spends in the system is higher when machine delays are considered. As more messages are transmitted, so that the network utilization increases, the delays become more pronounced. Rather than increase linearly as the service time formula suggests, there's a nonlinear increase, as shown in Figure 14-7.

**Figure 14-7:
System Service Time vs.
Message Load**

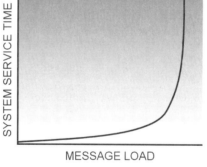

MESSAGE LOAD

The graph shows that as the number of network messages increases, the longer it will take to service each message. A point is reached where the delays increase sharply, and the network is said to contain a **bottleneck**. The performance function tracks the system service time so that when the bottleneck threshold approaches, an alarm is set that initiates fault management to issue interrupts.

Delays

Delays in a network cripple efficiency. The lower the efficiency, the poorer the performance. The network media, software, buffers, memory capacity, and the time needed to read and write files are all examples of network delays. Consider a network in which five users send files to a printer. The printer can print only one file at a time, so a line, or queue, is formed. For those files waiting in the printer queue, delays are introduced on the network.

Throughput describes the number of delivered messages when delays are considered.

The most commonly quoted indication of a network's delay characteristic is **throughput**. Throughput is the actual number of messages sent in a given time. It's calculated by:

throughput

$$TP = C/T$$

where TP = throughput, C = the number of messages sent, and T = the total time of the transmission.

The benefits of measuring throughput can be oblique. As in an earlier example, consider a network with a data rate of 1 kbps. Again, the time to transmit a single bit is 1 ms. But suppose we're sending 7-bit ASCII characters with 1 start bit, 1 stop bit, and 1 parity bit. Then, one character contains 10 bits. Our 1 kbps data stream has 100 characters (1000/10 = 100). The time needed to transmit one hundred 10-bit characters is 100×1 ms = 1 s. If there were no delays in the network, 100 characters could be transmitted in 1 second.

In fact, there are delays. Assume these delays consume 1.5 s. The total time of the transmission is 1 s + 1.5 s = 2.5 seconds.

$$TP = 100/2.5$$
$$TP = 40$$

The throughput is 40 characters/second rather than the transmitted rate of 100 characters/second.

The throughput rate represents an average of the ideal transmitted time (called **burst rate**) and the **delay time**. It's a very good performance indicator to consider when vendor literature places so much emphasis on network speed. A network may be capable of very high data rates, but if the delays are also high, the throughput will be low. Throughput is a much more meaningful tool for analyzing the system's response time for delivering services to users.

burst rate

delay time

Response time is the time required to deliver a message.

Response time is actually the reciprocal of throughput. As throughput describes the messages that arrive as a function of system delays, response time describes how much time is consumed in delivering a message. Mathematically, it's stated:

$$R = T/C$$

where R = response time, T = total time messages are required to wait in the network, and C = total completed messages.

The performance software will generally determine how much time messages wait in **queues** by averaging the length of all queues in a network. It's determined by:

queues

$$Q = W/T$$

where Q = average queue length, W = total time messages wait in a system, and T = total time of a message run.

objective data

subjective
information

The ultimate justification of performance management is to maximize network resources. The LAN manager has analytical and empirical data available in the performance database to draw conclusions about the performance. This is **objective data**.

Equally important is **subjective information**, particularly the complaints of users. It is the network users who are employing the resources of the network. The users' lack of technical understanding of the network results in vague, nonspecific observations of the tools they're working with.

In addition to interpreting performance database information and user concerns, the LAN manager should possess a thorough understanding of all aspects of the network environment. If the network delays are excessive due to heavy loading, should the network be taken apart and reassembled in a different topology? Is the problem in the twisted-pair transmission media, and is it time to upgrade to coax cable? Is the file server inadequate? Strong technical competencies of network managers provide intuitive insight to solutions that should ensure that the network resources are maximized.

KEY POINTS REVIEW

An overview of network troubleshooting strategies has been presented in this chapter.

- To determine the extent of network problem:

    1. Determine whether the entire network is affected.

    2. Localize the extent of the problem to an area of the network.

    3. Attempt to duplicate the problem.

    4. Apply proven troubleshooting techniques.

- The steps used in the CompTIA troubleshooting approach are:

    1. Establish the symptoms.

    2. Identify the affected area.

    3. Establish what has changed.

    4. Select the most probable cause.

    5. Implement the solution.

    6. Test the result.

    7. Recognize the potential effects of the solution.

    8. Document the solution.

- The following steps are used to resolve operator versus system problems:

    1. Identify the exact issue.

    2. Re-create the problem on either a mock network or isolated and unaffected nodes.

    3. Isolate the cause of the problem.

    4. Formulate a correction.

    5. Implement the correction.

    6. Test the correction.

    7. Document the problem and the solution.

    8. Give feedback.

- Typically, SOHO failures involve workstation and remote access problems.

- Remote connectivity problems typically involve physical, configuration, or authentication problems.

- Nearly all hardware devices have some type of light to indicate basic functions.

- Physical and logical connectivity refers to the hardware, cabling, connectors, and protocols running on a network.

- A wide range of test equipment is available to network technicians to troubleshoot network problems.

- Performance management is a means of objectively qualifying the performance of a network.

REVIEW QUESTIONS

The following questions test your knowledge of the material presented in this chapter:

1. To determine whether wires are shorted in a CAT5 cable with RJ-45 connectors, which piece of test equipment is used?

2. What is the purpose of a crossover cable?

3. A software program can't be loaded to a client across the network. It loads to all other clients, however. The cabling to the client checks out. What should be done next?

4. You receive calls from numerous users on a single LAN that their server is running very slowly. Where is the first place to look for information?

5. A user complains that he can't log in to the server. When another user tries the login at a different workstation, he is able to log in. What should you do next?

6. You've determined that a network-wide problem is centered at the hub. What is your next step?

7. In researching a login problem, you've determined that it affects all users in a single workgroup. What is the next step in identifying the extent of the problem?

8. What is a hardware loopback?

9. Describe how link lights can be an indicator of a problem.

10. List each of the eight steps that CompTIA recommends.

11. Describe how EMI can affect wire-based networks.

12. Why is it important to document proven solutions to network problems?

13. What is a TDR tester?

14. What is the purpose of a BERT tester?

15. What type of network infrastructure will be immune from noise generated by motors and generators?

1. A hub port is marked MDI-X. What does this mean?
   a. The port is unavailable.
   b. A crossover cable is required at the port.
   c. A coaxial cable is required at the port.
   d. A separate transceiver is required at the port.

2. A workstation NIC link light isn't illuminated. After replacing the NIC, the light still isn't lit. What should be done next?
   a. Reboot the server.
   b. Replace the cable connecting the NIC to the hub.
   c. Replace the hub.
   d. Replace the workstation.

3. Which of the following are three steps used in a systematic approach for identifying the extent of network problems?
   a. Determine whether the problem exists across the network.
   b. Determine whether the problem is caused by the system or user.
   c. Determine whether the problem is workstation, workgroup, LAN, or WAN.
   d. Use standard troubleshooting methods.

4. Using the steps listed in the previous question, select the next step after considering the following scenario:

   > A user complains that he can't connect to a server. You check his level of access and determine that he has login rights to three different servers but only one is causing a problem. To determine whether the problem exists beyond this user, you check several other clients that have access to the server in question and determine that they aren't having problems.

   a. Determine whether the problem is consistent and replicable.
   b. Determine whether the problem exists across the network.
   c. Determine whether the problem is workstation, workgroup, LAN, or WAN.
   d. Use standard troubleshooting methods.

5. Which of the following represent the first two steps used to troubleshoot network problems?
   a. Establish the systems.
   b. Re-create the problem.
   c. Identify the affected area.
   d. Formulate a correction.

6. You receive a call that the printer on a network isn't working. After confirming that all users sharing the printer are experiencing the same symptom, you attempt to re-create it by setting up a share from your computer. The results are consistent in that the printer won't print a test file you sent. What is the next step?
   a. Formulate a correction.
   b. Re-create the problem.
   c. Identify the affected area.
   d. Isolate the cause.

7. Which of the following represent three steps used as a systematic approach to determining whether a problem is attributable to the operator or the system?
   a. Have a second operator perform the task on another workstation.
   b. Have a second operator perform the task on the original workstation.
   c. Determine whether operators are following standard operating procedures.
   d. Formulate a correction.

8. A user complains of connectivity problems to the server and other members of his workgroup. You have him ping the local server but he doesn't receive a response. Thinking he may be entering the ping IP incorrectly, you ask him to have another operator enter the ping IP at a second workstation. The ping echoes the correct response. What is the next step?
   a. Have a second operator perform the task on another workstation.
   b. Have a second operator perform the task on the original workstation.
   c. Determine whether operators are following standard operating procedures.
   d. Formulate a correction.

9. Determine response time for a network in which 500 test messages were delivered in 2 seconds.
   a. 4 seconds
   b. .4 second
   c. .04 second
   d. .004 second

10. What is the value of NIC card LEDs?
    a. They tell you whether the network is operational.
    b. They are a good indicator of the status of a router.
    c. They tell you whether the workstation system board is working.
    d. They tell you whether the NIC is sending and receiving.

NETWORK+ OBJECTIVE MAP

The Network+ certification, covering the 2002 objectives, certifies that the successful candidates knows the layers of the OSI model, can describe the features and functions of network components, and has the skills needed to install, configure, and troubleshoot basic networking hardware peripherals and protocols. A typical candidate should have A+ certification or equivalent knowledge, but A+ certification is not required. In addition to A+ certification level knowledge, candidates are encouraged to have at least 9 months of experience in network support or administration.

The 2002 objectives update the Network+ certification exam on new technologies such as wireless networking and gigabit Ethernet. The scope of networking systems are broadened somewhat by placing an increased emphasis on Linux/UNIX, Windows 9x, Windows NT, and Windows 2000 and including AppleTalk as a network protocol. There is also more of an emphasis on hands-on experience needed in the areas of network implementation and network support, including troubleshooting scenarios.

The CompTIA organization has established the following objectives for the Network+ Certification exam.

DOMAIN 1.0 MEDIA AND TOPOLOGIES

The topics covered by this domain are approximately 20% of the questions in the Network+ Certification exam. This domain requires the ability to apply knowledge relating to network topologies. The ability to specify network characteristics, media type and connectors, and network components is also required.

1.1 Recognize the following logical or physical network topologies given a schematic diagram or description.

- Star/hierarchical - Chapter 1

- Bus - Chapter 1, Lab Procedure 2

- Mesh - Chapter 1

- Ring - Chapter 1

- Wireless - Chapter 1

1.2 Specify the main features of 802.2 (LLC), 802.3 (Ethernet), 802.5 (Token Ring), 802.11b (wireless), and FDDI networking technologies, including the following.

- Speed - Chapter 1, Lab Procedure 6

- Access - Chapter 1

- Method - Chapter 1

- Topology - Chapter 1

- Media - Chapter 1, Lab Procedure 3

1.3 Specify the characteristics (e.g., speed, length, topology, cable type, etc.) of the following.

- 802.3 (Ethernet) standards - Chapter 2

- 10BASE-T - Chapter 2

- 100BASE-TX - Chapter 2, Lab Procedure 3

- 10BASE-2 - Chapter 2

- 10BASE-5 - Chapter 2

- 100BASE-FX - Chapter 2

- Gigabit Ethernet - Chapter 2

1.4 Recognize the following media connectors and/or describe their uses.

- RJ-11 - Chapter 1

- RJ-45 - Chapter 1, Lab Procedure 3

- AUI - Chapter 1

- BNC - Chapter 1

- ST - Chapter 1

- SC - Chapter 1

1.5 Choose the appropriate media type and connectors to add a client to an existing network. - Chapter 1, Lab Procedure 11

1.6 Identify the purpose, features, and functions of the following network components.

- Hubs - Chapter 3, Lab Procedures 9 & 22

- Switches - Chapter 3, Lab Procedures 9 & 22

- Bridges - Chapter 3

- Routers - Chapters 3 and 5, Lab Procedures 25, 26, & 27

- Gateways - Chapters 3 and 5

- CSU/DSU - Chapter 3

- Network Interface Cards/ISDN adapters/system area network cards - Chapter 3, Lab Procedure 7

- Wireless access points - Chapter 3

- Modems - Chapter 3, Lab Procedures 4 & 5

DOMAIN 2.0 PROTOCOLS AND STANDARDS

The topics covered by this domain are approximately 25% of the questions in the Network+ Certification exam. This domain requires the ability to identify layers of the OSI model. Also, knowledge of protocols, routing, addressing, interoperability, and naming conventions is important. This domain also requires the ability to work with different protocols within TCP/IP and the ability to apply knowledge relating to network services, subnetting, gateways, public networks, private networks, WAN technologies, remote access protocols, and security protocols.

2.1 Given an example, identify a MAC address. - Chapter 2

2.2 Identify the seven layers of the OSI model and their functions. - Chapters 4 and 11

2.3 Differentiate between the following network protocols in terms of routing, addressing schemes, interoperability, and naming conventions.

- TCP/IP - Chapter 5

- IPX/SPX - Chapter 5

- NetBEUI - Chapter 5

- AppleTalk - Chapter 5

2.4 Identify the OSI layers at which the following network components operate.

- Hubs - Chapter 4, Lab Procedures 9 & 22

- Switches - Chapter 4, Lab Procedures 9 & 22

- Bridges - Chapter 4

- Routers - Chapter 4, Lab Procedures 25, 26, & 27

- Network Interface Cards - Chapter 4

2.5 Define the purpose, function, and/or use of the following protocols within TCP/IP.

- IP - Chapter 5

- TCP - Chapter 5

- UDP - Chapter 5

- FTP - Chapter 5

- TFTP - Chapter 5

- SMTP - Chapter 5

- HTTP - Chapter 5

- HTTPS - Chapter 5

- POP3/IMAP4 - Chapter 5

- TELNET - Chapter 5

- ICMP - Chapter 5

- ARP - Chapter 5

- NTP - Chapter 5

2.6 Define the function of TCP/UDP ports. Identify well-known ports. - Chapter 5

2.7 Identify the purpose of the following network services (e.g., DHCP/bootp, DNS, NAT/ICS, WINS, and SNMP). - Chapter 8

2.8 Identify IP addresses (Ipv4, Ipv6) and their default subnet masks. - Chapter 5

2.9 Identify the purpose of subnetting and default gateways. - Chapter 10

2.10 Identify the differences between public vs. private networks. - Chapter 5

2.11 Identify the basic characteristics (e.g., speed, capacity, media) of the following WAN technologies.

- Packet switching vs. circuit switching - Chapter 9
- ISDN - Chapter 9
- FDDI - Chapters 2 & 9
- ATM - Chapter 9
- Frame Relay - Chapter 9
- Sonet/SDH - Chapter 9
- T1/E1- Chapter 9
- T3/E3 - Chapter 9
- Ocx - Chapter 9

2.12 Define the function of the following remote access protocols and services.

- RAS - Chapter 7
- PPP - Chapter 7
- PPTP - Chapter 7
- ICA - Chapter 7

2.13 Identify the following security protocols and describe their purpose and function.

- IPsec - Chapter 7
- L2TP - Chapter 7
- SSL - Chapter 7
- Kerberos - Chapter 7

DOMAIN 3.0 NETWORK IMPLEMENTATION

The topics covered by this domain are approximately 23% of the questions in the Network+ Certification exam. This domain requires the ability to apply knowledge relating to server operating systems, client operating systems, VLANs, attached storage, fault tolerance, and disaster recovery. The ability to configure a connection in a given situation is required. The outcomes also include identifying the properties of a firewall and proxy.

3.1 Identify the basic capabilities (i.e., client support, interoperability, authentication, file and print services, application support, and security) of the following server operating systems. - Chapter 10

- UNIX/Linux

- NetWare - Chapter 10, Lab Procedures 23 & 24

- Windows - Chapter 10, Lab Procedures 8 & 20

- Macintosh

3.2 Identify the basic capabilities of client workstations (i.e., client connectivity, local security mechanisms, and authentication). - Chapter 10, Lab Procedures 10 & 12

3.3 Identify the main characteristics of VLANs. - Chapter 10

3.4 Identify the main characteristics of network attached storage. - Chapter 13

3.5 Identify the purpose and characteristics of fault tolerance. - Chapter 13

3.6 Identify the purpose and characteristics of disaster recovery - Chapter 13

3.7 Given a remote connectivity scenario (e.g., IP, IPX, dial-up, PPPoE, authentication, physical connectivity, etc.), configure the connection. - Chapter 10, Lab Procedure 13

3.8 Identify the purpose, benefits, and characteristics of using a firewall. - Chapter 13

3.9 Identify the purpose, benefits, and characteristics of using a proxy. - Chapter 13

3.10 Given a scenario, predict the impact of a particular security implementation on network functionality (e.g., blocking port numbers, encryption, etc.). - Chapter 13

3.11 Given a network configuration, select the appropriate NIC and network configuration settings (DHCP, DNS, WINS, protocols, NETBIOS/host name, etc.). - Chapter 10, Lab Procedure 33

DOMAIN 4.0 NETWORK SUPPORT

The topics covered by this domain are approximately 32% of the questions in the Network+ Certification exam. This domain requires the ability to apply knowledge relating to TCP/IP utilities, identifying problems and failures. The ability to configure clients and servers is required. This domain also requires the ability to implement wiring and diagnostic tools. An understanding of troubleshooting network problems is also required.

4.1 Given a troubleshooting scenario, select the appropriate TCP/IP utility from among the following:

- Tracert - Chapter 6, Lab Procedure 34

- Ping - Chapter 6, Lab Procedure 34

- ARP - Chapter 6, Lab Procedure 34

- Netstat - Chapter 6, Lab Procedure 34

- Nbtstat - Chapter 6, Lab Procedure 34

- Ipconfig/Ifconfig - Chapter 6, Lab Procedure 34

- Winipcfg - Chapter 6, Lab Procedure 34

- Nslookup - Chapter 6, Lab Procedure 34

4.2 Given a troubleshooting scenario involving a small office/home office network failure (e.g., xDSL, cable, home satellite, wireless, POTS), identify the cause of the failure. - Chapter 14

4.3 Given a troubleshooting scenario involving a remote connectivity problem (e.g., authentication failure, protocol configuration, physical connectivity) identify the cause of the problem. - Chapter 14, Lab Procedure 19

4.4 Given specific parameters, configure a client to connect to the following servers.

- UNIX/Linux

- NetWare

- Windows - Chapter 10, Lab Procedures 12, 14, 15, 16, 17, 18, 20, & 23

- Macintosh

4.5 Given a wiring task, select the appropriate tool (e.g., wire crimper, media tester/certifier, punch down tool, tone generator, optical tester, etc.). - Chapter 14

4.6 Given a network scenario, interpret visual indicators (e.g., link lights, collision lights, etc.) to determine the nature of the problem. - Chapter 14, Lab Procedure 9

4.7 Given output from a diagnostic utility (e.g., tracert, ping, ipconfig, etc.), identify the utility and interpret the output. - Chapter 6

4.8 Given a scenario, predict the impact of modifying, adding, or removing network services (e.g., DHCP, DNS, WINS, etc.) on network resources and users. - Chapter 10

4.9 Given a network problem scenario, select an appropriate course of action based on a general troubleshooting strategy. This strategy includes the following steps:

1. Establish the symptoms. - Chapter 14

2. Identify the affected area. - Chapter 14

3. Establish what has changed. - Chapter 14

4. Select the most probable cause. - Chapter 14

5. Implement a solution. - Chapter 14

6. Test the result. - Chapter 14

7. Recognize the potential effects of the solution. - Chapter 14

8. Document the solution. - Chapter 14

4.10 Given a troubleshooting scenario involving a network with a particular physical topology (i.e., bus, star/hierarchical, mesh, ring, and wireless) and including a network diagram, identify the network area affected and the cause of the problem. - Chapter 14

4.11 Given a network troubleshooting scenario involving a client connectivity problem (e.g., incorrect protocol/client software/authentication configuration, or insufficient rights/permission), identify the cause of the problem. - Chapter 14 (see objective 3)

4.12 Given a network troubleshooting scenario involving a wiring/infrastructure problem, identify the cause of the problem (e.g., bad media, interference, network hardware). - Chapter 14

GLOSSARY

A

Access Protocols: The class of protocols in the LLC and MAC sublayers of the Data Link layer of the OSI reference model. Media-access protocols include CSMA/CD, CSMA/CA, Token Bus, and Token Ring.

Accounting Network Management: One of five ISO functions of network management; the cost-effectiveness of the network, tariff rates, and new equipment-needs analysis are among the areas included.

Active Satellite: A repeater satellite that includes amplifiers for increasing the signal strength before retransmitting it to an earth station.

Adaptive Equalization: The dynamic sampling and evaluation of data transmitted through the telephone network. An adaptive equalizer compensates for intersymbol interference as it occurs.

Address Resolution Protocol (ARP): A wide-area network routing protocol used to map the MAC addresses of nodes to logical network addresses.

Administrative Utilities: Tools for network managers to set up or change user accounts.

Algorithm: The steps used to solve a problem. Error-detection fields, such as cyclic redundancy checks, are organized under a specific algorithm.

Alternate Mark Inversion (AMI): A digital encoding technique used with long distance telephone systems. Logic 0's are represented with 0V, and logic 1's by alternating the channel voltage between +V and –V.

Amplitude Modulation (AM): A method of superimposing data on a carrier in which the carrier amplitude is directly proportional to the data amplitude, and the rate of carrier amplitude changes is directly proportional to the data frequency.

Analog Loopback Test: A test carrier generated by modems to simulate reception and detection of analog carriers.

Angle of Incidence: The angle at which light enters a fiber-optic cable.

Angle of Inclination: The angle of a satellite's orbit, as referenced to the equator.

Answer Modem: The modem receiving data from a transmitting modem. The answer modem responds on a specified answer channel.

Antenna: Antennas are used in the transmission and receiving of microwaves and other radio waves. A satellite contains separate transmit and receive antennas, as well as a telemetry antenna for communicating with the ground control station.

Anti-Tinkle and Speech Muting: The section of a telephone responsible for preventing high-voltage spikes from entering the speech circuitry.

Antivirus Software: Software used to detect and/ or clean known computer viruses.

Apogee: The end of an ellipse orbit of a satellite furthest from the center of the Earth.

Apogee Thruster: A small thruster mounted on the body of satellites that ensures the satellite can be moved and remain in its orbit.

Application Layer: Layer 7 of the OSI Reference Model. The only layer in which users have direct contact with the model, it's the user interface for initiating application software programs such as FTP or HTTP.

Approvals: Approvals are formal authorizations provided by a designated individual for certain activities. They are normally provided in the form of passwords and network access permissions, as well as standard operating procedures.

ASCII: A 7-bit terminal code capable of producing 128 unique characters.

Asynchronous: A transmission method that uses start and stop bits to separate frames. It is typically used with personal computers.

Asynchronous Balanced Mode (ABM): An alternative form of the asynchronous response mode for configuring HDLC exchanges. In the balanced mode, network stations are peers and may initiate as well as terminate exchanges.

Asynchronous Response Mode (ARM): One of two modes for configuring HDLC exchanges. In the ARM mode, stations retain the primary/secondary designation, but the secondaries may transmit without first receiving permission from the primary.

Asynchronous Transfer Mode (ATM): A fast packet service capable of carrying voice, data, and video.

Atmospheric Noise: Noise that is the result of lightning and sunspot activity. Atmospheric noise tends to distort large segments of data.

Attenuation: The undesirable weakening of a signal.

Attitude Stabilization: The process of properly positioning and orienting a satellite.

Automatic Gain Control: A modem circuit that provides a flat response of the received data.

B

Backbone: A primary network segment from which subnetworks branch off in a tree configuration.

Backoff Delay: The condition a transmitter enters following a collision on a CSMA/CD network. Backoff delays are variable, and may occur up to sixteen times before an error is generated.

Balancing Network: A telephone circuit connected across the hybrid that samples the caller's voice, and applies it to the receive circuit. This provides the voice feedback necessary for the caller to adjust the volume of his voice.

Bandwidth: A range of frequencies in which nodes transmit and receive data. Since channel capacity is directly proportional to bandwidth, large-bandwidth channels carry more information than narrow-bandwidth channels.

Baseband: Refers to networks that communicate without carriers. Generally, baseband networks transmit at data rates of less than 10 MHz.

Baseline: Statistical data that shows the normal operation of a network.

Baud Rate: The number of data symbols transmitted per second. Baud = bps/N, where bps is bits per second, and N is the number of bits per symbol.

Baudot: An older terminal code, commonly representing up to 32 characters with a 5-bit code.

Beamwidth: The physical size of a satellite's footprint on the Earth.

Best Effort Service: Refers to protocols—particularly internetworking protocols—in which errors are checked in the header, but not in the data field of the message.

Binary Synchronous Communication (BSC): A character-oriented protocol developed by IBM. The size of the data field varies, by multiples of eight, with 128 bytes being common.

Bit-Error Rates (BER): A measure of the bit errors per transmitted symbol.

Bit-Error Rate Tester: Network test equipment used to check for individual bit degradation.

Bit Interleaving: The system used with time-division multiplexing in transmitting channel data in alternating bits.

Bit-Level Protocol: A class of protocols in which synchronization between stations is achieved at the bit level. HDLC and SDLC are common bit protocols.

Bit Rate: The frequency of the data; also referred to as bits per second (bps).

Bit Stuffing: A method of achieving text transparency with HDLC, also called zero insertion. For any data stream in the information field containing six consecutive logic 1's, a 0 bit is inserted after the fifth bit. The inserted bit is removed at the receiver.

Block Character Check (BCC): A one- or two-byte error-detection field, associated with the BSC protocol frame, and based on longitudinal redundancy checks.

Block Cipher: A class of substitution ciphers in which blocks of plain text are replaced with cipher text taken from block-cipher dictionaries.

Bootp: The Bootstrap Protocol defines how to determine the IP of a diskless system when bootstrapped. It's used when an IP is assigned to a remote node from a server.

BORSCHT Functions: An acronym that describes the control, management, and use of the telephone system. BORSCHT stands for Battery, Overvoltage Protection, Ring trip, Supervision, Coding, Hybrid, and Testing.

Bottleneck: The critical point in which network message delays have increased until data flow is at a standstill.

Breakout Box: Network test equipment used for loopback tests, clock, and signal monitoring. Breakout boxes are connected in parallel with the cable under test.

Bridge: An internetworking machine that connects networks (LANs) of different access methods. Operating at the Data Link layer, it is independent of Network-layer protocols such as TCP/IP.

Bridge Protocol Data Units (BPDU): Encoded signals used with Spanning Tree Protocol that specify the configuration of the topology or serve notice that the topology will change.

Broadband: A method of transmitting in which the data modulates a carrier frequency. Typically, broadband networks operate in excess of 10 MHz.

Brouter: A bridge/ router is used to interconnect LANs at the local level, as well as route packets to different network addresses.

Browse: Refers to read-only access to files.

Buffer Overflow: A condition in which the temporary storage of a receiver, i.e., multiplexer, receives more data than space exists to store it.

Buffer Pools: A method of organizing multiplexer memory. All terminals compete for storage space.

Bus Topology: The most common method of arranging network nodes, a network bus is characterized by the use of a network interface for connecting each station to the bus.

Busy Signal: A telephone signal indicating the called number is occupied. A busy signal consists of a dual tone of 480+620 Hz, 2 seconds on, and .5 second off.

C

Cable Labeling Conventions: A scheme used to label the entry and exit points of network cable, that can be resolved to the attached device.

Cable Tester: Network test equipment used to check cables for opens, shorts, and continuity.

Callback: A data security measure in which a host computer calls the modem of a station user who has initiated a network sign-on. If the dialed modem responds as expected, the station is assumed to be in a valid location.

Carrier Recover: The section of a modem that aids in calculating the amount of phase distortion in a received signal.

Carrier-Sense Multiple Access/Collision Detect (CSMA/CD): The IEEE 802.3 standard for bus networks, based upon the original Ethernet, and functionally the same.

Carson's Rule: A method of calculating bandwidth of an FM signal. BW= $2(\Delta F_c + F_m)$, where F_c is the deviation produced by the modulating signal, and F_m is the modulating signal frequency.

Central Office: The central point where all telephones within an exchange are connected. Each office can serve up to 10,000 subscribers.

Centralized Network: A network in which control and management of the network lies in a central computer. The attached workstations are forbidden to make changes to the network. LANs with a file server are centralized networks.

Channel Bank: The equipment needed to combine the channels of T-carrier facilities, referred to as digital banks.

CHAP: Challenge Handshake Authentication Protocol, used with PPP. The server generates a random string of bits and sends them, along with its hostname, to the client.

Character-Level Protocol: A class of protocols in which synchronization between stations is achieved with data characters. BSC is an example.

Character Stuffing: The method used with BSC for achieving text transparency. Within the frame, all control characters are preceded by DLE. In the data field, any character similar to a control character is prefaced with two DLE characters. The additional characters are removed at the receiver.

Characteristic Impedance: The value of pure resistance that a cable is to be terminated with in order to transfer the maximum amount of signal strength to a load. It is dependent upon the effective capacitance and inductance of the cable, and is calculated by: Z_o = the square root of the inductance, divided by the capacitance of the cable.

Cheapernet: A term describing 10Base-2 type LANs, using RG-58 coaxial cable.

Cipher text: Encrypted plain text.

Circular Orbit: Geosynchronous orbit, located 23,280 miles above the Earth.

Cladding: The portion of a fiber-optic cable encircling the core material.

Class-A IP Address: The first three digits of Class-A networks are numbered 1-126.

Class-B IP Address: The first three digits of Class-B networks are numbered 128 through 191.

Class-C IP Address: The first three digits of Class-C networks are numbered 192 through 223.

Clear-to-Send (CTS): An RS-232C signaling pin, initiated upon completion of the modem training time.

Client Configuration Documentation: Set of data that describes configuration parameters of a workstations. It includes IP, COM port assignments, IRQ assignments, amount of RAM, type of CPU, as well as other information pertinent to the operation and interface of the client.

Coaxial: A transmission cable consisting of two conductors insulated from one another, and enclosed in a polyethylene jacket.

Code Violation: Indicates that the bit transitions on a CSMA/CD network are too long or too short. This occurs when there's a collision between stations.

Collision Window: The first 464 bits of data transmitted on a CSMA/CD network. If there is to be a collision, it will occur within this window.

Command Assembly: The section of a satellite responsible for monitoring factors that may affect the satellite's operation, as well as providing management of the other sections.

Command State: The condition noted by a modem detecting a dial tone on the telephone circuit.

Compander: A compressor/expander used in the PCM encoding process that ensures both small- and large-amplitude signals will produce an identical coding change.

Concentrator: A network device that serves as an interface between stations, particularly in situations in which networks may be interconnected by a backbone.

Conditioned Lines: Fee-based telephone data channels that contain specific phase-delay and signal-attenuation characteristics.

Configuration Network Management: One of five ISO functions for network management; includes the physical architecture, selection of hardware, protocols, interface and access methods, and the level of service provided to users.

Congestion Signal: A telephone signal indicating a busy network. The congestion signal is a dual 480+620-Hz tone that's on for .2 second, and off for .3 second.

Connection-oriented Transport: A protocol that assigns sequence numbers to frames passed into the LLC, and tracks them at the receiving node. At the Data Link layer, it's the same as Type II LLC.

Connectionless Transport: A protocol that doesn't track the sequence of frames or packets of frames. A connectionless service, at the Data Link layer, is Type I LLC. See Connection-oriented Transport.

Consultative Committee for International Telephony (CCITT): An international standards organization responsible for developing the telecommunications standards.

Contention-based Systems: A general term describing CSMA/CD-type networks, in which stations vie for access to the network. Ethernet is a contention-based protocol.

Conversion Time: The time required for an analog-to-digital converter to reach full-scale resolution.

Convolutional Coding: Refers to error-detection schemes noted for the use of continuous feedback in producing the error-detection field of data frames. An example is cyclic redundancy checks.

Core: The center part of a fiber-optic cable that carries data in the form of light, and is constructed of glass or plastic.

Critical Angle: The angle at which light propagates along the core of a fiber-optic cable.

Crosslink: A satellite-to-satellite communication path for transmission in the Geosynchronous orbit.

Crossover Cable: A cable used to directly connect two computers, or hubs, in which the receive and transmit wires of a twisted pair, or other cable, have been reversed.

Crosstalk: Electromagnetic distortion resulting from two conductors, lying in close proximity, in a parallel plane. Crosstalk is generally associated with twisted-pair cables.

Cryptography: The process of writing secret messages so that the intelligence of the message is hidden.

Cyclic Redundancy Check (CRC): A widely used error-detection technique, based upon convolutional coding of the data stream.

D

Data Analyzer: Network test equipment used to identify data rates, protocol types, and number of bits in each character.

Data-Communication Equipment (DCE): Any device directly involved in transmitting and receiving data. Examples are modems and multiplexers.

Data Compression: The process of encoding data so that the data is transmitted with fewer bits. Examples of data-compression techniques are the Huffman and Dictionary methods.

Data-Encryption Standard Cipher (DES): The official encryption technique of the National Bureau of Standards. The DES is based on a 56-bit key from which sixteen 48-bit keys are derived to encrypt 64-bit blocks of plain text.

Data Link Layer: Layer 2 of the OSI Reference Model. The Data Link layer provides for point-to-point exchanges between network nodes. Frame formatting, error control, and access to the network are functions of the Data Link layer.

Data Rate: The frequency at which information is transmitted across a communication channel.

Data Set Ready (DSR): An RS-232C pin that, when initiated, tells the host DTE that the connection between two modems is active.

Data-Signal Rate Selector (DSRS): Designated as pin 23 on the RS-232C interface, it is used in modems that have the ability to automatically shift to varying data rates.

Data Terminal Equipment (DTE): Any device whose primary purpose is the manipulation of data. Examples are computers and terminals.

Data Terminal Ready (DTR): An RS-232C interface pin initiated by the answer DTE to indicate it will accept an incoming call.

Database: A large collection of similar data, usually stored in a host computer.

Datagram: The unit of measure of a TCP/IP transmission; it consists of a maximum of 65,535 bytes.

DC Shift: The gradual build-up of voltage, caused by the capacitive and inductive reactance of transmission cables.

Decibel: The standard criteria for evaluating the distortion performance of signal quality. The common method for evaluating power losses, and gains, is with the formula: $dB = 10\log (P_o/P_i)$.

Decimal Dotted Notation: The process of dividing the 32-bit TCP/IP addresses into four 8-bit groups. The groups are separated by a decimal point, and expressed in base ten.

Decryption: The process of recovering the intelligence from encrypted data.

Default Gateway: The term is taken literally to mean a "gateway to other networks," and not as a device that performs protocol conversions. In this context, it's the same as a router. See Gateway.

Delay: Refers to frequency or phase delays in data transmission that are undesirable.

Delta Modulation: A variation of pulse-code modulation. The DM output consists of positive and negative pulses that correspond to the quantized amplitude variations.

Demand Assignment Multiple Access (DAMA): A method of configuring TDM or FDM for satellites, in which channels are made available on an as-needed, or demand, basis.

Descrambler: A section of a modem responsible for removing the scrambling algorithm initiated at the transmitting modem.

Despin Axis: A device connected to the antennas of a satellite, that keeps the antennas pointed at a fixed position on the Earth.

Despin Rotor: A device that permits satellite antennas to be adjusted, so as to point to a desired ground location.

Detect and Fix: A technique for balancing the workload among network stations; it's characterized by a historical orientation, in that the problem is corrected after it's been identified.

Dial Tone: The telephone dial tone that originates from a 350/440-Hz oscillator at the local office.

Dictionary Concentrator: A data-compression technique that establishes unique bit patterns, based upon the content of the data to be transmitted.

Differential Phase-Shift Keying (DPSK): A modulation method used in modems, in which the symbol phase encoding is based upon the phase position of the previous symbol. Up to 16 bits-per-symbol have been used with DPSK.

Digital Loopback Test: A modem check that is used for testing the transmit and receive sides of both modems, as well as the connection between the two.

Distortion: The degradation of signal quality, usually measured in decibels, and referenced to a standard value.

Distributed Network: A network in which control and management of software is shared by the work stations.

Domain: An element of the Organizational Model of the ISO network management function; refers to a group of similar subsystems consisting of objects.

Domain Name System or Service (DNS): A database system used to map host names, IP addresses and e-mail routing.

Downlink: The modulated carrier transmitted from a satellite, the satellite transmit antenna, and the receive equipment at the ground station.

Downside: In a Token Ring network, downside is the side of the receiver the data enters; the upside is the side of the receiver the data exits.

Drive Mapping: The process of creating a drive letter to connect to another network resource.

Dual-Tone Multifrequency (DTMF): A method of tone dialing using a twelve-button keypad, and dual tones representing each of the twelve buttons.

Duplexing: Used in RAID implementations to provide a dedicated hard drive controller for each hard drive.

Dynamic Host Configuration Protocol (DHCP): A protocol used to dynamically assign IP addresses to clients and nodes. It's gradually replacing the Bootp protocol.

Dynamic Routing: Routers that advertise updates and collect updated routing addresses are called dynamic routers.

E

Earth Station: The source of satellite transmissions, also called the ground station.

EBCDIC: An 8-bit terminal code capable of producing 256 unique characters.

Electronic Industry Association (EIA): A professional trade organization that develops many standards.

Elliptical Orbit: A satellite orbit tilted at an arc in reference to the equator, and in which the Earth is off-center in the ellipse.

Encapsulation Bridge: A bridging method in which the MAC frames of the transmitting stations are placed in the information field of a transmitted network frame. The access methods of all nodes must be the same to use this method.

Encryption: The process of transforming data into a secret code.

Energy Detector: A section of a modem that samples the output of the automatic gain control to determine if the data signal meets the minimum requirements for successful data exchanges.

Environmental factors: A reference to the physical surroundings of network equipment such as temperature, humidity, electrical interference, and security measures.

Equalization: The process of compensating for phase-jitters and frequency attenuation. Data may be equalized at the transmitter (pre-equalization), or dynamically (adaptive equalization).

Ethernet: The forerunner of the IEEE 802.3 standard for bus networks. Ethernet was developed jointly by Xerox, Digital Equipment, and Intel. It is functionally identical to CSMA/CD, and often used interchangeably in literature.

F

Fairing: Metal skin placed over the nose of a rocket, protecting it from the heat during launch.

Fast Packet Services: A version of X.25 packet switching that transports messages at much higher data rates. Includes frame relay and ATM.

Fault Analysis: Refers to established procedures for locating and correcting malfunctions.

Fault Network Management: One of the five ISO functions of network management; concerned with detecting, diagnosing, and correcting problems.

FDM Hierarchy: An organizational structure used by the long-distance carriers, primarily for analog systems. The system is based on a group of 12 channels, each occupying a 4 kHz bandwidth. Five groups comprise a super group; ten super groups are included in a master group; a jumbo group contains 5 master groups; and a multiplexed group consists of 3 jumbo groups.

Fiber Distributed Data Interface (FDDI): The ANSI standard for transmitting 100 Mbps data over fiber-optic cable in local-area networks.

Fiber Optics: Transmission cable in which data is transported as light. Fiber-optic cable is noted for high data rates and wide bandwidths.

File Server: A network station dedicated to managing a local-area network. A LAN with a file server is a centralized network, and all exchanges between nodes are under control of the file server.

File Transfer Protocol (FTP): The protocol used to transfer files by copying the files from one system (computer) to another.

Fix: An interim solution for bugs that have been discovered either during beta testing or after the product was formally released. See Patch.

Folder Replication: Method used to back up data. Typically associated with copying a database from server to client so that more than one copy of the database exists.

Footprint: The geographical coverage of a satellite transmission.

Forward Delay Timer: Set by the root bridge of the Spanning Tree Protocol, it specifies the length of time the bridge will remain in each of the port states (disabled, learning, blocking, listening, or forwarding).

Forward Error Control: Error correction that occurs at the receiver, such as the Huffman Code.

Fractional T1: A portion of the 24-channel T1 facility for lease to small- or medium-size companies.

Fragmentation: The process of dividing TCP/IP datagrams so that the length is smaller. This may be necessary to pass the datagram over LANs that have smaller frame requirements than TCP/IP.

Frame: The collection of fields containing link control and management, as well as user information.

Frame-Check Sequence (FCS): The error-detection field of HDLC frames, one or two bytes long.

Frame Relay: A fast packet service that is similar to the X.25 interface. It provides variable data rates.

Frequency-Division Multiple Access (FDMA): A modified version of FDM for satellites that allocates the total bandwidth to a number of transponders.

Frequency-Division Multiplexing (FDM): In an FDM system, a wide bandwidth is divided among many dedicated channels.

Frequency Modulation (FM): A modulation method in which the carrier frequency changes in direct proportion to the data amplitude, and the rate of carrier frequency change is directly proportional to the data frequency.

Frequency Noise: Noise that is of a constant period, but of varying amplitude. A common source of frequency noise is the 60 Hz radiated from wiring.

Frequency-Shift Keying (FSK): A modulation technique used with modems, in which the phase of the carrier is shifted higher, or lower, to represent a logic 1 or 0.

Full Duplex: A system that permits simultaneous data flow between nodes.

G

Gateway: A wide area network interconnection machine that converts from one type of data communication system to another.

Generator Polynominal: In error-detection techniques, the organization of shift registers and exclusive-OR operations under the control of a specific algorithm.

Geosynchronous Orbit: A circular satellite orbit located 23,280 miles above the Earth's surface, also called the Clarke orbit.

Groups: The practice of organizing individuals into related groups, all of whom have a general need to a class of information.

H

H88 Loading: The practice of installing 88 mH coils every 6,000 feet along the telephone network. H88 loading attenuates the signal, providing a flatter frequency response.

Half Duplex: A system that permits data flow between nodes, in only one direction at a time.

Hamming Code: A technique for detecting and correcting errors, requiring a significant amount of overhead.

Handholding: An initial response to a problem in which you devote time, usually on the telephone, to working with the user on the problem.

Handshaking: The dialog exchanged between communicating stations that sets up the link.

Hardware Loopback: The ping utility and its many variations.

Header: All fields of data frames that do not include user information. While the header is necessary to establish and maintain the link, it also reduces the efficiency of the exchange.

High-level Data-Link Control (HDLC): The official Data-Link protocol of the International Standards Organization. HDLC is a bit-oriented protocol suitable for most network environments and topologies.

Hub-1: A high-speed switch at the center of a star network.

Huffman Code: A forward error-correction technique.

Huffman Concentrator: A data-compression method in which the data is sampled, and those bit sequences with higher occurrence rates are given abbreviated bit patterns.

Host: Any machine that communicates on the network. It normally refers to a device that has a dedicated or assigned IP address.

Hybrid: A transformer interface that provides for full-duplex operation of the telephone system. A telephone includes a 2- to 4-wire hybrid, and the central office maintains a 2- to 4-wire hybrid.

HyperText Transfer Protocol (HTTP): The protocol used to link files on the Internet.

I

Ideal Signal Point: A predetermined position in the signal-point constellation of a modem modulator. The ideal signal point is separated from the position of the received signal by an amount equal to an error signal.

Idle Token: The state of a token-ring network when the token is in transition between stations.

IEEE 802 Standards: A series of standards approved by the IEEE to address the implementation of recommendations of the ISO at the Physical and Data Link layers of the OSI Reference Model. The standards are not all completed, but encompass:

802.1 High-Level Interface
802.2 Logical-Link Interface
802.3 CSMA/CD
802.4 Token Bus
802.5 Token Ring
802.6 Metropolitan Area Networks
802.7 Broadband LANs
802.8 Fiber Optics
802.9 Integrated Voice Data

Information Transfer: An initial response to take when a problem is first reported. Information transfer is appropriate in a situation where reference material will address the problem as effectively as if you were going to the client and doing it yourself.

Impulse Noise: Sporadic noise resulting from relays, motors, generators, and switches. It is usually of short duration, and in close proximity to the affected equipment.

Information Frame: An HDLC frame type used to carry user information. Information frames are represented with a logic 0 in the frame-identifier field of the control field.

Information Service: A large database. Usually, access to an information service is made available for a fee.

Interconnect Transport Service: Software overlaid on the protocols that addresses the performance of a network.

Interface: Describes the physical connection between dissimilar devices. A common example is the RS-232C interface connection between PCs and printers.

International Direct-Distance Dialing (IDDD): A worldwide telephone numbering system that allows the direct dialing of any number in the world, without the assistance of an operator.

International Standards Organization (ISO): A large professional trade organization responsible for many standards.

Internet: A WAN used for education and research that uses TCP/IP protocols. The Internet is the largest of wide-area networks with controlled access.

Internetworking Protocol (IP): A Network-layer protocol used in conjunction with TCP to route between logical addresses.

Intersymbol Interference: The blurring together of data symbols caused by distributed channel reactance.

Iteration: The sixteen rounds of ciphering in the Data-Encryption Standard.

J

Jam: The state of a CSMA/CD network following the detection of a collision, in which the transmitters continue to send data for 32 bits.

Jam Pattern: A series of logic 1s generated after a collision is detected on a CSMA/CD network.

Jitter: The unavoidable delay in arrival times of symbols. It's created by harmonic distortion of the logic levels carried by the symbols.

K

Key: Specifies the parameters of a secret code, and is used to encrypt and decrypt the data.

L

Learning Bridge: Also called a transparent bridge. It is a bridging method that utilizes source-address tables for compiling a map of all addresses on the network.

Line Interface: The RJ-11 telephone jack that couples data onto the telephone network.

Line of Sight: Communication method associated with microwaves. The transmit and receive antennas must be arranged in a straight path.

Link Access Protocol-Balanced (LAPB): A subset of HDLC used with X.25 packet-switched networks. All stations on a LAPD network are peers.

Load Balancing: The even distribution of network processes among the nodes of a peer-to-peer LAN.

Local Area Network (LAN): A LAN is characterized by a collection of nodes connected together in a limited geographical area and operating under a single protocol.

Local Exchange Loop: The two-wire circuit from the telephone to the central office, and the wires connecting the two.

Logical Indicators: Network management software used to identify problems. Examples include TCP/IP utilities, Network Monitor, or Performance Monitor.

Logical Link Control (LLC): A sublayer of the Data Link layer of the OSI reference model. The LLC is responsible for frame formatting and the conventions necessary to establish a reliable link.

Login Account: A script that specifies the privileges of an individual or group access to the network resources.

Longitudinal Redundancy Check (LRC): A parity-based error-detection method in which the bits in blocks of data are arranged in columns and rows, and a block error field is generated.

Loop Length Compensation: A circuit in a telephone that regulates the speech levels of callers, regardless of the distance separating them.

Loopback Test: Modem tests that check the operation of local and remote modems, as well as the connection between the two.

Low-Noise Amplifier (LNA): The output power amplifier of a satellite earth station.

M

MAC Address: All nodes, or stations, on the network have a unique address. A 6-byte length is permitted, as the original version of Ethernet specified a 6-byte address. IEEE 802.3 permits a 2-byte alternative, but this is seldom used.

Major Axis: A satellite orbit that parallels the equator.

Managed System: A component of the Organizational Model of ISO network management; managed systems are logical groupings of objects.

Manchester: A common encoding method in which logic 1s are represented by the high-to-low mid-bit transition, and logic 0's are represented by the low-to-high mid-bit transition.

Mark: The steady state condition of a channel represented by a logic 1.

Max Age Timer: A parameter set by the root bridge of the Spanning Tree Protocol that specifies the length of time a bridge will wait to receive a BPDU.

Maximum Port Speed: A setting that allows you to specify the port speed for a modem.

Media: The type of physical connection used between network nodes. Examples are twisted-pair wires, coaxial cables, fiber optics, and microwaves.

Media Access Unit (MAU): A hardware device associated with coaxial cable. An MAU contains circuitry that allows a workstation to access the network media.

Medium-Access Control (MAC): A sublayer of the Data Link layer of the OSI reference model. The MAC is responsible for ensuring that network stations gain access to the network.

Mesh: In a pure mesh network, each node has a physical link (coax, twisted pair, microwave, fiber optic) connection to all other nodes.

Microwave: A type of transmission media. Data is modulated onto a carrier, and transmitted through the atmosphere.

Minor Axis: A line intersecting the equator at a 90-degree angle.

Mirroring: A RAID method of backing up hard drive data. In a mirrored configuration, the data on one disk is duplicated to another disk.

Modal Dispersion: Distortion found in fiber-optic cables that results from the light arriving at the receiver at different times.

Modem: An acronym for modulator/demodulator. Modems are required to transmit data between stations separated by 50 feet or more.

Modulation: The process of superimposing data onto a carrier. Examples are AM, FM, and PM.

Multiplexer: A device capable of transmitting more than one signal over the same channel.

N

Name Resolution: System for reconciling Internet names, IP addresses, and physical addresses so they point to the exact location of the destination node, no matter where it's located.

Network: A group of computers and peripherals connected together so that data may be exchanged between them.

Network Availability: The amount of time that network services are available: $A = (TB - TD)/T$: where A = availability; TB = time the network is busy; TD = time the network is down; T = total time the network is available.

Network Drawing: A sketch of a network. A network drawing is used to identify network components as well as the cable labels.

Network Interface Card (NIC): A network interface card contains a transceiver for sending and receiving data frames on and off a network, as well as the Data Link layer hardware needed to format the sending bits and to decipher received frames.

Network Layer: Layer 3 of the OSI Reference Model. The Network layer implements the virtual connection of the upper layers, by mapping a data route among the point-to-point links.

Network Management Model: The ISO description of network management; includes an organizational model, an informational model, and a functional model.

Network Utilization: The ratio of the time a network is used, to the total time the network is available. $U = TB/T$: where U = utilization; TB = time the network is busy; T = total time the network is available.

NIC Diagnostics: Tools used to assist in troubleshooting connectivity problems.

Node: A generic term describing any device that is connected to a network.

Noise: Undesirable interference of data signals that distorts the data.

Noise Factor: The ratio of noise at the input of a communication system to noise at the output. It is calculated by: $NF = 10 \log ((S_i/N_i)/(S_o/N_o))$

Nonreturn To Zero (NRZ): An encoding technique in which logic 1's are represented by $+V$ and logic 0's by $-V$.

Nonroutable Protocols: Protocols that aren't routable because they don't contain enough addressing information in their headers. MAC layer protocols such as Ethernet, Token Ring, or FDDI are examples of nonroutable protocols.

Normal Response Mode (NRM): One of two modes for the configuring of HDLC protocols. All stations are designated as primary or secondary. Secondaries are forbidden to transmit without first receiving permission from the primary.

Nyquist Rate: The Nyquist Channel Information Theory states that if the data is sampled at a rate of at least twice the highest transmitted frequency, the original data will be accurately recovered at the receiver.

O

Object: Refers to any network resource, such as software commands or network interface cards.

Off-hook: A term describing the handset lifted from the cradle of a telephone.

On-hook: A term describing the handset resting in the cradle of a telephone.

On-line State: The condition a modem enters when it has access to the telephone network.

Open System Interconnection (OSI) Reference Model: The standard model, developed by the International Standards Organization, which describes a complete data communication system. The model includes a hierarchical relationship between seven distinct levels: layer 1, the Physical layer; layer 2, the Data Link layer; layer 3, the Network layer; layer 4, the Transport layer; layer 5, the Session layer; layer 6, the Presentation layer; and layer 7, the Application layer.

Operator Versus System Model: A model used for determining whether a problem lies with the client or network operator, or the network.

Originate Modem: The modem that initiates a call. The originate modem communicates with the answer modem by transmitting over the originate channel.

Overhead: The portion of a data frame that does not contain user data. Overhead reduces the efficiency of communication exchanges.

P

Packet Assembly/Disassembly (PAD): The process of organizing data frames into packets of frames, sometimes used to refer to the synchronizing flags preceding BSC frames.

Packet Switching: The process of dividing data into packets for transmission over a WAN. X.25 is the conventional method of packet switching, in which data travels at 64 kbps in MAC-like packets.

Parity: An error-detection system based on an odd, or even, count of logic 1's in a data word.

Passive Satellite: Also called a reflector satellite, it is characterized by the absence of a repeater.

Password: An encrypted and secret word entered at the sign-on screen of a work station; usually used in conjunction with user IDs. If the password and ID match the password for the user, maintained in the computer files, access is granted to the network.

Password Authentication Protocol (PAP): Protocol used with PPP. The client is authenticated by sending a user name and password to the server.

Patch: A software enhancement that addresses a weakness in the original release of hardware or software. See Upgrade and Fix.

Payload: The weight of a satellite, including the satellite subassemblies and instrumentation.

Peer-to-peer Networks: Control of the network is distributed among the nodes, meaning there is no server connected to the network. All nodes are servers as well as clients.

Performance Network Management: One of five functions of the ISO network management responsible for collecting data, so that the integrity and efficiency of the network can be analyzed.

Perigee: The end of an elliptical orbit nearest the Earth's center.

Period: The time of a data bit. Period = $1/F$: where F is the frequency.

Permanent Virtual Circuit: A leased channel in which stations at each end are assigned permanent addresses, so that they may communicate at any time without the normal exchange of dialogue.

Permutation: The complete encryption process. In the DES system, up to 256 permutations may be imposed on the same plain text.

Phase Modulation (PM): A modulation method in which the amount of phase distortion is proportional to the data amplitude, and the rate at which phase shifts occur is proportional to the data frequency.

Phase-Shift Keying (PSK): A modulation technique used with modems in which the phase of the carrier is shifted for each change of logic levels.

Physical Indicators: Lights, LEDs, error messages, etc. that provide messages related to network problems.

Physical Layer: Layer 1 of the OSI Reference Model. The Physical layer includes hardware interfaces and the connection medium. It is the only layer at which data bits are actually transferred.

Plaintext: The data to be coded into a secret message.

Point-to-Point: A network topology in which data is exchanged between only two stations.

Point-to-Point Protocol (PPP): A communication protocol used to send data across serial communication links. It's the most widely used wide area protocol for accessing Internet service providers.

Point-to-Point Tunneling Protocol (PPTP): A protocol used to securely transport PPP packets over a TCP/IP network (i.e., the Internet).

Polarization: Refers to the orientation of an antenna in reference to the Earth. Antennas positioned perpendicular to the ground are vertically polarized, while antennas positioned parallel to the ground are horizontally polarized.

Policies: System configurations that affect all users.

Post Office Protocol-Version 3 (POP3): An e-mail protocol used with SMTP.

Precedence: Part of the Type of Service field of a TCP/IP datagram; it provides an indication to the network routers and bridges as to the significance of the datagram.

Predecessor: A method of referring to stations on a token-ring network. The station sending the token is the predecessor to the station receiving the token.

Pre-equalization: The process of compensating for known distortion at the receiver.

Presentation Layer: Layer 6 of the OSI Reference Model. The Presentation layer is responsible for determining the syntax used between communicating stations. This includes screen formats, terminal codes such as ASCII and EBCDIC, and provisions for language conversions.

Printer Port Capture: The process used to connect to a printer on a network.

Print Server: A computer used to queue requests to a printer. It's used in a network in which several users utilize the same printer.

Problem Extent Model: A systematic approach to identifying the boundaries of a problem.

Product Cipher: A class of encryption systems that combines substitution and transposition techniques.

Profiles: The configuration settings made for each user.

Protocol: A set of rules describing the exchange of data on a network. Examples include BSC, HDLC, and TCP/IP.

Protocol Analyzer: Network test equipment that identifies and decodes the common protocols, such as HDLC, Ethernet, and TCP/IP.

Public Key Cipher: An encryption technique intended to authenticate the message sender, as well as to perform encryption and decryption. In this type of cipher, a public key and a private key are used, but neither may be derived from the other.

Pulse-Amplitude Modulation (PAM): A variation of analog pulse modulation. A PAM signal consists of a series of pulses whose amplitude corresponds to the amplitude of an analog signal.

Pulse-Code Modulation (PCM): A form of digital pulse modulation. PCM is produced by quantizing an analog waveform to a series of pulses, then converting the pulses to a binary-encoded signal.

Pulse-Duration Modulation (PDM): A form of analog pulse modulation. A PDM signal is achieved by varying the width of sampled pulses in direct proportion to the amplitude of the modulating analog waveform.

Pulse Modulation: The most common technique of modulating signals within the telephone system. Pulse modulation includes Pulse-Amplitude Modulation, Pulse-Duration Modulation, Pulse-Code Modulation, and Delta Modulation.

Q

Quadrature-Amplitude Modulation (QAM): A modulation method used with modems. The data is represented with amplitude and phase shifts in the carrier.

Quantization Error: The amount of error produced in the analog-to-digital conversion process. It's typically expressed in 1 or 1/2 bit.

Queue Length: The time a network spends waiting in a queue: $Q = W/T$; where Q = average queue length, W = total time messages wait in the system, T = total time of a message run.

R

Random-Key Cipher: A cipher that uses logic circuits to generate a large number of keys. The number of possible keys discourages potential code breakers.

Received Line-Signal Detect (RLSD): An RS-232C command that modems exchange following the training period.

Receiver: The data-terminal equipment that accepts data from a sender.

Redundant Array of Inexpensive Disks (RAID): Consists of five levels of fault tolerance practices that are used with servers for protecting data, or improving the read/write performance of the server.

Refraction: The bending of a light wave when it is passed through materials of different densities.

Remote Loopback Test: A modem test in which a local modem instructs the remote modem to perform a digital loopback test and provide the local modem with the results.

Repeater: An interchannel amplifier that not only increases the signal amplitude, but also removes noise and distortion.

Request-to-Send (RTS): The RS-232C pin that initiates an exchange between modems.

Response Time: The amount of time consumed in delivering a message in the network, $R = T/C$: where R = response time; T = total time messages are required to wait in the system; C = total completed messages.

Rights: Refers to the ability to perform specific actions on the network.

Ring: One of two wires connecting the telephone to the central office. The ring wire is typically the red wire.

Ringback: A telephone signal sent back to inform a caller that the called number is ringing. It consists of a 440/480-Hz tone that's on for 2 seconds, and off for 4 seconds.

Ringer: The circuit in a telephone that signals an incoming call with a 90 V, 20 Hz signal that's on for 2 seconds, and off for 4 seconds.

Ring Indicator (RI): An RS-232C command sent to the DTE from the modem, indicating that a call has arrived.

Ring Topology: A network topology arranged with the nodes connected end-to-end, in a daisy-chain manner that resembles a circle.

Ring Wrap: The process of bypassing a failed station or link segment on an FDDI network.

Rocket Thruster: The section of a satellite that lifts it into its orbit.

Rotator: A device found in modems that generates an error signal equal to the phase delay of a received signal.

Routable Protocols: A protocol that can be transmitted across an internetwork. IP, TCP, UDP, IPX, and DECNet are all routable protocols.

Router: An internetworking machine that operates at the Network layer of the OSI model. It is protocol-specific to internetworking protocols.

RS-232C: An EIA interface commonly used to connect personal computers to peripherals. It supports one receiver and one transmitter at data rates up to 20 kbps. A logic 1 is specified at –3V to –25V, and a logic 0 at +3V to +25V.

RS-449: An EIA interface that offers balanced and unbalanced modes of operation. The unbalanced mode is described in RS-422 and specifies up to 10 receivers and one transmitter at data rates up to 100 kbps. The balanced mode is described in RS-423 and supports 10 receivers and one transmitter at data rates up to 10 Mbps. The logic 1 for both modes ranges from –3.6V to –6V, and a logic 0 falls between +3.6V and +6V.

RS-485: An EIA interface designed for a multiuser environment. Up to 32 transmitters and receivers are supported at data rates up to 10 Mbps. A logic 1 is represented by –1.5V to –6V, and a logic 0 by +1.5V to +6V.

S

Satellite: An orbiting communication system characterized by wide bandwidth capabilities and global coverage.

Scheduling: A network management technique used to balance the workload between nodes; it is a future-oriented system that attempts to anticipate problems and correct them before they occur.

Scrambler: The section of a modem that encodes the data to be transmitted in order to avoid distortion, such as intersymbol interference.

Server: A powerful computer on a network that contains a network operating system (NOS) and manages the flow of data on the network.

Security Network Management: One of the five functions of ISO network management; includes factors affecting physical security, file and record access, and the use of passwords and user IDs.

Serial Line Internet Protocol (SLIP): The forerunner to PPP. It has the same function; to connect nodes in a point-to-point configuration. SLIP only transports TCP/IP.

Serial Network Interface (SNI): An SNI is found in the network controller cards used with CSMA/CD LANs. It serves as an interface between the interface controller and the transceiver by Manchester II-encoding the data.

Serial Protocol: Point-to-point, physical communication protocol. Examples are PPP and SLIP.

Session Layer: Layer 5 of the OSI Reference Model. The Session layer is responsible for managing the end-to-end dialog of the network stations. This may include half- or full-duplex operation, and the inclusion of synchronization headers attached to data frames.

Signal Noise To Quantization Ratio (SQR): A general indication of the quality of a quantizer.

Signal-to-Noise Ratio (SNR): The measure of desired signal power to the amount of noise contained in the signal. It is found by: $SNR = P_s/P_n$.

Simple Mail Transfer Protocol (SMTP): Used to route outgoing e-mail, and in some applications, incoming e-mail.

Simple Network Management Protocol (SNMP): This protocol defines packet exchanges.

Simplex: A system of one-way communication.

Socket: A software abstract used to communicate processes. It's used as a programming interface to the communication protocol (TCP, for example).

Source Routing: An IBM bridging method used with Token Ring networks.

Space: The condition of a channel represented by a logic 0.

Space-Division Multiplexing (SDM): A multiplexing technique common with the telephone system. In an SDM system, a single channel is dedicated to a single receiver and transmitter.

Spanning Tree Protocol: Used with bridged networks to determine network paths for data messages. It prevents the messages from circling through the network endlessly by establishing fall-back routes.

Speech Channel: The portion of the telephone channel used for speech. The speech channel has a frequency range from 300 Hz to 3,300 Hz.

Spin Stabilization: A method of controlling the attitude of a satellite. The spinning action is initiated by thrusters mounted on the side of the satellite.

Spot-Beaming: A method of focusing satellite transmissions that sends a narrow beam to small, ground-based antennas.

Standard Operating Procedure (SOP): A document used to maintain control and consistency on a network. It's an approved document that is designed to convey knowledge, as opposed to data, to the reader.

Star Topology: A topology for arranging network nodes, characterized by a central hub that serves as a switch for connecting the stations.

Start Bit: The first bit in an asynchronous data frame that signifies the beginning of the frame.

Static Routing: A static router has its routing tables updated manually.

Statistical Time-Division Multiplexing (STDM): A modified version of TDM. An STDM multiplexer collects and stores data at the aggregate rate of the terminals feeding the multiplexer, enabling the data to be processed at very high rates for short periods.

Stop Bit: The final bit in an asynchronous data frame that signifies the end of the frame.

Stripe Parity: Used with disk striping by adding redundant data in the form of parity blocks. The parity may be a dedicated drive, or the parity blocks may be spread across multiple hard drives.

Striping: The process of spreading data on hard drives across more than one drive.

Subnet Mask Number: The decimal 255, then, is used to mask the network portion of an IP and only leave open the host portion. The subnets for each class are: Class A: 255.0.0.0, Class B: 255.255.0.0, and Class C: 255.255.255.0

Subnetwork: Identified by a default network mask (or natural mask), which is the decimal number 255. Subnetworks use the subnet mask in order to extend the use of a single IP address. There are class-A, -B, and -C subnetwork masks.

Subscriber Line-Interface Card (SLIC): An interface circuit between the analog local loop and the digital switching centers of the telephone system.

Subscriber Loop: Another term for the local loop that contains the telephone, central office, and the two wires connecting the two.

Substitution Cipher: A ciphering technique in which substitute alphanumeric characters replace the alphanumeric characters of the plain text.

Successor: A method for identifying stations on a token-ring network. The station receiving the token from the transmitter is the successor.

Supervisory Frame: A control-field frame type of HDLC, represented by the dibit 01 in the frame identifier field. Supervisory frames are used to inform a station of various conditions existing on the network.

Switch Hook: The telephone switch that connects the telephone to the central office when the handset is lifted.

Switching Hub: Includes a switching backplane that allows any port to be connected to any other port on an as-needed basis. In other words, a switching hub assigns ports dynamically and under control of the hub.

Synchronous: A method of transmitting data frames in which each bit, or frame, is tracked in unison by the receiver and transmitter. Typically, synchronous transmission is used at higher data rates.

Synchronous Data-Link Control (SDLC): An IBM Data Link protocol. SDLC is the forerunner of the OSI protocol HDLC. The two are functionally the same.

Synchronous Optical Network (SONET): Fiber-optic system used to interconnect wide-area networks at speeds from 54.84 Mbps to 2.5 Gbps.

Synchronous-to-Asynchronous Converter: The section of a modem that converts received data into the format suitable for personal computers or peripherals.

System Service Time: The average amount of time that a message spends in the system, $S = B/C$: where S = system service time; B = busy time; and C = the number of completed messages.

T

Tape Backup: Method used to back up hard drive data on a server or client.

Target Token Rotation Time Value: An FDDI number generated for the purpose of assigning a single station to initiate the transmission token.

T-Carrier: The TDM digital hierarchy of the long-distance telephone carriers.

TCP/IP Utilities: UNIX-based tools that can be used to provide a considerable amount of information about your computer, its place in a network, and other devices you're connected to. Typically used in troubleshooting. Examples include ping and ipconfig.

TDM Hierarchy: The digital multiplexing scheme used by the long-distance carriers, often called the T-Carrier. The T1 system contains up to 24 64 kHz channels at a rate of 1.544 Mbps; the T2 consists of 96 channels transmitting at 6.312 Mbps; the T3 includes 672 channels transmitting at 44.736 Mbps; and the T4 includes 4032 channels transmitting at 274.176 Mbps.

Technical Service: An initial response to a problem in which you must apply your expertise. This may be in person, or may require your hands-on involvement at a remote terminal.

Telemetry: Refers to the telemetry antenna on a satellite. Control signals passing to the satellite from a ground station, and data signals passing from the satellite to the ground station, are transmitted via the telemetry antenna.

Terminal Code: Binary numbers representing alphanumeric characters and special control functions. Examples are ASCII, EBCDIC, and Baudot.

Text Transparency: The practice of ensuring that user data remains separate and distinct from frame header data. Two common techniques for achieving text transparency are character stuffing and bit stuffing.

Throughput: A general term describing the ratio of frame header to user data contained in the frame. High throughput indicates a network is operating with high efficiency, and is calculated by $TP = C/T$: where TP = throughput; C = the number of messages sent; and T = the total time of the transmission.

Time-Division Multiple Access (TDMA): A satellite multiplexing scheme, in which ground stations are provided alternating time slots for sending data to the satellite.

Time-Division Multiplexing (TDM): A multiplexing technique in which a single carrier frequency contains the data from many channels. Each terminal is assigned a time slot in which it has access to the full bandwidth of the channel.

Timing Recovery Element: A device in modems that measures the synchronization between the receiver and transmitter.

Tip: One of the two wires connecting the telephone to the central office. The tip wire is typically the green wire.

Token: A network signaling element used by stations to gain access to a token ring or token bus network.

Token Bus: The IEEE 802.4 local area network. Stations connect to the network through interface adapters, and gain access to the network when they possess the token.

Token-based System: A ring or bus network that uses a signaling token for station access.

Token Recovery: Describes the process used in token-based networks for recovering the access token when a station node fails.

Toll Exchange: A series of centers used by the long distance carriers to route long distance calls. The toll exchanges consist of a class-4 toll center, a class-3 primary center, a class-2 sectional center, and a class-1 regional center.

Tone Generator: Test equipment used to generate an audible for locating wire pairs in UTP cable.

Tone Locator: Test equipment used to identify wire pairs in UTP cable.

Topology: Refers to the physical architecture of a network. Examples are ring, star, and point-to-point networks.

Training Detector: The section of a modem responsible for establishing compatibility between the modems during handshaking.

Training Period: The process of exchanging data streams between modems that establishes a common dialog.

Transceiver: A network component that simply receives and transmits signals. It lacks the sophistication to manage or massage the signal.

Transceiver Interface: A circuit associated with 802.3 CSMA/CD protocols that provides isolation between the network cabling and the network interface. Collision detection is monitored by the transceiver interface.

Translation Bridge: A bridging method in which the MAC frames of the transmitting station are converted to the frame type of the destination station.

Transmission Control Protocol (TCP): Used to establish a reliable connection between client and server, or other network devices.

Transmission Control Protocol/Internet Protocol (TCP/IP): A widely used internetworking protocol that's independent of vendor hardware and is characterized by a 32-bit addressing scheme.

Transmitter: The network device that sends data to a receiver.

Transparency: A general term describing the degree to which user data remains separate from header data.

Transponder: Contains the receiver and transmitter of a satellite.

Transport Layer: Layer 4 of the OSI Reference Model. The Transport layer ensures a virtual communication path by assigning node addresses. In addition, five classes of network service are specified that describe the robust nature of the network.

Transposition Cipher: An encryption technique in which the sequence of the plain text is rearranged.

Troubleshooting Model: A process of systematically identifying and correcting a network problem.

Trunk Line: A common pathway between telephone company central offices. Trunk lines are reserved, and are not available for direct subscriber connections.

Twisted Pair: A communication medium consisting of two conductors insulated from one another and twisted together. Twisted pairs comprise the majority of installed telephone cables.

U

Unauthorized Access: A phrase referring to security measures in which a user is denied access to a file or directory.

Unbreakable Cipher: An encryption technique in which the key is used only once.

Universal Asynchronous Receiver/Transmitter (UART): An integrated circuit that formats data characters to be transmitted as well as received. UARTs are found in personal computers.

Universal Name Convention (UNC): Microsoft method of naming computers. It follows the convention \\computername\filename.

Unnumbered Frame: An HDLC control-field frame type. Unnumbered frames are responsible for initiating and terminating station links, and are represented by the dibit 11 in the frame identifier field.

Unreliable Service: Refers to protocols, particularly TCP/IP, in which there is no end-to-end acknowledgement of received messages.

Update: Refers to a type of security access in which the user is authorized to write to files; the changing of such files.

Upgrade: An interim solution for bugs that have been discovered either during beta testing or after the product was formally released. See Patch.

Upgrade Maintenance: The process of comparing the software or hardware version of an installed component to the latest version available from the component vendor.

Uplink: A satellite transmitter carrier frequency, the transmitter ground equipment, and the satellite transmit antenna.

Upside: Refers to the side of a station on a ring network that data exits.

User Datagram Protocol (UDP): A simpler implementation of TCP, but without the reliability of TCP.

User-Defined Buffer Allocation: A technique for organizing multiplexer buffer-pool memory. With this method, all terminals are assigned dedicated buffer space based upon their estimated need.

User ID: A security measure consisting of a word, or combination of letters and numbers, entered at the sign-on screen by the user. Usually used in conjunction with a password.

V

Variable-Gain Amplifier: A modem amplifier used to increase the level of weak signals.

Virtual Connection: A logical connection that appears to the user to be independent of data frames, encoding, protocols, and all of the underlying mechanisms of data exchange.

Virus Signature: The known viruses that antivirus software detects. It's usually referenced by the release version of virus detection software.

Voice Channel: A telephone channel that extends from 0 Hz to 4000 Hz. Included in the voice channel are the 3 kHz speech channel, called the in-band signaling range; and the ranges from 0 Hz to 300 Hz and 3300 Hz to 4000 Hz, called the out-of-band signaling range.

W

Well-known Port Number: A 16-bit number that refers incoming messages to an application that will process them. An example of a well-known port number is 80, used for HTTP.

Wide-Area Network (WAN): A network encompassing a large geographical area. Usually, WANs are considered to cover distances beyond a metropolitan area.

Windows Internet Naming Service (WINS): Contains a look-up table used to resolve computer names to IP addresses; associated with Windows NT and 9x clients.

Word Interleaving: A process used to transmit time-division multiplexed channels in the T-Carrier system. Each channel is separated into 8-bit words, and the channel words are transmitted one after the other.

Workstation: A stand-alone computer, or a computer that has application programs stored on it that can be launched from it. In many cases, a client and a workstation are the same.

Workstation Backup: Method used to back up user and operating system information of a client computer.

X

XMODEM: A simplified modem protocol used with many personal computers for accessing large databases.

Z

Zero-Dispersion: Refers to commercial grades of fiber-optic cable in which the light is transmitted at 1.3 microns and 1.5 microns, with very low losses.

INDEX

Network+ Certification

Network+ is a CompTIA vendor-neutral certification that measures the technical knowledge of networking professionals with 18-24 months of experience in the IT industry. The test is administered by NCS/VUE and PrometricTM. Discount exam vouchers can be purchased from Marcraft. Earning the Network+ certification indicates that the candidate possesses the knowledge needed to configure and install the TCP/IP client. This exam covers a wide range of vendor and product neutral networking technologies that can also serve as a prerequisite for vendor-specific IT certifications. Network+ has been accepted by the leading networking vendors and included in many of their training curricula. The skills and knowledge measured by the certification examination are derived from industry-wide job task analyses and validated through an industry wide survey. The objectives for the certification examination are divided in two distinct groups, Knowledge of Networking Technology and Knowledge of Networking Practices.

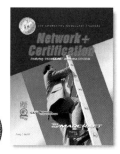

CompTIA seal of approval

i-Net+ Certification

The i-Net+ certification program is designed specifically for any individual interested in demonstrating baseline technical knowledge that would allow him or her to pursue a variety of Internet-related careers. i-Net+ is a vendor-neutral, entry-level Internet certification program that tests baseline technical knowledge of Internet, Intranet, and Extranet technologies, independent of specific Internet-related career roles. Learning objectives and domains examined include: Internet basics, Internet clients, development, networking, security, and business concepts. Certification not only helps individuals enter the Internet industry, but also helps managers determine a prospective employee's knowledge and skill level.

CompTIA seal of approval

The Complete Data Cabling Installers Certification provides the IT industry with an introductory, vendor-neutral certification for skilled personnel that install Category 5 copper data cabling. The Marcraft Complete Data Cabling Installers Certification Training Guide provides students with the knowledge and skills required to pass the Data Cabling Installers Certification exam and become a certified cable installer. The DCIC is recognized nationwide and is the hiring criterion used by major communication companies. Therefore, becoming a certified data cable installer will enhance your job opportunities and career advancement potential.

Server+ Certification

The Server+ certification deals with advanced hardware issues such as RAID, SCSI, multiple CPUs, SANs, and more. This certification is vendor-neutral with a broad range of support, including core support by 3Com, Adaptec, Compaq, Hewlett-Packard, IBM, Intel, EDS Innovations Canada, Innovative Productivity, and Marcraft. This book focuses on complex activities and solving complex problems to ensure servers are functional and applications are available. It provides an in-depth understanding of installing, configuring, and maintaining servers, including knowledge of server-level hardware implementations, data storage subsystems, data recovery, and I/O subsystems.

Fiber Cabling Installers Certification prepares technicians for the growing demand for qualified cable installers who understand and can implement fiber-optic technologies. These technologies cover terminology, techniques, tools, and other products in the fiber-optic industry. This text/lab book covers the basics of fiber-optic design, installations, pulling and prepping cables, terminations, testing, and safety considerations. Labs will cover ST-compatible and SC connector types, both multi- and single-mode cables and connectors. Learn about insertion loss, optical time domain reflectometry, and reflectance. This text covers mechanical and fusion splices and troubleshooting cable systems. This text/lab covers the theory and hands-on skills needed to prepare you for fiber-optic entry-level certification.

Wireless Networking Certification technology is one of the hottest technologies available today, used in electronic devices, such as cell phones and Personal Digital Assistants (PDA), to enable access to e-mail and the Internet. Wireless technology is also utilized in wireless Local Area Networks (LANs). With Marcraft's Wireless Networking Certification, you learn the entire process of designing, building, configuring, and managing a wireless network. This text combines in one place everything needed to successfully design, install, and troubleshoot a simple wireless solution. Keep on the cutting edge of wireless with Marcraft.

Security Installers Certification is an expert introduction to the security alarm industry for those who have limited or no previous knowledge of the industry. After successfully completing the Security Installers Certification program, you'll be prepared for employment in the security industry as a technician or a field installer.
This manual is also beneficial to sales reps for enhancing their technical knowledge. No matter what your background may be or what your educational intentions are, this manual offers you a wealth of information and will answer all of your security installation questions.

The Complete Introductory Computer Course is an entry-level course. It prepares students for the more challenging A+ Certification course. It also provides a careerport™ into the fast-growing IT industry. The MC-2300 is a 45-hour, easy-to-understand exploration of basic computer hardware, software, and troubleshooting. This course helps build students' confidence and basic computer literacy. The fully illustrated 198-page Theory Text/Lab Guide provides an easy-to understand exploration of the basics of computers: basic computer architecture and operation, step-by-step computer hardware assembly, computer hardware and functions, common software packages, consumer maintenance practices, and troubleshooting a "sick" computer. The reusable MC-2300 Intro Computer Trainer comes with all the necessary hardware, software, and tools to perform over 30 hands-on Lab Explorations.

The Complete Introductory Networking Course is a superbly illustrated theory text and lab guide all in one. It not only provides a great way for students to explore over 45 hours of easy-to-understand basic networking topics, but also develops job skills for starting them on the path towards a new high-tech career!
This manual guides you through such activities as: installation and configuration of local area network hardware, peer-to-peer networking functions, sharing computer resources, mapping to remote resources, and consumer-level network troubleshooting. The Complete Introductory Networking Course provides an excellent starting point for IT Certification including Microsoft's MCSE, Novell's CNA, and Cisco's CCNA.

The Complete Introductory Internet Course takes advantage of the growing demand for qualified Internet technicians. This 45-hour course explores easy-to-understand basic Internet topics and helps develop Internet skills.
This manual guides you through such activities as: configuring e-mail accounts, designing a basic HTML page, setup of a basic firewall for security, and establishing Internet connection slaving. The Complete Introductory Internet Course provides an excellent starting point for IT Certification including CompTIA's i-NET+ and Prosoft's Certified Internet Webmaster (CIW).